Praise for *Augustine*

A 2015 *New York Times Book Review* Notable Book

"This book revisits one of the most influential and prolific authors in western thought, a man whose preoccupations with sin, evil, bodily pain, longing, and love lie at the heart of this scintillating analysis. In brief, the book is about one man's lifelong search for heaven in a world of abundant evil, and his strivings to make some sort of contact with that heaven in his daily life. . . . But unlike so many interpretations of works of philosophy and theology, this study is grounded in the man's direct experience of the world around him—the people he knew, those he loved, his emotions and intense physical experiences, whether of pain, lust, pleasure or anger. . . . Beautifully written in a crystalline prose where not a word is out of place, it's a book to read in a garden, or the shady courtyard of a Mediterranean villa, as well as in the study or library."

—Julia Smith, PhD, University of Glasglow,
Wolfson History Prize judge

"Mr. Fox traces with clarity the development of Augustine's thought, but also of his character. . . . [He] succeeds in offering us a figure whose inner and outer struggles, whose strengths and weaknesses, do somehow reach across the centuries and touch something profoundly human."

—*Wall Street Journal*

"This book interweaves political, military, and personal history to describe in detail the first four decades of Augustine's life. . . . Fox explores everything that is known about the great teacher's life and social world, including his various lovers and intellectual partners."

—*The Economist*

"Robin Lane Fox has now done [Peter] Brown [author of *Augustine of Hippo*] one better. . . . Fox is such a good writer that interest never flags, and you always feel that you are there."

—Mark Lilla, *New York Times*

"This biography of the Church Father displays an eclectic, discursive approach. New delights, such as an exploration of Cicero's lost Hortensius, beloved by Augustine and pieced together by scholars through scattered mentions in the ancient record, add surprising shadings to Augustine's personality. Lane Fox sees his subject in intimate yet global terms: Augustine's disenchantment with politics, the dubious powers of rhetoric, and his own skill at navigating the system draws comparisons with Tolstoy, Byron, and Joyce. Most engaging is the portrait of Augustine's complex relationship with his lively, wine-drinking, social-striving mother, Monnica, from whom he 'imbibed the name of Christ,' and learned to 'retain it deeply within.'"

—*New Yorker*

"It is a profound understatement to observe that it was appropriate for Robin Lane Fox, at last, to tackle a biography of Augustine."

—*Financial Times*

"*Augustine: Conversions to Confessions* is a compelling read. . . . A page-turner that might last the whole winter long, come spring you'll be all the more enlightened."

—*Chicago Tribune*

"Fox has written an attentive, rich, and compelling book about Augustine which will reward scholars and edify non-specialists. It will also entertain both."

—*Catholic World Report*

"The universe of Augustine scholarship is a supremely crowded one and anyone who essays a new biography must, above all, distinguish himself from the magisterial works of Peter Brown. . . . Lane Fox does this in several ways. The first is a remarkably unsentimental take on his subject. . . . The most significant distinction is to frame the study entirely around Augustine's *Confessions*, which Lane Fox gracefully describes as 'a prayer which no pagan could have produced and which no Christian, before or since, has equaled.' . . . Lane Fox deploys an astonishing amount of newly discovered material."

—*New Criterion*

"[*Augustine*] is an engaging, respectful, and highly erudite yet readily accessible study worthy of its glowing commendations."

—*Choice*

"*Augustine* may be informative to the nth degree, but it's not dense. . . . Lane Fox describes everything engagingly."

—*National Catholic Reporter*

"This is an impressive resource for classicists, theologians, and historians of the late Roman Empire, who will enjoy chewing over the argument that the *Confessions* were written in a single burst, in 397."

—*Independent (UK)*

"Lane Fox's book is undoubtedly a watershed in Augustinian studies."

—*New Statesman (UK)*

"*Augustine* [is] a work of scholarship as readable as any historical novel."

—*Literary Review (UK)*

"Lane Fox's work is the fruit of intense study of Augustine's *Confessions* in its rhetorically forceful, rather jingly Latin, and modern scholarship on the topic. . . . Any reader interested in one of the early church's most influential figures, a saint we know more about than any other from the ancient world, will find this stimulating biography a pleasure to read."

—*Times (UK)*

"It is a compelling emotional drama. . . . This is a richly detailed and well informed book, which is written with skill and style. It will provide many with a rich feat of insights and information, and will doubtless find its place beside Brown, Chadwick, Marrou, and other scholars of the past."

—*Irish Catholic*

"Lane Fox presents a fascinating portrait, showcasing a vast knowledge of antiquity that allows him to explore and contextualize the themes of confession, conversion, and salvation. . . . [He] captures the drama—and at crucial moments the melodrama—of Augustine's emotional wrestling, his battles with being 'in love with love,' his self-proclaimed inner lack of God."

—*Wichita Eagle*

"Highly intriguing is the exposition on the role of Platonic philosophy in Augustine's metamorphosis, his allegorical biblical exegesis, and his mystical ascent toward divine union."

—*Library Journal*

"Readers pious and skeptical alike will recognize Lane Fox as an exceptionally insightful and probing biographer."

—*Booklist, starred review*

"Fox guides readers on an epic journey through the book and the life that inspired it. . . . [He] systematically explores his subject's well-documented life and provides in-depth background and commentary capable of assisting even seasoned scholars in a deeper understanding. . . . [Lane Fox] provides a true service to readers . . . [his] writing is coherent and approachable. . . . [*Augustine*] represents a close analysis of both *Confessions* and of Augustine himself, leaving few stones unturned. An erudite and ordered reading of Augustine's *Confessions* and a worthy addition to any library on early Christianity."

—*Kirkus Reviews*

"*Augustine* vividly retells the gripping story of Augustine's serial self-reinventions with both sympathy and shrewd insight. Robin Lane Fox brings to life the world of late Roman antiquity, and one of its most compelling personalities: *Augustine* is a perfect alloy of great scholarship and great storytelling."

—Paula Fredriksen, author of *Augustine and the Jews: A Christian Defense of Jews and Judaism*

"In this new book on Augustine, Robin Lane Fox brings his customary wit, verve, and insight to bear on the record of a passionate and complicated man. Author and subject are well-matched, and readers can freshly savor Augustine's intelligence and ambition, as well as his depth and his devotion, as Lane Fox generously allows us to follow every move of the man whose conversions and conflicts sired most of the children of Western Christianity."

—Robin Young, Catholic University of America

"In this book, Robin Lane Fox weaves imaginative parallels with figures like Libanius, Ambrose, Jerome, Sinesius, and others into his telling of the story of Augustine from his youth to the time when he wrote the *Confessions*. Thus is a reader drawn into Augustine's life by giving wide-ranging attention to the classical context for the *Confessions* and to many of the questions that continue to be asked about that book. All thirteen books of the *Confessions* are treated, attending at length to aspects of Augustine's life that others barely touch."

—Allan Fitzgerald, OSA, Villanova University

"Robin Lane Fox's *Augustine* is a masterpiece. Here, Lane Fox erects in splendid prose his very own trinity by reading Augustine's *Confessions* in the company of two other ancient literary lions, the pagan rhetorician Libanius and the Christian Platonic philosopher and bishop Synesius, whose lives share what many have considered quintessential Augustinian qualities—conversions and autobiographical confessions. As a result, Augustine emerges fully as a man of his very own time, the later Roman empire, deeply formed from the beginning by the intellectual concerns of his day to which he formulated his own brilliant, unique, and lasting responses."

—Susanna Elm, professor of history,
University of California, Berkeley

Augustine

AUGUSTINE

Conversions to Confessions

Robin Lane Fox

BASIC BOOKS
New York

Basic Books
Hachette Book Group
1290 Avenue of the Americas, New York, NY 10104
www.basicbooks.com
Printed in the United States of America

First US edition published in 2015 by Basic Books, an imprint of Perseus Books, LLC, a subsidiary of Hachette Book Group, Inc.

First US paperback edition: October 2017

Library of Congress Control Number: 2015949890

ISBN: 978-0-465-02227-4 (hardcover)
ISBN: 978-0-465-06157-0 (e-book)

First UK edition published by Allen Lane,
an imprint of Penguin Books, Penguin Random House UK.

Typeset by Jouve (UK), Milton Keynes

ISBN 978-0-465-09385-4 (paperback)

LSC-C

10 9 8 7 6 5 4 3 2 1

IN MEMORIAM

Peter Carson
(1938–2013)

'SCRUTATORIS ACERRIMI'

'Hoc et illud ultra in aeternum'
Augustine, *Confessions VIII, 11.26*

Contents

PART IV

PART V

PART VI

List of Illustrations

Introduction

Augustine is the person about whom we know most in the ancient world. Sixteen hundred years later, he can still be followed in changing detail through his own voluminous writings. For that reason alone, he is a fascinating study, inexhaustible evidence for a world both like and unlike our own. It still amazes me that we can read the very words of himself and his debaters on exact days as far away as 13 November 386 or 28 August 392. The ancient world is suddenly very close to us.

Augustine is also a Christian and is immediate to many readers for that reason too. When I began this book, both the Pope and the Archbishop of Canterbury were distinguished scholars of his thought and context. I do not share their, or Augustine's, faith, but, like them, I am intrigued by his restless intelligence and his exceptional way with words. My greatest debt, therefore, is to Augustine, who is always articulate about himself and his beliefs. I have often wondered how he would write to me, belittling my worldly multiplicity, but failing, I think, to dislodge it.

Like many others across the world, I have been inspired and sustained in my interest in him by Peter Brown's superb biography, first published in 1967. As he is the first to realize, the continuing flood of modern studies and even, remarkably, some newly found evidence alter some of its viewpoints after nearly fifty years. He has outlined in a second edition how he would adjust to them and I have remained aware that he would have done so in ways which I am not even able to see. I have said less on guilt and more on mysticism and I have presented differently Augustine's relation to Neoplatonism and to a 'lost future' in his middle age. I have had the luxury of much more space, as my book stops with the *Confessions*. I have therefore given more attention to the disputed details of his conversions and much more to the next eleven years of his writings and actions before he began to confess. I have a different view of the immediate context of the *Confessions*, their genre and their length of composition. I also have more to say about the last three books, ones which perplex initial readers but which I have come to value most.

There are many fine short books on Augustine, from Marrou to

Chadwick, Trapé to Te Selle. I saw no reason to add another, so I opted for a long book, based on my own reading of all Augustine's surviving writings until September 397. I have deliberately minimized my use of his writings after that date, partly for a practical reason, my relative ignorance, partly because myopia has advantages, as he himself composed the *Confessions* without knowing what he would write later.

I have planned the book with a clear structure for which a musical analogy may be helpful. Throughout, it is composed as a biographical symphony whose theme is Augustine's life up to the age of forty-three. The first half, or movement, is mostly about conversions, with confessing as an undercurrent. The second half is mostly about confessing, with conversions now the undercurrent, his conversions of others rather than himself. Throughout, I allow pagan Libanius and Christian Synesius to play variations on some of the chords. Neither of them had Augustine's intelligence, but, behind their rhetoric and complex style, I have found myself sympathizing with each of them too, at least over what they present as the most important items in their lives.

Augustine is the subject of a yearly torrent of scholarship across the world. I owe it a debt which readers, I hope, will bear in mind throughout. The challenge is less to say something which has nowhere been said before than to decide what to believe and why and what to work into a new whole. I have been helped by many lifelong experts who have looked kindly on yet another Augustine book. Two visits to Villanova University and the kindness of Fr Allan Fitzgerald at its Augustinian Institute have been most helpful. So has much modern scholarship across Europe and America, in particular the incisive writings of Henry Chadwick, the detailed commentaries by the great expert J. J. O'Donnell and the French tradition, old and new. At every turn I have learned from its past masters, Aimé Solignac, Pierre Courcelle and Jean Pépin, more recently from Georges Folliet and above all Goulven Madec, whose cigarette, at least, I once lit, before receiving a terse answer to a question about Augustine's ideas about 'weight' and the soul. The exact writings of Martine Dulaey and the brilliant studies by Isabelle Bochet have continued to make me see much which I would otherwise have missed. Augustine's writings have long been scrutinized for allusions to the pagan classical authors, but although his use of Christian authors began very soon after his conversion, it has only recently been studied in similar detail. 'His learning is too often borrowed,' Gibbon slyly remarked in a note to his great *Decline and Fall*, 'his arguments, too often his own.' We are now better placed than

Gibbon to test this remark against Augustine's early years, thanks especially to the work of Dulaey, Bochet and Nello Cipriani.

In Britain, the expertise of Gillian Clark, Carol Harrison, G. J. P. O'Daly, Roger Tomlin and Neil McLynn has been invaluable, accompanied by the kindness of many colleagues across the world who have sent me articles, books and helpful references, including A.-I. Bouton Touboulic, John P. Kenney, Paula Fredriksen, Christoph Markschies, Sigrid Mratschek, Michael Williams, Jason BeDuhn, Frisbee C. Sheffield and Peter Brown. I am particularly grateful to those who have read and criticized all or part of the book. My American publisher, Lara Heimert, made penetrating comments on its shape and structure. My English publisher, Stuart Proffitt, read it with the closest attention to its phrasing and intellectual blind spots. Mark Edwards commented acutely on my chapters on the Platonists and Neil McLynn on the two about Rome and Milan. It is a special pleasure to me that Samuel Lieu found time to comment on the Manichaean chapters forty years after I read his important thesis on Mani and his mission in Asia which revived my interest in that subject. Sigrid Mratschek read the last six chapters with her exacting eye and tightened their contents with her unrivalled knowledge of the exchanges of letters between the protagonists. In Oxford, Matthieu Pignot has helped invaluably with the notation and correction of the text and has given me encouragement on many of its topics, especially Augustine's catechumenate, on which his research is particularly important. Jonathan Yates of Villanova University then read most of the book at short notice with kind patience and expert attention, a masterclass which has improved it in many ways. None of these readers would have written as I have, but I have responded carefully to what they have corrected and adjusted. Their own views of Augustine would often be different.

My fellow classicists tend either to be cool towards Augustine or else to be unsure what his confessions and conversions really are. I have written to be intelligible, whatever the reader's prior knowledge of the subject. The effort requires more exposition than a book written for hard-pressed scholars only. I have been helped on the way by many able Oxford pupils who were encountering this subject after the insights of Herodotus, Thucydides, Aristophanes, Plato and many others in the classical world which we love. Jonathan Fowles, Caroline Halliday, Michael Blaikley, Joshua Horden, Joseph Diwakar, Isabel Sunnucks and Christopher Micklem have all made me rethink some of my views, as has Ella Grunberger-Kirsh, while adding a dossier, fit for the modern social worker, on the case of Augustine, his mother, his home and the elusive Father with whom, he believed, he had briefly established contact.

A full bibliography of all that I have read for each chapter would make the book unwieldy. Instead, I have picked out a few studies on each one, emphasizing them in prefaces to the notes on each chapter so as to orient readers. In a general preface I have given the bibliographical aids which are most helpful, especially in this digital age. I am exceptionally grateful to Matthew Lloyd for his skilled and dedicated typing, a far cry from Iron Age Greece, and above all to Henry Mason for his meticulous typing, formatting and criticisms which have made this book possible. William Golightly began by encouraging me with early notes and Katie Hager continued, but here too I pay special thanks to Matthieu Pignot for checking my references to Augustine, especially in the second half of the book. I am extremely grateful to Eugene Ludwig and his fund at New College, Oxford, which made a grant to me for the costs of preparing the book with such excellent helpers. I would have liked to thank the Bodleian Library after its many years as my working home, but it is no longer a pleasure to work on patristic authors in it after the upheavals imposed in 2013 and the breaking by the former Librarian, Sarah Thomas, of the carefully planned link between pagan and Christian worlds which had underlain its lower reading rooms productively for many years. Research into Augustine now means crawling on hands and knees to find essential journals in a sub-basement. Recent major books on Augustine have gone unordered and I am especially grateful, therefore, to New College's Librarian, Naomi van Loo, and her skilled detection of essential books and articles elsewhere in Europe. She and Rebecca Hutchins have been typically helpful to me in many ways.

I first encountered Augustine on an April Sunday in 1966 in the then-unspoilt Tuscan town of San Gimignano while wallflowers tumbled in red and yellow down the medieval towers beside the small central square. My uncle, Christopher Loyd, had taken me and my sister there from Florence and, after lunch and my first encounter with brandy, showed us the Gozzoli frescoes of Augustine's life in S. Agostino. I owe a conversion to that enchanted day, to Italy and its art, which have remained a yearly part of my life. The cover image of this book is chosen as a tribute to it.

I
Confession and Conversion

I

At the end of the fourth century AD a man in his early forties began to compose an intimate prayer to God. What emerged from his hours of solitude was a long Latin text, half of which revisited 'what I once was', the sins and errors of his early years. He told of his thefts as a boy, his remarkable mother, his concubine, his membership of an outlawed religious group, his love of sex, his worldly aspirations. He then undertook to set out 'what I [now] am', but the autobiographical details disappeared. He reflected at length on the nature of memory and the sins which still tempted him, whether the pleasure of hearing praises of himself or his idle delight in watching a spider catch a fly. He then began a complex meditation on the first two chapters of the Book of Genesis and its story of Creation. He found hidden meanings beneath the surface of many of its verses. He reflected on eternity and discussed our awareness of time in an argument whose brilliance still impresses philosophers. After thirteen books, only nine of which discuss 'what I once was', he concluded with praises of the goodness of God and an expression of man's hope for future rest in heaven.

This work, the *Confessions*, is like none other before or since. It is a Christian masterpiece, but its spell has spread far beyond the Christian Church. Its author, Augustine, composed it as a newly appointed bishop in the north African city of Hippo. He had been born in November 354, the child of a pagan father and a Christian mother in what is now eastern Algeria but was then proconsular Africa under Roman rule. Like his family, the world into which he came was not predominantly Christian, even forty years or so after the Emperor Constantine's unexpected support for its Christian minority. Augustine was baptized at Easter, 387, in his thirty-third year and then lived on to share

Christians' hopes of a new Christian era, keenly anticipated in the closing years of the fourth century. In 397, when he started to compose his confessions, wandering Huns were invading Greece, but they lay far beyond the subject of his book. Thirteen years later he had to make sense of the unimaginable, the sack of Rome by barbarian invaders in 410, the city which had been described as 'eternal' by Virgil, the beloved poet of his youth. After twenty more years as a bishop, he confronted yet another crisis, the invasion of barbarian Vandals who crossed from Spain and besieged Hippo, the city of his Christian community. He died there in August 430 at a critical point in what is still regarded as the fall of the Roman Empire in the West. It was a change which he had never contemplated in his early life.

These worldly changes did not interrupt his awesome flow of writings. They range from treatises on Christian conduct to philosophical dialogues and works of abstract theology and polemic. More than 400 of his sermons survive, some of which would have lasted for at least two hours when delivered in church, but the survivors are barely a fourteenth of those which he preached, some 8,000 in all. We have nearly 300 of his letters, but they are only a fraction of those he exchanged with correspondents. Amazingly, ever more of his sermons and letters continue to be found, preserved in manuscripts in which later Christians copied his and other contemporaries' works: four of his sermons were discovered as recently as 2007.[1] Not since the first philosophers after Alexander had anyone written so many books, far exceeding the 'metrics' of the professors who now study them. They make the last forty-four years of Augustine's life the best-known in the ancient world.

Even so, the *Confessions* transform our knowledge of him, not least by revisiting his early years, from which nothing written by or about him survives. They contain autobiographical detail, but they are not an autobiography, as books on 'the self' or 'life-writing' still tend to classify them. From start to finish they are a prayer, addressed by Augustine to God, but intended to be overheard by readers.

This unusually lengthy prayer does not reveal how it was being composed: was it written or was it, perhaps, dictated? Some ten years before, Augustine had composed *Soliloquies*, a novel sort of dialogue between himself and his own Reason.[2] In it, Reason told him to write down his thinking and not to dictate it, because such intimate matters require 'solitude'. Most of the confessions address even more intimate matters: was Augustine still obeying Reason and writing his prayer?

Was he perhaps speed-writing it, as shorthand was a widely practised skill? In another work, Augustine described it as useful so long as it does not divert its users from God. He might perhaps have learned it as an aid to his former career as a public speaker. He even refers to his 'pen'. When he turns to analyse 'what I am', he tells God how he is wanting to 'do the truth' in his heart 'in Your presence, Lord', but 'in my pen, before many witnesses'. He is not confessing, he says, in 'words and voice of the flesh', but in 'words of the soul and in the cry of my thinking'. His prayer is 'silent in clamour, but calling out in emotion'.[3] Was he writing a silent shorthand version, to be passed on to a secretary for a longhand copy which he could check and revise?

These hints are not as decisive as they may appear. Augustine refers to what 'we have written', but in antiquity 'writing' could include dictation. He describes himself as praying 'with my mouth and pen', but the 'pen' may be metaphorical: it refers to our Psalm 45, whose psalmist describes his tongue as the 'pen of a scribe writing swiftly'.[4] When he refers to his prayer as 'silent in clamour' and composed in 'words of the soul', he may be referring only to its silent preliminary formation. These two stages are described by Augustine in his own sermons. 'I have thought out what I will say,' he tells a congregation, 'I would not speak unless I had previously composed in my mind.' The confessions' 'words of the soul' may allude to this first, inner stage, which has been well described as the 'silent, dry run'.[5] Like others in antiquity, he would then dictate the result to a copyist. Augustine was already a practised dictator of expositions of the Psalms or sermons in church which were taken down by shorthand secretaries. As a bishop, he had expert secretaries in his household.

If he was dictating his long prayer, would he be standing or perhaps sitting down? Augustine had discussed the correct position for prayer scarcely a year before beginning his confessions and concluded that there was no one answer. However, Christians often prayed on their knees with their hands held upwards or, in North Africa, out sideways: writing then became impossible.[6] If Augustine was kneeling while he prayed, he could have dictated the *Confessions* in pre-formed passages to a secretary in the room who was using shorthand.

An oral method of composition helps to explain why the *Confessions* are a joy to read, and above all to recite, even for those who find it easier to believe in style and words than in their intended audience, God. Their account of his early years resonates with words from the non-Christian poets and authors whom he was studying at that time.

These echoes charm modern classicists, but in the second half of the work they disappear when he leaves his non-Christian schooling behind. He then encounters Platonist philosophy and in due course builds one long sentence, an entire paragraph in our modern texts, around language of the philosopher who most influenced him.[7] Similar philosophic language abounds in his concluding meditation on the biblical Creation. His main resource, however, is his command of scriptural phrases, especially words from several psalms combined into one.[8] His aim was not to cite scripture, as the identifying notes and brackets in modern texts imply. He was praying, and he would not stop to look up the phrases which he used. His memory of them was not always word-perfect. He was praying, and they came as readily to his mind as poetic phrases or 'formulas' once came to Homer's. The great writings of antiquity may thus describe a circle across more than a thousand years. Homer composed by drawing on earlier oral poets' traditional phrases and in many scholars' opinion, including mine, by leaving an 'oral dictated text' of his poems. Augustine, I believe, composed by weaving scriptural phrases into a long prayer, the greatest oral dictated text of Latin prose.

Nobody had called a book 'Confessions' before, but in the Hebrew scriptures confessions of sins were already well represented. In Jerusalem, Ezra had prayed and made confession while weeping. He also called for the assembled 'men of Judah and Benjamin' to 'confess publicly' their sins to the Lord, their marriages to foreign women. They were prevented from confessing by heavy rain. The psalmists, meanwhile, confessed their sins and God's greatness, and, in the 'Greek age' after Alexander, even the legendary Jewish patriarchs were said to have confessed on their deathbeds. In fictional 'testaments', each one was presented as confessing his dominant sin, in Dan's case anger, in Simeon's jealousy, in Reuben's sexual temptation: 'concerning women', a male author made him say, 'the angel of the Lord has told and taught me, that women are overcome by fornication even more than men, and in their hearts, men are what they plot against'.[9] Even the scriptures' supreme royal idolater, King Manasseh, was made to confess, repent and praise the Lord Almighty in a fictional prayer. It fills half a page in the apocryphal section of modern Bibles, but in the early sixth century AD it was copied in red and purple letters at Hierapolis in ancient Phrygia (inland, in modern Turkey). Recently rediscovered in a small room, it had been copied so that the houseowner could call on God whenever he read it. 'Thou wilt save me that am unworthy, according to thy great mercy. And I will praise thee for ever, all the days of my life . . .' Augustine's confessions have a similar scope.[10]

In pagan texts too, confessions of misbehaviour are well attested. In Roman law a confession before a judge usually sufficed for the confessor to be sentenced without more ado. In the Hellenistic world it became a commonplace to confess that wrongdoing was only human: 'I'm a man, I did wrong . . .' Confessions to a god were not so frequent and were thought by philosophers to be a sign of excessive fear before a divinity. They looked more favourably on confessions by students of philosophy: in the small groups of Epicurus and his friends, *c.*300 BC, 'mutual confession was a way of . . . self-improvement between members of the beloved community', made to one another, not to God.[11] In Latin literature, confession to a god proliferates in the least likely place, Petronius' scandalous fiction, the *Satyricon*. Its narrator in the age of Nero (*c.*AD 60) has been aptly credited with 'confession-compulsion'. He even confesses in prayer to the sexual divinity Priapus: 'I come to you, pure and a suppliant . . . forgive me . . .' and then he specifies the animals which he will offer to Priapus in return. Inland in western Asia, in the Roman Imperial age, inscribed texts in Greek bear witness to a similar practice in real life. In villages in Lydia or Phrygia, people testified to their misdeeds, their punishment by a deity, and their offerings to propitiate them (including the little monument on which their words are inscribed). They conclude with praises of the god or goddess concerned. Loosely classified as 'confession-monuments', they have also been understood as 'inscribed monuments (*stelai*) of exaltation'.[12]

Augustine's confessions are quite different from these faraway pagan practices. Whereas Petronius' hero or people in Anatolia promised gifts to the gods who had punished them, Augustine praises God's gifts to himself (including punishment) and promises nothing material in return. His relationship to God is one of love and humility, not the practical reciprocity which typified pagans and their gods. For him, as for the Hebrew psalmists, confession had two aspects: a confession of sins and a 'testifying' to God's works and goodness. In pagan literature, such a two-sided confession is very rare, but it is exemplified, strikingly, by a Roman emperor. In 177/8, Marcus Aurelius added a first, prefatory book to the 'meditations' which he had addressed to himself. In it he looked back on his life in terms of the care which the gods had taken of it.[13] He thanked them for giving him virtues and a well-timed impulse to practise philosophy. He also thanked them for his not having 'made himself a man' before the due time, for having 'even postponed sexual relations for a while', for not having been brought up 'for too long with my grandfather's concubine' and for the fact that 'I did not touch either Benedicta or Theodotus', two unknowns whose names suggest a Jewish or even a Christian presence in the young Marcus' household. 'Even when I later took up erotic passions, I was soon cured of them.' Thanks and confession coexist here: 'the helping gods', the emperor writes, 'and Fortune are needed for all such things.' Two centuries later Augustine came to a similar conclusion, but by a very different route.

Augustine often mentions 'conversion', but what does he mean by it? Long before him, pagan Greeks and Romans had described conversions, but they were mostly conversions to philosophy and its accompanying way of life. Such a conversion had already been presented by Plato in his marvellous story of the darkened Cave, whose inhabitants could see only reflections of images being carried behind them. As they sat there, they even gave prizes to those who best recalled the reflections in the right order, the first 'Oscars' for judges of 'special effects' being projected onto the wall before them. When one member of the audience escaped to the world of sunlight beyond, it was such a 'change', or conversion, Plato tells us, that he no longer wished to return to the dark. Less dramatically, the philosopher Seneca could write to his friend Lucilius about his own progress. 'I realize I am not only being converted, but transformed . . . it is a sudden change and I want to share it.' It was expressed in short sayings, the Roman equivalents of 'thought for the day': for example, 'I am beginning to be a friend to myself.'[14]

In the Bible conversions proliferate, in the sense of turning exclusively to one God and away from all others. The Greek word for such a turning, *epistrophē*, occurs more than 550 times in the Greek translations of the Hebrew scriptures. In the Latin translations which Augustine used, the word became *conversio*.[15] Only in a Latin fiction did a pagan convert to the cult of a divinity and regard it as his one cult before all others. Even if Augustine perhaps knew this forerunner, the *Golden Ass* by a fellow north African, Apuleius, his confessions owed nothing to it. Unlike its fictional hero's conversion, his own occurred in real life. As many as fifteen conversions by other people are mentioned in his confessions' text. Conversions to one and only one God were happening all around him, as men and women converted to Christianity from pagan worship. They were also occurring within Christianity when individuals converted to a life of sexual and worldly renunciation.

The Latin word *conversio* had a more general scope. It could mean a re-turning to God by someone who had 'turned away' (*a-versio*). Literally, it could refer to the turning round of a congregation in church, as we learn from one of Augustine's most recently found sermons. Its hearers were told to 'turn', facing away, it would seem, from the apse and also, by analogy, to 'turn' to God in their own lives. Less familiarly for our English usage, *conversio* could refer to God's own 'turning' to His universe or to individuals in it. This sense, a turning 'towards' us by God, is the sense of the word *conversio* when it first occurs in the *Confessions*. In their concluding meditation on Genesis, turning, or *conversio*, is the first turning of formless matter, the basic constituent of the universe. It 'converts' away from dark chaos towards God's light.[16]

The *Confessions* are not merely what a highly intelligent man thought about God. They are about a turning from Him (*aversio*) and a turning towards Him (*conversio*) by Augustine, his friends and contemporaries and the universe during Creation. They are a prayer which no pagan could have produced and which no Christian, before or since, has equalled.

II

In older age Augustine reviewed his writings, usually in the chronological order in which he had begun them. The beginning of the *Confessions* can therefore be placed securely in the year 397. The date of their ending is more disputed, sometimes being placed as much as six years later. Augustine does not tell us why he began to confess only at that particular time. Some have linked his decision to his age, as if a man's early forties are a good time for him to review his past. Others link it to a sudden change in his theological outlook, causing him to rethink his previous life, or even to a 'spiritual crisis'. Something specific, surely, made him begin, although no one event can account for the passion which surges through the work. In my view, the *Confessions* are not the result of a sudden change in Augustine's view of God and man. Their roots can be traced back through the previous eleven years, especially the five years of his priesthood before he became a bishop. A 'biography' of the confessions, therefore, requires study of Augustine himself up to the point when they are finished. They are a prayer, I believe, which had long been waiting to happen, but which was touched off by quite other events in his life.

In the text, conversions soon become apparent, but their number and nature remain disputed. Some of Augustine's modern scholars have credited him with at least four, a conversion of the mind, the heart and so forth. Other estimates extend to as many as thirteen. Nonetheless, one of his greatest modern scholars, Goulven Madec, has doubted that Augustine ever converted at all.[17] Problems of definition are important here. A vocation is not necessarily a conversion, nor is a deeper understanding or newly gained knowledge. On a strong definition, which some dispute, a conversion requires a decisive change whereby we abandon a previous practice or belief and adopt exclusively a new one. It involves a 'turning which implies a consciousness that the old way was wrong and the new is right'.[18] This strong definition is the one I accept, but, unlike Madec, I do not restrict conversions to changes from one religion to another. Conversions are possible within one and the same religious commitment, as historians of early and medieval Christianity recognize. It is here that Augustine's most famous conversion belongs, but the process does not stop with himself. Before and after his own conversion, Augustine was also a committed converter of other people.

Biographers of his early life face a notorious problem. Only one remark about the young Augustine survives from anyone else, although it recalls him, significantly, 'converting'. For a critical biography of him, his one-sided evidence would be a fatal obstacle, but for a biography of the *Confessions*, it is less of a problem. When they are built up from the past, it is only from the past which they choose to set before God and their readers. There may also be silences: some of them can be identified and filled from his other writings, but others necessarily elude us. A more tractable problem is the vividness of the language in which Augustine recalls and lays his past before God. Modern readers find it hard to remember that much of it may have been less startling in the context of its time. I will therefore present it against two near-contemporaries' lives. My aim is not to write a biography of all three persons, but to place Augustine, with the *Confessions* in his hand, as the central panel of a triple set of sketches, like a triptych on a medieval Christian altar. On the left side stands a sketch of his older contemporary Libanius, casting a look of profound disapproval up at Augustine, not least because he himself was a pagan and a committed Greek teacher, one who detested Latin and the technical skill of shorthand. On the right side, looking up with tempered adoration, is a sketch of his younger Greek-speaking contemporary Synesius, a Christian, a bishop and a fellow lover of philosophy. He would, I believe, have appreciated many of Augustine's writings between his conversion and his confessions, had he been able to read Augustine's Latin.

We have no idea of the physical appearance of these three men. My sketches are based only on their writings, which present a limited, but carefully crafted, impression of them as individuals. Libanius was born in 314 in the Greek-speaking mega-city of Antioch in Syria. Like the young Augustine, he devoted his life to the practice and teaching of oratory. He taught only in Greek. Sixty-four of his speeches survive, and were characterized by Edward Gibbon as the 'vain and idle compositions of an orator . . . whose mind, regardless of his contemporaries, was incessantly fixed on the Trojan War'.[19] Gibbon's judgement was misplaced. Libanius also addressed contemporary events and emperors and spoke up constantly for ethical values. He was the devoted champion of Greek culture and his own pupils, supporting them in abundant letters, 1,607 of which survive. His career reminds us of what Augustine, if unconverted, might have remained. Above all, Libanius has left his reflections on his own life, cast as a long speech. When first delivered, it concluded with the events of his sixtieth year. He, too, recited it, but not in solitude to God: he addressed it to select audiences, in my view including ex-pupils, probably in a lecture-room. Over time he added yet more to it. Gibbon dismissed this work as a 'vain, prolix, but curious narrative', but in pagan literature it is most unusual. Its account of Libanius' earlier life is a pagan counterpart to Augustine's Christian account in his confessions of 'what I once was'. Both authors write with great style about selected items in their past, from childhood onwards, and both reflect on their divine guidance, but they leave us with the same intriguing question: why ever did they suddenly decide to speak at such length about themselves?

Synesius, the youngest of the three, was born in Libya in the ancient city of Cyrene, probably in 374. Like Libanius, he wrote only in Greek. Although he never wrote his life, nor anything like the *Confessions*, he wrote a text, very different from Augustine's, which addressed the topic of conversion. He also left nine hymns and 156 letters, some of which were composed just before Augustine began to confess. Like Augustine, he was schooled in a demanding, classicizing style: it enabled his letters to live on as literary models in Byzantium for the next thousand years. Like Augustine, he became a fervent student of philosophy, but, unlike Augustine, he expressed it in hymns which he composed in complex, traditional metres. His subsequent life as a bishop then lights up, by contrast, the aspect of Augustine's life which neither he nor Libanius attempted: celibacy among 'brethren'. One of his letters then reviews aspects of his past life and his aspirations for the future: why did he, too, compose and circulate such a personal text?

The lives of Libanius and Synesius do not overlap with all of Augustine's early career, but they help to bring out aspects of it, his social class and the demands which it imposed on him, the pressures of his schooling and his worldly ambitions, his relations with close family members and the ideals of friendship which he projected onto those around him. Like Augustine, Libanius and Synesius write about ascents to a divine presence. More mundanely, they illustrate the social perils of travel abroad to great cities, followed by a return, like Augustine's, to a home town. They address their own and others' sexual lives in ways which contrast with Augustine's. They also illumine the bitterness which appointments to prominent jobs could ignite, especially, as ever, in a Christian church.

None of the three men ever met, except in later fiction, where each has had a notable after-life. In his florid novel *Hypatia*, Charles Kingsley (author of *The Water Babies*) made Synesius meet Augustine in Libya in the context of a hunting party, complete with the hounds which Synesius loved.[20] Here, Augustine was imagined impossibly far from home across an intervening desert, but was described as impressing Synesius and his companions nonetheless: 'Resolve, gentle but unbending, was expressed in his thin close-set lips and his clear quiet eye; but the calm of his mighty countenance was the calm of a worn-out volcano . . .' The Anglican hymn book still contains one of Synesius' hymns ('Rise up, my soul'). His most recent reappearance has been as the devoted pupil of his female teacher, Hypatia, in Alejandro Amenábar's film *Agora*.

Libanius' main fictional after-life has been owed to Gore Vidal. In his fictional *Julian*, Vidal used Libanius as one of the two main commentators on the Emperor Julian's unpublished memoir. 'My memory plays me odd tricks these days,' his Libanius complains. 'Even worse, I tend to mislay the notes I jot down as reminders, or (terrible confession!) when I do find them, I am often unable to decipher my own handwriting. Age spares us nothing, old friend. Like ancient trees, we die from the top.'[21]

Augustine, likewise, has continued to have a fictional life, in Catholic films of his biography and recently through Jérôme Ferrari's *Le Sermon sur la chute de Rome*, the winner in 2012 of France's major literary prize, the Prix Goncourt. He has even been made the subject of a fictional memoir from his concubine, who bore him a son but whom he dismissed after fourteen years together. His serious after-life has had a different scale and depth. His thinking and writing were to become rooted in Western Christianity, to a degree which would certainly surprise him. He formalized his values for a Christian community in a written Rule, one which still guides members of Augustinian monastic Orders throughout the world. His new genre, 'Confessions', continued to find notable followers, whether St Patrick in Ireland, Rousseau in France, or the modern novelist William Boyd. Above all, there is also Tolstoy, who published his *Confession* (in the singular) in 1884. He shows no awareness of Augustine either in its text or in his previous life. Nonetheless, a convert himself in older age and a master-novelist of conversion in his fictions, he covers ground in his *Confession* much like some of Augustine's, as he proceeds through an early life of 'dissipation' to an engagement with philosophers and abstract thinkers and an increasing sense of the worthlessness of his social milieu and its participants, who in Tolstoy's opinion were 'parasites'.

Admirers of the *Confessions* include Petrarch and Pascal, the poets George Herbert and John Donne, the mystical Teresa of Ávila, the Catholic convert and thinker John Henry Newman and the philosopher Ludwig Wittgenstein. Petrarch was given a copy by a friar in 1337 and kept it as his constant companion. He even considered writing confessions of his own. In 1347, he began writing his *Secretum*, in which a fictional 'Augustine' reproaches a fictional sinner who is modelled on Petrarch himself. He ends by rebuking him for 'love for a woman' and 'glory', two of the main temptations which Augustine had confronted.[22] There is a greater depth in Wittgenstein's engagement with the book. He first met it in 1919 through a fellow Austrian prisoner of war in Italy. He alludes fourteen times to Augustine and the *Confessions* in his subsequent writings and uses a quotation from them as the preface to his Philosophical Observations. He considered the *Confessions* to be perhaps 'the most serious book ever written'. There is an affinity of temperament between Augustine and Wittgenstein's own paradoxical questioning of accepted opinion and his belief that, in order to understand, 'the edifice of your pride has to be dismantled. And that is terribly hard work.'[23]

In the twenty-first century, most readers turn to psychology, not philosophy, to assess Augustine's presentation of 'what I once was' and 'what I now am'. Explicitly, Augustine analyses his own self, but it is he who puts questions to himself. We cannot transpose this self-scrutiny into a clinical study as a modern psychoanalyst would recognize one. Our relationship with him cannot develop dynamically through his responses to our continuing questions. Nonetheless, therapy is an idea which Augustine fully embraces. He refers frankly to the therapists, two of them, who 'heal' him. He is aware of their love, his dependence on it, and his 'transference' onto them and their mercy. They are costing him nothing: they are God and Christ. He addresses his analysis to them, although they know it all already, so that its readers, he hopes, will be stirred to a similar love. Just as he intended, he indeed causes us to reflect on ourselves. 'He saw his own story as that of Everyman,' one of his great modern scholars, John O'Meara, first observed, but there is no ordinary limit to the extraordinary range of his mind. Readers have credited him with discoveries about the human personality, with a 'discovery of the self', that hardy perennial, or a discovery of the will, though not unique to him, or even of the unconscious mind very long before Freud. Above all, Augustine is a human being, constituted exactly like you or I. He is intensely introspective, but, in fascinating ways, his understanding of himself and his constituent parts is no longer ours.

After sixteen hundred years, a post-Christian age has begun to wonder if we have finally 'finished with' Augustine's ideas. His confessions of sins, he himself tells us, 'rouse the heart and stop it sleeping in despair and saying, "I cannot"'. He hoped to encourage Christian readers to share his high ideals, but even those who do not share them and whose hearts say 'I cannot' are still moved to think, 'Why not?' We will never finish with his confessions because they will not finish with us.

2
Worldly Ambitions

I

'You have made us for Yourself,' Augustine tells God at the beginning of his confessional prayer, 'and our heart is restless until it rests in You.' He calls on God as 'always active, always in repose', but he admits that he can never know Him adequately. 'Do not hide Your face from me,' he prays, 'let me die . . . so that I may see it.' In the Bible, God tells Moses that to see Him is to die, but Augustine says that he will die if he fails to see God. From the start, therefore, he expresses a mystical aim.[1] Around him in his fourth-century world there were many thousands who had never considered this diagnosis of restlessness or expressed this fervent hope. Augustine needs to be considered briefly against their worldly context, one which his confessions dismiss as pride and wretchedness but which formed him in his youth and continued to surround him in later life.

He was born in November 354 in the little town of Thagaste, now Souk el Ahras in modern Algeria. For more than 500 years Thagaste had been under Roman rule, belonging to a common Mediterranean culture which stretched along north Africa's coast and linked it to nearby Italy in a way which we no longer imagine to be possible for what has become a Muslim region. Thagaste belonged administratively to the province of proconsular Africa, which included much of what is now north Tunisia, including the great city of Carthage 175 miles away on the Mediterranean coast. Carthage was the Roman governor's seat and Latin was the language of its educated classes and also those in the province's main towns. Latin-speaking Thagaste had a pre-Roman name, but it proudly used the title of 'municipality' (*municipium*). It was a status originally conferred by the Romans on towns whose upper class of magistrates, and sometimes councillors, thereby received the privilege of Roman citizenship. By the fourth century AD, Roman citizenship was common to all inhabitants of the Roman provinces and *municipia* had lost their former privileges. Nonetheless, Thagaste maintained its title as a mark of honoured status.

Proconsular Africa's prosperity was still evident in the fourth century, suggesting no imminent decline or fall. Its abundant olive oil and grain were still being shipped overseas in mass-produced containers. In the province itself, local surveys confirm that olive trees and olive presses extended way beyond the modern zones of cultivation.[2] Unlike Synesius in southern Libya, Augustine never lived or travelled in a landscape dominated by deserts: he happens never to mention a camel in Africa. Rather, it was through the sales of grain and olives and the rents from their owners' landholdings that the buildings and amenities of towns like Thagaste were financed. Augustine's corner of north Africa was thickly dotted with such towns, some 160 being known to us in proconsular Africa alone. In the 350s, the more westerly parts of north Africa had been troubled by invaders from the south, but Augustine's region had not been affected. In his youth, he was not living in a province in crisis, let alone one which was 'waiting for the barbarian'.

In Thagaste and the other towns around him, civic life depended on a donor-culture. A few rich notables paid for the buildings, shows and festivities which were enjoyed by crowds so much less fortunate than themselves. Some of Augustine's writings are excellent witnesses to their lifestyle, especially a philosophical dialogue which he dedicated to Romanianus, Thagaste's richest local benefactor and his own patron in early life. In it, he imagines the likes of Romanianus at the height of their public careers, putting on 'shows never seen before' in the amphitheatre, including bloodsports with those African rarities, wild bears. Their names would be listed in 'municipal tablets', where they would be accompanied by the details of each honour in their career. As the 'patrons' of Thagaste and neighbouring towns, they would uphold their interests with Roman governors and officials. The crowds would acclaim them as 'philanthropic' and 'generous' in return for the shows they financed. In a recently found sermon Augustine deplores lavish donors who 'refuse to break bread for Christ and yet leave hardly any bread for their sons', having bankrupted their families by their extravagant displays.[3]

These shows included gladiatorial combats long after Christian emperors' laws had supposedly banned them. The settings for them were the games which were still given in big cities by the *sacerdotales*, the holders of non-Christian 'priesthoods' in honour of the ruling emperors, as if the pagan worship of emperors had continued in the Christian Empire of Constantine and his sons. It continued only because Christian intervention had ensured that the honours no longer involved the offering of animal victims to the emperors as divine beings.[4]

Augustine refers Romanianus to the mosaic floors in grand people's houses, and indeed they are our most vivid evidence of their worldly culture. They show symbols of the circus arena and its beloved chariot racing; they depict teams of horses captioned fondly with their individual names; they outline scenes of hunting, both in nature and in the enclosed spaces of the cities' amphitheatres. In the great city of Carthage, big mosaics in town houses gave a splendid, but stylized, impression of the country life which their owners enjoyed in large 'second homes' on their rural estates. The finest such scenes adorned a floor in the house of one Lord Julius, shown in mosaic with the domed roofs of its private baths. Hunters set out for a day's sport: Julius rides to his house in grand official dress. Items from each of the four seasons are offered to him and his wife. Roses and jewellery are brought by servants to Her Ladyship; grapes and a hare are presented to Lord Julius and he is handed a scroll inscribed with his initials, ensuring that viewers will recognize him.[5]

These mosaics do not show country life or landscape for their own sake. Always they relate them to rich landowners and their families, the mosaicists' patrons. On some of them, hunters and horsemen appear against pillared loggias and big fortified houses set in country estates. Towers are shown on either edge of the houses' high facades, pierced by windows or balconies for the rooms on the first floor. In Libya, Synesius grew up in, and later owned, such a towered country home, locatable near Balagrae in the hills about ten miles from Cyrene. His family had another, close to the sea nearby, in which his brother later lived. These big rural houses were centres of an alternative world to urban Cyrene, one which Synesius relished. One such house existed near Thagaste, but it was owned by a family of absentee landlords who controlled entire villages in the country beyond the town and belonged in the highest social circles of the Roman Senate.[6] Augustine's family were not at all of this class. Augustine later refers to his family's 'poor little fields' and also calls his background 'poor' or 'modest' in a sermon in which he wished to emphasize his relative lack of riches. In fact, Patricius, Augustine's father, and his family had enough property to rank as town councillors, a status, however, for which as little as twenty acres sufficed. Their resources were poor when compared with the likes of Romanianus, but not poor in terms of most of Thagaste's other inhabitants: later in life, Augustine implies they amounted to as much as a twentieth of the income of the church in Hippo, his coastal city as bishop.[7] However, service as a councillor brought expensive public obligations and Augustine's family, like many lesser councillors, would find them a burden.

Promptly after his conversion and then for the rest of his life, Augustine belittles worldly splendour and ambition. He regards it as evidence of 'pride', the root of sin, and as a diversion of the soul to fleeting and unsatisfactory pleasures. Status mattered nonetheless, and complex legal categories marked out those around him under Roman rule, as his own letters well exemplify. Some of the most recently found reveal that slave-dealers still existed in north Africa and drew on powerful backers in urban society. They would buy children for a period of years and sell them on into slavery abroad, a contract to which the children's parents consented. One town councillor is described by Augustine as 'comfortably off', but was 'so excited', Augustine comments, 'by the fervour of this pestilential practice' that he even sold his wife.[8] At every social level the legal treatment of individuals varied according to social class, and there was explicitly 'one law for the rich, another for the poor'. The 'humble' free could be flogged, tortured and executed under Roman law, whereas 'the more respectable' were supposed to be exempted from the most extreme types of maltreatment and 'enhanced interrogation techniques'. Yet, nobody was entirely secure, as Libanius and Synesius well attest, deploring the flogging, torture and executions which governors might inflict even on members of their own upper class. As a Christian bishop Augustine spoke and wrote firmly against the practice of torture irrespective of the victim's social standing. He was also an opponent of capital punishment, the governors' prerogative.[9]

Libanius and Synesius both belonged among the big benefactors of their home cities, the Romanianuses of the Greek world. If they had ever met Augustine and his mother, they would have considered them decidedly common. In Antioch, Libanius' family had had many generations of important councillors, lessened only by early deaths or losses of property in times of political turmoil, losses which had been especially severe in his grandfather's generation.[10] Synesius' family history was not so turbulent. He traced his ancestry back to the first Greek founders of his native Cyrene a thousand years before, and beyond them, to supposed links with ancient Sparta. He was a truly local aristocrat.[11]

The two men's home cities, Cyrene and Antioch, were very different from Thagaste. They were predominantly Greek-speaking, and Synesius' Cyrene was much the most ancient. In mid-career, Synesius described it as if it was an impoverished ruin, and although he was pleading for benefactions from the emperor, his comments were not made without reason. On its limestone plateau, inland from the sea, Libyan Cyrene had been a frequent victim of local earthquakes, especially a big one in 365 to which a decline of its main temples and public buildings should probably be traced. The best-excavated big house in the city's plan is the house of a certain Hesychius, a prestigious 'Libyarch', quite possibly the Hesychius who was Synesius' father. It has Christian inscriptions among its decoration and befits his high birth, but, after a peak in the mid-fourth century, it seems to have declined during Synesius' adult lifetime, perhaps because of the earthquakes.[12] However, the civic spirit of Cyrene's leading families was not extinguished. In schools in the city, there were still teachers who could make Synesius write literary prose and learn to compose verse in the difficult metres used by lyric poets in the remote Greek past. His letters confirm that when he grew up, councillors in Cyrene were still capable of funding the shows and horse races for which the city had long been famous.

Libanius' Antioch in north Syria was a very different place. Three hundred years younger than Cyrene, it had become one of the empire's biggest cities, with a population in Libanius' lifetime which is estimated at perhaps 150,000.[13] With this status came political dangers, as never in Augustine's Thagaste. From the 350s onwards, it was the scene of recurrent political crises which were a terror to its upper class, including Libanius' own family. They are the background to much that his autobiographical speech discreetly avoids saying. As Antioch stood open to the eastern trade and travel routes of the nearby Persian empire, it was the natural base for Roman armies, commanders and emperors on their eastern campaigns. Libanius refers euphemistically to the clamour caused by their presence, the troops, the horses and the camels who flooded in 'like rivers flowing to the sea', the shields and weapons which covered the walls, the 'clash of arms, men bustling around, and horses neighing'.[14] Unlike Cyrene, let alone Thagaste, Antioch was a seat of governors, generals and their staffs, bringing hundreds of ambitious outsiders into its orbit. Antioch held the honorary Latin title of *colonia*. It was a grander title than 'municipal' Thagaste's, but Libanius, the champion of Greek culture, never mentions this Latin distinction in his writings.

Unlike Thagaste's, Antioch's straight streets were dignified by colonnades and were so long that residents needed a carriage to travel down them in comfort: they 'ran like rivers in flood', said Libanius 'with alleys leading off them like streams'. They were even lit by street lamps, whose olive oil was provided by the adjoining property-owners as a civic obligation, one which fell on widows and orphans too.[15] The city's regular plan is still visible in modern Antakya, but it included an island, now silted over, on the city's main river which reflected the new Imperial age and its religion. Joined by bridges to the main streets, it was the site of the emperor's palace, a big hippodrome for horse racing and the great Octagonal Church, which had been begun by the first Christian emperor, Constantine. Libanius, a traditional pagan, never mentions this church, either, in his orations.

Instead, his letters give a vivid picture of the pressures on the city's councillors. They were ranked according to three grades of eminence and, as in Thagaste, they differed widely in property and assets. The plight of the most 'modest', people like Augustine's family, is graphically presented by Libanius as they struggled to meet the expensive duties imposed on them and the dreadful duty of collecting tax from their fellow citizens. The number of councillors decreased in his lifetime to as few as sixty active members, far fewer than the former, ideal number of 600.[16] Those in the lower ranks could only envy the life of the richest members, for which the sunniest evidence survives, once again, in their house-mosaics. Their imagery of the four seasons in harmony idealizes Antioch's climate and pleasant hillsides. Their imagery of water relates to Antioch's fortunate assets, the River Orontes and the many springs on the nearby hills. The most famous of the big mosaics dates from the mid to later fifth century and shows the central figure of *Megalopsychia*, the Greeks' 'Generosity of Spirit', holding a basket in her left hand and distributing items from it with her upraised right hand. When first published, the items were wrongly considered to be roses. In fact, they are coins, positively jumping off her right hand as a largesse for the onlookers.[17] 'Generosity' is accompanied by images of captioned hunters who are attacking various wild animals. The reference is to the generosity of a donor who gives freely to pay for shows of animal bloodsports in Antioch's public arena.

High-principled Christians abominated these shows, as Augustine eventually did too, but disapproval was not a Christian monopoly. Pagan Libanius also avoided them from his youth onwards. However, unlike Augustine, he never deplored the ideals which their donors publicized. 'Generosity of Spirit' is repeatedly cited as a virtue in his civic speeches.[18] It is exactly similar to the generosity which Augustine belittles when addressing his patron Romanianus. In Antioch, the scope for it was much greater and the crowds of spectators much bigger. The city had its own athletic Olympics and teemed with bath-houses whose mosaics cheerily included the abstract female image of 'Joy'. In real life the heavy costs of heating such baths fell on the councillors as a far from joyful obligation. In Antioch, actors and dancers flourished and in Libanius' speeches we have the best prose description in all Greek literature of the pleasures and sexual temptations of a Greek *symposion*, or male drinking party, held on couches for the participating drinkers.[19]

The city's crowning glory was the enormous hippodrome next to the Imperial residence. The intense rivalry of its chariot races has recently been dramatized for us by an inscribed tablet, discovered in the very drain beside one of the racecourse's two turning points. The bend was a supreme danger-point for the chariot-drivers. The text invoked disaster on every single horse, name by name, in the teams which were to be entered by the Blue racing-faction. Strikingly, the divinities named in the curse are all pagan, ranging from Poseidon the horse-god to the shady figure of the goddess Hecate.[20]

On an evening before the races somebody had crept out and buried this deadly appeal to the ancient gods at the very point where the chariots whom it cursed would be most at risk. The text may even originate from Libanius' own lifetime, although its publishers have suggested a later date in the mid-fifth century. In Christian rhetoric the hippodrome was execrated as the 'Satanodrome', and this tablet reminds us why. As the race days approached, sorcerers and astrologers were active for and against each competing team. They tried to mobilize the pagan gods against their rivals and to summon them to their own defence because those rivals would be using similar spells. The races were run in an atmosphere heavy with spells and counter-spells, complicating the betting which they elicited.

When the young Augustine went off to study in Carthage, he encountered occasions of a similar scale. In Carthage, similar curse-texts have been discovered, naming and cursing every single horse in the opposing competitors' team. 'Tie down their running, power, spirit, impetus, speed,' one such spell prescribes, 'take victory from them, impede their feet, hamstring them, cut their muscles so that tomorrow in the hippodrome they cannot run, walk or come out of the starting gates.'[21] In Carthage too, horses with names like Zephyr, Dareios or Victor had to struggle against the supernatural odds before as many as 80,000 spectators on the major race days.

While teaching rhetoric, like Libanius, young Augustine already deplored the misplaced vanity and striving of the races, but accepted that the power of the spells and sorcery was real: he merely ascribed it to non-Christian demons. Under their unseen presence vastly more people watched the horses in Carthage and Antioch than would ever hear his sermons, let alone read a word of his confessions. Happy in their restlessness, they would look on his exalted ideas of rest and happiness as decidedly unpersuasive.

II

While he confesses to God, Augustine also addresses a human audience, people whom he calls 'slaves of God, my brothers', who 'rejoice on account of me when they approve me, but grieve together for me when they disapprove'.[22] They are Christians like Augustine, aspiring or actual celibates, and are called 'brethren'. He is not consciously addressing women, half of the human race, although the most prominent human presence in the *Confessions*' first nine books is a woman: his mother. He is not writing a critical social history, either, and so he refers only in passing to people of a lower social background than himself.

Most of Libanius' voluminous letters and speeches are even more narrowly focused. They refer by name only to some 720 adults in all Antioch, about 0.25 per cent of the population. Almost all of them are people of rank or power, city councillors, people too grand for council service, and powerful people in the Roman hierarchy, military men, governors and officials from the emperor's court. On two famous occasions, Libanius indeed addressed the plight of prisoners and victims of torture, but we can best supplement the social myopia of his writings from the sermons of one of his former pupils, Antioch's bishop in the 360s, John Chrysostom ('Golden Mouth'). He gives us his impression of the city's general social order: 'one tenth,' he states, 'were poor who had nothing' and four-fifths were 'middling', the band, surely, into which Augustine's family fitted.

Libanius and his Christian pupil John cast very different eyes on the poorest 'tenth'.[23] Libanius' most detailed reference to them is in a short speech which he addressed as if to his students and intended to be paradoxical. 'Yesterday evening,' he claims, 'someone was pained . . . while counting the beggars', some of whom were 'standing, some not able to do even that, some not even able to sit . . . while some were more emaciated than the dead'.[24] The onlooker was saying that it was 'piteous' that these people were dressed in rags or nothing at all in such cold, while from each passer-by they 'implored repeatedly "Give us something"'. Meanwhile, others passed by on their way from the baths to dinner, lit by torches and having everything 'except heavenly ambrosia and nectar'. 'How happy they are,' Libanius' man in the street remarked, and then described these rich men's gold 'which produces ever more gold too'. To tease his hearers and readers, Libanius went on to argue that among this golden minority were people who were 'even more pitiable' than those who 'extend their hand as beggars all day'. At least there was always someone to give something to the beggars, and as beggars they enjoyed one great relief: no judge in this world or the next would bother them for their accounts. Among the rich, by contrast, there were people who had prospered from ill-gotten gains and risked being called to account for them. Such people were 'even more worthy of pity than the poor, even if the poor swear on oath they are dying of hunger'.

On occasion, Libanius was capable of intervening humanely for people outside his own social class. He was not the only pagan in Antioch to do so: monthly contributions to the destitute, he tells us, were made by shopkeepers in the city. Nevertheless, thanks to his schooling and high social position, he could be unashamedly 'incorrect' in what he wrote about the rich and poor. No Christian would have dared to float such paradoxes in public, least of all John Chrysostom or the adult Augustine. Where Libanius represented people 'happily' starving, John saw the very image of Christ present among the ranks of Antioch's poor.[25] He was present there, appealing for much-needed charity, as John's sermons emphasized. Conditions were no different in the streets or around the churches of Augustine's north Africa. At least a fifth of his sermons characterize the plight of the poor in similarly bleak terms and contain encouragements to give them alms. In winter, during Lent and at major Church festivals, his appeals for such help are most frequent. His most recently found sermons include three which were grouped together in the library collection of his church at Hippo under the title 'alms-giving'. They stress that the intention with which the act is done matters more than the act itself. One of them answers some decidedly narrow-minded Christians, people who argued that alms should not be given to sinners and supported their case with words of scripture (Ecclus. 12.4–6). Augustine insisted in reply that alms should be given to anyone in need, because they are fellow humans.

In the *Confessions*, his only reference to poor people is to a drunken beggar in Milan whose apparently carefree manner made him reflect on his own careworn existence as an orator at the Imperial court. This paradox reminds us that his literary training had included moralizing similar to Libanius', whose profession he was following at the time.[26] In later life, however, his Christian appeals for charity and his uses of it are differently motivated. By giving gifts, Christian givers would 'lay up treasure in heaven', helping the poor, who were their equals in God's eyes. There were good social reasons for the appeal of the Christian churches in the towns around Augustine and elsewhere.

In Antioch or Carthage, when contemporaries referred to the poorest tenth in society, they may not even have been considering the ultimate non-possessors: slaves. They were regarded as human objects whom free persons bought and sold, whipped and used for casual sex. They were still ubiquitous, as late Roman laws and Augustine's own writings show. In Augustine's youth, slavery was still conspicuous on north African farms and in households of quite modest riches, including his own family's. A few of these slaves might rise to control slaves beneath them, like a pyramid, and, as ever, there were problems caused by sex across social boundaries: what was the status of a child who had one slave parent, especially if the mother was a free woman who had mated with a slave?[27] However, no mainstream thinker ever proposed slavery's abolition in antiquity. Our three protagonists accepted it, while discussing it and reacting to it in different ways.

Once again, deploying his education, Libanius explored a paradox which was far from unprecedented among free, cultured men: masters are 'enslaved' too, to their anxieties and desires, and cannot fully control their own lives. Slave ownership is such a bother to the master, as it is he who has to bury his slaves. How wisely one slaveowner used to say, 'There is only one slave in this house: the master.'[28] It was enjoyable for masters to hear, but outrageously untrue. Yet, Christians could also be hard-headed about slaves, their equals before God.[29] When one of the slaves of Synesius' sister ran away and took up with another master, he wrote to a close friend and professed that he himself, as a lover of philosophy, would of course rise above this loss. It was better to be rid of a 'bad' sort. However, the slave was not strictly his own and so, after professing the philosophy which his friend shared, he commended to him the slave-catcher whom he was sending with his letter. He had promised that his friend would give this volunteer every assistance. He even named the runaway's new master and whereabouts so that his friend would intervene. He himself, he then explains, is always on the closest terms with the slaves who have been brought up with him. This desertion was all a 'bad' slave's fault, one who had been carelessly brought up, he said, and could not tolerate a fine old 'Spartan' and philosophical education. Despite Synesius' disclaimers about 'philosophy' and his stress on his own humanity to 'good' slaves, he was writing to reclaim his sister's runaway in the most practical way.

In Augustine's view, slavery was not 'natural', as Aristotle and others had once tried to argue: it had not existed in Paradise. It was, however, 'just'. It was God's just punishment, visited on all Adam's descendants for his sin in the garden of Eden.[30] Augustine was not an abolitionist, but he was not blind to the individual suffering which slavery could cause. As a bishop he would use his church's funds to buy the freedom of slaves with especially harsh masters. It was hard to overlook them, because the cities and towns were socially stratified to a degree which would appal us nowadays. So would the constant cull of childbirth and the early age of girls at marriage, at least in prosperous households: Augustine was not exceptional in becoming engaged to a girl aged ten or eleven and intending to marry her when she first became fertile.

Among their social diversity, Antioch, Cyrene and Thagaste and their surrounds were linguistically diverse too. Aramaic was a widely spoken language in Antioch and its countryside, but Libanius refers to it only once. When he calls someone 'Syrian', he means they are an inhabitant of the Roman province of Syria, not that they are ethnically Syrian rather than Greek. In Antioch, Latin was the language of the governors, soldiers, generals and the many others in Imperial service or with aspirations to join it. Unimpressed by it, Libanius presents the permanent appointment of a Latin professor in the city as a catastrophe. His own cultural horizons are magnificently Greek.[31]

At school, the Latin-speaking Augustine was taught Greek, although he did not take kindly to it. Others in proconsular Africa spoke a different language, what Latin-speaking onlookers called 'Punic'. It was a

Semitic language with its own script which derived from settlers who had come from the Levant to the north African coast in the eighth century BC. Augustine never calls it 'barbarian'. Punic was used in the harbour town of Hippo, itself an old Phoenician foundation, where Augustine was to serve as priest, then as bishop for more than thirty years. In a sermon, he notes that Punic was the language of farmworkers in rural areas of Numidia, including those in his own diocese. Augustine was hindered by a lack of Punic-speaking clergy to serve in these rural areas, as one of his recently discovered letters makes all too clear. He never spoke it, but his writings show that he at least knew some Punic words. Recent studies conclude that his knowledge was slightly greater than previously thought.[32]

When Augustine refers to 'the Libyan tongue', the reference is always to Punic. In some of north Africa's inscriptions we meet another language, what we call 'Libyan'. For us, 'Libyan' is a language attested just to the east of Hippo in the wooded and mountainous district of La Cheffia, where truly Libyan inscriptions are found, although sometimes accompanied by a Latin text.[33] Historians now ascribe it to inhabitants of north Africa before any Greek-, Punic- or Latin-speakers arrived among them. Augustine is aware of it in general terms but he is not interested in its details. It is tempting for us to identify this 'Libyan' with the language of the people who are still known as Berbers, the post-Roman name for them in north Africa. A direct continuity is not proven and, in the context of Augustine's own life, the later term 'Berber' is better avoided. He was conscious of his identity as an *Afer* or 'African', but like Libanius' 'Syrian', it was used by him in a regional, not an ethnic, sense.[34]

III

The religion around Augustine, Synesius and Libanius was no less diverse than the language. Libanius, a staunch pagan, writes as if Antioch was overwhelmingly pagan, but we know from the writings of its bishop, John Chrysostom, and the city's many churches that the Christian presence was extremely strong throughout his lifetime. Augustine's texts are less one-sided. They show us from time to time that pagan cults, temples and philosophy were still significant in north Africa even ninety years after the Emperor Constantine's support for the Christian Church. In Augustine's youth there were as yet no laws from the emperors ordering the closure of pagan shrines. Not until 399 did such a law arrive, causing local riots and attacks on pagan buildings with cries of 'Away with the pagan gods.'[35]

As well as pagans, there were strong Jewish communities in Antioch and north Africa, relatively well protected by the legislation of the emperors during Augustine's youth. Libanius corresponded with individual Jews, including their Patriarch, and even taught the Patriarch's son, but his writings never comment on their religion or differences of belief.[36] Unlike Libanius, Augustine shows knowledge of some Hebrew words. He even knows that Jewish teachings are called 'repetitions', using a Greek word which translates the Jews' 'Mishnah'. There was an obvious reason for his scraps of linguistic knowledge: as a Christian he needed to be sure of the meaning of scripture. One way was for him and others to ask Jews what the Hebrew meant. The collective role of 'the Jews' around him was another matter. In his writings they usually serve as a historical example, a people whom God has preserved for His own purposes. 'Slay them not,' Augustine quoted influentially from the Psalms, 'lest at any time they forget thy Law. Scatter them by thy power.' The realities of Jewish life and worship were of less concern to him.[37]

The Christian communities were also diverse. In each of the three regions, the Christian faithful had exemplified their frequently low level of 'fraternity' and split into opposing groups. In Antioch, they were split between a Christian majority and a 'Eustathian' minority (named after their leader, Eustathius) who were credited with radical views on riches and the ownership of property. In Libya during Synesius' youth, there were heretical 'Arians', Christians whom other Christians accused of stressing Christ's humanity at the expense of His divinity. In Augustine's north Africa the bitterest division was not doctrinal: it was a schism which had split the Church into two opposing communities. In many of the towns and settlements there were two bishops, one for each community, each with its own church. By the end of the fourth century each community could mobilize some 400 bishops.

This devastating schism was a constant presence in Augustine's life, one which he began to address in writings and letters before writing the *Confessions* and which became a centre of his activity in the early fifth century. It went back into the tensions of the last pagan persecution of the Christians nearly fifty years before he was born.[38] During it, Christian leaders had been under constraint to hand over their churches' copies of the scriptures to pagan officials: those who obliged were regarded as treacherous compromisers by those who did not. The issue was divisive everywhere, but in north Africa it became focused on the hasty election of a deacon, Caecilianus, to the crucial bishopric of Carthage. One of the few bishops who consecrated him was subsequently alleged to have 'handed over' scriptures, making Caecilianus' consecration invalid. The charge turned out to be false, but remained the focal point for extreme ill-will and slander. Opponents of Caecilianus contrived the election of a separate Bishop of Carthage and refused to acknowledge Caecilianus' legitimacy.

The split was then compounded by appeal to the Emperor Constantine, who was newly supportive of Christianity. In 312, he accepted the senior candidate in Carthage and favoured Caecilianus as bishop of the 'universal' (or 'catholic') church. Money, then force were used to uphold this fateful decision, and within five years, opponents of Caecilianus' followers had been killed by fellow Christians, dying as 'martyrs' for their cause. The victorious self-styled 'universal' catholics then labelled their opponents dismissively as 'Donatists', naming them after their second schismatic Bishop of Carthage. These 'Donatists' could fairly have labelled the 'universal' catholics 'Caecilianists'.

The schism became deepened by subsequent aggression. In the 340s, the Donatists began to deploy groups of rurally available thugs, the feared Circumcellions, who entered the fray with clubs in their hands called 'Israels'; in reply, the emperor sent agents to distribute charity and try to restore unity. The result was even more bitter fighting and more martyrdoms throughout the 350s. The schism then gained momentum from events outside Africa. Against expectations, in 361 the new emperor, Julian, was a pagan and supported the Donatists, if only to cause trouble to the other Christians. In his early youth, therefore, Augustine saw a brief period when the alternative Christian group in Africa was being officially tolerated. In the 370s they became involved with rebels against Rome inside the province, a fact which did them no favours, but in general the 380s and early 390s would be decades of relative quiet for Donatists' churches. Profound tensions persisted, but the storm of forced conversions to the 'Catholic' Church still lay in the future.

Strikingly, the *Confessions* never allude to this schism at all. Augustine's home town, Thagaste, had once been a 'Donatist' community, but it had abandoned this allegiance before he was born, probably during the times of terror in the late 340s. Young Augustine was brought up to be one of the 'universal' Christians (a 'Catholic' only in this sense of the word). However, the existence of another Church was a fact which confronted him at every turn. The name 'Donatist' was never a name which such Christians used of themselves or their martyrs. Augustine's Christians were deliberately marginalizing their opponents' long history by calling them 'Donatists' and naming themselves the universal Catholics. In Augustine's youth, however, 'Donatists' were still the majority Church in north Africa.

The conflict was not caused by a heresy. Neither side held aberrant beliefs. They practised the same liturgy in their respective churches and read the same scriptures. Both Churches worshipped martyrs from the past, but the Donatists also worshipped martyrs of their own Church, people whom the Catholics had killed. Both groups looked back with respect to the great Cyprian, Carthage's martyr-bishop in the 250s. However, by (allegedly) lapsing during pagan persecutions, the self-styled 'Catholic' leaders had defiled their fellow Christians' 'pure' community. As a result, any Catholics who turned to the Donatist Church had to be baptized all over again, a 'sacrilege' which affronted Catholic opinion. Catholics regarded the sacraments as valid whoever administered them, because they were validated by Christ. Donatists, by contrast, considered the purity of the ministering priest to be essential to them. All the subsequent layers of aggression, slander and outright crime between the communities only deepened this basic indignation. Donatist Christians could never overlook what the Catholics had betrayed in the time of the Great Persecution, thereby making all their priests 'impure'.

This profound split drew on historic grievances, but it was also rooted in these differing views of the Christian Church. Modern historians once tried to explain Donatism as a movement of social protest which was particularly attractive to the rural poor in the outlying north African areas of Numidia. Donatists' churches were even identified with all the simple churches of these rural areas, the 'movement's' real heartland. In fact, there is now no agreed criterion by which archaeologists can distinguish the churches of one side of the schism from those of the other. At most, the remains of three Donatist churches may be identifiable, one of an impressive size and construction in the city centre of Timgad, another out at Vegesela (modern Ksar el Kelb), where a Donatist hero, Marculus, and his associates had been martyred. A third may be the big church in Hippo, for long accepted to be Augustine's own as a bishop but now assigned by recent study to the Donatists, not the Catholics. This reassignment, on Augustine's doorstep, shows how difficult it is to distinguish the church plans of one group from those of the other.[39] Although Donatist leaders used the assistance of violent rural 'terrorists', thugs from the countryside were not the central core of their Church. 'Donatists' were served by bishops and priests from backgrounds similar to those in Augustine's 'Catholic' minority. They were to be found in the major towns and the countryside alike. They existed prominently in Carthage. In Augustine's eventual seat at Hippo, they greatly outnumbered his own 'Catholics', even when he was composing his confessions.

In the minds of its members, the Donatist Church was a body 'unpolluted', kept 'pure' from persecutors, traitors and those who had compromised with persecutors in the past. This purity was not dependent on the members' ethical, let alone sexual, behaviour. It was the quality of a community which was united like a 'true Israel' before a God who, therefore, heard its prayers. Scriptural texts on purity and self-contained sanctity were applied to it in this sense. Its members saw themselves as the upholders of the scriptures old and new as a holy 'Law'. Their Church was 'gathered in' or 'collected': it was as pure as the Bride in the 'enclosed garden' which is described memorably in the ancient Song of Songs. Their Church was like the Ark of Noah, but it was waterproofed twice over, once to keep the baptismal waters inside for its living members, once to exclude the polluting waters of the outside world.[40] Their Church stood against that world, just as its founders had once stood apart from the pagan world around them. Its sense of separation was intensified by the fact that the 'Catholics' had split off and persecuted it and by the fact that Roman emperors and governors had frequently helped them do so. 'Donatists' considered their Church to be catholic in a different sense, 'comprehensive' in its rites and purity before God. It was not a 'Church Universal', with ambitions to spread through the world. Although it had members in Rome, they were Africans by origin and had been forced out by the troubles in their homeland. Essentially, it was the Church of Christians in north Africa, their 'ark'.

Already when composing the *Confessions*, Augustine took a very different view of the Christian Church. On earth it was not a society of saints. It was a mixed community of unreformed sinners among whom there were only a few aspiring 'stars', or perfectionists. A society of saints exists, but it lies hidden in the future, in God's heavenly community of those whom He will choose, inscrutably, by love.[41]

At a mundane level, this schism is a major reason why bishops proliferated in Augustine's surroundings. Many of the towns of the province, 'proconsular Africa', had small territories, separated by only seven or eight miles from the next town, but most of them had their own bishop. Often a town had two bishops, one for each half of the schism. Bishops were also sometimes attached to villages or landowners' estates in order to counter activity by bishops from the other party. Bishops tended, therefore, to be small-town people with a small territory as their responsibility. They attended mostly to religious business and the property of their own local church. Secular business in the towns, meanwhile, was the sphere of the magistrates and councillors and, above them, the province's governors and their staff.[42]

Augustine's north African church had a different profile to Synesius', settled to the east in Libya. In 'upper Libya' archaeologists have found more than fifty churches in the country villages, but most of them, perhaps all, belong after Synesius' lifetime. Even then, they would not all be the seat of a bishop. No more than twelve upper Libyan bishoprics are as yet traceable.[43] Bishops were spaced more widely in the Libyan landscape than in Augustine's province. The two men's circumstances therefore differed as bishops. Whereas Augustine became and remained only one bishop among very many in proconsular Africa, Synesius was appointed to his province's main bishopric. He had a noble family and a previous secular career on his city's behalf, assets which Augustine lacked. This difference of status and setting was to distinguish the two men's relations with the secular governors in their province.

IV

Despite the social barriers, Augustine, of all men, was not blind to the lives around him. His sermons are full of passing references to them. In Hippo, he even knows the true value of manure: gardeners in the suburbs, he observes, would vie for the 'contemptible scourings' of the town, the dung and rubbish, pay a good price for it and carry it away. By birth, education and social rank, Synesius might seem more likely to exemplify the 'social distance' which, so far, I have sketched among members of his upper class. However, his letters show something else, his close social contact with people outside the urbanized world. It is worth dwelling, finally, on the scope for it.

Far to the south of Cyrene, in Libya's inland deserts, Synesius describes how his beloved sport of hunting brought him into contact with the local tribesmen who lived far beyond the world of cities. He heard their music and shared their songs, having entered their company through his favourite field sport.[44] Neither Libanius nor Augustine hunted or had personal experience of such remote people: they are marginalized in their surviving writings. The bond of the hunting field was equalled only by the close contacts which could result from sea journeys. When Synesius returned from a fearful sea journey, probably in 401, he sent his brother the letter which does most to remind us how barriers between classes and communities might find themselves thrown down.[45]

Synesius had set off for home, he tells us, from Egypt's Alexandria in a boat burdened with debt, captained by a Jew and manned by a crew half of whom were Jews too, a 'perfidious race', in Synesius' opinion, 'who are convinced that they are being godly when they bring about the deaths of as many Greeks as possible'. The other sailors were a 'bunch of rustics who had not touched an oar for at least a year', all of them disabled. They even called each other by names relating to their incapacity: 'Lame', 'Left-hander', 'Squinty' and so forth. The passengers numbered more than fifty, including some Arab cavalrymen travelling west to Libya. A third of the company were female, 'mostly young and good-looking'. 'Don't be jealous,' Synesius told his brother: a curtain made from a length of torn sackcloth 'walled us off from them'.

This boatload of social diversity soon ran into serious trouble. The ship just missed the rocks on leaving port, whereupon the captain steered far out to sea. A fearful gale then broke, intensifying at nightfall. Even so, the captain refused to hold on to the steering, because the Sabbath was just beginning. As he could not work, he sat reading a book, presumably a book of the scriptures. He resumed his duties only when human lives were in danger and the Jewish Law permitted him to intervene. The ship's sail was soon torn in the gale, but there was no replacement on board as the reserve sail had been pledged against a debt, probably by the captain. The ship's second anchor had also been sold.

Synesius fell back on his deeply embedded culture: he looked in terror at the sea and recalled relevant verses, he says, from Homer's poems. Death by drowning, he rightly remembered, was the worst of all deaths for Homer's heroes, and so he thought that he understood why the Arab soldiers on board had drawn their daggers. They must have been wishing to kill themselves instead of dying unheroically in water. Somebody called out that anyone with gold should hang it round their necks, and the women promptly obeyed. They were reckoning, Synesius believed, that anyone who found their washed-up bodies on shore would trouble to put some sand on them and grant them rest in the next world in return for taking their treasure. In an extreme crisis Synesius describes neither the soldiers nor the female passengers nor himself as showing any concern for Christian teachings about death.

The gale passed, the ship put into shore and the passengers at last offered hymns of thanks to God. However, when they put out to sea again a few days later, the storm resumed. Once again they feared death, but after a fearsome day and night they were guided safely into a cove on the Libyan coast by an old man of the region 'dressed in rustic fashion' who kindly came out with a crew in a small boat and indicated the safe passage to a natural harbour nearby. He shipped off the passengers and showed them where to feed themselves by fishing among the rocks. Synesius describes him as a 'religious worshipper', surely a Christian hermit. The fishing turned out to be extremely good.

Other ships put into the bay, avoiding the storm, and matters improved further when women of this remote region arrived with yet more food, chickens, eggs and so forth. One of them even brought a bustard, a bird which 'a countryman would mistake at first sight for a peacock': Synesius was not the first Greek, when abroad, to discover that the bustard's meat is 'extraordinarily sweet'.[46]

Down by the seashore, one more act of social intermingling then took place. The local women's generosity, Synesius inferred, was not unmotivated. They were characterized by their enormous breasts, so long that they could push them up to their shoulders and suckle the children whom they held there. What they wanted to know was whether all the other women who visited them were as top-heavy as themselves: they would give presents to visiting women in the hope that the recipients would then show them their breasts. A young slave girl from the Black Sea region had been travelling on board whose figure was as 'neat and nipped in as an ant's'. She was kept very busy by the native women, who repeatedly sent for her in order to have a good look at her slender body. She was 'so extremely eager', Synesius remarked, 'that she would even undress for them'.

Without its detailed framework, manifestly one of real life, this entire narrative would be dismissed as the Homeric fiction of an overeducated male author who fantasized about 'primitive savages' and their female naked bodies. In fact it is told with excellent wit, a pearl among ancient Greek letters. It raises issues which are central to understanding the *Confessions*: sex, philosophy and the relation between experience and a subsequent 'fictive' memoir.

Sea storms were always a graphic subject for late antique letter-writers.[47] Christian Synesius retells his with the typical imagery and references of an educated man: he cites Homer, Zeus, rare mythology and even the sexually rampant pagan divinity Priapus. Yet such was his grounding in Homer that Homer's poems could indeed have come to his mind in a crisis. As for sex, he was a married man at the time. Wittily, he claims to be making his brother envious, what with all those female passengers on board and big-breasted women bringing presents of food. 'Of course I did not strike a bargain with them,' he claims, 'as I would then be untrue to the oath I would later have to swear', presumably to his Christian wife back home.

He called on God, he says, 'who gives Philosophy'. Here, he is referring, as ever, to the Christian God.[48] He writes in this way because he is writing for a cluster of educated people to whom he expects his brilliant letter to be shown, above all his great female philosophy teacher, Hypatia, in Alexandria and the lovers of philosophy around her. This language is no more 'pagan' than his Homeric references. While retelling his great adventure, Synesius wants to present himself to his intended audience with respect for the philosophy which they all admire, pagans and Christians alike. In November 386, the newly converted Augustine would present himself similarly to the fellow lovers of philosophy whom he had just met in Milan.

In wars, in sea storms or even during field sports, social distinctions could be briefly broken by circumstances. On his travels as a cleric through his diocese Augustine was made aware of the rhythmic singing of labourers in the north African cornfields and vineyards. He used them as examples in his sermons. Unlike Synesius he never camped with them for weeks on end but he admired them, nonetheless, for the way they sang 'from the heart'. Rhythm and emotional response appealed to him, hallmarks of his humanity. As for the sea, at Thagaste he grew up among hills about 200 miles from it and never travelled on it in his youth. As he later told a close friend, he tried as a boy to imagine what the sea must be like, by looking into a bowl of water.[49]

PART I

Erskine and I sauntered up and down some hours. I should have mentioned some time ago that I said to him that if venereal delight and the power of propagating the species were permitted only to the virtuous, it would make the world very good. Our pulpits would then resound with noble descriptions of conjugal love. Preachers would incite the audience to goodness by warmly and lusciously setting before their imaginations the transports of amorous joy. This would render the pleasures of love more refined and more valuable, when they were participated only by the good. Whereas at present, it is the common solace of the virtuous and the wicked, the man of taste and the man of brutality.

James Boswell, *London Journal* (1762–3),
Saturday, 26 March 1763

3
Infancy, Order and Sin

In this unequal society, united by shows and spectacles and the fear of intermittent violence, Augustine allows us like no other author to focus on an individual's inner and outer life. His analysis is not concerned with legal fine points or details of worldly status. It goes far deeper and addresses basic elements which are common, he thinks, to us all.

'I began to smile, first in my sleep; then, when awake . . .' Augustine's revisiting of his first months is unique in ancient biography.[1] 'All ancient philosophers,' Cicero remarked, 'turn to the cradle, believing that it is in early childhood that we can most easily recognize the "will of nature".' They observed that, unlike the young of other animals, a child comes naked into the world. It cries, surely a sign that it is terrified, but is its natural will to preserve itself or to seek its own pleasure? Pagan thinkers had been interested in such general questions, but never in relation to themselves and a personal God.[2] Augustine begins at the beginning for a very different reason. It is a phase which exemplifies the Christian dynamic of his confessions, the interplay between his own abject sinfulness and God's mercy and order in the world. They are linked by a heritage which we all share.

He begins with a blunt appeal to God which no pagan would have made. 'Hear, O God. Alas for the sins of mankind!' God, he says, has 'created man, but not the sin in him'. His revisiting of his infancy is not to be a sweet recall of love and attention and their effects on his innocence in the cradle. Who, though, can commemorate his sinful infancy, he wonders, as he himself cannot remember it?

God showed mercy to him in his sinfulness, he believes, and 'took him on' when he was first born. God provided the 'consolations of human milk', filling the breasts of Augustine's mother and his nurses with just as much milk as he wanted and seeing that he wanted no more than they gave. Augustine's rosy view of breast-feeding is based, surely, on watching wet nurses for whom it was never a painful struggle.[3] In Augustine's view, God even arranged the 'well-ordered' affection of those who suckled him. They are the first example in the confessions of a constantly important element in his thought, the 'order' which God has imposed on a good world.

Augustine deploys the imagery of suckling throughout his Christian texts and sermons. Christ on earth fed the 'little ones' with the 'milk of faith': Paul described himself as doing the same, and 'mother' Church, Augustine once states, has continued to suckle us with the Old and New Testaments, her breasts.[4] Augustine applies the image later in the *Confessions* to his own relation to God: 'what am I, when all is well with me, except someone sucking Your milk or enjoying You, the food which is not corrupted?' He has derived this imagery not from a subconscious infantile longing but from scripture, from Isaiah's words on God as a mother ('As a mother comforts, I will comfort you') and from a psalmist's words on the Lord God 'taking him up' after his father and mother have abandoned him (Ps. 27.10). He uses it because it is the supreme imagery of care and love, leading to growth. When expounding a psalm, he enhances his interpretation with the image of a mother in the small hours, breast-feeding her baby by moonlight.[5]

Even so, babyhood was not a time of innocence. Augustine cried, he realizes, 'avid for the breasts'. Since then, he tells us, he has witnessed and experienced the jealousy of a small baby who watched 'pale and with a bitter look' while another baby was breast-fed by his nurse instead. Despite the care and love extended to it, a baby resorts to tears and jealousy. It kicks against its elders and superiors even when they know that its demands are not in its best interests. This behaviour is proof indeed that no baby is ever free of sin. Augustine has observed it in others and can assume it of himself thanks to words of scripture. As the psalmist said, 'I was conceived in iniquity, and in sins my mother nourished me in the womb' (Ps. 51.5). In the Book of Job he had read: 'None is pure of sin before you, not even an infant of one day upon the earth' (Job 14.4–5).[6] Augustine is enabled to understand his infant self by understanding scripture about that forgotten phase of life. It is the first example of his understanding himself through scripture, a pattern which will run through the entire *Confessions*.

If God did not create this sin, where did it come from? At the very start of the *Confessions* Augustine is alluding to 'original sin', the sin which we all as 'Adam's children' inherit from Adam's first sin of disobedience and pride in the Garden. This sin has made us all mortals, programmed thenceforward to die, but it has not only affected our bodily frame. Augustine is quite clear, despite some of his modern interpreters, that the sin of a baby is in its 'mind' or 'spirit'. He says it four times in the course of his discussion.[7] Neither 'custom nor reason', he tells us, could 'reprehend' him as a baby because he could not yet understand a person who was 'reprehending'. Nonetheless he was acting reprehensibly, he insists. He puzzles, typically, over the implications. Is it really so sinful for a baby to cry while 'gaping for the breasts'? Indeed it is, he answers, because he would be reprehended for behaving in this way for food as an older man. The baby's practice is soon outgrown and given up, but we only 'purge away' what is bad, only what is good. A baby's limbs are feeble as it kicks and strikes out, but its mind is sinful. Few parents in the front line nowadays would disagree. Was there ever indeed a time when a baby was innocent, even in its mother's womb? Having no personal knowledge, Augustine draws on the psalmist ('conceived in iniquity') to refute the notion. He cannot recall such a period, but he accepts its sinfulness from observing others and from scripture. He ends with a rhetorical question which arises from the words of Psalm 51. ' "In sins my mother nourished me in the womb." I ask you, my God, I ask You, Lord, where or when was your slave innocent?' The implicit answer is, 'nowhere' and 'never'.[8]

The confessions begin, therefore, with a statement of the original sin which many interpreters have minimized in the text. The Latin phrase for it, *peccata originalia*, is indeed Augustine's innovation, one which is first used in his writings in the year before he began to confess. However, the idea had not dawned on him only then, causing him to compose his confessions in order to relate a new understanding to his own self. He was to develop it with particular force in the polemics of his older age, but it was not his own idea. It was present, he believed, in scripture (Job and the Psalms). It was implied in his Latin text of two letters of Paul (1 Cor. 15.22 and Rom. 5.12). Previous Latin Christian writers had already stated it. The revered north African Bishop Cyprian (*flor.* 250) had commented on a baby's 'alien sins', derived from Adam's original sin, about a hundred years before Augustine was born. So had Ambrose, the bishop who had baptized him eleven years before the *Confessions* and had symbolically attended to the traces of original sin in each candidate.[9] It was also acknowledged, I believe, in north African practice. When recalling his boyhood, Augustine says that he 'was being flavoured with salt from the very [leaving of] the womb of my mother'. In Christian practice, salt put on the tongue was an antidote to the demons and was given elsewhere in the Latin West to Christians when they were first under instruction from a priest as 'catechumens'. Many modern scholars therefore take this reference to be to Augustine's time as a child-catechumen. However, I take 'from his mother's womb' literally and understand him to mean that, from his birth onwards, he was regularly being given salt against the demons by his Christian mother. As he recalls, he 'imbibed the name of Christ with his mother's milk'. She also gave dashes of salt to the son whom she regarded from birth as a little Christian in the making.[10]

We can now understand why Augustine says at the very start that God created man but did not 'create sin'. Indeed He did not: from Adam onwards, man has chosen it. In his religious journey, as we will see, Augustine was to be seduced by two types of thinking, one which considered that moral evil relates to a necessity running through the universe, the other that it is an eternal substance, separate from God. Even as he begins to confess, his words implicitly refute these views, but he does not state that babies are 'guilty' as a result of their inherited sinfulness, nor that they will be haunted by guilt ever after. He realizes that they cannot speak or use language. They can no more experience guilt at what they are doing than understand that they are being reprehended for it. They have a remedy if they turn to Him: Christ their redeemer, who has taken away the sins of the world.

Infancy, which Augustine has forgotten, then passed into boyhood with the onset of the ability to speak. Typically, the mature Augustine wonders, forty years later, how? Grown-ups did not teach him words in an orderly system, as they later taught him letters. He tried, he assumes, to express the 'feelings of my heart', so that his wants, or 'will', should be obeyed, but although he was expressing them with 'the very mind you gave me, God', he could not make others do everything he wanted. So 'I used to grasp in my memory' when they called something and moved their body towards it and showed by the 'bodily movement, their expression, the inclination of their eyes, the movement of their limbs, the sound of their voice' which object was being named. Those expressions and movements, he writes, are the 'natural word, as it were, of all peoples' and show our minds' 'impulse' to whatever it 'sucks, possesses, rejects or avoids'.[11] By repeated watching and listening, Augustine believes, he collected up words 'set in their places in various sentences' and 'tamed' his own mouth to repeat them. With them 'I communicated signs of the wants which had to be enunciated'.

Famously, this account caught the interest of Wittgenstein:

'Augustine describes the learning of human language as if the child came into a strange country and did not understand the language of the country: that is, as if it already had a language, only not this one. Or again: as if the child could already *think*, only not yet speak. And "think" would here mean something like "talk to itself" . . .' In fact Augustine's view is more cautious. He does not think that he was trying to express propositions in his own private baby language. He was expressing the 'feelings of his heart' or 'concepts of his heart', which were prior to language. He gives due credit to others' gestures and non-linguistic signs; he correctly credits the role of memory; he denies that he learned from rebukes, for the sound reason that he could not have understood what a rebuke was. In the *Confessions* he does not consider how a child goes on to build sentences from words. In Wittgenstein's view, Augustine wrongly believed that each individual word comes with a ready-made meaning subordinated to it. Yet Augustine had already shown himself aware of the difficulties in such a belief and had discussed them in his dialogue *On the Master* ten years before.[12]

In modern terms Augustine is an innatist, believing that babies have an innate ability which is triggered by signs and pointing. On this controversial topic, some, but not all, linguistic philosophers consider Augustine to be 'precisely and demonstrably right', except that he credits the innate ability to God, not genetics. Throughout his discussion he continues to point out that he has no memory nowadays of what he is describing, at least until he began to speak. However, he does not make the error of equating his personal identity only with his consciousness.[13] His infancy is still a part of him, he realizes, even though he cannot remember any of it. This awareness of the hidden depths in a person is one of his confessions' exceptional strengths.

So is his awareness of the problem of his own reliability. His infancy confronts him with it as soon as his confessing begins. He is cautious about 'believing much about oneself on the authority of weak women (*mulierculae*)', mothers and nannies. Intriguingly, he considers he has learned more about his infancy by watching 'unknowing babies' nowadays than by heeding 'knowing wet nurses' about his past. He had evidence in his own household, we might add: he had a bastard son in his youth. By watching others, he has been able to infer his own first smiles, his little rebellions, his jealousies.

This awareness of the limits of memory runs through the *Confessions*' books about 'what I once was'. Quite often, Augustine admits that he has forgotten this or that or that he is unsure. His chronology is sometimes vague. When he recalls a public event out of sequence, he comments that he has overlooked it hitherto and simply does not know why. He is not reconstructing his past from written sources, his own or others. He kept no diaries at the time. Nor is he giving a complete account of all he knows, as we can see from his earlier works, which sometimes supplement what the *Confessions* include. Rather, he picks on memories which relate to his prayer's dynamic, to the depths of his sinfulness and its counteraction by God's inexhaustible mercy. His choice of what to discuss is driven by his sense of this interplay. If he omits something, or focuses on something which seems to us less significant, he is not necessarily being evasive: his confessing prayer imposes its own relevance.

A major theme is 'conversion', present at the start of his account of his life: it was first exemplified by God. God 'turned' to Augustine as a baby.[14] As an adult, it was then up to Augustine to be 'turned', or 'converted', decisively to God. Babies, he thinks, are created through God's 'ordering' of their person and their form, their senses and their limbs. All is done for their unity and safety and their bodies are formed with beauty. Augustine differs from the pagan Platonist philosophers, whom he had read, because he attributes the body's form, beauty and unity to a personal God. 'Where can a being like a baby have come from if not from you, God?' Like his contemporaries, he has no idea of genes, nor even of the female's eggs.[15]

From the very start, babies' impulses are disorderly and sinful. Their wilful turning away or 'a-version' must become a 'con-version' despite the fact, expressed in scripture, that each of us is inherently sinful as a descendant of sinful Adam. The terms in which Augustine examines his infancy will run through his entire analysis of his past. Throughout it, he sees the problems of 'growth and development'. His Latin expresses them in clauses set one beside the other, a style which he learned from reading scripture.[16] The style and the subject complement each other in a way which has struck literary theorists as 'unthinkable' previously. He presents his infancy in prayer to a God whose relations to time past, present and future, he says, are beyond our full understanding. However, they will recur twelve books later and draw a reply which he will ascribe there to God Himself.

4
Family Scars

After learning to speak, Augustine embarked on what he describes as the 'stormy society of life'. No memoir of childhood by a child survives from antiquity. Adult Augustine looks back on his own while confessing his 'straying' and testifying to God's mercy, care and correction during it all. Once again, he sets his propensity to sin beside God's hidden order in the world, themes which no pagan memoir ever interrelated.

His parents play very different parts in what he recalls. He does not name either of them until much later in the *Confessions* and then only so that his Christian readers can include their names in their prayers. Mentions of them are more significant than naming, but, even so, Augustine hardly mentions his father. He died in Augustine's seventeenth year, but, unlike his mother's death, the event is only noticed obliquely during the *Confessions'* discussion of Augustine's later reading habits. The silence is not evidence that father and son had been unusually distant or on bad terms. It relates to the *Confessions'* theme, Augustine's relation to God. As Patricius was a pagan until his last days, he was irrelevant to it.

Even so, a few remembered details give readers a sense of the man. Patricius was 'impulsively benevolent', Augustine recalls, as much as he was 'quick-tempered'. In a famous scene, Augustine recalls how his father was delighted when he saw at the public baths in Thagaste that his own son, bathing naked, had reached puberty, aged fifteen. He told Augustine's mother the good news, happy because he could now look forward to grandchildren. Augustine describes him as 'rejoicing in the effects of wine', the 'invisible wine', however, of this worldly hope. Patricius did not go off after the discovery and become literally drunk, as modern translators imply.[1]

Fathers had overwhelming power in Roman families, but although Augustine recalls being beaten by schoolmasters, he never recalls that

Patricius beat him too. Beating, rather, was for slaves. He recalls that early in his marriage, Patricius beat some of the household's slave girls at his mother's request: they had been slandering his wife to her and endangering the harmony of the family. The incident reminds us of the perils of a young wife, watched by slaves at her every move, and their scope for trying to turn a mother-in-law against her.[2] As for the marriage itself, Augustine describes his mother tolerating 'wrongs of the bed' so that she never quarrelled with her husband on 'this matter'. These wrongs are usually taken to be Patricius' infidelities, at least with slave girls in the household.

To Augustine, Patricius' temper was more evident than his adultery. Other women, Augustine remarks, had milder husbands, but Monnica dealt with angry Patricius by submitting to him until his rage had died down. Revealingly, Augustine recalls that these other wives marvelled that Monnica did not bear the marks of her husband's aggression on her face or person. The implication is that even the wives of 'milder' husbands bore their physical imprint. In Libanius' Antioch too, wife-beating husbands were a fact of life. We hear them echoing in the sermons of Libanius' Christian pupil, John Chrysostom: 'loud cries and wailing travel through the streets', John reminded his Christian audiences, 'as though an animal is rampant inside the house' at times when husbands are thumping their wives.[3]

Patricius' impulsiveness showed in another, more positive way. His name is attested for only two people in all our evidence from north Africa and its social resonance ('patrician') matches Augustine's own. The name 'Augustinus' is attested for only one other person in the province and has 'august' connotations like the emperors (*augusti*).[4] They fit the social ambitions which Patricius soon showed for his son. Despite the cost, he aimed to pay for his prolonged schooling, necessarily at his own expense in the absence of any 'state system'. Augustine also had a sister, whose name is unknown to us, and at least one brother, Navigius (probably older), but Augustine's were the talents which represented the family's best hope of advancement.

Prolonged schooling was not for all his family: two of Augustine's cousins were never financed beyond the first elementary phase. As Patricius was not rich, his decision to pay for it was admired by his fellow townsmen. Augustine acknowledges that it was due to 'bold nerve'.[5] It was to be the making of his son and after his death would be continued by Augustine's resolute mother, Monnica. She is an unforgettable presence in the *Confessions* and also, therefore, in Augustine's life.

When she dies, Augustine describes his own 'life as torn apart, for it had been one life, made up of hers and mine together'. The very structure of the *Confessions* is a witness to her importance. His autobiographical memories stop with her death and burial. He then moves on to confess his own inner life 'as I now am', omitting the intervening ten years.[6]

Facts about her early life emerge only from Augustine's praises of her before and after her death. Monnica had been born *c.*331/2 into a Christian household, almost certainly one in Thagaste. Was she perhaps closer than Augustine to a 'Libyan' or 'Berber' pre-Roman past? Support has been found in a possible derivation of her name, Monnica, 'from the pagan goddess Mon worshipped in the nearby town of Thibilis'.[7] However, all of Thagaste's inhabitants had once had non-Roman ancestors and, after many centuries of spoken Latin and Roman rule in the town, such a name would not represent a living non-Roman identity. An alternative derivation is 'Ammonica', a name based on the pagan god Ammon of Libya, who had been widely known in the Greek and Roman world for nearly a thousand years. So far as we know, Monnica always spoke Latin, with no evidence of being bilingual in any 'Libyan' speech. Neither her name nor anything known about her culture suggests she was 'basically' Berber. Nor was she black-skinned, as if Augustine was the child of a black African.[8]

The more tantalizing questions are her baptism and its timing. If her home town was Thagaste, it was still largely a town of 'Donatists' when she was young. It is a fascinating possibility, which Augustine never mentions, that his mother may have begun life and probably been given her first instruction, or 'catechism', in the Christian community which 'Catholics' regarded as schismatic. He never states that she had been baptized as a child, but, if so, it would probably have been by a Donatist priest. In a later letter, he turns out to have a relation who is a Donatist, probably through his mother's side of the family.

Like many other girls at the time, Monnica was married early, perhaps when she was only fifteen or sixteen. Aged twenty-three, she bore Augustine, and he leaves us in no doubt of her exceptionally loving concern for him throughout his life. She 'loved my being with her, as mothers do', he remarks, but 'much more so than many do'. Throughout, her Christianity was simple, unquestioning and true to the basic faith of her north African Church: later, as a widow, she would go to church at least twice a day. She prayed fervently and was prone to see visions of God and His angels. She could even distinguish, she said, between illusory dreams sent by demons and genuine visions from heaven: she could tell the demonic ones by their smell.[9] As visions were not unusual in Latin Christian culture, her visionary gifts are not the result of a 'pre-Roman' or distinctively 'African' temperament.

When recalling her death, Augustine looks back on her as an ideal Christian widow, true to the model described in the Pauline epistles. We can humanize her a little from other glimpses in the *Confessions* and from her very words, recorded in Augustine's earliest Christian works. His confessions recall a revealing story about her youth, perhaps so as to counter gossip about her character.[10] As a girl, she told him, she had been brought up very strictly indeed by a 'decrepit slave woman', trusted by her family. The slave's 'command' and 'authority' saw that Monnica was not even allowed to drink water on demand, a measure to stop any future tendency in her to drinking too much wine. Nonetheless, when sent to the cellars to draw wine for others upstairs, Monnica used to sip it, then drink an entire cup. In anger, another slave girl insulted her as a 'little boozer' (*meribibula*, a word known nowhere else in Latin and remembered by Monnica ever after). Monnica promptly gave up. Augustine dwells on the story as if it shows that a person, speaking angrily, cannot take the credit for correcting another's habits: God, he insists, had acted on Monnica here because she herself wished to change. To us, it seems more likely that the angry rebuke did indeed reform her, as Monnica never forgot its insulting word. Monnica herself told Augustine this story of 'conversion', but why did he retell it at such length in the *Confessions*? Later readers picked on it: did Augustine retell it to counter allegations that his mother had become too fond of drink?

The strictness of Monnica's upbringing connects with other, more evident characteristics. She could be stern, as she showed when a young Christian once affronted her sense of propriety. She herself was obedient to superiors, just as her own upbringing had taught her. She deferred to her bishop and even to the irascible Patricius. 'She used to tell other wives in Thagaste that when they heard what is called their "marriage-contract" being read out to them, they should think of it as if it was a legal document by which they had become slave girls (*ancillae*).' In order to avoid a servile beating, she advised that wives should wait, as she did, for their husbands' tempers to blow over before saying anything in reply.[11]

Perhaps Monnica could read and write, but as her son later reminded her, she was not educated. Nonetheless, she could show quick common sense, as the *Confessions* recall, explaining how she contradicted young

Augustine about the meaning of one of her dreams. Significantly, he did not forget what she said, even twenty-five years later. The best evidence of her directness survives in the first dialogues on philosophy which Augustine published. Her interventions were exactly recorded and were brief, but effective. Happiness, she remarked, is getting what one wants, but not if it is wrongly wanted. Clever minds who argue that they can prove nothing struck her as 'sick'. Her contributions amazed and delighted her son, who praised them as proof of an almost 'manly' intelligence. Once, she capped them by singing a Christian hymn.[12]

Her directness went with other qualities. She was a respected and discreet mediator for women who were at odds with one another. She could also deploy persistent emotional entreaty. Augustine recalls her in a deluge of tears about the critical choice in his life: she 'wept and wailed' at the prospect that he might be about to go abroad. Such an outburst was not in itself unusual: Libanius describes his mother as weeping profusely when he resolved to study abroad. The difference is that he was aged only about twenty, whereas Augustine was thirty and, before long, Monnica came after him to join him and intervene in his life.[13]

Unlike a pagan mother, Libanius' or anyone else's, Monnica deployed weeping during her daily prayers. Tears, a sign of contrition, intensified her claims to be heard by God. Augustine's religious straying in his late youth drove her to persistent weeping, to the point where others found it too much.[14] In retrospect, Augustine considered his mother's daily tears had been crucial for his rescue from ruin. Here, he misunderstood his past, crediting her with what had occurred for quite other reasons. It was a misunderstanding in her favour, a revealing type of mistake which he repeats elsewhere.

Monnica's blunt practicality was probably not unique to her. In many African households, so Augustine later observed, it was the wife who looked after the daily money.[15] In another sphere too she was dominant: her son's religion. She was causing him to 'imbibe the name of Christ, my Saviour, with my mother's milk and retain it deeply within'. His confessions are certainly not the story of a progression from paganism to Christianity, nor has Augustine reshaped them on this point to fit his later Christian identity. In one of his first writings, within months of his famous conversion, Augustine remarked to his patron, Romanianus, that the Christian religion had been 'inserted into us as boys and had become entwined in our very marrow, our innermost part'. There was a progression in Christians' lives. They might be born nominally Christian to a Christian mother or a wholly

Christian family, but the name 'Christian' would only gain content when they were presented as catechumens, or 'ones being instructed', and received their first lessons in the faith from a clergyman. They would then be called Christians by the clergy, but they were not allowed to take the eucharist. For that final step they would have to put in their names for baptism. Then they would be instructed during Lent by a clergyman before being baptized by a bishop at Easter. Thenceforward, they would be called not just 'Christian' but one of the 'Faithful'.[16]

Augustine does not happen to dwell on his earliest knowledge of Christ and the Christian faith. Surely Monnica talked to him constantly about its general nature, but he never recalls her reading the scriptures to him. Few, if any, mothers at the time would have done so, and quite possibly Monnica could not even read. Nor does he look back on being presented with 'gentle Jesus', that Victorian ideal, as a model for good little children. If children are especially blessed, it is, he says in his adult writings, because they exemplify humility.

When he was taken to church, he would have heard sermons and prayers, but not hymns or sung psalms as they were not yet the custom in Africa. Like many of us while still very young, he would not understand all that he heard. As a boy, he recalls, he had 'heard about eternal life, promised to us by the humility of our Lord God descending to us', but he does not say from whom he had learned it.[17] He makes it very clear later in the confessions that he had no idea about the Incarnation in the sense of the Word made flesh. In later life, Bishop Augustine composed a charming short text for the clergy on how to 'catechise the unlearned'. A first lesson, he proposes, should be about eternal life: when the *Confessions* say 'I was hearing about eternal life', was he hearing about it as a boy-catechumen?[18] If so, the instruction was oral, because Augustine did not try to read the scriptures by himself until some ten years later.

The *Confessions* do not dwell on his catechetical teaching, probably because it was not the sort of hard-won conversion, or 'turning', in which they are primarily interested. All he chooses to recall is that he was 'being signed with the sign of the Cross', a practice which we know to have been observed for catechumens. He was aware, therefore, that Christ had been crucified and that He was a Saviour. He also tells us that he enjoyed the Easter services very much indeed, at least in later boyhood. Through them too he would be aware of the crucifixion and the Resurrection.

Monnica would have brought her little boy, aged perhaps eight or nine, to his first lessons in the faith. This role helps us to understand why sometimes Augustine presents her in language which seems a free gift to post-Freudian analysis. Whenever her sons sinned, he says, she 'would go into labour-pangs' to bear them again for God. She strove that 'You [God] should be father to me rather than him [Patricius]'. Once again the language is scriptural, echoing Paul's 'birth pangs' for his sinful Christian converts and Jesus's advice to 'call no man your father on earth, for one is your Father, which is in heaven'.[19] Augustine's words are a comment on Monnica's concern for his religion, not on her subconscious concern to claim him from Patricius as her own. She is his mother, but so is 'mother Church', the mother whom Augustine will join fully at baptism. Through mother Church, the two of them then become brother and sister. Their shared Christian identity supplants their familial ties as mother and son.

Just as Monnica prevailed in Augustine's early religious formation, so she eventually prevailed on his pagan father. Patricius became a catechumen, apparently when Augustine was about sixteen, and died after being baptized near the end of his life. Again, Monnica had fulfilled Paul's advice to the Christian wives of non-Christian husbands: she had brought her pagan husband to believe. With an aggressive, impulsive father and a morally exemplary mother, Augustine is a tempting son for modern analysts who are alive to models in literature.[20] Like D. H. Lawrence's Paul Morel in *Sons and Lovers*, Augustine grew up in a violent paternal home and continued to idealize the values and place of the pious mother in his life; like Paul, he was a son who ultimately lacked commitment as a lover; as Lawrence himself explains, Paul was 'urged on' by his mother, and so, like Augustine, he casts off his mistress and, again like Augustine, attends to his mother as she is dying. The context, however, is different. Unlike Paul Morel's mother, Augustine's mother had not married beneath herself. Although Augustine abandoned his 'mistress', he did so for social reasons, with his mother's approval. There is never said to have been Lawrence's 'battle between the mother and girl, with the son as object'. When Augustine then abandoned his fiancée, he did so despite his mother's plans, not because of them. He opted dramatically for celibacy, not because of his mother, but because it was a high Christian ideal at the time.

Lawrence's friend and defender Rebecca West went further. In her biography of Augustine she suggested that 'in her religion [Monnica] had a perfect and, indeed, noble instrument for obtaining her desire that her son should not become a man . . . Monnica could have put him into the Church as into a cradle. He would then take vows of continence and annul the puberty she detested.'[21] This insight is acute about some mothers, but not about Augustine's. Again, the *Confessions* give enough detail to correct it.

As a little boy, Augustine fell acutely sick with a stomach illness and begged to be baptized. Emergency baptism was indeed a possibility and if little Augustine was already a catechumen, it was a natural step for him to request and expect to receive. It was also not unknown for a Christian mother to vow a sick child to God as a future monk or nun in return for a swift recovery from ill-health.[22] However, Monnica did not vow little Augustine to chastity and make the Church his celibate 'cradle' for the future. She began to arrange his baptism, but when he recovered from the illness, she promptly dropped the preparations. He begged her to continue, but instead she kept him as a Christian catechumen.

Why, he wonders with hindsight, had Monnica not had him baptized at once? Delayed baptism, it seems, was not unusual in Augustine's churches: 'even now', he remarks, 'about this or that person, this saying sounds on all sides in my ears, "Leave him alone, let him do it: he is not yet baptized . . ." ' There were risks, however, in postponement. In case of an early death catechumens were second-class Christians, awaiting God's judgement.[23]

Monnica delayed, Augustine believes, because she feared he would go on to commit serious sins, the most serious of which would be adultery with other men's wives. Certainly, the possibility of these sins soon concerned her. When she heard from Patricius of her son's physical maturity, she received it with 'pious fear and trembling'. Augustine remembered well enough that she actually told him with 'enormous solicitude' that he must not now sleep around. He was not haunted with guilt as a result: he dismissed her warnings as 'women's fears'.[24] However, when he looks back on this distant past, he considers that these warnings explained her delay over having him baptized. At baptism, all sins, even sins of adultery, would be washed away. If such sins were repeated after baptism, the result would be hell after death. So, a young man should wait until he settled down and married, before coming forward for baptism with a better chance of staying chaste.

Monnica's reasons were only a part of the story, Augustine considers. Prompt baptism would have been 'better', he reflects, but he recognizes God's role in its postponement. By being made to wait, he would undergo the tempting 'delights' of sex and ambition, and then renounce them from a position of insider knowledge before his baptism took place. Already Augustine looks back with a strong sense of a 'guided life', shaped by God's long-term plan for the best. As we will see, a sense of divine guidance is also present in pagan Libanius' presentation of his life. Sometimes, like Augustine's, it was a sense of guidance by a divinity who caused him apparent harm and difficulty, but, as later emerged, had done so for his long-term good. Unlike Augustine, Libanius had no sense of original sinfulness and his need for chastening and rescue by a merciful God. His 'autobiography', therefore, gives no space to his infancy.

Why, though, when sexually mature, was Augustine not found a wife at once? The reasons, we can infer, were his excellence at school and his chance of a good career. He must not be wasted too soon on a local bride from a modest family. Only when his career blossomed could he be married to someone with money in the higher social order. Meanwhile, he could have 'concubines', or pre-matrimonial sexual partners. Baptism, if delayed, would then wipe out those youthful sins. He could be channelled into the font before taking on marriage, fidelity (at least as an ideal) and the fathering of legitimate children.

This family planning is born out by his subsequent career. As Patricius had initially welcomed the prospect of prompt grandchildren, it is likely to have been Monnica's idea. However, even with hindsight, Augustine does not credit her with the calculation which changed his life. When he begins to recall and confess his adolescence, he tries to make sense of his predicament with a cluster of biblical phrases and a long complex sentence about his mother's priorities.[25] He realizes that although she had warned him to be chaste, she did not take care to shackle him with what he memorably calls the 'fetter of a wife'. A wife, he sees, would have been an 'enemy of promise'. The 'promise', he clarifies, is not the promise of a future life, in which Monnica believed, but the promise of his literary studies. Both his parents, he recalls, were 'too keen' that he should know his studies well, but his father wanted him to learn them for 'empty' reasons, his future career. Monnica, he thinks, must have wanted him to excel because she believed that these 'customary studies' would be some help for Augustine in 'acquiring God'. He means that she must have thought that they would help him to read the scriptures. He therefore misses her true motive, her hope, as much as Patricius', for his future career as a public speaker and teacher. He does not think of crediting her with the same pushy ambitions as all the other parents of children in his school. Even in his mid-forties, he does not fully realize what his life owed to his mother's social climbing.

Here, Libanius' family life makes a telling comparison. He was the middle son of three and, like Augustine, lost his father when he was young, in his case at the age of eleven. Like Augustine, he looks back and praises his mother's care for his progress, morals and schooling, although she also believed that a 'loving mother should in no way ever distress her son'.[26] Unlike Augustine's, Libanius' mother was a pagan and the family was socially well established. As a pagan, she was not in the least anxious about heresy or fornication, those major concerns for Christians. She remained in Antioch, content with her son's religion, and as a woman of property had no need to follow him and strive to find him a rich bride. In due course Libanius' intended bride was a close kinswoman, as befitted the marriage patterns of established well-off families in the Greek-speaking world. Their concern was to preserve status by keeping property within their family group.

Despite Augustine's puzzlement at the delay, neither he nor Libanius was unusual in waiting a while for marriage. Delay often accompanied a talent for public speaking and teaching, as we can best see from stories of Augustine's near-contemporaries in Latin-speaking Bordeaux. The lives of its literary careerists were vividly recalled by Augustine's older contemporary, the Christian poet and orator Ausonius. Several of Bordeaux's brightest men of letters, he recalls, rose through careers as teachers to make a rich marriage, exactly the aim which Monnica had for Augustine. However, the route to it would sometimes have appalled her. One of Bordeaux's 'talent', Dynamius, was a living reminder that adultery is not only a mortal sin. His reputation, Ausonius says, was 'wounded by a charge of adultery', which forced him to leave Bordeaux and take refuge in Spain. There, he used a different name and became a public speaker, whereupon a 'Spanish wife enriched him', Ausonius tells us, 'while he skulked abroad'.[27]

In later life Augustine still describes the tablets in which the tricky matter of the dowry was specified as 'instruments of purchase'. In his view they make the wife the 'slave girl' of the husband and him, in turn, her 'master'. He presents these tablets to Christian audiences, not so as to revile them, but to emphasize their force: 'every good wife calls her husband "master". Indeed, she not only calls him so: she knows it, she resounds it, she bears it in her heart, she professes it with her lips. She considers the marriage contracts to be the instruments of her purchase.'[28] This equation of the marriage contract with a slave contract was exactly what Monnica had told her contemporaries, the battered wives in Thagaste, during Augustine's youth.

5

'So Small a Boy, So Great a Sinner . . .'

I

'Who would not shudder in horror and choose to die,' Augustine later asks, by then nearly sixty, 'if offered the choice between undergoing death or undergoing childhood all over again?'[1] His own childhood was lived with an irascible father and a strict, but always loving, mother. It was made into a fate worse than death by the elementary teachers in Thagaste to whom his parents first sent him when aged about seven.

'Reading, writing and reckoning,' Augustine recalls, were the elementary school's syllabus, number being taught by recitation ('one and one is two') which he remembers as 'hateful chanting'. Above all, he remembers the beatings. Some of the other boys used to pray to God to escape a thrashing, so Augustine followed suit. They are his first attested prayers. Even his parents used to make light of the marks which the teachers delivered by strap or cane.

At elementary school Augustine learned only because he had to, whereas his hopes and dreams were all of games. He avoided whatever work he could and describes his ears being tempted by 'false stories' and his eye by spectacles, the 'games of adults'. These stories were poetic recitations and mimes in the theatre, but the spectacles would be horse races and bloody contests in the arena of a big city. In Thagaste the latter were known only by repute.

Augustine is clear about the motives of other parents: then, as now, they looked on education as a means to worldly, material ends. They dreamed that their boys might become admired men of riches and rank who would grow up to donate to their lesser townsmen some spectacular shows of bloodsports. Boys were beaten, Augustine muses, for daydreaming of the very games and sports which were the supreme ambition of their parents.

Augustine began his education in Thagaste with a teacher of reading, writing and number, the tasks he tried to dodge. He then recalls a grammar teacher who taught classic texts and the correct usage of words. Then, he moved on to a teacher in the art of public speaking. They were not a neat progression, nor are they evidence for a 'typical' three-stage process in ancient education. In Antioch, Libanius took them in an even less tidy sequence.[2] Augustine's confessions are more interested in the value of his schooling than exact chronology or the schoolmasters' names.

Memorable evidence of such teaching survives in texts from the Latin West which give the very exercises which young pupils had to copy out.[3] They would write a description of the school routine: 'I entered into school and I said, "Greetings, master; greetings, teacher", and he greets me in turn. He gives me a manual and orders me to read five pages in his presence, and I read accurately and finely . . .' Accurate and fine reading was not easy, because ancient manuscripts were not friendly to readers. Words were run together without much punctuation and their quick separation was a matter of long practice. No wonder Augustine disliked it. These copy-texts assume that boys and girls would sometimes be learning together, yet Augustine recalls no such thing. Throughout his schooldays he never hints at any daily contact, play or discussion with a girl, not even with his sister. Like his contemporaries', his masculinity formed in a one-sided setting.

Augustine is not describing his schooling for its own sake. Like his infancy, it is being presented to God in a complex pattern of God's correction and order, mercy and long-term love. Augustine confesses his resentment and idleness over the first part, the 'reading, writing and reckoning', but they were justly punished, he now thinks, because the whipping by his teachers was part of God's planned care for him. It forced him to learn and it taught him to read, write and count, skills which he nowadays uses in God's service. With their help he was made able to read the scriptures and be turned to God.

As the copy-texts show, pupils of a *grammaticus* might also have to learn the Greek alphabet. Augustine was expected to go on to read Homer, the true human miracle. However, he hated learning Greek and duly wonders, 'Why?' The question and its answering are clear evidence of his confessions' manner of composition.[4] He begins by remarking that the question has not been 'sufficiently explored' by him even now. It has occurred to him, therefore, on the spur of the moment, that what he has so far said does not answer it. So, he proposes an answer; then he digresses; then, he returns to the question and gives another answer, although it addresses a different aspect of the topic. He works in this way because his confessions are a prayer which is addressing God with words as they occur to him. He is not reworking them as a text according to hidden patterns and cross-correspondences. If we read them in that way, we are not reading the *Confessions* as he composed or planned them.

First, Augustine blames the difficulty of learning basic Greek 'letters', the grammar, therefore, as well as the alphabet. But, he remarks, basic Latin 'letters' were difficult and painful. He resented learning them, he thinks, because of the inevitable sinfulness and vanity in all human life, another implicit reference to original sin. He then explores how he was seduced by a further vanity, the fictional tales of Virgil's Aeneas. He then returns to his initial question from a new angle, not basic Greek grammar, but Greek literature. Was Homer not just as delightful as Virgil? He answers in terms of a deeper difficulty, that of applying words which have not been learned as one's mother tongue. Whereas he learned Latin orally from others, his Greek was learned only in books. So, the reason for his difficulties was psycho-social. He continued to dislike Greek, a prejudice which Libanius, its lover, would have deplored. In fact, Augustine's writings in later life reveal that his Greek improved until it was far from rudimentary.

Augustine observes how souls still turn away from the basic labours of learning words and grammar, but love the next stage, seductive stories in pagan authors, and thereby fall into sin. In the grammarian's classes, what he most enjoyed was Virgil. In all antiquity, Augustine is the reader whose love for the Latin poet we can best follow. He used to weep, he recalls, over the parting of the hero, Aeneas, from Dido, queen of Carthage, the scene in the *Aeneid* which has most moved readers since. He would have been distressed, he remarks, if he was ever prevented from reading what caused him so much sorrow. He was touched, therefore, by the sad plight of a woman dying for love, a rare glimpse of his responsiveness to a female's vulnerability. His response raises the wider possibility that Virgil's poetry remained a lifelong influence on his way of thinking.[5] Some of his choices in life indeed seem to match choices made by Virgil's Aeneas. Just as Aeneas underwent loss and personal trials on his flight from Troy, so the *Confessions* show Augustine losing friends and family. He went to Carthage and, like Aeneas, fell into temptation there. He then left the city against a woman's wishes (in Augustine's case, Monnica; in Aeneas', Dido) and dismissed his sexual partner, just as Aeneas deserted Dido. He then regained (like Aeneas) his wavering sense of purpose. Both men feel guided by divine providence; it is in Italy that both attain their destiny against their will. Both the *Aeneid* and the *Confessions* trace the journey of a man who is aware of the past, but living in the present and yearning for a future as yet unknown.

The Virgil of Augustine's grammar classes remained with him as an adult. Some twenty years later, when he began to teach a small group of boys, he took them daily through a book of the *Aeneid*, especially those same Books 2–4, explaining what they needed to know about the language and context. Like the young Augustine, one pupil became so impassioned about the story of lovelorn Dido that he 'seemed to me to need even to be restrained somewhat'.[6] It is not, then, surprising that Augustine continued to use phrases from Virgil throughout his writing life, more than 42,000 times according to a recent count. In the *Confessions*, even Monnica receives one. As a young lady, her son recalls, she was 'marriageable, now, in the fullness of years', Virgil's exact words about a nubile Latin heroine in his *Aeneid*. It is a touching, retrospective compliment, but it is the only one which he pays to her of this type.[7]

As a boy, he empathized with characters in the *Aeneid* and learned from teachers who shared the grammarians' view that Virgil was 'infallible'. They also treated him as a source of correct vocabulary and pronunciation. In north Africa, everyday speakers of Latin did not distinguish long and short vowels, a point which outsiders held against them.[8] Usefully, Virgil's Latin hexameters required boys to learn the correct quantity. There were also pedantic quiz questions which teachers set and then competed to answer. They were endemic in classrooms across the empire, whether from Virgil's Latin or Homer's Greek. In Synesius' Greek-speaking Cyrene, somebody wrote on the wall of a prominent building, 'What was the name of Priam's father?' The graffito parodied the typical quiz question of a schoolmaster when teaching Homer. It was even written in the cursive script of a school text.[9]

As a boy in Thagaste, Augustine recalls, he was obliged to compose a prose speech about the wrath of Virgil's goddess Juno against the Trojans: it won the first prize in the school competition. Again, this type of exercise was not peculiar to the Latin West. In the Greek East, speeches on topics from the classics were a staple diet for Libanius' pupils. While confessing, Augustine dismisses his speech as 'empty trifles', nothing more than a 'shameful prey for birds on the wing'. These words are a sarcastic echo of Virgil's *Georgics*, a measure of how far he has moved on in life. He looks back on pagan literature as full of lies: it was as worthless, he thinks, as those 'husks' for pigs on which the Prodigal Son had fed while exiled from his father. Only if it expressed something which related to an aspect of Christian teaching was it worth studying. For Christian readers, Virgil indeed had moments of insight. The older Augustine remarks how often he has marvelled that Virgil anticipated an ethical issue about alms-giving which is otherwise stated in the Gospels. No doubt he also noticed how 'pride' (*superbia*) and the 'proud' are always negative words for Virgil, as they are in his own Christian writings. In a remarkable sermon, delivered on news of the fall of Rome in late 410, Augustine defends the verses of the *Aeneid* in which Jupiter promised Roman 'rule without end'. Jupiter, he explains, is a false pagan god, and so far from believing what he wrote here, Virgil was flattering his contemporaries. He was 'selling words', a phrase which Augustine applied to his own early experiences as a public speaker.[10] Elsewhere, words in Virgil's own voice show that he realized that Rome's rule would one day perish, as indeed it now had: the 'infalliable' Virgil of his schooldays still weighed with him.

In the *Confessions*, Augustine declares to God that he was wandering from Him by enjoying Aeneas' wandering and was dying to Him by engaging with Dido's death.[11] He does not recall two other Virgilian subjects which would have seemed much closer to Christian teachings: the afterlife and a nativity. In the *Aeneid*'s sixth book, Virgil alludes to the punishments and reincarnations of human souls after death. When the adult Augustine discusses them, he assumes, like others, that Virgil was drawing here on Plato, and he points out how widely Virgil differs from Christian belief.[12] In his famous 'Messianic eclogue', Virgil had hailed the start of a new age related to the birth of an unnamed child. Like others before him, Augustine points to the similarities with Christian teaching, but never identifies the child with Christ. He stresses that Virgil was repeating the words of the ancient prophetic Sibyl, and so it is she (not Virgil) who may have anticipated Christianity before its time.[13] By Augustine's lifetime, some of the *Aeneid*'s most intelligent readers were interpreting the poem as an allegory about the human soul's progress through the world. Augustine never explores this approach. His own sense of a spiritual journey towards a future as yet unattained is not a legacy from Virgil and his 'shadow'. It took root from his impassioned study of philosophy, begun in his early thirties, and his subsequent engagement with the Psalms.[14] The Psalms, not the *Aeneid*, are the classics by which the mature Augustine interprets his past life.

Like every other Latin schoolboy, Augustine also studied the comic dramatist Terence, another lasting presence in his repertoire. To the mature Augustine, Terence posed the problem of the value of the classics even more acutely than Virgil. In his comic plays Terence wrote engagingly about serious sins like adultery, above all in his *Eunuch*, the play which had proved so popular in his lifetime that it made him a fortune. Notoriously, a young man in it uses tricks to seduce his beloved, whom he wrongly believes to be a slave girl. He dresses like a eunuch; he implies that he has actually raped her; he has even been looking at a painting in her room which showed the god Jupiter doing likewise to the young Danae. 'What a god! The one who shakes the heavens as a thunderer . . . !', he says, words which the *Confessions* quote from memory.[15] The play presented all that the older Augustine came to hate most about pagan literature: sex and bogus, immoral gods. As a Christian celibate, he wonders why he had had to learn stuff which is so corrupting.

His fellow Christian celibate and contemporary, Jerome, cites the *Eunuch* and its famous scene so often that he has been called a '*Eunuch*-freak'. Unlike Augustine, he found a good use for its language: he used it to denounce 'randy pseudo-monks', the arch-seducers of his own times.[16] Augustine was not addressing his confessions to 'pseudo-monks'. Gravely, he concludes that God had guided him to study authors like Terence because such study had one lasting value, the learning of words and letters. Like the painful basic studies of 'vocab', they could be applied to reading scripture.

He then wonders why pious Monnica had encouraged his schooling in such vain, immoral literature. Again, he mistakes her motives. He concludes that it must have been her roundabout means of teaching him to read and thus to read God's word. He does not reflect that like every other mother at the school, Monnica wanted her bright little boy to get on in society. Nor does he consider his other gains from what he read. It taught him to memorize and recite by heart, talents on which his literary style drew ever afterwards. His emotions were engaged by what he read, thereby opening that important element, his 'heart'. One hopes that, at the time, Terence made him do something which is missing from the *Confessions'* later books: laugh. Nor does he consider the lasting importance to him of the method by which grammar and vocab were imparted. Even thirty years later, as a Christian bishop, he would expound scripture in his sermons by taking its words individually and dwelling on each one's associations. This method was exactly the method he had learned from his schoolteachers, the *grammatici* who beat the classics into the little boys of Thagaste.

II

Schooling filled only the earlier part of young Augustine's day. There were also the boys' pastimes which modern biographers recover from passing remarks in his other works: 'in the fields around Thagaste', Peter Brown well puts it, Augustine 'stalked birds, watched the writhing tails torn off lizards; he thought of thunder as the rattling of the heavy wheels of Roman coaches on the rough flagstones of the clouds'.[17]

Unlike Tolstoy, adult Augustine did not regard a child as closer to ideal harmony than a grown man or school education as the ruin of innocence and therefore resented by its recipients. Original sin was in all boys, and they compounded it by their choices and the seductive pleasures which they preferred. Yet, Augustine also recalls what was good in his young self. He loved truth; he did not wish to be deceived; his memory was becoming strong; he was learning skill with words; he was soothed with friendship; he avoided pain, despair and ignorance. He was also alert about his own safety. With this touching little sketch, unrivalled in pagan literature, we can still compare the best about ourselves as children. In Augustine's view, these good features were all gifts of God. Even his instinct for self-preservation arose from the 'unity' which was part of God's hidden order in the world.

The darker side of his confessions needs to be kept in proportion. Like everyone else, he feared his schoolmasters' beatings and became anxious when he had to make a competitive speech in public, but he does not seem to have been unusually fearful or nervous, as if made so by pushy parents. Nor was he unduly scared by his Christian religion. As a boy, he may have had little idea of 'original sin'. He recalls, once, a 'childish superstition' in his past, but it may only have been a childish idea of God as an unpredictable old man.[18] In his confessions, he emerges rather differently, as keen and competitive. He wanted to win in every public contest. He would even steal bits of food from the household to sell or swap with other boys. He would cheat, he tells us, in order to be the victor in their games. Only later does he look back on childhood in general as the time of 'lies, perjury and theft'.[19]

The beatings at school have been seen, nonetheless, as profoundly formative for his idea of God: 'the irate schoolmaster of Augustine's infancy,' Leo Ferrari has written, 'becomes the scourging God who purifies his soul through the many punishments of life.'[20] However, this 'scourging God' was abundantly evident in scripture, whether or not its audience had ever been beaten themselves. The biblical God was the Great Chastizer of Israel's history and Job's plight, a text of particular interest to the confessing Augustine. The Epistle to the Hebrews stated clearly: 'Whom the Lord loves he corrects. He scourges every son whom he receives' (Hebr. 12.6). In Greek-speaking Antioch, Libanius' similar comments on the classroom make it hard to look on Augustine's schooling as especially traumatic. All over the empire, boys were in it together, a fact which conditioned their reception of the harshness. As Libanius reminded his young defectors, what had been good enough for him as a boy was good enough for them: 'canes will be active and straps too'. In his late sixties he composed a typically evasive speech to rebut the charge that he himself was 'harsh'. Beating, he claims, was not his practice, whereas other teachers have 'used up thousands of canes'. In fact he had been a willing beater.[21]

There was nothing exceptional about Augustine's classical education, either. Just as he loved Virgil, so Libanius, Synesius and their schoolfriends loved Homer. Augustine then devoured the orator Cicero, much as Libanius and Synesius pored over the Athenian orator Demosthenes. It was from his early youth onwards that Synesius' 'Attic' literary style took root.[22] The one difference is that, unlike the older Augustine, Libanius and his pupils never looked back and regretted their studies. As a grown man, Libanius continued to appreciate pupils 'who shed tears onto their texts of the Greek tragedies'. When he spoke on Euripides' tragic Hippolytus, he drew tears from his audience 'as if I was present and had witnessed his sufferings'.[23]

Boys being boys, distractions were not only confined to Thagaste. In Antioch, Libanius' widowed mother paid for him to go to a grammar teacher at the age of seven, but he went off to play in the fields and enjoyed his beloved pigeons instead. Unlike Monnica, his mother did not fuss too much about these absences. From a richer and socially established background, she could afford to allow her son to roam. A civic career in Antioch would be his for the taking.[24] In later life he had to deal with pupils who were much like young Augustine and his friends. They used to ignore his fine set speeches, he tells us, and intercommunicate only about 'charioteers, mimes, horses, dancers and past or future gladiatorial combats' when he was teaching them oratory.

Far the best insight into the similarities of grammar teaching and 'discipline' in Augustine's Thagaste and Libanius' Antioch is visual. It emerges from a set of mosaic panels, fifteen in all, which once edged an even larger mosaic floor. They were laid out in north Syria, most probably in or near Antioch, possibly during Libanius' lifetime.[25] Recently reassembled, the scenes and captions follow the schooling of a young boy, Kimbros. Kimbros is shown with his pet dog and then, face down, being caned on his bare bottom by his tutor. In another panel little Kimbros goes on to elementary school and meets his teacher, Marianos, while receiving gifts, apparently a pen and tablets. Another panel takes him on to the grammarian Alexandros, whom he greets formally with a kiss. 'Alexandros' is a very common name, but it is tempting to identify this one with Alexandros, a grammar teacher whom Libanius mentions in a letter of the mid-360s. If so, Kimbros' grammar schooling took place in Libanius' Antioch in exactly the years when the young Augustine was undergoing it in Thagaste.

In his grammar class, Kimbros makes a friend, Priscos, while the personified figure of Education gestures approvingly towards Alexandros' lips. The teacher, we conclude, is doing a good job, but not so Kimbros, who is denounced and consigned, it seems, to be whipped. He falls ill, but eventually returns to school accompanied by the captioned figure of Progress. The importance of these panels is that they were designed to run round a bigger mosaic, surely one in the house of a close family member or the adult Kimbros himself. When seated round them or when walking round the floor, their patron and his visitors could follow the trials of schooling as if in a cartoon strip. They saw none of Augustine's dynamic of sin and misapplied freedom. They did not discern God's 'orderly' punishment, recalling boys to the basic skills which, as future 'turners' to God, they needed to know. They were amused, not appalled, adults looking back on the horrors of their past.

There is one hazard, vividly presented by Libanius, which neither Kimbros nor Augustine recalls: child abuse. Little boys were accompanied to school by slave guardians, or pedagogues, who escorted them to the classroom and even kept an eye on the teachers' own behaviour. After school the pedagogues escorted their boys home. Libanius' speeches are the most vivid testimony to the hazards which these schoolboys faced.[26] In one speech, he expresses outrage at the innovation of allowing young boys to share couches with older men at parties connected with Antioch's Olympic games: their presence was a sexual temptation, gruesomely described. In a remarkable speech late in life, Libanius reproaches his older students for having agreed to toss a troublesome pedagogue in blankets when he brought his young charges to school. The pedagogues' job, he says, is to be 'guardians of youth in its flower . . . they are to repel unpleasant admirers and send them packing . . . they frustrate such people's advances like dogs which bay at wolves'. By carpeting a pedagogue, the older boys hoped to scare him off from guarding a handsome young boy. Then they would 'indulge themselves to their heart's content'.

Augustine refers to his own pedagogue, but says nothing about such wolfish harassment in Thagaste. He says nothing about Monnica being his chaperone, whereas Libanius praises his widowed mother for guarding her young sons from undesirable visitors. They were surely visitors with predatory, sexual aims, as Antioch was a big city with a strong Greek tradition in its schools. Sexual sins are not ignored elsewhere in the *Confessions*, but perhaps the young schoolboys in smaller, Latin-speaking Thagaste were not plagued by it.

By different routes to one and the same end, Libanius and Augustine then moved to the study of rhetoric, the underpinning of their future careers. Libanius appears to have started to study it before his fourteenth birthday, while also applying himself to the grammar studies which he had shirked. Such an early start in rhetoric has been considered typical of the Greek school tradition, but in north Africa Augustine also started early. Aged fourteen, he left his home town and went off to study 'literature and oratory' in nearby Madauros, about fifteen miles to the south. 'Literature' did not mean literary study as we understand it nowadays: it meant more of the grammarians' teaching. Libanius, catching up, and Augustine, edging forward, combined grammar and rhetoric at the same age.

Augustine must have lodged in Madauros, but only in two later letters does he recall it. On the main square, he remembered, there were two statues of the war-god Mars, one armed, one unarmed. The town's councillors were all pagans, and in a revealing exchange of letters, probably *c.*390, one of them gives a most powerful sense of what these traditional gods still meant. The letter-writer, Maximus, was by then an elderly man, but he had known young Augustine in the town, not necessarily as one of his teachers.[27] His reasons for writing are not stated. They have been suggested to arise from an assault by intolerant young Christians on some of the city's statues of pagan gods, but nothing in the letter is explicit, and if violence was the cue for it, the letter's tone is remarkably oblique. The myths of the Greeks about the gods on Olympus, Maximus states, are not true. What is true is the presence of the gods, publicly visible in town squares like Madauros'. 'We see them, we acknowledge them as tried and tested.' Behind their apparent multiplicity is only one God, of whom all these others are parts, like 'limbs' or like 'virtues'. Under these parts' many names, the one unnamed God is worshipped. He is 'without beginning'; he is like a 'great and magnificent father'; he has no 'natural offspring', an implicit rebuke to the Christians' 'Son'. He is honoured in a 'thousand ways' by the cults which are paid to many parts of him, what we now call the 'pagan gods'. They combine in 'discordant concord'. Christian martyrs with outlandish Punic names are as nothing against the power of Jupiter.

This letter is a telling expression of an educated pagan's beliefs during Augustine's lifetime. Whatever its cue, it implicitly challenged Christian practice and theology. Unlike the pagan gods, the Christians' God is invisible. Christians worship Him not in the main square but away from the public eye; their cults include worship of those human martyrs with preposterous local names. Augustine's reply picks only on marginal details, but it shows that he understood little about the pagan worship around him.[28] He regards the ancient Greek myths as items from a 'sacred history', as if pagans knew them from a sort of scripture book. He remembers Madauros' statues of Mars, but claims that they were neutralized by a third statue in the square, one which commemorated a man making a sign with his fingers towards the other two. Augustine misunderstood this statue as if its subject was casting a magical spell against the nearby 'demons'. In fact, it was the statue of a civic dignitary, holding his hands in an oratorical pose.

In Madauros he could also have seen a statue to the town's most famous citizen, the second-century orator and 'philosopher' Apuleius. He was author of the *Metamorphoses*, or *Golden Ass*, the novel which culminates in the nearest that pagan literature ever comes to a story of religious conversion. Throughout the tale and its subplots, Apuleius warned readers implicitly about the desire for misplaced knowledge, whether about magic or the gods. It was *curiositas*. To us, as to Conrad in *Lord Jim*, curiosity seems 'the most obvious of human sentiments'. To Augustine in his confessions, *curiositas* is sinful, one of the three basic 'lusts' affirmed in the New Testament (1 John 2.16).[29] The word was used repeatedly by Apuleius, but, like his Christian predecessors, Augustine applies it in a new way. 'Curiosity' is no longer the urge to have intimate knowledge about a god or his power: it is the urge to know and experience whatever distracts us from knowledge of God Himself. The young Augustine, returning from Madauros, was about to indulge it to the full.

6
Unfriendly Friendship

At the same early age of fourteen, the two future public orators, Augustine and Libanius, were already combining grammar studies and rhetoric. Their response to them was significantly different. Libanius presents his as a true conversion. In July 328, just after his fourteenth birthday, 'I was gripped,' he recalls, 'and a keen love for the subject entered me . . .' The charms of the countryside ceased to matter; he sold his pigeons, items 'which enslave a young man' and which are still familiar to us from their representations on the gravestones of young boys in the Greek world. He even gave up attending the horse races, theatres and gladiatorial shows. In July, his uncle attained the supreme honour of presiding over Antioch's quadrennial Olympic games. Even so, young Libanius stayed away from the occasion.[1]

This conversion grew from his previous months of rhetorical study and was helped by an outstanding teacher in Antioch, probably Ulpian of Ascalon, though Libanius does not name him. Augustine, by contrast, spent little more than a year in Madauros and then gave up his studies, but not his taste for games and shows. He had to give up because his father lacked the money to pay the next year's fees. He underwent a distraction, not a conversion. While he was still in Madauros, his voice broke and he matured sexually. He returned to Thagaste in his sixteenth year, underemployed and teeming (we might say) with hormones. As a pagan, Libanius pays no attention to this change, which is due neither to 'good' nor to 'bad' fortune, the themes of his speech, but is an inevitable fact of life. Augustine recalls it very differently, with the appalled hindsight of a celibate Christian adult. He dwells on the torrid effects in three vividly expressed chapters of his prayer. 'I want to put on record my past foul acts and the fleshly corruptions of my soul not because I love them, but so that I may love you, my God.' He 'burned', he 'boiled', he was 'swept over the cliffs of desire' and 'drowned in a whirlpool of outrageous lust'. He favours an imagery of floods and river currents, one which his confessions have already applied to the seductions of the pagan classics and which they will later apply to the abyss and chaos around the newly created matter of the universe.[2] He fixes his individual flood tide of disorder to two words for the underlying drive: concupiscence, or *concupiscentia* (a word invented by Christians), and *libido*, lust. *Libido*, by origin, was not used only for sexual lust, as early pagan authors remind us, but in the Christian Latin Bible it had meant nothing else. Augustine at first used these words more flexibly, but the sexual reference then predominated. He has influenced our vocabulary for sexual desire ever since.[3]

Driven by lust, he burned to be 'sated with the satisfactions of Hell below'. He 'dared to become like a wild wood, with varied and shading loves'. Sexual lust, he realizes, will transform a loving friendship. A loving friendship, he sees, can exist between one person's 'affection' and another's and is defined by a 'boundary' which is 'clearly lit'.[4] It is a fine image, the boundary fence of pure love and friendship, like the limit of a rural village lit up by the glare of street lights against the dark woods beyond. Sexual lust takes us disruptively beyond this boundary into the forest which it darkens. Augustine describes how 'I was boiling over, because of my fornications'. The implication is that, aged fifteen, he was already 'fornicating' with women (perhaps slave girls?). He recalls how his male friends in Thagaste would boast of these outrageous acts, the more so, the more vile they themselves were. 'It was a pleasure' (evidently, for Augustine himself) to do something outrageous not only out of 'lust for the act, but also for the praise [it brought]'. Even more vilely, 'when there was not the opportunity for something which I could admit and equal them, ruined as they were, I used to pretend that I had done what I had not done'. The 'brambles of lusts', meanwhile, were growing 'beyond my head'.

These complex metaphors are hard to translate, but they make it clear that Augustine himself went beyond 'impure thoughts'.[5] He actually did things, aged fifteen, and was as 'wicked' as possible. His loves were 'varied', whether varied with different people or varied in different ways, he does not clarify. They were 'shading', not in our sense of 'shady' or 'disreputable' but as part of his metaphor of a wild forest of lusts casting shade. He then lays emphasis on acts as outrageous as possible which 'it was a pleasure' for him to do. Modern readers therefore wonder if same-sex acts were involved, slave boys and adolescent male friends being available.

Later in the *Confessions* Augustine cites the 'men of Sodom' as examples of sinners 'against nature, everywhere and always to be disliked and punished', but as a young man he had not yet read about them. Is he passing over an actively homoerotic phase? It might seem unlikely, because the darker the sins which he confessed to God, the more he could thank Him for His loving pardon. Human readers, however, might slander him if he dwelt too specifically on an 'unnatural' past. He is not specific about what he did, and so we cannot know.[6] God anyway knew it all already.

He confronts another difficult question instead. What was his dear God, so loving, so merciful, doing for him while this sexual flood tide swept him away? He has already addressed this question when confessing his idleness in grammar classes and his seduction by the likes of Virgil and Terence. He answers in a similar way. God, he decides, was 'silently' aware of it all, 'sprinkling all my illicit pleasures with the bitterest discomforts'. He did not escape God's 'scourges', he now realizes, and God's plan was to bring him to chastity. God was needling, guiding and waiting to assemble all the pieces so that Augustine could 'turn' and make a decisive choice. Meanwhile, the 'discomforts' and 'scourges' were not an underlying dislike of sex: Augustine himself says that he loved it. Nor were they pangs of guilt, let alone a 'guilt' induced by Monnica's warnings against promiscuity. They turn out to be 'jealousy, suspicions and fears', as painful as the 'hot iron rods of torture', no mean pain in a late Roman law court, and 'angers and quarrels', words which echo words of St Paul. These 'scourges' would arise from the insecurities of young lovers. Before long, Augustine was to suffer them himself.

It was a tumultuous time, but 'what was it that delighted me', he asks unforgettably, 'except to "love and be loved"?' Here, he is using words which had a sinister past, the very words with which the stylistic model of his schooldays, the orator Cicero, had characterized the most dissolute young men in pagan Rome more than 400 years previously, supporters of the supremely 'wicked' and depraved aristocrat Catiline.[7] On returning home from Madauros, Augustine had been thrown back among friends and family in Thagaste. For many of them, education had ended altogether. The dark example of Catiline recurs in his most famous memory of this phase, when he was aged, as he remembers exactly, fifteen.

Once, at the 'dead of night' (like Catiline's conspirators), Augustine and some young friends raided a pear tree on a property near his family's vineyard. They stole masses of pears, but ate very few of them. They even threw some of them to pigs. This sin is analysed in greater length than any other in the *Confessions*, but Augustine is not exactly the first or last to steal fruit off a tree in a bout of poaching.[8] In 1888, the artist van Gogh was exploring in the south of France with a new-found friend, the officer Milliet, a man respected otherwise for his military discipline. 'I have come back from a day on Mount Majour,' van Gogh wrote to his brother, Theo, 'and my friend the second lieutenant was with me. We explored the old garden together, and stole some excellent figs.' Like the young Augustine, van Gogh had endured a year in which his schooling was abruptly discontinued. At the time of the theft, he too was pondering questions of God and the human condition, but the theft of the fruit prompts no comment. Instead, he remarks on the garden. 'If it had been bigger, it would have made me think of Zola's Paradou, high reeds and vines, ivy . . . scattered fragments of crumbling walls here and there among the green . . .'[9]

Augustine's analysis of his theft, by contrast, is long, and when first encountered may seem disproportionate. Is it a diversion, perhaps, in which he focuses at length on a lesser sin in order to distract his readers from wondering too much about his sexual misbehaviour? In his 'autobiography' his fellow orator Libanius shows himself to be a master of this sort of artful distraction. Or has he patterned it implicitly round a biblical prototype, Adam in the Garden of Eden, eating forbidden fruit, or the Prodigal Son, wandering among swine, so as to give the sin greater scope and make it symbolic for all mankind? Or is he merely repeating an analysis which he had given at length to others in earlier phases of his religious life?

In fact, the analysis goes to the heart of the *Confessions*. It makes their eventual account of 'what I am' seem less perplexing. While analysing this sin of theft, Augustine poses more than thirty rhetorical questions, some of which are addressed to God. One question arises loosely from another and, once, he even wonders out loud why he is 'considering and examining' the particular question which has just occurred to him. At three points he marks a sudden flash of realization: *ecce!* ('lo and behold!'). Remarkably, we are listening in to him in the unrevised process of analysing his past. As ever, he is analysing it in a prayer to God which we, its readers, overhear.[10]

This 'prayer overheard' is not a rehearsed narrative, representing what he has often confessed before. At no stage in his previous life had Augustine confessed individual sins to a priest or superior. Although his analysis includes words from scripture, they are arising spontaneously in the course of his praying. They have not been shaped by hours of checking and rewriting around a hidden pattern which we must work hard to extract. His confessing-prayer is not cryptic. There was no point in being cryptic when addressing God: God knew it all already.

As part of a prayer overheard, the story of the stolen pears is a literary curiosity which has deceived unwary readers. Three years before van Gogh's theft, the philosopher Nietzsche remarked in a letter that he had been reading the *Confessions* for 'relaxation'. 'Oh this old rhetor! How false he is and how distorted his vision! How I laughed (e.g. about the 'theft' of his youth, basically a student story).'[11] Certainly, the 'old rhetor' used skills from his years of training. He played on words which two of his school authors, Cicero and the historian Sallust, had used about 'wicked' Catiline. He used philosophy, especially Platonist philosophy on the 'deficiency' in evils and the apparent 'attraction' in worldly aims. He wove together words from the Psalms, Paul's letters and the Book of Job. He was not looking up these texts in a library. In each case he was drawing on what he knew by heart. He then combined these varied allusions into a paradoxical whole. Paradox was a technique which orators like himself and Libanius were taught to deploy in school. He deployed it, however, to a deeply serious end.

His analysis proceeds in stages, just as each one occurs to him. He begins by stating the absolute wickedness of theft: it breaks God's 'law', his Ten Commandments, the law 'written in our hearts'. Even a thief hates having something stolen from him. We did not do it, he tells God, because we needed the pears: they were not even especially good. The object, therefore, had not seduced them. We did it for the sheer pleasure of doing something illicit. His 'heart', his inmost being, he exclaims, is telling the truth now: 'look, God, my heart,' he repeats. 'Right now, let my heart tell you what it was seeking' in the deed: it was done 'so that I would be gratuitously wicked', the very words which Sallust had applied to Catiline. The only cause was 'my own wickedness'. We begin to see the special wickedness in the theft, although the items involved appear at first to be trivial. 'It was foul, and I loved it': three times in one sentence he repeats the word 'love', emphasizing the strength of his misplaced response. His soul 'leaped away from God's firmament to ruin beyond the boundary', words which echo Satan's fall from heaven. He sought 'disgrace 'or 'notoriety'.

Catiline and Satan are implicit models for what might otherwise seem a trivial sin. In the world of our senses there are many lesser delights and 'lower beauties': was Augustine excessively attracted by one of them? To find an answer, he runs through the 'attraction' which exists in other worldly desires. Only if we pursue these desires in the wrong way do we fall into sin, but, even then, these sins are undertaken as a means to an end, the 'good' which they appear to offer. Murders, he observes, are very seldom committed only for murder's sake. Even Catiline was evil for a further end, the honours, commands and riches which he hoped to obtain by seizing Rome and remedying his debts. Thieving young Augustine had no such aims. So he was worse even than Catiline, the language of whose enemies he has been echoing: he did not do it for some apparent 'good' at all.

Earlier in the *Confessions*, Augustine had described how he used to steal food as a boy from his parents' household. He never stopped to analyse those thefts in detail, and now we see why. He stole the food, he explains, as a means to winning favour among his friends. The theft of the pears was quite different. It was not done for a purpose: it was wickedness for wickedness's sake. Only a few of the pears were eaten and the others were fit to throw to pigs. So, what, he asks, was it that 'delighted' him in the crime?

Again, his mature philosophy of sin comes into play. Sins, he believes, are evil because of a 'deficiency' of good. As a result they have a sort of specious beauty, a view which he supports by reviewing a range of sins and their related deficiencies, fourteen in all: again, some of these sins recall vices ascribed to Catiline. In keeping with his philosophy he gives them a new explanation. Each sin, he claims, is a 'perverse imitation of a quality which God has to perfection'.[12] Curiosity, for example, aspires to knowledge, but 'God knows all things supremely.' How does his theft relate to this pattern?

In stealing the pears, he now realizes, he had loved to 'do what was illicit' in a show of misplaced liberty. Here, then, is the 'perverse imitation' in the sin. It was a shadowy 'likeness' of omnipotence, but omnipotence is the quality of God. Augustine has now reached down to an answer and so he rounds it off with words from the Book of Job. 'Look!' he says, writing down what has just occurred to him: 'Like a slave fearing his lord and seeking the shadow!' In his *Notes on Job*, which were being written just before the *Confessions*, he explains this verse as signifying Adam's hiding in the garden of Eden and seeking the covering, or shade, of leaves (the fig leaves) which marked man's first abandonment of God.[13] The verse's primary allusion is to Job, not Adam, but Augustine's understanding of it is present in the *Confessions* too. He is not identifying his theft exactly with Adam's theft. Unlike Adam, he had not been beguiled into it by a woman and he had not been tempted to seek knowledge, let alone immortality. He is not presenting himself as a 'new Adam'. He is presenting himself as Adam's descendant, an heir to the original sin which he has already assumed to be present in every baby.

While analysing his theft, Augustine poses a question, digresses and answers it from the 'heart'. He then moves on to another aspect of the same experience. He has already analysed in a similar way his distaste for learning Greek, but this time he thanks God explicitly for enabling him to recall his sin without fear. He thanks Him for forgiving it and 'dissolving it like ice', an image he has been using in his near-contemporary writings about 'sin' and 'habit'. Once again, his awareness of the depths of his past sins intensifies his sense of God's love, pardon and mercy.

His next question is posed in words from St Paul: what 'fruit', or profit, did he have from these evils? He has already accepted that no such profit was his motive, but might there have been some consequential profit nonetheless? 'Alone, I would not have done it,' he realizes: did he act out of love for the company he kept? Then, he remembers: together, he and his friends had laughed at how they had cheated the pear tree's owner. Sometimes we laugh when alone, he observes, but 'I would not even have been doing that all alone.' A new aspect has occurred to him, and so he lays this 'lively recollection' before God: 'look, God, here it is before You!' All by himself, he would never have stolen for the pleasure of stealing. 'Friendship' was essential to the crime, but it was an 'unfriendly friendship', one which seduces the mind and supports the desire to harm someone else. 'When someone says, "Let's go, let's do it", it ashames us not to be shameless.' It still does.

In Freud's view, vandalism is encouraged by pre-existing guilt and is undertaken so that this guilt has something external on which to focus. Augustine's self-analysis is very different. To have held back would have been to incur shame, not guilt at all. Nor was it a casual, babyish mischief. It arose from our human propensity for purposeless evil.

Sexual transgressions and theft for theft's sake, we now see, share a similar root: misapplied friendship. Augustine is the first Christian writer to explore friendship, rather than love, for a neighbour or for God. He knew very well the texts in which Cicero had explored friendship's nature and value: in the Greek tradition too, Synesius and Libanius took a straightforward view of friendship as a Hellenic good, best expressed by reciprocal actions and loyalty. However, unlike them Augustine had developed a sharp eye for friendship's dangers. They mattered profoundly in small Christian groups of celibate 'brethren', groups like his own before he composed the *Confessions*. His analysis of his theft is the self-scrutiny of a Christian who is accustomed to a monastic way of life. It is the longest such 'honesty about the heart' hitherto composed in the Latin West. Augustine's innovation is to have linked friendship to the human heart, that central item in the Psalms. He then analyses the depths of his sin so as to present the scope of God's mercy and grace in forgiving it and allowing him to recall it without fear. So, too, he hopes, his readers will not mock him, but will thank God for what they have not done themselves. He envisages them as 'called by God' and as already granted the gift of chastity: he is thinking of celibate strivers like himself.[14]

Where we would see only a theft for the hell of it, he sees a sinful claim to omnipotence, the quality of God. He is not a consequentialist, judging his act only by its consequences. He is aware of the crucial role of *camaraderie*, which encouraged the looting and stealing by the gang, but he focuses on the theft because it was evil for evil's sake. Whereas Adam ate the forbidden fruit for a purpose, Augustine did not. He has not focused on the incident in order to distract his readers from his sexual sins. He would never consider that sexual acts are done and enjoyed simply because they are illicit. As the theft was enjoyed solely for that reason, it warns us about something even darker in ourselves. Its analysis is 'what matters'. It relates to the sinful, original core which is in us from birth onwards as descendants of Adam and Eve.

Within a year, Augustine had left his friends and orchards and gone off to be schooled elsewhere. None of those friends ever dreamed that their misbehaviour one midnight would still be analysed nearly 1,700 years later. Yet, teenagers still lapse into 'orgies of looting', urged on by others, although the goods which they loot have next to no value. Distorting friendship went forward with Augustine, soon to beset him with new temptations.

7
'To Carthage I Came . . .'

I

In his seventeenth year Augustine left Thagaste again and resumed his studies in Carthage, the second greatest city in the Latin West. His enforced 'year out' was ended. He was able to resume because he was helped by Cornelius Romanianus, one of Thagaste's richest men.

Romanianus was to assist Augustine's progress for the next sixteen years of his life. Augustine then thanks him in a text which he dedicated to him in November 386: 'you took me on as a poor little young man going off to his studies, with a house, expenses and what is even more, with the support of your mind'. Romanianus, it seems, helped Augustine to lodge in Carthage and contributed to costs which were beyond Patricius' means. It appears from words written later by Romanianus' son that the family were of 'one blood' with Augustine's, presumably through kinship with Patricius.[1] Romanianus recognized young Augustine's promise. When the boy had trained as a speaker, he would be useful in the legal battles which beset a rich man's life.

In late 370/71, Augustine arrived in the city, which was the seat of the Roman governor. Years later, one of his deacons would recall how the names of governors were written on ivory tablets and read out as a roll of honour on prescribed days in front of the crowd. People would call out their support for honest governors of the past and shout insults and hiss at the names of those who had been corrupt and rapacious. Other attractions have been memorably evoked by his modern biographer, Peter Brown. 'Its marvellous artificial harbour was ringed with colonnades; its regular avenues shaded with trees; its waterfront open to the wide world. On the "Maritime Parade", Augustine could see the skeleton of a whale large enough to shelter twelve men; a mosaic showing the Sciapods, the weird inhabitants of the lands far beyond the Roman Empire; in the bookstalls that lined the street, he could pick up centuries-old writings of Gnostic heretics, a source of distress, later, to the older bishop, but an exciting discovery for the crowds of curious browsers.'[2] Now at last he could see the sea rather than imagining it from a bowl of water.

Augustine's *Confessions* are equal to the occasion. 'I came to Carthage (*Karthago*) and round me crackled a frying-pan (*sartago*) of outrageous loves. I was not yet in love but I was "in love with love"', words which once again echo the young friends of wicked Catiline.[3] 'I had an inner, more secret lack, and I disliked myself less, though I was actually lacking.' Augustine is not saying that he had been plunged into self-hatred, let alone into a hatred of his sexual desires. His 'hidden lack', he goes on to explain, was his inner lack of God and God's 'food' (available through the scriptures, which he had not yet digested).[4] Once again, he is not recalling a guilt-ridden youth. He is looking back on himself as someone who was looking for love without the slightest awareness of what he really lacked. To find it he plunged mistakenly into 'sex and the city'. He aspired to be 'elegant and urbane'; he rushed into a sexual affair. He was also 'carried off' by 'theatrical shows'.

In Carthage, there was no escaping shows and spectacles. Even in antiquity they were known to abound in the city, as its archaeological record attests.[5] They took place, as often, on the edges of the urban centre. To the north was the theatre, and just beyond it a smaller odeon for fewer spectators. To the south lay the big circus for horse and chariot races and to the west the huge amphitheatre, scene of the gladiatorial fights and the combats of wild animals of which Augustine had dreamed as a schoolboy. If a church service coincided with one of these shows, people would walk out of the congregation. Among the crowds of spectators, Augustine observes, there would no doubt be some future bishops. When the crowds poured out of the arenas they might happen to see a Christian celibate, a 'slave of God', passing by in distinctive dress and hairstyle. He was as unusual as a 'white blackbird'. 'You miserable wretches!' Augustine imagines the spectators calling out. 'What a lot you are missing!'[6]

As he is confessing his sins and thanks to God, Augustine has no reason to give his human readers a clear idea of how he spent a normal day. Instead, his focus is on his straying: the shows, sex and the seductions of heresy. Once again, 'friendship' and its perils underlie them. To see why, we need to consider the sort of shows Augustine sampled. He went to the gladiatorial shows which were still being given by rich donors, despite an Imperial ban on them. He also went to the theatre, but not for the plays in our Greek and Latin classics. He watched Latin extracts in which a single actor sang a classic scene, and he also watched mimes and pantomimes.

Ancient pantomime was an art form closer to our ballet. In it, a skilled lead dancer acted out the various parts in a story, usually items from an ancient myth, while a chorus of male and female singers backed him. The dancer, usually male, was masked and costumed and admired for the softness and flexibility of movements which were based on traditional positions for the feet and hands. Extracts from Virgil's *Aeneid* might be danced, not only the story of Dido and Aeneas but also, Augustine later remarks in a sermon, the fine scene in Virgil's Underworld in which Aeneas' father 'showed the souls of the great Romans who were to come into bodies'.[7] These 'souls' were presumably represented by the chorus behind the dancer. 'Only a few of you,' Augustine tells his congregation, 'know this story from a book, but many of you know it from the theatre', much as many nowadays know Dickens' novels only from televised versions. The wondrous skill of the lead dancers rightly impressed him. They could 'almost talk with their eyes' and could communicate by conventional movements, not words, a skill which fascinated him.[8]

Mimes, by contrast, were spoken sketches of everyday life, performed by men and women together. They not only wore no masks: sometimes, the women went topless, or less. Favourite mime plots involved adventures among brigands and the troubles of adulterous lovers. For Christian moralists, mime actresses ranked as low as prostitutes. In fact, the two skills often went together. Christian bishops therefore refused baptism to actresses. In due course their refusal caused a casting shortage for the very spectacles which their Christian audiences were not willing to forgo.[9]

Besides these stage plays, there were plays and dancing in connection with cults of the gods. Nearly forty years later, Augustine still recalls how he used to watch dancers and musicians in Carthage performing in honour of the goddess Caelestis (Goddess of Heaven) or mother Cybele. In mid-March the latter was honoured with tales of self-castration by her devotees, while Caelestis was typically honoured by 'a company of prostitutes', mime dancers who (Augustine claims) celebrated obscene acts in the presence of the virgin goddess's statue. Unsurprisingly, the audience packed in, watching 'with the utmost attention'.[10] As in theatre shows, there were dirty songs, lost to us nowadays but sung with gusto by the crowds.

Characteristically, Augustine recalls his emotional responses. He 'rejoiced together' with the lovers 'when they enjoyed themselves through their wickednesses' and he 'shared their sadness' when they had to part and 'lose each other'. In school he had wept while listening to Aeneas' parting from Dido: now, in the theatre he wept 'vehemently' whenever the actors elicited his tears, above all by performing the parting and sadnesses of unhappy lovers. 'At that time I loved to be distressed,' he recalls, but he also asks why we wish to be pained by watching 'distressing and tragic things' which we would not wish to suffer ourselves. He answers his question in another complex sequence of paradoxes which play on the differences of 'misery' and 'mercy', distress and delight. He is not primarily answering the classic question, 'Why does tragedy give pleasure?' As his answer proceeds, it becomes plain that he is thinking primarily of the pleasure we take in disreputable pantomimes and mimes.

He asserts that he and we enjoy them the more we 'suffer' from similar 'miseries' ourselves as we watch. He has just recalled how he was suffering the jealousies and quarrels of his own love affairs and so he is now considering primarily the fictional presentation of such scenes in mimes. A man, he believes, is 'all the more moved by them, the less he himself is healthily rid of such affections'. He does not consider a modern answer to our pleasure in watching tragedy, that it allows us to anticipate what may one day befall ourselves. He takes an opposite view, that the pleasure in watching is even greater if we ourselves are already victims of the emotions which we are watching. He then considers the merit, or otherwise, of the spectator's apparent 'sympathy'. It is misplaced because it is sympathy for what is 'false', a category which he does not distinguish clearly from the 'fictitious'.[11] It is especially misplaced if the scene being watched is 'filthy', a reminder that he is thinking especially of mimes. 'Sympathy', he concedes, is a good form of 'distress' and indeed it arises from 'friendship'. However, it can tip over into seething, boiling lusts, another instance of friendship misapplied, and be the beginnings of an acute and unhealthy 'itch'. Like a modern critic of sex scenes on the internet, Augustine deplores our reactions for being provoked by fakes and for preparing us to be beset by a more intense lust.

Augustine's analysis, often misunderstood, is unique to him, but his disapproval is not. In Antioch, Libanius' Christian pupil, Bishop John

Chrysostom, is even more outspoken about the sins of watching theatre, especially mimes, while showing how well he remembers the hairstyles, the make-up and the naked bodies of the actresses on stage. He and Libanius went against popular taste, exemplified by the two big theatres in the city and the many items from mimes and drama which are shown in mosaic floors in houses of the rich.[12] Theatre was only fit, Libanius considered, for the vulgar crowds who attended it. Men of culture would keep away, especially because it distracted serious students from their work. Whereas the young Augustine enjoyed it, Libanius claims that he stayed away entirely from the age of fourteen onwards. In all his letters, he never alludes favourably to the theatre or praises any of his friends' interest in it.[13]

Once, for rhetorical effect, Libanius crossed this self-imposed boundary. Unlike the adult Augustine, he spoke in favour of pantomime artists and relished the paradox in a choice of topic which allowed him to challenge previous orators' dislike of their morals and influence. His rhetorical tour de force made points, nonetheless, which Augustine never considered. Theatre, Libanius realizes, provides a space and a time for relaxation from public affairs. The viewers are not corrupted into repeating in their own lives what they watch on the stage. Lovers of wild-beast shows do not promptly take up hunting, so why will a pantomime provoke adultery?[14]

Neither Libanius nor Augustine considers theatre's capacity for widening and sharpening our sensibilities through dramas which we have not confronted in life. Neither engages with Aristotle's famous judgement about 'purging' the audience by pity and fear. Both discuss the theatre's effect on the spectators, but never on the fighters and dancers. It was they who were required to strip naked or to risk their lives.[15]

II

In Carthage, 'friendship' was also misapplied by students. Augustine was no exception. He joined a group of boisterous harassers, the aptly named 'Overturners', who would set upon shy and innocent freshmen.[16] 'Brazenly' they would go after modest unknowns, like Oxford's Bollinger Club in the fiction of Evelyn Waugh. Augustine soon realized that this company was not his natural milieu, but it was hardly the choice of an overanxious student. He had acted, he later believed, out of 'impudent shame' and had gone along with the horseplay without really endorsing it. Newly arrived, he may well have been somewhat adrift. The names of significant friends are linked to his time in Carthage, but several, perhaps all, of them belong only to his later years there as a teacher. The Overturners were probably his first attempt to fill a gap.

'Friendship', he admits, was also distorted by his hunt for sex. 'It was sweet to me to love and be loved, even more so if I enjoyed the body of someone who loved me.' As a result, 'I was polluting the spring of friendship with the filth of lustful desire.' The language, as ever, is metaphorical and not specific, but Augustine is not saying that he polluted 'male' friendships with same-sex lust. 'Friendship', he means, is an ideal state, which he perverted by lust in general, but the further sin of lust for a male is not specified. The imperfect tense is significant: 'I *was* polluting', not once, but continuously, at the level of 'lust'. He then 'rushed into love', because he badly wanted to be caught by it. He was duly 'loved' and 'reached the chain of enjoyment', physically, but it brought 'jealousy, suspicions, fears and rages'. Manifestly, he had sex with a lover, surely a female, as he does not, with Christian hindsight, call it 'unnatural'.[17]

Soon afterwards, he refers to an actual incident, again in unspecific language. 'I dared even in the celebration of Your solemn rites', a church service, 'to lust within the walls of Your church and to conduct the business of procuring the fruits of death.'[18] This reference to deadly sin has been much discussed ('did he masturbate in church?') but one of his recently found sermons has now clarified it. While preaching in Carthage more than thirty years later, Augustine urged his Christian congregation to 'obedience' by reminding them of improvements made since his time in the city as a student. At that time, he tells them, he used to 'keep vigil', presumably at night-time, in congregations in which the sexes were mixed, the 'women mixed in with the wicked importunings of the males', and where there was an opportunity of 'tempting even their chastity'. The means, perhaps, were messages sent or called out during the sermon by 'ambushers of chastity'. In the past, the entries to church had been unsegregated, and so the men, 'wicked and impudent', also used to 'say such things, face on, to married women (*matronae*) as they passed through'. Subsequently, the Bishop of Carthage segregated the sexes inside the church building. He also introduced separate entry channels, one for women, one for men, so as to 'stop them confronting each other in narrow entrances and beginning what they later would strive to complete'.[19]

These two memories recall the memory in the *Confessions* and help to explain it. The 'business' which Augustine dared to conduct, thereby procuring 'deadly' sin, was the arranging of a sexual date, to be concluded elsewhere, in a mixed night-time congregation. He had been an 'ambusher of chastity'. His sermon's second memory, the brazen propositioning in the narrows of a church porch, may also be one which he had realized as a young man. He recalls men accosting *matronae*, married women. As a result of his own conduct, he confesses, God 'thrashed him with heavy punishments'. They match the punitive 'iron lashes of jealousy, suspicions . . . rages', which he has already mentioned. If his date was a married woman (*matrona*), these punishments of jealousy and quarrelling are more readily understood.

The 'varied loves' and 'fornications' in Thagaste and this propositioning inside a church and (probably) on the way into Carthage's basilica refute modern characterizations of Augustine as shy and timid. However, in late 371, during Augustine's first autumn in Carthage, his father, Patricius, died. His mother, Monnica, was left to cope with the financing of Augustine's studies. Again, Romanianus' help proved to be crucial, but sex soon compounded the circumstances in a new way: Monnica had to accept a third party in the relationship, a *concubina*, or 'partner', whom Augustine had taken on by spring 372. She came from a humble family and was probably already a Christian. She was not married, so she was not one of the 'matrons' whom Augustine remembers being pestered by young men in the church porch. It is not even clear that she was a girl whom he picked up at night in a mixed congregation inside the church itself.[20]

Recent social changes have made this concubine seem less startling than she seemed to scholars in the 1950s. A pre- or post-matrimonial concubine was not at all unusual in a man's life. Like Augustine, Libanius also took one, but only in his late thirties after the death of the girl, his cousin, to whom he had been betrothed. Unlike Augustine, he remained faithful to the woman until her death and continued to care deeply about their son. However, his social position was tellingly different. As he was well-born and well-off, he had no need to marry above his station. He was quite blunt about the virtues of a concubine in older age. Of her death, he simply remarks, 'She was worth many serving-maids.' After her death, she 'no longer came running to me and I was simply left to shout'.[21] Concubines solved life's perpetual problem, housekeeping.

As a couple, Augustine and the girl 'lived together', like many nowadays, but did not marry, because their prospects and social standing were too disparate. Although marriage was more highly regarded, concubinages were recognized in Roman law. In the very year when Augustine began his affair, a concubine's rights of inheritance had been legally specified. If there were legitimate heirs from the male's marriage, the concubine and any children from the relationship received only a twelfth part. If he had no children by a marriage, she and her children by him received a quarter.[22] Such rules only concerned well-off members of the propertied class, but Augustine, from a councillor's family, was at a level to be affected.

The Churches' views of such relationships were necessarily relaxed. Soon after Augustine began his, a Church Council ruled that unmarried men who had a concubine could receive the eucharist. The Council, admittedly, met in Spain, but even in Spain men who had both a wife and a concubine at the same time were excluded from the rite. Higher-minded bishops continued to wish for more, but young Augustine would have paid no attention to a denunciation of people like himself.[23] His relationship was a 'pact' agreed for 'lust', he frankly recalls, but it also involved mutual fidelity. In old age, as a celibate bishop, he still recalled the experience of the male orgasm. He does not consider it 'proper', he writes then, to be 'inanely curious' about what women 'feel in their hidden entrails when the seeds of either sex are mixed with pleasure in the womb'. He is not 'feigning ignorance of female sexual pleasure', here.[24] He believes, like others, that both the man and the woman produce 'seeds' when making love, but he leaves it to women to consider what a woman may feel, not while doing so, but afterwards, when the seeds are mixing in her womb for conception. Meanwhile, his concubine may have taken as much pleasure in the sex as he did.

The relationship was not planned for legitimate offspring, the goal of marriage, but by early summer his concubine was pregnant. She bore Augustine a son, whom they named 'Adeodatus', or 'Given by God'. The name had originated from the Punic name Iatanbaal, which it translated, but by the fourth century it was simply a common name among Latin-speaking Christians. It was especially apt for an unintended child 'given' by God out of wedlock. The choice of name suggests that the mother, like Augustine, had Christian sympathies. 'When a child is born against one's wishes,' Augustine well remarks with hindsight, 'nonetheless it compels itself to be loved.'[25] Adeodatus was much loved, but he also had to be accepted by Monnica. She had good reasons to be tolerant. Concubinage before marriage was recognized to be a temporary arrangement, at least until the man found a rich enough wife. The girl would be no obstacle to Monnica's long-term social aims for her son. Meanwhile, she and Adeodatus would help to deter young Augustine from the deadly sin of adultery. As a strict Christian, Monnica could never have agreed with young Tolstoy's memorable aunt. 'My kind aunt, the purest of beings, with whom I lived, always used to tell me that there was nothing she wished for more than that I should have a liaison with a married woman.' She said so in elegant French, but she shared Monnica's aims: a job for Tolstoy at court, 'and the supreme happiness, that I should marry a very rich girl and as the result of this marriage have as many serfs as possible'.[26]

In later life Augustine came to regard this topic differently. He considers that a man who takes a concubine 'for a time' until he finds a wife worthy of his rank and assets is an adulterer by his very intention. However, if the concubine remains unmarried and gives up sex when the relationship ends, there is some hope for her. In his later writings, Augustine finds it hard to call such a woman adulterous, especially if she has had a child in the relationship.[27] Augustine's own concubine was to be just such a person. In later life, she perhaps never knew what her former partner was so generously preaching about her circumstances.

In older age Augustine denounced sex during pregnancy as a sin. No doubt the young Augustine had indulged in it. Precautions against pregnancy were also sinful, but for another thirteen years Augustine continued to have sex with his concubine without any more children. In antiquity, there were herbal antidotes, not all of which are now thought to be inefficient. There were also 'times of the month', miscalculated in ignorance of the female's ovaries.[28] Plainly, the young Augustine lived in what the old Augustine regarded as sin and compounded it in widely practised ways.

III

Augustine's sinful memories are luridly presented to God, but they are not a full record of his student days. He worked hard; he lived with his young family; he survived the competitive life among fellow students which the writings of two other keen pupils, Libanius and Synesius, help us to appreciate. Like Augustine, they lived their years of higher study in big cities away from home. When they recall their higher education, Synesius in carefully constructed letters, Libanius in his 'autobiography', they differ from Augustine's confessing. They present themselves and their studies in a favourable light.

Unlike Augustine, Libanius already had a history of rhetorical talent in his family. It was evident in one of his uncles and in his grandfather. Nonetheless, he broke with family tradition by leaving his home in Antioch and opting for higher studies abroad.[29] Whereas Augustine's parents backed such a plan and paid for as much of it as they could, Libanius' plan divided his kin. His rhetorically gifted uncle favoured it, but his other uncle considered it 'impossible'. His mother wept and lamented her imminent loss, like Monnica at a later stage in Augustine's career. At the age of twenty-two, Libanius went off to Athens, the ultimate centre of higher study on which a friend had inspired him to set his sights.

Whereas Libanius, wanting to study rhetoric, opted for Athens, Synesius, wanting to study philosophy, sailed off to the mega-city of Alexandria in Egypt. Their friends in both places differed notably from those whom Augustine made in Carthage. Augustine's fellow students were mostly drawn from Africa's Latin-speaking towns, but Synesius' in Alexandria came from cities outside Egypt and Libanius' in Athens came from all over the Greek-speaking world, from the Black Sea to Palestine.[30] Life among them was cliquey and aggressive nonetheless, as Libanius vividly reveals. Like Augustine, he never names his teachers, but his letters allow us to trace personal links between his admired teacher Ulpian in Antioch and the teacher who was his preferred choice in Athens when he first arrived. Athens' local version of the 'Overturners' upset these links, nonetheless.

Libanius and his contemporaries have left memorable descriptions of the organized kidnapping of newly arrived students in Athens and the ordeals of a 'freshmen's initiation' in the public baths.[31] Gangs escorted the new intake while mocking and threatening them according to their levels of accomplishment. There was said to be a playful element to it all, and perhaps with hindsight the new boys realized it, but there was more to it than brutal ebullience. Both Carthage and Athens maintained a teacher of rhetoric with an official salary (Athens maintained three), but even these 'public' teachers charged fees from their students. Around them other teachers simply set up classes where best they could and competed for pupils. The more pupils they had, the longer their classes survived. In Athens, the local Overturners were recruiting new pupils for their own particular teacher. On arrival, the young Libanius thus found himself obliged, he claims, to swear an oath of loyalty to a professor whom he had not even wished to frequent. As he only swore under duress, he was not obliged, he also claims, to join in the fights which were launched by the professor's gangs.[32] As in Augustine's Carthage, violence broke out between classrooms while the pupils of one professor fought those of another. Like Augustine, Libanius claims that he stood aside whenever outsiders vandalized a rival teacher's room and pupils. This violence was the consequence of a market in higher education run wild. Competition ruled, heated by faction and vicious slander. As the competing pupils and teachers were keen to sabotage one another, the dark arts of sorcery and astrology also flourished among them. They were deployed to harm rivals and assist success as freely as in the city's hippodrome, that other competitive setting. In Athens, but not Carthage, the gang warfare of the students once came to all-out war, requiring intervention by the Roman governor.[33]

Instead of joining in this chaos, Augustine and Libanius worked at the rhetoric which they had already begun to study. So did Synesius, to judge from his mature literary style, although he never says with whom he continued to absorb it in Alexandria. The subject imposed punishing demands on its students, still visible in the vast range of classic Greek authors whom Libanius' prose style can echo, including Plato and the great historian Thucydides. These authors had to be memorized remorselessly. Both Augustine and Libanius recall how they or a friend would pace, after lessons, in the city's centre with a writing tablet or a text in hand. The classes were sometimes held in the heart of the city, in the forum or main square in rooms screened only by curtains from the hustle of the real world, but often in the teacher's own house or any available public space.[34]

Thanks to their studies, Libanius and Synesius became able to write and speak classic Atticizing Greek, based on texts written seven centuries before their own time. It was as far away from them as Dante is from us. Similarly, Augustine learned to compose in a Latin which was not at all the Latin of everyday speech. In these antique languages, practice speeches had to be improvised and delivered in which great decisions of past history were revisited or the implications of episodes of myth were teased out. These studies had already been pursued for many centuries in Greek and Latin higher education. Young Augustine, Libanius and Synesius are examples of what modern literary scholars now call the 'Third Sophistic', heirs to two previous phases of 'sophistic' public speaking, the most famous being one in the second and early third centuries AD. Libanius' model was indeed a sophist from this 'second' phase, Aelius Aristides, whose portrait, even, he would try to acquire. He wanted to research a vital question, the nature of Aelius' hair. For public orators, baldness and flowing hairstyles were both a topic for sparkling lectures and an aspect of their own 'personal grooming' before their audience. Synesius's role model, Dio, had spoken against baldness, but Synesius, himself bald, wrote brilliantly in praise of it. Libanius may not have been bald too, but he wanted to know exactly how his hero, Aelius, had styled his hair.[35]

Aelius and his contemporaries had also represented a verbal mastery of rhetoric and the old Greek classics, but this education was not irrelevant or socially pointless. It marked out its best exponents as especially hard workers. As performers they could compete, like young Augustine, for the many prizes for public speaking which were offered at public festivals. Much in life depended on well-spoken words. They could sway the favour of a governor or even an emperor, people who had the power to make big grants or to resolve disputes. As a classical education was shared by other men with influence, it enabled speakers to engage with them as if on common ground, despite what were often wide differences of home or background. It dignified its exponents and listeners while they engaged with a subject agreed to be much greater than their own selves. Synesius once lengthily assured a prominent courtier at Constantinople, who liked to be thought of as a philosopher, that he was indeed the worthy heir to Plato's pupils in Sicily a mere 750 years earlier. Likewise, Libanius began a letter to the Jewish Patriarch with an allusion to Euripides' *Telephus*, a favourite of Athenian comic poets some eight centuries in the past.[36] Whereas Synesius learned the complex, but delightful, metres which he later used for his Christian hymns, Augustine's main training was in the arts of prose rhythm and style. It is disputed how far his confessions use sentence endings which are shaped by the quantities of their vowels, like those of his admired Cicero. The most thorough recent study concludes that they are, and certainly they are full of turns of speech which his rhetorical schooling had taught him.[37]

None of the three chose to study what might seem the most relevant subject: Roman law. Aged fourteen, Libanius had already 'converted' to the rhetorical art and had no wish to struggle as an advocate in a law court. Instead, he presents himself as a young man determined on rhetoric and teaching because they were his passions. For Augustine, they were a natural way of extending his talent profitably beyond his small town. If he progressed, he might find himself addressing judges and Roman governors abroad, but he would mostly be involved in teaching rhetoric in classes. Neither public role was for the timid. In the court-room or the forum, orators would battle for victory, and the classroom was no comfortable ivory tower, either.[38]

In Athens, Libanius describes all the teachers as low-grade and insists that his poor health prevented him from performing loud declamations in their presence. Critics claimed that in fact he had never enrolled with the city's top teachers, that he was afraid of being obscured by their crowds of pupils and their fame, and that, so far from being kidnapped, he chose a dim teacher quite freely. Whatever the truth, these allegations are evidence of the competitive, personalized gossip which swirled among pupils.[39]

In such a setting, intensive study spawned its own anxieties. Aged twenty, before leaving for Athens, Libanius suffered a physical shock which grew to seem a turning point in his life. He had been reading that pearl among classical texts, Aristophanes' comedy *The Acharnians*. Its humour and crudeness would have intrigued the young Augustine as much as they would have appalled the old Augustine twenty years later. While Libanius read, a thunderbolt struck the ground beside him, an evident sign from the god Zeus. It induced dizziness and headaches which went on to plague him throughout his career. They were not, as he later thought, a legacy of this one event. They were constant side-effects of the strain in a rhetorical career.[40]

Aged eighteen, among the classes in Carthage, Augustine underwent a shock of a different kind. For the first time in his life, he was converted. He became fired with the love of 'wisdom', ignited by a very much older book.

IV

The book in question 'changed my emotional direction', Augustine recalls, citing, typically, its impact on his feelings. He 'burned', he says, and 'all vain ambition became vile to me all of a sudden'.[41] He 'lusted' for something else, with an 'incredible blaze' in his heart. In the 'usual course of study' he had encountered a book which others used to read mainly for its style. It was the *Hortensius* of Cicero, a text which had been written more than four centuries earlier. As the original is lost to us, scholars still struggle to recover parts of it from later authors' citations, including those by Augustine himself.[42]

Cicero would have been delighted by his short work's impact. In late 46/early 45 BC he had written it as an encouragement to the study of philosophy. It was the first of a cluster of philosophical works which he was to write while Julius Caesar was dominating Roman political life, Cicero's primary love. He composed it as a dialogue, and set it in the grandest of houses, the villa of the immensely rich Lucullus in the idyllic scenery of the Bay of Naples. The dramatic date of the discussions was significant, the late 60s BC when Cicero had stood briefly at the height of his political career. He chose as his fellow participants three of the greatest men of Rome at that time, Lucullus, Catulus and Hortensius. Cicero gained lustre by associating himself with these elderly giants of the past.[43]

This grand social setting cannot have been lost on the young Augustine, a boy from Thagaste who was aiming to progress socially. Here were the noblest Romans of a golden era discussing the merits of philosophy before his very eyes. Catulus, it seems, began by speaking up for poetry. Next, Lucullus spoke up for history, fittingly, as he had written a history book. Hortensius, the famous orator, then spoke at length for oratory. After some further disagreements, Cicero, finally, spoke up for philosophy. Hortensius was 'profoundly moved' and was probably won over to philosophy (though this outcome is still disputed, as the end of the dialogue is not known to us). In his own speech, Cicero exposed pseudo-philosophers but praised philosophy as a whole, not any one school of it nor even the sceptical school which he himself favoured.

Reconstructions of this work from others' piecemeal citations have now helped us to realize what Augustine saw in it. Cicero defined philosophy as the 'love of wisdom' (*philo-sophia*), words which struck home to his young reader. He also stated a basic ethical truth: 'everyone wishes to be happy', words which would become a guiding principle of Augustine's later writings.[44] However, humans do not agree on what happiness is. It cannot be lost to the random turns of fortune, as instability is the mark of a false good. False goods are sought by a 'wickedness of will', a notion which would become central to Augustine's thinking.[45] The sole source of happiness is philosophy, which persists despite the ups and downs of fortune.

In life, there are four basic, cardinal virtues which help the search for it. The aspiring wise man must exercise them all, but his mind must be cultivated first like ploughland. The pursuit, or seeking, of wisdom is essential, even though its finding is not guaranteed.[46] Here, appropriate studies will prepare him. The love and pursuit of truth make the vulgar ambitions of riches, fame and pleasure seem trivial. Sex, too, is a distraction. Like a flame on oil, bodily pleasure ignites youthful passions, but a 'great pleasure of the body cannot be compatible with intellectual thought'. It prevents us from 'paying attention, embarking on reason, thinking of anything at all'.[47] Augustine was much impressed by this point, made in the text of an elderly Roman orator who was over sixty years old at the time of writing. Even so, Cicero had just married a rich young wife. His first wife, divorced from him, ascribed this brief-lived second marriage to sexual infatuation.

Near the end of his speech for philosophy, Cicero presented the likely nature of an immortal soul's life in the 'isles of the blessed'. Eloquence and the cardinal virtues would no longer be needed and happiness would be purely contemplative, like the life of the gods.[48] This idea of contemplative, god-like bliss in a future life will be the hope, many years later, with which Augustine's *Confessions* end. Philosophy, Cicero also wrote, is the one means of escape from the miseries of human life. Some thinkers, he remarked, propose that eventually the cycle of years will go round and after 12,954 years the world will return to its initial position. Others, respected poets, have been more sombre. We are born, they say, in order to pay off punishments because of crimes committed in a previous life. Souls have been joined as a dire punishment to bodies, just as Etruscan pirates used to tie living prisoners to corpses and then throw them into the sea. 'If our souls are eternal and divine, then the more they engage in reasoning and the keen desire for research, and the less they become implicated in human errors and vices, the more easily will they ascend and return to heaven.'[49] For the first time Augustine was reading a drastic theory of pre-existent sin and punishment and rewards after death: as a boy, he may never have thought much about Adam's original sin.

Aged eighteen, he devoured this book, one to which he would repeatedly return. It shows up particularly clearly in two phases of his life. In November 386, when he began to teach philosophy, he used it for the very purpose which Cicero had envisaged, the training of young pupils. His own early writings draw heavily on it too. Then, some thirty years later, from *c.*418 onwards he reread it and singled out sentences which seemed to hint at his particular concern at that time, original sin. The *Hortensius* was to prove extremely fertile for him. Its statement that 'everyone wants to be happy' is mentioned no fewer than eight times in the *Confessions*' discussion of happiness when he analyses his present self, 'what I [now] am'.[50]

When he first met Cicero's text, it impressed him with three things above all: a burning desire for 'wisdom', defined as 'the knowledge of things human and divine', the need for an indifferent attitude to riches, and the merits of sexual abstinence.[51] Riches are not to be sought unduly, Cicero explained, but if they happen, they are to be used without restraint. This advice blunted for ever the material aims of Augustine's boyhood daydreams. As for sex, Augustine's most famous prayer to God is 'Give me chastity . . . but not yet.' The *Confessions* do not refer to it at its moment of origin, but they give the necessary clue to its date.[52] Before mentioning it, Augustine recalls how he had just read the *Hortensius* at the age of eighteen, but was still putting off the 'investigation' of wisdom whose 'very search alone, not even its finding' is to be preferred to earthly riches and kingdoms and the pleasures of the body. Here, he is quoting the *Hortensius*' own words, and he goes on to recall how as a 'wretched young man', even more wretched at the beginning of 'adolescence itself', he had prayed for chastity from God, but 'not yet'. The 'beginning of adolescence' might seem to belong at an earlier point in his life, but in texts written before the *Confessions* Augustine already linked it with his encounter with the *Hortensius*.[53] He also confesses that the *Hortensius* changed his prayers to God, and now we can see why. He no longer prayed for riches. For the first time, aged eighteen, he prayed for sexual chastity. Chastity, but not just yet . . .: meanwhile, his concubine had recovered from childbirth, and sex with her was irresistible.

Is the impact of the *Hortensius* Augustine's first conversion? Certainly, it was not a religious conversion. He is quite clear about his faith when he read the book. In Cicero's text, he failed to find the name of Christ, and so, in search of wisdom, he turned to the scriptures instead. He had perhaps heard of Christ as 'wisdom' from Christian friends or in such parts of the Christian service as had caught his attention when he was in church as a young catechumen. However, he had not bothered to read the scriptures before, and they disappointed him. They were written in such painfully unstylish Latin. Their translators had been struggling to stay as close as possible to each word of the scriptures' Greek text, not because they were ill-educated, but because they believed it to have a divinely inspired authority.[54] As yet, Augustine had no idea that this unstylish jumble could be read allegorically. Only later in his life did he reinterpret such curiosities as the four named rivers of Paradise and understand them as the four cardinal virtues which the *Hortensius* praised.[55]

His priority was no longer rhetoric: it was philosophy, a type of conversion which pagans had long recognized.[56] However, unlike an impassioned philosophic convert, Augustine did not promptly abandon his way of life or adopt a philosopher's typical cloak. He simply changed his priorities, and here Synesius helps us to see if 'conversion' can be fairly ascribed to him. Crucially, when Augustine was fired with his new passion for 'wisdom', nobody was at hand to teach him it. Synesius, by contrast, was a rich young man, easily able to pay for further studies in the big city of Alexandria. There, he encountered philosophy, not in a book, but from his chosen teacher, none other than the revered Hypatia, the lady whose command of rarefied Platonism, geometry and astronomy made her, he believed, the 'authentic president of philosophy's mystic rites'.[57]

For her French admirer the poet Leconte de Lisle, Hypatia had 'the spirit of Plato and the body of Aphrodite'. The daughter of a notable mathematician and astronomer, she carried on her father's work and became a magnet for pupils, visitors and the city's dignitaries. She was already (probably) in her late thirties when Synesius came to study with her, but she became his idol ever after, a 'blessed lady', 'divine' in spirit.[58] Unmarried, she dressed in a philosopher's simple cloak and impressed her virtue and self-control on her circle of pupils and admirers. She did not hold a public position. Instead, she was one of the big city's many private teachers and attracted hearers to her family house. She gave them the intense experience of exclusive 'mysteries' and otherworldly teaching. Her small group proclaimed lasting 'companionship', as if bound by a shared secret history. Synesius presents it in many of his letters precisely because philosophy is the ideal against which he wishes himself to be seen.[59] Unlike his fellow Christian Augustine, he learned philosophy in a class with a celebrated teacher, and not only a teacher, but a woman.

In his letters Synesius insists that this teaching resulted in his conversion. Like Augustine's, it was not religious: Hypatia was a pagan, but Synesius never let her teaching weaken his Christian faith. Instead, just like Augustine, he equated 'wisdom' with Christ. In a metrical hymn, perhaps composed for Hypatia's study group, he even prays, 'May wisdom attend me, Good at attracting the young, Good at attracting the old, Good for being the queen who dominates riches.'[60] After reading the *Hortensius*, Augustine would have endorsed Synesius' every word. Like him, however, Synesius continued to practise rhetoric. He had a new ideal, not a new way of life, but he still presents himself as a 'convert'. He matches himself with a famous orator-philosopher from the past, the Greek-speaking Dio of Prusa (AD 50–*c*.112). Synesius credits Dio with a philosophic 'conversion', even if it seems a lukewarm one to us: Dio compared himself artfully to Socrates, but also continued to practise rhetoric.[61] If Synesius could call himself and Dio 'converts', we can fairly apply the word to the young Augustine when struck by philosophy for the first time. Like Synesius, he did not yet give up his rhetorical studies. Thirteen years would have to pass before he opted for philosophy alone. His values, meanwhile, had been altered.

On his own initiative, he became caught up in Cicero's ideal, the 'love of wisdom' (*philo-sophia*). When the Latin scriptures repelled him, he turned elsewhere to find it. He joined a group whom Cicero had never imagined, people whom Augustine calls 'Manichaeans'. They were a most drastic choice: they had been outlawed by Imperial laws on pain of death. They exemplified, again, the perils of friendship and set a 'twisted rope' of it, Augustine confesses, around his neck.[62] However, they were to retain him for the next nine years. Were they yet another conversion, or did they attract him because of beliefs which he already had? The answers take us into times, lands and texts which make Thagaste seem very small indeed.

PART II

The lady, who more than half a century ago was my Sunday-school teacher, tried to teach me that the world was created innocent, and that evil sneaked in, but even then, at eight or nine, I was a Manichee and thought her more innocent than the garden she had faith in. Evil lay underground in Paradise before life ever appeared. It was part of the mud life was made with. It awoke the moment life awoke, like a shadow that leaps up rods long when a man stands up at sunrise. Though we may not like it, we had better not forget it.

Where you find the greatest Good, there you will also find the greatest Evil, for Evil likes Paradise every bit as much as Good does. What makes the best environment for Clematis armandi *makes a lovely home for leaf-hoppers.*

Wallace Stegner,
All the Little Live Things (1967) 54

And this is the message which we have heard from him, and announce unto you, that God is light, and in Him is no darkness at all. If we say that we have fellowship with Him, and walk in the darkness, we lie and do not the truth: but if we walk in the light, as He is in the light, we have fellowship one with another . . . If we say that we have no sin, we deceive ourselves and the truth is not in us. If we confess our sins, He is faithful and righteous to forgive us our sins . . .

1 John 1.5–9, one of the New Testament
passages which most resembles what Mani taught

8
Apostle of Christ

The sect which Augustine was now to join had a history of more than a hundred years. In 216, its founder, Mani, had been born in Mesopotamia (nowadays, Iraq) to the north-east of Babylon. From the age of twenty-four onwards he travelled widely in the Middle East through Iran and into western India. He taught and wrote prolifically until, aged sixty, he was imprisoned and killed on the orders of the ruling Shah of Persia.

Mani never visited north Africa and the young Augustine is unlikely to have known as many traditions about him as we do. As Mani's followers were a persecuted sect, their texts were often torn, discarded and burned by their opponents, leaving only fragments to survive on scraps of papyrus, parchment or Chinese paper. These fragments have been found in desert oases from Egypt to central Asia and have been brilliantly studied in recent decades. They allow us to amplify the long summary of Mani's life and writings which was written in Arabic in the 980s by a Muslim bookseller, Ibn Nadim, who had access in Baghdad to Manichaean texts now lost to us.[1] As these texts' many languages show, Augustine was not joining a sect which was peculiar to Latin north Africa. Our increasing knowledge of Mani's life has put his origins in a clearer context. Like his father, he was a convert. In the *Confessions*, Augustine is dismissive of the sect's 'delusions', but conversion and 'calling', we now know, were integral to it.

Mani's family and the significant dates and events of his youth were remembered in stories among his followers, some of which go back to Mani himself, and many others to a time soon after his death. Even those which are not factually correct are evidence for perceptions of him in the years before Augustine joined the sect. Mani's father was called Pattek ('Pattikios', in Greek). He was described in later tradition as a man of noble birth from Ecbatana (Hamadan) in central Iran. He was a pagan and in due course moved south, it was said, to the much bigger city of Ctesiphon in Mesopotamia. There, he was said to have heard one day in a pagan temple a voice repeating the dreaded command: 'Do not eat meat; do not drink wine; do not have sex with anyone.' Pattek had already had sex with his wife, whom some of the later traditions called 'Maryam', perhaps to compare her with Jesus's mother, Mary.[2] She was pregnant, but Pattek joined a strict sect of Baptists in Mesopotamia who lived by a junction of the Tigris and Euphrates rivers and observed the commands which he had heard. It was in their company that his son grew up.

The boy's name, Mani (in Greek, Manichaios), is still much discussed by scholars. It may be an abbreviation of the Aramaic *mnyhy'*, meaning 'Mani the Living', and he may have assumed it, not at birth, but as a young man because of its religious resonance.[3] Aged twelve he indeed believed he had a divine revelation. It was a vision of his heavenly Twin, to be followed by other such visions during his youth. Thanks to an important Greek text, preserved in a tiny book of parchment and skilfully recovered in 1969, we can now read long-lost traditions about Mani's earlier life. They were assembled from his disciples some thirty or forty years after his death, but include quotations from writings by Mani himself. One gives a Greek translation of Mani's own words about his visions. 'I was protected through the might of angels and the powers of holiness which were entrusted with my protection. They also brought me up with the visions and signs they showed me, which were short and very brief, just as I could bear. For sometimes [he came to me] like lightning.'[4] Such supernatural contact was not, of course, unprecedented. It was ascribed to Jesus in the Gospels, among others. Aged twenty, pagan Libanius was also visited by thunder and lightning, those signs, he believed, from the god Zeus and the cause of his lifelong susceptibility to migraines.

At first the teachings of Mani's Twin were to be kept secret, but they sat awkwardly with life in the Baptist community. Its members lived by rules which prescribed the strictest purity. They respected many biblical laws of the Jews, except for the offering and consumption of meat (they were vegetarians) and the use of fire in their rites (they used water). They practised circumcision and observed the Sabbath, but abstained from sex and washed very frequently for ritual reasons. They ate only the special bread and vegetables which they grew and prepared. They 'baptized' each vegetable before they ate it. However, they were not an isolated, local group. In Augustine's lifetime like-minded

Baptists were recognized to be a significant presence in the Holy Land. They persisted long after Mani, spreading into southern Arabia, where they are probably the enigmatic 'Sabians' whom Muhammad mentions with esteem in the Koran.[5]

The Baptists were not restricted to Jews, but they respected many Jewish laws and revered many apocryphal Jewish texts. It is of the first importance that the recently discovered Greek 'biography' has confirmed that Mani was born into a community which was considered Christian, although its practices and many of its beliefs were not those of most Christians in the Latin West.

Fortified by his visions, the young Mani began to challenge the Baptists' rules in the name of the 'Saviour', Jesus Christ. Jesus, he observed, had never taught that repeated washing made the body holy. Mani argued that in the very soil which the Baptists tilled, there was a divine substance, the spiritual Jesus who was imprisoned in it. Here, Mani appealed to Elchesai, a past figure of prophetic authority whom the Baptists honoured and who was also believed to have had a vision of angels. One day, Mani claimed, as Elchesai prepared to plough the earth, it had spoken to him. 'Why do you make your living from me?' it asked him. Elchesai wept, kissed it and realized, 'This is the flesh and blood of my Lord.'[6] Water had also spoken to him and taught him that he should not pollute it by washing in it. These and other visions ran contrary, Mani realized, to the relentless washing and tilling of the Baptists in his own day. While appealing to Elchesai, a past authority whom they professed to respect, Mani began to look to a new future. Enlightened by his heavenly Twin, he refused to eat the Baptists' special bread. Inevitably, the Baptists began to interrogate him and tried to discipline him.

In spring 240, when he was aged twenty-four, his Twin appeared to him again and completed the lessons about his origin and parentage, 'how I was separated from my Father on high and was sent according to His will, what orders and teaching He gave me before I clothed myself with this mortal body, before I fell into error in this loathsome flesh'.[7] Mani learned that his 'spirit' had existed long before his earthly birth. His father, Patticius, had merely 'built the house' (Mani's body), but 'another came and moved into it' (the Twin). This extreme dualism divided the 'spirit' from the 'loathsome' body and was certainly taught to the young Augustine in north Africa.

Nowadays, scholars can match many parts of Mani's teachings to an undergrowth of earlier Jewish and Christian writings, many of which are best known in languages other than Greek in the Christian East. The presence of Christ in the very earth of the material world was not a novel idea in this febrile thought-world, one in which the historical Jesus of the four Gospels had been replaced by a 'cosmic' Jesus, a spiritual redeemer in a drama about the universe which extended way beyond Galilee and Judaea.[8] Mani must have read widely in such texts, but in his view his knowledge derived directly from his 'blessed father': the Twin 'revealed to me the secrets about himself and his undefiled father and the entire universe'.[9] Mani's account of his calling emphasizes that he was sent to those like himself whom his Father had already chosen. It also emphasizes his Father's 'grace'. Grace and election were at the centre of his theology, far though he was from Augustine's Western Christian heritage.

Aged twenty-four, Mani learned truths about the time before the universe was founded, truths about the foundation of 'all good and evil deeds' and truths about their intermixture in the present time. He also learned that the world was soon to end, and so there was an urgency for him to go out and preach 'secrets hidden since the world began'. Secrecy must give way to a universal mission.

When Mani broke with the Baptists in 240, only a very few followed him, but they included his father, to whom, Mani said later, 'abundant grace will be given, on account of me'. According to Ibn Nadim's sources, Mani had a deformed foot, but some modern scholars consider this detail to be a slur by his critics. The prospects for this small group of wanderers were not bright. Mani recalls how he told his Twin, '[My enemies] are great in number, but I am alone. They are rich, but I am poor. How, then, will I who am alone against all be able to reveal this mystery among the great number which is [caught in] error? [How will I go] to [kings and] governors?'[10] Nonetheless, with the assurance of divine guidance, he was to become the most successful travelling missionary in all Asia.

On leaving the Baptist community, Mani first travelled and taught in peripheral kingdoms within the Persian Empire. The sequence of his journeys is uncertain because the evidence is fragmentary, but a likely order is that he went up to Azerbaijan in western Iran and then returned to take ship in a port on the Persian Gulf. He then travelled east to towns along the coast as far as the mouth of the river Indus (nowadays, south Pakistan). Central to his Gospel from its very beginning was the absolute opposition of Light and Darkness, good and evil. This dualism was familiar to those of his Iranian hearers who were already

Zoroastrians, but Zoroastrian religion was not his source for it. Mani also upheld a strict vegetarian diet and the total renunciation of property and sex: he preached against the killing and eating of animals. Even so, he is said to have won an audience in the highest princely society of the Iranian world. They included men who were impassioned lovers of hunting, as Mani himself recalled: Mani was the first 'anti', or teacher opposed to bloodsports, whom they had ever heard. Despite this obstacle, we are told, they were persuaded by him, helped by their belief that he worked miracles of healing. He is also credited with an early encounter with Buddhism in a sub-kingdom in the east which turns out, from recently published evidence, to have been ruled by a prince of the Persian Empire's ruling family.[11] According to another recently published text, he met 'many sects and castes' in the Indian subcontinent (or at least its western regions, now Pakistan) and was believed to have distinguished carefully between them. He looked closely at Brahmins and their rules and noted their 'prophecy and rigorism' and their distinctive hairstyles. They were unwilling, he is said to have found, to listen to any teachers except their own.[12]

In south-west 'India', Mani would have seen Buddhist monasteries. They would not have been entirely strange to him. As a young man in Mesopotamia, he had already known a simple community life in small organized subgroups: his father, Patticius, had been a 'house-master' in the Baptist sect. He was impressed by stories of Buddha and soon regarded him as one of his Gospel's forerunners, but I do not believe that in his lifetime his Gospel owed a significant debt to what he saw and learned about living Buddhists.[13] A newly studied text in Coptic from Egypt shows that, very soon after his lifetime, he was represented as disputing at the Persian court with a figure whose name was based on Buddha's ('Iodasphes', or Bodhisattva). Mani is said to have prevailed over him and is even honoured in the text as a 'Buddha' himself. This story shows that Mani's relation to Buddhist teaching was soon an important issue, not only in India. However, only after his death, in predominantly Buddhist contexts, did his followers adapt some of their practice to their Buddhist surroundings.

Returning into the Persian Empire, Mani found a new and accommodating Shah to be on the throne, Shapur I (242–73). He had already impressed a member of the dynasty, the prince in the Indian region, and soon he was taken into Shapur's court entourage. He was reputed to be a healer and had a useful expertise in astrology. In due course, he addressed a special text to Shapur, his only one in Persian, which set out ten reasons why his Gospel was superior to all previous ones. Fragments of it survive in two translations and emphasize that Mani's Church will endure until the end of the world, despite persecution and the deaths of its leaders, and that Mani himself has written down his teaching, whereas Jesus and other previous 'apostles' had written nothing.[14] Mani even illustrated his teaching in pictures, in a volume entitled *Picture Book*. He was a man of many talents, an artist, a prolific writer and the composer of at least two rhythmical psalms.

He was also good at planning a coherent mission. Early on, he began to appoint 'apostles' and leaders of his communities. His religion was self-consciously a 'religion of the book', held together by canonical texts composed by himself. Except when writing to Shapur, he wrote in Aramaic, his first language: each of the twenty-two sections of his written Gospel began with one of the twenty-two letters of the Aramaic alphabet. His epistles were also numerous (seventy-six were known to Ibn Nadim, making him Asia's most prolific religious correspondent: he wrote one to India and another to the Syrian city of Edessa). He composed many other texts, but in Asia seven came to be regarded as especially important, including a Book of Mysteries, a Book of Giants and the Gospel of Life. 'The older religions,' he wrote to Shahpur, 'were in one country and one language, but my religion is of the kind that will be manifest in every country and in all languages, and it will be taught in faraway countries too.'[15] His view has indeed been vindicated. He never wrote or spoke Greek or Latin, but nowadays a full study of his writings and their impact needs a grasp of Greek, Latin, Coptic, Syriac, Persian, Middle Iranian dialects and Chinese, languages in which their fragments and legacy survive. After his death, his Gospel was to be carried through central Asia and its oases along the Silk Road, eventually reaching China by the year 694. Until the early twentieth century, followers of Mani survived in Fujian, where one of their hill-top shrines is preserved as a monument at Jinjiang, about twelve miles west of Quanzhou. Many paintings which represented Mani and his followers existed in the Far East, where up to ten of them have been identified in Japan within the last ten years. One, painted in south China, may well be based ultimately on Mani's *Picture Book*.[16]

When his protector, King Shapur, died in 273, Mani was no longer secure. In Babylon, he recalls, 'I proclaimed the word of truth and life . . . The [kings and the leaders] and the sects of that place were set against me . . . they waged some great wars with me. The lawless judges took me, they watched . . . they would not permit me in Babylon a single day to journey in their land . . .'[17] The sequence of events is not clear from the texts which have so far been published, but it may well be that at first Mani was exiled into Armenia. There, he came into contact with another local prince, Prince Bat, and converted him. In early 276, he was summoned to a hearing before the Persian king, Vahram I, and insistent members of the Zoroastrian priesthood. A Persian text later recalled for a Persian audience that king Vahram was eating and about to go out hunting. To Mani, he said, 'You are not welcome.' He had sworn, he explained, never to let Mani into his land. In anger he told him, 'What need is there of you, since you go neither fighting nor hunting?' He then complained about Bat's conversion.[18] To the relief of his senior Zoroastrian clergy, he ordered Mani to be put in heavy chains and imprisoned and left to suffer. After twenty-six days, so his followers later claimed, Mani began to fail: 'his eyes were fixed and still. Three female [Hearers] of the faith went to him,' they said, sitting by him and 'closing his eyes because they were swollen'.

While Mani was dying, they kissed his mouth and begged him to give a sign of his 'love which is full of mercy and restraint'. He is said to have died on a Monday and, if so, the date was 26 February 276. His body's fate is disputed. Some said it was flayed, a regular Persian punishment for enemies, and hung on the city gate. Whatever happened to it, his followers promptly began a springtime festival to commemorate his death. At it, they sang psalms of mourning as if he had been crucified: 'they loaded me with iron, as they do to sinners; they fettered me as they do thieves . . . Lo, the sky and the earth and the two sources of light [the sun and the moon] bear witness of me in the heights that I did good among them, but they in their cruelty crucified me.'[19]

Mani had already envisioned missionaries like those in Jesus's Gospel and had chosen twelve apostles of his own. Some of them were sent westwards into the Roman Empire, including Addai and one Pattek (not his father). They entered Egypt and also Syria, where their teaching was well received at the desert city of Palmyra, perhaps even by the famous Syrian queen, Zenobia.[20] In east Iran the mission fell to the adept Mar Ammo, who made a notable use of interpreters and took the Gospel into central Asia, where missionaries exploited an alphabet closer to the Iranian spoken language and wrote with it in a distinctive, uniform style. After Mani's death, his Church continued to be persecuted, but the teaching mission persisted. It spread across to Rome and Roman north Africa, where in 302 the governor petitioned the Emperor Diocletian on how the sect was to be treated. Diocletian learned that members had recently come from hostile Persia and were causing, he believed, 'the most serious injuries to the civic communities'. They might well infect the 'innocent and orderly' Roman people and the entire empire with the 'damnable customs and perverse laws of the Persians' as if with 'the poison of a malign serpent'.[21] The leaders and their books must be burned and if their followers persisted, they must be put to death. In 373, young Augustine was committing himself to a sect which was a long-standing object of persecution in both the Persian and Roman empires.

Officially outlawed, its members were harmless, except to their own persons, on which their inner group, the Elect, imposed a rigorous diet and style of life, including a ban on sex. The wider group of Hearers was excused these restrictions, but both they and the Elect included women. Inevitably, they drew the attention and insinuations of male outsiders. Soon after Mani's death, a bishop in Egypt composed an epistle for his churches which circulated in papyrus copies, carefully folded and therefore better able to survive for posterity. In it, he denounced the sect's women as deceitful infiltrators whom male worshippers only honoured, he claimed, because they needed their menstrual blood for their ceremonies. While Augustine was in the sect, a Christian scholar in Rome warned of its appeal to females. The teachers seek them out, he wrote, 'because they always want to hear something only for its novelty'. They then persuade them to do the foulest things. The 'women are longing to learn', he claimed, 'but do not have the power of discrimination'.[22]

Libanius, as a pagan, regarded the group very differently. In one surviving letter, written in 364, he is almost certainly pleading on behalf of its members when he addresses a request to an Imperial official in Palestine. They 'venerate the sun', he says, 'without offering blood sacrifices; they honour it as a god of the second rank; they chastise their natural desires; they consider their last day as their gain'. They are to be found, he knows, in many places of the world, but 'everywhere they are only few in number. They harm nobody, but are harassed by some people.' He wishes those in Palestine to be protected from harm, to be able to turn for refuge to his correspondent and to be 'free from anxiety'. Libanius misunderstood them as if they were philosophic pagans.[23] If he had been approached ten years later by the young Augustine, he would have written a reference for him without any fuss. Synesius would have been less amenable. As an orthodox Christian, he would detest Mani's heretical teaching and would hate it for being opposed to that joy of his life: hunting.

Young Augustine's response was wholehearted. Mani's 'Church' was to retain him for at least nine years, and even later was to claim significant time and energy. Within two years of abandoning it, he began to write books against it and its teachings. By the time he wrote the *Confessions* he had already written nine such works, and the *Confessions* continue the polemics. After leaving it, he calls its members 'Manichaeans', using the dismissive term ('Mani-ists') which outsiders customarily applied to them. He also attacks a claim which Mani's Gospel and letters openly asserted. Mani described himself as the 'Apostle of Christ by the will of God'. His missionary role model was the Apostle Paul, another great letter-writer who had broken with the Jewish Law: Paul too had had heavenly visions and had been an active missionary in high society. Mani's Gospel also referred repeatedly to Jesus Christ, but its Christ is a spiritual being, only briefly in an earthly body. Mani did not see his Gospel as 'parasitic' on Christianity, as modern Christians might misdescribe it, nor did he relate Christ to it simply in order to persuade Christians among his hearers. Young Mani's belief in his heavenly Twin was based on the 'Twin' among Jesus's disciples, Thomas the 'Twin' (in Greek, Didymos). It was probably in imitation of this Thomas that Mani had gone promptly to India, the land of Thomas's mission in East Christian tradition. A spiritual Jesus Christ had long been worshipped by other East Christians and was integral to Mani's Gospel from its very beginning. Above all, in Mani's view, he himself was the 'Paraclete' or Holy Spirit whose coming had been promised by Jesus. He referred to a long chain of forerunners, from Adam to Buddha, but he was not teaching only their wisdom. There was one exception to the list: after breaking with the Baptists he was for ever opposed to Jewish practices and traditions. He never related himself and his message to their patriarchs and national heroes. Nonetheless, he referred to God the 'Father' and to a spiritual Jesus, the Saviour, and to the Paraclete or Holy Spirit, himself. His Gospel, he thought, had been promised by the true Jesus Christ, one who was no Jewish 'Messiah'.[24] It was the ultimate Christianity. In north Africa, his followers in Augustine's lifetime sometimes state openly that they worship a Trinity of Father, Son and Holy Spirit.[25] To us, this 'Trinity' is complicated by accompanying 'powers' and 'emanations', but if Mani's followers presented it to the young Augustine, they may have told him more about a Trinity than he had ever discovered from his mother or his early years as a 'Catholic' catechumen.

To an everyday Christian like Monnica, Mani and his followers were hateful 'Manichaeans', the most loathsome of all heretics. They were not Christians at all. To Mani, Christians like Monnica were only 'semi-Christians'.[26] His Gospel revealed what the four Gospels of the 'semi-Christians' had misunderstood or enlarged with false 'Jewish' padding. Unlike most 'semi-Christians', Mani and his Elect followers lived up to the poverty and chastity which Jesus Christ had taught to His disciples in the Sermon on the Mount, most of which Mani considered to be authentically preserved. When the young Augustine joined this group, therefore, he did not see himself as converting away from Christianity. The change was a conversion, but in a much less dramatic sense: one, he thought, within Christianity. He was joining the true Christians, who had the truth about the Christ whose name he had imbibed with his ignorant mother's milk.

9
The Living Gospel

I

In the *Confessions* Augustine scornfully recalls the Manichaeans and their 'madness'. Their words, he remarks, were 'snares of the devil' and they mixed the 'syllables of your name [God's] and our lord Jesus Christ and the Paraclete'. Their tongues, Augustine claims, were 'empty of truth' and 'they went on saying "Truth, Truth" . . . but truth was never in them'.[1] Even these brief dismissals are evidence of the detailed knowledge which he had retained. 'Snares' were a favourite image in Manichaean writings. In their Greek and Coptic texts Manichaean scribes indeed mixed and shortened the names of God and Christ, and Mani called himself the Paraclete. A recently found text, preserved in Egypt from a book made of wooden boards, has confirmed that in their daily prayers Manichaeans uttered 'praise with a pure heart and truthful tongue'. The word 'truth' occurs no fewer than twenty-two times in the recently found Greek text of Mani's 'biography'.[2]

The *Confessions* do not present God, or us, with a full catalogue of all Augustine thought and did while a member of the sect. It was behind him and he did not wish to dwell on it. However, he persisted in it for nine years and it accounted for his first conversions of others: he convinced several of his friends in north Africa to join. It formed part of him and, even after he abandoned it, his confessions are still in dialogue with its views of God, Christ and the world. The difficulty for modern scholars is to assess what he knew while still a member. Nothing he wrote at the time survives. When he encountered Mani's teachings, they had been translated into Latin through at least two languages from their original Aramaic.

We have bits of only three texts by Manichaeans which were current in Latin in Augustine's lifetime. One is a fragmentary codex, found near Tebessa in north Africa, which is mostly concerned with relations between the two groups in a Manichaean community, the Elect and the Hearers. Another is a long book by Faustus, a Manichaean leader, which is preserved for us only in short extracts quoted by Augustine himself. The third is an extremely polemical text about Manichaeans and their teaching which was originally composed in Greek *c.*340 (the 'Acts of Archelaus') and was translated into Latin, and which used a letter now recognized to be by, or close to, the hand of Mani himself.[3] We can supplement these texts with the actual words of two Latin-speaking Manichaean teachers, transcribed by secretaries, when Augustine, by then a 'Catholic' priest, interrogated them in public. Should we also add details from the various texts which he later wrote against Manichaeans, or had his knowledge grown by the time he wrote them? Should we supplement them with items from Manichaean texts in Eastern languages or did the teachings differ too much from place to place?

It is seductive for modern critics to emphasize the 'flexibility' of Mani's Gospel, as if it varied, like a myth, between many cultures and contexts. Peripheral details varied from place to place, but the central doctrine was not an orally preserved myth at all. As Mani emphasized, it was 'the Truth', the very truth which he himself had written down in order for it to be spread and preserved in its correct wording. The more we discover from papyri, the more striking are the parallels between items mentioned by Augustine and items attested in Egypt's Coptic language or even in the east Iranian dialects which were used on the Silk Road to China. A recently found text in Egypt gives the wording of a long Manichaean prayer, but much of it matches evidence preserved by Augustine and even more of it matches evidence preserved by later Arabic sources. Mani's followers, it is now clear, prayed in much the same terms in north Africa, Egypt and the Near East.[4]

As a young Hearer, how much of Mani's teaching did the young Augustine really know? To the relief of some of his modern Christian readers, he was never one of the inner Elect. The recent Pope, Benedict XVI, has been a serious scholar of Augustine's thought, but once claimed that Augustine had only a slight knowledge of Manichaean literature while in the sect and that the important authors for understanding him at that time are Cicero and Virgil.[5] The same point had already been argued by one of Augustine's contemporaries, Secundinus, a Manichaean Hearer in Rome. When Augustine had long since left the sect, Secundinus wrote to him and asked if he had ever really understood it, professing with feline irony all due respect to Augustine's 'egregious sanctity' and 'admirable and sublime prudence' as a 'Catholic' Christian bishop. Secundinus was an educated man who knew Augustine's *Confessions* and his other writings against Manichaeans. He also knew Cicero's *Hortensius*. Would it not have been better, he asked, if Augustine had joined the Academic philosophers or 'interpreted the wars of the Romans who conquered everything'?[6] He was not innocently suggesting that Augustine would have made a good ancient historian. In the *Hortensius*, Lucullus spoke up for the value of writing history before, finally, Cicero spoke up for philosophy. Secundinus was insinuating that Augustine should have followed one of the other options in the *Hortensius* rather than trying to pursue its ideal of 'wisdom' by taking up Mani's 'true Christianity' and failing to understand it.[7]

As a committed Manichaean Hearer, Secundinus is a fascinating, but decidedly tendentious, correspondent. He wrote to Augustine because he was aggrieved by Augustine's defection from his sect and by his many attacks on it since leaving. So far from losing interest in it, Augustine had actually increased his knowledge of Manichaean writings while continuing to attack them. In 394, he wrote a refutation of the 'book of Adeimantus', Mani's disciple Addai, which dwelt on inconsistencies in the Old and New Testaments. Augustine recalls that when he refuted it, it had 'come recently into our hands': he may not have known it while a Hearer in the sect.[8] Another useful source of new knowledge was his interrogation of Manichaean opponents. In December 404, a prominent Manichaean, Felix, brought five Manichaean texts with him but they were confiscated by the authorities before the debate with Augustine started. On the first day Augustine began by handing Felix his own copy of the *Letter of Foundation*. Felix appealed to another, the *Book of Treasures*, which Augustine tried to exclude. The interrogation then broke off for four days, and when it resumed, it was Augustine who cited the text of the *Book of Treasures* for a refined point about free will. During the break, it seems, he had gone to the authorities and read Felix's copy of the book. In the same year, in his *On the Nature of Good*, he then quotes verbatim from *Treasures*, Book 7.[9]

Such encounters may have refreshed, or increased, adult Augustine's knowledge, but he had not lacked it as a younger man. Much of what he then knew had been orally based. As a young Hearer, he listened to the Elect, sang with them and prayed with them. Like other educated young men, he was trained to retain what was read aloud to him. Now that we know words of the Manichaeans' daily prayers, we can see how much knowledge they presupposed: a Hearer was expected to recite them four times a day. As we will see, there was also a close connection between members' beliefs and actions. What Augustine did every day made sense only in terms of Mani's more general teaching about the universe.

As a Hearer, he himself read Manichaean texts. They were not restricted to members of the Elect, and Augustine says in the *Confessions* that he studied them closely. He also tells the story of a previous young member, a future Christian bishop, who 'read and often copied out their books' after his mother had given him to the sect.[10] We can compare him with young Matheos, who is attested in recently found Manichaean letters from Egypt. Matheos was urged to 'study psalms whether Greek or Coptic' and to study 'the Sayings and the Prostrations', evidently the Manichaeans' daily prayers. He was to 'write a little from time to time, more and more'. Literate members like Matheos were very useful. They could copy the texts and especially the psalms, copies of which were needed for a basic purpose: they would teach the members what words they had to sing. Papyrus texts of their psalms include copies written in simple, everyday handwriting.[11]

Above all, the young Augustine knew the sect's *Letter of Foundation* in Latin. It was a crucial source for the world's prehistory and the nature of Adam and Eve. He himself tells us that 'it contains almost everything which Manichaeans believe' and is 'usually very well known indeed to almost all of them'. Augustine was one of the 'almost all', because he tells us that 'it was read to us' while he was a Hearer. He recalls that he was someone who 'sought curiously and heard attentively and believed rashly all these fictions which hold you Manichaeans trapped and bound in your daily practice'.[12] This attention and 'rash belief' enabled him to convert a cluster of his friends to the sect.

Attempts to deny him much knowledge while spending nine years in the sect fail before this evidence.[13] To reconstruct what he learned, I will use words from the Manichaean texts which his later writings cite, especially the *Letter of Foundation*. However, they imply a much wider knowledge and depend on a broader context to have any sense. I will restore this context to Augustine's knowledge by drawing on the Syriac and Coptic texts which are most explicit about it. I will exclude later Chinese or central Asian texts, many of which have been elaborated after their authors' contact with Buddhism. My summary is one which I believe that the young Augustine knew, though it is not given word for word in his later writings.

II

Mani's Gospel was comprehensive because it explained everything. 'By his preaching,' one of his followers in north Africa later told Augustine, 'Mani taught us the beginning, middle and end: he taught us about the fabric of the universe, why it was made, whence, and who made it; he taught us why there is day and why night; he taught us about the course of the sun and moon.' The lesson was new and convincing. 'Because we did not hear this in Paul nor in the writings of other apostles, we believe this, because he [Mani] is the Paraclete [the Comforter, the Holy Spirit].'[14]

At the centre of his teaching was a radical dualism, the absolute opposition of Light and Darkness, Good and Evil. This opposition existed before the universe; it is still embedded in it; it is rooted in every one of us and in everything else which lives. Mani gave a drastic answer to religion's hardest question: why does evil exist? His answer was an 'axis of evil', central to what we still call a 'Manichaean' view of the world. I will discuss it in three of its aspects: Creation, evil and our own human nature. Each remained at the centre of Augustine's thinking.

Nowadays, Mani's cosmology strikes what he would call 'semi-Christians' as a teeming myth, more like *Star Wars* than their own Christianity. However, most of it can be matched with items in earlier texts whose authors called themselves Christians, most frequently authors in the Near East.[15] They had 'secret' Gospels and a 'secret history' of the material universe. They regarded it as evil and in need of redemption by a hidden God and his many 'powers' or 'aspects'. Among them was a spiritual Christ, whom modern scholars have well called the 'apocryphal Jesus'.[16] Unlike the Jesus who is known from the four Gospels, He was not born from Mary. These 'knowledgeable' fringe Christians, Mani's predecessors, turned the Gospel story into a general sort of myth. Members of the 'apostolic' Churches soon vehemently attacked it and labelled it dismissively after its human preachers, denying their claims to be Christian at all.[17]

In the beginning phase of time, Mani taught, there were two separate kingdoms before our universe existed. One was the Kingdom of Darkness. The other, lying above it, was the Kingdom of Light. Each was eternal and uncreated, but their natures were very different. While a member of the sect, Augustine had sung about the Kingdom of Light in a 'Song of the Lovers', whose words he could still quote from memory some twenty years later. It was a landscape of sweetness and 'salubrious breezes'.[18] It was composed of scented fields of flowers: flowers were especially prominent in the Manichaeans' imagery of paradise. They lay among 'hills and trees and seas and rivers flowing for all time with sweet nectar'. The Kingdom was ruled by God the Father, eternal by nature, true and glorious. He gave off twelve Ages 'clothed in flowers and full of songs' who were made of His same divine substance. In turn, these Ages 'throw their flowers at God the Father's face'. The Kingdom echoed with music and song, just as Mani's own Church echoed on earth with music and psalms. It was not characterized by dancing, a distinction, rather, of Jewish communities, from which Mani sharply differentiated his 'Church'.[19] Apart from Light, four other good elements were present in the Kingdom: Air, Wind, Fire and Water. Crowned with wreaths of fire, the Father reigned with a blazing countenance. According to the *Letter of Foundation*, he was placed slightly above this 'clear-lit, blessed land' in 'realms that cannot be moved or shaken by anyone'. He was to be imagined, Augustine explains in the *Confessions*, as a vast mass of physical light.[20]

The Kingdom of Darkness lay beneath this kingdom, but thrust into its underside 'like a wedge'. It was inferior in quality to the Kingdom of Light, but, crucially, its Darkness was eternal and uncreated. In that fact lies Mani's answer to the origins of evil: it has always existed as an independent realm. Its kingdom is of 'immense magnitude', so the *Letter of Foundation* tells us, and in it 'dwelt fiery bodies, pestilential kinds'. There were 'infinite darknesses, streaming with their offspring' and beyond them were 'dirty and turbulent waters with their inhabitants; inside them were horrible winds'. There was also a 'fiery and corruptible region with its own leaders and nations. Inside it, likewise, was a race full of darkness and smoke in which the awful Prince of all things passed his time, a leader with countless chiefs around him.'[21] Augustine and our Latin sources say little about this awesome Prince of Darkness, but his profile has been brilliantly reconstructed from Coptic, Syriac and Chinese sources.[22] Significantly, he is never called a god. His kingdom was 'a pestilential land with five natures' and in the *Confessions* Augustine alludes exactly to its 'five elements, variously coloured because of the five caves of darkness'. Perhaps he is recalling one of the pictures for which Manichaean books were famous. A copy of the *Letter of Foundation* might have shown him a picture of each of the five elements in a different colour, and, if so, such picture books were indeed known in the Latin West as well as in Asia.[23]

The five elements in these 'caves' produced five Trees from which other princes of darkness arose like worms. Smoke produced two-legged creatures, including a primitive type of man; darkness produced serpents, because snakes cannot see clearly; water and wind produced creatures which swam and flew; fire produced four-legged animals, 'because', Augustine claims, 'they were insatiable and hottest of all for sex'.[24] Life in the Darkness was a life of constant combat and copulation. From the very beginning, therefore, sex typified the kingdom of evil.

The Kingdom of Darkness's trees were bad trees, whereas the Kingdom of Light's trees were good trees. This opposition is most fully developed in Manichaean texts from Asia, but like other themes of Mani's teaching, his followers believed it was already known in the genuine scriptures which the 'semi-Christians' of their day preserved, among many 'Jewish' additions. 'A good tree cannot bring forth evil fruit, neither can a corrupt tree bring forth good fruit' (Matt. 7.18).[25] The letters of Mani's admired forerunner, Paul, were particularly well-informed. They referred to Light and Darkness and 'principalities and powers'. The First Letter to Timothy even recognized the 'Lord of Lords who only hath immortality, dwelling in the Light which no man can approach, whom no man hath seen nor can see'.[26] Unlike modern scholars, the Manichaeans (and Augustine) regarded this letter as Paul's own.

The Kingdom of Darkness was made up of 'matter' which had its own random movement. Importantly, it was not only a material realm. It was animated by a 'thought of Death', which is best known to us in Asian sources but was known to the young Augustine, as a detail in his very first text against the Manichees shows.[27] Evil, therefore, is not merely an evil substance: it has a driving principle which can plan and affect other creatures' inner life. Made restless by it, inhabitants of the Kingdom of Darkness moved to a position from which they caught sight of the Kingdom of Light. At once they began to covet its peaceful idyll. To protect it, God the Father staged a pre-emptive strike, the first in a series of cosmic battles. The Beginning now ended and, on most reckonings, the Middle phase began.[28]

In his Kingdom of Light, God has many attributes and offshoots. He contains 'wisdom and the living forces of the spirit' and 'twelve limbs, or Members, of his Light', the *Book of Treasures* explained, in each of which 'are hidden thousands of countless and immeasurable treasures', from which the book presumably took its name. There are also twelve Aeons, or Ages, as Augustine knew, and five mental powers, equated with five good elements, light, air, fire and so forth. These powers and qualities are not 'begotten' by God. For Mani and his followers, sexual reproduction is not at all consistent with the divine. They are better thought of as 'partial aspects' of God. They proliferate in the Manichaean Gospel but are not unique to it, as they also proliferate in other radical East Christian texts and teachings.

By using some of his 'powers' God began a battle against the powers of Darkness, knowing that He must lose it in order to win the war. As the *Letter of Foundation* told, He released a 'splendid and brilliant divine power, rich in virtue' to attack and 'destroy the offspring of darkness so that perpetual peace, after its extinction, might be prepared for the dwellers of Light'. God's envoy to the Darkness was Primal Man, who was armed with the five good elements from the Light Kingdom. Before leaving, the other divine powers gave him the 'signs of truth'. They wished him 'peace'; they kissed him and shook him by the right hand; they bowed down and laid their hands on him.[29] These 'signs' in the Kingdom of Light are precedents for the 'signs' with which new members like Augustine would be welcomed into Mani's Church on earth. As elsewhere, Manichaeans' everyday practices were grounded in practices which their Gospel ascribed to prehistory.

Like a master spy, God knew that His envoy into enemy territory must suffer, but that his capture, ultimately, would assist His own Kingdom. As the Manichaean psalms well put it, 'by a single lamb he saved his sheepfold', an image which Augustine would remember for many years.[30] Again, 'semi-Christian' scripture seemed aware of this drama. 'The Light shone in darkness,' the Fourth Gospel said, 'and the Darkness comprehended it not.' The Fourth Gospel even knew of the Good Shepherd who laid down his life for his flock. Of all the Gospels, the Fourth was the one which Mani valued most, thinking that it was the least distorted by 'Jewish' additions.

Primal Man brought the very substance, Light, for which the demons of Darkness had lusted from afar. The Prince of Darkness duly conquered Primal Man, and his own demonic agents devoured the Man's panoply of powers, just as the God of Light had planned. Primal Man was then put to sleep, until he awoke to give seven prayers for his rescue. In his Kingdom, God the Father then released yet more powers to help him. Their leader was Living Spirit, who went to the edge of the Kingdom of Darkness and, in a crucial initiative, greeted Primal Man with a call. Captive Primal Man gave a reply and Living Spirit held out his hand to receive him. Augustine certainly knew this episode because it set a lasting pattern for believers. They had been born captives, but, by assenting to Mani's Gospel, each of them, like Primal Man, heard the 'call' and 'replied'. Aged eighteen, young Augustine had 'replied', and so he would exchange a shake of the right hand, like Primal Man's, whenever he met a fellow member of the sect.[31] Just as Primal Man had prayed seven times for his rescue, so Mani's Elect followers were expected to pray seven times a day. Hearers like Augustine were expected to pray four times.[32] It was probably as a Manichaean that Augustine first made regular daily prayers to God the Father. As a catechumen in the 'Catholic' Church he would not have had to pray daily and his visits to a church were probably only sporadic.

The rescue of Primal Man was partial. Behind him were left bits of his light-armour, the 'five powers' which the demons of darkness had shredded, swallowed and imprisoned. From now on, the purpose of 'middle time' is to free and recover them, the 'bait' with which the demons of darkness have been ensnared. In the battles to recover them, their Kingdom's 'thought of Death' will be repeatedly outwitted by the Light Kingdom's 'thought of Life'.

First, Living Spirit and his helpers defeated and captured most of the ruling demons in the Darkness. Living Spirit then used them to create a universe, one of eight earths and ten heavens. In the process, the captives were forced to release much of the light which they had acquired. If they had polluted it, it became a thousand stars, ones which are still visible to us as the Milky Way. Purer light, only slightly contaminated, became the moon, while the purest light of all became the sun. Nonetheless, the demons retained some of the light in their possession. Some of them, therefore, were flayed and their skins were stretched to make the heavenly firmament. Their bodies, male and female, were fixed onto this firmament as planets and signs of the zodiac. From other demons, the bones were pulled out and used to make the rocks and mountains of our world. Their excreta were made into its earth.

Once again, the primeval combat has had lasting, practical consequences. On earth, Mani and his followers, including the young Augustine, prayed daily to the sun and moon, not as gods in their own right, but 'glorifying the great luminaries', so their prayers said, 'which conquer the enemies and enlighten all creation . . . and escort victorious souls into the greatest Aeon of Light'.[33] The Milky Way is made of pure light in transition and is known as the 'Column of Glory'. The demonic zodiac and planets, meanwhile, exercise malign influence on bodies which are beneath their sphere. These bodies include humans, whom they influence limb by limb: Manichaeans therefore believed in astrology, an art which was also practised by the young Augustine. In the *Confessions*, he discusses the Book of Genesis's 'tunics of skin', worn by Adam and Eve, but explains them as the skins of the scrolls of scripture which have been rolled out by God as a firmament above our world. Augustine first met this connection between skins and the heavenly firmament in his time with Mani's followers.[34] In the *Confessions* he is implicitly dissenting from their lurid role for them.

Our world, at first sight, seems extremely evil, because its rocks and soil are made of demonic bones and excreta. However, Mani did not follow the extreme theories of many other fringe Christian groups, who professed total alienation from the material world. Mani's Living Spirit made a universe with a beautiful form and proportions. Its Architect was a divine Power and the universe, therefore, is a work of art. It is planned for a purpose: the recovery of particles of Light which are trapped inside it. After leaving the sect, Augustine continued to praise the universe's 'design' and 'beauty', God's providential work. It runs through the *Confessions*, supported by philosophy and words of scripture, but it had already been sung and praised by his Manichaean friends.[35]

The design of Mani's universe is held firmly in place. Five supporters care for it, the 'sons of Living Spirit' or 'Porters' in the Manichaean psalms: Augustine remembers their names in Latin. Atlas supports it on his shoulders; 'Splenditenens', Augustine tells us, steadies it with his hand; the King of Glory flies around it, extracting Light where possible.[36] The King of Glory has devised three 'wheels' to help him in his task, wheels of fire, water and wind.

To shake out the captive Light, the universe had to be set in motion. God therefore provided another agent, the 'Third Envoy' (or 'Elder'), who set the three wheels moving so as to draw up the Light which they would dislodge. Then, He teased the captive demons to release yet more. As the *Book of Treasures* described in Latin, God the Father arranged that the shapes of 'beardless boys' and 'beautiful virgins' should appear in the sun.[37] Asian Manichaean sources are more detailed. The Third Envoy himself appeared in the sun as a beautiful naked girl, causing the male demons who were bound in the zodiac to ejaculate towards him. Their sperm fell back without reaching its target and landed on the earth and sea. In the sea it produced a sea monster which one of the Porters speared to death. On the dry earth, it soaked in and then sprouted as fir trees, from which all other vegetation developed. The

Third Envoy also appeared as a lovely young male, naked against the sun. At the sight of him the female demons on the zodiac miscarried the offspring they were carrying. Their abortions fell to earth, where they copulated freely and gave birth to the animal kingdom. As they had been conceived before Darkness had intermingled with Light, their children were wholly evil and demonic. However, they grazed on the new sperm-born vegetation and from it absorbed particles of Light. Animals, therefore, are not made entirely of evil. However, none of them, not even a dog, ranks as 'man's best friend'.

Augustine refers to this 'disgusting' purgation and liberation of Light, but does not go into detail.[38] If he knew that the 'purgation' was 'disgusting', he knew the full sexual story. Our most detailed source for it is a later one, surviving only in Syriac as late as the 760s, but its author, a Christian doctor, based his summary on a text by Mani himself, quoting actual extracts from his book of 'Legends'.[39] It is from this good source that we also learn of the next battle with the captive demons in heaven and earth, perhaps caused by their rebellion. To frustrate them, God released a fourth warrior, the first 'Jesus' to feature in the story. He is not the historical Jesus of the 'semi-Christian' Gospels. He is Jesus of Light, or 'Jesus the Splendour'. He has no connection whatsoever with the Virgin Mary, human flesh or the crucifixion. He forces the demons to release yet more light, but does not end their plotting.

These stirring events explain facts of our material world. When Atlas, supporting the world, shifts it occasionally from shoulder to shoulder, we experience the effects as earthquakes. When the demons on the firmament shake with fury at the loss of their Light, we hear their anger as thunder in the heavens. There are important consequences for our daily diet, as we will see, in the fact that animals are evil, light-poor creations and that flowers, trees and vegetables have sprouted from a light-rich demonic orgasm. At the very end of the *Confessions* Augustine attacks the 'madness' of this view of Creation, one which his own explanation of Genesis has contradicted at length.[40] As a young man, he had also learned that sometimes the sun or the moon hide their light from the continuing combat of Light and evil in the world below. This 'hiding' explains the eclipses which darken the sky. Meanwhile, God does not wish to contemplate the struggle which He is shaping. He has hidden Himself in His Kingdom behind a veil to 'soothe His pain' at the sufferings of His Light. Eventually, He will remove it, but before He does, the struggle must spread to one more battlefield. One element remains to be created and involved in the war: ourselves.

III

As the *Letter of Foundation* states, the precise origins of Adam and Eve, our ancestors, are a 'mystery', in the sense of a secret. The *Letter* was written to explain it.[41] One fact is clear: we descend from creations of the demons, powers as evil as the 'Thetans' of modern scientology.

After losing the 'third war', the demon of Lust, or Sin, decided on a counterattack. He (or in Persian, 'she') released two demonic powers, Saclas (whose name Augustine knows in Latin) and his mate Nebroel (in Greek, 'Nebrod'). Young Augustine knew the sequel from the Latin *Letter of Foundation*, read out while he was in the sect. In it, the ruler of Darkness is heard speaking from his bad eminence to his attendant demons, the first such address to be attested in Christian literature. 'It is fairer for you to give over to me the Light which you have in your might,' he tells them, 'thus I will imitate the image of that great figure [Living Spirit] who appeared so gloriously, and through that image we will be able to rule, freed eventually from association with Darkness.'[42] The demons confer and agree, partly from lust, partly from fear. They are afraid that otherwise they will lose their remaining Light. They also lust for another sighting of the beautiful naked male and female forms by whom they had been aroused in the previous war.

To centralize their Light, their Prince ordered them to copulate and produce yet more children. They then had to bring their babies to him so that he could eat them and absorb their qualities. After eating them, he sent for the female demon Nebroel, who had 'emanated from his same stock', and inseminated her, passing into her all the Light which he had amassed and digested from the babies. He added 'some of his own thinking and virtue'.[43] She conceived, and the offspring were first Adam, then Eve.

This vivid story presents Adam and Eve as microcosms of the intermingled Kingdoms of Light and Darkness. Adam was born with a body of evil matter, 'the garment of sickness', as Manichaean psalms call it, made from 'the filth of demons', but this matter was formed 'in the image' of something far more lovely, the image of the male and female, Third Envoy's creations, who had been seen naked against the sunlight. Adam and Eve, though children of demons, were not entirely evil. Inside them was some Light, a part of God, captured from the heavenly kingdom. However, evil impulses and influences teemed inside them too and, limb by limb, they were subject to the malign astrological powers of the demons on the heavenly firmament. They were also seething with the Prince of Darkness's mental evils, ones which he had superimposed on the powers of Light. They lead the soul to 'bad deeds', as Mani was said to have explained to questioners, 'to all the sins of desire, to idolatry and the assertions of deceit'.[44] Our combat against them is continuous.

Behind this potent variation on Genesis lie previous Jewish and Christian interpretations of the story of Creation, plainly known to Mani.[45] Again, where he seems to be most non-Christian to modern readers, he was drawing on texts and traditions accepted by previous thinkers from the Christian 'fringe' who had regarded themselves as Christians in the East Christian world as far as Mesopotamia. For Mani, as for them, insight and self-awareness are agents of redemption which rescue us from the hostile, material world. 'Jesus the Splendour', he teaches, gives off another power, Light Mind, who will transmit such awareness to all believing humans, His descendants. A main theme of Mani's Gospel is the descent of a divine element into mortals and their world, in which it lives as particles of Light and awaits release by mortals who are aware of its presence. However, Mani then differs from many East Christians' use of this theme. Once we have regained this knowledge in a sudden awakening, it can still be overpowered, he thinks, by a contrary surge of desire. Other heterodox Christians considered themselves permanently freed from everyday moral restraints by the mere fact of their superior insight. By contrast, Mani's Adam and every human after him are never so free.[46]

In a hostile world, among evilly created animals, Adam and Eve were created for a diabolic purpose. They were to copulate and scatter their particles of Light through their offspring so that Light would be spread too widely for God and His agents to recover it. Through their human creations the demons would then rule the world. Mani described this plan in a context which is related to the Book of Genesis of the Jews and, in his view, 'semi-Christians'. However, he rejected any words in Genesis which might contradict it. He owed more to Jewish and East Christian non-scriptural texts, ones which had elaborated the story of Creation in their own way.[47]

Just as the Book of Genesis describes, Adam lay at first in a 'deep sleep', but Genesis failed to mention that God had foreseen the danger. He sent envoys to awaken him, led by Jesus the Splendour, who drove off Adam's demonic guardian and encouraged Adam to eat from the Tree of Knowledge. Adam duly ate (Augustine even says that according to the Manichaeans this Jesus took on the form of the serpent) and when insight and self-knowledge were granted to him, he lamented his predicament. This cardinal moment is best expressed in a Syriac text, again based on original Manichaean sources. 'Adam cried and wept: he raised his voice terribly like a roaring lion, tore his hair, beat [his breast] and said, "Woe to the maker of my body, the chainer of my soul, and woe to the rebels who have reduced me to servitude." '[48] Aware of his double nature, Adam reawakened to his true self, the divine Light which was being opposed by his foul flesh, blood and desires. By this single moment of realization, his divine self regained the awareness which it had formerly had in God's Kingdom of Light. From Jesus the Splendour, Adam then learned the whole story and became a 'new man', a phrase which the Apostle Paul had used without fully realizing its scope. Each one of us can follow Adam's awakening. As Mani promised in the *Letter of Foundation*, his Hearers will be 'instructed by this divine knowledge' and, by it, they 'will be liberated and dwell in eternal life'.[49]

This awakening and self-awareness were not easily expressed in Augustine's Latin. With hindsight, he criticized Manichaeans for believing in two 'souls', one being composed of particles of God, the other from particles of the Prince of Darkness. Yet, there is strictly only one 'soul', the Light-particles within us, and an 'evil soul' seems false to Manichaean teaching. Nonetheless, Augustine's language may be more at fault than his understanding.[50] The Manichaean body and its matter are not inert 'filth'. Through them, as through the Kingdom of Darkness, runs an evil impulse, the 'thought of Death'. There is also the simple sense of 'being alive', our unenlightened consciousness, and there is Reason, or *nous*, the separate intellectual power by which this consciousness becomes aware. We can try to express these layers by words like the 'ego' or 'psyche', but, like Augustine's two 'souls', they import a misleading resonance. Rather, Mani knew Jewish texts which wrote of the contrary 'impulses' in man. His followers also knew a text by the early Christian visionary Hermas in which the existence of these contrary impulses is explicit. Secundinus, an intelligent Hearer, uses the phrase 'two spirits'.[51] Augustine is not, then, wrong to see more than a simple opposition between 'body' and 'soul' in Manichaean man. He is aware, correctly, of layers of consciousness. They will be an important legacy to his own future progress. However, the phrase 'two minds', which he also used, was closer than 'two souls' to Mani's original teaching.

Aware of the truth, Adam could either live by it or relapse. In him and his descendants, therefore, the 'foundation' for good or evil deeds was laid. The scope for unenlightened evil was made brutally clear by Eve. Jesus the Splendour had ordered Adam, as 'new man', to abstain completely from sex, although the 'old man' was still living on in him among the seething temptations of his fleshly nature. Eve meanwhile had sex with a senior demon and gave birth to Cain. Then she had sex with Cain and bore Abel. After two more births she was ready to seduce Adam, an event which is best described by the bookseller Ibn Nadim, drawing ultimately on early Manichaean texts.[52] Eve learned magical syllables to enslave Adam; she gave him a garland from a flowering tree; when Adam saw her, garlanded, gorgeous and stark naked, he had lustful sex with her and made her pregnant. She bore him Seth, the ancestor of the human race, but promptly wished to kill the child. Adam saved him, but through Seth and his descendants Light became scattered through humanity, thereby realizing the demons' aims.

Once again, items in the world's early history are still crucial for our own selves. Lust and desire are rooted in our fleshly nature and at any moment, they and their myriad 'demons' may again cloud the Light of the soul. 'Desire seeks to occupy and submerge the field of clear thinking,' wrote Henri-Charles Puech, one of Mani's greatest modern scholars. 'I am very much inclined to interpret this myth – the assault of darkness on the realm of light – as a projection of the individual Manichaean's sense of sin.'[53] There was ample scope for this sense. The enlightened members of the Elect were to live by the most demanding standards, including absolute chastity throughout their life. The supremely dangerous desires inside us are sexual.

The fates of our first parents differed according to their awareness or lack of it. Despite his one sexual lapse with Eve, Adam had 'awoken' and acknowledged his true self, the particles of divine Light within him. When he died, therefore, his soul ascended back to the Kingdom of Light. Eve, by contrast, remained unaware and unrepentant. When she died, she ended in hell, together with her incestuous children. She is not a role model for female members of Mani's Elect. Unlike her, they are aware, awakened and sexually turned off. Instead, she is the prototype of unenlightened women, sexy, wicked and dangerous to men.

For the rest of 'middle time', Light is being scattered far and wide by sexual reproduction. Animals copulate and so do humans. However, as humans descend from such Light-rich ancestors, humans are the agents who can best set Light free. To do so, they must follow a strict rule of chastity and diet which we will confront in the next section, but they follow it in a world of exceptional poignancy. In every plant and tree, fragments of the divine Light, the very Light from God's kingdom, are still entrapped and suffering. Our true selves, our Light-elements, are suffering likewise inside us from the pulls of lust and pleasure. This Light is the true 'suffering Jesus', a phrase used by Augustine but attested now in east Iranian texts: it is not a north African peculiarity.[54] This truly 'suffering Jesus' never suffered as flesh on the Cross: Manichaeans would never make the sign of the Cross in daily life. They denied that His suffering ever took place briefly on what they regarded as a footling little hillside called Golgotha. It is universal in time and space and is still going on within and around each one of us. Jesus suffers in every plant we touch or tree we cut or fruit we eat. He is the Cross of Light, made up of all the particles of divine Light which are scattered through the world.

Pagan friends of Libanius or teachers of Synesius would be incredulous of this claim, but not wholly unfamiliar with the idea. They had an approximate parallel in their pagan Orpheus, the singer whose blood and body were said to have been scattered by his female murderers. The 'fragments, Orpheus's life', his modern interpreter Ann Wroe has well written, 'shone scarlet on the bushes or hung . . . like bloody rags through the woods. In the autumnal Rhodopes [Orpheus' haunt in modern Bulgaria] they still flare out, red leaves of dogwood or sycamore among the pines.'[55] Whereas Orpheus' blood and limbs show up locally, and only in nature, Mani's 'suffering Jesus' is present in our innermost being, as well as in all nature and in every animal throughout the world.

Before Mani, Christian teachers in the Near East had compared their Gospel to a pearl, a comparison used by Jesus in Matthew's Gospel. Mani gave it a new, exquisite range.[56] The pearl in a seashell, he believed, resembles in colour the opalescent Light which resides within each of us. The divers who seek out a pearl are like the apostles of Mani's Church who reawaken the pearly Light within their hearers. Just as the divers bring their pearl to merchants, so Mani's apostles restore Light to the heavenly 'merchants', the sun and moon. The merchants then take the pearl to kings and nobles, just as the sun passes Light to the Aeons who attend the Father in His Kingdom. Every night, we can see the ascension of the Light which has been set free. First, it goes to the 'Pillar of Light', what we now call the Milky Way, and passes up by this 'Column of Glory' which the Third Envoy has set between heaven and earth. Then, some of the Light passes on to the moon, which grows ever fuller with it for the first fifteen days of the month. Then the moon passes the purest Light on to the sun: the loss of this Light causes the moon to wane for the rest of each month until its Light-supply is refilled.

When most of the Light has been freed in this way from evil matter, the End will begin. Mani had already emphasized it in his text to the Persian King Shapur and like Jesus's disciples, his followers were quick to believe that it was already upon them. They, too, equated it with the persecution which they were suffering, first in the Persian Empire, then also in the Roman Empire.[57] Augustine and the Latin sources knew about a final Judgement and perhaps they also knew the details, that the two Porters who support the earth and heavens (Augustine's Atlas and 'Splenditenens') would release their grip, causing the 'highest and lowest' to collapse into one. A fire will then blaze up and consume the universe in order to free as much remaining Light as possible. It will burn for '1,468' years, a number known in other heterodox Christian texts: it represents the cyclical 'Great Year' of the Egyptians' calendar-reckoning, 1,461 years, with an extra apocalyptic 'week', or number 7, added to it.[58]

The adult Augustine is our best surviving source for what happens next. The demons will be thrown into perpetual prison, the females into a tomb, the males into a globular mass (*globus horribilis* or *bōlos* in Greek): their sexes will be segregated to stop them reproducing and proliferating. Onto the females' grave, so the bookseller Ibn Nadim learned from texts by Mani, a stone will be fixed 'as big as the world'.[59] Onto the globular mass of males, any souls who have refused to follow Mani will be 'affixed' as guardians of the demons inside the lump. They will be a 'cover', Augustine writes, fitted on the outside of the *globus horribilis*.[60] Evil, therefore, will not be destroyed. It will be separated and dumped under protection, like nuclear waste. Despite the adult Augustine's polemic to the contrary, the souls of unbelievers will not be 'damned' or condemned to hell. As they still contain Light, they will be fixed as sentinels on the exterior of the evil mass. Then, at last, the Father will remove the veil which has hidden Light's suffering from Him, and as Paul had already predicted, He will be seen 'face to face'. What began as a catastrophe will end as a victory, but not a perfect victory. We are still waiting . . .

10
Becoming Martha

I

When Augustine joined the sect, deeply serious men and women from the oases of central Asia to the busy company of Rome and Carthage were singing, reading and believing this powerful Gospel of Life about themselves. From the beginning, Mani's Church was characterized by a split-level structure, familiar in other East Christian communities in the Syriac-speaking world.[1] There was a small inner core, the Elect, and there was an outer circle, the Hearers (or catechumens), of which Augustine was one. Yet, each group depended on the other. The Elect depended on the Hearers for their daily food and donations, while the Hearers depended on the Elect for the liberation of their imprisoned Light. Hearers helped to support the Elects' 'overachieving' way of life but did not have to obey the same rules.

By Mani and his early followers, the Elect and the Hearers were connected to one of the most memorable of all Gospel stories, the presence of Jesus in the house of Mary and Martha.[2] This scriptural text was certainly applied to them in north Africa, as the Latin Manichaean codex, found at Tebessa, confirms.[3] While Jesus talked, Martha had been 'cumbered with much serving', whereas Mary sat and listened. Martha, Jesus reminds her, is 'anxious and troubled about many things', but 'one thing is necessary', as Mary exemplifies, having 'chosen the good part'. Like Mary, Mani's Elect chose 'one thing', a single-minded life focused on the rescue of scattered Light. The Hearers were Marthas, living in multiplicity but serving the Elect at mealtimes, just as the pragmatic, admirable Martha had once served Mary and Jesus while he talked and talked and did nothing to help with the chores.

As a Hearer, Augustine was a Martha, serving and obeying the Elect. He knew very well that the conduct of the Elect was controlled by three 'seals'. One seal bound the 'breast', essentially their sex life. Another bound the 'mouth', above all their diet. A third bound the 'hands', their permitted handiwork. These seals defined the Elect's rigorous way of life which enabled them to save bits of Light imprisoned in the world.[4]

Sealing their breast, the Elect were forbidden marriage and concubines and lived in strictest chastity. Hearers like Augustine were not so sealed: they could continue to be sexually active. However, they must not produce children, because they would thereby scatter the Light into ever more flesh and blood. Its recovery would then be even more difficult. Already a father, Augustine could enjoy sex with his concubine so long as he did not fertilize her. As he recalled, he enjoyed sex enormously. He was not a 'hypocrite' in doing so: as Mani already explained, an illuminated soul was awakened to the Truth, but would still be frequently and unavoidably befouled by carnal lust. What he could avoid, he duly did and for nine years in the sect he fathered no more children. Even so, his Light-particles were fortunate, given the ignorance, which Mani shared, of which days were safest in a month.

The seal on the mouth limited believers' diets. The Manichaeans believed more literally than anyone before them that 'we are what we eat'. The Elect were forbidden to eat meat because it was the flesh of animals and was minimally endowed with Light. It was 'filth'. It fuelled lust and desire and it bogged down the Light which was present in its consumer. Selective quotations of words by the Apostle Paul were used to endorse these limits: 'I will eat no flesh for evermore' (1 Cor. 8.13) and 'it is good neither to eat meat nor drink wine' (Rom. 14.21). Mani rejected wine as the evil bile of demons. He also rejected the eating of fish (they had to be killed) and eggs (they had to be broken). He even banned the Elect from drinking milk. Hearers were less restrained. They could eat meat, but they should not personally kill it or butcher it, as they would be going against the commandment 'not to kill'.

Since the demons' cosmic orgasm, Light has been scattered into the earth and taken up by every plant and tree. The Elect, therefore, must consume as much vegetation as possible and free this Light from its material coverings. Bright exteriors are the signs of copious Light within: 'so far as a thing shines,' Augustine recalls, 'it is from God'. Olive oil glistens and is especially rich in light, and so are lettuces, but apples are to be avoided because they are the fruits which led Eve astray. Grain contains the seeds of life, but best of all are juicy fruits and watery vegetables like cucumbers. In central Asia, Manichaeans encountered water-melons, hitherto unknown in the classical world. As they were supremely Light-rich, melon patches were planted beside Manichaean settlements in the region.[5]

There was an obstacle, even so, which was marked by the third seal, the 'seal on the hands'. In the earth and all its fruits, the 'suffering Jesus', or the Cross of Light, is present. Anyone who digs the earth, prunes a tree or picks a fruit causes pain to the Light which is imprisoned in it. The Elect can never be gardeners. The Hearers, therefore, must grow, pick or bring the Light-rich food to them. Thereby, they wound the Cross of Light in the soil, the trees and the produce, but if they are digging or picking it to sustain the Elect, they will be forgiven their sin by the Elect themselves. In the *Confessions* Augustine refers scornfully to the belief that even a fig, when picked, will 'weep' and ooze from its 'wounds'.[6] Yet he himself had shared this belief for nine long years. This 'sin' was avoided by traders, bankers or rhetorical teachers, Augustine's own way of life, but it was very hard for a Hearer to be a farmer. A life of hunting and gardening, the charmed life shown by mosaics in Africa's great houses, was absolutely denied to Mani's 'true Christians'. They had cut themselves off from this secular heaven on earth.

In Coptic and other Eastern texts, 'commandments' are mentioned which regulate believers' behaviour, five commandments for the Elect and ten, even, for the Hearers. Augustine never mentions commandments for Hearers, but he probably knew all or some of them nonetheless: not to lie, not to kill, not to steal, not to commit adultery and so forth.[7] The Hearers' life was not a free-for-all. Although Mani explicitly described his followers as a Church, they were not able to build specialized churches, because the sect was illegal. Hearers were encouraged to give alms from their income and to provide a house for the Elect and their meetings. They were also encouraged in the most explicit terms to give a human being to the sect, a slave or, better, a child.[8] Letters found recently in the Egyptian oasis of ancient Kellis confirm the Elect's precise, material requests to their Hearers. They are unabashed seekers of donations.[9] Gifts of oil and grain allowed the Elect to live and conduct their saving work, while gifts of people enhanced the sect's domestic staff and future members. After all, the Elect could not perpetuate it by natural reproduction.

Every day, several times, the Elect and the Hearers would pray to the sun and moon 'with a pure heart and a truthful tongue'. If the night was cloudy and the moon was invisible, they would pray to the north, the direction in which they believed the sun was circling before rising again in the east. Libanius was wrong to conclude that Manichaeans therefore worshipped the sun and moon. They were worshipping the divine Light, a part of God, which the moon and sun sheltered. In north Africa, some of them also believed that God's Son was present in the sun. They were encouraged to wash before praying. In Eastern texts the prayers are to be accompanied by prostrating the body, but Augustine only mentions prayer on bended knee.

Every day, not before the late afternoon, members would meet in rooms in private houses, like 'cells' in a mobile, secret group. Only after Augustine's lifetime would they build special monasteries and then only in the faraway havens of central Asia. Into the room Hearers would bring a Light-rich meal for the Elect, the only meal which they ate. Hearers were expected to fast on Sundays, whereas the Elect fasted on Mondays too. In the West there was a two-day fast for Hearers during the annual spring commemoration of Mani's martyrdom. In the East, the Elect might fast then for twenty-six days to match the traditional time of Mani's imprisonment.[10]

This fasting was not a symbol of negative alienation from the world. Positively, it reduced the entry of evil matter into the body and prepared the stomach to go to work on Light-rich food. Mani was said to have observed the digestive outcome. It made no difference, he explained, whether or not food had been ritually washed: its bulk was separated and excreted equally in either case. What mattered was the state of mind of the eater and the nature of the food he swallowed.[11] The meals which were brought to the Elect were therefore selected for their richness in Light. By eating fruit and grain, they killed nothing. Instead, their stomachs separated out the waste matter (perhaps in visibly greater bulk, as they were vegetarians): it was then excreted, but never into water as it would pollute it. For the Elect, a modern lavatory would be an abomination. After digesting it, the Elect then breathed out the remaining Light from their mouths, especially while praying and singing. They also sweated it, hiccupped it or even, so the older Augustine mocked, farted it out to set it on its way back to heaven. Manichaeism is the only world religion to have believed in the redemptive power of farts.

The bodies of the Elect were not, like modernist houses, 'machines for living'. They were highly tuned 'machines for liberation'. The special food which they received from the Hearers was not food to be offered as alms to any old beggar, a point which Augustine later emphasizes, even at the start of his most recently found sermon on 'alms for all'. The Hearers' charity was channelled solely to those who could go to work on it. The more the Elect devoured, the more Light they set free. They were not aspiring to holy anorexia. In a semi-desert oasis in Egypt or central Asia, they were heroic munchers, trying to liberate Light from an almost impossible number of trees and blades of greenery.

When the meals were brought in by the Hearers, probably in an orderly procession, there was no urgent need to cook or wash them. Prayers were said and hymns were sung and, according to Augustine, individual Elders, leaders of the Elect group, laid forgiving hands on Hearers, who knelt as suppliants.[12] There was confession by Hearers to the Elect and perhaps by members of the Elect to one another, but its scope in Augustine's era is still uncertain. In later texts from east Iran and central Asia, individual confessions of specific sins are attested, but by then the influence of Buddhism and its 'confessions' had become much stronger in the local Manichaean groups.[13] In north Africa, however, the nature of such 'confession' is an open question. If Hearers confessed individually, they may only have confessed a list of general sins. There is no evidence that each of them confessed their specific sins to the searching eye of an individual Elect. They may only have confessed in a collective prayer, recited in unison. One evident sin to confess was the picking of the Light-rich meal and the damaging of the Light in fruits, plants, trees and vegetables. The Elect then said words of 'apology' to the bread placed before them: 'I have not reaped you, nor cast you into an oven. Another has brought this to me. I am eating without fault.' Then, we are told, the Hearers would depart.[14]

Confession also occurred at the annual spring Festival of the Platform, or 'Bēma', at which it cleansed the Elect and Hearers for the coming New Year. The elderly Augustine could still recall some of the details: a platform, approached by five steps and 'adorned with precious linen cloths', was placed so as to face the worshippers. For other details we have to look to the Coptic psalms which were sung at the festival in Egypt.[15] The room was bathed in the light of lamps and sweetened by roses which had been picked and brought by Hearers: Mani was said to have specified the most 'Light-rich' flowers, among which, charmingly, were violets.[16] On top of the platform stood a big portrait of Mani himself and around him, on the steps, were placed copies of his books, especially his Gospel. In the Coptic psalms, the five steps to the platform, or Bēma, are presented as five steps for the ascent of the soul as its Light goes up to heaven. In Augustine's post-Manichaean writings, he frequently exploits the idea of steps, or stages, in the ascent of the soul to God. He found it in texts by Platonist philosophers, but the imagery may already have been known to him in psalms and prayers at the Bēma Festival while a Manichaean Hearer.

Before the Bēma, psalms were sung in honour of Mani himself, the 'apostle of Christ', the one who had truly suffered and died. The spiritual Jesus had not suffered on the Cross, and so Manichaeans did not celebrate Easter. Instead, the Bēma Festival was held in the Easter period 'and,' recalls Augustine, 'we used to desire this festival day with greater fervour because the other [Easter] had been removed'.[17] Before joining the sect he had evidently enjoyed Easter's church services very much.

At the Bēma Festival, psalms appealed for mercy and forgiveness. They survive only in Coptic: 'We pray to you, our God full of mercy, forgive us our sins. We pray to you, God, You the Father, first of Gods, the One who is hidden but whose Light has been revealed. We cry to You, hear us.' Mani himself, they said, had instituted the day of the Bēma as a day for this purpose. In his recently found 'biography', Mani is said to have received from his heavenly Twin the power to 'pass on pardon for sins to sinners who accept repentance', but it was a particular sort of repentance.[18]

To understand what it meant in the Latin West, we can best turn to Secundinus, the Hearer who later wrote to Augustine from Rome. Secundinus explains that an unenlightened person sins without self-awareness and is ignorant of the 'two natures' inside him, the 'soul' of divine Light, made from particles of God's own substance, and the opposing impulses of evil Darkness.[19] Only those who have been enlightened by Mani's Gospel and become self-aware will sin 'voluntarily': they 'consent to evil', but only in the weakened sense that they are not 'arming themselves against the enemy'. They must be 'ashamed that they have erred' and then they will find a ready 'author of mercy'. Crucially, a sinner is not 'punished because he has sinned, but because he has not grieved about his sin'. After leaving the sect, Augustine emphasizes the difference between this limited notion of 'confession' and a repentance for truly voluntary sins. The Manichaean says sorry and acknowledges what has happened because of the warring elements in his own nature. By saying sorry, he helps to arm his soul, or divine Light, in its future struggles against the 'lust of Darkness' within himself. 'Conscience' is only awareness. Augustine, by contrast, insists that all sins are by definition voluntary, but some may live on and escape our conscious mind: they can be remitted only by true repentance and the grace of God.[20] His confessions recall such hidden sins, his theft of the pears being one, and lay them before God so that they can be 'melted' in a detailed, individual prayer unlike any group confession during his Manichaean past. 'Conscience', for him, could nag and be bad.

At every meeting, every day, the Elect would eat their meal after the Hearers departed. The giving of the food for it was called the *agapē*, or love-deed, but the meal itself was not, strictly, a eucharist. It was not 'done in remembrance' of Jesus, let alone with sacraments or symbols of his body and blood, those evil items in Manichaean thinking. It was done simply to liberate bits of the inherent 'Cross of Light'.[21] As a Hearer Augustine was never allowed to witness the meal itself, but in later life he knew rumours of the proceedings which circulated among hostile outsiders. It was said that flour was scattered on the floor and a male Elect and an Elect girl were required to have sex on top of it.[22] Both produced 'seed': their lubricating fluids, which would drip onto the flour. The male was then said to interrupt the act and release his own sperm onto it. Mixed together, the sperm-seasoned flour would then, supposedly, be eaten as Light-enhanced bread, because sperm is intensely rich in light. By digesting it, the Elect would be enabled to release an exceptional concentration of Light.

In the first Christian centuries, sexual slanders had assailed the Christians' innocent eucharist. The transfer of such stories to the Manichaeans' meal may deserve no more credit, but in older age Augustine refers to testimonies which were extracted from Manichaean females. When on trial in Carthage before the 'prefect of the palace', one girl, Margaret, testified that she had undergone this sexual ritual when aged only twelve. Another, Eusebia, a female Elect, denied it and claimed that she was herself still a virgin. She was then physically examined and found to be no such thing, whereupon she was 'compelled, with difficulty', to confess that she too had had sex on a scattering of flour. Augustine even adds that others had admitted as much to Church leaders, as was revealed by the 'Episcopal Acts' which had been sent to him by the trusted Christian Quodvultdeus, the recipient of Augustine's text *On Heresies*.[23]

When 'compelled, with difficulty', a terrified female, on pain of death, might confess almost anything to the likes of Quodvultdeus. A male Manichaean also admitted that such behaviour went on, but only in splinter groups from the main Manichaean Church. We will probably never know, but the eating of Light-rich sperm had a clear physical logic for Manichaeans, whereas it had none for the other Christian groups who were accused of it. What matters is that this shocking rumour was known in north Africa in Augustine's lifetime and was sufficiently convincing for judges there to try to confirm it. It was to rebound on Augustine himself, as we will eventually discover.

Meanwhile, it was in this sect that Augustine first experienced a religious group which strongly professed love, friendship and a sense of community based on a shared relation to God. These values never lost their appeal for him. As a Hearer, he was part of a community which was steadily accumulating good deeds. With characteristic precision, a senior Manichaean was said once to have reckoned, 'in the church over which I became the head, fifty Elect were with me. They stood before me while they fasted every day.' By each fast, he calculated, 'each one of them had engendered seven angels', making 350 in all. 'I [was grateful] on account of the great profit and go[od] I had achieved . . .'[24] In the *Confessions* Augustine refers to the munching, digesting Elect as 'breathing forth angels'. If we apply the same calculation to his nine years in the sect, each Elect, fed by Augustine, engendered no fewer than 3,276 angels and sent their Light on its way back to heaven.

Munching and serving, neither the Elect nor the Hearers had an incentive to hasten their own deaths. The Elect were assisting a great cosmic process. They were not aspiring to inner mystical visions of God in this life. God, the Father of Light, was veiled and hidden from them, they believed, and there was no possibility of ascending temporarily to His presence. However, when death was near, they should prepare for it and 'burn with desire to rejoin the Kingdom of Light'.[25] For Manichaeans, a 'resurrection of the body' was an appalling notion. Only the Light in them would ascend into heaven, waiting in transit before passing from the sun to the Kingdom of Light, which it had first left with Primal Man. Hearers could look forward to a slower progress. Dutiful Hearers' Light would be reborn in the Elect of the next generation and would then be passed up to Heaven. The Light of less dutiful Hearers would be reborn only in plants and vegetation, from which some future Elect might perhaps liberate it by eating it. Unbelievers like you or me will pass our Light down the chain to animals from which no Elect will ever rescue it. Unlike the young Augustine's, the best for which our particles of Light can hope is to live on inside a sheep or cow.[26]

II

Young Augustine's prompt transition from reading Cicero's *Hortensius* to praying and singing in a Manichaean group now becomes much clearer than he troubles to explain in the *Confessions*. In the sect, he met an appealing combination of 'insider' knowledge and detailed cult. The *Hortensius* had inspired him with a love of wisdom, but wisdom, he tells us, would never satisfy him unless it included the name of Christ. Mani, he now found, was teaching the 'true' Christianity and was the source of all wisdom. In his text for King Shapur, Mani actually wrote that 'wisdom and knowledge are what the apostles of God constantly bring, in one era after another'. They 'have added to the wisdom which I have revealed, just as water adds to water and becomes many waters'.[27] In the *Hortensius*, Augustine had met the idea that the soul might be punished by being joined to the body, that it might suffer for its previous life and that at the time of death immortal souls return to the heavens. Cicero had even praised philosophy as 'the knowledge of divine and mortal things'. Augustine now discovered that nobody knew more about such things than Mani, the expert on the soul's descent and ascent and its troubles from being joined to the body, that 'nest of filth'.

The *Hortensius* had first dimmed Augustine's ambition for riches and first set before him the ideal of sexual abstinence. Mani's Elect, he now found, renounced sex, but Hearers could respect the ideal without following it, thereby conforming neatly to his recent prayer to be chaste, but 'not yet'. The Elect exemplified the neglect of riches and abandoned all worldly goods, 'taking no thought for the morrow', but Hearers did not have to give away their property.

In the *Hortensius*, Cicero had presented wisdom as an ideal for which we must strive. 'I was led on gradually,' Augustine observed, 'little by little', with the enticing belief that there was yet more to learn and that the Elect were keeping it from him meanwhile.[28] Cicero had also praised the rational pursuit of wisdom: Manichaeans emphasized strongly to potential converts that their 'Truth' was rational. As Augustine's later writings make clear, they presented the whole exotic doctrine as based on 'reason', not 'authority'.

Mani also stated that his Truth was not something new. What his heavenly Twin had revealed to him and he then revealed to the world had been partially revealed by previous apostles, of whom he was the last. His disciples explained that these apostles included Adam, Enoch and Seth in the Jewish tradition, Hermes in the pagan tradition, and Zoroaster, Buddha and Aurentes in Asia: Aurentes probably derived from a misunderstanding of the Buddhists' word *aurent*. Pagan Hermes was the so-called 'Thrice-Great Hermes' of Egyptian tradition, some of whose writings indeed anticipate Mani's teachings about the demonic powers of the planets and the zodiac and the origin of vegetation from an ejaculation of heavenly sperm.[29]

The most important of all Mani's acknowledged forerunners was the Apostle Paul. Mani and his followers were close readers and interpreters of Paul's epistles, in which they picked on phrases which supported their own teachings. Whatever did not suit their case was dismissed as Jewish padding, added to Paul's original text. This 'critical theory' was applied to all scripture. After his youth in the Baptist sect, Mani set no value on the Jewish Law or the Old Testament books, which were full of dissolute behaviour by the Jewish patriarchs. The New Testament had some value because its core was the teaching of an earthly, mortal prophet, Jesus, who had been a forerunner of Mani himself. The claim of the 'semi-Christians' that their Gospel had been predicted by texts in the Old Testament was entirely false, as indeed historians consider it to be nowadays.

Mani knew the four Gospels in a harmonized single text, but was aware that other texts contained discrepancies, including two contradictory genealogies of Jesus.[30] These contradictions were further evidence of 'Jewish padding'. By such claims Manichaeans evaded whatever did not suit their case, never more so than when they rejected all the biblical psalms and the entire Acts of the Apostles because it stated that the Holy Spirit had first been bestowed on Christians at Pentecost. According to Mani, it arrived on earth only later with himself, the 'Paraclete'. Instead, he and his followers accepted books of apocryphal 'Acts' which purported to describe the doings and sayings of each of Jesus's major Apostles. They added 'enlightened' material to them, as we can best see from surviving texts of the 'Acts of John'.[31]

In his new company, Augustine was still a 'catechumen', just as he had been called in the 'Catholic' Church. His previous catechizing had not taught him properly about the Incarnation or the spiritual nature of scripture. The Elect, however, taught him proof-texts from scripture for the first time. With their help, he had new weapons for winning arguments and much liked winning, he tells us. He also found his ear flattered. Whereas the literal translation of the Latin Bible had repelled his sense of style, the Latin translations of Mani's writings had a flowery, abundant manner. Although they used clause after clause without subordination, they sounded much better than a book like Exodus in Latin. There was also the pleasure of singing the Manichaeans' own psalms at group meetings. Augustine responded strongly to rhythm and music and had known no such singing in his 'Catholic' Church.

The obvious loser was his mother, Monnica. At first she broke off close relations with him, refusing to have him with her at the same table and considering him spiritually dead. Nonetheless, she prayed for him persistently, weeping as she did so. In due course, as she told him, she saw a dream.[32] She saw herself standing on a wooden ruler while a shining, joyous young man was coming towards her in her sorrow. He asked her the cause of her daily tears. She explained, and he told her not to worry, but to pay attention and see, for where she was, there Augustine was too. She then saw Augustine next to her, standing on the same rule.

When she told her dream to Augustine, he had the nerve to tell her that of course she should not despair of being where he was: she should become a Manichee. Manichaean texts indeed stress the scope for widows to join their Church, but 'No,' Monnica promptly replied, 'it was not said to me, "Where he is, you are", but "Where you are, he is too."' In the *Confessions*, years later, Augustine still recalls his amazement at her swift realization of what her vision meant.

When Augustine recounts this dream in the *Confessions* fifteen years later, it is not one which he has invented with hindsight. As he specifically comments, he is telling us what his mother told him and he says that he 'often' talked of her reaction. From 373 onwards, therefore, there were different daily prayers in the family. Monnica continued to pray and weep for her Augustine at 'every hour of her prayers'. Meanwhile, Augustine, four times a day, offered the prayers of a Manichaean Hearer: 'I worship and glorify the great Light-givers, both sun and moon and the virtuous powers in them, which by wisdom conquer the antagonists and illuminate the entire order and oversee and judge the world and conduct the victorious souls into the great aeon of Light.'[33]

III

Mani's 'true Christians' did not only profess love and friendship in superlative language between themselves: their groups provoked questions and discussion among their members. In the *Confessions*

Augustine shows us some of these questions, but mostly as questions between himself and friends whom he converted to Mani's Gospel. In fact, Hearers were not the passive, unquestioning people whom modern studies of Mani and the sect tend to present.

For their concerns and debates, we can turn, finally, to some of the most fascinating questions and answers to have survived from a religious group in late antiquity. They are superb evidence that Hearers were as capable of doubt, depression and uncertainty as any other people who are told to commit themselves to exceptionally demanding rules. They are set out in the *Kephalaia*, or 'Chapters', which survive only in Coptic collections from Egypt but whose core goes back to the fourth century.[34] Some of them purport to give the unprompted teaching of Mani on difficult points of doctrine; others give his answers to questions supposedly posed by the Elect, the disciples and even the catechumens (Hearers). It is not so important whether each question was really put to Mani in his own lifetime or answered in exactly the words which we read. What matters is that they address topics which were considered to be in need of answers in the communities after Mani's death. Some of them are explicitly ascribed to Hearers. These remarkable sources show that their concerns were precise and poignant. They are an insight into what Augustine and fellow Hearers in north Africa will have wanted to discuss and sort out.

Like the Hearers and Elect, we share the need for further enlightenment about items in Mani's cosmic story, the workings of the Wheel of Salvation, perhaps, or the exact activities of the Light Mind. However, the Elect and Hearers also needed reassurance about the continuing combat which they felt in their inner selves. 'You have told us that the Light Mind is the one who shall come and assume the saints . . . You have also told us, "When he enters in the body of the flesh, he binds the old man" . . . [So] n[ow], where is he? In [the fact] that the old man is chained in the body? For I see how rebellions arise there despite his bondage . . .'[35] Another Hearer put a direct question about mood-swings: 'Sometimes I am peaceful in my heart, and my considered thought is constructive . . . Even my body is carefree, and my soul [rejo]ices in wisdom and true knowledge. There are also times when I will be troubled. My doctrines are confused. Gloom increases with them, and grief and anger and envy and lust.' Where does all this trouble come from and why?[36]

An observant Hearer could even have problems in accepting the Elect's credentials.[37] 'A catechumen once stood before my master [Mani], the apostle. He said to him, "When I see a righteous one being angry and resentful as he quarrels with his friend, turning his anger on him and [utterin]g ugly words . . . it is obvious that they are not righteous . . . Directly, I find fault, s[a]ying, "If these are righteous, why are they angry?" ' Above all, Hearers had questions about their alms-giving, their prayers and the future of their own souls. If they picked fruits or trampled on plants or cultivated the earth when they were trying to help the Elect, were they really wounding trapped Light? What was going to happen to them? Why did Mani's *Picture Book* not show anything about the souls of the Hearers, people on the 'middle way', when their bodies died? Would a Hearer really have to be reborn and have his soul sent into another living being? Crucially, what about Hearers' prayers for the souls of those already dead? Are they effective and, if so, how?[38] Perhaps, as a Hearer, Augustine had moments of praying for the soul of his dead father, Patricius.

In reply to this important question, the Master emphasizes the role of prayer and intercession in cosmic prehistory. Prayers had worked to save Primal Man; they had worked to rescue Adam; they will work, therefore, to help the souls of the dead, but only if they are offered by an observant group member. As these repeated questions show, ordinary Hearers, like early Christians everywhere, wanted to know if their prayers would help their own 'friends and family'. As for themselves, if they had sinned in the past or again during their lives as Hearers, would they be wholly forgiven? In reply, Mani the Master is made to be remarkably precise: four-fifths of a Hearer's sins, his answer says, will be forgiven with the help of the prayers of the Church, but one-fifth, even if he or she has been virtuous, will have to be punished and purified in the next existence.[39] Augustine the fruit-stealer, fornicator and Overturner would only ever be 80 per cent clean.

As the patterns of worship and conduct were the same in each Manichaean community, they would provoke similar reactions, whether in Egypt, Syria or Carthage: the *Kephalaia* show us the questions which Hearers would raise. Like Augustine and his friends, they had problems caused by conversion. The remarkable fact is that Mani is made to answer them in terms which are strikingly similar to those attained by the mature Augustine and his post-Manichaean thinking.

One of the Elect, we are told, 'stood up before the Apostle', Mani, and asked him the penetrating question:

> 'You say there are 15 paths related to a person's actions, three of which lead to Hell for actions of lust, desire and injury to the suffering "Cross of

> Light". What, then, about the catechumen? How does his end come out? For, from the first, before he receives the faith of God, these three paths draw him on: the appetite in his bones; the appetite of his fornication; and the damaging action that comes from the wounding [of trapped Light-particles]. Before he becomes a catechumen, do these three paths lead to Hell? Then, does he go, following after his limbs, to bondage? Will his "richness" as a believer fail to outweigh his previous sins? If indeed this will happen, according to me, it is very difficult for him to live. For, there is a multitude of catechumens set in the world, walking in error and derangement before they receive the faith of God. To where will their end come?'[40]

Augustine, up until now, had been one of them, a traveller on these three paths.

The apostle (Mani) gives a 'great lesson' in reply. Before any apostle is born into human flesh, he explains, God chooses the 'forms' of His entire Church, Elect and Hearers alike, in Heaven. After choosing them and freeing them in heaven above, He and His Word of light come to them on earth below. Everything which the Hearers have previously done will then be guided by angels to 'places wherein they will be purified'. Because a believer's 'form' has been chosen before his birth, none of his sins before he joins the sect will be held against him in perpetuity. As soon as he becomes a Hearer and fasts and gives alms, 'at that moment, he can receive this grace . . . immediately, all his first deeds which he did before he received the knowledge shall be freed'. They will no longer drag him down.

Conversion is explained here in terms of a prior, heavenly election, leading on to grace whereby all pre-conversion sins are forgiven. The Hearer's prospects are explained by a fine comparison. He is 'like a royal horse stamped with the seal of the king, which someone will stealthily muzzle and take to his own house because of the mark that is on it'.[41] Branded in heaven with 'the mark of faith and seal of truth', Hearers like Augustine will 'assent' on earth to the call and will then, through grace, believe and prevail. They assent because they have come from the right stable.

As we will see, the mature Augustine will have to follow a long scriptural and theological path to an acceptance of God's prior election of individuals, His gift of grace to them and His unfathomable mercy towards their past sins. These ideas will then be central to the *Confessions'* view of the human predicament. Yet, as this question and answer show compellingly, a similar core of beliefs addressed similar concerns among Manichaean converts. Modern studies of his thought have sometimes moved between two extremes, Christian scholars tending to say much less about Manichaeism and its relation to Augustine's later thinking, specialists in Manichaeism tending to see it persisting, as if Augustine remained deep down a believer in it. By surveying the scope of its teaching and practice, we have restored what Augustine heard and believed for nine long years. We are also better placed to understand what follows.

For eleven years, between his culminating conversion and his confessions, Augustine returns repeatedly to close readings of the first two chapters of Genesis and its story of Creation. He continues to address the great questions of evil and humans' free choice, the nature of the soul and our human composition. He engages ever more closely with Paul's letters, texts which he heard repeatedly in extracts in his Manichaean group. He looks for the unity and hidden depths of scripture, both of which were denied by his former 'true Christians'. He engages with the force of 'concupiscence' in each of us, having heard as a Manichee about the evil of sexual desire, what was sometimes called by them a 'disorderly movement'. Augustine does not keep on returning to these questions because 'Manichaeism was the one truly impassioned religious experience of his life.'[42] That experience was yet to come. Nonetheless, Manichaean teachings set questions which remained a constant influence on his own journey. Without them, we cannot understand him.

11

Selling Lies for a Living

I

For nine years Augustine was to combine his public life of studying and teaching with life as a Hearer in this 'secret group'. He even won most of his friends over to Mani's true Christianity. 'We were seducing and being seduced . . .': already, the future convert was proving himself to be an active converter.[1] Presumably, he converted them intellectually by 'reasoned' arguments just as Mani's followers had converted him. He was someone whose intelligence they already respected. None of these aspects would be present in his own decisive conversion, some thirteen years later.

Meanwhile, his private life was divided. Augustine never states that he encouraged his concubine to join Mani's Church: was he, perhaps, afraid of the law? The meetings of the 'true Christians' in Carthage were held secretly and the continuing legislation reminds us why. In March 372, in the year before Augustine joined the sect, the emperor had addressed an order to the prefect of Rome, stating that Manichaean teachers must be heavily punished wherever an 'assembly of Manichaeans' is found, that the members must be segregated as 'infamous and ignominious', and the houses for their meetings must be confiscated.[2] However, official orders were slow to translate into action and as our record of these laws is incomplete, we do not know if similar orders were extended to Carthage. Augustine was evidently not too worried as he continued to persuade male friends to join the sect. Fear of the law would hardly have dissuaded him from recruiting his concubine. Fear of the Elect may have played a bigger part, because, as we have seen, they encouraged Manichaean Hearers to give a child to the sect. If Adeodatus' mother stayed out of it, Augustine could perhaps cite her as an obstacle, likely to denounce him if he gave up their little boy.

In these years there was a gap between his religious beliefs and his public studies. It did not hold him back, any more than it held back Lucius, hero of his compatriot Apuleius' *Golden Ass*, who became the devoted worshipper of the goddess Isis, even shaving off all his hair, while continuing to be a successful barrister in the law courts. Our one and only impression of young Augustine which is not by Augustine himself relates in part to this phase. Years later, in *c.*407, someone who had known him very well in Carthage wrote him a letter, the feline opening of which is quoted in Augustine's reply. The author, Vincentius, had become bishop of a schismatic community about 400 miles west of Hippo. He recalled young Augustine in Carthage as someone 'dedicated to literary studies' and a 'devotee of peacefulness and honourable behaviour'. He had reason to emphasize Augustine's quiet nature, but his memory of him is not as a libertine or an idling mind.[3]

In his confessions, Augustine also recalls his literary labours, but for him they seem like talent misapplied. He has not forgotten the mental triumphs and literary prizes of his youth, but 'What good did it do me?' he asks of each one in turn. Looking forward, we can give an answer which he misses. In this period he stored ever more furniture in the chambers of his mind. It was to persist there, ready to shape his work as a new sort of teacher twelve years later. He was studying and training in the exact equivalent to the world of Libanius and his fellow pupils in Athens. Trained rhetors had no specialized legal training, but would sometimes use their skills at speaking to plead a case in court. Augustine did likewise, because he insists that although he helped guilty people to escape, he did not wish to have innocent people condemned.[4] A trained orator might also become a teacher, the route which was to shape Libanius' entire career. The same route appealed to Augustine, his conversion to philosophy still being an ideal more than a reality.

To secure a career, he was studying hard. He was top of his rhetorical school, he tells us, and 'aged about twenty' he grasped a text which is still too much for many of us, the text by Aristotle which its readers had entitled the *Categories*. Latin translations of the *Categories* existed, but it is unclear which of them Augustine read. Augustine's teachers also regarded it as extremely difficult and his fellow pupils had to pay a tutor to take them through its contents. Augustine understood it without any assistance, a fact on which the *Confessions* remark proudly. He was formidably able. The *Categories* could be read as a text about words and their relations, the aspect which was most relevant for aspiring orators. However, it was also important for logic and questions of definition, leading into deeper questions about what something 'is' and how words refer to it. Its underlying method uses dialectic, or logical reasoning, a subject which Augustine continued to regard favourably throughout his life. Later in the *Confessions* he will distinguish four types of 'priority' and apply them to God's order of the world. These distinctions draw on ones which he had first read in Aristotle's *Categories*.[5] At that time he had no doubt applied them to Mani's Gospel, although logical rigour was not a quality of Mani's writings.

Augustine also studied the 'liberal arts', both the grammar and rhetoric which his schoolteachers drummed into him and, beyond them, the music, astronomy, geometry, dialectic and medicine which he found for himself in other texts. Again, he studied them on his own. His north African predecessor, Apuleius, had described his own progress through a syllabus similar to Augustine's as a series of sips from cups, one after another, but to take the final draught of liberal arts, he had had to leave north Africa and go off to Athens.[6] Augustine went to the local booksellers instead. 'I read as much as I could,' he tells us, and we can deduce that the crucial books were those which Rome's pagan polymath, M. Terentius Varro, had written on the 'Disciplines' more than four centuries earlier. They were nine in number, like the Muses.[7]

These books, mostly lost to us, reinforced Augustine's remarkable erudition for the rest of his life. They deepened his interest in word roots, or etymologies, and multiplied his range of arresting anecdotes and curious facts about the world, items which he shared ever after with educated men, pagans and Christians alike. In the Greek East, pagan Libanius and Christian Synesius were similarly furnished from manuals of poetry, 'marvels' and myths. Like these manuals, Varro's nine books were not austerely scientific. For Varro, music included a theory of harmony, as well as the study of poems' metre. Number meant 'numerology', not the brilliant theorems of the earlier Greek mathematicians, but a mystical theory of number. Varro considered that the study of these disciplines could lift the mind upwards on a mystical path to God, even that the universe sings and dances for its supreme God. He duly honoured the great Pythagoras, the authority on the 'music of the spheres'. Through Varro, Pythagoras began to interest Augustine.[8] In Alexandria, by contrast, Synesius read actual texts ascribed to Pythagoras' pupils during his lessons in 'divine philosophy' with his teacher, Hypatia. Unlike Augustine, he read them in their original Greek.

Varro had been Cicero's younger contemporary, active while the *Hortensius* was being composed. Like others in north Africa,

Augustine was maturing in dialogue with Varro, Cicero and Virgil, classic Roman authors some four centuries in the past. In spring 374, his horizons were then lit up by something contemporary, our Halley's Comet, which we can calculate to have been visible in Carthage at that time.[9] For pagans like Libanius, comets were omens, sent by the gods to warn mortals. For Augustine, already a Manichaean Hearer, this comet will have been a flash of divine Light. What he had so far learned from Varro about astronomy did not persuade him otherwise.

While educating himself, Augustine had taken up the study of astrology. Mani taught that astrological power was exerted over each limb of the human body, a belief which he had taken from pagan astrologers. Unlike them, he linked it to demons who were fixed on the heavenly firmament. Even without Augustine's Manichaean studies, astrology was an ideal subject for him. It was a textual expertise, practised only from written sources, and it befitted his bookish skills. Like every astrologer, he had to make a personal collection of previous horoscopes and use them as a database. He would also need to scour old texts on the meaning of planetary conjunctions, the zodiac signs and their movements.[10]

Although specialists practised astrology, many educated people accepted it. In his autobiographical speech Libanius refers optimistically to a prediction by astrologers that he would recover the sight in an eye weakened in old age. He did not study astrology himself, but he never implies that it is nonsense. For many thoughtful people, the question was simply how far the power of the stars extended.[11] Are the stars signs, but not causes? Do they govern the body only or do they also determine the soul and its decisions? The young Augustine read Latin texts which lacked the Greeks' finer points about the universe and its laws and which could therefore be combined more easily with a Manichaean account of the world. He did not hesitate to extend the power of the stars to humans' decisions as well as to their bodily movements.

This type of astrology fitted very well with his views on blame and responsibility at the time. As a Hearer, he tells us, he thought that 'it is not we who sin, but some other nature sins within us', the powers of the Kingdom of Darkness. It 'delighted my pride that I was set outside blame, and when I had done something bad, I did not confess that I had done it'. 'Confession', he recalls, was not his practice. Instead, 'I loved to excuse myself and accuse something else', the dark power 'which was with me', in the material body.[12] He was not being troubled by some pre-Freudian guilt about himself. Astrology fitted his Manichaean sense that another sinful element was in his make-up and quite beyond his control. It could also predict what its influence would be.

In his later, post-astrological years, Augustine reiterates that astrology denies free will and personal responsibility and makes punishments superfluous. This objection to it was traditional: why, he asks, do some husbands believe in astrology and nonetheless beat their wives for gazing provocatively out of a window? On an astrological view, the women cannot help it.[13] As a student, however, Augustine would welcome predictions about the daily course of his intensely competitive career. Unlike other forms of divination, astrology did not involve the sacrifice of animal victims or prayers to named gods. It was therefore compatible with Manichaeism, which execrated the killing of animals and did not recognize such gods at all.

After ten years or so, wiser minds would succeed in talking him out of it, but his writings persist in attacking it, testifying to its appeal in the world around him. It was a widespread rule that astrologers were not to be prepared for Christian baptism unless they renounced their art. Nonetheless, Christians would sometimes ask an astrologer about the best timing for their own baptism. If pagan astrologers recanted and burned their books, he observes, they would often aspire to become Christian priests. In his own case much more would have to intervene between his abandonment of one system, astrology, and his priesthood in another, the 'Catholic' Church.[14]

Meanwhile, he was engaged with lessons and competitions, recitations in the theatre and frequent sex with his concubine. The *Confessions* have no reason to give a full autobiography, but if we strip away Augustine's hindsight, he seems to have been a hyper-intelligent young man, sociable but serious, who now thought he knew better than the old wives' tales of his uneducated mother. His spare time, as ever, was filled by friendship. In the years between 373 and 383 Augustine was to make the important individual friendships which we know best, but each of them, significantly, was based round his studies and his authoritative role as a teacher. Perhaps he had previously kept company with people in groups, whereas his close individual friendships arise only now, and then most often with people who looked up to him as an older guide. Naturally, they were all male. Augustine did not find close individual friends only through his 'secret group', although its members would fulsomely profess 'friendship' between one another, as recently found Manichaean letters in Egypt exemplify.[15] He does, however, refer to special friendships with two male members of the Elect, surely in Carthage, men of 'good repute, ready intelligence, leaders in their debates'. One, especially, became a close adherent of Augustine 'because of his liberal studies', a tribute, again, to Augustine's love of learning.[16] These friendships are another reason for not minimizing his grasp of Mani's teachings.

He contrasts here, significantly, with Libanius and Synesius. As students, they already made enduring friendships, ones which they could exploit as part of an important 'old boy network' in later life. In Athens, Libanius befriended two members of well-born families from the Levantine coast, one of whom would become prefect of Egypt under the pagan Emperor Julian and send his sons to study rhetoric with Libanius himself. The other would encourage Libanius' first return to Antioch. On news of his early death, Libanius paid a touching tribute to their shared student days, when they had 'whetted each other by criticisms' back in Athens. Another friend, Clematius, would go on diplomatic missions to the frontier with Persia and would stay on the way back with Libanius, then sick in Antioch, and prove himself 'better than medicine, as he sympathized, joked and was serious about "the old days"'. He then became one of the new pagan high priests whom Julian appointed.[17]

Like Libanius himself, these 'old boys' were all pagans, whereas Augustine's closest known friends were Manichees, converted by himself. In Alexandria, Synesius' fellow alumni are even better known, because ten of them feature in letters which present their shared love of philosophy. In later years, several of them receive requests from him to use their influence as he wishes. Another early friend, Hesychius, became governor of upper Libya. Another became a 'first-class grammarian', known for a book on verbs and nouns.[18] None of Augustine's university friends became a governor or a person of worldly influence or wrote a book, although one or two later became local north African bishops. In Athens and Alexandria, the students included young men from top families and faraway Greek cities. Synesius and Libanius came from well-connected, well-born backgrounds quite unlike Augustine's, and were young men whom others from abroad with similar backgrounds wished to know. In Carthage, Augustine befriended only north Africans.

In 374/5, aged twenty, Augustine left his studies in Carthage and returned home to Thagaste. There was no graduation ceremony. One reason for his return was money, as he had been relying on Romanianus to pay his fees. Another, in the background, might have been legal pressure. The Roman authorities were opposed to 'eternal students' who stayed abroad and thereby avoided civic obligations in their home towns. In Rome, visiting students had recently been ordered to return to their towns when aged twenty: 'if any student should neglect to return home of his own accord, by the administrative act of the prefect he shall be returned even more disgracefully to his *municipium*'.[19] African students in Rome were specially mentioned. We do not know if similar orders were addressed to the big city of Carthage, but it was at this very age, twenty, that Augustine returned to his *municipium*, Thagaste.

As his father, Patricius, had served as a councillor there, his sons, Augustine and Navigius, would be expected by their fellow townsmen to fill his vacancy. For an aspiring teacher, the burdens of council service were extremely daunting, as Libanius' life in Antioch exemplifies. Libanius was to become ever more harassed during his efforts to remain exempt from its expensive and time-consuming duties. As a student in Athens, he had already accepted his mother's sale of part of the family property, a sale which reduced the risks of his being enlisted for council service in his native city. Nonetheless, he soon ran into problems. In 361, one of his uncles died, leaving him additional property, liable to council services, and promptly Libanius' immunity was contested.[20] In Augustine's absence, by contrast, Monnica had sold nothing. On his return to Thagaste, his brother may have already begun to serve first as a councillor on the family's behalf, while Romanianus, the local big man, helped Augustine once more with his 'favour, close friendship and the sharing of his house'. He made Augustine 'famous and prominent, almost on a par with himself', surely by backing him when he set up as a teacher in the town.[21]

According to his later biographer Possidius, Augustine taught only as a *grammaticus*, one of those 'guardians of the language' who had beaten correct usage and grammar into his younger self.[22] However, the *Confessions* imply that he taught rhetoric, a higher art. As the boundaries between each stage were not fixed, Augustine probably taught grammar, like the teachers of his own adolescence, but offered rhetoric to any who were capable of it. He had no salary. He earned only the free-market fees which he could coax from those who chose to study with him rather than with the teachers who had once taught him. Meanwhile, he continued to pass on Mani's Gospel to his close friends. Manichaeans emphasized the value of winning over the rich and cited Jesus's advice at Luke 16.9, 'And I say unto you, Make to yourselves friends by reason of the Mammon of the Unrighteous.'[23] Nobody in

Thagaste was more of a servant of Mammon than Romanianus. Before long, Augustine had converted him too.

II

During his first year back in this lowly capacity, Augustine developed a friendship on which his confessions dwell at special length. It exemplified new perils beyond the 'brightly lit boundary'. It involved a young man whom Augustine had known at school, where they had played together and studied. Only now, in their early twenties, did they become exceptionally close. Augustine never names him, but explains that he won him over from a half-hearted Christianity to Mani's Gospel of Light. Their friendship was 'heated by the fervour of similar studies and aspirations'. Augustine was probably the young man's teacher. As Hearers, they would profess warm friendship in the Manichaean manner, but in this case there was so much more. During almost an entire year, this friend became 'sweet to me beyond all sweetness in that life of mine'.[24]

If we compare Libanius, there was nothing unusual in such intimacy at this phase of a speaker and teacher's life. Libanius recalls two special friends from his first 'idyllic' years as a teacher in the city of Nicomedia: Celsus (destined, yet again, for a high career under Julian) and Aristaenetus (unusual in his reluctance to take up an official post). 'The greatest impulse to happiness,' Libanius writes, 'is the acquisition of sound friends.'[25] Intense expressions of friendship were conventional between educated men in the fourth century, but none is more fervent than Augustine's memories of his unnamed 'coeval'. The question has been raised by modern readers, but nothing in Augustine's language suggests a sexual relationship between the two men. The friendship was not to be long-lived. The young man fell ill; Augustine sat daily by his bedside, but when the patient lost consciousness, others surreptitiously gave him the Christian sacraments, the first attested instance of a Christian ambush with the last rites. When the friend briefly recovered, Augustine expected that, as a Manichaean, he would enjoy a joke about this phoney 'baptism'. However, he 'recoiled in horror' and told Augustine not to make fun of it, if he wanted to be his friend again. Augustine withdrew, dismayed, but before the friend could relent, he died in Augustine's absence.

Nowadays, we know that there are patterns, clinically observed, in humans' responses to bereavement. In antiquity, Augustine's intense memory of this loss can be set beside another such 'grief observed', the grief of his idol, Cicero, at the death of his beloved daughter, Tullia. Augustine's response has been written up years later with rhetorical hindsight, whereas Cicero describes his reactions in letters to his friends which begin about a month after the initial shock of his bereavement.[26]

Augustine dwells on the uncontrolled tears, the power of places and objects to provoke grief for his absent friend, the loss of all pleasure in previously pleasurable pursuits and his 'huge burden of misery'. Life became a 'horror' for him. There is no mistaking the agony, what Tennyson later expresses at the death of his beloved friend Arthur Hallam: 'He is not here . . . On the bald street breaks the blank day.' Unlike many modern grievers at a sudden loss, Augustine does not recall an initial phase of detachment from what had happened. He recalls only the consequent obsessive misery. 'I hated everything for not having him.'[27]

'Books and poems' were Augustine's attempted distraction, but they failed him. Cicero was more purposive. At first, he went to a close friend's house in Rome and, as a remedy, fell back on literature and read everything he could find which had been written in the genre of consolation. When the city crowds and the political impact of Caesar's dictatorship unnerved him, Cicero planned another strategy for recovery. He withdrew to a series of villas outside Rome, where he remained largely alone. Augustine was younger and less well-connected and had no such safety net of houses around him. Cicero then started to write a 'Consolation' himself, the text of which survived in north Africa into the fourth century. 'I can tell you there is no consolation like it. I write for days at a time, not that I get any good by it, but for the moment I am distracted.' Whereas Augustine found no respite in pleasant places and landscapes, Cicero adopted a routine of near-solitude. 'Early in the day,' he writes, 'I hide myself in a thick thorny wood and do not emerge till evening.' He took books with him, but, even so, he was interrupted by the inevitable 'weeping with which I struggle as best I can, but so far' (nearly a month after his loss) 'it is an unequal fight'.[28]

Augustine was not yet a practised author. Nor was he of an age or financial standing to seek solace in arranging a memorial. Cicero, by contrast, quickly found a project which became an alternative focus for his grief: he planned to buy land and build a shrine for his dead daughter. In other times, he remarks, people of whom he had read would have found distraction in public affairs. It was denied to him because

Caesar was suffocating free political life. Augustine was too lowly even to consider such a remedy.

After writing the Consolation, Cicero began to write more demanding philosophy. Three months passed and although the sadness persisted, he had begun to re-engage with the world, having managed the stages of bereavement with commendable maturity. So, too, Libanius was to lose his dearest of friends, Aristaenetus, in a fearful earthquake that ruined the city of Nicomedia in north-west Asia Minor, the place which he recalls as one of the happiest venues of his life and dignifies with a most charming urban description. The shock of this earthquake, in August 358, was to turn Libanius' hair grey and he writes how 'I disregarded food, I threw away all speeches, I rejected sleep, I lay mostly in silence.' But then, like Cicero, he countered depression by writing. He composed a literary Lament for the city, 'the dearest of all cities, fallen with the dearest of all men'. Like Cicero, he was helped by composition: 'I grieve now, but in a steady-minded way.'[29]

Augustine was much younger and less fortified, and found relief only by a total change of scene. Missing his friend all over Thagaste, he tells us, he transferred himself to Carthage and escaped the painful reminders. Remarkably, he had been offered a job as a teacher of rhetoric, nothing less than a public job with a proper salary at the city of Carthage's expense. It was extremely unusual for a mere *grammaticus* to jump so far up the ladder, as unusual as for a schoolmaster nowadays to become a university professor. Romanianus' patronage had not even been relevant. At first, Augustine recalls, Romanianus opposed the move 'out of love for his home town', but as he could not stop a young man's desire to better himself, he changed from 'dissuader to encourager' and arranged 'all the essentials' for Augustine's journey. The move was not undertaken simply out of grief: it was also done for the sake of this 'more illustrious' job.[30]

If there were particular patrons behind this appointment, we are not told their names. It marks the first big break in Augustine's career, a job on exactly the same public ladder as Libanius'. Like Augustine, Libanius was to be offered a public teaching post in the city of his studies. However, when he was denied it, he simply left with a well-placed 'old boy' to take a job in his friend's city further away. Family and university contacts continued to mould his early career.[31] Augustine's movements, by contrast, will owe more to his Manichaean network.

In Carthage, the consolations of friendship gradually reasserted themselves in Augustine's life. He found new friends and continued to enjoy existing ones. Through them and the passage of time, he recalls, he surmounted his loss. Like Cicero, but by a different route, he re-engaged with the world and began to compete again in public. His confessions then return to dwell at length on his recent grief and friendship. His analysis addresses in sequence God, himself, his soul and then sinners in general, and moves from one level to another in ways which challenge those who read the *Confessions* only for biographical details. During this analysis, major themes of the work are touched on more powerfully than before. They are propelled, as ever, by his spontaneous act of prayer.[32]

At one level Augustine reflects on friendship in literary terms which were conventional for pagans and Christians alike. He draws on Cicero's ethical writings and repeats some of their platitudes. In a friendship, Cicero had stated, the essential ingredients are truthfulness, virtue and benevolence: friendship must be a not-for-profit relationship. Augustine even describes his friend as his 'other self', a view which is known through Cicero to trace back to Pythagoras. In Cicero and in Varro's books on the liberal arts, Augustine also met the idea of friends becoming 'one from many', *e pluribus unum*, a phrase with a long afterlife. Again, this idea was believed to have begun with Pythagoras.[33]

These phrases idealized 'perfect' friendship, but they were not peculiar to Augustine. In Alexandria, as a student, Christian Synesius applied Pythagorean number theory to ideal friendship, an idea which Hypatia, surely, had introduced to him. Two of his friends make a trio with God, he writes, and so he himself makes up a fourth with them, four being a specially mystic number.[34] At the time of his own intense friendships, in the late 370s, Augustine may indeed have seen them in terms which Cicero and the Pythagoreans had taught him. As he was reading these two authors while these friendships formed, the *Confessions*' phrases may be carefully chosen to echo his thoughts at the time.

'My treasure,' Alexander the Great was believed to have said, 'lies in my friends.' In Carthage, Augustine tells us beguilingly how he found solace once more in friends: 'we would talk together and laugh together and in turns do one another kindnesses; together we would read sweetly styled books, now joking, now being serious; we would disagree from time to time without rancour, just as a man might disagree with himself . . . we would teach or learn something by turns, pine with distress for those absent, welcome those returning with joy . . .' These friendships came from the 'hearts' of people who loved one another. They set 'hearts and minds' on fire.[35]

Such reflections on friendship show Augustine at his most charming, but they are not unique to him. In the Greek tradition they were strong and Libanius was no less open about them. He sustained this type of friendship with his old university friend, Clematius, even when Clematius had a career in the Imperial service: if either of them was seen without the other in Antioch, even in their early forties, the prefect would ask jokingly, 'And where is your other half?', the very phrase which Augustine uses of his friend. When Clematius became a pagan high priest of Palestine, Libanius sent him a letter in which he imagined the reception of another old friend, its carrier: 'I can see and hear it, though absent: the gestures, the jokes, the laughter flowing from you both, the remembrance of old times, the reports about the present time, the charmingly witty stories and' (being Libanius) the 'story of me and my affairs'.[36]

In Carthage, while teaching and recovering from his loss, Augustine developed two new friendships which were to become the two dearest in his life. Once again, both were with people whom he taught, but this time both younger than himself. He began to know Nebridius, a young man from a rich landed family outside the city. When Augustine met him, Nebridius was a pagan. Intelligent and inquiring, as Augustine recalls, he was never content with a superficial answer to a difficult question, and before long he was framing a radical objection to Mani's views. In later life, his letters to Augustine show his questioning, philosophic mind in action. It remained a sounding board for Augustine's own until his premature death in 391.[37]

The other friend, Alypius, was from Thagaste, where his parents were upper-class citizens. Like Nebridius, he was much better off than Augustine's family: he was related to Romanianus, possibly as his nephew. Like Nebridius, he was a younger man, perhaps as much as nine years younger than Augustine. He was another of Augustine's pupils in Thagaste, but when he moved to Carthage a quarrel between Augustine and his father caused him to break off contact. His commitment to Mani's Gospel is the likeliest culprit. In Carthage, Alypius then resumed his attendance at Augustine's classes and the friendship re-emerged. Augustine does not bestow on him the language of intense love and mutual delight which he uses of his unnamed friend, perhaps because Alypius was so much younger. However, he lets us know something of his sexual history: Alypius had been put off sex by his first unfortunate attempt with a girl. Was she to blame, or, deep down, was he homosexual? He never married and, befitting his natural gravity, went on to study law. Neither Augustine nor Alypius imagined that thirty years after their meeting they would both be celibate bishops in the 'Catholic' Church.[38]

Augustine's confessions then turn to dig deeper into the friendship he had lost with his unnamed coeval in Thagaste.[39] Why, he wonders, had weeping appealed to him so much in his bereavement? For Christians aspiring to the 'perfection' which Jesus had proposed in the Gospels, tears raised questions of selfishness and loss of control, failings which they analysed as sins. Once again, Augustine proceeds by raising questions as he prays to God. Is 'bitter weeping' sweet because we hope to be heard thereby by God? Surely not, if it is caused by loss. Such weeping is not the same as the weeping which sometimes accompanies prayers and which aims to attract God's notice: Monnica, we know, practised such strategic, tearful prayer. Is it, then, that 'weeping is a bitter thing, but out of disdain for things which we formerly enjoyed, at a time when we are recoiling from them, it [can] delight us'? Augustine leaves this tortuous question unanswered, but he had surely not been 'disdaining' his friendship when he wept for it. He had merely lost it. He does not consider that weeping is the inevitable consequence of a loss of psychological control. Cicero, by contrast, writes graphically of the impact of the 'fangs of grief'.

Typically, Augustine returns and worries at the question again. What did I feel, he wonders again, in that 'bitterness'? Then, he remembers: he had felt the 'most heavy tedium in living on' but also a 'fear of dying'. As death could suddenly take away his friend, he had thought that it would 'suddenly take away all men too'. Once again, he feels that he has worked back psychologically to the truth. 'That is how I was, entirely so! I have remembered. Look, my God, my heart! Look! The inside of me!' Yet again, we are listening to his self-analysis in progress, unrevised and written down as it happens. It was well said, he continues, that a 'friend is half of one's soul', as poets and others had put it. If so, he himself had surely been weary of living because half of his soul was gone, but still afraid of dying, because then all traces of his other half, his friend, would be extinguished. He does not know, he says, if he would have been willing to die for him, 'as is said about Orestes and Pylades, if it is not a fiction'. These two devoted friends had been made famous by Euripides' classic Greek dramas and were known in the Latin-speaking world through a Latin play, named after them, by Pacuvius: Cicero had made it even more famous by remarking on its spellbinding effect on Roman audiences. Augustine would know of it from Cicero's text but also, perhaps, from theatrical stagings in

Carthage. Only a Greek text on love, much later than Cicero, had discussed the love of Orestes and Pylades in erotic terms. Augustine did not know this text and certainly did not think of the two men as sexual lovers.[40] His own friendship, he merely wishes to say, lacked the extreme self-sacrifice of theirs.

In older age, Augustine rightly criticizes this analysis for being superficial. It plays with phrases and the paradox of 'bitter-sweet' tears. 'I had become a great puzzle to myself,' he remarks, in the context of the effects of bereavement, 'and I kept asking my soul why it was so sad.' The truth was that he had been depressed, the natural response to such a bereavement, but he had not been suicidal, a more extreme response to loss. As a public speaker he would have practised formal speeches of lament, exemplified among Libanius' Greek speeches. Whereas they lamented the dead persons and the loss of their many gifts, Augustine's analysis is self-centred. He does not consider the impact of the loss on his friend's family or other friends in Thagaste. Above all, he never considers whether guilt was deepening his depression. His friend had been appalled by Augustine's flippancy about his deathbed baptism and had died before the quarrel could be made up. Augustine blames his false Manichaean view of 'God' for preventing him from finding rest. At the time, he believed that God was within him, in particles of Light, but not above him, he reflects, and so he could not refer his troubles to One beyond and above himself.[41] His attempts to do so collapsed on a vain illusion. Actually, Mani's teaching would have intensified the loss for a different reason. His friend had renounced Mani's Gospel, become a 'semi-Christian' and then died. According to Mani, therefore, his Light would not ascend to the sun. It would be reborn in a meaty animal and no member of the Elect would ever eat it and set it free.

Though consoled by friends, Augustine observes that he did not yet understand friendship's true role. It is here that his confessions embark on a remarkable burst of prayer, one which addresses God, his soul, then sinners and the 'sons of men'. The core of it explores what he has already stated, that a stable, well-adjusted friendship depends on loving God too. Between two Christian friends, three is never one too many in a relationship, but the third must always be God. God alone is stable, eternal and a source of repose. As scripture commands us to love both God and our neighbour, we must love the one in the other. In due course, this high ideal of friendship will underlie Augustine's ideals for the life of monastic 'brethren'.[42]

At the time, in Thagaste and Carthage, he was misled by a 'huge fable', which seduced and 'itched' his mind by 'advancing irritation'. It was not his false Manichaeism. It was his love for friends as if they would live for ever. In Carthage, he recalls, he repeated the same error. His confessions therefore return to analyse its roots. Through God, we are parts of an orderly whole, although, mostly, we fail to see it. As mortals, we must die, because death is our due limit, but our fleshly senses cannot fully grasp this ordered process: they have their limits too. Through God's creating word, nonetheless, they can hear what resounds so finely in the Book of Job: 'From here to there, and no further.'[43]

Our souls, then, must not be deafened by 'vanity', a crucial word in Augustine's denouncement of fleeting, worldly objects of desire. They must turn back to God, the one and only point where love and quietness endure. If we ever love a soul or body on earth, we must realize that it is being loved by God too. 'See where He is – wherever there is a taste of truth.' He is 'innermost, in our heart, but the heart has strayed from Him'. Sinners, meanwhile, seek the happy life in the 'land of death, but He is not there'. They ignore that, once upon a time, God descended to us, in the Incarnation, so that we too might 'turn again to our heart and find Him'. Instead, sinners fall low by trying to ascend in opposition to Him. 'Gather them with you to God,' Augustine addresses himself, 'because you speak with His Spirit when you speak this, burning with love.'[44]

His confession has now soared into an impassioned, inspired sermon, preaching the need for conversion back to God. It is not addressed specifically to Manichaeans, his former companions in error. Instead, it addresses all 'foolish sons of men' and expresses ideas which will become much clearer as his confessions proceed. They include God's presence within us, our inner 'heart', the 'limits' of each created thing and the existence, once again, of a hidden order behind perceptible changes through time. Augustine also declares his impulse. It is not only penitent confession. It is also a burning fire of love, a force, he states, which is propelling his prayer.[45]

These ideas are complex and, as he well says, 'I did not know them at the time.' Yet, the *Confessions* have now traced three perils in friendship: the herd impulse to steal and sin, the sexual impulse to cross 'brightly lit boundaries' and the heedless impulse to love a friend as if for ever, without loving God too and discerning our place as parts in an ordered whole.

12
Guided Encounters

I

When Augustine arrived to take up his public teaching post in Carthage, the governor of the province of north Africa was living proof that culture could propel a family ever further up the ladder of the Roman Empire. He was the son of Ausonius the poet, who had been the tutor of an emperor-to-be and then, in old age, was rewarded by his former pupil with nothing less than a governorship and the high honour of the consulship at Rome. When Ausonius' son left Africa, the next year's governor, in 376, was Ausonius' son-in-law. They exemplified jobs for 'friends and family' at a level of which young Augustine could only dream.[1]

In 380/81 he had recovered sufficiently from grief at the recent loss of his friend to make his own bid for patronage in higher society. For the first time, he wrote a book. It arose from talks with his friends in Carthage, thereby giving us a glimpse of what they 'would teach or learn' in long afternoons. 'I used to say to friends,' he recalls, '"Surely we do not love anything which is not beautiful? . . . So, what is beauty? What attracts us to the things we love?"'[2], perennial questions that would later engage another young verbal 'artist', Joyce's Stephen Daedalus and his student friends in Dublin.

His answer became *On the Beautiful and Apt*, which he composed in two, perhaps three, books. By the time he wrote the *Confessions* he had lost track of them, and so they are lost to us too, but he had been very pleased with them at the time. Bidding for attention, he dedicated them to Hierius, a famous thinker and speaker in Rome. He had never met Hierius, and the *Confessions* reflect austerely on why he had admired someone whom he knew only from hearsay: perhaps his critics had later alleged that Hierius was another Manichaean friend. He was by birth a Greek-speaker 'from Syria' and was surely familiar there with Antioch and Libanius. However, he had gone on to master Latin, a feat which Libanius would have deplored, and had migrated to Rome, in Libanius' eyes, the last straw. He also engaged with philosophy. Perhaps he never read this youthful book from an unknown African, forced on him like a young man's unsolicited thesis. Already, it shows, young Augustine was looking for connections in Rome. In Athens, young Libanius saw no need to write and make such a pitch. Friends and his existing network would suffice to get him a job.[3]

Augustine could recall only the outline of his book, but its special interest is that it belongs in his committed Manichaean phase. 'I had been reading many things of the philosophers,' he tells us, and his memories of the book bear him out. Its question about beauty is typically Platonic, the sort of topic which Augustine would find in a short handbook of philosophical theories. His main answer, he recalls, distinguished between beauty as a part of an orderly whole and aptness as a quality relating to a specific part. This distinction anticipates the important distinction in his writings some ten years later between 'enjoying' something as an end in itself and 'using' it as a means. He explains what is 'apt' in terms which match what Cicero had written about 'aptness' in a composed speech. As a teacher of orators, Augustine had no doubt read this view of aptness.[4]

The work's second book moved on to discuss the nature of the soul. Revealingly, it traced an opposition between virtue and peace and reason on the one hand and lust and passion and vice on the other. Here, his Manichaean beliefs are interestingly relevant. Augustine could not treat Hierius to a basic statement of Mani's outlawed Gospel, but he could blend its ideas into a philosophical form. Virtue in the soul, he therefore argued, reflects unity, whereas vice reflects division, discord and multiplicity. The principle of virtue is a 'monad', without sex, whereas vice is opposed to it and is a 'dyad' riven by lust. Here, Augustine was casting Manichaean beliefs in Pythagorean terms. He related goodness to a sexless Monad and lust to a seething Dyad, two Pythagorean terms which he set, as Pythagoreans did not, in opposition to one another.[5] It was not unusual for a young man to apply Pythagorean concepts to theology. In Alexandria, Synesius learned such terms while studying with Hypatia and then applied them to the Christian Trinity, whose God, he wrote, is a 'monad' and whose persons are a 'triad'. Augustine stopped with two items, a monad and dyad, because they were apt for Mani's dualism.[6]

Hopelessly speculative, this book shows two important ways of thinking nonetheless. Although Augustine was reading non-Christian wisdom, he was willing to believe it could be consistent with 'true Christianity', in his view Mani's teaching. There were indeed some impressive similarities. Pythagoras was believed to have been a vegetarian: so were the Manichaean Elect. He was even considered to have taught that the souls of the just ascend to the moon. Here again, he was very compatible with Mani.[7] While looking for harmony between two different types of wisdom, Augustine was also assuming that 'unity' existed behind the diversity of the world. This idea was leading him to believe in a hidden 'order' in the universe, a belief sustained in the *Confessions* from his account of babyhood onwards.

His belief in a hidden 'order' is reinforced by his reflections on three encounters Like Tolstoy in his own life and novels, Augustine and his friends will be brought to change away from their former pattern of life by the impact of others and their words Whereas Tolstoy typically presents chance meetings in which a past acquaintance causes himself or a fictional character to awake and to realize a truth about the person and then about himself and the need for a change of life, Augustine presents encounters which, with hindsight, are providential, guided by God, and in which words sometimes have on him an impact that is the very opposite of their utterer's intentions. The first, a simple one, was an encounter with Alypius. Unlike Augustine, he had thrown himself into the excitements of watching the horse races in Carthage's huge circus stadium. After the quarrel between Augustine and his father, he was staying away from Augustine's classes, but one day he entered the room while Augustine was reading a text with his pupils. By chance, Augustine illustrated a point by comparing the 'vileness' of the races and the circus games. Earnest Alypius took the comparison to heart and gave up attending such shows thereafter. With hindsight, Augustine ascribes this happy chance to God's underlying ordering of the world. God, he believed, had used him as His instrument for changing Alypius' ways and had made him effective in a way he had never intended.[8]

Around him, meanwhile, Carthage was teeming with non-Christian sorcerers and fortune-tellers, prophets and diviners, all of whom promised to reveal the future. One of them, Albicerius, was scarcely educated and was known for a life of frequent debauchery. He was a 'soothsayer', or *hariolus*, and his predictions were famous for being accurate. Even Augustine was moved to appeal to him. He sent Romanianus' young son on a mission to ask about a missing silver spoon, and Albicerius obliged with a correct answer, as he did in other cases put to him. Augustine even heard that Flaccianus, a member of Carthage's upper class, had once asked Albicerius which verses of Virgil he himself had on his mind. Not only did Albicerius identify them. He recited them, although his own schooling was thought to have been minimal.[9]

This mind-reading continued to puzzle Augustine, just as it puzzled, later, the young Synesius. Pagans ascribed it to the aid of *daimones*, or divine intermediaries, whereas 'semi-Christians' ascribed it to demons. Augustine was never so certain. Years later, he refers to people who are not mad or in a trance but who are 'acted on by some hidden instinct and are inspired with thoughts that become prophecies when they speak them'.[10] Perhaps he remembered here the impact which his chance words had had on Alypius, and surely he also remembered Albicerius' uncanny clairvoyance. Both items implied the existence of an ordering power in the universe, but how would Mani explain it?

Out of class Augustine and his fellow Hearers still liked to trouble 'semi-Christians' with a battery of set-piece arguments. If man is made 'in God's image', they would ask, is God a being like one of us, with hair, teeth and fingernails? If God has created the soul, why does it do wrong? If God is so good, why does He create evil?[11] Contradictions could be extracted by the dozen from the scriptures of the 'semi-Christians', whether in the bad behaviour of the patriarchs or the Gospels' conflicting family trees for Jesus. Augustine admits that he did not bother to check these points. He liked to advance them and win arguments as a result.

In Carthage, Alypius was spending the time necessary for a young man of his class in attending on grand, potential patrons. Augustine, though socially inferior to Alypius, was not confined to his schoolroom, either. Surely he talked personally with Flaccianus and thereby heard his story about the soothsayer. Flaccianus was from the highest social class in Carthage: educated members of it would like to meet and talk with such a bright young man in their city. They did so again when Augustine won the prize for a 'theatrical poem', verses, evidently, which he recited on stage in a public competition. In 382 the prizegiver was the provincial governor, Helvius Vindicianus. Augustine comments on Vindicianus' medical learning and, indeed, he is still known to us as the author of texts on anatomy and gynaecology.[12] Like Augustine, he had studied rhetoric and had dedicated a work to a much grander recipient, in his case the reigning Western emperor. Unlike Augustine, he had translated texts of the older Greek masters into Latin and become a doctor at court. He then received the governorship of Africa, perhaps the province of his birth. After honouring his young prizewinner, Vindicianus talked to him at more length, and showed a style of speaking which Augustine, ever the vigilant young connoisseur, recalls that he admired: he spoke in an 'unadorned way' which was 'delightful and serious, with a liveliness to the points he expressed'. In conversation, he discovered Augustine's taste for astrology and warned him off it. As a young man, Vindicianus said, he had considered following a career as an astrologer: if he could understand difficult medical books, he had thought, he could surely understand difficult astrology books too. He then discovered they were 'utterly false'. Augustine should follow his advice. He had rhetoric to teach and he should leave this other delusion alone.

The young Augustine countered by pointing out that astrologers' predictions quite often come true. Vindicianus did not deny the fact. Instead, he ascribed it to the power of 'fortune', which is 'diffused all about in the nature of things'. It was not surprising, he said, if apparently random verses or words then turned out to be true predictions. This power of 'fortune' worked on the human soul 'by a higher instinct', although the soul might not know it, and it allowed the soul to predict truly. Augustine did not forget the older man's opinion: he would repeat it as his own, years later, when trying to account for soothsayers like Albicerius.

There was a reason for Vindicianus' opinion. His father, we happen to know, had written about the 'reason of the entire universe'.[13] Evidently, his son had warmed to the idea. Anticipating Wordsworth, Vindicianus thought 'of something far more deeply interfused . . . A motion and a spirit that impels All thinking things, all objects of all thought And rolls through all things . . .' A pagan like Libanius accepted the goddess Fortune and believed she was providentially active on his own behalf. With hindsight, Christian Augustine detected the loving guidance of a merciful God in his every move. God, he believed, had carefully provided Vindicianus for him, although he was not yet ready in his inner 'heart' to accept and act on the great man's advice. Nonetheless, God had deliberately 'traced' it on his heart and left it as a 'memory' for future impact. Helvius Vindicianus, like his father, saw a hidden power of 'fortune' in the universe and even thought that it might act on an individual's soul and inspire truth. One day, this 'divine power' in apparently random words was to have a drastic effect on Augustine's own life. More immediately, it was to feature in yet another encounter in the city.

II

Vindicianus is the only provincial governor whom young Augustine met personally. His social centre still lay elsewhere. Between 373 and 382 he was one of a group of Hearers who offered 'soul service' of approved food more than 400 times to the male and female Elect. They were giving him his first experience of a small religious group whose members professed friendship and 'love' between themselves. When off duty, he continued to read, as ever without a teacher, absorbing 'many things of the philosophers'. However, they were found to say things which did not match Mani's Gospel.

A clash thus emerged between two different views of the heavens. It is valuable, here, to compare Synesius' response to similar teaching. As Hypatia's student in Alexandria he engaged keenly with the classic views of previous Greek astronomers. She herself wrote an *Astronomical Canon*. She edited the text of a book of Ptolemy's astronomical *Almagest* and also his *Handy Tables*, where many of her insertions still survive in the text.[14] Whereas Augustine was about to be rid of a false god thanks to Greek astronomy, Synesius was taught astronomy as a step towards the true God, the One who could best be expressed in Platonist terms. Although Hypatia was not a Christian, he remained passionately true to her lessons ever after, praising her 'sacred geometry' and even devising an astronomical gift for an important courtier at Constantinople on the back of what she had taught him. It was a 'planisphere', made of silver, with a complex celestial map and a rotating section. Expert opinion has judged it harshly as 'a very expensive but completely useless showpiece', but the letter in which he describes and presents it is not an exact scientific manual. Hypatia's father, Theon, had written a book called *The Little Astrolabe*, and it is therefore he who deserves the credit for the world's first astrolabe.[15] Synesius' letter and gift were based on Hypatia's teaching of her father's text. His 'planisphere' was a carefully chosen gift for a courtier who liked to think of himself as a philosopher. For such people, scientific astronomy and religious philosophy coexisted. Augustine, by contrast, was working in Carthage only from short surveys of 'many things of the philosophers' which he bought and read in his spare time. He had no classes with an expert teacher. As a man might read nowadays about evolution and genetics in a 'guide to modern thought' and then realize that the Bible's stories of Creation are untrue, so Augustine began to find from his own reading that Mani's view of the universe was very hard to justify. Since the sixth century BC, Greek philosophers and astronomers had been correctly predicting the timing of eclipses of the sun and moon. They even explained why they happened. Mani's own explanation seemed most implausible. According to him, eclipses occur when the two Light-ships, sun and moon, choose to hide their orbs from the distressing sight of the battle with evil in the world about them. If eclipses depend on emotional choice, how could Greek astronomers predict them accurately?

In 381 and 384, partial eclipses of the sun were visible, we can calculate, in Carthage. They made this question particularly pertinent.[16] There were also questions about Manichaeans' treatment of the 'semi-Christian' scriptures. As one such 'semi-Christian', Elpidius, observed to Augustine, it was not convincing to claim that wherever the scriptures were mistaken or opposed to Mani's Gospel, they had been padded out with 'Jewish' interpolations. What if these passages were genuine?

Augustine's new thoughts on 'aptness' contained potential problems too. Manichaeans liked to attack the immoral behaviour of many people in the Old Testament, especially the oversexed Hebrew patriarchs. In the *Confessions*, Augustine defends them by arguing that their conduct was appropriate for the time in which they lived. Had this point already occurred to him in Carthage when he focused on the notion of 'aptness' in his first book? 'Aptness' could also be brought to bear on the idea of 'absolute evil'. When somebody denied that evil was a substance, a Manichaean teacher replied that if a scorpion was put in the man's hand, he would withdraw his hand soon enough. Augustine reflects that this answer can nonetheless be queried. The poison does not kill the scorpion which contains it. Perhaps it is not a wholly evil substance. Perhaps it is 'apt' for a particular purpose, self-defence.[17]

To cap all these doubts, there was the question posed to him one day by his tireless, inquiring friend Nebridius. God, by definition, is incorruptible, so why did the Manichaean God ever fight against invading Darkness? If God is incorruptible, Darkness could never harm Him. If He is not, then He is not God. The question impressed his hearers, especially Augustine, with whom it was to remain, nagging at his faith. Many years later, he himself would deploy it insistently in his public disputes with Manichaean leaders.[18]

There were moral problems too. As questions in the Coptic-Egyptian *Chapters* remind us, Mani's Elect were not always a 'perfect family'.

It is revealing that some of them split off from the main Church and classified themselves as the true, observant core. Within five years of leaving their Church, Augustine was giving precise details of some shocking behaviour by members of the Elect in Carthage, people whom he knew well. He had watched an inglorious scene when some Elect members met on a main public square in Carthage and made catcalls at young ladies who were passing by. None of these Elect showed any remorse, suggesting that they made a habit of such sinful conduct. There were also reports of sex abuse. Augustine says that he reported to the leaders of the sect the distress of a lady who told him that she had been sexually harassed when the lights were put out at a group meeting. Again, the authorities did nothing, fearing that the law would become involved. Similarly, they refused to discipline an Elect whom Augustine had heard arguing in one of Carthage's typical shopping quarters, the 'district of the fig-sellers'. The man then made a female member pregnant, but the Elect did nothing and it was left to her brother and his friends to take revenge.[19]

When Augustine claims that he and others complained about such conduct, he deserves to be believed. Nonetheless, these bad examples did not destroy his loyalty, no more than a few bad priests cause modern Catholics to renounce their faith. Augustine still believed that an even greater truth was being kept back from him and that one day the good Elect members would reveal it. Meanwhile, they tried to reassure him. He should wait until their most learned teacher paid a visit, the famous Faustus, one of their Church's seventy-two bishops throughout the world. Augustine kept back his questions, 'waiting for Faustus' and preparing for discussion.

Faustus arrived in Carthage in late 382/early 383 and at one level made a very good impression. He had been born in Milev, some way to the west of Augustine's Thagaste. Many of the Manichees were from 'semi-Christian' families, but Faustus was the child of two pagan parents. He was not from a rich home, but he had had some education, enough to be considered a man of the 'liberal arts'. Now in his forties, he was a bishop, but, like the seventy-two missionaries of Luke's Gospel, Mani's seventy-two bishops were not tied to any one district. Faustus himself had just travelled to Rome. As a bishop, he was one of the Elect, without a wife, family or worldly goods. He depended on Hearers like those in Carthage for food and maintenance.[20]

Augustine recalls that he found Faustus agreeable and that his manner was seductive. As ever the critic of others' speaking, he observed that Faustus delivered a speech every day and had acquired an easy style, the result of his organized and graceful nature. For a sense of Faustus' strengths, we can look forward to his *Capitula* (or 'Chapters'), the work which Faustus later circulated, having written it, probably, while under sentence as a criminal. From 386 to 387 Faustus was to be condemned to an island by anti-Manichaean legislation, a sentence which gave him time to write. His book is our longest known work in Latin by a Manichaean: we know bits of it because Augustine later wrote thirty-three books against it. He cited each chapter (there were thirty-two in all) and then attacked it at six times the length of his quotations from Faustus' text.[21]

Augustine wrote this refutation in the early fifth century. When composing the *Confessions*, he was still ignorant of all that Faustus had published, but the *Chapters* help us to see how Faustus is likely to have been thinking at the time of their meeting. Written three years later, they were designed to help existing members of Mani's Church, people, on the surface, like Augustine. They were cast as answers to objections raised by a fictitious opponent and were useful weapons, therefore, for winning converts and defeating counterarguments. Faustus focused on four areas. He attacked the 'Old Testament' of the Jews and 'semi-Christians' by exposing its immorality and its irrelevance to true Christian beliefs. He realized, correctly, that it predicted nothing about Christianity. He denied the incarnation of Christ and His suffering on an earthly cross. He denied that Mani taught the worship of two gods. The 'Father of Light' was God, but the Father of Darkness was not. Faustus exposed, point by point, supposedly 'Jewish' additions to the genuine core of the New Testament. He was a self-aware biblical critic. He would accept only statements which were 'carefully investigated and found to be true, decent and not corrupted'. However, the test of the truth of a statement was whether it agreed with Mani's Gospel. Like Mani, Faustus considered that pagan prophets were more relevant to Mani's truth than biblical ones. He therefore cited texts by 'Thrice-Great Hermes', 'Orpheus' and the Sibyl, authorities who would impress a pagan listener.[22]

Faustus could also appeal powerfully to his own way of life. After all, the Elect were the only people in north Africa who really did live by the precepts of Jesus's Sermon on the Mount. There, at least, was a text which 'Jews' had not interpolated. 'Do you ask if I believe the gospel?' Faustus wrote. 'Perhaps you do not know what is called the gospel. The gospel is nothing other than the preaching and precept of Christ. I have parted with all gold and silver and have ceased to carry money in my purse; I am content with daily food; I have no anxiety for tomorrow and I am without care about how I shall be fed or wherewithal I shall be clothed; and do you ask if I believe the gospel? . . . You see me poor, meek, a peacemaker, pure in heart, mourning, hungering, thirsting, bearing persecution and hostility for the sake of righteousness, and do you doubt my belief in the gospel?'[23]

As the *Confessions* recall, Faustus indeed spoke fluently; his character came across well; he talked to the Hearers as a group. Young Augustine, teeming with questions, regretted, typically, that he could not 'press' him. He raised his problems about astronomy and the heavens, but Faustus confessed with appealing modesty that he did not know the answers. The *Chapters* show that Faustus was best when dealing with disputed scriptural texts and points within Mani's system itself.

Faustus, it transpired, knew only one of the 'liberal arts', or disciplines: grammar. He had never even studied astronomy. As a result, young Augustine ended up meeting individually with the very man he had hoped would solve his problems. However, he found Faustus to be rather narrowly read. He knew only some bits of Seneca, some Latin poets and some speeches of Cicero. He knew the main Manichaean texts, albeit in Latin: the comment implies that Augustine had expected more from a Manichaean bishop, at the very least some Greek. Augustine's teaching pride was stirred. Though only a Hearer, he began to take his middle-aged bishop through texts which Faustus had heard about and longed to know or which 'I considered to be fit for a mind such as his.'[24]

Once again, a visitor had become an unintended agent of change. Faustus had been meant to re-establish Augustine's belief, but, instead, he had weakened it. With hindsight, Augustine sees God's 'hidden providence' at work in this encounter too. 'Your hands,' he tells God, 'in the hidden course of Your providence, were not deserting my soul.' The 'snare' around him, he reflects, was beginning to be undone. There was also the fact of Monnica's daily tears, her 'sacrificial offering', day and night, from the 'blood of her heart' on Augustine's behalf.[25] With hindsight, many years later, he realizes that God was paying attention throughout and dealing with him 'in wondrous ways'. Meanwhile, his doubts about Mani's universe remained unanswered. They were serious, because Mani's cosmology was not an optional extra, like a frill on the ethical core. It was part of a closely knit whole which linked

Light and Darkness, the make-up of each living being and their proper response to the material world. As if he had read Darwin and found the first chapters of Genesis shot through the head, Augustine was left with an ethic and a cosmology which did not add up. For the moment he persisted with Mani's sect, but his belief that the Elect were hiding further truths had been dashed. He continued, however, to revere the 'sanctity' of Mani himself.[26]

Soon after Faustus' visit, probably by early summer 383, Augustine formed a new plan. Without his child and his concubine he would sail to Rome and try to teach there. If the plan worked they could come over and join him. It sounds bold, but travel from Carthage to Rome was quick and unsurprising. Already Augustine had dedicated his book to a senior orator in Rome; Faustus had just been visiting the Manichaean group there and Alypius had already left for Rome to pursue his legal career. Fellow Manichaeans in Carthage also encouraged him and would probably have had some useful contacts in the city.

Augustine's decision became an item of personal attacks on him in later life, one of which was revived by his enemies just before he wrote the *Confessions*. 'You acted with me,' he tells God there, 'so that it was persuaded of me . . .': like other sensitive decisions, it is one which Augustine presents in the passive voice. He gives two reasons: the prospect of greater gain and honour, and escape from the behaviour of the students in Carthage. He disavows the first, but then admits that it carried some weight.[27] The second was much more important, but his critics later added a third, his wish to dodge strict new laws against Manichaeans. Elsewhere in the empire, the laws indeed intensified from 381 onwards: in one case, Manichaeans' wills and business deals were invalidated, and the ban was made retrospective. In late May 383 the Emperor Gratian then sent out an edict for the Western provinces, including Africa. It ordered 'constant and perpetual pursuit' of converts from Christianity to Manichaeism and those who 'deflected unstable minds to their society'. There was no greater deflector at work than Augustine. However, by the time this edict reached Carthage, Augustine had almost certainly decided to leave for other reasons. The edict would anyway not be applied until a governor took it seriously and in Carthage its enforcement had to wait until 386. It is not, then, the missing link in Augustine's decision to migrate.[28] Although 'Manichaean friends', he tells us, surely including Faustus, encouraged him to transfer to Rome, they felt no legal pressure on themselves to leave Carthage too. It was not until 386–7 that Faustus himself was arrested.

The law became involved, but only later. In 386, when Augustine was still in Italy, he was denounced *in absentia* to the governor, who was at last applying it. The governor even gave a decision on Augustine's guilt.[29] When Augustine composed the *Confessions*, this blot on his record had recently been recalled and used against him by his enemies. When confessing his departure, Augustine does not mention these subsequent charges. Instead, he stresses yet again God's plan and hidden 'providence', as if his departure was divinely guided. God, we are to infer, was working through Augustine's ambitions.

Boisterous students were the visible cause of his decision to leave. Whereas the Overturners, Augustine's former company, targeted new arrivals, the existing students of a teacher would form partisan groups and break into a rival's teaching room. They would then turn the place upside down. They were not a new hazard, but they were particularly harassing to Augustine at this time. They are the reason which he confesses to God for his departure and their menace is indeed confirmed by his fellow orator Libanius.[30] In Athens and Antioch, Libanius deplores the rowdiness of the student population. In Athens especially, it led to battles between followers of one or other professor: Libanius even recalls how one professor had had his face pushed into the mud and another found himself hauled out of bed and threatened with drowning in a well. Augustine had heard that Rome's students were better behaved, a belief which may owe something to recent laws to control them: in the 370s, the city prefect at Rome had been ordered that any 'student in the city who does not conduct himself as the dignity of liberal education requires, must be publicly flogged, at once put on a ship, expelled from the city and sent home'.[31] Augustine looks back on these students just as he looks back on Faustus: they were unwitting instruments of God's plan, ones whom God had used 'secretly'. Laws against Manichaeans, to be sure, had nothing to do with his departure.

At the time a different instrument became involved: Monnica. Evidently, she had moved to live near or with her son in Carthage. When he set out for the harbour, she sensed what he might be planning. She went with him, trying to dissuade him. She was not bewailing the possibility that he might go specifically to Rome: she was bewailing that he might go anywhere whatsoever without her. She clung to him 'violently', he recalled. She begged and wept 'fearsomely'. He told her a lie. He was merely going, he said, to bid goodbye to a friend who was sailing away. His confessions do not conceal the lie and as he later wrote a book on lying, the ethics of it will not have escaped him in later life.

'With difficulty' he persuaded her, though she was 'refusing to go back without me'. He advised her to spend the night in a chapel dedicated to St Cyprian, Carthage's famous third-century bishop. She spent it there in 'praying and weeping'. Meanwhile, his ship was waiting, 'not in the town's main port', the archaeologist Serge Lancel has concluded, 'but in the little bay at the outlet of the modern "Hamilcar's ravine", on the heights of which the ruins of the so-called St Monica's Basilica can still be seen. At that time, a chapel to the memory of St Cyprian stood there.'[32]

'That night,' Augustine writes, 'in secret, I set out, whereas she did not . . .' The wind filled the sails, the shore disappeared from view and Monnica awoke next morning to find him gone. 'She was insane with grief', he tells us, 'and complaints and loud lamentation.' She accused him of 'deceptions and cruelty'. Classical scholars cannot help comparing Virgil's Dido, whose beloved Aeneas abandoned her and sailed likewise to Italy from Carthage. Aeneas' departure, too, was divinely guided. However, the comparison is not one which Augustine's language evokes and the details of the two occasions differed.[33] Aeneas was obliged by the gods in a vision to leave against his will: Augustine was not at all unwilling. He only detected God's guidance long after the event. Aeneas left in winter on an early morning and Dido, unlike Monnica, watched the ships depart. She knew his plan already and there had been no deception about it. At the time, it was not Virgil who made sense of the decision for Augustine, but Mani. The lying to his mother, he could tell himself, was caused by an inevitable flicker of the 'axis of evil', prevailing over the Light within him.

Unlike Dido, Monnica lived on. She returned to pray for her son and in due course she too would come to Italy. In her case, her role in God's plan was not to be fulfilled in ignorance.

13
Eternal Rome

I

When Augustine reached Rome, he found lodgings through the network of Manichaean 'true Christians'. There were many of them in the city, including a bishop, and in order to be trusted, he must have continued to undertake 'soul service' for the Elect. Despite his doubts, he lodged in a Hearer's house, but fell seriously ill and came close to death. Modern readers cannot help wondering if guilt at his deceitful parting from his mother was a cause. Augustine looks back and considers that he was very sinful at the time, not specifically to Monnica but to God, to himself and to 'other men' and also because of the 'chain of original sin whereby we all die in Adam'. As a Manichaean, he had not been believing in redemption by a crucified Christ and so God, he concludes, had not yet forgiven him his sins. Nor had they been washed away in baptism. The sickness, he concludes, was God's 'scourge' on his sinful self. If he had died, he would have gone to burn in hell.[1]

Nonetheless God had not been willing to let him die. With hindsight, he considers that He had brought him to Italy to fulfil His orderly plan and to restore him eventually to the 'Catholic' Church. As ever, God had been showing mercy and 'concern for the salvation of my soul', even though Augustine was an errant Manichaean. What, though, about pious Monnica? Her prayers and weeping had failed to keep him in Carthage: why had God ignored her? Here, as elsewhere, Augustine distinguishes between two types of tears. Monnica's 'maternal lamentation' at his departure had been a symptom of the 'relics of Eve'. She had succumbed to 'fleshly pining for her son'. These tears had been selfish tears, to detain him for herself. However, when he had gone, she continued to weep and pray for him twice daily, as she no doubt later told him. These tears were different. They lamented his religious 'death' as a Manichee and were shed for his salvation, begging God to restore him to the truth. 'Wherever she prayed, the flood of her tears would soak the ground.' Augustine respects these tears, comparing Monnica to the Gospels' 'widow of Nain', whose tears moved Jesus to bring her child back to life.[2]

This daily weeping posed a problem for him: how could God have ignored the tearful prayers of such a chaste and virtuous widow? With nearly fifteen years of hindsight, he found an answer. In visions, God had already shown Monnica that one day her son would be standing faithfully beside her as a Catholic Christian. He therefore had to be made to leave for Italy, where he would have the encounters necessary for this result: he also had to recover from his sickbed. At the time, Monnica had probably not known that Augustine was very ill, but, nonetheless, God had heeded her prayers, he concludes, and restored him to health. If she had not been praying, what did he think that God would have done to him?

A realist, leaving God out of the matter, would conclude that Augustine had left Carthage for his own ambitions and recovered from illness through his own stamina. His confessions' sense of a 'guided life' is again very strong here, and, as ever, it is shared by pagan Libanius in his autobiography. Despite their religious differences both men are providentialists, especially when they discuss their travels. By Augustine's age of thirty, Libanius had already moved to be a teacher in four separate Greek-speaking cities. His progress, he tells us, was dogged by accusations of magic and astrology and by two narrow escapes from death. He was the victim of persistent slander from his rivals, caused by 'distress, fear and jealousy'. Thirty years or more after the events, he recalls them in a way which seems evasive at crucial points: he credits the goddess Fortune with guiding him throughout, even though he had blamed her, he says, when his troubles began. In two successive summers in the early 350s, he cut short visits to Nicomedia, the place where he claims to have spent years as happy as any in his life. First, an epidemic was besetting the city and after falling ill he had to leave in haste. Next, he returned to find a famine, which forced him to change his plans. The goddess Fortune, he claimed, had been guiding him on both occasions. She stopped his second visit, providentially, by sending storms and thunderbolts. As for the first one and his illness, 'by causing me these pains, she bestowed salvation on me'. Fortune foresaw, as Libanius did not, that Nicomedia would be flattened by an earthquake.

She worked through misfortune to save him, although the 'salvation' was physical, not spiritual.[3]

Augustine's baptism was indeed to occur after his journey to Italy, but not for four years. Nicomedia was indeed to collapse in an earthquake, but only seven years after Libanius' failed visits. Like Augustine's God, Libanius' goddess put him through 'testing trials' and then granted 'graces' which seemed greater as a result.[4] However, unlike Libanius' goddess, Augustine's God was the Creator of a 'good' universe. He was the only god in it, whereas Libanius' Fortune was one goddess among many. Unlike Libanius, Augustine would become convinced while in Italy that the universe and all life in it are governed by God's hidden 'order'. God, therefore, had 'predestined' young Augustine's course in conformity with His hidden 'justice'.[5] Libanius' Fortune could be bountiful, but unlike God, she was not concerned to be just to one and all.

II

In Rome, Augustine entered a city of more than half a million inhabitants which was still one of the wonders of the world. It had been the city of Aeneas and Cicero and can only have impressed the young arrival, their student. The *Confessions* do not dwell on it, because Rome's impact was unimportant for the *Confessions*' subject, Augustine's turning back to God. However, it was the scene of options and controversies which were soon to have important consequences for him elsewhere. By dwelling on them in Rome, we can put this future into a fuller context.

The 'eternal city' was a historic city, but no longer a regular seat of the Roman emperors and their court. Military priorities had drawn them northwards to cities like Trier and Milan which were nearer the routes from Rome to the Balkans. Their feared praetorian guards were long gone, but Rome was still a necessary residence of the senators, all 2,000 of them, although most of them had large estates in the provinces too. Within this class, the palatial villas of the true aristocrats rose on Rome's hills above the hotter, seedier districts of the city below. The villa of one of the grandest families, the Anicii, has recently been located in the gardens of the Villa Medici on the Pincian Hill. Beneath this ultimate layer of grandeur spread lesser families of the upper class, senators who owed most of their superior standing to recent appointments in the emperor's service. In the words of an eloquent member, the Senate was 'the better part of the human race'.[6]

Augustine was ill advised to ignore any chance of this 'better part's' patronage. He still needed to attract paying pupils in a competitive market. He recalls that he began to teach 'at home', in the house of his Manichaean host, therefore, and to gather pupils there 'through whom' he would become known. There were plenty of people from north Africa in the city, but, for the first time, he did not have Romanianus to help him. Meanwhile, his friend and ex-pupil Alypius was living proof of the value of good contacts. He had secured a job as 'assessor' to an important official, a position for which his legal studies in Carthage made him eligible.[7] Augustine, by contrast, was offering rhetoric, a crowded field in which he could not expect his talents to prevail at once. Libanius could have warned him. 'Each spring,' he wrote, 'brings some of our young men from Antioch to Rome.' Libanius never advised a father to encourage this exodus and he never talked up the value of the Latin language. The migration was caused, he wrote, by 'stupidity which anticipates what it most wants'. The young hopefuls ought to be warned that most of them are 'given back' by Rome to their cities and return 'not much different from flocks of sheep'.[8] Augustine, a fellow migrant, risked returning to Thagaste with his tail, too, between his legs.

Libanius had never seen Rome but he recognized that it was special. 'I envy you,' he wrote to Marcellinus, one such migrant from Antioch, 'for having Rome, and Rome for having you: you have something which is unlike anything in the world.' It would be good for Marcellinus to pass his time 'in silence' there and attend to 'speeches delivered by others'. Rome, to be sure, 'nurtures many orators who are following in their fathers' footsteps', people from whom a young visitor can learn.[9] Ever the stylist, Augustine would be keen to hear how such people delivered a speech. Marcellinus was also being invited to literary gatherings, as Augustine would hope for himself if his pupils and contacts increased. Marcellinus was reciting bits of his literary work in this company: 'do not stop composing,' Libanius urged him, 'because you must become more famous' and reflect glory on Antioch. As yet, Augustine had written nothing except *On the Beautiful and Apt*.

Libanius' letter may address a very famous Marcellinus, the great historian Ammianus Marcellinus, who was present, unknown to Augustine, in the very years, 383–4, while he was in Rome.[10] Ammianus is one of two visitors to whom we owe brilliant satirical attacks on people in the city at this time. The other is none other than the famous Christian

Jerome, such a sparring partner in Augustine's future career. Their caricatures are one-sided, but rooted in first-hand observation.

Like Ammianus, Augustine would have seen the grand carriages of Rome's rich in the streets and the gestures of their occupants, whose silk robes billowed in the breeze. Sometimes, they would career through the broad avenues of the city as if they were 'driving post-horses with hooves of fire'. Their one idea of a cultural evening, Ammianus complained, was a banquet with topless dancing girls or music on the water-organ and 'lyres as huge as carriages'. 'Instead of an orator', or someone like Augustine, the 'teacher of stage-mimes is summoned', while their 'libraries are perpetually shut like tombs'. What is known of pagan senators' reading and study in this period excuses only a few of them from this criticism.[11]

Like Augustine, Ammianus had arrived as an outsider who needed to win patrons. His comments on the pitfalls are relevant to Augustine's social prospects. 'If as an honest stranger,' he complained, 'you enter to pay respects to someone well-heeled and swelling with pride, you will be asked many questions and forced to tell lies. You will then marvel . . . when such a grand person is paying such effort and attention to someone as humble as you and you will regret that you had not visited Rome ten years earlier.' On the following day, this same grandee 'will have forgotten your very name: when you repeat your call, he will keep you waiting and humiliate you for years'. The exceptions were those perennial bonds between Rome's upper and lower classes: dancing girls, charioteers and dice-players, forerunners of the 'pussy contingent', jockeys and professional backgammon-players of 'eternal Rome'.[12]

The common people of Rome, in Ammianus' view, were little better. They would spend the nights in wine bars, play 'pugnaciously' at dice, 'snort' through their noses and stand gaping 'in rain or sunshine' at the performances of racehorses and charioteers. Augustine comments tellingly on Rome's 'vagabonds', the so-called *passivi* who would collect their free bread and give or throw away any surplus after sating their hunger.[13] Even so, these *passivi* were privileged members of the plebs, no more than a fifth or so of the total number. They were among those eligible for distributions of free grain, whereas the rest of the plebs had to buy what little they could. A preoccupation with 'bread and circuses' was understandable in a city where most people's livelihood was very vulnerable. The 'bread' depended on grain imported yearly from Augustine's north Africa. The 'circuses', meanwhile, linked Christian and pagan, rich and poor in a calendar of fun and excitement. No fewer than 1,580 horse races have been calculated to be the annual minimum on offer in Rome's Circus Maximus, more than the annual provision of horse racing in the whole of modern Britain.[14]

There were also bloody shows of gladiators and animal combats. As a Manichaean, Augustine would not go near such bloodshed, but the *Confessions* give a brilliant picture of its appeal even to the grave, principled Alypius. Urged on, significantly, by friends, Alypius accepted an invitation to attend a gladiatorial show in Rome, but only on the understanding that he would keep his eyes shut. The roar of the huge crowd caused him to relent and have a look. 'As soon as he saw blood,' the mature Augustine writes, 'at the same time he drank down hideous cruelty.' He did not 'turn himself away, but fixed his gaze and kept drinking in the very Furies and not knowing he did so . . .'.[15] He succumbed to the raw fascination of violent viewing, like another visitor to Rome long after him, Lord Byron. In May 1817, while witnessing the public execution of three robbers, 'the pain seems little,' Byron wrote, 'and yet the effect to the spectator,' he admitted, is 'very striking and chilling. The first turned me quite hot and thirsty, and made me shake so that I could hardly hold the opera-glass . . .' Alypius 'looked, shouted and was inflamed'. Unlike Byron, he was not sated by his first sight of blood. 'The second and third,' Byron wrote, ' . . . I am ashamed to say, had no effect on me as a horror, though I would have saved them if I could.'[16] Alypius, however, 'took madness back with him and by it, was roused to return again and again'. In Carthage, he had taken to heart Augustine's rebukes of the 'vile' horse races. In Rome, these scruples disappeared before public bloodshed and its activation of a human 'thirst'.

When Augustine arrived in Rome, the city, like Carthage, was far from a Christian society. A majority of the senators still worshipped the traditional gods, 'pagans' as Christians called them, though it is far from certain that public sacrifices of animals continued in these gods' honour.[17] There were also many Christians who ignored their preachers' ideals. Some of the richest patronized the crowds with gifts at the very games which their bishops execrated. Others in high office showed the most callous disregard for Christian ethics. It was exemplified in a shady affair of land-grabbing at the expense of a social inferior by a former consul, a member of Rome's grandest Christian family, precisely during Augustine's time in the city.[18] As in Carthage, Augustine was living among people who felt there was much more to life than the liturgy. Around them, in the city's traditional centre, almost all the main public and religious buildings still belonged to a non-Christian past.

During Augustine's stay, the bishop, or 'pope', of the city was the ageing Damasus, a veteran of twenty years' leadership of the Christian community. His first initiatives had addressed a lethal rift between Christian factions in the city but he had then addressed an issue on which they could unite, the division between those who upheld the 'Nicene' creed of 325 and those, dismissed as 'Arians', who did not.[19] This division would soon confront Augustine elsewhere. Damasus had also striven to extend his Christian leadership in the city's urban profile. Outside the city walls he had patronized the popular burial sites of Rome's Christian martyrs and had advertised their presence in the cemeteries, or 'sleeping places', and the catacombs, or 'lie-downs', for the city's dead. Here, Damasus' monuments, buildings and finely cut verse inscriptions reached out to the entire Christian community, but his austere morals were not shared by most of those to whom he appealed. Every day, as Augustine discovered, riotous drinking parties were held near St Peter's and its surrounding burial sites on the Vatican Hill. Christians revelled in this 'hideous pest', afforced by crowds of pilgrims who brought their local customs with them. These celebrations, too, would impinge on Augustine elsewhere.[20]

As ever, Christian counterweights were set beside practices which strict Christians deplored. Near the popular festival site of old Imperial Rome, the Campus Martius, Damasus had patronized a gleaming new church for the Roman martyr St Lawrence. Deliberately, he sited it in the district where the rival racing-factions had their stables. He placed it near the yard of the most populist clique, the 'Greens'.[21] Of all the martyrs, Lawrence was the one who was said to have reached out most widely to the poor. Now he could reach out to race fans, Christians and pagans alike.

III

During Augustine's time in the city, the political news was urgent. In August 383, the reigning emperor in the West, Gratian, was defeated by a military challenger, Magnus Maximus, who had crossed from Britain into Gaul. Gratian fled, only to be killed by Maximus' supporters. The title of emperor passed to his twelve-year-old half-brother, Valentinian

II, whose court remained anxiously in Milan. To pagan polemicists, the Christian Gratian's murder seemed providential. It was due to the anger of the pagan gods, they later said, who had sent a new Maximus (the usurper) to take vengeance on the non-Maximus (Gratian) who had refused to take the traditional title of 'Maximus' and be Pontifex Maximus as an emperor should.[22]

Behind this splendid polemic lay a ruling by Gratian which had caused outrage among pagan senators in Rome and some of their Christian colleagues too. Gratian and his advisers had stopped the traditional public support for pagan cults at Rome.[23] If Gratian had indeed refused the usual title of Pontifex Maximus, there would be nobody to fill vacancies in the public colleges of the pagan priests. Over time, these priesthoods would diminish. Certainly, he had abolished privileges for Rome's seven Vestal Virgins, including their right to free grain and their exemption from public secular duties. He had also ordered the removal of the ancient altar (but not statue) of Victory from the Senate house, one on which pagan senators swore oaths and offered incense before beginning their debates. Above all, he had announced the confiscation of the temple estates which publicly supported pagan cults at Rome. The Vestals were one such cult and were especially vulnerable because, as virgin girls, they did not have big estates of their own to support their expenses.[24]

These measures did not mark the 'end of paganism', but they were a very serious blow against it. Pagans considered the public cults to be promoters of the community's 'safety', and therefore to need public support. Their plight has remained famous because of a petition and a polemic which it promptly provoked. This battle of words involved Pope Damasus with Ambrose, Bishop of Milan, and the pagan prefect of Rome, Symmachus. Although these latter two protagonists were soon to shape Augustine's career, Augustine as a Manichaean had no interest in such 'semi-Christian' battles. They made an impression on him only through a well-expressed phrase which they generated. Two years later, in his first personal text, Augustine would echo the wording of a sentence in Symmachus' artfully written plea, the one which is nowadays the most famous in the entire dispute. 'It is not possible,' Symmachus wrote, 'to arrive by one route at so great a secret . . .' As a teacher of rhetoric, Augustine, it seems, studied the published text of the plea and fastened on these words. In Rome, style and good speaking were still his particular interests.[25]

The other protagonist, Damasus, had not only built up shrines in honour of Rome's martyrs. He himself engaged in excavations to rediscover them. In the cemetery off the Via Salaria one of his most elegant inscriptions testifies to his success: 'The tomb was hidden under the hill's furthest mound,' it proclaims, 'this, Damasus reveals, because he preserves the bodies of the pious.'[26] This sort of 'revelation' would also soon recur in Augustine's future.

Meanwhile, in the city's grand houses, bodily integrity was provoking an even sharper debate, three years before it was to obsess Augustine and his friends. Pope Damasus had written in prose and verse on the merits of the virginal life. It is probably he who ruled that all senior clergymen should remain celibate, something which 'the Roman Church especially guards', and be pure when handling the sacred vessels in the liturgy.[27] Not everyone was persuaded. In 383, when Augustine arrived, a former Christian ascetic, Helvidius, had responded to Christians who championed celibacy by writing a text to uphold the Christian value of marriage and childbearing. Helvidius even denied the virginity of Mary, because she was the mother of Jesus and those 'brothers of Jesus' whom the Gospels mention.[28] This sound little text and the reactions which it provoked are known to us through another visitor to Rome, the Christian Jerome. He was to be both a critic and a correspondent of Augustine, but, as yet, the two had never met.

Like Augustine, Jerome had been born in a minor provincial town, in his case Stridon in Dalmatia. He, too, had been schooled in the liberal arts. However, unlike Augustine, he had spent time at the Western emperor's court; he had lived briefly as a Christian solitary in the desert landscape of the Holy Land; he had studied with Greek commentators on the scriptures in Alexandria; he even studied the original Hebrew of the Old Testament. When he arrived in Rome in summer 382, he too needed to make his reputation. He used avenues which Augustine, as yet, could not: a skilled way with the text of scripture, the example of his own hard-won chastity and an exceptional talent as a letter-writer. As his family was richer than Augustine's, he had no need to make his way upwards through a paid teaching career. Instead he pressed his claims on Damasus. He earned the bishop's patronage and then set about serious biblical scholarship, revising the translations of scripture and addressing problems in its Hebrew. Through personal contacts, he also struck up friendships with a cluster of high-ranking Roman women in their grand households.

To us, Jerome remains famous for his barbed and highly pitched letters. They survive, however, because he himself preserved and circulated them, not least to enhance his own profile against rivals in the city. Damasus himself has remained on record with a letter which put scriptural problems to Jerome, but they are problems which one of Jerome's Christian rivals in the city had also tried to address. By answering them, and ignoring him, Jerome's letter established his own superiority. His letters to female contacts also advanced his profile as much as theirs. They presented him as their Christian counsellor, their guide, as widows, in the ultimate overachievement, a sexless way of life.[29]

The Gospels contained sayings by Jesus in support of the existence of a higher ethical standard, 'if you would be perfect'. To live without sexual activity was to 'live like angels'. Those who pursued this aim believed that they were aspiring to the highest Christian ideal. Some wanted to focus on God without the distraction of earthly loves. Others wished to avoid the dangers of childbirth and what the Younger Pliny, centuries before, had once called the 'bother' of bringing up children. Among the egalitarian values of the Christian communities, the sexless option was an approved avenue of competition. No single motive can explain the choices of its takers at different stages of life, but modern scholars have well categorized this Christian minority as 'virtuosi' or, in my less exalted phrase, 'overachievers'. The worldly Christian majority were content for the most part to let them get on with it. In 384, a husband in Rome prepared to bury his latest wife: he had already had twenty previous wives and she herself was the veteran of twenty-two previous husbands. Jerome witnessed the occasion and, as Peter Brown presents his evidence, 'the husband led the procession around her bier, "crowned and carrying a palm of victory, with all the people of the City in attendance, to the chant of 'Lay 'em out in hundreds.'"'[30]

Sexual renunciation was soon to be a major theme of Augustine's life, but it was not new among Roman Christians. There had been isolated cases at least since the early fourth century and already in the 350s the Bishop of Rome had ceremoniously veiled a well-born young Christian virgin and marked her out as the 'bride of Christ'.[31] The classic text for Christian 'virtuosi' was Athanasius' *Life of Antony*, which was available, by the 370s, in a Latin translation. As a result, its Christian hero, self-mortifying in the Egyptian desert, had begun to impress high-society women in Rome. They were not short of teachers. One was none other than Augustine's future opponent in later life, the burly, talented Pelagius, active in the 380s in some of Rome's great houses, where he, too, taught a message of chastity, emphasizing free will and linking it to the renunciation of riches and the corrosive power of bad habits. In my view, he was already known to Jerome, who, predictably, scorned him as a potential rival.[32]

Meanwhile, Jerome was making his separate pitch to a group of grand Christian widows and their Christian daughters, concentrated in big villas on the Aventine Hill. His surviving letters are brilliant presentations of these women's lifestyle and the rewards of a virginal life. Some of the most memorable are addressed to the family of Paula, herself in her mid- to late thirties. Paula's father, a rich Greek, claimed descent from King Agamemnon, no less, and had owned the entire city of Actium in north-west Greece. Paula's mother, a Roman, claimed as her ancestors the Scipios and the famous Gracchi of Rome's distant free past. Paula herself had married a husband 'in whose veins', wrote Jerome, 'ran the noble blood of Aeneas and the Julii'.[33] After an unbroken run of four daughters, she finally produced the necessary son and, as long planned, gave up sex. Her husband then simplified her choice by dying. Avoiding the usual social pressure to remarry quickly, Paula remained a widow, an ideal item for Jerome's letters and advice.

Her third daughter, Julia Eustochium, was an even more promising target. As a young girl, she had shown interest, Jerome purported to remind her, in a life of perpetual virginity. In 384, while Augustine was in Rome, Jerome courted her by his most dazzling letter on the merits of the non-convergent life.[34] Aged thirteen or fourteen, when a female of her class would be preparing to marry, Eustochium had already appalled her pagan aunt and uncle. In desperation, Jerome claimed, her aunt had tried to brighten up the girl's drab style of dress and even to enliven her awful hair-do by 'weaving her neglected hair into a wavy quiff'. Jerome claimed that this no-nonsense aunt had been punished by a vision and, soon after, by death. With his eye on a wider public, he dwelt unforgettably on the worldly temptations which surround the life of a determined virgin. Damasus had already asked him to translate into Latin two of the perfectionist Origen's homilies on the biblical Song of Songs. Despite its erotic origin, they had reinterpreted the Song as a text in praise of Christian virginity. Jerome used phrases from it to welcome young Eustochium as an aroused 'bride of Christ'. He urged her to live within the walls of her parental home, renouncing all face-to-face contact with men.

Jerome's letter to her drew a chorus of enraged complaints from less extreme Christians, 'sham' Christians in Jerome's unforgiving language.[35] One reason was that his sketches of them were not wholly inaccurate. Pagans gleefully sought out copies of the text and Augustine himself soon read it. In high-society gossip, an heiress who opted for virginity was as much of a social disaster as a daughter nowadays who drops out on hard drugs. However, young volunteers for the sexless option were very few, the majority of them being widows like Paula whose childbearing was already in the past. To avoid family damage, their property could usually be re-routed to their previous children or siblings.[36] Lifelong renunciation by a young virgin, innocent of the male touch, was a very rare event, and, even then, most families would have a brother or sister who could inherit her property instead.

After dazzling the young Eustochium, Jerome turned his attention late in 384 to a second target, her eldest sister. This lady, Blesilla, had married at the age of twenty, but had been bereaved of her young husband after only seven months. She was expected by her worldly friends to remarry soon, but caught a serious illness and on her recovery announced her conversion to celibacy. Jerome evidently saw his chance to encourage her to renounce worldly adornment, restrict her diet to a minimum and live henceforward without sex.[37]

Upper-class girls inside Roman mansions were not part of Augustine's life in the city. Their talents would have greatly surprised him. The widowed Marcella was honoured by Jerome as someone who persistently posed questions about the meaning of transliterated Hebrew words. In her fifties, she was said to know the Psalms intimately and to be reading them closely with Jerome by her side.[38] The psalms which young Augustine knew by heart were psalms of the Manichaeans. He had never even taught a female pupil. His concubine and son had joined him in Rome, but his only other female company was Manichaean, the female Hearers and Elect whom he still met for 'soul service', singing and prayers. Socially, they were a very mixed bunch, but the Elect, at least, kept the ideal of chastity before him. His friend Alypius, meanwhile, was continuing to praise it after his bad early experience with a girl. However, his views made no impact on Augustine, who continued to tell him how delicious sex was with a woman and urged him to try again.[39]

Jerome also addressed letters in praise of celibacy to men: if he had somehow met Augustine in Rome and written to him, would he have caught his interest? It was still too early ('Chastity, but not yet . . .'), and personal exposure to Jerome might have put Augustine off for good. The more tantalizing question is whether Pelagius, his future opponent, might have been more successful. His teaching about celibacy and free will was in part a reaction to the Manichaean presence in Rome, and Augustine's Manichaeism was indeed fading away. However, he was in no mood for a commitment. Instead, he was drawn to a new philosophy: scepticism.

The doubts about Mani's truth which had formed in him in Carthage had still not been answered. They were now reinforced by a theory of doubting, one which Augustine encountered while continuing to read 'many things of the philosophers'. These sceptical philosophers were Greek thinkers of the Hellenistic age and were known as the Academics, after their links with Plato's Academy. With Varro's *Disciplines* and Cicero's *Hortensius*, their writings were to become a third pillar of the young Augustine's mind.[40]

Augustine does not specify what he read in Rome, but the likeliest answer is that he read the sequel to Cicero's *Hortensius*, the book which had enflamed him ten years before. In spring 45 BC, after the *Hortensius*' success, Cicero composed another dialogue, the *Catulus*, in which, once again, the participants were prominent men from the late 60s BC, the zenith of Cicero's own career. Once again, the scene was a luxury villa on the Bay of Naples, this time Catulus' own. Probably, it stood at the fine vantage point of Cumae, a place which was famous in Virgil's *Aeneid*.[41] The dialogue does not survive, but references to its contents prove that Catulus asserted that the philosophers who succeeded Plato in the Academy had held a sceptical view of knowledge. Cicero then argued in favour of the sceptical views of these 'Academics' and supported them with allusions to philosophers before Socrates and with observations on the unreliability of the human senses. Probably, he spoke last, as in the *Hortensius*, but this time his speech was for a specific, sceptical view. Augustine would thus find a ringing defence by Cicero, his hero, of the sceptical doctrine that nothing can be known for certain.

Once again, philosophy was confronting him in a dialogue which was set among great names of the Roman past. Socially respectful as ever, Augustine would admire these past grandees all the more while present in their capital city. The doctrine that only the probable and 'truth-like' is a basis for our actions is one which he says that he himself 'sold'.[42] He began to teach it, therefore, when pupils asked him for his views on truth and knowledge. The theory fitted well with his career. Teachers of rhetoric are concerned to show how one view can be made more plausible than another, but they are not concerned to teach the truth.

Meanwhile, Augustine's friendship with Alypius deepened. Alypius took up sceptical philosophy, again following his older friend and teacher's lead.[43] Augustine's Manichaean host was not spared the sceptical challenge, either. Augustine began to question Mani's Gospel: 'I was not defending it with my former animosity,' he tells us, throwing an incidental light on his previous commitment, 'but nevertheless, my familiar dealings with them – for Rome secretly contained many of them – made me lazier about seeking out anything else . . .'[44] With a marvellous clarity about his beliefs, the *Confessions* recall that he still held to two essential Manichaean items. One concerned the problem of evil. Like many before and since, he could not believe that God could have created anything truly bad. This conviction led him to accept evil's separate origin as a 'sort of substance', a separate 'mass' opposed to the 'mass' of God, but smaller. It was either thick in form, like earth, or thin, like air, and it was a 'malignant mind creeping through the earth', an exact allusion to the 'thought of Death' which we know from Manichaean texts in Asia.[45] Christ was only imaginable as an extension 'of the mass of your most shining substance', the Kingdom of Light. An incarnation and a birth from a human virgin were impossible for such an entity.

If Augustine was so taken with scepticism, why did he not doubt Christ and the entire existence of God? It was not only that he had imbibed them with Monnica's milk. As a working rule, most types of sceptic, even Greek ones, would go along with the 'custom of the country' and observe its existing religious rites and festivals. Sceptics were not sure of their validity, but they were not sure of their invalidity, either, and so their compliance in everyday rites, they said, did not commit them to statements of certainty about the gods.[46] The overall aim of their suspension of judgement was tranquillity. In a memorable image, one of the Greek masters of scepticism had advised fellow sceptics to copy the practice of the master artist Apelles when he had wished to represent the foaming sweat on a horse.[47] The more Apelles tried to paint it, the more it eluded him. So, he gave up striving, threw the sponge at the canvas and found that he had hit it off exactly. Suspend judgement, regard all beliefs as provisional and then, like an action-painter, this sceptic said, you will hit on peace of mind.

Temperamentally, Augustine could not behave like an Apelles. In 391, six years before writing the *Confessions*, he already looked back on this sceptical phase as an exceptionally turbulent one for his mind. 'Great deliberation I had . . . by what method Truth could be found, for love of which I sighed . . . Often it seemed to me that it could not be found, and the great waves of my thoughts were bearing me to support the Academics. But the human mind is so lively, acute and perspicacious and if I did not think that Truth was hidden . . . a method was needed, and that same method must be taken from some divine authority.'[48] It is a fine insight into his intelligence and seriousness. He was engaging with hard philosophical reasoning, but his only teachers were whatever books he could buy and read in his hired lodgings. As Alypius was discovering, good copies of books, in his case law books, were not cheap.[49] Augustine continued to think hard, drifting on with bits of Manichaeism for want of anything more certain. In autumn 384, he then applied for a new and much more prestigious job.

Once again he explains his candidacy by a complaint about students' bad behaviour. At Rome they were artful non-payers. They would take lessons and instead of paying for them would transfer to another teacher. The menace was endemic in a free market and, once again, is attested in the Greek East by both Synesius and Libanius.[50] Within two years of Augustine's problems, elderly Libanius was speaking publicly on exactly this issue, one which had bedevilled his career for the past forty years. His students, he explains, had to swear an oath of loyalty to him, but they paid little respect to it. Some would move from one tutor to another; rich boys would spend their father's allowances on drink and sex and then be high-handed to their teacher about paying his fees at all; poorer ones might not pay anyway. Libanius tried various remedies, including a call for solidarity among the teachers in the city. He justified his own practice by claiming that he did not charge fees but requested 'contributions' from those who wished to pay.[51] Augustine had no public salary in Rome and relied on fees in order to live. He would have hated the threats and arrogance of well-off pupils.

To escape the bother, he canvassed for a position which suddenly became available. Milan was the seat of the boy-emperor, Valentinian II, and his court. In late autumn 384, the city, not the emperor, sent to Rome to find a candidate fit to be its public orator. The job carried an assured salary and would require speeches on specified individuals and public subjects, the business of much of Libanius' career in the Greek East. As if to justify it, Augustine recalls that it came with a promise of transport at public expense, an 'extra' as rare as the offer of transport in a black limousine to a professorial interview nowadays.[52] Augustine lobbied for the job through his Manichaean friends in Rome. It had been submitted to the recommendation of the prefect of the city, Q. Aurelius Symmachus.

For the first time, Augustine's career intersected with someone independently famous to posterity. In 384, Symmachus was in his mid-forties, a self-styled 'lover of his fatherland', Rome, and a worshipper of the traditional pagan gods. He was a prominent senator and had been the governor of Augustine's African province ten years earlier. His family's palace was on Rome's Caelian Hill, but it was backed up by estates in the hinterland of Naples and on the Bay and by other domains in Africa itself.[53] When Augustine's friends contacted him, Symmachus was well practised on the hub of the worldly chariot wheel. He was a master of writing Latin letters in order to commend hopeful candidates. He addressed them to officials whom he professed to know well, artfully calling them by their name, not their faceless titles. He stood for a 'scrupulous regard' for friendship, a *religio amicitiae*.[54] This friendship was not the idealized friendship of an Augustine and the 'other halves' of his soul. It was as frankly based on mutual favours as the 'friendships' of a modern business leader. Symmachus wrote with discreet care for people whose claims appealed to him and whose success would benefit himself.

From candidates for the Milan job, he required a presentation, a speech to be delivered in his presence on a prearranged topic. Unfortunately, the subject is unknown to us. Symmachus shared Augustine's admiration of Cicero as a speaker, but Augustine may never have realized that his assessor was the very son-in-law of the man who now owned Hortensius' villa on the Bay of Naples.[55] It was irrelevant to Symmachus, if he even knew, that the young man before him happened to be a Manichaean. Augustine was one more example of a north African for whom he might write in support, befitting his own contacts with the province. Symmachus had already served often enough as a facilitator for people at Rome who were passing on up to Milan.[56] One of his correspondents in Milan was the important military commander Bauto, a pagan and someone, it seems, whom Symmachus had tried to involve in his recent petitions on behalf of Rome's public cults. Bauto may well have encouraged the city selectors in Milan to draw on Symmachus' knowledge of likely candidates for their job.[57]

We do not have Symmachus' letter for Augustine among his copious surviving correspondence, but Libanius shows what a letter from the great man could mean. Libanius had known Symmachus' father as a young man and in 391 Symmachus obliged him with a letter which Libanius describes as a dream come true.[58] After an interpreter translated it from Latin into Greek, he gave it to three of his friends to take through Antioch and show to those friendly to him, 'so that they should rejoice', and to those who were not friends, 'so that they would choke' (with envy).

Augustine evidently spoke well and on Symmachus' recommendation was appointed to the job. It was a fortunate escape, for other reasons which he does not mention. In summer and autumn 384 Rome was troubled for the second year running with a serious food shortage. As city prefect, Symmachus simply ordered all foreigners and 'pursuers of the liberal arts' to leave the city. According to the historian Ammianus, 3,000 dancing girls in the city were exempted: better to be a stripper than a teacher.[59] Lacking the right attributes, Augustine would have had to return home to north Africa had Milan not made its fortuitous request. He would have been lost to intellectual history, a casualty of a bad harvest and the city prefect's crass response to it.

The Milan job also restored to Augustine something valuable: renewed exemption from any claim by Thagaste for his services as a local councillor. As there was no poll tax on the residents of towns, he could look forward in Milan to a rare tax-free existence. If he chose to break decisively with the Manichaeans there, he would at last have a proper salary of his own to support him. As a result, he had no need for them to continue to give him lodgings. However, the Manichaeans' own texts help us to see what they would think of him if he did in fact desert. 'The Mind which was formerly in [such a person] turns away from him and returns to the Apostle who sent it. He is filled with evil spirits and they swell in him, dragging him hither and thither . . . he changes and grows like a person of the world, like a bird whose [feathers] are being torn out.'[60]

When Augustine set off north in late autumn 384, Jerome was too busy to notice. He was cajoling the young Blesilla, Paula's eldest daughter. After a brief marriage, she had recently been widowed and had turned to a celibate life. Encouraged by Jerome, she gave herself up to fasting and penance, prayer and the close study of scripture. She quickly acquired Hebrew, but Jerome treated her nonetheless to a gross misreading of worldly verses in the Book of Ecclesiastes.[61] After four months of voluntary mortification, she died in November 384. Her early death provoked a storm against Jerome, her 'personal trainer'. Be thankful, Jerome wrote to her mother, who had fainted at the funeral: remember that Blesilla keeps company now with Mary and the saints; she will be tortured to see her mother conducting herself in a way so displeasing to Christ.[62]

In December, Jerome's patron, Pope Damasus, died too. Jerome entertained hopes that he might even be appointed as the next Pope, but in summer 385 his numerous enemies attacked him with a malicious accusation. Paula was said to be preparing to sail off with him and settle in the Holy Land: surely he had seduced her? A Church court met to hear the charges, a 'Council of the Pharisees', Jerome called it contemptuously. 'They gossiped that I was a sorcerer,' he wrote in self-defence, claiming that his accusers included 'semi-Christian' women and a slave who changed his story under torture.[63] Nonetheless, enough of the case stuck for him to be obliged to leave Italy. In August 385, in the port city of Ostia, he wrote his own reply for posterity and dedicated it artfully to Asella, the most reclusive and impeccable of Rome's elderly virgins. She had been devoted to celibacy for forty years before Jerome even arrived.

The letter was intended to circulate, presenting him as an innocent victim, not least to his celibate female contacts. 'I write in haste, Asella, as I board ship, grieving and in tears': despite modern doubts, perhaps he did. He presents himself in terms of scriptural analogies and role models so as 'to dramatise his expulsion', Andrew Cain has acutely observed, 'as an event of epic biblical proportions'.[64] Jesus, Jerome points out, was also called a sorcerer and as a 'soldier of the Cross' he must suffer slander in order to attain knowledge of heaven.

Two years later, in Ostia, Augustine would also prepare to leave Italy, having undergone something very different, a shared vision of God. Ten years later, he too would implicitly answer critics, after a similar charge of sexual harassment in connection with a promotion in the Church hierarchy. He too would cast himself in terms of scriptural role models. He too would write for celibate readers, males, however, not females. He had no idea of this letter of Jerome, the confession of his most famous celibate predecessor.

PART III

He constantly spoke of his mother in later years, with affection and amazement . . . 'My mother accepted the Bible, every word of it, as in every respect the inspired Word of God, and for many years I was never allowed to come into contact with any other view' . . . Her son, by contrast, insisted that he was never able, even as a small boy, to form a mental image of the being to whom he was required to pray.

Robert Parker, *Proceedings of the British Academy* (2007) 448–9, in his obituary of the great Marxist historian Geoffrey de Ste Croix, whose predicament recalls the Augustine whom he later detested, except that the young de Ste Croix's uncertain mental image of God was a mark of his religious doubt

. . . with fire in him forge thy will
Or rather, rather then, stealing as Spring
Through him, melt him but master him still:
Whether at once, as once at a crash Paul,
Or as Austin, a lingering-out sweet skill,
Make mercy in all of us, out of us all
Mastery . . .

Gerard Manley Hopkins, *The Wreck of the 'Deutschland'* (1876), contrasting the conversions of Paul and Augustine ('Austin')

14
Milan and Ambrose

I

In Milan, the poet Ausonius wrote, 'all things are wonderful'. The city has 'countless smart houses' and its pillared squares are filled with marble statues. There are temples, 'palace citadels and a rich mint', the one whose coins we still appreciate. There is a big enclosed theatre and a circus for horse races, 'the people's pleasure'. The city is guarded by a double wall and is not cowed by 'Rome's proximity'. From personal knowledge, Ausonius ranked it as the third city in the West and the seventh in the Roman world.[1] It was to be the scene of two decisive years in Augustine's life, memorably presented in the *Confessions*.

By autumn 384, Milan already had a long history. The richness of its north Italian hinterland was famous and its pork had been particularly admired. Since 381, it had undergone a major change: it had become the seat of the Western emperor, his court and army. The army's arrival opened new opportunities for suppliers, contractors and, therefore, corruption, and imposed new burdens on the city's territory. The court's arrival changed the city's networks of power. It brought to Milan careerists and top office holders whose patronage of 'friends and family' overshadowed the local councillors. A new type of pork barrel soon typified the city: 'the parvenu capital,' Neil McLynn has acutely explained, 'looked south to Rome for talent and to borrow the lustre of its cultural credentials; the senatorial aristocracy in turn needed its outlets', for power, profit and the advancement of their concerns as the self-styled 'better part of the human race'.[2]

Despite Ausonius, all was not exactly wonderful when Augustine took up his new job within easy reach of the Alps. In late August 383, when the Emperor Gratian had been killed in Gaul, the army with him had promptly changed sides to Maximus, the successful usurper.

Gratian's body had still not been returned to Milan more than a year later. His title had passed to his half-brother, the twelve-year-old Valentinian II, whom Maximus had invited to come to him 'like a son to his father'. It had required an important embassy in winter 383/4 from Milan to evade the request and deter Maximus from following up with military force. Backers, meanwhile, gathered in Milan for the new child-emperor and in spring 384 the Eastern emperor, Theodosius, declared his support.[3] For the moment, Maximus remained at bay in Trier, but the likelihood was that he would attack before long. The court in Milan was now one of three, caught between Trier and Constantinople.

Soon after Augustine's arrival, in November 384, he had to deliver a panegyric on the occasion of young Valentinian II's 'tenth' anniversary as holder of an Imperial title. Prescribed flattery was to be expected in his job, as Libanius, another public orator, exemplifies. Among his speeches for emperors, he had to praise two of the sons of Constantine, keen Christians: he passed over their Christianity in silence.[4] Augustine's brief was no less awkward. Little Valentinian was not the fit age for a ruler, as contemporaries well knew, unless he was to be kept 'shut in at home'. While speaking, for the first and only time Augustine saw an emperor face to face. He would have seen a young boy, seated on a throne and attended by eunuch-chamberlains and his resolute, bejewelled mother, Justine. 'In a speech to the emperor,' he recalls, 'I had to tell many lies and be approved by people who knew I was telling them.'[5] The situation in Milan made the lies painfully obvious.

After Gratian's death and the defection of most of the troops with him, the military command in Milan had passed to Flavius Bauto, a pagan and a Frank. He had restored military credibility, but only by recruiting barbarian Huns and Alans and Gothic contingents from further east. On 1 January 385, he began to hold the consulship, its one non-Imperial holder in Valentinian II's reign.[6] Again, Augustine was paid to make a speech of praise, to be delivered before a big audience in full public view, perhaps in the Circus beside Milan's palace. At this very time, his fellow orator Libanius was also delivering panegyrics for military men. In 384, aged seventy, he composed one for the consulship of Richomer, also a barbarian, and in 385, the year of Augustine's oration, another for Ellebichos, a German. Both men had come to Antioch as military commanders and although Libanius befriended them, flattery was required. In a letter to Richomer, Libanius laid it on: 'you took your pleasure in action, covering the plains with the corpses of enemies, whereas I took mine in hearing about the victories from messengers'. As pagans, they were congenial to Libanius and both of them exercised important patronage on his behalf.[7] For Augustine, by contrast, Bauto's paganism was most unappealing and his patronage was never a help. Before speaking, he would have been taken through what he must say. To judge from Libanius' two speeches, he would have had to applaud Bauto's culture and character. After its delivery, the text of the speech would be circulated. He is lucky that it does not survive.

Time in a court city could be demoralizing for highly educated outsiders. In Constantinople, capital of the East, Libanius and Synesius illustrate the problems. Libanius first visited as a trained speaker in his late twenties. He had no publicly paid job, but within a year he acquired fame and many pupils through his talents. He also attracted vicious hostility from rivals and the city's established professor. When he returned, seven years later, he held a prestigious professorship, paid in kind by Imperial funds, but, even so, he was unhappy, hating the uncultured audiences and the need to attend important patrons' dinners. Again, matters ended badly.[8]

When Synesius visited Constantinople, he too was in his late twenties. Unlike Augustine and Libanius, he had not come to teach and practise oratory. He had been sent as an ambassador to plead for a remission of taxes for his home city, Cyrene. For three years, he endured frustrations which young Augustine would soon recognize, waiting for access to persons of power and fretting, meanwhile, at the distraction from 'philosophy', the ideal which he had been professing since his studies with Hypatia. In a florid poetic hymn, he looked back on his experiences, deploring the 'labours' he had endured and the 'pains, prompting so many tears'. The 'pains' and the 'labours' were caused by concern for his diplomatic mission, 'bearing my motherland [Cyrene] on my shoulders'.[9]

In the 380s, Milan, like Rome, was far from being a Christian society, but its Christianity is all that the *Confessions* recall. At their centre is a bishop, the first Christian of enduring fame whom Augustine ever met. 'I came to Milan to Bishop Ambrose, known to the world as among the best of men . . .' In modern Milan, his name still dignifies a bank, a choir and a library; Milan's church retains the unique privilege of celebrating its own form of the liturgy, the ancient Ambrosian rite. Augustine credits God, as ever, with bringing him to Ambrose.[10] It is, then, tempting to credit Ambrose with decisive interventions in Augustine's life.

II

In 384, when Augustine arrived, Ambrose was in his mid-forties and had been bishop of the city for ten years.[11] It was not the career which his father would have predicted. Ambrose had been born into the senatorial class, though not into the effortless dominance of Rome's true aristocrats. After his father's death, he had been educated at Rome, where he studied, inevitably, the 'liberal arts'. He had risen to a provincial governorship in and around north Italy, centred on Milan. In 374, when the city's Christians were divided on choosing a new bishop, Ambrose had found himself in the city's main basilica in an attempt to restore order. Instead, he was acclaimed bishop by the crowd. To disqualify himself he is said to have engaged in some profoundly un-Christian activities, at least according to his later biographer, one of his deacons. He is said to have gone to his seat of judgement and ordered several people to be tortured. He announced, we are told, that he wished to become a philosopher. He is even supposed to have invited prostitutes to come to his house. When torture and the threats of sex and philosophy failed, he is said to have attempted to leave Milan altogether. Refusals of the crushing 'burden' of a bishopric were familiar enough, but the stories of this one went to extraordinary lengths.[12] There was ample reason. Ambrose was not even a baptized Christian at the time. He was only a catechumen, or 'hearer', unable to take the eucharist.

Later, Ambrose recalled that he had been called to his bishopric 'from the noise of civil quarrels and the terrors inspired by public administration'. Jerome, predictably, was more forthright: 'yesterday, a catechumen, today a bishop; yesterday, in the amphitheatre, today in the church; previously, a fan of actors, now, a consecrator of virgins'.[13] Nonetheless, Ambrose had two highly prized assets: he was rich and he was unmarried. His sister had become a dedicated Christian virgin and his brother had not married, either. This brother then died only four years after Ambrose began his bishopric. If Ambrose chose to remain celibate, he would have no heirs or siblings who would inherit his fortune. He could therefore spend it freely on Milan's Christian community. It was a major factor, no doubt, behind its acclamation of him for the job.[14]

As elsewhere in north Italy, Milan's Christians were badly split. The rift was theological and turned on the precise relation of Jesus Christ to God. The question had been a minefield since the attempt by

Constantine, the first Christian emperor, to impose unity and a creed at the Council of Nicaea (AD 325). Before Ambrose, for twenty years the Bishop of Milan had not been one of the 'Nicenes', Christians who considered that the Son is 'of one substance' with the Father. More precisely, he had been one of the 'Homoeans', holding that Christ was 'similar' to the Father. In their enemies' rhetoric, these Homoeans, the 'Similar Party', were yet more 'Arians', followers of the heretical Arius, who had been excommunicated and exiled at the Council of Nicaea.[15] In the Greek East, however, Homoean bishops had been numerous, and in north Italy in the 380s they were a significant presence. In Milan, when Augustine arrived, they had an important focal point: the boy-emperor's mother, Justine, was a Homoean, as were the Gothic soldiers in the boy-emperor's guard. The Homoeans also had a preacher and a minister of note: Auxentius, an arrival from the East.[16]

To an ambitious young orator, an alignment with the Homoeans at court might have seemed the shrewd career move. His own view of Jesus, he recalls, was still hazy. As his faith in the Manichaeans' spiritual 'Jesus of Light' had faded, he had been left more or less with the view which he had held when encountering Cicero's *Hortensius*: Christ was a man of exceptional wisdom. He had been born miraculously from a virgin, thereby 'despising worldly things', pre-eminently sex, for the sake of a greater good, immortality. He showed 'divine care' for mankind, but he was not God on earth: he had an 'exceptional excellence of human nature' and a 'more perfect participation in wisdom'.[17] The 'Similar Party' was far closer to this view of Christ as a god-like man than was Ambrose's 'neo-Nicene' theology. However, Augustine was not concerned with rarefied details of Christology.[18] Rather than attend the Homoeans' services in a palace room, he took himself off to hear Ambrose preach in the city's big basilica. He did not go because he wanted to pray there. Ambrose was reputed to be a good speaker and, as the new public orator, Augustine simply went to hear him and assess him.

Ambrose 'received me in a fatherly way', he recalls, and asked about Augustine's travels. As hospitality was part of a bishop's role, this reception need not have been a prearranged interview. Augustine never says that he had come with a letter of introduction to Ambrose, still less with one from Symmachus. Although Symmachus and Ambrose corresponded over people of mutual concern, their letters were not unduly cordial. Augustine's job in Milan was for the city, not the Church.[19] Their first meeting was perhaps only after a Sunday service. Ambrose, it seems, asked a routine question, but Augustine thought that Ambrose 'loved' him as a Christian loves a stranger and promptly 'loved' Ambrose from the heart. He was alone in an unfamiliar city, yet he felt he had experienced the personal touch of a great and good man.

By 384, Ambrose was indeed a major presence in Milan. Since his appointment, he had risen to ever greater prominence through connections with the Emperor Gratian and through deploying strategies which he had observed in Damasus' Rome. Like Damasus, he had been involved in Church Councils against the Homoeans and their appointments, culminating at Aquileia in 381.[20] Inside Milan, he had advanced a unified profile for his own Christian community and had emphasized it, like Damasus, with plans for strategic buildings. In 384, at least two churches were already being built with Ambrose's encouragement at cardinal points outside Milan's double wall, where the roads led out to Italy's major cities. Beyond the 'people's pleasure' of a racecourse, he had commissioned the church beneath whose altar he would eventually ask to be laid to rest (the modern Sant' Ambrogio).[21] It was interrelated with one of Milan's Christian martyrs, a type of asset which Ambrose, like Damasus in Rome, would carefully enhance in the city during his bishopric. He also began to process out to the sites of existing martyr cults and to transform the rowdy festival days of their martyrs into celebrations of the eucharist by his priests.[22] This initiative was also to be most influential for Augustine.

When Augustine went to hear him, Ambrose was about to preach in Milan's 'New Basilica', the enormous church which he had inherited from his Homoean predecessor. Capable of holding some 3,000 hearers, it lay beside a second basilica, the Old Basilica (which has been built over, nowadays, by Milan's cathedral, San Giovanni). As an educated senator-governor, now turned bishop, Ambrose was exceptional in north Italy. In winter 383/4, it was he, remarkably, who had been sent as the Milan court's ambassador on the crucial mission to the usurper Maximus in Trier, the first bishop ever to take on such a prominent diplomatic role. He was an accomplished speaker and, unusually for a cleric, had a background in the upper reaches of non-Christian public life.[23] As a bishop, he would also be considered to be above bribery. It was a vital asset on the mission because most of the emperor's troops and officers had already changed sides in Gaul and joined the winners. To prevail, Ambrose had had to be highly economical with the truth. He succeeded well enough at it.

As Augustine would have noticed, virgins and widows were a

prominent presence in Ambrose's church, where they made up a special order. Here, Ambrose had developed another Roman innovation, a ceremony of 'veiling' which received young, committed virgins into a new life. In Rome, Ambrose's young sister had undergone the ceremony and Ambrose himself continued to live virginally.[24] However, he had not renounced all worldly pomp. In his church, he dressed in fine silk robes, a type of dress of which big fragments have survived in Milan. They are datable between the fourth and sixth centuries and may well relate to Ambrose's own. Some of them are woven with scenes of a lion hunt.[25]

In the *Confessions* Augustine gives only one reason for his coming to the church services: Ambrose's oratorical style. He listened 'studiously'. 'I was delighted by the sweetness of this speaking,' Augustine tells us and adds, 'more erudite, but less soothing, than Faustus the Manichee'. Ever the judge of words, the young Augustine had not lowered his standards. 'Sweetness' is the quality which Ambrose ascribes to the music of the heavenly spheres and the song of angels before God. In his own letters Ambrose urges newly appointed bishops in north Italian towns to deploy 'sweetness' and 'soothe' by the grace of their words. Ambrose's surviving works bring a poetic mannerism into Latin prose, but are far from soothing to our taste, as he moves from one topic to the next in a loosely connected sequence. The erudition shows in echoes of Virgil and Cicero or his allusions to 'wonders' in the natural world, items so rare that they survived in the texts of medieval bestiaries. Unlike Augustine, Ambrose read Greek with ease, including bits of Platonist philosophy. Through it, he had absorbed a way of interpreting Christian scripture which was new to Augustine and was to change his understanding.[26]

On Sundays, Augustine recalls, he would come to listen attentively to Ambrose's sermons. People talked and interrupted, as we can infer from Ambrose's own words, but Augustine was not troubled. He was not there to take in the contents, and yet as he listened to the style, his 'heart', typically, opened to what was being spoken. He does not recall that he was influenced by Ambrose's rhetorical training, one which he shared. Instead, he is clear, as we should be, that Ambrose was the first person to show him that concealed other meanings, or allegories, could be discerned in awkward verses of scripture. They did not have to mean what they appeared to say on the surface. Ambrose's use of allegory was derived from Greek authors, the Christian thinker Origen (*c*.185–254) and the Greek-speaking Jew Philo in Alexandria in the early to mid-first century, from whose books Ambrose took whole patterns of interpretation while claiming that, as a Jew, Philo had not been able to 'discern the mystery' himself.[27]

Hidden meanings and 'mysteries' beneath the surface of a text were not new for Augustine. During his literary training he had learned that allegory could be applied to verses by Virgil.[28] Now, beneath the clumsy style of the Latin scriptures, a deeper meaning was being shown to lie hidden. Ambrose could reveal its depths because a key had been made available by Christ. 'You have read in the Apocalypse,' Ambrose later wrote, 'that the Lamb opened the sealed book which nobody thitherto had been able to open . . . by means of His Gospel: Jesus handed over the key of knowledge and gave it to us so that we may open.' Faith in Christ, Ambrose believed, guides scripture's readers to the hidden meanings which unify it and to which they are linked by the Holy Spirit. In this sense, so Ambrose would preach, 'the Letter kills, the Spirit gives life', words of St Paul to the Corinthians which greatly struck his hearer, Augustine.[29] They were a sort of 'rule' for understanding scripture whose depths of meaning made it like a 'sea'. One level might be natural, but another might be 'moral', discernible with the help of allegorical keys. A third level was mystical, which only allegory could unlock. Ambrose did not name his source, but, like the 'rule', these three levels had been formulated in Greek by Origen.[30]

Augustine's acceptance of Ambrose's allegorical approach marks a cardinal point in his development. As a priest, and then for the rest of his life as a preacher, he himself would apply allegory to the scriptures and weave patterns of meaning from their raw material. He would not see them as subjective ingenuity. Over time, he developed the 'rule' which he first heard from Ambrose, 'the Letter kills, the Spirit gives life'. 'Veils', he learned from Ambrose, had been laid across words of scripture, and only in Christian humility can we draw them aside. We can then grasp with love, a gift of the Spirit, what the Spirit 'gives life to' beneath.[31]

These beliefs were extremely rich for him, but neither Ambrose nor Augustine understood the Bible's origins as a historical critic would understand them nowadays. Although Ambrose used Greek translations too, his main resource was a Latin translation which a modern critical eye would regard as often untrue to the original Hebrew and Greek.[32] However, as the scriptures and their translators were 'divinely inspired', it was right, Ambrose believed, to read them as if verses in the Old Testament foretold verses in the New. Where the four Gospels differed, it was also right to look for an underlying harmony. Critical readers nowadays recognize no such harmony in the Gospels, nor that the authors of the Hebrew scriptures had consciously predicted anything in the Christian New Testament.

From a modern critical perspective, Ambrose's allegory is an example of creative misunderstanding. Having no such perspective, his hearer, Augustine, was most receptive to it. The relation between an author's intention and a text's meaning is one which will greatly interest him when he begins, five years later, to write on the scriptures himself. He believes as firmly as a modern literary critic that an author may be unaware of the truth in what he has written. A gap between what is written and what is understood is inevitable, he thinks, especially when a text is obscure and difficult. A reader who finds a valuable truth in such a text is reading its author with love. If he reads in 'error', he is making a human error, but if he finds a worthy truth, his error is one 'most worthy of a human being'.[33] In Augustine's next conversion, a year and a half later, 'creative misunderstanding' of words both spoken and read will be crucial.

Fascinatingly for Augustine, Ambrose's allegories countered the Manichaean attacks on the Old Testament. They showed that difficult bits of the 'law and prophets' appeared not to mean what Manichaeans said they did. Nonetheless, Augustine's recent scepticism did not desert him. He concluded merely that the 'Church Universal' had teachers who could answer the travesties which others ascribed to them. He did not yet conclude that this Church's way was the right one to uphold.[34]

From this point until his culminating conversion, two and a half years later, the *Confessions* set out the progress, 'step by step', through which Augustine will come to know God and adopt a 'stable' relationship to Him. Like no other early Christian, he traces with exact clarity each intellectual step by which his understanding changes. Being Augustine, he also recalls exactly his emotions: first, 'despair', as if in an impasse, then, repeatedly, 'hope', as progress is made. The first step, he insists, led him away from the Manichees, but not yet to Ambrose's Christians. The Manichees had attracted him by their emphasis on reason, not authority, and on their own repeated 'Truth'. Both claims, he realized, were now damaged. Their reasoned criticisms did not address the hidden depths of scripture. Their true cosmology was increasingly open to refutation. With the help of his manual of philosophers' theories, Augustine continued to examine Mani's views of nature and the 'body of the universe'. From his sceptical viewpoint, he tells us, he did not want possibilities: he wanted 'proofs that were certain'. Once again, he found counter-arguments in the theories of past Greek thinkers which he read in summaries in Latin. Their opinions, he concluded, were 'much more probable' than Mani's, but, even so, he did not consider them 'certain', because the sceptic in him, he recalls, was still wary.[35] Nonetheless, there was a positive result. With so much against them, the Manichaeans, he decided, must be abandoned once and for all.

Essentially, Augustine had thought his way out of them. He recalls this phase as one of intense mental effort. He does not refer to the arguments of his friends Nebridius and Elpidius, back in Carthage, about God's 'incorruptibility' and the Manichaeans' arbitrary dismissal of the scriptures. Instead, the decisive arguments, he tells us, were those which he found in the philosophers about the 'very body of this world' and the whole of nature which is perceptible by the 'sense of the flesh'.[36] They extended, therefore, beyond his earlier discoveries about eclipses. They were 'highly probable'. Importantly, Augustine admits that he could not refute Mani's other teachings by 'arguments which were certain'. Here, he means Mani's teaching on imperceptible matters, the nature of evil, the soul and the nature of God. He still had no idea, he recalls, of a 'spiritual substance'.[37]

Augustine was already inclined intellectually to doubt because he was continuing to study scepticism in texts by Cicero and others. Consequently, his abandonment of Mani's Gospel did not entail an immediate commitment to the 'Church Universal'. To a sceptical mind, he recalls, that Church's teachings were not certain, either.[38] Yet, crucially, he did not extend his scepticism to the Christian Bible or to Ambrose's allegorical method. In Milan Augustine never applied his lessons from the 'many things of the philosophers' to the Bible's cosmology. Nor did he extend his scepticism to Christ. None of the philosophers whose views he was reading had even mentioned Christ, but, for that reason, Augustine still refused to go over to them. His stance here is basic to an understanding of his next conversion. It was not to be a conversion from doubt or agnosticism to Christian faith. Since his earliest boyhood, he had believed firmly in Christ, from whom neither Cicero's *Hortensius* nor Mani's 'true Christians' had ever removed him. Aged thirty, he was still seriously underinformed about Christ's teachings and the intractable problems of His nature, but he was as unshakeable as ever in his faith in Him. His problems, rather, were problems of intelligent understanding. He did not know how to imagine God and how to relate God and Christ to the world and to his own self. This gap existed because the Manichaeans' teachings about the world had turned out to be such a pack of lies. The 'suffering Jesus' was not scattered all over it and the plants and animals were not demonic. Every night, the moon looks very different to a post-Manichaean eye. After being caught by such misplaced 'certainties', Augustine was shy about accepting yet more theological beliefs. He was wary, rather than disillusioned, but he was still passionately keen to find truth.

To many of his modern readers, his abandonment of Mani's Gospel seems to be a conversion, albeit a negative one, a 'de-conversion' or a 'disenchantment'. At the time, outsiders might also see it in this light. Again, the letter of his old acquaintance in Carthage, Vincentius, is illuminating.[39] In Carthage, he says, he had known Augustine as someone who was 'set far apart from the Christian faith'. To Vincentius, therefore, Mani's Gospel did not seem at all like 'true Christianity'. However, outsiders like himself had no idea of Augustine's own reception and understanding of the steps on his journey. Vincentius did not know that Augustine had imbibed the 'name of Christ' with Monnica's milk, that he had been a Catholic catechumen from boyhood and that he had adopted Mani's teaching as the 'true Christianity'. In Augustine's own view, the view which matters, he was not converting by resuming his status as a catechumen. He was merely reverting, going back within a Christian faith which, in his view, he had never left.

Like many previous sceptics, including Cicero, he decided to fall back on what he had inherited without questioning it with the same intensity as other beliefs. As a catechumen in the Church Universal, he would attend services, be called a Christian, but not be a baptized 'faithful' Christian. Matters were made easier for him by his presence in a city far from home whose clergy had never known him as a committed Manichee. There would be no need, unless someone informed them, for a ceremony of renunciation before he was received again. He would pray and listen to the scriptural readings and the sermons of Ambrose, from which, he says, he was learning step by step. He would then leave before the eucharist was given, a 'mystery' which he would not see: he had not witnessed the meal of the Manichaean Elect, either, during his nine years in their community. At some point in the future, he would become a 'seeker' and put his name forward for pre-baptismal instruction and baptism. There was no question of his turning to the 'Similar', so-called Arian, party at court. The 'Church Universal', he observes, was the Church which had been 'commended' to him by his parents. So, he would remain there, he recalls, on that 'step', until 'something certain dawned by which I would steer my course'.[40]

While he hesitated, an unhesitating force reappeared in his life: Monnica arrived to be with him again in Milan.

III

There were no doubts in Monnica's mind. On the sea journey from Africa, storms had scared the 'simple' sailors, but she had carried them through the panic, insisting that she would be safely brought to Italy.[41] She knew it because of that vision in which God had shown her that, one day, Augustine would be beside her, standing on her same Christian 'rule'. She knew, therefore, that she would survive to re-meet him.

When she duly found him in Milan, she heard that he had given up his dreadful heresy and she 'rejoiced'. She was not surprised, and as 'such a great part' of her prayers and vision had now been fulfilled, she was calmly confident: she told him that she 'believed in Christ' that she would see him as a baptized Christian before she died. 'This, she said to me, but to You, God', she kept pouring out 'yet denser prayers and tears' so that God 'would accelerate His help and enlighten my darkness'.[42]

This 'river of tears' was not so exceptional nor even so feminine as it seems to us. Also in a court city, Synesius, in his late twenties, recalls how 'night after night' in Constantinople his bed was soaked with his tears and lamentations and how, before Christian shrines, he would 'soak the ground with the dampness of my eyes'. He was bearing his 'mother' on his shoulders as he toiled and wept, not his physical mother, but his 'motherland', Cyrene. Whereas Monnica wept in prayer for her son, Synesius wept on behalf of his overtaxed city. He mentions his tearful prayers as extending for three whole years.[43]

In a culture accustomed to sobbing before God, Augustine looks back on his mother's tears as effective agents of his salvation. In their first phase, he thought, her tears had helped to save him from virtual death, like the tears of the 'widow of Nain' in the Gospels with whom he had already identified his mother. Those tears prompted God to bring the widow's son back to life, just as Monnica's tears had now prompted God to bring her son back to Himself. In the second phase, so Augustine thought, Monnica's tears would finally bring him to baptism. They encouraged other gifts too. Less than two years later, in one of his first works after his conversion, he states that Monnica's prayers have 'indubitably' encouraged God's gift to him of a mind which makes him 'prefer nothing whatsoever to finding the Faith'.[44] Later in life, he then refers opponents of his views on God's grace to the *Confessions*, which show that 'it was through the faithful, daily tears of my mother that it was granted to me not to go to my ruin'. This 'ruin' was his near-'death' in Manichaean company, averted in Milan.[45]

In the *Confessions*, Augustine emphasizes the role of Monnica's tears, the very 'blood of her heart'. Nonetheless they present a sequence of events which is coherent and explicable without them. In it, Augustine heard some people's objections, failed to find answers from others and read philosophy texts which undermined Mani's teachings about the visible world. Just as his confessions have misjudged Monnica's reasons for putting him through a schooling in pagan poetry and rhetoric, so they misjudge the role of her sobbing and weeping in his 'pilgrimage' back to God. As she was so pious, and the tears were so prolific, how ever, he thought, could God not have heeded her?

In Milan, Augustine's progress might seem more easily explicable by Ambrose's personal interest, as if the most famous of bishops deliberately converted the future's most famous Christian thinker. In 385–6, the two men's personal relations were more oblique and therefore even more interesting.[46] They were mediated by a third person. It was Monnica who made the greater impression on Ambrose, and Ambrose, at first, on Monnica.

After hearing that Augustine had dropped Manichaeism, Monnica did not ascribe her son's new 'doubting' state to the influence of Cicero and the sceptics, philosophers whom she had never read. She credited it to Milan's bishop. She was even keener than before to 'run' to church and hang on Ambrose's every word.[47] Ambrose's writings show that communion in his churches was given around midday, after a service of psalm-singing and readings. There were also morning and evening services when psalms were sung and lessons read, and there was a vigil in the night for prayer and readings. Every day, Monnica took communion, at noon therefore (except on days of fasting), but she also went to church 'in the [early] morning and evening', the times for separate services without the eucharist.[48] All the while, she loved Ambrose 'like an angel of God' because it was Ambrose, she believed, who had brought Augustine to his present state of 'doubting fluctuation'. Ambrose himself had no idea of that state or his own impact on it.

Reverently, Monnica even adapted her Christian practices to

Ambrose's rules. In north Africa, she had been accustomed to go out to 'martyrs' memorials' in the local burial grounds and celebrate the festivals there with her fellow Christians. Like them, she would bring wine, bread and 'cakes' and distribute whatever she did not consume to others who were in need. These festival days of 'rejoicing' could turn into days of Christian rowdiness, even drunkenness, vices which were much in evidence in their celebrations on Rome's Vatican Hill. In the *Confessions* Augustine insists at some length that Monnica watered the wine which was drunk in the martyr's honour; she took only one cup; she sipped only from that one cup, even if several martyr memorials were to be visited.[49] Once again, he is implicitly answering critics who had alleged that his mother had been much too fond of drink.

In Milan, she found the rules were stricter than in Africa. Monnica turned up to honour the martyrs, probably those who were commemorated in the burial ground around Ambrose's emerging new church, the 'Basilica Ambrosiana', but the door-keeper of the burial ground told her that Ambrose forbade offerings of food and wine. The bishop did not wish to give those present the slightest chance of becoming drunk. He also did not wish the cult of the martyrs to resemble the pagans' annual festival, February's *parentalia*, which was held for several days in honour of dead family members. Christian martyrs were the 'very special dead' and were to be honoured differently.[50] Monnica obeyed, though Augustine doubts if she would have obeyed this order from anyone except Ambrose. Consequently, she learned to bring a pure heart and prayers to the martyrs' memorial shrines and to give 'what she could' to the Christian poor who came there while the eucharist was celebrated. Henceforward she obeyed Ambrose's refocusing of the 'cult of the saints' from turbulent crowd occasions to celebrations of the liturgy.

In north Africa, Monnica had been accustomed to fast on Saturdays. When she found that the church in Milan differed on this point, Augustine went to seek Ambrose's guidance on her behalf: an unaccompanied visit by a widow would not have been acceptable. He recalls it not in the *Confessions* but in a letter nearly contemporary with them.[51] Ambrose's answer was brusque at first: 'he could teach Augustine nothing except what he himself did, because if he knew anything better he would do it'. Ambrose, it seemed to Augustine, was merely imposing his views without further authority. In doing so, he disappointed Augustine's intellectual values. Then, as Augustine clearly remembered, Ambrose 'followed him', because, surely, Augustine had begun to walk away, and added a second reason. 'Follow local custom in Church matters', and then, he added imposingly, 'you will not be a scandal . . .' It was a crushing comment. Nearly twenty years later, Augustine still recalled it as words 'like an anvil from heaven'. However, it showed that the great man did, after all, have a principle behind what he did. Of course Monnica obeyed it. The advice to 'follow local custom' had long been a principle of Roman governors in their provinces. Formerly, Ambrose had been one of them.

This ruling, hardly an inspired one, continued to impress both Monnica and Augustine. The 'custom of the country' often guided his own rulings as a bishop, except, significantly, on the matter of partying in honour of local martyrs. At the time, however, Ambrose was answering a question posed for Monnica's sake: when Augustine asked it, he was only a catechumen, not interested in the niceties of fasting. Even when Ambrose happened to speak to Augustine on other occasions, it was Monnica whom he mentioned. Augustine was fortunate, the bishop 'often' said, to be the son of such an exemplary widow.[52] Again, it was the sort of comment which the bishop might make when greeting Augustine and his mother on the way out of church. He was seeing her in church up to three times a day and she was an assiduous giver to the poor.

Ambrose, meanwhile, had no idea of the 'turmoils' which were affecting Monnica's son, once a Manichee, still a believer in Christ, but uncertain what the 'Church Universal' believed or what God was really like. Augustine's mind was 'intent on seeking' and 'restless in debating'. Meanwhile, he considered Ambrose 'a happy man, according to the standards of this world' because 'so many great powers in it honoured him': he was aware, therefore, of Ambrose's high standing in Milan and, surely, of his recent diplomacy on Milan's behalf. The one point which struck Augustine as 'burdensome' was Ambrose's remarkable abstinence from sex.[53] Ever since reading the *Hortensius*, Augustine had admired the ideal of chastity, but as yet he could not possibly inflict it on his own life.

'At that time,' Augustine recalled in a text written six years later, 'nobody was more open to being taught than I was.'[54] The *Confessions* repeat this memory and ask rhetorically, surely Ambrose might help, but when would Ambrose have time to do so? For us, the chronology of Ambrose's movements is uncertain. After Augustine's first meetings with him, Ambrose, we can best infer, went back to Trier on another diplomatic mission to the usurper Maximus in winter 384/5. He was sent to ask for Gratian's remains to be returned to Milan, but his plan failed, and the mission left him with very bad memories of Maximus' brusqueness and anger.[55] In spring/early summer 385, Monnica's arrival in Milan was a tiny speck on Ambrose's busy horizon. Recently, he had faced criticism for his second embassy's failure. He had even written a careful, justificatory letter on the topic and addressed it to the boy-emperor, Valentinian.[56] During Holy Week 385, from 6 to 13 April, he had yet more on his mind. The emperor's mother, Justine, had demanded the use of a church in Milan so that she and her fellow Homoeans could hold an Easter service inside it: they wished to use the Basilica 'of the Gate' (Portiana), which one of Ambrose's predecessors, probably a 'Homoean', had built by the city's south wall. Ambrose boldly refused the request, claiming sole authority over Milan's churches. Soldiers were sent to keep the peace, but Ambrose mobilized a crowd of his own supporters and had them scared off. In the aftermath, there were even threats of kidnapping him or removing him from the city.[57]

All the while, Ambrose was a bishop. He was beset, therefore, by the requests and disputes of the thousands of Christians in his care, the crowd of 'people with business', whom Augustine recalls as keeping him from meeting Ambrose face to face.[58] Nonetheless Ambrose maintained an 'open door' policy when he withdrew to his rooms. Augustine and his friends 'often' went in the hope of a hearing, but when Ambrose was not taken up with petitioners, he was found either to 'be refreshing his body' with essentials or 'his mind with reading'. Augustine and his friends were too overawed to disturb their superior: they could see him through the door 'reading silently'.[59] Silent reading was not unparalleled in antiquity, but it was sufficiently odd to prompt their curiosity. Why did the great man do it? Was he afraid that a waiting visitor would pick on a passage which he was reading aloud and then draw him into a long exposition of it? Was he, they wondered, resting his voice? Ambrose's own writings refer to the merits of silence over speech and observe that they are exemplified in scripture by the likes of Job or Moses.[60] The happy result of his Job-like silence was that pesterers left his doorway, admiring him all the more. Augustine, revealingly, 'came often', but always left without bothering the great man. Ambrose's immersion signalled 'do not disturb', the envy of many since.

Ambrose's silent reading has attracted attention, then and nowadays, but the very fact of his reading is illuminating: in a fine modern study of his spirituality and preaching, Goulven Madec imagines him 'reading a [Greek] work by Origen, the commentary on the Song of

Songs, for instance. He would be impregnating himself with this interpretation so as to prepare his own homilies.'[61] As his surviving sermons in Milan show, he was indeed more of a reader than an original thinker. Meanwhile Ambrose little knew what a trial he was missing, a tortured debate with a former Manichee who had become obsessed with the standards of truth as expressed by the sceptical Cicero, the author 'of whose shrine Ambrose was the sacristan'.[62] Augustine recalls how he needed to catch Ambrose 'fully at leisure' so that his 'turbulences' could be 'poured out to him'. However, the bishop was too preoccupied to be caught. So, Augustine went on coming to church with Monnica on any given Sunday and listening to Ambrose at a distance 'discerning the mystery' in scriptures whose literal meaning was nothing of the sort.

Meanwhile, the *Confessions* describe Augustine's progress towards understanding: it was his attempt to be 'honest to God'. He learned 'step by step' from such sermons by Ambrose as he heard. A major obstacle for him had been Genesis 1.26. When it said that God made man 'to His image and likeness', did the text entail, as Manichaeans taught, that God was shaped like a man? Augustine found this anthropomorphism ridiculous. For years, it had prevented him from taking the 'Church Universal' seriously. Ambrose's preaching now explained that the 'image and likeness' was our soul, or 'spiritual substance', not our flesh or body at all.[63] Augustine would later see other problems in the Latin text of the passage, but in 385 it was enough for him to learn the basic point, that 'flesh' was not the 'image' in question.[64] Many in Ambrose's audience, let alone in the churches in north Africa, probably assumed, as nowadays, that it was. Most of them imagined that God was a sort of man, only bigger.

Ambrose's exposition of this verse was not one which came naturally to the Christian majority, but it was the answer which Augustine wanted. From Ambrose's surviving writings, we can see that it was indeed a prominent theme in his sermons. 'Our soul,' he preached, 'is "to the image of God". In this, man, you are in your entirety, because without this, you are nothing: you are earth and into earth you will be dissolved . . . What exchange will a man give for his soul in which there is not just a small part of himself, but the substance of his entire human totality?' Yet again, 'The soul is "to the image of God", whereas the body is to the form of the beasts. The body, therefore, cannot be to the likeness of God, but our soul is . . .'[65]

Here, once again, Ambrose was helped by his lack of a modern text-critical understanding of the Bible. The Book of Genesis describes two separate Creations, using two separate Hebrew sources of different dates which are contradictory. As Ambrose had no idea of the text's history, he explained the first one (1.26) as the creation of the soul, the second (2.1) as the creation of the body. Even his frequent resource, Philo's writings, had not taken this particular line of error. It survives very clearly in the later part of Ambrose's published sermon *On the Six Days of Creation*, raising the problem for us of its date of delivery. None of Ambrose's surviving sermons dates itself, but this one was certainly delivered before 388, when Augustine drew on it.[66] In my view, it originated in Holy Week 387, but Ambrose preached many other sermons while Augustine was in Milan and we can tentatively accept that some of them contained themes which we also find in undated survivors, those likeliest to have originated between 385 and 388. We cannot be sure that we have the very sermon which Ambrose preached in Augustine's presence, but, in my view, we can form a compelling idea of what he may have said from those few which survive.[67]

Still wary and sceptical, Augustine reckoned that Ambrose's explanation of 1.26 was 'probable', but no more. Unlike Augustine, Ambrose knew about the immaterial soul ultimately from Plato and his later followers: their ideas may have reached him indirectly, through Jewish and Christian sources which he read. He was eloquent about this 'image' within us. 'Our soul is free and wanders in diverse thoughts, hither and thither,' he told audiences. 'Look, we are now in Italy, and we are thinking of what seems to cover the east or west; we seem to range with those who are settled in Persia and we see those who pasture in Africa.' This inner traveller within us 'is joined to God . . . it adheres to Christ'.[68] We are capable, therefore, of being transformed or remade. Ambrose had no interest in Plato's belief in the reincarnation of the soul. Instead, he preached the remaking of the 'inner man', as stated in Paul's Letter to the Colossians. By focusing on the soul, or inner man, we can 'gaze on the glory of God and be remade to the same image'.[69] This connection would soon prove very fertile for Augustine.

The body, by contrast, is 'mud' from which the soul must be purified and separated. While God created the body, Ambrose's view of it was unusually negative, although the resurrection of the body was not ignored in his sermons.[70] From Ambrose the diplomat and worldly manoeuvrer, this intense other-worldliness may seem surprising. However, he was also a committed celibate whose soul was striving to dominate the body. By despising the body as 'mud', he assisted this self-imposed struggle.[71] For Augustine the ex-Manichaean, this dualism was not so startling as it is to us. For years, he had accepted that particles of Light from God's Kingdom were within him and were being constantly threatened by his body's urges, those implants from the Kingdom of Darkness. Ambrose's preaching applied a dualism of body and soul, but with a very different reference. For Ambrose, the soul is God's image, and God, therefore, is not a substance. He is a spiritual being.

Even so, Augustine hesitated to commit himself. Ambrose's preaching, he thought, was possibly true, but might it not be as illusory as Mani's? Whatever Augustine read or discussed, he tells us, he was looking at this time for a truth as certain as '7 plus 3 equals 10'.[72] As his subsequent attack on sceptical theory will show, he was continuing to read widely in sceptical philosophy in these months, engaging with yet more dialogues by Cicero in which sceptical views were expressed. Like the young generation of Christians around the poet Tennyson in the 1830s and 1840s, Augustine and his friends still wished 'to let the uncertain remain uncertain, but to learn how much and what we could honestly regard as true, and believe that and live by it'.[73]

Rethinking the matter, Augustine began to realize how much we do, in fact, treat as certain, even without the evidence of our own eyes. We accept that we are our parents' children, although we never saw their act which set us on the path to life. Augustine reflected that, nonetheless, he was certain about the identity of his parents, something which 'I could not know unless I believed what I heard.'[74] He also began to re-evaluate the books of scripture. Ambrose had shown him that the Holy Spirit had placed deep-sea meanings below the surface of the text. He now reflected that these inspired books were being trusted by people all over the world. This universal credence seemed another strong argument against scepticism. Here he was on Sundays, sitting in the church which was called 'Universal', hearing scripture which, he learned, was 'universally' revered. The literal Latin of the biblical translations had repelled him at the age of eighteen, but now he realized that it existed to suit the simpler sort of Christian. The hidden meanings were there for the clever minority like himself. The Bible, he was discovering, truly had something for everyone, himself included.[75]

Once again, an interplay of books and people was helping him to move forward, the books of the Bible and the preaching of his admired Ambrose. Significantly, 'I was beginning to be turned (*convertebar*),' Augustine remarks for the first time in the *Confessions*, echoing Psalm 6.11.[76] He was 'turning' to a true appreciation of God's nature and His presence in the world. 'I was rejoicing,' he recalls, at what he had found out.

15
'Torn from My Side . . .'

Outside Ambrose's church, Augustine was living through a crisis of a different type. His career seemed worthless, utterly at odds with his ideals. Every day he was teaching rhetoric and declaiming half-truths, even lies, but what fascinated him was philosophy, or the love of wisdom. It was not that he had once studied it, as Synesius did, with a university teacher. In the next months, we can look in on something much rarer, a man who has been teaching himself to think logically and has come to think that his public career, by comparison, is futile. At the court of the Emperor Nero, Seneca had once written as if he was similarly disenchanted, but unlike Augustine he was someone who had been schooled in the philosophy which re-oriented him. It is still arguable how serious his commitment to it really was. For Augustine, it is not arguable. Across the distance of time and background, he touches us by his awareness, a hallmark of the 'happy few', that a life of public relations and public speaking is superficial. Even eleven years later, this awareness still brought the best out of his writing.

In Milan, he was being pressed from two directions. He longed to find the philosophical ideals of 'certain' knowledge and the 'happy life', but at the same time he was still striving for the next round of glittering prizes to which his hard-won career could lead him. The holder of a paid civic job could expect friends and family to cluster round him, hitching themselves to his income and success. Monnica was now with him in Milan, and so were hangers-on like his brother Navigius and two of his dimly educated cousins. Alypius had come up from Rome to pursue his legal career nearer the court. There were other independent friends in town, also from north Africa. Romanianus had come from Thagaste to try to prevail at Milan in a dispute which was involving him in a lawsuit. There was also Marcianus, 'my oldest friend' as Augustine later called him, a man either now, or later, of senatorial rank. Above all, there was the acute Nebridius, who had travelled specially from Carthage to be near Augustine so as to continue to talk and dispute with his clever friend and pursue truth and wisdom. As he was rich enough not to need a job, he was acting as the lowly assistant to a grammar teacher in Milan. In turn, this teacher, the amicable Verecundus, became another member of Augustine's 'significant group'.[1]

Except for Monnica, none of these people was a baptized Christian. Far from it: Romanianus was still a Manichaean Hearer, but his generous friendship persisted nonetheless. Neither Alypius nor Nebridius was baptized, and Augustine continued to talk and argue with them about scepticism and the nature of what philosophers called the 'happy life'. Everybody wants to be happy, Cicero's *Hortensius* had taught them, but the question was, how? In Milan, Augustine had to teach until noon, taking pupils who paid him to teach them public speaking. He had to compose exemplary speeches for their benefit and to deliver others whenever one was needed on the city's behalf. In the afternoon, he had to attend, like Alypius, on 'greater friends', potential patrons who might help him up the ladder to a salaried job in the government or send him rich pupils for his benefit. He was courting them for their intercession on his behalf, their 'suffrage', as he calls it, a word which had slid, significantly, from its earlier meaning of 'vote' to one of 'patronage'. He would have to wait on them, 'dangling away life in an ante-chamber', as a patron in eighteenth-century London neatly describes the process.[2] It was so distasteful to his fellow seeker of wisdom, Nebridius, that he had taken his lowly teaching job in order to avoid it. Augustine was not rich enough to follow suit.

It is at this time in his life that the externals of his public career can be most tellingly compared with his autobiographical counterpart, Libanius in the Greek-speaking East. Like Augustine, Libanius taught classes of pupils the arts of public speaking until late midday. He too looked forward to summer 'long vacations' from July until September. He held publicly paid positions, although in his case the salary and allowances appear to have been paid by the emperor, not by the city to which he was attached. In his early thirties, he too had to speak and teach for a parvenu court, the one at Constantinople, even grander than Augustine's Milan. He was no more happy there than was Augustine, his fellow orator, in Italy. In Constantinople, the 'new Rome', Libanius disliked the military men, their frightful use of Latin and their detachment from the Greek classics. He dreaded the long days of dining and drinking among the high and mighty, those 'greater friends' whom Augustine felt obliged to court. He did not slacken in composing and performing speeches, but 'most' of those who came, came only to watch his movements and gestures, because 'most of the council there' (the Senate) was drawn from men-at-arms, not 'men of the Muses'.[3]

Unlike Augustine, Libanius dwells constantly on the malice of his rivals. Wherever he taught and spoke, they beset him with slander, charges of alleged malpractice and even, as we shall see, black magic. In the big cities of the Greek-speaking East, bitter competition between rhetors had long been endemic. In the Latin West, it seems, Augustine faced less competition and from him alone we would never guess that so much backbiting could attend teachers in a free-market system. In Milan, he seems to be without any rivals for his public role.

Libanius, meanwhile, was spared the doubts which beset Augustine's philosophical mind. Besides his continuing 'turbulence' about God's nature and the origins of evil, Augustine continued to fear judgement after death, a topic on which Mani's psalms had been chillingly precise. Libanius had no such anxieties. He knew very well who the gods were. Like Monnica, he communed freely with them in his dreams. While asleep, he envisaged them in the very forms in which he saw them every day in sculptures all over the cities. He had no haunting fear of a judgement in hell after death: he had been initiated into the mysteries at Lerna, near Argos, while he was a student at Athens, and these pagan rites would promise him a safe passage after death through the Underworld. He might even go to the fields of the blessed, where his disembodied soul could re-meet the soul of his former hero, the Emperor Julian. As for worldly misfortune, it was sent either by a disaffected god, one among many in the heavens, or perhaps by an intermediary evil spirit.[4] As the gods had not created the world, Libanius did not find the evil in it to be a theological problem.

Secure in his education, Libanius never pined for further wisdom. His firmly held values were grounded in the classics of Greek ethics and literature. In his early thirties he felt alienated in Constantinople, but neither there nor after his return to his native mega-city, Antioch, did he cease for one moment to believe in the value of his teaching career. Unlike Augustine in Milan, he was passionately committed to his profession and to his pupils, whom he called, admirably, his 'children'.[5] He taught what he believed, the importance of stylish speaking and the educative power of the Greek classics. Together, they formed men and built social bridges, as they still do, between people of very varied backgrounds. Their transmission was Libanius' heartfelt vocation. Unlike Augustine and his friends, he never pined to escape his career. He reminds us, however, of the financial rewards for a top teacher who could perform speeches of panegyrical praise on demand. In his mid-thirties, Libanius once had no fewer than 1,500 gold pieces, or *solidi*, in his possession: one of his slaves, he tells us, happened to run off with them. He had amassed this huge sum in less than eight years: it was an invaluable bastion against the continuing inflation of everyday coinage and would have bought, in Italy, at least 300,000 pounds of pork.[6]

'I was gaping for honours, marriage and gain,' Augustine memorably recalls, 'but You, God, were laughing at me . . .' Libanius' store of gold coins gives force to the 'gains', but 'marriage' strikes a new note. Augustine's brilliant presentation of the tensions of the next year is the pinnacle of his autobiographical confessing. At the centre, wondrously, stands a small group of friends in a court city where they were despairing of lives which had come to seem so futile. 'How much longer of this?' he recalls that they kept on asking, near a court which we know to have been poised on the edge of collapse. Once, when Augustine had been preparing a hypocritical speech in praise of the emperor, he passed a 'poor beggar', drunk in the street in Milan. 'I groaned' at the sight and 'spoke with the friends who were with me', as ever, about 'the many sorrows of our madnesses'. For only a few little coins, the beggar, though drunk, had acquired the happiness which was eluding them in their pursuit of so much more.[7] These memories are retold with touches of philosophic and rhetorical colour, but they are not therefore untrue.

Unlike Libanius, Augustine even treats us to a brilliant review of his life so far, a classic example of a man assessing all that has eluded him at the cardinal age of thirty. If he dies, he wonders, will he be punished in the next life for all he has failed to learn in this one? The sceptics, he remarks, doubt if anything certain for living a life can be 'comprehended', but we must therefore seek it all the more diligently. Yet 'Ambrose has no free time; there is no free time to read . . .' Where can we find the books themselves; 'where and when can we buy them? From whom can we take them?' As all texts had to be copied by hand, good copies were scarce and expensive. In Antioch, Libanius is a vivid witness to the limits of the book trade and the need for paid copyists. Augustine never had Libanius' luck, a rich friend who sent him a whole cartload of books just as his public career was beginning.[8]

Nonetheless, so many things, Augustine considers with hindsight, were being done on our behalf 'by divine power'. Why do we not abandon 'worldly ambition' and wholeheartedly seek the 'happy life'? But, then, he reminds us, brilliantly: 'wait . . . those things are pleasant too . . .' It is a 'great thing' if 'some honour is granted on request', a post, perhaps, in the Imperial service. There are those 'greater friends', and even a provincial governorship, albeit a lowly one in the ranking, might be given in due course. In the mid-380s, a minor provincial governorship was not an unrealistic hope for a professor of rhetoric, trained on the classics.[9] There was, however, something else. 'A wife must be married', one with 'some money of her own' so that she will not 'weigh down' Augustine's expenses. That much will be 'the limit of our desires'. Many great men, 'most worthy of imitation', he recalls, had been devoted to the study of wisdom even when they had a wife.

The pros and cons of marriage are an eternal topic and even Libanius, who was briefly betrothed, uses them as a rhetorical exercise, or 'preliminary', for public speakers. He found plenty to say in marriage's favour. The gods, after all, had married; children are a blessing to cities; a wife is a steadfast asset in times of sickness when she is 'adamantine' in her resolve, Libanius claims, and is up to every task, 'weeping, trembling, running around, beseeching the doctors, praying to the gods to divert the evil away from her cohabiting husband and onto herself'. A wife must be self-controlled, a virgin, of course, before marriage and ever-faithful. Fear of a wife's adultery, he argues, is not a valid counter-argument against marrying in the first place.[10] It was fun for Libanius to rehearse this sort of case as a test of his literary skill, deploying conventional points in the rhetorical tradition, but for most of his life he lived only with a servile concubine, the woman whom he prized for coming to him whenever he shouted out.

After his own three-year visit to Constantinople, Synesius, also aged about thirty-two, was to marry and continue to profess a supreme love for philosophy. Beside Augustine, meanwhile, Alypius was taking the opposite view. A wife, he argued, would be an obstacle to the leisure which was needed for the pursuit of wisdom. He himself was still having nothing more to do with sex. Augustine, however, was working on his younger friend's reluctance. He cited the example of philosophers who had also been married: they were a stock item in debates on marriage's pros and cons. Perhaps Augustine did not know that the philosopher Theophrastus and others, including Seneca, had written the opposite, that marriage was not at all fit for a wise man. Importantly, his discussion of the question was so far being driven by philosophical, not scriptural, concerns.[11]

More immediately, Augustine dwells on the pleasures which he could not possibly give up: without sex, he would view his life as a 'punishment'. What motivated him, he admits, were 'insatiable lust' and the delights of his sexual 'habit'. In due course, even Alypius became curious to have another try at what Augustine was plainly enjoying so intensely. Neither he nor Augustine, they admitted, cared much about having children, but nonetheless, Augustine claims, Alypius began to 'long for marriage too'. Augustine even says that if the 'honourable name of marriage' had been added to his continuing sexual pleasure, Alypius would have been 'obliged' to understand why he could not abandon his copulating way of life.[12]

The 'honourable name of marriage' reminds us that Augustine was still enjoying a concubine, but that concubinage, in some people's eyes, was not entirely reputable. In early summer 386, Augustine's years in marital limbo began to be brought to a close. As on other delicate topics, he recalls the change with verbs in the passive voice, but he does not entirely conceal his own agency. 'I began to seek a wife,' he writes, and requests for guidance were 'mine'.[13] The course which Monnica had set in his youth was now reaching its conclusion. He had risen up the social ladder; he could probably acquire a lucrative minor governorship with the help of a 'greater friend'; he could at last consolidate his social gain by marrying a woman of much higher status than any of the small-town girls of Thagaste. Once married, he would put behind him promiscuous pre-marital sex. He could then be baptized, and wipe out his past sins, the end to which Monnica had been weeping, praying and devoting her attention.

Augustine does not say that it was Monnica who pushed him into marriage or singlehandedly found him a suitable bride. Naturally, she would encourage what had long been her aim, but Augustine was independently keen to be married, as he himself tells us. He was sufficiently keen to ask his mother to pray daily to God for a vision concerning the outcome. Again, God's 'providence' was assumed by them both to be active in such matters: pagan Libanius, favoured by dreams of the gods, would have assumed much the same. However, Monnica received no clear vision on the matter. She saw only 'vain imaginings', which were of no help. Nonetheless, plans were 'pressed on' and a 'girl was sought'. Augustine was aged thirty and no longer in a father's legal power. His mother, therefore, had no formal right to find him a bride, but as the finding would involve dealings with a girl and her mother, she still had a useful role to play.[14] From Virgil's *Aeneid*, Augustine could have recalled the virgin Camilla for whom, as a potential daughter-in-law, 'many mothers' throughout Etruria yearned. Camilla, so keen on hunting, remained 'content with Diana alone', words which are perhaps not Virgil's most plausible long-term prophecy.[15]

A girl was duly found, not necessarily from the families of Monnica's group of church widows. She had money, and was perhaps more likely to have been found through Augustine's contacts with 'greater friends'. She was 'promised', but a delay of nearly two years was agreed, the legal maximum during which a betrothal could remain valid.[16] The girl was still under-age, needing the two-year delay to be capable of reproduction. She was probably only ten or eleven years old. 'Because she was pleasing she was being waited for . . .,' Augustine recalls again in the evasive passive voice.

While he waited, he had to sort out his existing life. His one-and-only 'partner' of the past thirteen years, the mother of dear Adeodatus, had to be sent away. It was not that a civic professor of rhetoric could not decently live with a 'concubine': in Antioch, Libanius kept one for many years, the mother of his son. However, Augustine's was of too lowly a status to be married to him in his present eminence. We do not know how lowly she actually was (Libanius' concubine was of servile birth), but she was well below the rank and fortune of Augustine's newly found child-fiancée. Even twelve years later, Augustine's language is eloquent about his intense feelings for the sitting tenant. She was 'torn from his side', he recalls (some readers see here an allusion to Eve, torn from Adam as a spare rib, but Augustine is not explicit).[17] His heart was 'cut to pieces', he recalls, and 'bleeding', and the 'wound' festered. It was worse for the woman. She returned, alone, to Africa, vowing she would never have sex with a man again. Perhaps we can conclude, without Augustine saying so, that she returned to her own family. Nonetheless, she left her son, Adeodatus, behind. It was unusual for a father to retain his illegitimate son, but the fourteen-year-old Adeodatus was clever, Augustine's prospects were much brighter and Monnica was there to help with him: evidently, Augustine's future parents-in-law had accepted the boy's existence. Meanwhile, his bereaved partner left for a life of chastity, anticipating the decision which Augustine himself would eventually make. As she made it quietly, and never wrote her confessions, her momentous choice remains the less famous of the two.

Augustine never names her. He does not even use the blunt word 'concubine'. He refers to her awkwardly as the 'one with whom I was accustomed to go to bed'. Even with the hindsight of a celibate

Christian bishop, this strategic rupture did not seem his finest hour. Monnica would have approved the breach, but nothing is said about her initiating it. Augustine was surely a prime mover.

Meanwhile, Augustine and his friends resolved, magnificently, on a different escape from their vexing way of life. They would withdraw and live in a commune. About ten of them would go, including those mainstays of such communes, people able to pay for the venture, especially the willing Romanianus. If he won his lawsuit, he had even told Augustine he would give him half his fortune for the pursuit of philosophy. They would live in one household and have all things in common. Two 'magistrates' would be chosen yearly to run the essentials, and the other members would be left in peace. The origins of this idea were not Christian. Patently, it was modelled on the reported practice of Pythagoras, the pagan philosopher whose wisdom the young Augustine had already incorporated into his first book, *On the Beautiful and Apt*.[18] Pythagoras had remained Augustine's ideal type of a sage, known to him at second hand through Varro's writings.

At the time, Romanianus amazed his fellow drop-outs in waiting. In a 'sudden thunderclap', he announced that he would give up sex and live as a celibate, the ideal of a Pythagorean but also of the Manichaean Elect, to whose sect he still inclined.[19] The announcement came to nothing, but the topic went to the root of the entire communal plan. Some of the participants were married, Verecundus the teacher being one, and others, like Augustine, were about to be so. Would their wives, the 'little women' (*mulierculae*), put up with the plan or not? The answer was 'no', so the plan collapsed, shipwrecked on feminine resistance.

Augustine was not the only self-taught enthusiast for philosophy in the group. Unlike Synesius and his friends, nobody in this potential commune had ever studied the subject in a school or with a professor. Nonetheless, they were ranking it above all the demands and prospects of their everyday lives. Augustine, Nebridius and Alypius were even disputing about the 'ends' of good and evil, a question which shows that they had been reading Cicero's long philosophical text on this very subject (his *De Finibus*).[20] Of the various philosophers' 'ends', Augustine's vote would have gone at this time to Epicurus' proposal, he tells us, if only Epicurus had believed in the immortality of the soul. Suppose, Augustine asked, in an Epicurean way, we could live in 'perpetual pleasure of the body' without any fear of loss: why would we not be happy? What else would we ever seek? The only brake on his hedonism, he recalls, was his abiding fear of death and God's judgement, topics which his years as a Manichaean had done nothing to dim. Otherwise, he tells us, he would not have held back from an 'even deeper whirlpool of carnal pleasures': one wonders what he would have tried.

Fearful or not, he was not faring too badly in that whirlpool already. While he waited for his underage fiancée to mature and marry him, he promptly replaced his former concubine with another. She was taken to fill the two-year gap, another girl 'with whom I was accustomed to go to bed'.

16
Greater Friends

I

At one level, at least, the way forward was now clear. After a delay of nearly two years, Augustine's marriage would be finalized and his religious status rounded off: he would be taken forward at last for baptism. The plan which Monnica had laid in his youth would be fulfilled. Augustine would emerge from the baptismal pool, a full and faithful Christian, in time for Easter, 387. Indeed he emerged then, but much which Monnica never expected was to happen meanwhile. Important though these happenings were to be, they were not to be the sudden making of a new Christian convert. If Augustine's restless mind had gone quiet between May 385 and April 387, if he had avoided reading new books and had never taken new conversations to heart, he would have been baptized anyway. His conversion was to address quite other problems.

His circumstances gain from a comparison, once again, with those of Tolstoy, centuries later. In his *Confession*, Tolstoy also recalls his utter disillusionment with his career, in his case the writings which have made him immortal. 'I considered writing to be nonsense, but I still went on writing', for money and fame and in order to suppress any troubling questions about the 'meaning of life'. Just as Augustine felt that he was 'selling lies for a living', Tolstoy felt that he was teaching 'without knowing what'. Just as Augustine was discussing the 'end' for which life is lived, Tolstoy was asking himself, 'why should I wish for anything, why should I do anything?' Both were aware that life is short and death inevitable, but Augustine held resolutely to the philosophers' ideal, the 'happy life', whereas Tolstoy ceased to believe that life could ever be 'happy' at all. He engaged in wide reading in his search for an answer, looking for 'mathematical certainty', just what Augustine had been looking for in his sceptical phase in Milan. He had the sense of being lost in a dark forest, just as Augustine felt that he was bobbing up and down in a sea of uncertainty. Tolstoy concluded from his reading that 'Happy is he who was not born; death is better than life: one needs to be rid of life.'[1] Never for one moment did Augustine consider killing himself.

At the time, he was thirty, a young man (*iuvenis*) and no longer a 'youth' (*adulescentulus*). The spiritual crises which follow are not crises of adolescence. Nor was he in a vacuum, doubting everything. He was 'certain' of Christ's existence. He was certain that God is 'unchanging'. This opinion had a long history in Greek philosophy but is best known to us from a fine discussion in Plato's *Republic*: Augustine had probably found the idea in one of his books of 'many things of the philosophers' and discussed it with Nebridius and others.[2] He was 'certain' that God is 'incorruptible': this view indeed came from Nebridius, who had advanced it forcefully against Mani's Gospel in Carthage. It was also stated in words by Paul which Augustine had probably known as a Manichaean 'Hearer'. He was 'certain' about the authority of the scriptures, which were supported, as he had learned through Ambrose, by the authority of the 'Universal' Church. He was 'most certain', now, that the Manichaeans were wrong. He was sure that God's judgement would occur after death. He was also sure that the scriptures, if understood, could save him from its punishments. He was as sure as ever that God was not shaped like a man, and he was 'gladdened' to have discovered that the Universal Church did not think so, either.[3]

He was not having a crisis of faith: he was having a crisis of understanding. His abandonment of Manichaeism had left him with the two big questions which it had claimed to answer. One was the nature of God. The other was the bluntly worded question which Manichaeans put to potential converts: the origin of evil. In the wake of his Manichaeism, his confessions describe brilliantly how vain 'imaginings' were still fluttering round him and obscuring his sight. He tried to drive them away with a single 'swipe', he tells us, but then they returned, like a cloud of mosquitoes, to block his view all over again. They were a 'crowd of uncleanliness', words which one of his modern scholars has traced to Virgil's words for the foul Harpies who prey on animal sacrifices in the *Aeneid*, Book 3.[4]

The problem was that Augustine still thought of God only in material terms. He looked on the world of objects, he tells us, and reasoned from what he could see to what he could not. He could imagine a sort of infinite space outside the world but not a space which was void. Augustine was using his mental power of imagining in images, but he still thought of this mental power as material.[5] Meanwhile, as a thought-experiment, he tried to compress the world and its contents into a globe in his mind's eye and imagine it surrounded by boundless space. God somehow permeated through it all, he imagined, like sea-water through a sponge or sunlight through the atmosphere.[6] This sort of pantheism is associated with the Stoics, but Augustine had heard something similar from the governor, Vindicianus, in Carthage. He may have enlarged Vindicianus' view on his own initiative. He then realized that it had a flaw. The bigger the body or object, the bigger would be the amount of God in it: there would be more God in an elephant than in a sparrow. So, the 'vain imaginings' continued to impede his sight.

The problem of evil, meanwhile, was beginning to be more tractable. He was absolutely certain that the Manichaeans were wrong to think of it as a substance from the Kingdom of Darkness, but, if not, where did it come from? He was 'hearing', surely in Ambrose's sermons, about the free choice of the will. Once again, Ambrose's published work *On the Six Days of Creation* (in my view, preached in April 387) has a striking statement of this point, the sort of argument, we may assume, which the bishop would have used in earlier sermons between summer 385 and spring 386. The 'choice' of evil, he preaches, 'which we are able not to do, if we wish not to, we must ascribe to ourselves rather than to others'. Ambrose even emphasized this point explicitly in opposition to the 'deadly Manichaean plague'.[7] Augustine now realized that it was he himself who chose to sin, not a force inside him which 'prevailed' rather than 'chose'. It was a complete change from Mani's views about human beings. It led him to a sense of having a sinful self, one which persists in a sinner's memory as part of his enduring identity. That sense is crucial to the *Confessions*.

What troubled Augustine, rather, was the evil which he did not wish to do: involuntary evil. Thanks to Nebridius and his conversations, Augustine was certain that God must be 'incorruptible' and superior, therefore, to corruption and the corruptible. So where does involuntary evil come from? If God is absolutely good and unchanging, how can it come from Him? Does it come from the Devil and his evil will, but, if so, why did a good God create a will which was evil? Augustine says that he began to ponder this question when 'carefree', but he describes it as soon causing 'turmoil' for him. He was inclined to explain involuntary evil-doing as a punishment from God, a 'just' one but, often, an inscrutable one. As a boy, surely, he had had the justice and judgement of God instilled into him in general terms by his mother. In Cicero's *Hortensius*, he then read, and perhaps remembered, the view of 'some' that the soul is being punished in this life for wrongs in a previous existence.[8] He does not, however, ascribe to himself in Milan any consideration of Adam's 'original sin' or its heritage.

Meanwhile, one explanation of the problem collapsed for him: he ceased to believe in astrology. His friend Nebridius had never credited it, but even in Milan Augustine had continued to consult texts and charts and give answers on demand. Another friend, Firminus, now approached him with a question about his worldly ambitions.[9] Firminus had been well educated, Augustine notes with his usual care, and spoke with refined eloquence, a proper gentleman. Before consulting the texts for him, Augustine commented that he was no longer sure if astrological theories were true: Firminus tried to reassure him. His father, he said, and a neighbouring friend had been passionately interested in the subject. They would observe the exact timing of the births of the animals in their keeping and then interpret them by astrological charts. Even the prenatal Firminus had been put under astral observation. When his mother was pregnant with him, a slave girl in the friend's household was pregnant too: her master knew it, Augustine says, just as he knew the canine pregnancies of the bitches in his household. Messengers had announced the exact moment of the two babies' births, and they coincided. Firminus then grew up to a gentleman's life, whereas the slave's child remained in slavery.

Firminus had never thought this story through, but Augustine took it as a challenge, not a reassurance. If astrology was true, why had two simultaneous babies had such different futures? Greek experts could have answered him: even a few seconds of time, they claimed, make all the difference, and the horoscopes of the parents at conception are influential.[10] Perhaps the latter was the point which Firminus meant to make. However, Augustine went on to consider the problem of twins: why do two babies, born to exactly the same parents in quick succession, go on to very different lives? Whereas Vindicianus in Carthage had tried to dissuade him from astrology, but left him convinced of it, Firminus in Milan tried to reassure him, but left him disbelieving. Once again, words worked in a way which was unintended by their speaker, but was shaped by their hearer's predisposition.

Now that the power of the stars no longer explained involuntary evil, Augustine was indeed in turmoil, wondering what did. He was bobbing up and down, he tells us, 'up' when he dwelt on God as good and incorruptible and in no way the source of evil, but pushed 'down' when he was overwhelmed by material, bodily images. All the while, 'God was inside while I was looking outside', words which will only become clearer in the sequel. 'What torments those were in my heart as it began to give birth and what groans, my God!' Augustine felt very agitated, but he was not moaning out loud. He was having 'tumults of the soul' which were heard by God alone. His false imaginings 'bit' his face, he tells us, like insects: they caused swellings which stopped him seeing clearly.[11]

While the *Confessions* vividly trace these efforts at understanding, Augustine passes over the external events of an entire year, from early summer 385 to early summer 386. As ever, his confessional prayer is not concerned with a full autobiography. In the mornings, nonetheless, he was continuing to teach rhetoric and in the afternoons to attend on those 'greater friends' in hope of their favours. It is to them that the next stage in his progress can be traced.

Milan's high society was one of military men and courtiers on the make, people who were thrown together for worldly reasons. As they had come from varied backgrounds, there was scope for them to have brought less predictable interests with them. In Carthage and Rome, Augustine had never met fellow 'lovers of wisdom', or philosophers, except for the few contemporaries whose interest in the subject he himself fostered. In Milan, he now hit on individuals with pre-existing philosophic interests of their own. We can recover three of them from the texts and letters which he soon dedicated to them: Zenobius, Hermogenianus and Theodorus, all of whose names had Greek roots, implying that they may have known Greek better than Augustine. Zenobius 'often' discussed with him the question of the 'order' in the universe. He even wrote a poem on the subject and urged Augustine, who heard it, to explore the topic more fully. Such 'order' was to become central to Augustine's thinking and would be upheld in the *Confessions* from his first analysis of his infancy onwards. Zenobius also rallied to the idea that worldly, perceptible concerns are fleeting and that our minds must aspire 'utterly' to an unchanging, higher realm. By November 386, he was known to be writing a poem which would eliminate the 'fear of death'. It was about the immortality of the soul.[12]

These interests show that Zenobius was an admiring student of Platonist philosophy, someone whom Synesius, his young contemporary, would have been thrilled to discover as a like-minded friend. Hermogenianus, it seems, was another, the man to whom Augustine would soon send the text in which he first refuted scepticism. Hermogenianus' quick letter of acknowledgement missed one of its main points. In reply, Augustine urged Hermogenianus to look more closely at his tentative account of the 'sceptical' Academy's history and comment on it. This request implies that Hermogenianus was a Platonist too, someone interested, therefore, in the Academy's succession of teaching.[13]

Of the three, the best known is Mallius Theodorus. He was a recipient of letters from Symmachus, no less, and, thirteen years later, of a long poem by the court poet Claudian which honoured him as the year's new consul. Theodorus was certainly 'learned', just as Augustine recalls. He wrote a book on Latin verse metre which still survives. He knew Greek, wrote on early Greek philosophers and their differing views of the universe, and discussed later Greek philosophers, probably in a book of 'many things of the philosophers', which he perhaps translated from a Greek source. He also wrote on ethics, on the 'end' at which life should aim and the 'rule' of what is good. Like Cicero, he cast the 'obscure skills of the Greeks' into eloquent Latin and presented them in dialogue form. He even pursued questions of astronomy and the nature of the world. Augustine remarks that 'sometimes' he had listened to Theodorus affirming that neither God nor the soul must in any way be thought of in bodily terms: the soul is 'closest' to God. It was a view which Augustine had also picked up from Ambrose's sermons. By autumn 386, Theodorus was undertaking a prose work on an even more difficult question, how souls come to be in bodies, whether by necessity, by God or by nature.[14] Once again, these questions were Platonist questions. As Augustine was soon to discover, Theodorus was 'most studious' of writings by Plotinus, the recent, and greatest, Platonist. Augustine recalls a certain Celsinus saying that Plotinus' books were 'full', or fertile. On one attractive theory, this Celsinus was another contemporary in Milan, a 'fourth man' with Platonist interests.[15]

Zenobius wrote poetry and Theodorus wrote on metre: there is now another witness to their interests, our most recently rediscovered Latin poem. It is more than eighty lines long and addresses the sort of person who denies that the world and its contents are by nature good: Manichaeans would be prime examples. It dwells on the world's four constituent 'elements', fire, water, earth and air, and their 'discordant concord' in a good and coherent whole. Ultimately, the idea of these elements and their unity in opposition goes back to the early Greek philosopher Empedocles. An interest in the elements, in Empedocles and his idea of unified 'opposites' is credited exactly to Mallius Theodorus by Claudian's poem in his honour.[16] This rediscovered Latin poem is a rare tour de force, as it is composed in a complex metre which is unparalleled in later Latin. Theodorus, we recall, wrote a book on Latin metre and is praised by Augustine for reviving the highest standards of literary style and eloquence. In Ambrose's sermon *On the Six Days of Creation*, the world's 'discordant concord' is cited precisely against people who deny the world is for the best.[17] The newly found poem states the same. Its theme and form well fit the milieu of Milan in the mid-380s: it is, I believe, a poem by Theodorus himself. If so, Augustine received a copy from him and kept it, like other bits and pieces, in a bundle of unpublished notes which was later preserved among his own writings.

Augustine professes bonds of friendship with these people, but expresses them in ways which show he is desperate to impress. Zenobius may perhaps be the Zenobius who would later rise high in the emperor's service, the brother of a learned young man whom Augustine would answer, years later, in an important letter about the history of philosophy. Hermogenianus has been linked, albeit uncertainly, to major persons of that name in the orbit of a very grand family indeed, Rome's Anicii. If Celsinus is one of this milieu too, there are bearers of the name Celsinus in Roman high society (including Symmachus' brother), although a firm identification is impossible.[18]

Theodorus' profile, at least, is known. He had strong local connections with the region of Milan. He had been born to a relatively modest family but had risen far up the ladder of rank and position. He held a minor governorship in north Africa, then another in Macedon (by the 'walls of Pella', among memories of Alexander the Great) and then the most important of the Western governorships, the one based on Gaul. In autumn 383, Maximus' usurpation was presumably the reason why Theodorus' career had halted. Like Cicero, he was living in hope, but in enforced retirement, and meanwhile was writing Latin verses and philosophy and spending days in a rural villa, in his case outside Milan.[19]

Nowhere else in the Latin West of the 380s can such a cluster of people with Platonist interests be identified. In the Greek East, young Synesius' experiences help to put them in context. Some thirteen years later, during tedious years of attending Constantinople's court, he too made literary and philosophical friends. As in Milan, people of varied backgrounds had congregated there. He refers to their meetings as a

'Panhellenion', giving them the name of the famous civic grouping which Hadrian had instituted at Athens three centuries earlier and to which Synesius' Cyrene had once belonged.[20] This 'Panhellenion' was not a formally recognized group, no more than was Augustine's 'Milan circle'. Rather, it was a range of friends who met and discussed poetry and literature, including older, classic texts. Synesius refers to some of them as 'philosophers', although their literary interests are the ones which are more evident to us. Perhaps, like Zenobius in Milan, some of them wrote poems on philosophic subjects, and certainly 'philosopher' was a name they liked to be given. Their equivalent to Mallius Theodorus was the elderly Marcian. Like Theodorus, he was the ex-governor of a province; he was praised for his divine eloquence and for being a student of older texts, a 'philosopher'. He presided over the friends' meetings just as Theodorus presided over those in Milan.[21] The philosophy of these 'Panhellenes' need not have been deep, but Synesius was familiar with Platonism by the time he visited the court and so he compliments them with Platonist phrases. He would no doubt read to them his own Christian philosophic poems. One of these friends, Simplicius, was a very highly placed military official, but several years later he was still asking to be sent Synesius' poems, probably his philosophic hymns.[22]

Synesius' relations with this group differed crucially from Augustine's with his 'friends'. Synesius had come to the court as a well-born aristocrat from a long-famous Greek city: his noble standing was one reason why it had sent him as an ambassador. He could easily pay for the costs of a long stay abroad. He could offer 'gifts' or bribes, to win people of importance: his silver 'planisphere' was one such 'gift'.[23] He was in the capital for a communal purpose, not simply as a young man who was hoping to make a career: he had been sent to plead for a change in his city's taxation. Beyond his 'Panhellenion' of like-minded friends, there were even grander and more powerful court figures, and, like Augustine, Synesius was well aware of that fact. His network of friends could be used to pass his letters on up to them. Like Augustine, he would eventually have the chance to speak in the highest company, the emperor himself. He was not being paid for the speech, but he wanted to impress, for the sake of his embassy and city. He delivered a complex, ingenious attack on enemies at court, composing it in a form which Augustine had met in Milan: an allegory, not from scripture, but from ancient 'Egyptian' myth.[24]

Synesius' Panhellenion of friends was probably a group of Christians like himself. Thirteen years earlier, in Milan, Augustine's 'greater friends' were more disparate. Nothing which Augustine says about Zenobius or Hermogenianus requires them to have been Christians, although Zenobius, he tells us, was someone unconquered by lust and polluting desire: evidently, he was celibate, albeit (probably) a pagan. A fourth 'friend', perhaps Celsinus, was pagan too. Only Theodorus was a Christian, but probably not yet a baptized 'faithful' one. His sister Daedalia, however, was a committed Christian virgin. When she died, Theodorus would compose an epitaph for her in the cemetery of Ambrose's newly built church: she was buried in honour beside Milan's long-dead martyrs. Theodorus praised her as 'mother of those in need', a tribute to her recognized charity, and his poem expressed themes associated with Platonists: Daedalia's soul, it said, had constantly aspired to 'return' to its origin in heaven.[25]

As her eminent resting-place shows, charitable Daedalia and her family would have been well known to Ambrose. In general, Ambrose shared the Apostle Paul's low opinion of the 'foolish philosophy' of this world, but there was one exception: Platonism, with its unworldly emphasis. In a series of brilliant studies, the late Pierre Courcelle showed that phrases adapted and culled from the Platonist Plotinus are present in surviving texts of several of Ambrose's sermons, those datable, probably, between 386 and 387.[26] Whether or not Ambrose ever read Plotinus directly, these statements relate him to the Platonist milieu which is traceable among Augustine's new 'friends'. Ambrose also lived beside a human link with Platonist teaching. His instructor before baptism had been an older priest, Simplicianus, who had come to Milan from Rome. There, he had been a friend of the learned Victorinus, the man who first translated Plotinus into Latin. Simplicianus, Ambrose writes, was a man who read widely every day and who considered 'intelligible things' with his 'sharp mind': 'intelligible things' were a Platonist concern, and so Simplicianus, too, had an interest in this sort of philosophy.

Bishop Ambrose and his priest thus seemed, to Courcelle, to emerge as important forces in Augustine's own imminent fascination with Plotinus' Platonism. There might have been a study group, he suggested, or even, as others later suggested, a 'Milan circle', meeting under Simplicianus' guidance and trying to construct a 'synthesis' between Platonist philosophy and Christianity: if so, Augustine's intellectual progress could be linked even more closely to the 'Catholic' Church.[27] However, Augustine is clear that he never spoke to Simplicianus at all until summer 386: by then, he had encountered Plotinus' books independently. Of his newly found friends, only one, Theodorus, was certainly a Christian, and he and the others were not meeting in a circle under Christian guidance. Away from the church, Theodorus presided over a much more traditional setting for discussions of philosophy among friends: dinner parties. In November 386, Augustine compliments Theodorus as the example to himself of how to host a strictly mannered dinner.[28] In the afternoons, while Augustine attended the houses of individual 'friends', there may have been individual conversations with them, but the focal point, as ever, for an exchange of views was a patron's dining-room. Augustine would have felt honoured to be invited by the great Theodorus. Perhaps some of the others first met him as a guest there. If so, they realized his intelligence and then sent him texts by themselves and others in order to feed his interest and impress him.

Ambrose was not a guest at these parties, but he was aware of Theodorus' interests, not least through Theodorus' sister Daedalia. His own use of Platonist phrases had other sources besides Plotinus: he also read Greek Christian texts in which Plotinus' words had already been subtly Christianized.[29] By contrast, Theodorus and the other contemporary laymen cited Platonists as their actual sources and took up Platonist questions explicitly. If Augustine detected any unattributed hints of Platonism in Ambrose's church sermons, it was only because Theodorus and his friends' table-talk enabled him to recognize them. The 'happy life', the 'order' of the universe, the nature and immortality of the soul were their intellectual concerns. A 'wisdom-agenda' had already formed for him, and in the Latin West in the mid-380s it could only have formed in the setting of Milan.

II

In these very months, Ambrose had even less time than usual for questions of other-worldly philosophy. At Easter, 385, he had denied the Homoeans, or Similar Party, at court the use of a basilica for their church service. His denial had not ended the problem. In January 386, a law was issued guaranteeing free rights of assembly to those who followed the Christian faith as approved at the Councils of Rimini (359) and Constantinople (360). These approved 'followers' included all those whom Ambrose and his fellow Christians in north Italy dismissed as heretical 'Arians'. Any 'turbulent opposition', the law also proclaimed, from Christians who claimed a freedom of assembly exclusively for themselves would be treasonable and punished with death. Ambrose, implicitly, was a turbulent priest. The law had him in mind and was plainly the result of pressure from Auxentius, the Homoeans' leader in Milan, and the boy-emperor Valentinian's like-minded mother, Justine. Ambrose was soon to call her 'that woman' and denounce her as a new Jezebel.[30]

In the 380s the public church-going of an emperor still centred on special occasions, especially Easter.[31] The law would thus become crucial as Lent ended. In the *Confessions*, Augustine says nothing at first about the momentous events which were to follow. He had stood to one side of them, and they were as irrelevant as a workers' strike to the theme of his confessional prayer, his progress to knowledge of God. Only two books later in the *Confessions* do the events of 386 return to his mind, and then only in connection with his mother, Monnica. She had been present at the main storm centre, which he presents, plausibly, as a persecution of Ambrose by Justine 'in favour of her heresy'. For more detail, we can turn to three great contemporary survivors: the sermon which Ambrose preached 'against Auxentius', a letter he sent to the young Emperor Valentinian II and another letter which he sent to his virgin sister Marcellina describing the days of conflict.[32] She was in Rome at the time and was the first recipient, although a female, of the news outside Milan.

The timing and sequence of these letters and the topography of events in Milan have remained a challenge to scholars, but, in my view, all three texts belong between Palm Sunday and Easter Saturday, 386. Until then, the impact of the law is obscure to us. As Lent ended, the emperor's court, as before, would claim to use the Basilica-by-the-Gate, the 'Portiana' church, which perhaps stood on the site of modern San Lorenzo. In late March, a few soldiers were deputed to guard it, but Ambrose's congregation continued to meet inside it for services. To sustain his congregation's morale and counteract any 'despair' and boredom, Ambrose introduced the singing in unison of psalms and hymns. It was a novelty for his congregation. Augustine recalls its fine impact and its role in passing the 'tedious' time during the congregation's long occupations of the church building. He was not there himself, but his mother, Monnica, was inside, singing heartily with the rest of Ambrose's congregation. The unified singing may have begun only shortly before Holy Week, 386: Augustine considers it to be an introduction from the East.[33]

On 27 March, the Friday before Palm Sunday, 'illustrious' members of the emperor's court raised the stakes: they demanded use of the big 'new' basilica in the central city as well as the Portiana, the Basilica-by-the-Gate. Soldiers were sent for a vigil in order to make the point clear. On the next, day Ambrose's congregation rejected this demand by uttering concerted shouts, cast as 'acclamations', or organized chants, at which fourth-century crowds were well practised. The praetorian prefect then came back with a revised demand: 'at least the Portiana'.[34]

On Palm Sunday, Ambrose preached the remarkable sermon whose text we still have. In it he insisted, 'the poor of Christ are my riches', whereas 'the emperor is within, and not above, the Church'. He shaped his speech round the chants and acclamations with which he expected his hearers to support it. Examples from scripture dramatized his predicament: he compared himself with Job and alluded to Naboth's loss of his vineyard. He also alluded to Peter's martyrdom, known from the 'Quo vadis?' story in Rome. Throughout, he drew on the famous fourth speech against Catiline which Cicero had composed as if for delivery to the Roman plebs. Whereas Cicero's speech had been a literary invention after the event, Ambrose's sermon was delivered 'live'. Inside the big basilica, Ambrose assured his congregation that they were not alone and unnoticed in their struggle. Like Elisha before the Syrian army, they were being attended by hordes of angels, summoned by their prayers. 'Those we cannot see do more to protect the servants of Christ than those we can see': an invisible presence hovered in church above Monnica and her fellow Christians.[35]

Down in the Portiana, meanwhile, hangings had been brought in to decorate the church for the court's imminent use. There was a violent encounter on the way to the church, which Ambrose tried to check, and throughout the Sunday night before Holy Week his congregation stayed put, 'under siege' in the (big) basilica. On the Monday, big fines, payable in gold, were announced to have been imposed on the companies of traders in the city, people who were believed to be largely on Ambrose's side. A few of them were even arrested in advance of payment. Palace staff were forbidden to go over to Ambrose, and senior figures repeated the demand for use of the Portiana.[36]

The fines, the arrests, the sit-ins and the increasing presence of soldiers mean that Augustine cannot possibly have missed this drama in the heart of the city. Ambrose then sent a cool letter to the emperor, refusing, as before, to appear in a hearing with the 'Arian' bishop,

Auxentius: he also refused the alternative offer, to leave the city. Wednesday, 1 April, was to prove momentous. By early morning, one of the basilicas, probably the big 'new' one, began to be occupied by the soldiers who had been surrounding it. On hearing that Ambrose had denied them the eucharist, some of them defected nonetheless to Ambrose's congregation, which had gathered across the way in the smaller 'old' basilica. They were greeted there with glee, and so was a message which had been sent by Christian supporters, asking Ambrose to come down to the Portiana. Ambrose began to preach on the scriptural reading for the day, verses from the Book of Job. Again, he identified his trials with Job's, insisting that 'trials and temptations from women are particularly severe'.[37] News then came that envoys had come to take down the Imperial hangings in the Portiana and fold them away. It was an implicit admission of defeat, and Ambrose sent clerics down to the Portiana to follow up. That night, the Imperial hangings were torn, supposedly by 'children at play'.[38]

Repeatedly, during these and other encounters, Augustine could have joined his mother in Ambrose's congregation. He did not do so, and one of the reasons may be that the struggle was a struggle with the court, the major customer for his public rhetoric. Still an unbaptized Christian, Augustine decided to avoid the troubles. The praetorian prefect who had tried to win over Ambrose had recently been the governor of north Africa, and if Augustine cared for such personal ties, they may have pulled him in the prefect's direction.[39] On Thursday, 2 April, Ambrose was vindicated. When he had just preached a sermon on Jonah, news came that the emperor had ordered his soldiers to withdraw and the merchants' fines to be repaid. 'Imagine the happiness of all the congregation at this moment,' Ambrose wrote, 'the cheers of all the people, the thanksgiving!' Within days, the court had withdrawn briefly from Milan, but not before the chief eunuch in the Imperial household had threatened Ambrose: 'do you treat Valentinian with contempt while I am above ground? I will have your head.' Undaunted, Ambrose replied, 'I will suffer as befits a bishop, you will behave as befits a eunuch.'[40]

The immediate sequel to Ambrose's victory is not known to us. At least we know that he did not drop the link between himself and real martyrs: he preached on the heroism of the Maccabees, brave martyrs in scripture. In June, this link between himself and martyrs was exploited again, before the dedication of his newly finished church, the modern San Ambrogio. His congregation urged him, again by acclamations, to 'consecrate it as you consecrated the church [of St Nazaro]'. 'I will,' replied Ambrose, 'if I find relics of martyrs.' At once, he writes, I 'felt a thrill, as if of foresight', and in a remarkable episode he carried out a hunt for the remains which he required.[41]

For once, a 'cult of the saints' survives as described by its inaugurator in words which he wrote very soon after the event: we have the very letter which Ambrose promptly sent to his virginal sister in Rome. The 'hunt' for the martyrs is also embedded in one of his hymns, in carefully chosen words which keep the excitement of the discovery alive. They, too, were written in its immediate aftermath.[42]

Ambrose admits that 'even his clergy were anxious' about his initiative. Determined on a 'find', he chose to dig in front of the very altar which honoured two known martyrs, the two saints whose memorial shrine stood in his new church's adjoining cemetery. It was a near-certain 'find', and indeed 'two men of amazing stature, such as were brought forth in the old days, were discovered', the bones intact. These martyrs had already made their power felt by causing a possessed woman to be thrown down beside their burial place. Crowds gathered and the bones were found 'arranged in order, the heads torn from the shoulders'. There was even, Ambrose insisted, an 'abundance of blood'. Whoever were they? No text explained, but old men usefully recalled hearing these martyrs' names in the past and reading stones on which their names had been inscribed. They were Gervase and Protasius, they said, as 'demons' then testified during a spate of exorcisms which accompanied the discovery. During these rites, the demons protested that they were being 'tortured' inside the people whom they possessed and that they were being 'forced' to declare the truth. The entire episode was alive with a sense of heavenly powers, the demonic and the saintly in judicial confrontation.[43]

On the following day, the relics of the martyrs were laid carefully on a couch and escorted by crowds to the new basilica. Contact with them caused miraculous healings, culminating in the healing of a beggar, Severus, who had been blind from birth. The two martyrs were then deposed under the new church's altar, where Ambrose himself would one day be deposed too. The 'Arians', naturally, dismissed the entire episode as a fraud and the martyrs as nothing of the sort. In a sermon to refute them, Ambrose was adamant. Even the exorcised demons had testified to the martyrs' identity. They had also insisted that the Holy Spirit was divine, thereby refuting 'Arians', who denied the 'all-encompassing power of the Holy Trinity'. The martyrs,

Ambrose preached, had long been the true Christians' invisible protectors. Now, Christians' eyes were opened: 'we used to have patrons, but we did not know it'.[44]

As Ambrose's contemporary hymn stated bluntly in its very first verse, 'we cannot *be* martyrs; we *find* martyrs'. He means that Justine had denied him martyrdom in April, but now, in June, Gervase and Protasius had emerged to fill the gap.[45] Eight years later, in a 'Jewish cemetery' in Bologna, he was to repeat his martyr-hunting and find yet another long-lost couple, Agricola and Vitalis. Like Damasus in Rome, from whom perhaps he had learned, he was consciously linking the long-buried power of martyr-'patrons' to his own episcopal patronage. In Milan, the discoveries of the martyrs' bodies, the healings and their 'transfer' were a powerful reassertion of the unity and triumph of the 'Catholics' after their beleaguered days at Easter. The martyrs whom Ambrose rediscovered have remained patron saints of Milan and neighbouring churches.[46]

Such clashes with an 'Arian' faction were not confined to Milan. Some fifteen years later, they were to erupt, far more bloodily, in Constantinople in Synesius' presence. Again, a leader's demand for a church in which to celebrate mass was the impulse for a riot and, again, it involved Goths, an 'Arian' element in the city's troops.[47] The result was a massacre, leaving thousands dead, and reminding us of the caution, in fact, which Justine showed in pursuit of her wishes. It was a point which Ambrose could not recognize. In the East, however, his subsequent actions would have been illegal. In February 386, a law had reiterated harsh sanctions against anyone transferring a buried body or breaking up and selling a martyr.[48]

In the *Confessions*, Augustine does not recall the finding of the martyrs while referring to his time in Milan. He recalls it later and does not give every detail correctly, probably because he did not witness them. When found, he claims, the martyrs' bodies were still 'incorrupted after so many years', whereas Ambrose states explicitly that he found the bodies' heads severed. Augustine was indeed caught up by the noise and the shouts of praise, but he did not see the most famous healing, the cure of the beggar Severus, at close quarters.[49] It is not that philosophically minded Christians were always above the lure of 'special effects'. While in Constantinople, the philosophic Synesius attended every martyr shrine on either side of the city, praying, weeping and pleading to their individual martyrs, through their relics, to help his slow-moving embassy on behalf of Cyrene.[50] Similarly, Augustine credits the reports of the martyrs' finding and the resulting 'fervent praises of God' as the reasons why Justine abandoned the 'rage of persecution'.[51] He was over-interpreting their role: she had surely given up the 'rage' since Easter anyway.

The reason why at first Augustine passed over these tumultuous events is that the new-found martyrs did nothing to bring him closer to God. He had had quite other preoccupations. At this very time in Milan a pagan gave him some novel reading: 'books of the Platonists'. As ever, Augustine looks back on this personal encounter as one 'procured' on his behalf by God. By it, his horizons were to be changed for ever. Through these books, he was to make personal contact, not with a long-dead martyr, but with the God he sought.

17
Plato Reborn

I

The 'books of the Platonists' were made available to Augustine by a 'man puffed up with the most enormous pride', a pagan, therefore, not the Christian Mallius Theodorus or anyone in Ambrose's church. This person is the 'fourth man' among Augustine's known philosophic friends in Milan, but Augustine does not name him. The best guess, in my view, is Celsinus, because Augustine writes six months later that 'Celsinus says' the Platonist books are 'full', or, as we might say, 'rich'. Here, Celsinus seems to be a contemporary, known to Romanianus, to whom Augustine is writing, and not an author from the past.[1] As usual, Augustine looks back on this chance encounter as one 'carefully arranged' for him by God. It was to transform his thinking about the nature of God, the nature of evil and the nature of himself. It also touched off something in him which has not always been fully appreciated: mystical experience.

Augustine never tells us which books he read, but within a year he mentions especially 'books of Plotinus', the brilliant Platonist philosopher who had died more than a hundred years earlier. At first, he tells us, he read 'very few'. The *Confessions* allow us to infer that they included Plotinus' text *On Beauty*, his *On the First Good and the Other Goods*, *On What are Evils and Their Origin*, and probably his *On Providence*. After Augustine's first encounter he continued to read more, including *On the Soul* and *On the Presence of Being, One and the Same, Everywhere as a Whole*.[2] Phrases from them became embedded in his mind. They resurface with the Psalms, Paul's letters and the opening chapters of Genesis in the *Confessions*' soaring last three books. While confessing, he did not stop to look them up. They had become woven into his thinking since this first encounter in Milan.

II

Plotinus' life is known through his devoted pupil Porphyry, who wrote admiringly on his master. He was a more recent thinker than Augustine's other formative mentors, Cicero and Varro. He had been born in Egypt in 204 and began to study Greek philosophy at the age of twenty-eight. He continued to do so for many years in Alexandria and, in due course, became 'eager to acquaint himself with the corresponding practices of the Persians and the "way" that was followed in India'. In 243/4, he joined the Roman Emperor Gordian's eastward campaign into Persia, and if it had succeeded, he would have been in the further East during the very years when Mani's Gospel was being carried there. Instead, the campaign came to grief in Mesopotamia (modern Iraq) and Plotinus eventually made his way back to Rome, where he arrived aged forty. He taught and studied in Rome and near Naples for another ten years and began to write philosophy only when he was fifty. 'When he had written something, he could never bear to revise it,' Porphyry recalls: he would not even correct the spelling. Plotinus was always kindly and ready to assist others, but he maintained a strict mental concentration, eating and sleeping very little, until he died in 270, aged sixty-six, after a painful disease with complicating symptoms which suggest facial lymphodoema.[3]

Like Cicero, this remarkable thinker spent his mature philosophical life in the comfortable world of grand Roman houses, especially near the Bay of Naples, where the hearers of his teaching included prominent members of the Roman Senate. Unlike Cicero, he also taught upper-class ladies, including one, perhaps two, of the ladies who were married to Roman emperors of the mid-third century. Once again, through reading, Augustine was leaving behind his modest north African background and sharing discussions set in the grandest Roman society of the past. Unlike Cicero, Plotinus wrote in Greek and used abstract terms which already had a long history. Augustine could read him only in a Latin translation which had been made by the philosophically minded Marius Victorinus as recently as the 350s. It does not survive, but any translation faced difficulties because Plotinus, unlike Cicero, was a profound and independent philosopher. His writings remain extremely difficult, both for their thought and for their compressed style. As Porphyry recalled, Plotinus preferred to think, not write, and even when he was talking in a continuous flow, he was thinking in a focused way.[4]

Thanks to Porphyry's biography of him, we are able to read his surviving texts in a sequence arranged by theme or date of composition. In Milan, Augustine followed no such order. We are aware, as Augustine was not, that Plotinus' views sometimes vary on central questions, whereas Augustine's first reading was not scholarly, in this sense. On a first encounter, Plotinus' writings still baffle newcomers. They seem to rely on unargued postulates and elliptically stated starting points. In fact, they often arise from statements in Plato's classic writings, especially his *Phaedrus*, *Timaeus* and the difficult *Parmenides*, engagement with which is the hallmark of a true 'Neoplatonist' thinker. Augustine had not read much Plato, let alone in Greek, and most of what he knew came from his little book of 'many things of the philosophers', but his reading of Plotinus was to be very acute indeed. Although Plotinus' mind often seems to begin halfway through an argument, it is capable of rigorous reasoning as it excludes alternatives and circles round a central question from different aspects. On the way, Plotinus helps his readers with apt metaphors and analogies, rivalling Plato, their acknowledged master. These analogies refer freely to the gods in Homer, the Greek myths and the imagery of pagan cults and mystery cults. Augustine would at once be aware that he was not reading a Christian text.[5]

Some 600 years after Plato's death, Plotinus thought of himself as Plato's expositor: soon after reading him, Augustine called him 'Plato born again'. It is only we who call him a 'Neoplatonist'. Two bits of Augustine's previous reading would have helped him follow the arguments. Plotinus' views on 'Being' develop the idea of a 'dyad' which Pythagoras had explored: Augustine had already developed this idea in his very first book, *On the Beautiful and Apt*. Plotinus also engaged closely with some of Aristotle's statements. Like others in his tradition, he believed, wrongly, that Aristotle had simply agreed with Plato. Plotinus had absorbed Aristotle's *Categories* and even criticized it. It was the book which Augustine had mastered on his own at the age of twenty. The *Categories* was prescribed by Plotinus' pupil Porphyry as the first text in the philosophy syllabus for new students.[6] Quite by chance, Augustine came well prepared.

When Plotinus wrote, he was implicitly taking issue with two types of thinking, both of which happened to be urgent concerns for Augustine in Milan. One was scepticism, from whose stonewalling Augustine had just emerged. The other was dualism, which Plotinus knew through fringe Christian thinkers, people who regarded the world as an evil creation, at odds with the inner nature of enlightened mortals. Augustine himself had just broken with the extreme dualism of Mani, but had not yet answered the difficult questions which Mani's Gospel posed. Plotinus insisted on a particular answer and Augustine was ripe to be convinced by what he read.

While interpreting Plato, Plotinus developed Plato's most difficult views in a new and powerful direction. I will sketch them only in areas which are central to Augustine's engagement with what he read: Plotinus' ideas about God, about the origin and nature of the universe and its inhabitants, the proper modes of human behaviour, and the turning 'inwards' which can unite each one of us with the divine world above.

Unforgettably, Plato had emphasized the difference between two worlds. The world of visible existence and change misleads us and denies us certainty: in our 'shadowland' on earth, we are deceived by illusions, the flickering images on the wall of the Cave which we short-sightedly inhabit. We cannot rely on what we see or infer from the objects around us. Behind their deceptive multiplicity, there must, so Plato argues, be a higher world, the world of Forms which gives our changing world meaning. To take an example dear to Plotinus and already considered independently by the young Augustine: in this world, there are many instances of what is beautiful, but if items as diverse as a face or a work of art or a way of life can be called beautiful, surely there is a higher 'Form' of beauty from which all these instances of the beautiful derive?

In later life, Plato had also puzzled over profound problems of identity and difference, themes of his *Parmenides*. If we say that A is the same as B, must there not be a difference between A and B for the statement to be worth making? This question did not preoccupy Augustine, but it underlies the structure of Plotinus' universe. Plotinus argued that the invisible world culminates in three principles: the One, Intellect and Soul. This 'supranormal threesome' has an obvious resonance for Christians who think of a Holy Trinity, but when Augustine first met it, he admits that he had no clear idea of a Christian Trinity at all. The first abstract 'Triad' which he encountered was Plotinus' pagan one, much more coherently argued than Mani's complex of divine powers and 'Light Mind'.

Plotinus writes of the One as 'God' or the 'Good', but he is distinctive in believing that thinking and reasoning cannot express it. Insofar as the One can be known, it is known only through a mystical intuition and a 'presence superior to knowledge'. Language, he states, cannot explain what the One is: it is also the Good, but human terms like 'One' and 'Good' refer defectively to the One's reality. We 'are taught about it by comparisons and negations, by knowledge of things which come from it and by certain methods of ascent'. The use of negations about God leads to negative theology, the time-honoured method of being more precise about God by saying what He is not. The Platonists had been the first thinkers to develop this austere approach.[7] The 'methods of ascent' were to be grasped with exceptional rapidity by Augustine. They lead to mystical awareness, as Augustine very soon realized.

By a mixture of statement and tight argument, Plotinus described the One as perfect, self-sufficient, infinite in power and extent, and utterly simple. 'There must be something simple before all things and this must be other than all the things which come after it . . . it is also said to be beyond being . . .' This One is the most unusual postulate in ancient thought. It is completely removed from caring or communicating, in sharp distinction to Augustine's solicitous Christian God. Once, in a late text, Plotinus describes it as 'capable of love', but this love is strictly love for itself. It is utterly different from the Christian God's love for His creatures: 'I have yet to find,' remarked Plotinus' modern connoisseur E. R. Dodds, 'a text which suggests that it is interested in the salvation of the individual or even aware of it.' Instead, the One's 'love' for itself is a mark of its essential 'simplicity'. Nonetheless, a trio of 'love, power and Being' is present in the One which is 'boiling' with creative power, like a vibrant rhythm or a fountain.[8] By a sort of overflowing, it continually brings about lesser entities, but it has not the slightest personal interest in anything which it causes to exist. The first of the 'supranormals' in the succession from it is Intellect, which takes its nature from the One. Plotinus describes Intellect as 'turning back' towards the One in a sort of 'pause' which makes it 'Being', and also looking towards the One, in a 'gaze' which makes it 'Intellect' at one and the same moment. Plotinus means that by looking at the One, this entity thinks about the One, and so Intellect is in existence. At the same time, thinking involves a duality, both a thinker and an object of thought, and so, beyond the duality which is Intellect, there must also be a single, simple One.[9]

Like Plato's, Plotinus' upper universe is eternal. Time does not yet exist in it, a point which Augustine grasped well, developing it at the end of the *Confessions* when he interprets the first chapters of Genesis.

When Plotinus writes about Intellect 'thinking' or 'gazing', he appears to use words which presuppose time: we think one thing after another and when we gaze, we see what we did not see before. Perhaps he means only that these activities recur constantly. He also describes Being, or Intellect, as 'desiring' or 'loving' the One. This 'love' is not sought, or reciprocated, by the One, but it is impressed, like a 'trace', onto Intellect.[10] In Plato's heaven, the ideal forms were static and abstract forms of Beauty, Shape and so forth. In Plotinus', they are parts of Intellect and are thinking actively. They think about their interrelationships but they are also pulsating with 'love'. Plotinus' heaven is vibrant and alive.

From Intellect, Soul exists, 'proceeding' from Intellect, contemplating it and 'desiring', also with love. At two removes from the One, Soul has less of a trace of the One and so its thinking is not so concentrated. Soul's thinking, therefore, is accompanied by distracting activity. As a result, our visible world is brought into being, a spin-off of Soul's thinking. Soul also reasons discursively, following one judgement or argument with another, and this sequential reasoning occurs in time. Timeless eternity is thus left behind.

For Plotinus, the visible world is thought into being. It has not evolved or been created: it has 'proceeded' from an outward turning of the One's subsidiaries, Intellect and Soul. In his later philosophy, Plato had assumed that the Universe had had a Creator, but Plotinus agreed with the earlier Plato and insisted that the world had always existed. It would be a great mistake, he insists, to assume that the One or Soul had planned it or created it all of a sudden. Against this type of Creator, Plotinus even wrote: 'are we to imagine that he thought up this world all by himself, as well as the fact that it ought to be placed in the centre: and then he thought up water, and that it ought to be placed on top of the earth, and then everything else in order as far as the heavens? He thought up animals next, I suppose, and assigned specific forms to each of them, just as they have them today, and for each, thought up their intestines on the inside and their limbs on the outside? And then, once each thing had been properly arranged inside his mind, only then did he set about his task. Nonsense . . .'[11] How could he have thought it all when he had not yet seen anything? How could he have carried it out, when instruments like hands and feet did not exist? So much for the God of Genesis whom Augustine had accepted from boyhood and recently heard about in Ambrose's sermons. Plotinus dismissed basic Christian assumptions about the universe as impossible.

Plotinus advanced another less usual objection: a pre-planned creation would be much inferior to a consequence of the One's spontaneous, absorbed action. Sometimes, we think that we are doing something while we do it, making love, perhaps, or making conversation or reading a book like this one. Plotinus rated such self-conscious action far below unthinking creativity. The One, the Highest being in his universe, did not even plan at all: 'it was not because things had to be thus and in this way that it was decided to make them so . . . Consider . . . what we observe even in the case of plants: the lovely shape of their fruits and even of their leaves, the way they flower with generous spontaneity, their delicacy and their variety . . . Their arrangement is such that even if someone had the most excellent capacities for rational planning, he would be astounded, since rational planning could not have come up with any other way to make it.' Things must be as they are, he is saying, because they are what they are.[12]

Soul's upper part continues to contemplate Intellect, but its lower part, which Plotinus sometimes calls Nature, gives off an outward movement which runs out eventually into the universe which we can see. That universe includes the heavenly bodies, the stars and planets, in which a bit of 'Soul' is present: Plotinus thinks that the stars can see and hear. Several times, he engages with the claims of astrologers that the stars are primary 'causes' of our actions and other events on earth. He accepts that they may be 'signs' of what will happen to mortals, but, even in his later writings, he limits their 'causing' to a partial role in causing and then only the causing of physical events. He had studied the casting of horoscopes and was very critical of them. As Augustine had recently ceased to be an astrologer, he would find Plotinus' arguments that we ourselves, not the stars, cause evil to be most welcome. When he first read him, he did not read the treatises in which Plotinus allows the stars a little more power as 'causes'.[13]

Below the stars, the universe includes matter, solid things like rocks and metals. They have resulted from the turning-outwards of Soul, through which, ultimately, runs a trace of the One. A cardinal argument is that Soul also sometimes turns towards herself 'as if she is walking on emptiness'. She 'becomes more undefined' and 'makes what comes after her'. The outcome is a faint image and is 'non-being'. The lowest emanation of Soul is the 'soul' in plants, but it generates something 'totally other than herself'.[14] That something is matter, and matter, therefore, is characterized by the absence of good. This crucial point was seized on by the young Augustine, but, even so, he adapted it. In Plotinus' opinion, but not Augustine's, matter is utterly evil, although it is shaped and given form by a soul. In Augustine's, it is neutral, but shaped into good by God the Creator.

The arguments which Plotinus uses here relate to arguments in Plato's *Sophist* and Aristotle's *Physics* and *Categories*, none of which is familiar or tenable nowadays in a post-Darwinian world. Nonetheless, their result is important for Augustine's progress. With great subtlety, Plotinus deduced evil from the same process which leads ultimately back to the One. In Plotinus' universe, God had not gone to work on pre-existing matter, nor had evil confronted Him as part of a separate Kingdom of Darkness or realm of Satan. Instead, evil matter occurs at the point where all-pervading good runs out. Imagine, for instance, a garden from this point of view. Nearest the house the form and planting are most intense and concentrated: the pattern then merges into informality as it runs away towards the boundaries; it ends in evil weeds and nettles where good gardening runs out. In Plotinus' universe, by contrast, there is no gardener, no master plan: we can compare a musical chord, played to oneself in harmony, then rippling outwards into eventual indeterminacy.

The idea that there is a diminishing goodness and creativity in the visible world puts questions of aesthetics in a new perspective. Plotinus' writings on the Beautiful give a new twist to Plato's theories on art as a mere 'imitation' of reality. The exquisite play of sunlight on flowers after rain, the diversity of shapes and colours in a landscape, even the apparent beauty of symmetry in a human face: each is an effect very far removed from its underlying cause. Yet, through them all runs the outward-flowing dynamism of Thought and Being, a dynamism which is ultimately traceable to the One. Plotinus' novel emphasis on beauty's rhythm and movement is the point at which his theories live on for those who reach out to them with an open mind. They change the way we look on our world. 'Even in this world,' he wrote, 'we must say that beauty consists less in symmetry than in the light which illuminates the symmetry, and this light is what is desirable. After all, why is it that the splendour of beauty shines more brightly on a living face while only a trace of beauty appears on the face of a dead man? . . . Why is an ugly man, as long as he is alive, more beautiful than a statue?'[15]

Plotinus' universe is thus based on a single unifying principle. Here, it stands in direct contrast to dualists like Mani. Whereas they had the impudence to explain items in the world as the remains of evil demons from a Dark Kingdom, Plotinus argued that 'all things both are the

One and not the One: they are Him because they come from Him: they are not Him because it is by abiding by Himself that He gives them out.' In a particularly vivid manner he continues, 'it is like a long life, stretched out at length: each part is different from what comes next in order, but the whole is continuous itself, with one part differentiated from another: the prior does not perish in the subsequent . . .'[16] Being and the universe unravel like a life through time, as part of a single sequence. Crucially, this unravelling does not belong to a distant past. Unlike the Book of Genesis, Plotinus is not setting out a history of the early universe. He is describing a continuing process, without beginning or end, which is going on (he would say) around each one of us even now because of the continuing tension towards and away from the One. The continuous unravelling accounts for something else: the existence of man among the animals and plants.

Like Plato's man, Plotinus' man is a composite being, made up of a soul and a material body. The human soul in each one of us has descended from the greater Soul with whom it once used to contemplate Intellect. It has come down, but the explanation of its descent is not wholly clear. It did not 'fall' through choice or compulsion, although Plotinus in early treatises wrote of its 'arrogance' in descending. In his later writings, he views it from another angle: it departs at the moment which is natural, not chosen, and its descent is not consciously planned, but necessary. Its descent is inevitable, but it is 'like a natural leap, or like those who are moved, without reasoning, to the natural desires of sexual union . . .'[17] It does not make a choice. It leaps by necessity into an invisible world and a body which is formed from matter. Unlike the soul, this matter is inherently evil, lacking any impulse of goodness. By entering a body, therefore, a soul is at serious risk of becoming evil.[18] If it is 'too eager' for the pleasure and demands of the body, it will be perverted. Like Narcissus, it may be captivated by its own image, faintly reflected in its bodily setting. By diversion, or inertia, it becomes evil. The reason is not that the body is thoroughly evil in itself: rather, the body diverts the soul into excessive concern for itself and thereby perverts the soul's goodness. This view of moral evil was taken up and enlarged by Augustine, for whom it remained very important, but Plotinus' idea of the soul's punishment is different from a Christian view. Those souls who succumb and turn to sin are duly punished, but Plotinus accepts, like Plato, that souls migrate after death and return to another body and another life. Souls which have sinned in humans by making evil choices and following false priorities are reincarnated in animals or, worst of all, in plants. This view was familiar to Augustine after his years as a Manichaean Hearer, but he rejected it.

Unlike Plato, Plotinus accepts that in the upper universe there are not only ideal 'Forms' of universals, the forms of Beauty, Mankind, Justice and so forth. There also forms of individuals, of Monnica, Augustine or his concubine. Their existence requires Plotinus to confront extremely difficult questions about the scope and nature of memory (does a soul retain knowledge of its previous existence?). These questions were to exercise the mature Augustine for many years, but in Milan the question which most impressed him was different: what is the nature of the soul which is in our bodies here and now?

In a wonderful passage of the *Republic*, Plato had described how there lives within each of us our pure but cluttered self. It is like the sea-god Glaucus 'whose original nature could not easily be made out now by those who might see him' being tossed among the breakers and the swell of the sea. The waves have battered Glaucus' limbs, and seashells and seaweed have stuck to him 'so that he looks more like a wild beast than what he once was'.[19] Plotinus gave a new scope and dynamism to this powerful image of an encrusted true self. Within each of us, our soul exists at various levels. At its lowest level, it is closest to the body's desires, sensations and processes, not all of which may reach our conscious thought. In its middle level, it is self-aware. It is the agent of our discursive thinking, which is directed to external objects and to arguments which proceed in sequence. Plotinus is acutely aware of the problems which earlier philosophers, including Aristotle, had encountered in the concept of a thinking mind, one of whose objects of thought can be itself. He surmounted them, but added a third level to the soul, the intellect or 'undescended soul'. It is turned towards Intellect and the One and is contemplating the 'world which we have lost'.

This tripartite inner layering may seem quite unconvincing in an age which has, mostly, dispensed with the notion of a soul altogether. However, it touches on matters of lasting importance. At the lowest level of the soul, Plotinus had expressly noted what we now call the 'unconscious'.[20] Deep in us, we may have a disposition, or tendency, built up from previous experience, which is a more powerful influence on our thoughts and behaviour than any 'habit' which we acknowledge. At the highest level, by contrast, Plotinus believes that our soul shades into a superconscious. 'The Intelligible world is within us . . .': behind every unpromising face or person, behind narrowly focused athletes and even lawyers, there is this inner intellect, the upper level of the soul, contemplating the Intelligible world and its entities, even when our thinking, everyday selves are quite unaware that it is doing so. Within each of us, therefore, lies our true, upper 'self', the eternal Intellect's thought of our 'self'. Inside us, it is linked indissolubly to the divine world, ultimately to the One, but most of us are unaware of this amazing fact. Through the common element of a higher soul, we are present to each other, but 'since we look towards the outside', Plotinus writes, 'away from the point at which we are all joined together, we are unaware of the fact that we are one. We are like faces which are turned towards the outside, but also attached on the inside to one single head. If we could turn round – whether spontaneously or if, as in Homer, we were lucky enough to have "Athena pull us by the hair" – then all at once we would see God, ourselves and the All.'[21]

The One is omnipotent, even in each of our inmost souls. Yet, we ignore its presence, as a choir singing around a conductor 'may sometimes turn away, so that he is out of its sight, but when it turns back to him it sings beautifully and is truly with him. So, we are always around him . . . but not always turned *to* him: but when we do look to him, then we are at our goal and at rest . . .'[22] The imagery of 'turning' here will become fundamental to Augustine's use of the word 'conversion'.

Turning is only the beginning. Plato had written memorably of the capacity of the soul to ascend to the dazzling presence of the Good: Plotinus developed the master's words on how to reach it. We must not be a Narcissus, in love with the body's faint reflections of our soul. We must imitate Odysseus, and recognize the possible stages of our soul's inner journey homewards. We must then pursue them despite the body's Siren call. Here, Plotinus is the heir to a long Greek tradition of the ways of drawing near to God. They had been elaborated most fully in the wake of Plato's writings and remain one of the most powerful legacies of ancient thought. Either we can turn outwards and marvel at the wonder of the world, and reach out to God through contemplation of its order, its heaven, its stars, its beauty. Or we can turn inwards and follow the ancient advice to 'know yourself': we can then recognize God through the inner mystery of the soul. Plotinus wrote in a tradition which took these noble themes for granted: his preference was firmly for the introspective route.[23] Here, his thinking was to be transformative for Augustine. He grasped it, applied it and adopted it, making it a cornerstone of his spiritual life.

We must turn inwards, Plotinus tells us, but not simply to 'know ourselves', because this sort of self-knowledge still involves thinking and discursive reasoning. Our aim lies beyond thought. For Plotinus, it is a simple integration with the upper self, the 'layer' which is constantly contemplating within us. First, we prepare ourselves for this inward return with preliminary virtues, the social virtues of temperance, justice and self-control. With their help we can moderate the downward pull and deadening diversions of the body. Among these diversions, sex is particularly seductive, and so the aspiring wise man will resist it: 'for what can true self-control be, other than avoiding pleasures of the body as if they are unclean, from something unclean?' Plotinus writes memorably of the body as resembling the infamous bronze bull in which the Greek tyrant Phalaris was said to have roasted his victims.[24] Yet, those who practise the social virtues do not revile their oven of a body altogether. They live in it as a well-tempered composite, whereas those, like some of the thinkers on the Christian fringe, who blame it on an evil creator, cannot come to terms with it at all. In a memorable image, Plotinus suggests the difference between the two groups: 'it is as if two people were living in the same well-built house: one of them criticizes its structure and its builder, although he keeps on living in it all the same. But the other does not criticize it: in fact, he asserts that the builder has constructed the house with consummate skill, and he waits for the time when he will move on and no longer have need of a house at all . . .'[25] Mani had been the former; young Augustine was now reading an exponent of the latter view.

The next stage in our progress is to detach ourselves from this house, well-made though it is. To do so, we must practise three purifying virtues. One is courage, which prepares us to leave the body without fear; another is profound self-control or 'justice', which is a submission to reason; the third is intelligence, which is the soul's proper activity. With their help, we can separate ourselves from the body and its diversions and also 'turn' towards God. Potentially, while we do so, we still have the social virtues, but we are no longer concerned to exercise them. 'Leaving them behind, the wise man will choose another, the life of the gods . . .', to whom, as Plato wrote, we are to 'liken' ourselves as far as possible. 'At this stage, moral effort is no longer a combat, but a victorious flight . . .', as Plotinus' great scholar, Pierre Hadot, has aptly put it.[26]

How do we return to our inner true self? Not by reasoning, Plotinus tells us, nor even by philosophy: linguistic and analytic philosophy, exported far and wide since the 1950s, would be an utter hindrance at this level. Such reasoning has merely helped to prepare us by giving us grounds for accepting that the divine world exists. Moral effort has prepared us too, for 'without true virtue, all talk of God is words'. What remains is passive contemplation, after we have stripped away the cares and desires of the visible world and the body. We must now strip away the categories of time and space and 'awaken to our self'.

As this passive contemplation is hindered by thought and argument, it is not surprising that Plotinus' writings say very little about its achievement. Once, only, does he describe an experiment in the necessary non-thought. We are to visualize a simple, transparent sphere and to fill it with a mental image of the entire universe, the stars, the earth, the sea and all beings. We must see it as a unified whole, but we must also see the parts as distinct, 'in such a way that if one of the parts appeared, the presentation of the others would necessarily ensue'. Our point of view is from the centre of the sphere outwards, and we must abstract even more from this image. 'Eliminate its mass, then eliminate the presentation you have within you of its spatial extension and its matter.' By intense, inner contemplation, we then become our true superconscious self, after stripping down our perceptions to their underlying abstract Form.[27] It is all more intense than Augustine's recent attempt to imagine the world as a sphere and then explain it as a God-soaked sponge.

Reintegration of our upper soul with its divine origins requires practice after the long preliminaries and the exercise of virtues. Even then, Plotinus advises, we will need to pray for the Good to become present to us. There is more to it, clearly, than his written texts set out, but our progress is helped by an advantage: our superconscious self has an inherent love for the One, the divine source of Being, traces of which it contains, albeit at several removes. 'Since the soul is other than God, but comes from him,' Plotinus memorably observes, 'it is necessarily in love with him . . . The soul in her natural state is in love with God and wants to be united with Him; it is like the noble love of a girl for her noble father.' This powerful kinship draws our secret 'true self' up to the divine world: 'when the soul sees the beauties of the world flow away, she knows very well that the light which was shimmering on them comes from somewhere else. Then, the soul rises up to the other world, for she is clever at finding what she loves . . .'[28] For Plato, earthly love, between two people, is the starting point which propels the soul upwards on its intellectual progress to the world of Forms. For Plotinus, earthly love of beautiful things or of a person is a false turning, a distraction which we use only as a metaphor. Rather, the love of the

Ultimate is inherent in each one of our souls from the beginning.[29] The soul is at first unaware of her higher leanings, but like an inveterate gold-digger, he tells us, she directs her search, and then deftly attains what she loves. Her progress becomes a mystical, not an intellectual, ascent.

By turning inwards and passing beyond thought, we begin to look on the visible world as a transparent veil. We do not marvel at the wonder of the world or reach out to a 'god of the universe' by joyful extroversion: we see through it all, like the mythical Greek hero Lynceus, who, as Plotinus reminds us, 'could even see what is within the earth'. We must shed all earthly cares and anxieties and even shed the 'memories' which are implanted in our souls. We will then see beyond, to the form of Beauty and thence to the Good itself. It is made present as a light: 'Suddenly, a light bursts out, pure and alone. We wonder from where it came, from the outside or the inside? When it disappears, we say, "It was inside – yet, no, it wasn't inside." We must not try to learn whence it comes, for here there is no "whence".' The duality of seer and seen disappears and 'suddenly, the soul sees the Good appear within her. There is no longer anything between them and they are no longer two, but both are one.' In the zone of eternity, union with Intellect is not at all monotonous, because Intellect is thinking and so 'furiously alive'.[30]

We cannot expect to retain this joyous state for long. We may feel fear and weariness and 'gladly come down and fall away' into the perceptible world, as if our 'sight has become tired of [focusing on] small objects and gladly falls back among big ones'. Like old King Minos, as Homer briefly described him, we can nonetheless attain the closest company with God. Like Minos, we may then be inclined to legislate for others because of what we have understood.[31] Equally, we may not want to do so: we may simply want to describe what this mystical union is like. Here, once again, there is a difficulty: the experience is not expressible in words or thought and so, Plotinus tells us, 'whoever has seen, knows what I am saying', as we might say of the difference between loving and being in love. According to his pupil Porphyry, Plotinus attained a mystic union only four times in his later life: Porphyry himself attained it only once, at the age of sixty-eight. Such is the remoteness of the One in Plotinus' thinking, beyond Being and beyond Intellect, that modern scholars have sometimes doubted whether Plotinus even made this much contact with it. Yet there are passages in his writings which appear to refer to such a contact, beyond the lower stages of the soul's ascent. When the soul has reached the level of Intellect, 'it is there that one lets all study go; up to a point one has been led along, and as far as this, one thinks what one is in, but one is carried out of it by the surge of the wave of Intellect itself and is lifted on high by a kind of swell. One sees suddenly, not seeing how, but the vision fills one's eyes with light. It does not make one see something else by it, but the light itself is what one sees.'[32] This description is intensely relevant to Augustine's imminent experience after reading Plotinus for the first time.

Plotinus' spiritual life is characterized by 'tranquil confidence and peaceful gentleness'. It comes into being through moral preparation and mentally focused discovery. Only once does Plotinus use the word 'ecstasy', as if contact with undescended Soul involves an irrational penetration of the mind by an outside force. Suppose, nowadays, that he was given hallucinogenic drugs. He would not accept that they had opened new 'doors of perception' or reunited him with his true self. They would merely be distorting chemicals. The goal of touching or being smitten in the world of Intellect requires intellectual, not chemical, preparation and arises only from concentrated thinking. It is not a trip which an interfering substance can power.

Reintegration with our inmost self is unpredictable, but in Plotinus' view it is not at all a gift of divine grace. Each one of us has this inner level, but few use it, and yet, Plotinus states, it is accessible to us all: 'let those who are unfamiliar with this state imagine, on the basis of their loves here down below, what it must be like to encounter the being they love most of all'. We are part of a universe which is shot through with traces of a higher life and to which we are always straining, did we but know it. We cannot analyse this higher principle, nor break it down into propositions about this or that, but we can make contact with it, briefly. Access to it is quite sudden and leaves us with a sense of rest. 'There will be a time when the vision will be continuous as there will no longer be any bother from the body', after death.[33] This prospect, too, will become important in Augustine's developing thought as a Christian.

For the sake of 'blessed vision', we should even 'let go the attainment of kingship of the entire earth and sea and land, if by abandoning them and looking beyond them we can turn to That and see'. Such was the heart of the thinking which Plotinus expounded to fascinated hearers in Rome and near the Bay of Naples. Its highest aim was peace and contemplation. 'One feels of Plotinus,' John Dillon has concluded, 'that he would gladly have helped an old lady across the road – but he might very well fail to notice her at all. And if she were squashed by a passing wagon, he would remain quite unmoved.'[34] Plotinus chose to teach, nonetheless, and he did not only teach like-minded wise men who had aspired to the One. Having mastered his lower self, he encouraged other aspirants to do the same, well-meaning people, the 'middling' sort, people like the young Augustine who was reading him with fascination.

His own audiences included the Emperor Gallienus and his wife, some immensely grand senators, one of whom was a consul, and Gemina, the widow, most probably, of the Emperor Trebonianus, who had been killed in battle by his own troops. It was a profoundly challenging and romantic message, expressed to people whose chiselled eyes still stare at us from portrait-busts of antique marble. With a fine glance sideways, Plotinus reminds us, nonetheless, that many are not disposed to share it. 'When people are too weak for contemplation, they switch to action . . . Owing to the weakness of their souls their faculty of contemplation is insufficient . . . Yet they still want to see, and so they switch to action in order to see with their eyes what they could not see with their spirit. When they create something, it is because they themselves want to see it and contemplate it and when they propose to act, insofar as they can, it is because they want their act to be perceived by others.'[35] So they press on through life, unaware of their superconscious, the projects men of today in their grey suits or hard hats. Until summer 386, they included Milan's young professor of rhetoric, who had been striving for sexual pleasure and worldly advancement in his substitute for real life.

18
Inwards and Upwards

I

Among the turmoil in Milan, this Platonist philosophy was to change the way in which Augustine regarded God, the world, evil and truth. These claims are large, but we are lucky to have the impression which he set down within six months in a work dedicated to his patron, Romanianus. The 'books of the Platonists', he wrote, released 'a very few drops of the most precious ointment', like 'fine Arabian scent', which provoked an 'incredible fire, Romanianus, incredible, beyond anything perhaps you would even believe about me, incredible even to me about my very self'.[1] He had 'burned' when first reading the *Hortensius*, but this blaze was even greater.

In a Platonist context, this outcome was not as extraordinary as it may seem. Already in the mid-second century, the Christian thinker Justin had described his resort to Platonist writings: 'in my indolent stupidity,' he wrote, 'I thought that immediately I would see God, for this is the goal of Plato's philosophy'.[2] Augustine realized this goal not once, but thrice. Twice in Milan, and once, two years later, the *Confessions* describe and interpret his ascents to God's presence. They are the first detailed accounts of such an experience by a Christian in the Latin West, except for the visions of martyrs while awaiting their day of death. They have had a decisive effect on subsequent accounts of mystic visions and their interpretation in the next thousand years of Western Christianity. Yet, it is still disputed whether his experience has been obscured by his later interpretation and by the underlying purpose of the *Confessions*. In two of the three cases, the ascents have even been classed as 'failures', 'vain attempts of an ecstatic sort'.[3]

As a first step, Augustine was 'admonished', he recalls, by the Platonist books to turn inwards. By an inward turn, Plotinus was telling him, he could encounter divinity. As he was still unsure how to think of God, it is not at all surprising that he promptly tried to act on what he read. 'There is not much between,' Plotinus had written, 'not much between us and Divinity.' It sounded so seductive.

Already as a Manichaean, Augustine had been taught to think of three levels in his soul. One was *psyche*, the simple consciousness of being alive; another was 'spirit', or *pneuma*, which was at risk to the constant assault of evil impulses, the implants from the Kingdom of Darkness. The third was 'mind', or *nous*, the implant from the Kingdom of Light. All three could be supported by selective quotations from Paul's letters. Though Augustine had abandoned Mani's Gospel, he had been shaped by its account of man for at least nine years. Even if he had not reread Paul since leaving the sect, he would find Plotinus' notion of the three 'layers' of the self or soul easier to comprehend than we do. He would not, however, have been prepared by any mystical exercises among his Manichaean friends. They never attempted to ascend to their hidden God in their lifetimes or to imitate Mani himself by attaining a vision of their heavenly Twin. Mani once wrote that 'the sun and moon are our path, the door from which we march forth into the world of our existence [in heaven], as has been declared by Jesus'. The 'march', however, was only undertaken by separated Light-particles when released from the evils of the body.

Eleven years later, Augustine presents his spiritual experience in prose which is a complex masterpiece, rich in scriptural and Platonizing resonance. It describes two separate high points, the second of which is prefaced by a review of the first. When he turned inwards on the first occasion, he recalls that with the 'eye of the soul' he soon 'saw' a bright light. It was not a light like the 'common light of day', only brighter and bigger. 'It was not that,' he writes, 'it was different, different, indeed, from all others.' Here, Augustine refers back with great conviction to what he had never forgotten: 'it was not above my thinking mind, as oil is above water'. It was not spatially 'above': it transcended him spiritually. God, he believed, had shone on him 'intensely' and Augustine recalled that he 'trembled with love and horror', as well he might. He believed that he heard Him, 'as something is heard in the heart', but God thrust him away. As a result he returned to the mundane world, but that world seemed quite different.[4] He was absolutely certain now that God existed as a spiritual, not a material, being. God was both above him but also accessible very deep in his innermost being. It was from there that Augustine had come within range of Him.

Augustine's 'seeing' was not seeing with the eyes. It was what he later classifies as 'intellectual vision'. Such an experience has been known and described by other individuals, whether Christians, Muslims or neither, whether religious or not. Typically, they describe it as dazzlingly bright, like a sort of light, and very short-lived: it tends to be interpreted by them as knowledge. When Augustine had his experience, his belief in the Christian God and his Platonist readings would be influencing the direction of his mind. This mental content cannot be stripped away, as if to recover the 'basic' experience which he underwent: it was itself wrapped up with the experience.[5] In Platonist terms, however, it was most surprising. Young Augustine had not been practising the prescribed virtues of courage, justice and self-control. He was not in a quiet place. He was agitated by the surrounding clamour of Milan and his futile career. He was still revelling in sex and was roasting, Plotinus would say, in the 'bull of Phalaris'. He was a full-time teacher of rhetoric who had never tried to turn inwards before, but his very first attempt produced 'incredible' results. To account for this remarkable outcome, it is appropriate to invoke Augustine's temperament. Three times within two years, he was to undergo experiences of what he understood to be divinity. He does not relate the third one to a prelude of mental turmoil or hectic 'fluctuation', but the first and second emerged from a most turbulent context.

If a psychologist could persuade him nowadays that what he sensed was due to his mental stress, Augustine would readily accommodate this suggestion to his existing view of God. Yet again, in 'wondrous ways', he would conclude, God had used a secondary agent to prompt him and 'turn' him to a fuller realization of Himself. At the time, Augustine had no such diagnosis to hand. So far as his written account is grounded in his experience at the time, it is not in itself especially interesting: he sensed a dazzling light at a distance, an impression of a heavenly voice, and a sense of an abrupt falling away to the everyday world. What is accessible, and abidingly important, is what Augustine made of it when thinking it over and over.

Eleven years after the event, the *Confessions* give an orderly account of his progress. First, he has an experience, then the knowledge which resulted from it. Then he has a second experience, also related to new knowledge, and finally he addresses the moral questions with which it left him. The brief outline which he wrote for Romanianus within six months of the event calls the experience 'incredible' three times over, but then the manuscripts of its text give two different wordings: either,

'I looked back, *however*, I confess', or (surely correctly) 'I looked back *only*, I confess' ('only' suits the ashamed tone of 'I confess'). 'I looked back only, I confess, as if from a journey, onto the religion implanted in me as a child.'[6] He 'looked back only', as if over his shoulder while he travelled ahead in a Platonist direction and Christianity, his religion since childhood, seemed a distant point behind him. If he had continued on the road, he would indeed have undergone a conversion, one away from Christianity.

This phase lasted only briefly. 'Nonetheless', as he realized with hindsight, the Christian religion of his childhood was 'drawing me to it, although I did not know it'. However tentatively, we can reactivate this brief gap in his Christian commitment by relating what he recalls (I believe, correctly) to what he could have read in Plotinus. Then, we can proceed to what he made of it later in Christian terms and to the crucial ways of thinking in which he brought the 'Platonist books' and Christianity into line.

II

Plotinus stated that a contact with divinity could happen 'suddenly': none was ever more sudden than Augustine's. It was indeed as if Homer's goddess Athena had pulled him by the hair. Like Plotinus, Augustine looked inwards, then upwards with 'the eye of the soul'. Like Plotinus, he was seized by 'love' for what he saw. He was also terrified. Plotinus could have warned him: 'when the soul's eye is only just awakened, it is not at all able to look at what is brilliant . . .' Indeed, Augustine's recently awoken soul could not persist in looking. Plotinus implied that a well-tuned soul might hear 'the sounds of voices on high', but only after much training and spiritual exercise.[7] Augustine, however, 'saw' and sensed as if 'hearing in his heart'. Plotinus never wrote about sensing with the 'heart'.

Like Augustine, Plotinus considered the experience to be brightly lit, but the vision of light which he describes differs from Augustine's. Plotinus regarded the soul as divine and considered that a part of it was still lodged in the upper world. The soul, therefore, would not see a blazing light which was separate from itself. It must first make itself 'beautiful' by moral effort and prolonged self-shaping: then it would see, 'wholly itself, nothing but true light, not measured by size or bounded by shape'. Augustine, by contrast, saw a blazing light quite separate from himself: he was not permeated by it or reunited with it. What did it mean? He assumed immediately that it was absolute Truth: at once 'I would more easily doubt that I was alive than I would doubt that this absolute Truth existed.'[8] Manifestly, he is not introducing this notion long after the event. He had not been united with this light, but he had made some crucial discoveries. God, or divinity, is absolute and transcendent. He is both superior to, and within, the deepest recesses of our inner spiritual being.

In the *Confessions*, he describes the consequences as a new understanding of the universe. Neatly, perhaps too neatly, he discusses four aspects of it one after another: Being, then Truth, then Good and Evil, then Beauty. However, they relate exactly to the doubts which had been agitating him in Milan at the time and to the unanswered questions with which he recalls that Mani's sect had left him. Each of them was a concept about which he had just been reading in the Platonists' books. These questions, then, are highly likely to be questions with which he indeed engaged in early summer 386 in the 'light' of his inner experience.

This experience led to new knowledge, not to some mystic gift of tongues.[9] Thanks to it, Augustine realized as never before that there was an immaterial God beyond him, absolute, transcendent, eternal and unchanging. This God was infinite, but infinite 'otherwise' than he had previously thought. God, he realized, was infinite in power, not space. When he then looked at the world around him, he understood that the world's 'being' was relative to God's. The world existed, but in comparison with God it did not. Whereas God is unchangeable, the world is changeable. Necessarily it changes in time. This comparison between the time-bound world and immutable God will recur often in his writings, not least at the end of the *Confessions*. It drew on the Platonists' contrast between 'being' and 'not being', but it did not apply their contrast in quite the same way.

In the *Confessions*, Augustine then reflects on 'Good' and 'Evil'. Although he considers them in terms of 'corruption' and the 'incorruptible', they are not anachronistic concepts for his thinking in Milan. 'Corruption' was an idea which he had carried with him since his Manichaean days, when he would have heard the word 'corruptibility' in readings from Paul's epistles and had confronted it in the clever objections of his friend Nebridius to Mani's cosmology. 'Incorruptibility' suggested to him a simple, or too simple, argument. Something can be corrupted only because it is good and because corruption is depriving it of good. If it was deprived of all good, it would not exist at all.

Therefore, what exists is good, and there is no wholly evil substance, as the Manichees wrongly believed. Good and evil have both come from God and are part of His hidden 'order'. Perhaps even in summer 386 young Augustine remembered that, in Genesis, God is declared to have 'made all things good'. Reacting against Mani, he then went a step further than Plotinus. Plotinus thought that underlying matter, the basic stuff of the material world, is evil. For Augustine, it is not: God has created it out of nothing.

Augustine then addressed this cardinal problem. Previously, he used to say of unpleasant things that 'he wished they did not exist': no poisonous snakes, perhaps, no droughts, no slugs, no earthquakes. After his visionary experience, he tells us, 'I no longer yearned for better things. I was thinking of all things [together].' When judged by God's absolute standards, everything is good in relation to the whole, though some things rank lower in it than others. This view of the world presupposes an underlying 'order', both in space and in time. Six months after his experiences, Augustine was to devote an entire work to 'order' in the universe, one which helps us to grasp what his changed understanding meant. If the whole eludes us, it is because we are like statues in the corner of a great palace: we survey only a tiny fraction and ignore the architecture of the total building. Some things in the world are superior to others, but, even so, the whole is always better than those superior things alone.[10] Again, this holistic way of thinking could indeed have been dawning on him at the time of his encounter with God. His new friend Zenobius had written on 'order', and our recently found Latin poem on the universe develops the idea. Written, I believe, by Theodorus, it answers those who protest against parts of the world and fail to see them as 'harmonious discord' in a beautiful whole.[11] Previously, Augustine had been one of the worst protestors.

This new way of thinking in terms of a hidden 'order' affects how we look on evil and truth. For Augustine, the evil in the universe now seemed to be the result of a 'deficiency of good'. This view is Plotinus', and, tantalizingly, it is also stated by Ambrose in his published sermon *On Isaac*.[12] The sermon's date is uncertain, though early in 386 is the most attractive guess: if so, Augustine may have heard this new view of evil in a sermon before he read about it in Plotinus or heard it discussed by his 'greater friends' in Milan. For Plotinus, God is not a purposive creator or artist at all: evil is simply a part of the way the world is. By contrast, for Augustine, apparent evil is not 'evil' when seen in the totality of orderly creation. This idea of an orderly, created whole explained two previous questions in his mind, the 'beautiful' and the 'apt'. Whatever exists, he now realized, is good through its 'aptness' to its place in a beautiful whole. It is 'fitting', or 'convenient'. Augustine is most famous nowadays for his sombre views on original sin. However, he also believes that the world is orderly, ruled by God's providence and arranged for the best. This optimism was born in him in Milan and never lost.

After his first ascent to God, Augustine recalls that he also changed his views on truth and moral evil. Previously, he had been swayed by the relativism of the sceptical philosophers who argued that 'one man's meat is another man's poison' or that what looks straight or fine in one light may look bent or murky in another. Now, he grasped that an absolute Truth exists: the yardstick of Truth is divine and also eternal. God did not begin His work after time had passed: whatever exists is 'apt' for its time, and, like everything else, time is relative to God. Mani had written of a divine 'Splenditenens' who helps to hold up the world. Augustine now writes of God as 'Omnitenens', 'holding all' in Truth (or reality). In the wake of his new experiences, he repeatedly describes himself as 'most certain'.[13] Sceptical doubt, he is emphasizing, has been utterly routed from his mind. The hallmarks of his visions are love and a new certainty. Unlike his later admirer Luther, Augustine will never be beset by doubts again

If each soul is God's creation and the world is beautiful and good, what is moral evil? Inspired by words of Plotinus, Augustine sees it, crucially, as the 'perversity of a will, distorted into the lowest things and turned away from the highest substance, God'.[14] It is not Mani's contrary 'power of death', a force which had supposedly been rooted in our beings from a Kingdom of Evil. It is always the result of a choice, one made freely by the soul, which stands midway between God, who is above it, and the created world, which is beneath it. By a perverse distortion away from God, we choose to sink into sins such as sex or, nowadays, insatiable shopping.

Now, indeed, Augustine observes, 'I was looking for You, God, and not for a delusive imagining', like those which he had previously compared to a blinding swarm of mosquitoes. However, 'I was not standing firm in my enjoyment of You': he was not what Plotinus called 'established' in contemplation. So, he continued to turn inwards and try to ascend again. He describes the experience, not retelling the first one from a new angle, but recalling a second one which was distinct.

This time, his Platonist language is more pronounced.[15] He dwells on the ascent's 'stages', a word which Plotinus' pupil Porphyry also used for the process. They are inner psychological stages, not successive stages in his perception of the external world. Augustine describes the inner layers of his consciousness, just as Plotinus had distinguished them. He left perceptions behind, he tells us, the sounds and smells and sights of the world. He passed beyond the parts of the mind which are aware of perceptions (as animals' minds are, too) and the part which categorizes and judges them (this judging part is peculiar to humans: 'this rose is sweet'; 'that sound is a bell'). These levels of his mind were 'changeable', but, by going deeper, his mind then 'raised itself to its intuitive intelligence', what Plotinus called Intellect, or the upper part of the soul. It 'took thinking away from its habitual levels', he remarks, using words which Cicero had considered to be the mark of a 'great mind'. At the time of his ascent, Augustine would have known Cicero's phrase and might well have applied it promptly to his experience. He realized that the 'unchangeable' is preferable to the 'changeable', a realization which is a new item of knowledge. So, his own mind wished to discover 'with what light it was being flooded'. Here, we can compare Plotinus' words: 'suddenly, a light burst out, pure and alone. We wonder from where it came, from the outside or the inside?' Then, in a 'flicker of a trembling glance', Augustine tells us, his soul arrived at 'That which Is'. It could not fix its gaze and, once again, it fell away, longing for more.

This second high point differed from the first. It resulted in a brief contact with divinity, 'That which Is'. The word 'flicker', or 'beat', with which he describes it recalls Plotinus' language for a soul which is 'struck' or smitten.[16] By a simple 'gathered intuition', Plotinus writes, we grasp what 'transcends the nature of our intelligence'. Once again, Augustine surely wondered at the time, 'What did I reach?' or, as Plotinus would say, '. . . touch?' On the first occasion, he had gained knowledge, although he fell back without making contact with its source. On the second, he also attained knowledge, but then made brief contact with its source and wondered why he could not prolong it. Afterwards, as he followed briefly the Platonists' road, he began to talk and talk of what he had seen. 'I was inflated with knowledge,' he recalls, 'and I kept chattering on.'

Another, later, who 'chattered' after such experiences was the novelist Dostoyevsky. 'I have really touched God,' he wrote. 'He came into me myself; yes, God exists, I cried . . . I do not know whether this joy lasts for seconds or hours or months, but believe me, I would not exchange it for all the delights of this world.' Unlike Augustine, Dostoyevsky did not feel that his inner self was ascending. He felt that 'the heaven was going down upon the earth, and that it had engulfed me'. Unlike Augustine, he related his experiences to his physical state: he was epileptic.[17] Augustine's resources were quite different. After Plotinus' texts, he 'seized on the Apostle Paul', he tells us. 'I was tottering, hurrying, hesitating', in mixed metaphors of movement which well catch his uncertain predicament. 'These people, I said, could not truly have done so much and lived as it is evident that they lived if their letters and arguments were opposed to this great good . . .' In context, the first Christians are the plural group whom he is considering here: they, then, are 'these people', whereas the 'great good' is Plotinus' route to God.[18] With Paul's help, Augustine was now to interpret the experiences which had nearly set him on a different path.

III

Paul's epistles had first come to Augustine's detailed attention as a 'true Christian' in Mani's sect. We have no evidence that he had read them then in full, nor that he had continued to read them since abandoning the Manichaeans. Why did he turn to them now so promptly? In Mani's recently found 'biography', the question of heavenly visions and ascents is indeed prominent and Mani's followers cite Paul and his own experiences described at 2 Corinthians 12.2. In Ambrose's sermons, Augustine would also sometimes hear words from Paul's letters about the transformation of the 'inner man' and about an ascent towards God. Among Ambrose's surviving sermons, his *On Isaac* is again the most pertinent. It dwells on the capacity of the soul to 'seek within itself', to 'pursue the divine', to 'pass beyond intelligible things' and 'somehow pursue the divine', being 'strengthened and fed by it'. It then relates this process explicitly to Paul the Apostle, going on to quote his words to the Corinthians about his being 'caught up into Paradise', while 'out of the body' (Ambrose states).[19] Whether Augustine had recently heard this sermon or another like it, this sort of connection, heard in Ambrose's church, may have impelled him, like his post-Manichaean memories, to turn to Paul's letters and try to make sense of his own recent 'ascent'.

On reading Paul, Augustine rapidly believed that he had found the heart of the Platonists' teaching, and more besides. He read 'most intently and most piously', but it was a most remarkable rereading of the texts. By the Manichees, Augustine had been persuaded that the Apostle's views were inconsistent and that they conflicted with the Old Testament. Now, he recalls, they seemed to him to be harmonious both among themselves and with the rest of scripture. In the heat of the moment another aspect, surely, was more immediate to him. Among Paul's long exhortations on the Jewish Law and Christian behaviour, the end of the world or the status of male circumcision, Augustine believed he had found Plotinus' teaching on turning inwards and re-uniting the upper part of the soul with its divine analogue.

When relating the two, Augustine had surely fastened, like some of the Manichaeans and like Ambrose, on Paul's words to the Corinthians about his own ascent 'into the third heaven'. There, Paul had 'heard unspeakable words which it is not lawful for a man to utter' (2 Cor. 12.1–4). To the Colossians he had written, 'set your affection on things above, and not on things on earth' (Col. 3.2). To the Romans, he wrote that 'the mind of the flesh is death, but the mind of the spirit is life and peace' (Rom. 8.6). Augustine considered that Paul wrote our Letter to the Ephesians: in it, he could read, 'Be renewed in the spirit of your mind' (Eph. 4.23). Yet, Paul had never read a word of Plato. He had no grasp of logical or mental philosophy and had lived 200 years before Plotinus reshaped Plato's teachings. Paul 'saw through a glass darkly', and thought that only in the next life will we see 'face to face' (1 Cor. 13.12).

This turn by Augustine from one source of wisdom, Plotinus, to another, Paul, was not unprecedented in his career. Aged eighteen, he had turned from Cicero's *Hortensius* to seek 'wisdom' in the Bible. Then, his *On the Beautiful and Apt* had interpreted Mani's 'true Christianity' in the light of the Pythagorean wisdom which he had just encountered in Varro. Now, he was reading his new-found philosophy, Platonism, into a Christian text which, by origin, had never engaged with it. It was a most creative misunderstanding. He found it there because he wanted to.

Not until some thirty years later can we read Augustine engaging explicitly with, in my view, the crucial text for his understanding, Paul's words about his own ascent to heaven (2 Cor. 12.1–4).[20] There, Augustine distinguishes three types of vision, the bodily (sense-perception), the spiritual (to us, the imagination) and the intellectual. Just as in the *Confessions*, he identifies the contemplation of God with the last, the intellectual type of seeing. By it, the soul understands only what is true: if it is not true, the soul does not 'see' and grasp it. It gains it through the gift of God, but this mode of knowledge is a gift given to very few. Even after so many years, there is a hint here of what Augustine himself had found in this cardinal text by Paul in the wake of his own visions in summer 386.

When Augustine began to rethink his experiences, no doubt within hours of them, he was not an expert scholar of 'Neoplatonism'. Nor, in the *Confessions*, was he writing for readers who were. An apparently central similarity with Paul's thinking sufficed to convince him. Thanks to it, he promptly interpreted his visionary experiences in a profoundly Christian direction. Plotinus had written that the man who reunites with his higher soul will need 'none to guide him': Augustine, by contrast, quickly came to believe that he had been guided throughout by God. It was 'You', God, 'who took me up': like a doctor, God had been 'tending' his swollen vision and his head 'as if with a poultice'.[21] God had then seemed to speak with him in his inner being. Plotinus' higher Trinity had no such concern for individuals. The One, his God, was utterly beyond such actions as caring or cossetting or speaking. Moreover, Augustine's upper soul remained, on the first occasion, 'far off' from the divine light. When he thought it over, he decided, presumably within days, that his soul must have stayed 'in the region of unlikeness', a Platonist phrase. It is a phrase, however, which Plotinus applies differently, to the material world which distracts the soul before its ascent begins.

On further reflection, Augustine decided that words with a scriptural resonance correctly expressed his experiences, as if God had shouted them towards him, a spectator from afar. 'I am the bread of the full-grown: He seemed to say, grow, and you will feed on Me . . .' These words do not refer to the bread of Holy Communion, as if Augustine was being told by God to be baptized and take the eucharist before he could be 'changed in God'. In Augustine's later writings, this 'bread' is always the nourishment of the grown-up angels in heaven, which Christ brought down in a simplified form as milk and baby food to us novices on earth when He took on human flesh.[22] During Augustine's first ascent, when the 'weakness' of his soul was beaten back by the divine light, it had seemed to hear abiding Truth, 'as is heard in the heart'. In the *Confessions*, Augustine expresses this Truth as the very words which God had once spoken to Moses from the Burning Bush: 'I am who I am', or 'I am [the One who is]'. They are words about 'Being' which have resonated in many attempts to know God, whether Jewish, Christian or Muhammad's in the Koran.[23]

What Augustine 'heard in his heart' convinced him that God is an absolute Being. We can tentatively follow the steps by which he thought about this discovery and, later, expressed it. 'Being' was not one of Plotinus' 'supranormals', his highest Triad. It was placed there by his pupil Porphyry, but, in my view, Augustine had not yet read Porphyry when he first had these experiences. In Plotinus, however, he could already find a sufficient argument related to the One. As the One is eternal, it 'is', without the possibility of being the opposite, 'not being'. It is therefore Truth (as it cannot be contradicted). Augustine, helped by Plotinus, grasps this very point: God is absolute Being and absolute Truth. Where, though, does God say such elevated things in scripture? Much more is said there about His limbs and His bad moods, but apart from some statements in John's Gospel ('I am the Truth') or in Revelation ('Alpha and Omega'), His most existential statement is the one He makes to Moses from the Burning Bush. Augustine was not the first Christian, even in the Latin West, to have fastened on this challenging announcement, but not until 390/91 does it appear in any text Augustine writes.[24] With hindsight, manifestly, his confessions have interpreted in scriptural language what he first 'sensed' and then considered philosophically. Again, he differs from his guiding philosophers. Plotinus' One never speaks and Porphyry's 'Being' is impersonal. As Augustine thought over his experiences, it seemed to him that God had spoken to him as He once spoke to Moses, using personal terms (*I am . . .*). These sensed experiences are indeed mysticism, but not as Plotinus or his pupil Porphyry understood it. Above all, unlike Plotinus' One, Augustine's God is the creator of the human soul. Unlike Plotinus' soul, therefore, his Christian soul was not being reintegrated with the Soul which it had left behind. Instead, it saw from afar; it 'arrived' and briefly touched, but it was not itself divine. Promptly, it fell away.

In describing his experiences Augustine preserves these conspicuous differences. He was not at all concerned to 'baptize Plotinus' *Enneads*'. To a degree not always recognized by their scholars, the *Confessions* present exactly the opposite view.[25] With great force, Augustine prefaces his account of his experiences with careful comparisons and contrasts. He tells us, first, what he read in the Platonists, but also, pointedly, what he then read only in Paul and the Fourth Gospel. Plotinus, he emphasizes, said nothing about the Incarnation and man's consequent redemption by Christ. Plotinus ignored Christ's essential mediation between God and 'humble' men. As the Platonist soul 'falls' by necessity, not by choice, there is no place in Plotinus' system for a 'Son of God' to be sent into the world to redeem us from freely chosen sins. The Platonists' books, Augustine drives home, have some of the truth, but by no means all.

Their moral perspective, he thinks, is misguided too. Christ has shown 'humility' in His incarnation, and 'humility' is the all-important quality which Christians must make their own. The Platonists, he thinks, were much too arrogant. Despite Augustine, no member of Plotinus' circle would ever have described their master as proud: his entire mode of life strove for patient, gentle serenity. In Augustine's view, however, Plotinus was 'proud' because he presumed too much from unaided human nature. The 'presumptuous' Platonists stand in contrast to 'confessing' Christians, who are humbly dependent on God's gifts and guidance for their ascent.

Repeatedly, Augustine uses Paul's words to the Romans, that 'invisible things are understood through the things that are made': he takes them to be saying that we understand the spiritual and divine by transcending the visible, created world.[26] Paul's words belonged in an important context. He was claiming that God's eternal power is 'made manifest' in the visible world so that pagans, too, can grasp it. However, they have turned away from it into sexual lust and homosexuality. 'Professing themselves to be wise, they became fools' and exchanged 'incorruptible God' for idolatry. They 'have no excuse'. The words which Augustine applies to his experience were a stern rebuke to pagans.

Augustine combined his Christian understanding with an explanatory 'history of philosophy', one which is most fully stated by him in 396, just before he began to compose the *Confessions*. God, he believed, had revealed 'the one true wisdom'.[27] He revealed it to Moses and in due course the wisdom passed to other early Greek philosophers and to Socrates and Plato in Athens. Traditionally, philosophy was considered to have three sections: metaphysics (about God and reality), logic and ethics. In Athens, each of these sections met with differing treatments. Logic was categorized by Aristotle, who agreed, supposedly, with his master, Plato, in all things: logic was therefore subsumed into the 'one true' philosophy about God. Ethics were less fortunate. They fell into the hands of the hedonist Epicureans and the Stoics. Meanwhile, Plato passed on the true metaphysical wisdom to his followers in the Academy, but they concealed it as a secret doctrine. They needed to refute the new materialists, the Stoics, so in public they taught scepticism to confound the Stoic theory of knowledge. In private they kept the 'true wisdom' about God and reality to themselves. All the while, God's wisdom had become decreasingly clear to outsiders. In Greek and Egyptian hands, it had been contaminated by the false worship of idols, by blood sacrifices to demons and by astrology and sorcery.

God then sent Christ incarnate among men to re-teach the wisdom which the Platonists had almost lost. Christ made it available in simple detail to the uneducated crowd. When Paul described 'philosophy' as 'vain deceit', he did not mean the 'one true wisdom' of the Platonists and Christians. He meant the hedonist ethics of the Epicureans and the materialism of the Stoics. In the wake of Christ's teaching, Plotinus and his followers had tried to restate the 'one true wisdom', but they had entangled it with pagan rituals and magic. For modern scholars, this entanglement is evident in Porphyry, but rather less so in Plotinus. In Augustine's view, the Platonists' theology was much sounder than their religion.

From this perspective, Augustine did not find Christianity in Neoplatonism: he found a core of what to us (not him) is Neoplatonism in Christian scriptures. He had not, therefore, been 'converted' by his Platonic readings. They had simply deepened what he saw in Christian scripture, his existing faith. Before he tells us about his 'turning inwards', he places the Platonists by comparing them with the Israelites in the biblical Book of Exodus. From Egypt, as God willed, the children of Israel had brought objects of true gold, but they had muddled them with false idolatry, their cult of the golden calf, and with the lure of heathenism, the 'Egyptian' lentils for which Esau had sold his rights of inheritance. By reading the Platonists, Augustine was paying attention to the 'gold', wherever it came from, but was rejecting the false idolatry. In the Acts of the Apostles, Paul had reminded his Athenian hearers that 'we live, move and have our being' in God, as 'some of their own people' said. From Athens ('thence'), Augustine wrongly thinks, came the books of the Platonists: he himself, therefore, is using the wisdom of people who 'lived and moved' in the very same God as his own. God ('You') had explained this fact in Paul's own words, spoken in Athens, the Platonists' very own city.[28]

This wholly false history coloured Augustine's response to his new philosophy. He was not becoming a 'Christian Platonist', as many modern readers have wrongly inferred. Even less was he converting to Neoplatonism before he underwent Christian baptism a year later. Nor was he to remain a 'closet-Platonist' for the rest of his thinking life. He had, he believed, found Platonist wisdom implied and restated more clearly in Christian scriptures. It was there because it was part of the 'one true wisdom' which had filtered from God's first revelation down to latecomers like Plotinus. Augustine had dug out the gold from the Platonists' writings and abandoned their worthless, surrounding mud.

Importantly, this same 'history' of philosophy is attested for others present in Milan in the mid-380s, for Hermogenianus, one of Augustine's 'greater friends', perhaps for Zenobius, who had been writing on the immortal soul, and above all for Ambrose in some of his published sermons.[29] Ambrose even misquotes Paul's speech to the Athenians in exactly the same wording which Augustine gives. Ambrose fills the missing links in the 'one true wisdom's' history. In Egypt, he states, Pythagoras had heard it from Jeremiah, and Plato then took it from Pythagoras: Augustine's chronology could thus be improved. Once again, we cannot date securely the published sermons in which Ambrose expressed these views.[30] We can best conclude that such views were being aired in Milan at the time of Augustine's experiences.

How ever did the notion that the Platonists had a long-concealed 'secret doctrine' come to Augustine's mind? Was it, some have wondered, when he read texts by Porphyry, later in 386? A simpler possibility lies to hand. When the pagan 'fourth man' gave Augustine his bundle of Platonist texts, he might well have hinted to him that they contained the Platonists' hidden doctrine.

Once again, it is unlikely that Augustine could have come to these conclusions anywhere in the Latin West except Milan. Ever after, they remain a template for his spiritual life and writings. Ascent to God remains central to his first writings, and a progress to Him by stages, first by looking outwards, then by turning inwards, remains central to his aspirations. 'Often, I do that,' he tells us in the *Confessions*.[31] When they turn from autobiography to 'what I now am', he describes himself in terms of his preparations for a spiritual ascent to God. Then, when he discusses the 'heaven of heavens' in scripture, he identifies it as the ideal Heaven in God's mind. This Heaven is contemplating God in Platonizing bliss, in a way which a Christian individual can hope to realize only in the life to come. The *Confessions* thus cohere round the mystical core of vision and ascent which Augustine first elaborated to explain his inner experiences in Milan. The love which drives the *Confessions* is the love of God which these experiences left in Augustine's soul. God, he has learned, is transcendent, but He is also within each one of us 'more inward than our innermost part'. He is a spiritual being.

The *Confessions* rise to the challenge of this 'one, divine philosophy' by expressing it in a superb comparison. 'It is one thing,' Augustine says, 'to see the homeland of peace from the wooded peak of a mountain . . .' The Platonists had seen this homeland, a territory which they shared with Christian lovers of wisdom. It was presided over by a transcendent, spiritual God. But 'it is another thing to find the way there . . .' On the way to it, the Platonists became lost on impassable roads and tracks. Their own deserters ambushed them and preyed on their remaining number. They were led astray by 'the lion and dragon', demonic enemies. 'It is another thing,' however, 'to hold to the road which leads there', to the homeland itself. This road is the road of the Christians, fortified by their heavenly commander, Christ. Deserters from this heavenly army never rob the convoy which persists on the road: they 'avoid it like a punishment'.[32]

Unexpectedly, we can now hear Augustine, seven years later, enlarging on this very theme, the one which his confessions had memorably exploited. In Carthage, in early January 404, he preached a long sermon, recently rediscovered, 'against pagans' on their feast of the Kalends of January. The image of the 'homeland' and the two roads returned to his mind in fuller detail, as did the 'lion and dragon'. They are explained as the 'false arts of the Platonists', their magic and sacrifices, sorcery and astrology. He also enlarges on the Christian convoy.[33] Some Christians, he preaches, can see further and more clearly than others. They include any Christian who 'can transcend all created things in his mind and see the ineffable light of wisdom'. Such a Christian will see that 'all that is said from that source is unworthy of its magnitude', apt though such talk may be for the 'little ones' who are being nourished from that same source. Those who cannot 'transcend and see inexpressible truth' must hold fast to their mediator, Christ. So, he adds, must those who can see what is 'immutable'. Otherwise, they will have seen in vain.

Before a Christian audience, on a January day of traditional gift-giving, Augustine was returning obliquely to what he himself had discovered in Milan. The 'lion and dragon', he explains, are the arts of the Devil, who interposes himself as 'mediator' for those who stray from the high road. When they stray, they run into a 'baffling inextricable mountain'. Those who march onwards include those who 'transcend' and see the immutable. Augustine had been one such 'transcender' in Milan, nearly twenty years earlier. The experiences had certainly not faded from his mind.

Despite Augustine's fine imagery, Plotinus' ascents to God had not relied on magic and blood sacrifice, the black arts of the 'lion and dragon'. Despite Augustine's reinterpretations, the fact remains that it was Plotinus' books, not Paul's, which taught him to turn inwards, then upwards. He had reached 'That which Is' without relying at all on Christ. A year later he would return to It, but next time he would not be alone. His mother would join him on the road.

19
Sex, Ambition and Philosophy

I

After these remarkable experiences, Augustine no longer looked on the world and his place in it in the same way. More than ever before, lessons in the tricks of rhetoric and speeches on hard-faced commanders seemed a waste of time. The 'true and divine philosophy' had brought him into contact with God.

If Libanius or Synesius had promptly met him and heard him 'chattering' about his visions, whatever would they have thought of him? In fact, visionary experiences were part of the mental outlook of their friends, their teachers and themselves, in ways which put Augustine's into a wider context.

Libanius had a few friends and pupils who studied Platonist philosophy, but he himself had no personal interest in the difficult Neoplatonist teachings.[1] He would have found the inward-looking mysticism of Plotinus and Augustine very abstruse: only Gore Vidal, in his modern novel *Julian*, has ever misunderstood Libanius as a mystic. However, he would not dismiss the Platonists' visionary aim as ridiculous. In his pagan world, encounters with one or other of the gods occurred each night in the inner world of dreams. Libanius himself freely crossed this open frontier, dreaming of Heracles or Asclepius the healer, who seemed to communicate with him by words or symbols. No less than Augustine, he lived with the 'sensed presence' of the gods. Above all, he ascribed their visible company to his admired friend, the pagan Emperor Julian.[2]

Julian is the pagan who has written the nearest equivalent to Augustine's accounts of a divine ascent. In *c.*350, just before Augustine was born, he had the sense of a close encounter which was to divert his entire life. Like Augustine, he recalled it some twelve years later in carefully crafted language, in his case enriched by his beloved Homer.[3] Unlike Augustine, he presented it explicitly in the guise of a 'myth', leaving his readers to discern its inner truth. He describes it as predestined, an aspect which he expresses through the traditional imagery of the Fates.

Julian makes his 'myth' anonymous, but it is clear that it refers to his younger self. Like Augustine's God, Zeus, he says, took pity on him and made the sun-god, Helios, swear an oath to 'take special care of him, cherish him and cure him of his disease' (the 'disease' is his Christianity). Julian presents himself as Helios' 'son' in whom the god has implanted a paternal 'spark' of fire. Helios and Athena then transported the young man to a deserted place, where he met youthful Hermes, just as Hermes is met near the immortal ending of Homer's *Iliad*. Like Wagner's Siegfried, Julian was carrying a sword, but also a shield and a spear. With Hermes' guidance he proceeded through a divine landscape which was teeming with flowers 'such as the gods love' and with 'trees of ivy, laurel and myrtle'. Beyond this heavenly forest lay a high mountain, the seat of Zeus himself, to whom young Julian was told to pray.

In a 'sort of sleep or ecstasy' the sun-god Helios was then revealed to him. The young Julian clung to the god, reluctant to let go, but was ordered against his will to return to earth and engage in public affairs, a task in which he was to be guarded by a helmet from the goddess Athena and a 'torch' from the sun-god himself. 'Remember,' Helios told him, 'that you have an immortal soul which is our offspring and if you follow us, you will be a god, and, with us, see our father [Zeus].' These orders were given on a high mountain peak to which Helios had taken him up. It was 'filled with light from on high'.[4]

Augustine, too, felt 'taken up' by his God to a zone of extraordinary light from which he was unwilling to descend. Like Augustine, Julian was to convert after his experience, but his conversion took him away from Christianity to the pagan gods. They had been lingering in him since childhood, not in his mother's milk but inside him as an 'inner spark'. He became a deserter from the Christians' convoy, but so far from shunning their road ever after, as the *Confessions* claim that such deserters do, he continued to harass and persecute any Christians who persisted on their march.

Like Julian, Synesius was conscious of a 'divine spark' in his soul. In letters to a former fellow student, he urges him, 'philosophize and raise up the divine in yourself to the first-born God'. This first-born is probably Christ, expressed in language which Neoplatonists used for their heavenly Triad.[5] The ascent of the soul to the divine is a constant presence in Synesius' writings, in his letters, in his short book *On Dreams*, in two speeches which he composed for the court in Constantinople and, above all, in his poetic hymns. Even during sleep, Synesius states, 'the gift of prophecy in dreams can open for the soul a way to the most perfect visions of what exists, even if the soul has never desired it and has never been caused to think of such an ascent – the very summit, among what exists, is to peer out beyond one's nature and to be bound together with the Intelligible world'.[6] Dreams were a route to God which Monnica, but not Augustine 'peering out', explored in Milan.

In his hymns, Synesius expresses this aspiration in complex, metrical language which is heavily Platonist in range and imagery. He tells his 'lyre' to sound a 'Doric song', not about 'soft-skinned young girls and their sexy laughter', but about 'unpolluted Wisdom from God': in Milan, Augustine will soon confront this very priority.[7] This hymn is cast as if the singing of it will help the singer to ascend to God. 'Only confirm your impulse with songs which bring [you] to the Intelligible world.' Then, 'the Father will appear very close by, stretching out His hands, for a beam of Light will run before, and light up the paths'. Finally, 'Come there, my soul, entreating the Father, Ascend, do not delay, Leaving earthly things to earth. Soon, mingled with the Father, You will dance, divine in the Divine.'[8]

If Augustine, a decade earlier, could have read and sung this hymn, he would have been entranced by its call. He had 'ascended', encountered Light and abandoned earthly things. Actual union, or 'mingling', with the Father was not his experience, but his ascent was 'guided' by God, although God had concluded it by thrusting him away. Several years later, Synesius was still composing such songs of ascent: 'Ignite, king, the lights of ascent, and let the soul, fleeing the body, no longer sink into the blind folly of the world.'[9] Even more pervasively than Augustine, Synesius, a lifelong Christian, uses Platonist language to express his ideal. Its ascent is the ascent of a disembodied soul while it discards the evil accretions which accompany it. The natural world around it is not so much God's purposeful creation as an emanation from His abstract powers. Synesius' heavenly Triad comprises the One, His will and creative Wisdom.[10] The Son's, or Intellect's, role is one of 'cleansing', not redeeming, and His incarnation and bodily Resurrection are nowhere stated. Synesius can even write of plural 'gods'.[11]

This language, surprising to modern Christians, derives in part from

Plotinus' pupil Porphyry, the author whom Augustine went on to read within six months of his own ascents to God. Synesius also uses imagery, adjectives and abstract triads which he has borrowed from a most esoteric text, the *Chaldaean Oracles*.[12] It was a pagan poem, anonymous by origin, written in the later second century AD. Augustine was wholly unaware of this Platonizing 'holy text', but Synesius continued to draw on it, citing it repeatedly in his hastily written book *On Dreams*. These *Chaldaean Oracles* had become connected with controversial rites by which pagans claimed to force and manipulate their gods, an art which was detestable to thoughtful Christians. In *On Dreams*, Synesius writes nonetheless of rites which 'purify' the soul: probably, they are the 'rites' in his Platonist sources, ones which Christians like himself should, strictly, not accommodate.[13]

Where had he encountered these rarefied texts? The answer leads back to his revered philosophy tutor Hypatia, whose inherited interests included the *Chaldaean Oracles*.[14] Synesius' use of them is revealing. By a professional modern philosopher, he has been ranked as 'a philosopher of the most dismal stripe'.[15] Nevertheless, his writings present him as a fascinated ex-pupil, one who venerated his philosophy tutor, idolized the subject to which she had introduced him and held fast ever after to her tutorials. He was unable to advance the subject by thinking it through for himself. He simply added to his religious faith whatever his tutor taught him, a loyal pupil with an 'upper second class mind'. He did not engage in Augustine's impassioned comparisons with Paul and other scriptures or persuade himself of their core of shared 'wisdom'. Rather, he remained true to his tutorial syllabus, even while pursuing the active life of a landowner and a champion of his city's best interests. His robust life of action did not stop him from writing about the soul's divine spark and the invisible holy Triad. He saw no need to abandon worldly activities. He continued to write hymns of ascent, but, unlike Augustine, he shows no sign of a successful mystical ascent himself.

Both men were Christians. Before baptism, however, young Synesius had encountered philosophy and been converted to it by exclusive classes with a well-born lady. For him, therefore, philosophy was a secret 'mystery' fit only for the few. It was something for which the masses were wholly unsuited.[16] Augustine, by contrast, was self-taught outside any lecture- or classroom. In due course, while still professing their love of 'wisdom', both men became bishops. Augustine, however, believed that 'wisdom' had been restored to its true form and presented to one and all. He did not hesitate, therefore, to treat a Christian audience of farmers and harbour workers to an uplifting sermon on the essential being of God, 'That which Is'. It was not a 'mystery', it was not madness: it was the 'one, true *philosophy*', revealed for us all by God Himself.[17]

II

Now that his world-view had changed, Augustine had reached the point from which a break with his past, a conversion, was highly likely. Manifestly, it would not be a conversion to Christianity. Aged 31, he had been a Christian, in his own view of himself, throughout his life, apart from his very brief wobble in recent weeks. Nor would it be a conversion to baptism. He was already set on the path to the baptismal pool which would complement his marriage, his mother's long-laid plan. Baptisms occurred in the Easter season, and if none of the events of the next few weeks had happened to him, he would still have emerged from the pool at Easter, 387, a 'faithful Christian' after the customary classes of instruction from Bishop Ambrose. These classes would have put right his 'fuzzy theology' about the relation between Christ and the earthly Jesus. He and his friends were still wondrously out of line with the Nicene Creed. His patron Romanianus sympathized with the Manichees. Nebridius thought that Christ had only seemed to suffer on earth and that His humanity was no more real than the Manichees insisted. Alypius, meanwhile, had no idea what Ambrose and his Church really believed. Augustine was now 'certain' about God and evil, but still thought Christ had been a wise man who acquired immortality.[18] Like many baptismal candidates, Augustine needed teaching, but the result would be a correction, not a conversion.

His conversion was to be quite different, combining three interlocking levels. One would be a conversion from rhetoric to philosophy, a familiar pattern among intelligent pagans and Christians. Another is a conversion from 'worldly ambition' (*spes saeculi*), a conversion utterly alien to Libanius the lifelong teacher: the very phrase is one of Augustine's distinctive favourites. The third is the renunciation of the aspect of life which Augustine greatly enjoyed: sex. Christian 'virtuosi' engaged in other renunciations, restricting their diet, their drinking of wine, their sleep, their washing and their worldly possessions. The renunciation of 'worldly ambition' involved the renunciation of a worldly salary and worldly goods, honour and power. Sexual activity is classed by Augustine as part of the 'worldly burden', one which also led to children and descendants, those 'worldly' results. Emphasis on it is not a modern distortion of his concerns. Augustine himself is quite clear about what bothered him: 'longing for sex' (*desiderium concubitus*) and 'enslavement to worldly business'. Sex, he says, was the 'tightest chain' by which he was bound.

Each of the levels of his conversion had been burning slowly in him since he was first enflamed by reading the *Hortensius* and finding the love of wisdom, or *philosophia*, ranked far above rhetoric, riches, honours and sex. At the time Augustine had prayed, 'Give me chastity, but not yet . . .' Time had now passed and some old pigeons were coming home to roost. They were not based on what he had observed for many years in the Manichaean Elect. Augustine was not intending to restrict his food, his washing or, as yet, his ownership of property.

The three aspects to his decision are picked out in the very first text which he writes only a few months after the decisive changes in his life. In November 386, he dedicates it, *On the Happy Life*, to his 'greater friend' Mallius Theodorus, with due respect. In its preface he exploits the metaphor of seafarers who seek the 'harbour' of philosophy, as he and Theodorus both had.[19] In his own case, he says, he had been detained at sea by two 'anchors', the enticements of a 'wife and worldly honour'. His aim, he remarks, had been that when he 'had attained them, then at last, as is possible only for very few people, I would hurry under full sail and with all oars into that bay', the 'bay of Philosophy'. His aim, he means, had been to acquire an honorific post in the public hierarchy and marry the child-bride who was waiting for him. After he had profited from public office, her dowry would enable him to study philosophy for the rest of his life. However, he read the 'very few books of Plotinus' and compared them 'as best I could' with the scriptures. As a result he 'wanted to break all those anchors', but his 'considered esteem for certain people' weighed with him. He was then struck by a 'storm which seemed to be adverse', but was a blessing in disguise, he writes, because it caused him to cast away the burdens which had weighed down his 'ship'. This 'storm' was his affliction by pain in his chest which affected his speaking voice. It forced him to give up rhetoric, abandon his bride-to-be (implicitly, one of his 'burdens') and turn to philosophy instead.

Notoriously, the *Confessions*, eleven years later, tell a story to whose climax these problems of health are incidental. Nonetheless, at two of the levels of his conversion, they were highly relevant. Without any need to convert, they made his continuation as a public orator all but impossible. A voice failure would oblige him to renounce 'worldly ambition', his lucrative career based on public speaking. If he gave up rhetoric, he could then 'convert' to philosophy, a classic pattern. The change did not have to be total and permanent, as Libanius and Synesius well show. They faced similar dilemmas, but responded in a different way.

In this very year, unknown to Augustine, his rhetorical counterpart in the Greek-speaking world, elderly Libanius, was also suffering acute problems of health. They were compounded by the return of his migraines, which had been dormant since that thunderstorm fifteen years before. 'There was the fear that I would be laid low while sitting in the company of my young pupils.'[20] Unable to sleep, he was praying for death. Ominous dreams seemed to portend it and he could talk of nothing else. He could not read the classics and he could not even compose a speech. 'My speaking had been destroyed, even though the young kept on shouting their demands for it.'[21] To cap it all, he had two acute attacks of gout, as never before. People expected him to be dead by the morning, and in other cities the rumour spread that he had indeed already died.

In one and the same half-year, spring and summer, 386, the two public orators, Augustine and Libanius, were thus both suffering from the loss of their all-important voice. Augustine's condition was exacerbated by personal stress, by his sense of the futility of his career and its insecurities, but also by his mystical experiences and the feeling that big choices must soon be made. Libanius traced his ailments specifically to malicious magic. In his classroom, that 'chorus-space for speaking', a dead lizard, or chamaeleon, was found to have been buried with its head bent round, one front leg missing and the other stuck into its mouth 'to silence it'. The spell, as usual, was designed to be an exact enactment of the intended effect.[22] Like this lizard, Libanius suffered the effects in his head (the migraines), a leg (gout) and his tongue and mouth (his inability to speak in public). There was nothing in the least comic about it. The spell had targeted Libanius as meticulously as the spells which are preserved in papyrus texts or lead tablets.[23] Like everyone else, Libanius took for granted that such spells could have an exact, malign effect according to their construction.

Both orators look back on their health crises in the same way, as blessings in disguise. Augustine is quick to classify his chest pain as a 'storm' which fortunately freed him for philosophy. Libanius presents the entire episode of the lizard and his consequent illness in terms of providence and latent good fortune. Providential dreams helped him to sense the hidden cause of the problem; pagan prophets helped him to surmount it, and when the spell was uncovered, it was his good fortune, he writes, that it had been buried and not left to work more potently above ground.[24]

The two men's responses differed in one very important particular. The loss of Augustine's voice confirmed his existing wish to resign as a public orator. Despite his similar health problem, Libanius did not think for one moment of lessening his lifelong commitment to rhetoric and teaching. Somehow, aged seventy-two, he would continue. Indeed, he continued for another seven years, teaching, writing and speaking, resisting the rising tide of Latin studies and exerting himself on behalf of former pupils and their requests. His finest hour still lay ahead, in the notorious 'Riot of the Statues', which was to shake Antioch a year later and in which he was to intercede for those caught up in official reprisals.[25] Illness forced him to take time off, but it did not cause him to abandon his entire career.

Synesius, meanwhile, confronted one of Augustine's dilemmas and also responded differently. His tutor Hypatia had converted him to philosophy, but when he left her and returned to Cyrene, he was still a landed aristocrat, highly skilled in composing speeches and in writing poetry in complex metres. In response to critics, he even addressed the nature of 'conversion' in his *On Dion*, composed in *c.*404/5, long after he had left Hypatia's classes. 'The philosopher, according to us,' he states, 'will keep company with God and himself through philosophy, but with men through the underlying powers of [rhetorical] speech.'[26] The one, therefore, did not have to be given up for the sake of the other, despite his critics. Like Augustine, he had written youthful poems (now lost to us), light rhetorical works and even a sparkling essay *On Baldness*. As a result, he says, critics were attacking his pretentions from two corners, men 'in white cloaks', he tells us (surely Platonist philosophers), and others 'in brown cloaks' (Christian monks in Alexandria and also, perhaps, Cynic so-called philosophers, although a reference to them here is disputed).[27] They complained that he was only a frivolous 'sophist', but he defended himself by appealing to his role model, Dio of Prusa (*flor. c.*100). Whereas Synesius had written on baldness, Dio had written a speech in praise of hair. Dio, he insisted, had begun life as a practitioner of rhetoric, but then converted to philosophy after a reversal in his life and fourteen years of exile. Synesius' reading of Dio's life is not one which modern scholars share, but he applied Dio's example defensively to himself.[28] He even sent the text to Hypatia, implying that despite his youthful trivia, he was indeed a philosopher, just like Dio some three centuries earlier.

Like Dio's supposed 'conversion', Synesius' was not one-sided. He had become impassioned by philosophy as a student, but as his letters and speeches show, he had never abandoned his previous rhetorical training. He continued to apply his rhetoric to his civic duties. Could not Augustine do likewise, take time off, like Libanius, to recover and calm down and then, like Synesius, continue to philosophize while resuming a rhetorical and patriotic career? The obstacles were his class and his temperament. Libanius had many well-placed connections thanks to his upper-class family background, his 'old boy' network and his ever-multiplying ex-pupils. He could survive time off, whereas Augustine, precariously placed and much less well-born, could not. The relief of a short break would probably help his voice to heal, but by then he would have lost the public job which made him a plausible husband for his rich fiancée. After turning inwards and ascending to God, he could not simply go back to teaching 'lies' in another city at a lower rank.

Unlike Libanius, he had felt a conversion to philosophy smouldering in him for the past twelve years. He could not simply profess a 'love of wisdom' and continue like Synesius with his rhetorical trade. Rhetoric had lost its point for him, whereas philosophy was something he was burning to pursue, because he had the brain and the talent for it. Nonetheless, Synesius gave two apt warnings. Those who ascend to God without due preparation engage in a 'mad leap', a sort of 'Bacchic frenzy'. Their descent is especially brutal because they have no preparatory studies to which they can return.[29] Augustine had just made such a 'mad leap'. Even if he took up philosophy full-time, he would be advised to hold on to his preparatory studies in rhetoric and literature.

There was also the burning question: sex. Synesius greatly reproached Christian celibates who glorified in their sexual abstinence as an end in itself. Celibacy might help a philosopher, he considered, but it was not essential for philosophizing.[30] When Synesius wrote *On Dion* he had recently married, with the blessing of the Bishop of Alexandria. He even dedicated his views on rhetoric and philosophy to the son whom he and his wife were expecting.[31] The sexual dilemma of Augustine's conversion would have struck him as excessive. For Libanius, it went against the conventions of his rhetorical class. Pre- or extra-marital sex with a paid woman was no sin for an otherwise loyal husband, although it was impermissible for women. Not to marry at all was not only to withdraw from civic responsibility. Lifelong virginity went against the example of the gods: it was 'godless'.

III

Despite the 'turbulence' which he kept to himself, Augustine's intensified urge to convert to philosophy had not formed in isolation. His 'greater friends' were encouraging his interest with their philosophical poems and dialogues. There was also the daily presence of his friend Nebridius, the person with whom Synesius would have felt most at home. Like Synesius, he had enough of a landed income not to need a teaching career. In Milan he had agreed to help out the elementary teacher Verecundus, but the job was far beneath his intelligence, and he had only taken it out of kindness. He did not wish to become known to 'the great men of the world', because they would be a source of 'worry and anxiety'. Nebridius wished to keep his mind free for 'researching or reading or hearing something about wisdom in as many hours as he could'.[32] Here was an example, very close to Augustine, of someone who had already renounced 'worldly ambition' (*spes saeculi*) and converted to philosophy as the ultimate value in life. He was a crucial model for Augustine's decisions, even more than the *Confessions* happen to emphasize.

In the Milan of summer 386, worldly ambition was anyway tempered by the tense political situation. What would the usurping Maximus choose to do next? If he swept down from Trier and overthrew young Valentinian's court, Augustine would have to flatter him to have any chance of retaining his job as a public orator. If Augustine took his next step and successfully lobbied for a governorship of a minor province, Maximus might then take power and throw him off the ladder altogether. It might seem wise to anticipate the trouble, follow Nebridius' example and give up.

As older and wiser heads no doubt reminded him, such a retirement from 'worldly ambition' would deter his prospective parents-in-law. He was not nearly as rich as Nebridius. Why should they give a well-endowed bride to someone who abandoned his professorship and launched into a life of 'wisdom' without any training in the subject, any hope of a tenured position and any reason for polite society to take him seriously in his new career? He was not interested in being a philosopher in any of the recognized schools, Platonist, sceptic or Aristotelian, for which he would have to go east and teach in Greek. For him, there was only the 'true and divine philosophy', God's philosophy, which had been made widely available by Christ. This Christian starting point might deter fee-paying pupils in pagan families from taking his courses.

Should he, then, break off the demands of his engagement and choose the third level of conversion, the abandonment of sex? Since his mystical experience, Augustine had been studying Paul's letters 'most carefully' and it had not eluded him that in the letters to the Corinthians (especially 1 Cor. 7) the Apostle had written of sex and marriage as no more than a Christian 'second best'. He also knew the cardinal text in Matthew's Gospel in which Christ praises those who become 'eunuchs for the kingdom of heaven'. These texts were cited by Christian celibates everywhere, including Jerome to his noblewomen in Rome.[33] In the churches in Milan, Augustine saw their call at work among baptized Christians. Weeks before, his impulse to a communal life had been purely philosophical. Now, his impulse to selfless living was scriptural. 'I saw the Church full,' the *Confessions* tell us, 'with one going this way, another that way.' He is alluding here to Paul's much-cited words at 1 Corinthians 7.7: one way is sexual, the other, celibate. Some members of the Church were married, whereas others had renounced sex: should Augustine come forward for baptism as a sexually active candidate or not?

The question had always been present in Christian history, but it had gained urgency in parts of the Latin West precisely during Augustine's adult lifetime. We have seen it already at work in Rome. In Spain, it had recently become a challenging option through the teachings of the heretical Priscillian.[34] In northern Italy, by contrast, it had found few takers in the quieter worldliness of Milan's outlying towns. Publicly, it had been given a new emphasis by Ambrose only since the 370s and especially for female members of his church. It fitted well with Ambrose's image of the true, uncorrupted Church which he wished to uphold against its heretical 'Arian' rival. In honour of it, he had introduced his formal ceremony of veiling for young virgins. Girls were to be sent up to Milan from outlying churches and welcomed in a public reception as new 'brides of Christ': they took on vows and veils which Ambrose considered to be binding for their lifetime. Remember, Ambrose told their parents, that a 'virgin is your gift to God . . . a virgin is a victim sacrificed by her mother and by that daily act of sacrifice the divine anger is appeased'.[35] There was another, more practical aspect. 'The virgin is pledged without loss to her parents: she will not trouble them for a dowry . . .'[36] The inspiring example of the Virgin Mary was there to urge them on. In his later writings, Ambrose emphasizes Mary's perpetual virginity, which had been uninterrupted (so he claimed) by the birth of Jesus. Role models were also found among female martyrs of legend, Thecla, sentenced to a brothel in Antioch, or little Agnes, martyred at the age of twelve, when almost too small for the executioner's sword and yet, said Ambrose, many of the onlookers wanted her 'to come on forward' as their bride.[37]

Ambrose's gifts for imagery and storytelling ran freely on the topic of virginity, but he had to admit that his pleas won few converts. Even Jerome found them badly pitched: his own letters on virginity implicitly countered arguments which Ambrose had used.[38] Meanwhile, very few parents were prepared to surrender a daughter from the socially conditioned conveyor belt of marriage and childbirth, despite the garlands of praise which Ambrose wove from that erotic intruder in the Bible, the Song of Songs.

In one such sermon, Ambrose acknowledges the helpful presence of a fellow hunter for young 'brides' of Christ, his friend the Bishop of Bologna. He had come up to Milan to assist Ambrose's mission, but, even so, their catch had not been impressive. In Bologna, Ambrose remarks, the devoted virgins of the Church still numbered only twenty.[39] Ambrose's teaching was not directed only to women. He himself personified male virginity and at Christian baptism he stressed to each candidate, male and female alike, the higher merits of a celibate life. Baptism, he preached to them, was an opportunity for an ascent of the soul, for a transformation, for a 'flight' from the body and the world which Ambrose himself exemplified.[40]

In his own social circle, Augustine had other examples. His younger friend Alypius was no apostle of the sexual act, which he personally had disliked. He had been greatly impressed by the celibacy of the Manichaean Elect and only months before had been arguing that celibacy was an aid to philosophical study. Augustine now knew Zenobius in Milan, a 'greater friend' who was living with a mind free from 'the filth of lusts' and 'pernicious desires'.[41] He would also know about Mallius Theodorus' sister, the devoted virgin Daedalia. There was also an example very close to his heart, his dismissed partner, Adeodatus' mother. She had left for north Africa and was vowing never to have sex again. If she could give it up, could not he?

The lifestyle of those who renounced sexual activity resounds loudly in Christian texts, but, even so, they were a tiny minority. Christian virginity, like the virginity of olive oil, was a matter of degree. An elegant Latin text explains the nuances, while addressing the very uncertainties which were affecting Augustine in Milan. Of unknown authorship (a later friend of Augustine has been suggested), the *Consultations of Apollonius and Zacchaeus* was probably composed in the mid-390s.[42] This fiction describes how a Christian, Zacchaeus, supposedly won Apollonius, a pagan philosopher, to the Christian faith before a crowd of hearers and brought him quickly to baptism. Apollonius, the ex-pagan, then asked Zacchaeus about the prominent topic of celibacy, only to be told that marriage in itself is not sinful, but that it should be chaste and conducted without sex except for the conception of children.[43] Followers of this so-called 'middle way' (the long-suffering *mediocres*), he is told, will not rank among the 'brightest stars', as Paul had called them, of the future kingdom, but their failings will not influence the 'little ones' (*exigui*), people who are not prepared to be talked out of regular sex. As for the 'stars', some of them have never known marriage at all. They live apart, even when in a town; they share possessions and sleep on beds of rush matting before waking at dawn and singing psalms. Others live even more heroically in the desert as followers of a monastic life. These monks, Apollonius observes, are widely disliked by contemporaries. Zacchaeus assures him that this hatred is due only to a few wicked monks who 'mislead young ladies for the sake of foul gain or win them away from their proposed chastity'.[44] A few rotten apples in the celibate basket bring the whole crop into disrepute.

The ranks of celibate Christians, Zacchaeus explains, include various levels of age and experience. Some are virgin recruits, but others have had a first marriage and are avoiding a second 'since one of two things happen to those who are incautious: either they do not find in the second one what they lost in the first one or, second time round, they suffer what they lacked in their first one . . .'[45] These prudent veterans are seldom considered so frankly in a Christian text. Together with those couples who had had children and had brought themselves thereafter to agree a test-ban treaty in bed, they are a reminder that the 'bright stars' in a Christian Church were not all young ladies who were cultivating drabness, nor young men like Augustine who were trying to suppress the flood tide of their hormones. In support of the life of the virginal 'stars', Zacchaeus cites Matthew's Gospel on 'eunuchs for the kingdom of heaven' and Paul's 1 Corinthians 7, exactly the texts which Augustine cites as influencing himself in summer 386. 'Only a lazy and diffident soul,' the newly converted Apollonius answers, 'who hopes for nothing special from God's generosity will be slothful among little things, when the highest have been put to him.'[46] Augustine, ever the overachiever, was no such person. He was always responsive to exemplary people and he had belonged for years to a Manichaean group whose Elect were all celibate: his patron Romanianus, still a Manichee, had spoken recently of doing likewise. He also read that in his Letter to the Corinthians Paul called it 'good' not to touch a woman.[47]

Even so, it would be a drastic decision. Baptism certainly did not require it, nor, as yet, did the priesthood, nor even a bishopric, had Augustine been interested in either. Nor did philosophers have to give up sex. In Alexandria, Hypatia, Synesius' tutor, was famed precisely for being unusually obdurate. Pupils and hearers admired her virginal beauty, but when one young hearer, it was said, professed sexual love for her, she threw her stained sanitary towel at him and told him to look at it and see what he actually loved.[48] She remained a virgin, an awesome female tutor and an 'honorary man'. Her pupil Synesius professed the same philosophy, but married nonetheless, refused to give up sex and fathered no fewer than three sons. Like many others, Augustine was still tied to a woman, his second concubine, with no hint that she was anything other than a pleasure in bed. Yet the perfectionism of others was starting to trouble him.

So were two other items in what he was reading. 'I did not want to be more certain about You,' he tells God, 'but I wanted to be more stable in you.' In the Platonist books he could discover that bodily passion and sexual pleasure pull the soul away from God. They are the enemies of 'stability': was that why he had recently been thrust quickly from God's presence when he ascended towards it?[49] He was in turmoil. So he decided to go to Simplicianus, the elderly priest by whom Ambrose himself had been baptized. 'I had found the good pearl,' he recalls, 'and it had to be bought by selling all that I had . . . and yet I was hesitating.'[50] For Mani, his former guide, that 'pearl' had been the heavenly Light, glistening in each of our embattled souls. For Augustine, it was now chastity, a conversion from sex for the rest of his life.

20
Into the Garden

I

On arrival, 'I narrated to him the circuitous course of my wandering': elderly Simplicianus is the first person known to have heard the rehearsed narrative which Ambrose, reading silently, had escaped. It was the germ of what would one day become the *Confessions*, Books 3–7. Their meeting turns on two themes which develop powerfully. One is the telling of stories of conversion. Beginning with Simplicianus, the *Confessions* tell three such stories in sequence before telling a fourth, Augustine's own, and a fifth, Alypius'. The other, again, is creative misunderstanding. If read carefully, Simplicianus and Augustine converse at cross-purposes, but, nonetheless, the older man's words have an important effect. Creative misunderstanding then resurfaces in the culminating moments of Augustine's own conversion.

Simplicianus was a wise, experienced adviser, one whom Ambrose, his former baptismal candidate, still 'loved as a father'.[1] In Augustine he saw a brilliant public orator who had become enthralled, he learned, by Platonist teachings. Before Augustine could come to the crux of his problems, whether or not to give up sex, the older man embarked on a story suggested by an item which the agitated young man in his room had mentioned.

While telling his convoluted tale, Augustine said he had read 'some books of the Platonists', ones which Victorinus had translated into Latin. Victorinus, he had heard, had once been a teacher of rhetoric at Rome, but had died, Augustine believed, as a Christian. Wise Simplicianus saw his cue. First, he commended Augustine for not straying into other philosophers' writings: they were 'full of fallacies and deceits according to the "elements of this world" ', as Paul had written to the Colossians, whereas 'God and His word were insinuated into the Platonists in every possible way'. Ambrose's letters show that Simplicianus indeed had no sympathy with the sophistries of worldly philosophers.[2] Like Ambrose, he made an exception only for the unworldly Platonists.

Augustine's memory on this point is well-founded, but his *City of God*, at least twenty-five years later, gives a detail which the *Confessions* happen to omit. 'We were used to hearing Simplicianus say', Augustine remarks there, that a Platonist philosopher had greatly admired the opening of John's Gospel ('In the beginning was the Word . . .') and had considered that it should be publicly inscribed in letters of gold. Augustine is not necessarily referring to repeated meetings between Simplicianus and himself: he may be recalling what Simplicianus said to him at the time, and on other occasions said to others. The opening of John's Gospel had indeed been noticed with approval by a Platonist philosopher, Amelius, some 200 years earlier but Simplicianus may have been thinking of a more recent example.[3]

There was no need at the time for Simplicianus to go into theological detail. However, he was talking to a young man of the most avid curiosity. Augustine went away, took the hint and filled it in by reading John's Gospel when he returned to his own scripture books. Selected words in the Fourth Gospel's first chapter had been deployed by Mani and his followers to support their teaching on Light and Darkness. Augustine now came to it afresh and read it in the light of his newly found wisdom. 'In the beginning was the Word,' he read in the very first verse, 'and the Word was with God, and the Word was God': Plotinus referred to Intellect as the second of his supranormal entities and also mentioned a Word (*logos*). Victorinus may even have translated Plotinus' 'Intellect' as 'Word'. Augustine also read: 'All things were made by him . . . and whatever is made, in it is life': Plotinus considered 'Soul' to be the source of our visible world and here too he seemed to be groping for the Gospel. He seemed close to what Augustine read next: 'In him was life and life was the light of mankind and the light shines in darkness, but the darkness comprehended it not . . .' Here, some of the most suggestive treatises by Plotinus are those grouped together in his fifth Book. They refer to Intellect, or 'reason', as light, and they allow that our upper soul may make contact and be 'lightened' by light from the One.[4] As Augustine says in the *Confessions*, the verbal parallels between John and the Platonists are not exact. John's Gospel addresses the blindness and darkness of the world, whereas Plotinus argues that all the world, including ourselves, is yearning for the One. The more Augustine continued to read, the more parallels he may have found. From a Syriac source, published only in 1981, previously unknown sayings by Porphyry have emerged in which he states, 'The Radiance, the second Mind, who issued forth and descended . . . returned and was raised up. He is Light, then, even when he descends, for he illuminates the World by his ineffable Descent . . .'[5] Augustine was certainly reading Porphyry by November 386 and if he ever knew texts like these, they would have reinforced his belief that philosophy known to the Platonists was latent in the first chapter of John's Gospel.

What was not known to them, as the *Confessions* emphasize, were two pillars of Christian theology, the Redemption and the Incarnation. On reading John's first chapter, Augustine learned that the 'Word became flesh and dwelt among us'. Until that time, as he tells us, he had thought of Christ as a mortal man, endowed with exceptional wisdom. Four months later, however, he is clear in his first surviving writings that Christ had been God incarnate. He had not been instructed meanwhile in a baptismal class. The neat explanation of his change of perspective is that it resulted from Simplicianus' remark. In response to it Augustine went away and read the start of John's Gospel and found that, like Paul's letters, it amplified the 'true philosophy'. It stated the Incarnation very clearly. Father Simplicianus has thus been hailed by modern Catholics as the 'real architect of Augustine's Catholic conversion'.[6] Yet, it was not so much a conversion as a correction, and Simplicianus, I believe, was an inadvertent architect. He dropped Augustine a hint in passing, but it was Augustine who followed it up and made much more of it.

Simplicianus' impact was entirely oral, through well-aimed stories. When Augustine mentioned Victorinus, Simplicianus realized that his tale was worth retelling. He had known Marius Victorinus in the 350s and was aware that he had been born in north Africa. Like Augustine, he had been a public orator and a teacher of rhetoric, albeit in Rome itself. Much grander than Augustine, he had been the friend of senators. His name was well known in the 'eternal city' and he had even been honoured with a public statue in Rome's imposing Forum of Trajan.[7] For years, he had been a pagan, but then he began to read 'holy scripture and all the writings of the Christians' and to investigate them 'most studiously' and to scrutinize them thoroughly. One day, in an intimate moment, he told Simplicianus to realize that, now, he was a Christian.

Without becoming a catechumen, Victorinus had been converted by his own intense scrutiny of scripture. It was an unusual route in the mid-fourth century, and Simplicianus refused to believe it unless he saw Victorinus inside a church. 'So, do walls make Christians?' Victorinus retorted, memorably.[8] He was afraid to go to church and provoke a hostile reaction from the pagan great and good in Rome. Nonetheless he continued to read the scriptures and to gain confidence. In due course, he began to fear, Augustine tells us, that Christ would deny him in heaven if he was afraid to confess Christ among men. Such a denial can still be read as a warning in Luke's Gospel. One day, all of a sudden, he said to Simplicianus: 'Let's go to church: a Christian is what I want to become.' He put his name forward for baptism; he received baptismal instruction; he was prepared to profess his faith. In Rome, a sly compromise was offered to prominent converts who were afraid of public derision: they could profess their faith in private. Victorinus refused. He mounted a rostrum in public, to the amazed delight of the crowd. 'Victorinus, Victorinus,' they whispered in hushed tones, and roared with exultation when they saw him in person. He spoke his words, whereupon they took him to their hearts, Augustine says, 'in love and rejoicing'.[9]

The *Confessions* add brilliant, compelling colour to the story. As ever, Augustine draws on the Psalms, invoking God who causes the heavens to bow and the cedar trees to smoke: like a tall tree, Victorinus was touched, he says, by this smouldering power. The cedars, as elsewhere, symbolize pride. 'Come, Lord,' Augustine prays, 'do it, rouse and recall us, fire and seize us, be fragrant, grow sweet; let us love, let us run': with this amazing string of imperatives, his prayer of confession is plainly approaching a climactic point. For the time being, he tells us, he 'burned to imitate Victorinus', and 'that was why Simplicianus told the story'. The old man added that later, the pagan Emperor Julian had banned Christians from teaching literature and rhetoric, but Victorinus 'preferred to give up schoolteaching rather than God's word'. Augustine was doubly impressed. Victorinus, he thought, was 'more fortunate than brave, because he had found an opportunity to be wholly free for God'.[10]

Simplicianus' story struck home at several levels, but it had not addressed Augustine's most urgent problem. Certainly, there were similarities: Victorinus was an African and a public orator, 'most learned in the liberal arts', and like Augustine he was someone who had read 'so many things of the philosophers'. Like Augustine, he had been reading scripture intently. He had, however, been a pagan. Simplicianus described him in order to encourage the young public orator in his presence to take the plunge and be baptized. Victorinus was a fine example of Christian humility after public pride. Simplicianus also wanted to nudge Augustine to give up his career by showing him that even when under threat, Victorinus had put Christianity before secular teaching. These points were well made, but they did not solve Augustine's dilemma: sex or not?

Augustine's experience is a familiar one, a meeting with an old and respected figure of authority with a problem on one's mind which is never addressed directly during the time spent in his room. Simplicianus missed the main issue. Unlike Augustine, Victorinus had been married: we know from a Latin inscription that he had a granddaughter, Tulliana (named, therefore, after Tullius Cicero, his admired model).[11] Simplicianus mentioned Victorinus' abandonment of his career in order to encourage Augustine to do the same. Augustine heard it, but envied Victorinus for something else, for being entirely free for God. How was he himself to be free when he was pledged to be married and had little of Victorinus' social rank and riches? Simplicianus had not explained.

Augustine now felt an inner tension more strongly than before. One part of him wanted to give up his worldly career and concentrate on God; the other was still bound to sexual life with a woman. The *Confessions* present this tension in terms of a conflict described by Paul in his Letter to the Galatians: 'the flesh lusts against the spirit and the spirit lusts against the flesh' (Gal. 5.17). He tells us, 'I *had* read' this passage and as it is one which Manichaeans are known to have exploited, Augustine had probably first met it in their company. Since leaving their sect, however, he may have been rereading this letter as part of his renewed engagement with Paul in recent weeks.

Previously, he recalls, he had been putting off the decision to 'despise the world' and 'be a slave of God' because he still told himself that his 'perception of the truth was uncertain'. Now, since his mystical experience, he had a new certainty and his scepticism had been overturned. Nonetheless, he was still postponing a decision, like someone, he says, who is reluctant to wake fully after a pleasant sleep. He knows he should wake, but cannot quite do it. Likewise, Augustine was 'certain' that he should 'give himself' to God's love, but he could not give up his existing seductions. They were sex and worldly ambition.

He presents his predicament with two more allusions to words by

Paul. 'Awake, thou that sleepest, and arise from the dead, and Christ shall shine upon thee' (Eph. 5.14, which Augustine and the early Christians accepted to be a letter by Paul). Again, these words are ones which Manichaeans liked to cite: Augustine may have known them from his Manichaean past. He also presents his inner predicament in terms of a crucial passage in Paul's Epistle to the Romans (7.22–25). On one side, there was his 'delight in God's law according to the inner man', his longing to give himself up to God and the study of wisdom, but, on the other, there was the contrary pull of the 'law in his limbs', the attachment, surely, to sex. Again, these words were exploited by Manichaeans, but in summer 386 Augustine was reading Paul intently and carefully on his own account and was making his way through Romans. His understanding of his own conflict may indeed have been posed in these Pauline terms at exactly this time. Again, Augustine was understanding scripture through his own experience and his own experience through scripture.[12]

Just as Paul had written, Augustine felt himself being 'led captive by the law of sin which was in my members'. This 'law of sin', Augustine explains, was 'the violence of habit'. When confessing it eleven years later, he describes his 'will' as being held by 'the enemy', surely Satan, who had 'made a chain from it for me and had bound me'. He goes on to explain Paul's words, 'It is not I that do it, but sin which dwells in me' (Rom. 7.17). This in-dwelling sin, he states, is 'sin resulting from the punishment of a more freely chosen sin, because I was a son of Adam'. At its root, therefore, lies 'original sin', latent in his confessions since his reflections on his infancy, but present in us all nonetheless. It is not just that, since Adam, we all die as mortals. Nor is the sin lodged only in the 'flesh'. Like a baby's sinful will, it is a sinful will causing our 'flesh' to lust for other's 'flesh'.[13]

While confessing, Augustine emphasizes the difference between his predicament and the Manichaeans' view of sin and evil. It was he himself who was divided, not between two warring substances, one of which was the Manichaeans' 'deadly mind', but between two wills which weakened one another. He was not in an impasse. By his heritage he was sinful, but he himself had chosen to turn that heritage into habit. Lust and delight, habit and necessity, had formed a chain, but it was a chain which free choice could break. He is not still a Manichaean deep down, understanding himself in Manichaean terms. A resolution was drawing nearer, but no more than Ambrose was Simplicianus to be its master architect.

II

Not long after the meeting with Simplicianus, another friend came to call, one whose impact was to be more profound. He had come for a purpose which Augustine, when writing the *Confessions*, did not remember. What mattered was what he happened to say, a story which arose by chance.

Augustine recalls that 'his customary anxiety' was growing. He was frequenting the church, 'so far as there was time from worldly business', but he still resembled a man trying to wake from the 'depths of sleep'. As often as he roused himself to get up, he sank back, saying 'soon', or 'look, soon' and 'leave me for a little while'. His visitor, Ponticianus, was to jolt him to the core. The *Confessions* allow us to date his arrival quite closely: on or soon after 4 August 386.[14] Augustine remembered the timing, even after eleven years.

Ponticianus was a north African and an Imperial courier with a post, therefore, at court. Perhaps he is the same Ponticianus for whom Symmachus is known to have written a letter of reference. He was a baptized, 'faithful' Christian, given to 'frequent and lengthy prayers in church'. He happened to notice a book on the gaming table in front of Augustine and himself. He expected it to be a book connected with Augustine's work as a teacher, but opened it and found, to his surprise, that it contained the letters of Paul. Augustine explained that he was reading it intently.

Once again, books and people alternate importantly in Augustine's intellectual journey. Their alternation now reaches a climax, with interconnected pieces. It was to begin when a Christian book, Paul's epistles, was found on a gaming table, that hotbed of worldliness and chance. In turn, this book was to touch off the telling of a story about another book, one which had also been found by accident. That book told the tale of a conversion which had itself been caused by words read aloud from another book, also a book of scripture. This tale had then caused others to convert. In the wake of this story, Augustine himself would turn to a book for words of guidance and, on opening it, he would convert. His friend Alypius would look at the book and would convert likewise. One text after another was to change the lives of people as they appropriated the words for themselves.

When Augustine told Ponticianus that he was 'expending the greatest care' on Paul's writings, Ponticianus began to tell him about Antony of Egypt, the Christian desert father. There was a reason, surely, why their conversation took this turn: Augustine would have mentioned his particular concern of the moment, Paul's verses on the war of 'flesh' against 'mind' which he had been reading in the Epistle to the Romans. Weeks before, the charismatic Paul had reclaimed Augustine after his encounter with Plotinus' texts. The ascetic Paul now came to the fore. He prompted talk of Antony, the first great solitary in Egypt. Until that moment, Augustine and his friend Alypius did not even know his name.

Ponticianus developed his amazing story by telling of Antony's wondrous behaviour in the desert and of the thousands in Egypt who now lived there as his celibate heirs. Augustine and Alypius had never heard of them, no more than they had heard of Ponticianus' next astounding subject, a monastery, fostered by Ambrose, just outside the walls of Milan. There, too, the story of Antony had had an impact: Ponticianus proceeded to describe it.

Antony's life in Egypt was not a new arrival in wider Christian awareness. First, it had been written up in Greek by Athanasius, the great fourth-century Bishop of Alexandria so as to present an idealized Antony, hero of the desert, to his metropolitan Christians. This book then reached Rome with Athanasius in the 350s and, since then, had been translated twice into Latin in the early 370s. One of its translators, Evagrius, was a pupil, no less, of Libanius: Antony's story had thus reached Antioch too.[15] Antony, the *Life* said, had converted to the life of a celibate hermit when he heard words read aloud in church from the Gospel: 'if you would be perfect, go, sell all you have, give to the poor and follow me'. He then responded to another Gospel verse: 'take no thought for the morrow . . .' He understood commands in the Gospel as if they were direct 'oracular' commands to himself.

Anthony's *Life* then became an 'oracle' to others. To hear about his decision was, in turn, to be impelled to imitate it. The *Life of Antony* had already inspired copycats in the Latin-speaking world. Here, Ponticianus had an unforgettable tale to tell.[16] In the early 370s, he himself had been in Trier with the court of the Emperor Valentinian I. While the emperor was watching an afternoon show in the arena, he had gone out for a walk in the garden park, one of those green spaces which often adjoined the walls of an ancient town. Three men came with him, two of whom were members of the Imperial bureaucracy. On their walk, two of them strolled apart and 'fell on a cottage', another happy chance, in which, they found, were dwelling some celibate Christian 'slaves of God'. They discovered a book among the celibates: it was Athanasius' book, in Latin, in which Antony's life was narrated. One of the visitors started to read it, and then broke off. What was the point, he asked his friend, of their worldly ambitions and their perilous earthly career? Their best hope, he said, was to be 'friends of the emperor', but that fragile status was a short-lived favour beset with dangers. Antony's tale inspired an alternative: 'Look, here and now I can become, if I will it, a "friend of God".'

Ponticianus' friend read more of Antony's story, 'troubled with the birth of a new life': he 'kept on reading', Augustine tells us, 'he was changed within, where You, God, were watching'. As the friend was 'tossed on the waves of his inner heart, he groaned from time to time . . .' Then, he resolved on the better course. 'From now on, I have broken myself from that worldly hope of ours,' he declared, 'and I have decided to serve God.' He was joined in his resolve by his companion.

As it was growing late, Ponticianus walked back to find the two of them. When he reappeared, they told him of their decision to give up sex and their careers and 'how such a will had arisen in them'. Ponticianus and his friend regretted that they could not bring themselves to join the two budding celibates: they 'congratulated them, but wept at their own selves'. They went off to the palace, 'dragging their hearts on the ground', as Augustine memorably puts it, whereas the others 'stayed in the cottage, fixing their hearts on heaven'. The two in the cottage each abandoned a fiancée, and when the girls heard what had happened, they too vowed their virginity to God.

Ponticianus told a fine story, but it was not told in order to guide Augustine down a similar path. Once again, a story proved to be more apt than its speaker may have guessed. It addressed the very topic which Simplicianus had not discussed: how someone, feeling alienated from his public career, could become a celibate 'slave of God'. Such celibates, it emerged, were living in a cottage-commune almost on Augustine's doorstep, whereas his own recent plan for a commune had failed. In the story, the converts too had agonized before their will triumphed over their fleshly habit. They too had had fiancées and, like Augustine's abandoned partner, these girls had vowed themselves to a sexless life. 'You brought me face to face with myself, O God,' Augustine considers: crucially, he was being forced to a new sense of his identity.[17] 'If I tried to avert my gaze from myself, Ponticianus was telling what he was telling' and 'You, once again, were bringing myself before me . . . the more ardently I began to love those two men of whom I was hearing, the more detestably I hated myself in comparison with them . . .' Yet again, Augustine credits God with working through a speaker's words in a way which the speaker had not intended.

What then follows is his recollection of inner struggle and turmoil, a masterpiece of self-awareness. As Ponticianus spoke, Augustine tells us, he was 'gnawed inside', not with guilt, but with shame, shame that he had spent 'ten years and more' shirking the choice to abandon the world and sex and pursue wisdom and chastity instead. He was 'laid bare to himself' and reproached by his 'conscience', a crucial element. 'Now the day had come . . .'. Since the age of eighteen, the issue of chastity and 'love of wisdom' (*philo-sophia*) had been deferred by him, after his first impassioned reading of Cicero's *Hortensius*. Deeply disturbed, after Ponticianus left, he 'set upon' Alypius, he tells us, with a comment truly worthy of a trained professor. 'The uneducated are rising up,' he remarked, 'and seizing heaven by force . . .' Illiterate peasants like Antony and ignorant time-servers like Ponticianus' friends had opted for eternity, whereas he and Alypius, profoundly educated men, were 'rolling around in flesh and blood' with their 'teachings which lacked heart', that major failing in open-hearted Augustine's estimation. On first reading Cicero, he had remembered its impact on his 'heart'. Now, his own teaching seemed to lack 'heart' and to be arid. Heaven could not be left to nitwits: once again, human examples were encouraging him to make a change of life.

Ponticianus had not named the group in Trier's park and there is still a possibility that they were not quite as 'uneducated' as Augustine believed. In a brilliant combination of evidence, Pierre Courcelle conjectured in 1950 that one of the Imperial messengers with Ponticianus might have been none other than Jerome himself, aged perhaps thirty at the time. Jerome indeed took to a celibate life while in Trier and even cites as his inspiration the very same words of Christ which inspired Antony to celibacy.[18] They also inspired, he tells us, one of his friends: 'Go, sell all that thou hast and give to the poor . . .' This fine conjecture has fallen from scholarly favour, but it is still worth taking seriously. If correct, it adds to the gaps in Augustine's understanding.

'I withdrew into myself, and what did I not say to my own soul? I lashed it to make it follow me as I tried, now, to go after You. It kept on struggling back, it kept on refusing but not excusing itself.' Augustine spoke to Alypius, but his face, eyes and expression, he recalls, were much more eloquent than his words: evidently, Alypius told him so later. In Ponticianus' absence, the drama then moved to a familiar setting. Just as Ponticianus' friends had converted to celibacy in a garden park in Trier, so Augustine, anguished in spirit, now went out into a garden. He was followed closely by Alypius.

They were renting rooms in the house of an absentee landlord whose ground floor opened onto a garden space. There have been many such bits of ground since then, used carelessly by tenants in the owner's absence, where trespass alternates with casual tidying. Gardens also had a scriptural, symbolic history. Ambrose talked and wrote of scripture as a garden, the 'garden of the soul', and even of a 'drunken garden' whose green shoots grow like a Christian's well-ordered body.[19] In the ancient Song of Songs, the 'garden enclosed' was widely misunderstood to be a symbol of virginity. If Augustine wished to evoke these images, he was well able to do so. He did not do so, because this garden is only a factual presence in his story, the worldly scene of what followed.

In the ageing Tolstoy's great novel about conversion, *Resurrection*, his prince-hero also engages in what he calls 'a cleansing of the soul'. He reflects on the 'discord' between his past life and his new awareness. He begins to resolve to break off from his existing female attachment and the ties of excessive property. The 'tempter within' seems to murmur to him, 'But are you the only one?' He resolves to break the 'lie that binds me', and then he prays, 'asking God to help him, to enter into him and cleanse him'. He then begins to cry, both 'good' tears of contrition and tears which are 'bad', tears of 'tenderness at his own goodness'. He then looks out of the opened window onto the garden beyond. The shadow of a poplar tree in all its intricacy falls by moonlight on the gravel. 'Oh, God, how delightful,' he says, 'meaning that which was going on in his soul'. A tree, a garden, a resolve to break free of worldly ties, inner murmurings of past temptation, a prayer to God and tears will also occur in Augustine's imminent experience, but, unlike the prince, he will not reflect on the garden or its form and thence on his own soul. The garden is in his memory only because it was the factual setting at the time.

Augustine sat down with Alypius 'as far from the house as we could'. The setting is precisely recalled, and yet the sequel has been a battleground for modern scholars: is it fiction or history? Augustine introduces it with phrases based on Plotinus: here, certainly, he is giving us his own literary tour de force. However, it is naïve to class a story which has literary colouring as, therefore, pure fiction. The colouring, like Plotinus' writings, may have been in Augustine's mind at the time or it may be helping him later to express a historical chain of accurately recalled events.[20] Even so, he has left us with more problems than he resolves. When he first refers to his conversion, about three months after the event, he gives no detail of the turmoil which the *Confessions* will now present so powerfully. Until then, he has written up none of the details. Can we trust his hindsight after eleven silent years?

In the *Confessions* the prelude has been set with meticulous detail.[21] Nebridius, he recalls, was absent: only Alypius was present: Ponticianus had arrived on other business. Ponticianus' story about Antony became a story about events in Trier; it increased Augustine's inner anguish. Ponticianus left: Augustine berated Alypius and together they went into the garden. As the house was let, use of the garden was not confined to its owner. None of this detail is linked explicitly with a wider symbolic meaning. It is not phrased in language from scripture or related to theological reflection. It was all shared and witnessed at the time, because Augustine's famous conversion was also the story of Alypius' conversion. Alypius was still alive when the *Confessions* were made public and was well aware of what happened next.

Augustine begins by reflecting on his crisis of will. If the mind gives orders to the body, he observes, it is obeyed at once. If it gives orders to itself, but is itself divided, it is resisted. The resulting anguish, he believes while writing the *Confessions*, is a sign, once again, of our punishment as 'sons of Adam': it is our penalty for Adam's fall. A divided mind is divided because two wills, he believes, are in opposition in one and the same soul. He then dwells on the differences between this existential dither and the view of the Manichees, who explain it by two competing natures or substances, one good, one evil, within us all. This prolonged reflection will hardly have beset him at the time, but the digression does not affect the credit of the detailed story which he continues to tell.

The nearer he came to breaking free, the greater the 'horror' the approaching moment caused him. He presents it in a superb dramatization of the inner struggle by which he was being 'excruciated'. He was accusing himself more than ever; he was 'rolling and tossing himself in his chain until it would be broken entirely'; he was saying to himself within, 'Look, let it be done now, let it be done now' and was then 'going forward to what he had resolved'; he was 'almost doing it, but still not doing it'; he was 'falling back' but not to his former point. He was standing and catching his breath and trying again; 'a little more, and I was there, a little more and I was already touching it and holding it, and yet I was not . . .' The moment when 'I would have become something else' was still waiting and 'the nearer it was moved towards me, the greater the horror it was casting on me'. Such an intensely remembered struggle was not just a struggle to give up the externals of a career and its prospects. It was a struggle against a deep-seated instinct, sex.

Augustine dramatizes his inner drama in two superb images which make the root of his struggle quite clear. First, he recalls his 'long-standing girlfriends', his sinful urges. Those trifling vanities began to tug at his 'fleshly garment' and whisper quietly: 'Are you sending us away? . . . From this moment on, "this and that" will not be permitted to you, from now on, to eternity . . .' Their whispering was deeply shocking. 'What filth they were suggesting . . .': 'this and that' were therefore sexual acts, the pleasures of his past sixteen years. Yet, he heard them with less than half of himself as they murmured and tried to pull at him 'furtively': he was going nonetheless on his way. They were holding him back, but only while he hesitated to shake himself free. His 'violent habit', the strength of his sexual past, seemed still to challenge him. 'Do you think you can do without those things?' it asked. But already it 'was saying this very tepidly'.

Brilliantly written, this last tussle with temptation is true to the spirit of what happened. Temptation was then balanced, he tells us, and outweighed by what confronted him on his way forward 'to where, too, I had set my face, but was still fearful about going'. Augustine says that 'the chaste Dignity of Continence' was revealed, 'calm' and 'joyous' but not 'dissolutely joyous' as an enticingly promiscuous woman would be. She was stretching her pious hands out to receive and embrace him while sheltering 'clusters of good examples'. These 'good examples' were 'so many boys and girls, many young people, people of all ages, serious widows and elderly virgins': she was 'in no way sterile, but was the fertile mother of children'. Yet again, human examples were urging him to action. Continence mocked him, silently, with a wry but encouraging smile, and once again Augustine dramatizes the experience in words.[22] They pick up the words with which he has just dramatized his 'girlfriends', his sexual sins. They had seemed to say, 'Are you able to do without us?' It was 'as if' Continence was saying: 'Are you "unable" to do what those boys, those girls can do? Are they really able to do this in themselves, and not in the Lord their God?' Surely not, was the implied answer, because chastity, she seemed to be expressing, is a gift from God: it is not simply a matter of the human will on its own. 'Cast yourself on Him without care,' she seemed to be telling him, 'He will receive you and heal you.' This inference is a crucial element in the equation, and not, surely, one which Augustine has imposed on the story with hindsight. Augustine says he was blushing, because he was still hearing the murmurings of 'those trifling things', obviously his sexual past, as he would not have blushed about any other renunciation. He was set against himself. Meanwhile, Alypius waited in silence for the 'outcome of my unaccustomed movements'.

Continence is not described as a thought flashing vaguely in Augustine's 'heart' or mind.[23] She is presented as a vision, one who does not speak but whose expression conveys a message which Augustine dramatizes in his own well-chosen words. It seems unlikely that the vision itself is an expressive invention, introduced into the story to dramatize his choice. What 'was revealed' is distinguished clearly in his text from what Continence 'seemed as if' to say. It is only too likely that there was indeed a moment when he realized that the ability to be celibate would rest ultimately with God. Years before, it was to God that he had prayed to 'give' him chastity . . . but not yet. Now, he realized that if he took the leap, God would indeed receive him. In the group in Continence's care, one role model was left unspecified: a man in his early thirties, engaged to be married. Augustine was now to fill this gap.

A great storm of weeping welled up in him and he left Alypius sitting. Here, too, he notes the limits of his own memory: he can no longer recall exactly the words which he uttered while his voice choked with tears. Other details, by implication, are still within his recall. 'Extremely amazed, Alypius stayed where we were sitting', as well he might. Meanwhile, Augustine flung himself down beneath a fig tree, he tells us, and 'rivers of tears burst from my eyes'. They are the only flood of tears in the *Confessions* which has not been connected to prayer or bereavement. The fig tree has been a more controversial presence. Fig leaves play a part in the traditions about the biblical fall of Adam and Eve and a fig tree shelters Nathaniel in the Gospel when Jesus is passing by, but Augustine makes no allusion here to the scriptures, although they are frequently his verbal resource. In a sermon preached perhaps in the very year of his confessions, he interprets Nathaniel's fig tree as the symbol of man's sinful life in the flesh after Adam's fall. He even goes on to mention Paul's conversion.[24] In the *Confessions*, however, he makes no such reference. The fig tree is not meant to be the symbolic fiction which many of his modern readers have taken it to be. Fig trees grow in the back gardens of many tenanted houses: Augustine recalls this one because it was another detail at the time, the very tree under which he indeed lay down. Supporting his veracity, he notes limits to his memory: once again, he says, he can give only the gist of what words he said, although this time they were said to God. It amounted to: 'How long, Lord? Will you be angry for ever?', words of a psalmist. It was a highly significant moment. For the first time in his anguish, Augustine addressed God: he began to pray. How long, he wonders, would he go on saying, 'Tomorrow and tomorrow'? Why not now?

After praying, he recalls, he heard a voice repeating in singing tones the words '*tolle lege, tolle lege*'. His prayer, significantly, was being followed at once by an 'admonition', as if, perhaps, a response by the gift of God. The voice was coming from a 'neighbouring house' (*de domo vicina*), according to all but one manuscript of the *Confessions*: the exception traces back to the fifth century AD, and gives the words '*de domo divina*', 'from a divine house', presumably the house of God.[25] However, Augustine recalls that, at the time, he did not know if the voice was a boy's or a girl's and the whole drift of his story tells against the rogue manuscript's wording. His first thoughts, he is explicit, were that the voice was indeed human, a voice, therefore, from a 'neighbouring house'. What, he then wondered, were the words? His expression changed; his tears stopped; he began to think 'very hard indeed'. Were children in the habit of saying such a thing in a game? He did not think that he had heard it anywhere before. Having ruled out a human interpretation, he repressed his tears, stood up and inferred that he was 'being commanded from heaven', presumably through this child's divinely guided words. '*Tolle, lege*', the words which he heard, are ambiguous, truly like the words of an oracle. They can mean 'Take away, gather' or 'Pick up, gather'; they can also mean 'Take away', or 'Pick up, read'. Augustine took them in this last sense. He had just heard the story of Antony, who had responded to words being read from the Gospel as if they were addressed to himself. Ponticianus had then told another story in which reading had provoked a conversion. 'Read', not 'gather', was the sense which Augustine, so soon afterwards, would naturally give to the word *lege*.

He returned to where Alypius was sitting, the place where he had left his book of Paul's letters, the very one which had been lying on the gaming table. He opened it and read the first 'little chapter' onto which his eyes 'had been cast'. It was part of our Romans 13 and he quotes verses 13 and 14. In a recent 'brutally literal' translation by the Jesuit scholar Robert O'Connell, the words say 'not in rioting and drunkenness, not in chambering and [acts of] shamelessness, not in contention and rivalry but,' in my translation, 'put on the Lord Jesus Christ and make no provision for the flesh in its lusts' (these last words, '*carnis*' and '*concupiscentiis*', have a predominantly sexual sense, although O'Connell wishes to minimize it). Augustine tells us he had never read those verses before, he tells us. Evidently, his 'most careful reading' of Paul had not yet extended to the end of the epistle.

Augustine's searching of the scriptures for a personal oracle was a widespread Christian practice. 'Bibliomancy' was also practised by pagans, who consulted at random their classics like Homer and Virgil.[26] Years before, in Carthage, the governor Vindicianus had aired the possibility of a hidden force behind people's words. Now, Augustine's 'oracle' from Paul seemed to be speaking directly to his predicament, just as an 'oracle' from the Gospel had once spoken to Antony's and made him convert. Augustine, it seemed to say, must give up 'contention and rivalry', surely by abandoning the ambitious arena of a worldly career. If he must 'put on Christ', surely he must do so by being baptized? He must cease to 'make provision for the flesh in its lusts': here was a heaven-sent instruction, he assumed, to give up sex henceforward. 'All the darkness of doubt disappeared.' Augustine marked the page and shut the book. As he was calm now in his expression, he communicated with Alypius. Yet Alypius too, he tells us, was undergoing a new resolve. He asked to see the book; he read what Augustine had read and then he read the next verse, as Augustine had not: 'Him that is weak in faith, receive.' He revealed it to Augustine and took it as his cue to join his older friend and teacher in a new commitment to celibacy, to 'putting on Christ' and to being 'received', surely at baptism.

Regrettably, we do not have a comparable account by Alypius of what he experienced. As a result his conversion is unjustly overshadowed by Augustine's.[27] He was younger than Augustine, perhaps only twenty-two at the time. Like Augustine, he had recently been attracted by the sceptical philosophers, but unlike Augustine he had not then read some Platonic books. He had never ascended to God's presence and he had not had his doubts about evil and the universe replaced by absolute certainty. He had not had a chat with Simplicianus and perhaps he had not bothered greatly with Paul, except for such Pauline verses as he had known in his Manichaean phase. He had no idea, Augustine tells us, what the 'Church Universal' of Ambrose really believed about Christ. He had never even read the start of John's

Gospel with Platonic philosophy in mind. All, therefore, that Augustine presents as essential for his own conversion had passed Alypius by: he was indeed, by comparison, 'weak in faith'. Yet, he converted nonetheless. What convinced him was what he heard from Ponticianus, what he then observed in his respected older master, whose lead he tended to follow, and, above all, what he then found in Augustine's passage of Paul and the words which followed it. It sufficed for him to take the decision. He would stand firmly by it for the rest of his life.

Their conversion was twofold, a decision to abandon sex and a decision to abandon worldly ambition. They were much easier decisions for Alypius: he had no fiancée to support, no intermediary concubine and no experience of sex with a woman except for one disagreeable episode. His career was in a temporary lull while he waited for another appointment on the legal and administrative ladder in Milan. Unlike Augustine, he was not a teacher and would not disappoint any pupils if he gave up his worldly calling.

Like the two friends in Trier of whom Ponticianus had spoken, Augustine and Alypius had become a pair resolved on celibacy. Together, they went indoors. Monnica was in the house and she would have to be told the news.

III

If the scene in the garden, the voice's words, the text in Paul were so important, why does Augustine mention none of them when he touches on his change of life in texts written very soon after the event? Not until seven years later, in 392/3, do we find him citing the crucial verses of Romans 13 as an authority, but even then he cites them in a letter to his bishop only so as to support a ban on Christians' rowdy behaviour in north Africa. He gives not a hint that they had once determined his own course of life and he does not comment on the last verse, so crucial for him personally.[28] Two years later, in 394, he gives answers to questions from his celibate Christian brethren about problematic verses in Romans, but again he interprets the crucial verses differently from his subsequent interpretation in the *Confessions*. 'Provision for the flesh,' he writes, 'is not to be condemned if it concerns the needs of bodily health. If it concerns unnecessary delights or luxuries, then the person who enjoys them is rightly chastized. For he is making provision for the desires of the flesh . . .'[29] He does not specify sex within marriage as an 'unnecessary delight', nor does he relate the verses to his own decision.

The answer to this long silence is not that the *Confessions* are giving the retrospective fiction of an older, more 'theological' Augustine. Self-evidently, the exact and detailed framework of the garden scene has not been invented with hindsight. It was witnessed, after all, by Alypius, who was still alive in 397 but is never known to have challenged the story or denied that he had read Paul's words. The texts which Augustine had been writing since the event were not confessions: they belonged to very different genres. Prefaces to philosophical writings or polemical texts against Manichees were not the places for a precise account of a personal crisis of will. As for the exact text from Romans 13, neither a practical letter to a bishop nor an outline exposition, even for celibate readers, were appropriate contexts in which to dwell on its impact on him personally. When he eventually writes up the full story in the *Confessions*, he is confessing it to God, who knows it all already. God was not an audience to whom to tell conscious lies. Augustine also expects the story to be read by other aspiring 'slaves of God', perfectionist Christians for whom the details of a conversion to sexless living were of passionate, contemporary interest. The *Confessions*' detailed, step-by-step story is suited to this public.

The story which it tells is not of a sudden conversion, experienced in a blinding flash of light. It is a story of inner conflict, surmounted in stages and finally broken by interpreting words which happened to be heard and read. It is not a conversion to Christian faith, let alone to 'Catholic' faith. It is a conversion away from sex and ambition. Its grounds differ from the conversions which a younger Augustine had brought about in his African friends when converting them to Mani's Gospel. Then, he would have impressed them as an example, one whose intelligence they already respected. In turn, he stressed the 'reason' in Mani's teachings. In Milan's garden he himself was inspired by the examples of others, people, however, whom he had never met. He took the decisive step through his own interpretation of words, none of which made a reasoned case for his decision.

His conversion was also very different from Paul's conversion to Christianity on the road to Damascus: Augustine has certainly not reshaped his story to fit the model of Paul's.[30] In a blinding flash of light, God had forced the unbelieving Paul in a totally new direction: a crisis of will did not come into it. The whisperings of Augustine's former 'girlfriends', his sexual sins, and the sighting of Continence and her troupe are brilliantly presented, but the turning points in the story are told in narrative sentences which are as short as any in the entire *Confessions*. Since the event, Augustine has thought deeply about God's role in it all, but this thinking has not distorted the basic framework of events. He had not 'deserved' his conversion, he realizes, by his own merits, but, even so, he had not been forced into it abruptly, like Paul, without any choice. It was he himself who had interpreted the vision of Continence, the words of the child's voice and the words which he read in Paul. He tells the story with careful attention to his divided 'will', a legacy, he believes, of 'original sin'. God's grace presented a framework to him, the vision, the words, the passage of scripture, but Augustine considers himself as assured of its gifts only if he personally 'jumped across' and made the commitment. Unlike Paul's, his conversion had been a long slow process, requiring a final leap. He goes on to ask God in his confessions: 'from what lowest and deepest secret place was my *free choice* called forth in a single moment?'[31]

Had he, nonetheless, made mistakes at the time? This question is more pertinent than the question of subsequent fiction. What were the words sung by the child's voice? They remain as puzzling to us as they were to Augustine himself. Were they indeed the accompaniment to a game, as he had promptly wondered, perhaps words from a Milanese game which he did not know? Or were they directed to him, but with a different sense? Augustine was lying prostrate and weeping under the fig tree, and at a distance the child might have missed his tears and the reason for his posture. Seeing him lying beneath the tree, near, perhaps, to its fallen fruit, had the child started to chant a refrain perhaps sung by fruitpickers or harvesters?[32] 'Pick up, gather; pick up, gather . . .' Like Augustine, we do not know, but it is more likely than not that the singer did not mean 'Take up, read.' Rather, Augustine mistook '*Tolle lege*', sung for whatever reason, and gave it the wrong meaning.

When he then hit on Romans 13.13–14 in his book, did he misunderstand its words too? The order to 'put on Jesus Christ' is not self-evidently an order for an individual to be baptized. Fourth-century Christian commentators did not always take it in this sense and modern scholars, too, have read it as concerning all believers, whom Christ will enfold collectively.[33] However, Augustine says that he read a 'bit of a chapter' (*capitulum*) and, as Robert O'Connell has recently pointed out, his usage of that word elsewhere implies that he read Paul's preceding verses too: 'let us cast off the works of darkness and let us put on the armour of light'. The imagery of 'light' and 'darkness' was familiar to him from his Manichaean past, a reason, perhaps, why the *Confessions* do not quote this verse, but other Western Christians applied it to baptism, a rite which Manichaeans rejected.[34]

Baptism was not the central issue in Augustine's decision: the crucial points in his hard-won conclusion were the renunciation of worldly ambition and, above all, sex. However, 'not in chambering and wantonness' (or 'lying together and immodest acts') are not words which obviously refer to everyday sexual intercourse in a married relationship. Other fourth-century Christian readers took them, rightly, as a reference to sexual excess, fired by 'revelry and drunkenness'. They fitted the behaviour of guests at a drinking party, reclining among tempting slaves, young boys and one another, and they applied to adultery and other 'impurities'. Paul's 'make no provision for the flesh in its lusts [or 'desires and longing']' refers to undue lust, predominantly sexual lust, but it does not refer to all sexual desire in marriage. In the Greek East, even the ascetic Bishop of Antioch, Libanius' pupil John Chrysostom, explained that Paul was not forbidding sexual intercourse. He was opposing 'fornication', or promiscuity. He was 'not speaking of necessities, but of excess'.[35]

Only six years after the garden scene Augustine himself interprets these words in this more restrained way. They referred to sexual sins, he wrote, which would disqualify a Christian from taking the sacraments, not sex within marriage, therefore, but adultery and so forth.[36] This interpretation was widely, and rightly, shared and Augustine was well able to accept it. In the garden, however, he tells us of his more extreme reading. He was not the first Christian to adopt it. Before him, an ultimate overachiever, Origen (*c.*AD 250), had taken Paul to be equating the 'works of darkness' with 'chambering and wantonness', meaning all acts of lying together 'like animals', including marriage itself.[37] However, he was not Augustine's source, as his commentary on the passage was not available in Latin when Augustine read the text in the garden. In 386, before converting, he had never looked at it in Greek, either. It seems that, with chastity on the brain, he made a similar mistake to Origen's: he misread Paul as if he was commanding a total ban on sex. In a different context, six years later, he read it in a less extreme way.

Was he, perhaps, influenced by another text by Origen, one which was certainly available in Latin by 386? In his *Commentary on the Song of Songs*, Origen discussed the book whose 'enclosed garden' was widely read by Christians as symbolizing chastity. In it, Origen cited Paul's very words at Romans 13.13–14 in connection with another great encounter beside a tree: Abraham's meeting with a heavenly threesome by the oak tree at Mamre.[38] By putting off wantonness, revelry and so forth, a man, Origen explains, passes from 'night' to the clarity of day, and therefore Abraham saw his heavenly guests at 'noon'. He had attained 'purity of heart' and a noonday's 'light of the mind', and so he would be able to see God. In November 386, Augustine was indeed to show knowledge of this book by Origen, but he had not necessarily read it before his conversion in early August. Anyway, he had thrown himself down by a fig tree, not an oak, and had not been consumed with a vision of God at all. 'It was as if a light of security had been infused in my heart,' he recalls, immediately after he read Paul's words, and 'all the darkness of doubt fled in different directions'. He means that he had the clarity of certainty. His imagery of 'light' and 'darkness' alludes to Paul's accompanying words (Rom. 13.12): Origen's words about Abraham have not shaped Augustine's experience or his presentation of what happened.

Instead, he converted in the garden through his own creative misunderstanding. It was the final piece in the recent sequence. Like Ambrose, he had misunderstood words in the Book of Genesis ('the image of God') and believed that they referred to the soul, which Genesis never mentioned. Like Ambrose, he committed himself to understanding scripture by allegorizing its surface meaning. He then persuaded himself that the core of Plotinus' teaching was present in Paul, although Paul had never read a word of Plato, let alone of a Neoplatonist. He probably mistook the word 'gather' for 'read' in the singing which he heard in the garden and he then misunderstood what he read on opening his book of Paul's letters. However, he would not have minded if these errors had been pointed out to him. Soon after his conversion, he came to believe in the inadequacy of words in any communication of the truth. Their impact, he argues, depends on their hearer's inner 'heart' and its enlightenment by God within.[39] In the garden, he would say, he was at last ready for constructive misunderstanding. Since then, he came to understand his entire life as guided step by step by God. If God had worked through misunderstandings, Augustine would merely have said that He had worked providentially, as He had intended.

In human terms, was his conversion inevitable? At one of its levels, the conversion from rhetoric and worldly ambition, it had become so: his voice had failed him and his continuing role as a public orator was impossible, at least for a while. If he had never met Ponticianus, never heard a child's voice or never opened Paul's letters, he would have found himself unemployed, with only his temporary concubine to caress him. He could have pursued philosophy, but his 'worldly ambition' would have had to end for months, maybe years, before resuming at a lower level.

Would he also have given up sex? 'I had long been disposed to do so,' he later wrote, but the timing had never been fixed: 'Give me chastity, but not yet . . .' Only a few weeks before, he had learned from Paul and the Gospel that chastity was 'better', but even since then it had taken a chain of coincidences to make him take the hard decision. Without them, he might have continued to waver: he might have dropped his job and broken off his betrothal, but not dismissed his second concubine. Nor had his will been overridden in the matter. He had responded, finally, to 'providential' words of omen, found where the pagan Libanius would have recognized them, in words given by a child's voice and words found at random in a book. God, Augustine came to believe, would 'give' him chastity and sustain him in it, but even then God had not forced him to take the leap against his will or 'made him an offer he could not refuse'. Another Augustine is imaginable, one still dithering after talking to Simplicianus, one aware of the 'better' course of chastity, but still holding back from it, one responding to Paul's words about 'wantonness' by dismissing his intermediate concubine and then going on to marry his child-bride as arranged.

There was one further consequence. By his decision, Augustine had once again excelled his mother's plans. He had first done so aged eighteen when he had become a 'super-Christian', so he believed, and left her behind as a 'semi-Christian'. Now, he had frustrated her lifelong ambition on his behalf. She had been hoping and planning that he would marry above his social origins and promptly be baptized, leaving the stains of pre-marital sex behind. He had now overturned that plan by giving up sex altogether. Yet, she could not possibly object: her defeat was an even greater triumph. Just as she had dreamed, Augustine would stand beside her on the same solid 'rule of faith', but both of them would now be celibate, as she had never dared to hope. For Monnica, too, God had moved in mysterious ways. If God works indeed in human lives, He works through human error.

In Milan, nobody would have guessed that this 31-year-old man, to their eyes on the edge of a breakdown, would show himself within five years to be a thinker and writer with an assured Christian viewpoint. His contemporaries back in Thagaste remembered him very differently. While he had been living through his months of turbulence in faraway Milan, inquiries had begun behind him in north Africa. In summer

386, a new governor had started to apply the recently strengthened laws against Manichaeans. Augustine's name had been denounced to him and he had ruled on his guilt.[40] If his townsmen in Thagaste had heard that he had given up sex without being baptized, their memories of his Manichaeism would have seemed confirmed. They would not have known that the former converter was now himself a convert.

PART IV

Just the worst time of the year
For a journey, and such a long journey

T. S. Eliot, *Journey of the Magi* (August 1927), after his Anglican baptism in Finstock Church, Oxfordshire, in June 1927

Thanks to the advice of the priest in New York, I was now reading through the Psalms of David in my hours of sleeplessness. The more I studied the Psalms, the more I found them an incomparable treasure-house of hope and encouragement. One of their most compelling messages is that there is nothing new under the sun in the human condition. King David himself appears to have had more than his fair share of dark sins and darker periods of despair, yet his total reliance on God always pulled him through, often with a refreshed and quietened soul.

My starting point in these readings was that great penitential cri de coeur, Psalm 51, which had been recommended by the Manhattan pastor. It became a turning point in my journey because of its clarion call to face up to guilt, repent and accept God's promise of receiving forgiveness through faith.

The background to the Psalm is that King David had been caught out by Nathan the Prophet committing a series of reprehensible crimes which made mine look like pinching an extra lump of sugar at a vicarage tea party.

Jonathan Aitken, *Pride and Perjury* (2000), after his imprisonment for perjury in June 1999

21
Gentle Withdrawal

I

So far, we have followed Augustine's memories with a constant eye on his conversions. There have been three, to philosophy, to celibacy and within Christianity to the supposedly 'true Christianity' preached by Mani. Conversion has been the obvious theme to pursue in his early life because he himself looks back on it in terms of a turning from and towards God. It is also the theme which makes him special for modern historians. He is the only early Christian who has told us in detail about his conversions. They are not conversions to Christianity from non-Christian belief. They have emerged as conversions away from rhetoric, worldly ambition and sex.

After his decision in the garden many modern scholars continue to look for yet more conversions and make them a guiding theme in their accounts of the following years. Augustine continued to try to convert others, but in my view he underwent no more conversions himself. However, he is also special for being the author of a masterpiece, the *Confessions*. Confessing, therefore, is the thread which I will trace in the next eleven years until this masterpiece's beginning. Gradually, he will assemble in his mind the pieces which enable him to confess in a novel way. If he had confessed his sins to God after coming indoors from the garden, his prayer would have sounded very different. Eleven years later, he had written on deep questions of free will and grace, sin, faith and predestination, questions which were to become central parts of his legacy to Christian thinking. They are also the themes with which Luther, Calvin and many others would engage through knowledge of his writings and which would earn him his status as a Doctor of the Catholic Church. They are a far cry from his days as Milan's Libanius, 'selling lies for a living'.

'You broke my bonds,' Augustine tells God, drawing again on the words of our Psalm 116. Nonetheless, a fortnight of the summer term remained after the scene in the garden. If Augustine refused to go back to work, his pupils and others in Milan would put pressure on a decision which they would find selfish or bizarre. So he served out the last two weeks, saying nothing. Around 23 August, the term ended, to resume again in October after the holidays for the grape harvest. What was he to do meanwhile?

In the *Confessions* he describes his resignation as a 'gentle withdrawal', but he does not state exactly when he made it. His first published works, composed in November, are more helpful. After resigning his job he ended up at the country villa which his friend Verecundus had lent him near the foothills of the Alps, at least twenty miles from Milan. In early to mid-November he could describe himself and his companions as having arrived there only a 'very few' days before. The implications tend to be overlooked: Augustine did not withdraw to the villa in mid-August as soon as the summer term ended. In the *Confessions* he knows that he is still open to criticism for not having resigned at once from what he looks back on as his 'Chair of Lying'. There was a practical reason. On announcing his decision, he would be well advised to leave Milan, but in August and September Verecundus would be on holiday in his sub-Alpine chalet. He was married to a Christian wife and had stated frankly to Augustine and his friends that he did not wish to give up sex with her. He would not be a like-minded host or participant in the routine which the newly celibate Augustine was planning. Only when Verecundus returned to Milan would Augustine prepare to go up to the villa with his group of chaste companions. He waited and resigned in October, doubtless by letter, leaving when the term was about to begin.[1]

A conversion, like a wedding, is only a beginning and it might all go horribly wrong. We have no idea of the first few nights after Augustine's dramatic decision, but he had to battle with his sexual instincts and with what Shakespeare, in a similar context, well calls 'the huge army of the world's desires'. He was also still struggling with the pains affecting his chest and voice. At least he could continue to read avidly. The texts which he composed in November reveal that he had read more books by Neoplatonists, including texts by Plotinus' pupil Porphyry. He had also begun to read books by Christian thinkers other than the scriptural authors. Their first trace in his writings is an echo of a homily on the Song of Songs by the celibate Origen (*c*.AD 250). It had recently been translated into Latin and had probably caught his eye in Milan. There would not have been rare texts on philosophy and scripture in Verecundus' villa, as he was a *grammaticus* by trade.[2]

Meanwhile, there was the matter of his temporary concubine and his child-bride in waiting. Both now had to be dismissed. If he had already exchanged betrothal gifts with his fiancée, the law required them to be returned. Like his resignation, this rebuff was best left as late as possible to avoid weeks of hostile comment before he left. It was not that he was unsure of his next step. Before the garden scene, he had already been desiring to 'seek God and the happy life'.[3] As a practised teacher he now planned to seek them with a small 'school' of pupils by embarking on philosophy, not rhetoric. This venture was not one for his intellectual equals in Milan. None of the 'greater friends' would consider leaving their own lordly villas and accompanying a party of social inferiors into someone else's sub-Alpine 'chalet' so as to study with beginners. Romanianus could not go, either. After losing his legal battle over worldly affairs, he had left Milan for north Africa. Nebridius, recently emerged from Manichaeism, was sympathetic with the group's focus on philosophy, but chose to remain in Milan because he was committed to help Verecundus with his teaching. Before long he returned home to his mother in north Africa. Verecundus himself was 'sad' to see his new friends go, but felt unable for matrimonial reasons to join them in their celibate initiative. As Augustine and his group left, they 'exhorted [Verecundus] to the faith appropriate to his stage, one of married conjugal life'.[4] They were not expecting everyone who was close to them to follow their own conversion: it would be better for Verecundus to be baptized while still sexually active than not to be baptized at all. Of Augustine's other friends, only one, young Alypius, was a willing companion, after his parallel decision in the garden. Even he was not free from worldly obligations and had to go to and fro between the villa and Milan. None of the other males who had enthused about a philosophy-commune a year earlier was willing to join the new venture.

As the October term began, Augustine set out from Milan for the hills, accompanied by a small band of potential 'lovers of wisdom': his fifteen-year-old son, his untrained brother, the young son of his patron, Romanianus, a recently dismissed soldier-boy, two barely educated north African cousins, his elderly, uneducated mother, Monnica, and from time to time the legally trained Alypius. They were all part of a pre-existing north African cluster with links to Thagaste, Augustine's home town. Unlike the supporters of the previous commune, they were Christians. However, Monnica was the only one to have been baptized.

'You had pierced our heart with arrows and Your love,' Augustine memorably tells God in the *Confessions*.[5] Nowadays we think of God's arrows as the arrows of plague or sickness, piercing the bodies, not hearts, of protector-saints like Sebastian in Italian Renaissance paintings. In the scriptures, however, Job bemoans 'the arrows of God in my body' and, shortly before writing the *Confessions*, Augustine made a note on Job's words that the 'arrows' are 'God's words with which the soul is transfixed when it is compelled to confession'. For Jerome, likewise, God's arrows are words in scripture. In the *Confessions*, Augustine relates them to God's past actions, 'You *had* pierced . . .' By this past tense he was surely referring to the words of Paul which he had recently read in the garden and to any scriptural readings which he had attempted since then. He describes these arrows as 'transfixing our intestines'. Before his conversion, he had been pierced only in the 'forepart' of his heart, but now his heart, the centre of his feelings and thinking, was transfixed too.[6] Originally, the arrows were an image from the Psalms, not the arrows of God's punishment in Psalm 38 but 'the sharp arrows of the mighty' (Ps. 120.4). Later in life he comments on this passage and explains that 'when human hearts are transfixed by the arrows of God's word, the effect is not death, but the arousal of love'. The Lord, he thinks, 'is a skilled shot, with His eye on love'. Pagans credited their Cupid with shooting arrows of love, but his arrows were usually related to looks and glances. 'God shoots to turn us into His lovers,' Augustine was later to write, and He does so by His words, as Cupid never did. Plotinus and his pupils had written memorably of the soul's innate love for the One, but the One never spoke or shot verbal arrows at anyone. From now on, love will remain central to Augustine's religious life, but it is a differently grounded love to the love of the Platonists. Arrow-struck Augustine was burning with passion for a new lover: God.[7]

Augustine was also 'fired', he tells us, by the examples of others, 'slaves of God'. Ever responsive to role models, he had been citing different examples less than a year before: 'lovers of wisdom', philosophers, who had been married. Now his examples were Christian celibates, people like Antony or those friends of Ponticianus of whom he had recently heard.

Back in Milan the fee-paying fathers of prominent young sons had no idea of this change of horizon. They had been expecting yet more rhetorical tricks from their city's brilliant teacher when the school year began. They returned for the term to find that he had done something last-minute, resigned and disappeared. He had done it in Carthage and he had done it in Rome. Now he had done it again in Milan. Libanius, that devoted teacher of rhetoric and tireless supporter of his former pupils' interests, would have snorted in disgust.

II

Verecundus' sub-Alpine villa, or 'chalet', was set in a verdant farm at Cassiciacum. Its exact location is still uncertain, a matter of dispute for some 500 years, but the likeliest candidate is the modern Cassago Brianza some twenty miles north-east of Milan, because it is close enough for Alypius' visits to the big city and back again.[8] In this idyllic setting Augustine would continue doing what he had done before: teach. He would no longer teach rhetoric to the competitive sons of ambitious parents. He would teach a syllabus of his own devising which would prepare his little 'chalet' party for the devoted study of wisdom. Weeks before, on hearing of Antony's exploits, he had exclaimed that the uneducated were rising up and seizing heaven. At Verecundus' villa, he would go to work on the barely educated and stretch their minds. He was aiming to convert them to philosophy, just as he had been converted in his youth.

The students were to attempt philosophical argument, but they were not to plunge directly into Plotinus and Porphyry, although Augustine might treat them to some of their themes. We can follow the lessons, not through the *Confessions*, which avoids duplicating the story, but through the three books of dialogues which he published at the time. Some of the dates are uncertain, but the likeliest timetable is that in early November, perhaps on 10–12 November, the group grappled with what we now read as the beginnings of *Against the Sceptics*. While addressing scepticism, they addressed the problem of whether in order to be happy we must know and possess truth. On 13 November, Augustine's thirty-second birthday, they diverted to debate the happy life and continued with it for two more days, probably 14–15 November. It was probably immediately afterwards that they broke off for about seven days and read and commented on three books of Virgil's *Aeneid*. About

22 November they were diverted to debate problems of order, God's order concealed in the universe. They then paused and returned to finish their discussion of scepticism, a task which took another three days. Then they spent two more days on difficult questions of order.[9] This discussion ended with a long exposition by Augustine of the ethics by which young seekers of wisdom should live, the subjects which they should study and the questions which they should address, naturally in 'order' too.

These topics were no new departure. In Milan during the previous year, Augustine had thought his way through scepticism, had discussed 'order' and the 'happy life' with his group of friends and had debated the 'ends' of human life about which they had been reading in Cicero's philosophical works. His programme of study was now to be based on the texts which had formed his younger self, Virgil's *Aeneid*, Cicero's *Hortensius* and, above all, Varro's books on the liberal arts. Like Varro's, his teaching would revere Pythagoras, the most other-worldly of sages, and aspire to the heavenly realm. This aspiration had been intensified by Augustine's recent reading of Platonist books.[10] The garden conversion marked an absolute break in his professional, worldly and sexual life, but intellectually there was continuity.

There would also be continuities of character. The young Augustine whom the *Confessions* brilliantly recall had been competitive, emotional and exceptionally intelligent. He had prevailed in the battles to become a top public speaker. He had wept freely over scenes in Virgil or mimes in the theatre. His heart, he recalls so engagingly, had been touched by books, some of which even 'fired' him, and it had 'bled' after his dismissal of his concubine. His exceptional intellect, his natural gift for philosophy and his heart and tears would need to find new outlets. Hitherto, he had enjoyed praise, but had hated sham compromise and boisterous confrontations not of his own choosing. These patterns, too, would not disappear overnight. There was also his awareness of his recent ascents to God's presence which had left him with a sense of the potential of his soul, unstable though it was. Here also there was much for him to work on.

In the villa we can read Augustine arguing in his own words for the first time. They have puzzled some of his modern historians because they seem to have a minimal relation to Christianity despite his recent conversion. He does not refute scepticism by asserting the Christian faith. He refutes it philosophically. He never quotes the Gospel at length but he remarks that he praises Pythagoras every day.[11] He uses pagan figures like Hercules or the nymph Cyrene to illustrate his arguments. His subjects are the classic subjects of the philosophical schools: happiness, the 'end' of the good life, and truth. Even some of his careful readers have considered them peculiar hybrids, more non-Christian than not. This reading misses more than it explains. It is inattentive to the texts' genre and their intended primary audience and it overlooks the Christian convictions which are explicit and implicit in Augustine's arguments.

Surprised by the tone, many have thought that, like Cicero's dialogues, the texts cannot represent what was actually said. In fact, they are evidence for the best-known weeks in the entire history of ancient philosophy, a gift which their readers have not always appreciated. Shorthand secretaries accompanied Augustine and his fellow seekers of wisdom and took down the words of their debates. They are not a realistic touch of colour which Augustine added later. On the contrary, they play an unusual role which is not matched in any other text in this genre.[12] They oblige the debate to be cut short as darkness is falling and they can no longer see to write. Their record is authoritative. Despite one of the young participants' entreaties, Augustine refuses to allow him to have an ill-judged opinion erased from the transcript. It still stands there, with Augustine's words of insistence that it should. He tells Romanianus, recipient of *Against the Sceptics*, that thanks to the secretaries he will be able to read the subjects and opinions of the young participants, 'but words of myself and Alypius too'. He is not saying that all the words in the text are his own, but that words of himself and Alypius were among those transcribed.[13] Presumably he tidied up the shorthand record before sending off the text, but he did not introduce new topics and new arguments.

Shorthand secretaries were a luxury which Augustine would not have financed personally. When they are mentioned in the writings of a Latin Christian contemporary, they turn out to have been paid for by the author's mother.[14] Monnica had neither the motive nor means to pay for transcribers. They were provided, no doubt, by the person who had the most direct interest in the results: Romanianus. The texts could be sent to him in his absence to show him how the group was progressing in its search for 'wisdom' and especially how his own son was getting on. Copies also went off to impress others: Nebridius, who acknowledged them in letters with a philosophic thrust, and Augustine's 'greater friends', who did not. Before publication, Augustine added elaborate dedications in which he flattered these recipients' intellects and aspirations and related the contents to their current predicament. The *Happy Life* was dedicated fulsomely to none other than Mallius Theodorus, who was also extolled in *On Order* for his talent, learning and character.[15] *On Order* was dedicated to Zenobius with praises of his intelligence, love of beauty and purity from lustful 'filth'. In the course of the debate, he was credited with taste, poetic skill and such benevolence to the young group that Augustine disclaimed the compliments which he liked to pay them.[16] There is a modest wit in these praises, as if Zenobius was a closer friend than Theodorus. Both instalments of *Against the Sceptics* were dedicated lengthily to Romanianus. The preface to the first book evokes the grand public honours and household of a donor as rich and public-spirited as himself and presents his recent worldly setback as a providential blessing which allows him to concentrate on the 'divine' better part in his soul. The preface to the next instalment thanks him laboriously for his lifelong patronage and his potential as a fellow philosopher. During the debate, when Romanianus' son is invited to think that his father may one day join him in philosophical argument, the boy begins to cry and to pray to God that it may occur. Then, the other participants succumb to tears.[17]

Like Alypius, Augustine was well used to the cultivation of patrons, whether Hierius the orator, recipient of his first book, or 'greater friends' while in pursuit of their 'suffrage' in Milan. Reviewing these dialogues in old age, Augustine regretted their 'pride' and 'schoolroom' tone.[18] He was referring to their rhetoric and their use of pagan literary and mythological models. He might also have noted the tone in which he flattered social superiors.

III

This intended audience helps to explain the form which the texts take. Augustine and the participants presented their efforts as the fruits of 'leisure' in the setting of a rural villa, a 'leisure for philosophizing'. There were precedents for such 'leisure': Cicero and great senators from the Roman past in their grand villas on the Bay of Naples, Plotinus and his senatorial audience in similar settings, and Mallius Theodorus in the villa near Milan which Augustine had visited. Augustine and his group were to engage in philosophical dialogues, the very form which Theodorus had adopted for his intellectual writings. They were not to be 'slaves of God' like Antony, tales of whose exploits had helped to fire Augustine to his change of life.[19] They were not to become unkempt and subject themselves to prolonged fasting. Their meals were modest, but they would still drink wine. Unlike Antony, Augustine had not promptly given away his worldly goods. Moderate riches, he still believed, are not a priority, but if they happen to come along and are well used, they are fine.

Philosophical dialogues would present Augustine to his patrons as they had known him: someone with a passion for the one true wisdom. This context imposed restraints. Talk of a dramatic sex crisis was out of place, because philosophers did not have to undergo one in order to be free to philosophize. The reasons for giving up rhetoric, an inferior study, were more relevant. Hence, when Augustine's dedications describe his own circumstances, they dwell only on the pains in his chest which, he says, obliged him to give up teaching public speaking and concentrate on the pursuit of 'wisdom'.[20] There was very little direct mention of Christ. As Alypius told him, the name of Christ did not belong in philosophical dialogues.[21] Not that the recipients would miss Him too much. One of the patrons, Romanianus, was still a Manichee and another, Zenobius, was probably a pagan. When addressing Mallius Theodorus and Romanianus, Augustine even referred to personified Fortune, an idea familiar to pagan Libanius, his fellow orator. Nobody, he writes to them, can enter the 'harbour of philosophy' without Fortune, whose help is sometimes hidden in apparent adversity.[22] In Augustine's case, the 'help' had been ill health; in Theodorus', political failure; in Romanianus', the tiresome lawsuit. Already, within four months of the event, Augustine was understanding his conversion in providential terms. Libanius also perceived Fortune's 'grace' at work in his life, even when she seemed adverse at the time. Fortune cared especially for him, but was one divinity among many. In Augustine's view, Fortune was part of a general Divine Providence whose 'order' is often hidden from us, but is all-pervasive nonetheless.[23] For Augustine, but not Libanius, Fortune is subject to God's Providence by which He cares for His entire world. That world is His creation, an idea which Libanius never entertained.

Before going to the villa, Augustine had never studied with a philosopher and never given a class in the subject. He was still a 'boy' in it. 'Who is that man?' he imagined outsiders saying on picking up one of his texts.[24] The dedications to his 'greater friends' would answer them: he was a lover of wisdom, they showed, who knew distinguished lovers of the subject. By sending them the transcribed texts of his efforts, he even hoped that they might join in the debate and help to carry it forward.[25]

His long-standing patron, Romanianus, was in different circumstances. Whereas Theodorus and Zenobius were writing on philosophical subjects, Romanianus had never written a word on them. He had lost a lawsuit and gone back to Africa. In his prefaces, therefore, Augustine urges him to follow his mental talents and take up philosophy after this providential setback. Romanianus, he says, has been held back by two obstacles: uncertainty of finding the truth and the assumption that he has already found enough of it. This 'assumption' is his continuing Manichaeism, something which Augustine promises to address in a separate work. The 'uncertainty' is scepticism and will, he hopes, be dispelled by the arguments which he is sending 'against the sceptics'.[26] He sends him the first book in advance of the next two, because it shows his son's progress towards a conversion to the true philosophy and will encourage him, he hopes, in the same direction. In a florid moment, Augustine even ventures to hope that Romanianus' legal opponent will take a similar step. Like Augustine's 'greater friends', he is given some remarkable compliments on his natural gifts. He has a 'seed of spiritual beauty', although it is 'twisted and deformed' by surrounding vices as it tries to emerge to 'true beauty'. He is a 'lover of beauty', Augustine says, as his refined hospitality and surroundings show. It reads as if this man had been another one of his patrons. As a 'love of beauty' is close to the 'love of wisdom', Romanianus' enemy may rightfully entwine himself in the lap of Philosophy. Philosophy is like a mother from whose breasts, Augustine writes, we try to feed, and so Romanianus' opponent will be like Romanianus' very own brother, a part of Philosophy's family.[27] 'Are you amazed by this,' Augustine asks, as well he might, 'and perhaps you laugh?' We might expect Romanianus to find the notion irritating, as he had just lost a law case to this 'brother'. However, as Augustine well claims, we must 'never despair of anyone'. The capacity to live a virtuous life is hidden in many more people than we may think. So is the capacity to grasp the essence of wisdom. The teaching at the villa will help to explain what he meant.

22

Villa Life

I

When Augustine withdrew to the villa with his small 'reading party' he took with him many questions from his past which he would now have time to think through. His phase as a Manichaean Hearer was nearly two years behind him but it had left him with a whole cluster of unresolved questions. Mani's story of Creation was wrong, but what are the relations between God, Creation and human beings? Unlike the Manichaeans, Augustine had come to believe in a hidden order which unifies the world. How, therefore, should the opening chapters of Genesis be understood? What about the rest of the scriptures now that Ambrose had shown them to be full of hidden meanings? What about ourselves? We are not made up of two conflicting substances, one good, one bad, but we are nonetheless (Augustine believed) a blend of body and soul. How do these two interrelate?

Whereas Mani believed that he had made contact with his divine Twin, Augustine believed he had briefly 'touched' the presence of God Himself. Could he repeat it or prolong it and, if he did, should he keep it to himself? 'I kept chattering on . . .' he recalled after his first experiences in Milan, but self-persuaded mystics can become relentless company, as later examples show. In May 1908, on the River Euphrates, the great Christian scholar of Islamic mysticism, Louis Massignon, believed that he too had had a life-changing encounter with God. Feverish at the time and contemplating suicide, he continued ever after to talk of this transforming experience, 'combining force and sweetness, anger and pity, with such intensity that some who met him could not bear his presence', a fellow scholar has acutely recalled, 'but most were overwhelmed by a physical sense of the supernatural; always talking . . . and returning, even on the most unpropitious occasions, to the central moment of his own life, the drama of sin and contrition and the divine light in the face of the Stranger'.[1] Augustine, by contrast, would keep quiet about his experience in the texts which he wrote in the immediate aftermath.

On arriving at the villa, Augustine the convert aimed to convert his little group. He did not take them into the complexities of scripture, which, as yet, he little knew how best to approach. Instead, he took them through the *Hortensius* in the hope that it would affect them as it had formerly affected himself. In order to sharpen their grasp of grammar, language and hidden meanings, there were also the daily readings of Virgil's *Aeneid*. Augustine distinguishes three activities, 'hearing' Virgil's books as they were read aloud, reviewing them in a 'recension' word by word, just as his own teachers in Thagaste had once explained them to him, and 'considering them' (*tractatio*) in more general discussions of longer passages which might involve allegory.[2] It is no surprise that Virgilian phrases and mythical figures grace the group's debates. However, their underlying source was the *Hortensius*, especially during the discussions on scepticism and the happy life.[3]

The transcribed dialogues give a charming sense of how time was spent. On sunny November days, the group would go out with the secretaries and writing tablets and wrestle with philosophical questions in the meadows around the villa. The Virgilian qualities of its sub-Alpine setting cannot have been lost on them. On cloudy or rainy days they would stay inside and converse in the villa's bath-house, a recognized venue for lectures and discussions during the 'leisure' of well-off villa-owners. There was no fixed hourly routine. Of a morning, they might write letters. Once, they were not free to pursue 'wisdom' until late in the afternoon because they had begun the day by 'arranging business' with the rustics and had then reviewed in detail the first book of Virgil's *Aeneid*, pausing on difficulties. Every day before dinner they would listen to half a book of Virgil being read aloud, presumably by Augustine himself. Manual work on the farm was not in the programme. Verecundus' villa would be staffed by dependent labourers, including slaves, the 'rustics' with whom, twice, Augustine and the group arranged matters. The routine is not said to have included physical work, even for the boys. The priorities lay elsewhere. When a day dawned clear and blue, Augustine and the group had dealings with the workforce only 'for a short while' and then set off into the meadow to debate philosophically.[4] A fine day, ideal for farmwork, did not divert them. There is no mention of a garden, either. Indoors, it was much the same. The boys are never described as washing dishes and there is no evidence that Monnica was cooking or cleaning. She came in and out of the group's discussions and even announced that lunch was ready, but when she joined a morning debate, the announcement of lunch became the job of a designated slave boy.[5] He and others like him were evidently doing the housework all the time.

Meanwhile, Augustine's teaching programme was not at all mundane. Its mission was to explore the 'world of intellect', the invisible, spiritual world which lies behind and beyond the shadowland perceived by our senses. Augustine had learned this fundamental division from the Platonist books. Philosophy, he writes for Romanianus, 'teaches truly that everything must be utterly despised which is seen by mortal eyes or which any sense attains'.[6] In the villa, he convinced himself of the superiority of the 'world of the intellect' in short, logical arguments which he proudly communicated to his friends outside.[7] Ultimately, their subjects were 'God and the soul'. The mind, he believes, can rise to contemplate them both, but first it must recognize the higher unified truth which lies beyond apparent multiplicity.

Augustine taught his pupils that the world about them had a hidden dimension. If they looked carefully, they might see signs of God's hidden order in their daily experience. They were not simply looking for random signs of God's interventions, or 'providences', in the world. Their questions were more general. Where exactly does chance cease and order begin in the visible universe? One night, fallen leaves blocked a water channel near the boys' dormitory: was this blocking fortuitous, they wondered, or like everything else in the world did it have an orderly cause? On a fine morning they watched two cockerels fighting until one was victorious and the other was a bedraggled mess of feathers. The fight was not a lesson in 'nature red in tooth and claw'. Even the loser seemed 'beautiful' and 'in harmony with nature's laws'. 'We asked many questions: why do all cocks behave like this? Why do they fight for the supremacy of the hens subject to them?' The answer, no doubt, was lust, but the 'beauty' of the fight had briefly diverted the watchers with pleasure: why? What is it that we seek beyond the evidence of the human senses? What else do those senses help us to grasp? The cockfight could be interpreted as evidence of the existence of 'law' and orderly 'measure' whose elements are 'consistent'.[8] Augustine's former interest in the apt and beautiful now fell into place in what he had learned to be God's providentially ordered universe. There is no non-moral evil in it. If seen as parts of the whole, evils like snakes or floods are good in relation to their ordered position. Such optimism is not so persuasive to those whom such evil befalls.

Nearly ten years later, one of the participants, Romanianus' son Licentius, was to look back fondly on this time lived with 'the pure rules of good people'.[9] 'Leisure' was not idleness. There were prayers every morning, and although members of the group were given time to themselves, it was time for thinking hard. Beyond the logical wrestling and the questions on order and happiness, a bolder aim was at work: Augustine wished to raise himself and his pupils to nothing less than a sustainable vision of God. The hours with Virgil, grammar and logical argument were a necessary prelude, the 'cleansing' of the participants' vision so as to see beyond the material world.

This 'leisured' aim was not unparalleled. Fifteen years later it would have been entirely congenial to the Christian Synesius, a fellow devotee of philosophy. In his letters he relates 'leisure' constantly to the exercise of the intellect and the attempt to raise it to God.[10] He claims to have realized this aim, not in alpine hills but in the desert spaces of southern Libya, with a group of companions very different from Augustine's own. After returning home from his prolonged embassy to Constantinople, Synesius was to be found, once again, hunting with hounds and horses in the remote Libyan countryside. In an excellent letter he presents this setting to his former student friend Olympius. His companions, he tells him, are simple Libyan huntsmen who have never seen the sea and are unable to believe that edible fish live in such a thing. Together, they hunt and at night sing songs to a little lyre about animals and about the huntsman's life. To Synesius the desert gives 'leisure for philosophizing, but no time for bad behaviour'. He is truly enjoying the 'golden age of Noah'.[11] Unlike Augustine and his pupils, he was joining actively in the farming, the herding and, above all, the hunting for daily food. His friend Olympius was a carefully chosen recipient for the letter: he was both an excellent horseman and a former philosophy student with Hypatia. Synesius presented his 'outdoors' friend with an image of a truly idyllic life. He even reviewed the excellence of its locally sourced produce.

His hymns are further evidence of it. They present him as one who has returned from the grim labours of Constantinople and is visiting the 'pure deserts' of southern Libya away from the 'imprint of men beset by city-cares'. There, his soul, 'ceasing from labours, ceasing from laments', will render up to God the hymn which is due to Him. It is the hymn which follows, in which Synesius calls on God for mercy, praises Him as 'Monad and Triad', and prays for the ascent of his soul to Him beyond the material world. Like Augustine, Synesius was awaiting imminent baptism but aspiring nonetheless to a philosophic contact with the divine.[12] The desert was his Cassiciacum. Whereas Augustine argued for an ascent to god in rigorous masterclasses, Synesius expressed his yearning for it in philosophic hyms. He would have loved to receive copies of Augustine's villa dialogues, to read their allusions to myth and poetry, to think of 'wisdom' as a set of 'mysteries' which needed a guide if they were to be penetrated, and to participate by letter in the sessions' aims. He did not think that the hidden order of the world fully explained evil, because he also thought that there were demons in it, entities which Augustine was not discussing in his texts at this time. Nonetheless Synesius believed that God might use these demons as instruments of just punishment, and so it would be fun for him to argue with Augustine about their relation to 'order'. If he had ever been invited to the villa, he would have found the company socially beneath him, the daily lessons too elementary and Monnica's mind no substitute for divine Hypatia's. However, he could have escaped into the foothills for a day's boar-hunting and then enjoyed a masterclass with Augustine alone in the evenings.

In his first dispatch from Cassiciacum Augustine tells Romanianus that 'Philosophy promises she will show clearly the truest and most secret God, and now, already, deigns to show Him off as if through clear clouds.' In his second dispatch, he is 'confident' that he will 'come to the highest Measure itself', meaning God the Father. He is beginning to 'recognize, somewhat' experiences could be related Him to whom he has 'given his whole self'.[13] His own visionary experiences could be related to his programme of teaching, and yet in the classes he never describes them openly to his pupils. A capacity for an instant, unprepared vision, he acknowledges to them, is the gift of very few, but, even so, he does not name himself among them. Instead, he teaches that a long preliminary training, a sort of 'doctoral' period, is necessary. Since the summer, what had changed?

Even in Milan, Augustine's soul had been 'thrust away' and had made no more than a flicker of contact with the divine. To become 'stable' in God's presence, he had realized that he must abandon the 'chain' of sex, but, even then, renewed ascents would not be easy to prolong. Meanwhile, he had no doubt continued to 'ascend' beyond the material world, but his reticence suggests that attempts to make contact with God Himself had failed. Since August, his new commitment to celibacy had compounded his view of himself. It had set the standard of virtue very much higher and intensified his sense of his own imperfection: inevitably, he was continuing to struggle with his sexual dreams and instincts. Previously in Milan, he had turned inwards without any sense that he was morally falling short. At a time of personal stress he had promptly soared upwards and made fleeting contact, he thought, with divinity. The soul, he believed, was God's creation, and yet it had fallen away by misguided choices and was clotted with worldly sin. How could he rectify it and teach others to do the same?

Back in Carthage, when reading the old books of Varro, he had discovered that a syllabus of the 'disciplines', or liberal arts, could point the mind upwards and, as Pythagoras exemplified, cause the 'immortal soul' to follow a 'secret journey' to the heavens.[14] Here was the preparation he and his pupils needed. By November, he had found it amplified in writings by Porphyry, the Platonist who had written a long work against the Christians, which Augustine may not yet have known. Whereas he rejected Porphyry's paganism and his interest in magical rituals, Porphyry's translated writings, I believe, confirmed to him that 'disciplines classes' can purify the mind for a vision of God.[15] By the third week in November, Augustine was expounding this very plan of study. There were to be lessons in seven (not nine) disciplines. They would purify the students' minds and bring out the truth and order which were latent in them. Thanks to Varro and (arguably) Porphyry, Augustine had found a focus for his novel role: he would be a teacher of philosophy with a mystical aim.

He could speak lyrically to his students and readers about the end result. Ordinary words cannot describe it because 'they have all been filthied with the vilest things'. It is a vision of inexpressible beauty, but it also gives knowledge. It is not undertaken only for a sense of ecstasy. 'The person who lives well, prays well, studies well will see it.' In the villa the potential beneficiaries were more of a challenge. The dialogues show them at work, recorded in their own words. The two country cousins had little to contribute, except silent assent, to the first steps of mental exercise: one was even named 'Rusticus'. Augustine's brother, Navigius, had a sibling's wariness of whatever his brother tried to argue. He complained of a bad liver and, after a week, left briefly for Milan. Augustine's son, Adeodatus, was more promising. Though only fifteen, he was extremely intelligent. During the arguments he asserted the value of a chaste life, much to his grandmother Monnica's delight.[16]

The two older boys already liked books. Both of them loved Virgil, and Trygetius, the ex-soldier, had a winning passion for history. He showed a detailed knowledge of Cicero's speeches against Catiline back in 63 BC and even quoted one from memory. His main sparring partner was to be the young Licentius, Romanianus' boy. Together, they tussled mentally with puppy-like enthusiasm, exulting in victories, rueing defeats. Licentius' passion was poetry, not history. He was writing verses on the two unhappy mythical lovers Pyramus and Thisbe. This sort of love owed nothing to God's arrows.[17]

Unlike the steady Trygetius, Licentius was to progress from one position to the next in the course of a fortnight. Thanks to the secretaries' transcripts, we can follow his progress. When Augustine begins by asking if we can be happy without finding truth, Licentius argues that we can. A happy life, he states, is not a life in possession of the truth, but a life spent searching for it. He had merely taken this view from Cicero's *Hortensius*, the text with which Augustine had begun to train him. He held onto it with difficulty, but whenever he had to define a concept, his confidence deserted him. So far, his views were in keeping with those of the sceptics, but he had yet to endure an attack on them by Augustine himself.[18]

Before Licentius had to resume this argument, he changed his ground. In the night hours he was awake in the group's shared bedroom and was diverted by a mouse on the floorboards. The sound of water outdoors, blocked by leaves, embarked him on a decidedly non-sceptical discussion: is there a hidden order in the world? He began to argue that there must be. Extravagantly, he exclaimed at the bigger truth which was dawning on him, 'a divine thing which begins to reveal itself': Augustine then had to help him to express his 'theory of everything' in words. He was hardly able to do so: he maintained, nonetheless, that 'both good things and bad things' are in order. He became agitated; he loomed over poor Trygetius' bed; he alarmed him by demanding point blank, 'Is God just?' He then flung himself down on his bed. He even claimed to have lost his taste for poetry. He has had a flash of illumination from 'a very different light'. Philosophy, he now thinks, is more beautiful than 'Thisbe, than Pyramus, than that Venus and Cupid . . .' With a sigh, he then 'gives thanks to Christ'.[19]

In the morning he was to be heard singing a line from the Psalms: 'O God of hosts, convert us and show us thy face and we shall be saved.' To Augustine's delight he was undergoing a conversion, the very thing, to 'true, divine philosophy'. Augustine even took the chance to tell him how to treat the topic of Pyramus and Thisbe more appropriately.

When the two lovers are lying dead, he should mock the 'curse of unclean lust and burning passion' and praise 'pure and true love'. Sexless love, not carnal love, brings souls to wisdom and the happy life and enables them to escape from death.[20] Others before him had not imposed such a moral on this amorous myth.

In the first instalment which he sent to the boy's father, Augustine describes Licentius as being 'converted' to philosophy from 'youthful pleasures and enticements': would it really last? Augustine had already promised to subject the boy's sceptical arguments to harder questioning. When he did so, Licentius fell apart. When he resumed the debate about 'order', Licentius was again unable to hold the argument for very long. After a sudden illumination, he fell away. His mind needed more preparation with the disciplines, and even then it would have far to go.[21]

There was nothing so unstable about the oldest participant, Monnica. In these dialogues we still hear her own words, a rare female voice preserved in an ancient text with the help of shorthand note-takers: she is brusque and conspicuously shrewd.[22] On Augustine's birthday she intervenes in the debates on the 'happy life'. She makes a blunt point about the soul's 'nourishment' by wisdom, contrasting Trygetius' recent absent-mindedness when eating his breakfast. She insists that if anyone desires evil, he is wretched even if he 'possesses' what he wants. She has never read Cicero's *Hortensius*, but she has anticipated the very point which Augustine is about to make from it. Augustine compliments her for 'gaining the citadel of philosophy'. She protests, no doubt modestly. 'Entirely forgetting her sex,' Augustine writes, 'we thought that some great man was sitting with us.' He has understood meanwhile 'from how divine a source' her wisdom flows. Her mind, he says, is 'enflamed for divine matters', as he himself has long observed, not least from 'daily living together' and 'his attentive consideration'. She is devoted to God and is being guided by Him. When the dialogue culminates in Augustine's philosophical account of a Trinity, Monnica spontaneously sings the opening lines of Ambrose's hymn on the subject, which she had learned during the siege in Milan's basilica during Lent. It is an extraordinary ending to a dialogue which has such Ciceronian colour on its surface and so many engagements with the *Hortensius*.[23]

On being told what sceptics are, Monnica dismisses them curtly as 'sick' (or 'epileptic'). The debates *On Order* are much more to her liking, but when she intrudes in them, she is cautious. She asks that her name should be excluded from the record because women, she thinks, are never included in books of philosophy. Augustine declines, not only because women had indeed featured in the past (even Plato's Socrates conversed with Diotima). Monnica, he tells her, has a special claim. She loves wisdom even more than she loves her son: the word 'philo-sophy', he kindly explains to her, means 'love of wisdom' (a view he had found in the *Hortensius*). Monnica's 'wisdom' is such that she no longer fears death or disaster. As a result no truly cultivated reader, he remarks, will protest at finding her included in the book.[24] Cultivated Zenobius and Theodorus, we infer, might otherwise have wondered what on earth she was doing there. Augustine's spontaneous tribute to his mother is charming, and once again he is admiring and affectionate. Monnica 'gently and piously' disclaims the compliment, saying he has 'never spoken so much that is untrue'. In the sequel, however, she proves him more right than wrong. She continues to sit in on the debates and makes a penetrating point about the relation of evil to God's order and justice, thereby upstaging the two boys.

Monnica had not had any literary education: 'if I were to say,' Augustine tells her, 'that you could easily attain the sort of speech which is free from errors of expression and pronunciation, I would be lying'.[25] Nor had she had any training in the liberal arts, but she is more than able to draw acute conceptual distinctions. She goes straight to the point, stating 'obvious' commonsense distinctions, but she also respects the demands of logical reasoning: 'if reason compels this, I cannot say "no"'.[26] These dialogues show her innate shrewdness, whereas the *Confessions* will have more to say about her unswerving faith and obedience. In the villa, she could smile and parry compliments, but if basic values, in her view, were involved, there was no crossing her. On the night of his 'conversion' Licentius left to go out to the lavatory, where he sat loudly chanting his favourite line from the Psalms, 'O God of hosts, convert us . . .', set to Ambrose's new music. Monnica hammered him for singing these words in such an improper place. He tried to answer back: if an enemy was detaining him in the lavatory, surely God would heed his words? Monnica was not impressed with his facetiousness. It took Augustine on the following morning to show him that his singing about 'conversion' had almost been prophetic.[27] Even the time and place, Augustine observed, had been apt, whatever Monnica said. The night was dark, the lavatory filthy, and the conversion of which Licentius sang was a conversion from the 'darkness' of error and the 'filth of the body and its stains'.

Licentius and Trygetius arrived at the villa as Christian catechumens. In the first days Licentius freely invoked God and both of them argued combatively about Christ as God's son.[28] They did not need to be converted to Christianity: they merely needed to understand it more deeply. The only conversion in the villa, Licentius', was a short-lived conversion to 'wisdom'.

II

Nobody in such a 'chalet' party was on holiday. Lessons were all around them and expectations were high. The recipients and the participants are described as notably impassioned and expectant. Like Augustine in the garden, they have a chance to 'awake' from their previous 'slumbers'. They must 'cast off' their habits and allow a new truth to 'break out'. To assist them, the transcribed dialogues share a similar form. First come the tortuous arguments by which they struggle under Augustine's prompting to establish something true. Then he takes over and gives a monologue which takes the question into new ground. *On the Happy Life* is the most coherent, whereas *On Order* begins fitfully, stopping and starting no fewer than four times before changing topic halfway through. Why did Augustine publish such circuitous texts?

In his older age Cicero had published 'disputations', set in his villa at Tusculum, in which questions and answers in dialogue led on to long expositions by Cicero himself.[29] Augustine's are similar, but he was not simply following Cicero's genre. Unlike Cicero's, his dialogues record real teaching, and so their shape reflects what is still the form of a good tutorial. First, the pupils dispute under guidance; then the tutor speaks alone and carries them up to a new level. The preliminary arguments are 'exercisings' of the mind, but unlike a tutorial they are parts of a more general spiritual exercise: ultimately, they will prepare their participants' minds for a vision of God.[30] By having the words transcribed, Augustine could send them to fellow lovers of wisdom and exercise their minds too. Transcription also enabled his pupils to re-examine the arguments and see where they had gone wrong. *Against the Sceptics* ends with the wish that the boys should repeat its refutation of scepticism all over again with Alypius taking them through it. They could then master the refutation and be rid of obstructive scepticism once and for all.

Augustine's philosophical skill and dedication are more impressive than the results. *On the Happy Life* makes repeated use of phrases, arguments and imagery from Cicero's *Hortensius*, the young participants' lesson book. It dwells on false, transitory ends and the instability of riches and accepts Cicero's generalization: 'everyone wants to be happy'. It then concludes that the happy life resides in the 'perfect knowledge of God', assisted by that non-Ciceronian trio, 'faith, hope and charity': the question of whether any God exists to be known is not adequately addressed. The core of the book, briefly expressed, is its definition of happiness: 'the happy man is the one who has God'.[31] This conclusion may seem oddly expressed, but it rests on a combination of philosophy and Christian 'authority' which relates exactly to Augustine's interpretations of his visionary experiences in Milan. There is a continuity, easy to miss here, between his recent ascents and the thrust of *On the Happy Life*.

'Having God' means 'enjoying Him', not in the hedonistic sense of finding Him enjoyable, but in the sense which Augustine's later works make clear to us: 'enjoying God for His own sake', not using Him as a means to anything else, 'and clinging on to Him in love, for the sake of Him alone'. Happiness, therefore, resides in active contemplation. Its object is 'He who endures for ever'. The end of the dialogue helps to fill out what is meant.[32] Happiness, Augustine explains, is 'contemplating wisdom when it has been found', 'holding oneself to it' and not being dragged away by the 'weight' of other competing illusions. Wisdom is the Wisdom of God, and as God's Wisdom is His son and as His son is God, the happy man's intent contemplation of wisdom is the intent contemplation of God. As John's Gospel says, 'He is the Truth' (this verse, John 14.6, is implied by Augustine in a text written soon afterwards to have been much used by the Manichaeans).[33] God is also 'Measure', in the philosophical sense of being the absolute standard by which measuring is done.

This theorizing on happiness is shaped by Augustine's reading of Plotinus, but it also relates implicitly to his recent experiences and his Christian faith. The happy man is the one who remains secure and contemplative in God's presence. He is not thrust away or dragged down, as Augustine had been in Milan. God is expressed in the philosophical terms of Being, Truth and Measure, terms which were used in the 'wisdom' preserved by the Platonists. As Augustine's son, Adeodatus, observes, happiness is best attained by those who are chaste. They are not only those who abstain from 'illicit lying-together': they abstain from all other defiling sins.[34] Happiness, therefore, requires both the renunciation of sex and the maintenance of as sinless a life as possible. The proposal relates exactly to Augustine's new commitment: a chaste and virtuous life directed to sustainable contemplation of God.

At its core, therefore, *On the Happy Life* is mystical, the heir to what Augustine had read and experienced in Milan. *Against the Sceptics* also begins with phrases from the *Hortensius*, but is prefaced by the recognition that Romanianus may be held back from pursuing philosophy by 'despair' that he can ever find 'truth'. The dialogue, Augustine hopes, will help him to see that despite the sceptics, he can do so. It will demolish two fellow sceptics, his son Licentius and the worthy Alypius. It will show truths which are as certain as the truths of mathematics.

This dialogue continued to be valued in antiquity as a disproof of scepticism, but not all of its laborious arguments work. Some of its premises need to be supplemented and their scope is not always clear. The most successful is an argument against withholding assent from anything because the risking of error is unwise. Action and judgement risk error, Augustine argues, but we cannot abstain entirely from acting or judging. It is not unwise to risk error, therefore, and so it is not wise to withhold assent in every case. Augustine's longest argument is less successful. He discusses the conditions for knowledge, especially the ones upheld by Zeno the Stoic, but in the analysis of a modern logician, Christopher Kirwan, 'he doesn't win, because he doesn't keep his eye on the ball'. He also 'needs a reason for treating indubitability, or unrejectability, as a sign of truth. But unlike Descartes, Augustine offers no such reason: so the game goes to the Academics.'[35]

On Order engages with a particularly difficult question: is there a providential order in the world? Like *Against the Sceptics*, it fails to answer its own question, but for a different reason. Augustine's logic is not defective, but he abandons the question for another, the 'orderly' preparation which a mind needs if it is to succeed in addressing such a general topic. The soul has a potential which a harmonious training can unlock. It is said to depend on the 'disciplines' of the liberal arts and on aspects of 'number' which are latent in its structure. Neither point is established by hard logic: they depend on Augustine's underlying source, old Varro and his eccentric Pythagorean authorities.[36]

III

For historians, the aspirations in these weeks are more interesting than the answers. Within four months of their conversion Augustine and Alypius can be followed arguing in their own words. In the Milan garden Alypius had agreed to adopt his admired ex-teacher's new commitment, but in the villa we can see that he was still halted where Augustine had been standing in the previous spring, with a readiness to champion scepticism. However, his new Christian commitment was not shallow.[37] Although he encouraged Augustine to minimize all references to Christ in the transcribed dialogues, he did not do so as a half-hearted Christian: mentions of Christ would be generically out of place in a philosophical dialogue. He had come to the villa with philosophy in only one of the compartments of his mind: he had not allowed it to undermine his commitment to celibacy and, surely, to baptism ('putting on Christ'). Philosophy engaged him on a more abstract plane, in matters of argument but not action. When he takes the sceptics' side in the debates, he argues tenaciously, but his defeats are very much to his liking. In every point he defers to Augustine's superior talent. By the end of the dialogue he has abandoned whatever sceptical leanings he had brought with him and he concludes, as ever, in perfect friendship with Augustine, who has refuted them. Before the snows melt, he then proves his commitment by a personal act of overachievement: he walks barefoot on the Alpine mountains' ice. This type of trial was not unprecedented among keen Christians, although bishops in Italy disapproved of it.[38] In Alypius' case, it was a challenge which had been waiting to happen since the scene in the garden. As Augustine recognizes, it had been easy for Alypius to give up sex, as he had never liked it. If he wanted to shine as a new 'slave of God', he had to do something more demanding. A frost-bitten walk was a challenge for him in the way that celibacy was not. It was not that he became a convinced Christian only when embarking on this trial in late winter. In the previous summer, in the garden, he had already opted for baptism, but baptismal applications had to wait until nearer Lent, many months in the future. For that reason only, he had delayed his application.[39]

Augustine, his iconic teacher, is in a much more fragile state. He prays, he weeps, he considers himself 'wounded' and he cannot cope with a competitive contest. Still conscious of his own conversion, he states that people turn to God when 'admonished': just so, the words '*Tolle lege*' had recently admonished himself.[40] The dialogues are not the place for him to dwell on his choice to abandon sex and worldly ambitions. His expressed concerns are philosophy and its scope.

In late November he is already clear about the continuing programme for his pupils. He even tells them exactly which virtues they must cultivate in order for their minds to begin to be fit to 'ascend'.

Love of money and love of honour must not divert them. They must hate nobody and must obey the 'golden rule', to 'do as they would be done by'. They must also refrain from all 'sexual matters'. When Augustine concludes that they must embark on governing the state only when they are mature, he must be drawing on a pre-existing source: advice on 'government' was not exactly relevant to these young boys. Probably, he has drawn on rules ascribed by Varro to Pythagoras, but he blends them, revealingly, with Christian ethics. They are his first embryonic 'Precept' for members of a group. If they follow it, then God will hear 'most readily' their prayers. God's help, he believes, will be dispensed to those who deserve it by their virtuous way of life. At this point in his life he does not consider that God's grace will be granted irrespective of its recipients' merits.[41]

On first acquaintance the Augustine of these dialogues has seemed to some of his modern readers to be a Neoplatonist and to show little or no concern for Jesus, the Gospel or the Resurrection. Repeatedly he uses the language of flight. The soul must flee from the perceptible world of the senses: it must flee from worldly pleasures: so far as possible, it must flee from 'this body'. The spiritual world is what matters and the aim is to contemplate the divine.[42] Part of his ideal is to have no fear of death. This aim, at least, has an obvious Christian dimension. Among Jerome's coterie of noble Christian females in Rome, elderly Marcella had been presented by him as 'praising that saying of Plato's, that philosophy is a meditation on death'. She lived her life 'as if she always believed she would die'. She even dressed as if she 'remembered the tomb'.[43] Fearlessness about death was indeed a Christian quality. It was one which pious, elderly Monnica exemplified, as her son recognized.

If read closely, Augustine's other unworldly ideals are not those of a Platonist, either. He writes that he is praying daily for Romanianus' conversion to philosophy, imploring the 'virtue and Wisdom of the highest God', but this Wisdom, he remarks, is the one which the 'mysteries' (of Christianity) 'hand down to us as God's son' (in 1 Cor. 1.24).[44] It is not Plotinus' One, or Intellect. He states explicitly against the sceptics that he is 'certain and resolved nowhere to depart from Christ's authority: for I do not find one more valid', valid in the sense of powerful, both for Augustine and for many others in the world. The endings of each of the dialogues are manifestly Christian. *On the Happy Life* quotes Paul and the Fourth Gospel to establish 'on divine authority' that the son of God is Wisdom and Truth (1 Cor. 1.24 and

John 14.6). This God is three-in-one, a statement which causes Monnica to conclude the discussion by singing the words from Ambrose's hymn. About two weeks later, *Against the Sceptics* ends with praise for philosophy, not the philosophy 'of this world' which 'our sacred things most decidedly detest' (an allusion to Paul, Col. 2.8), but the philosophy of the higher world of the intellect. This world is accessible to us only because, in 'a sort of popular clemency', the supreme God directed down to the human body, no less, the authority of divine 'Intellect'. 'Not only by its teachings but by its deeds, it arouses our souls to return inwards and behold their fatherland, without concerted disputations.'[45] Augustine is referring here to the incarnate Christ who enables us to turn inwards and ascend to the spiritual world. In *On Order*, he is even more explicit. The only function of 'true, authentic philosophy', he states, is to 'teach the existence of the Principle of all things and the greatness of the Intellect which resides in Him'. These abstractions are not the supranormal entities of the Neoplatonic Triad. They include 'that which has emanated from there, without any degeneration, for our salvation'. This phrase refers to the Christian Word incarnate.[46] The text then goes on to state the 'sublime fact' of this Incarnation, again calling it a 'kind' act of God.

These statements are intermittent and have sometimes been missed by historians. To a Platonist, their firm assertions of the Incarnation as the key to philosophy would be repugnant. Unlike Augustine and his pupils, they could not call God's son 'Christ'. For Augustine, however, God's Wisdom is identifiable with Christ (1 Cor. 1.24 said so), and so the 'love of wisdom' (*philo-sophia*) is the love of Christianity, as others in the Greek world had independently concluded.[47] He cites Jesus's words in the Fourth Gospel that He is the Way, the Truth, the Life, and when he praises the 'Wisdom which is the right Way leading to Truth', he means Christ. The Platonists are useful only because they have retained some of the original 'wisdom' revealed by God and because they have worked through aspects of its abstract philosophy. Platonists explain how the soul can raise itself to a vision of God. They explain that God is both within us and above us, but that He is not contained in the external world. They help us to understand the all-powerful Trinity of Father, Son and Holy Spirit, a Trinity which the scriptures never mention as such. Augustine therefore states that God is the 'Principle' of all and the 'Intellect' is Christ who is Truth and Wisdom. He ends *On the Happy Life* by postulating a trinity of Measure (God), Truth (His Word) and an Admonition (surely he remembered his recent admonition in the garden) which 'acts with us so that we recall God and search for Him'. This 'Admonition' is evidently the Holy Spirit. It is like a sunbeam, he says, as it illumines us all. This unusual language for the Trinity is one which his studies of the 'one true philosophy' and his recent experience had suggested to him.[48]

For Augustine, this philosophizing does not stand in contradiction to faith: it helps him to understand faith. The relation of reason and authority is extremely important to him, and with good cause.[49] Once, the Manichaeans had promised him 'truth' based on reason, not on authority, but it had turned out to be entirely false. Now, while reinstating authority as a starting point, Augustine recognizes several ways to truth which interrelate, none excluding the others. Only a very few will begin from faith, he realizes, and then strive to understand it by reason. For them, philosophy is a nurturing mother, but this philosophy is not non-Christian. It is part of the single wisdom which God first revealed and Christ incarnate reaffirmed. Most ordinary people will only need authority and will rest content with that as the grounds for faith. Their minds will not be disciplined to ascend to God in their lifetime, but God will 'draw them to Himself' nonetheless by the 'chain' of faith, one of Augustine's favourite images for turning to God (the Latin text of John 6.44 spoke of 'drawing'). Already Augustine writes passionately about 'divine' authority and its superiority. It 'directs' a man and 'shows him how far it has humbled itself for his sake', a reference to the Incarnation. It teaches 'its power by its deeds, its clemency by its humility and its nature by its precepts'. All these things are handed on 'secretly and soundly' in the rites 'in which we are initiated'. This authority is Christian and it 'cleans the lives of good men most easily, not by tortuous disputes but by the authority of its mysteries'.

In the villa, therefore, Augustine's Christian commitment is beyond question. Within it, however, he adopts a split-level approach. He focuses his thought not on everyday perceptions but on the soul and the invisible world. He also believes that philosophy is for only a few. This approach would be extremely congenial to his fellow Christian, Synesius. Like Augustine at this time, he accepted some sort of resurrection, but would not accept it in a crude, literal sense. He was explicit that philosophizing is a mystery, fit only for the few, not for everyday Christians. He was willing to teach improving myths, if he must, in public to Christian audiences, but he would continue to practise philosophy in private.[50] Augustine was practising this very philosophy in private with a small pre-selected group. Like Synesius, he was aiming for his soul to ascend to God, freed from the restraining chains of the body and worldly desires which would try to pull it back. His insistence on soul, not body, was not as extreme as Synesius', but his language for God and His Son was as abstract and unscriptural as Synesius' philosophic poetry.[51]

There was one other way to truth, recognized once in passing by Synesius but daily exemplified for Augustine by someone at his side. Entirely chaste, his mother, Monnica, exemplified pure piety and a mind most intently 'enflamed' for God. Despite her accent and bad grammar, she could go straight to the 'soul' of a subject under study by Augustine's pupils without bothering with its 'body'.[52] She had had no classes in disciplines, but she drew her wisdom directly from God's 'fountain'. Synesius was aware that such a person might perhaps be found among holy monks, but he knew none himself: his female icon, Hypatia, was a pagan. Monnica, however, was considered by her son to have played a crucial part in his new thinking. Augustine affirms that he 'undoubtingly believes' that by Monnica's prayers God has given him a mind such that he will 'prefer nothing whatsoever, want nothing else, think of nothing else, love nothing else than the finding of truth'.[53] After saving him from Manichaeism, Monnica's weeping and praying, he believes, have helped to make him a 'philosopher'.

The dialogues philosophize, but Christian values, concepts and the Incarnation are interwoven in their philosophy. There are elements in them which are not yet harmonized but which lie side by side, in suspension. Among their emphasis on reason and the disciplines, there is a parallel awareness of the importance of divine aid and authority. Augustine had still not had any pre-baptismal instruction. He draws only sparsely on scriptural phrases, most of which, one suspects, he had first considered closely during his Manichaean phase. In the next few years, however, 'disciplines classes' will fade from his priorities. Studies in the liberal arts will give way to intense meditations on scripture. In the villa, he was about to make a start.

23

'Watering My Couch with Tears'

In later years Augustine looked back on his time in the villa not just as 'leisure' but as the 'leisure of a Christian life'. Its Christian scope becomes even clearer if we look beyond his philosophical dialogues with the boys. As the *Confessions* recall, it was in the villa that Augustine first engaged with a crucial resource for his future thinking, writing and confessing: the 'psalms of David'.

The Psalms had been thrown into special prominence in Milan earlier in the year. They were Ambrose's favourite book of the Old Testament and in spring 386 he had ordered them to be sung in church as part of his new musical initiative. Psalm 79 had been his brilliantly apt choice: 'O God, the heathen have come into thy inheritance; they have defiled thy holy temple . . .'[1] Indeed they had, and Monnica had been one of the psalm's singers in the face of 'Arian' harassment. She would therefore approve, and perhaps encourage, her son's engagement with these powerful texts. Powerful indeed they proved to be. As Augustine read them, he tells us, he cried aloud to God. He 'burned to recite them', his new discovery, throughout the world. He 'was inflamed by them towards You, God'.[2] His reading of the Psalms in the villa, his first ever, is a decisive correction to modern readers' doubts about the Christian depth of his conversion.

In a brilliant prelude, the *Confessions* recall God's 'flattening' of Augustine's proud thoughts to the level of humility in the aftermath of the garden scene. God 'thoroughly tamed me', he recalls, with 'internal pricks'. When he then recalls his reading of the Psalms, he observes that they 'exclude the swollen spirit', meaning pride and conceit. As the Psalms were among God's 'arrows', they would be prime agents of this internal pricking and and its consequent pangs. Then, as now, their surface meaning was a challenge. Puzzling headings – 'for the end, for the secrets of the son . . .' – introduce them. Words for musical pauses break up their texts. They are rich in metaphors and imagery, much of whose Hebrew is still very hard for us to understand. Augustine read only a Latin text which was itself translating a Greek translation of a Hebrew original. Without realizing, he confronted gross misunderstandings and yet more incoherence which resulted from them. A deep reading seemed to be needed to find the spiritual meaning beneath it, as Ambrose's preaching had taught him. Who, indeed, was speaking? Some psalms were headed 'psalms of David', but others were anonymous, although they used the first person singular. They addressed 'you' in the plural or 'men' in general.[3]

In Verecundus' villa he was already assuming that the Psalms were prophetic and that in them the Holy Spirit spoke. Psalms composed in the first person seemed particularly immediate to him because many of them were written, he thought, by someone newly converted to God. They spoke of struggle and joy, the opposition of other people and the temptations of the world, the very obstacles which he had known in July and August. Psalms of this type run through the entire collection, beginning with Psalms 3 and 4. Psalm 6 pleads with God to restrain His anger and to heal the psalmist, who nightly 'waters my couch with my tears'. It ends with a confident statement that God will hear the psalmist's prayer and confound his enemies. In the villa Augustine would have encountered such psalms as soon as he began to read through his psalter. Fittingly, therefore, the *Confessions* quote from Psalm 6 when they express the thoughts which, himself in tears, he had spoken to God while lying beneath the garden's fig tree: 'And then, O God, how long?' As he says, these exact words were not used by him at the time, but their impact on him is readily imagined when, tearful again, he read them in the villa less than four months later.[4] Other psalms addressed his ultimate aim, a vision of God. 'How long wilt thou hide thy face from me? [Ps. 13.1]. Look on me and hear me, O Lord . . . Illumine my eyes, so that I may never sleep in death . . .' Wondrously, the visionary ideal which the Platonist books had given him could be discovered in his new night-time reading.

Personal interpretation of the Psalms has a long history, one which still continues, and, at the time, Augustine's was not unique. It had been current practice for decades among monks in the Holy Land and Egypt. Their communities listened daily to psalms being sung and then identified the words with their own predicaments. In the Latin West Augustine's rapt response was not a novelty, either. In Rome, the well-born ladies in Jerome's circle were presented by Jerome as keen readers of the Psalms who applied the words to their own predicaments.[5] With Jerome, of course, at her side, Marcella welcomed allegorical readings. Her 'incredible ardour' for the holy scriptures caused her constantly to sing, 'These words have I hid in my heart that I might not sin against thee' (Latin Ps. 119.71). She posed detailed questions of Hebrew language which stretched Jerome, her mentor. Paula, he wrote, recited the Psalms in Hebrew with an excellent pronunciation. However, Augustine was not commenting on the Hebrew text and could not even understand it. His 'ardour' over an inaccurate Latin translation would not exactly have impressed Jerome's noblewomen.[6]

The *Confessions* dwell on his engagement with one psalm in particular, Psalm 4 (in English bibles, 'Answer me when I call, O God of my righteousness . . .'). Halfway through, after a musical annotation, it changes abruptly in tone, becoming, as its modern scholar John Day has observed, 'an individual lament in which the note of trust is particularly marked'.[7] It was therefore particularly apt for the contrite Augustine, newly embarked on a life devoted to God. His Latin translation took the opening words to be 'When I called on You, You heeded me, God of my righteousness'. However, the Hebrew text began with an entreaty ('*heed* me'), not with the Latin's past tense ('heeded'). The Latin's 'heeded' was an error, but it caused Augustine to think at once of his conversion in the garden. There, he had finally prayed to God, or 'called on Him', and promptly, he believed, God had 'heeded' him through the child's words and the text in Romans. As he read Psalm 4 in his room, he exclaimed aloud, referring its words to himself and experiencing 'what it made of me'. As he read, he tells us, he commented on each part which he was reciting.

The *Confessions* give a brilliant account of the meanings which he found, but are they meanings which struck him while he read in 386 or have they been elaborated by his re-readings in the intervening ten years? Two other interpretations of Psalm 4 by him survive, one, carefully weighing alternatives, among the expositions of the Psalms which he began to dictate about eight years later, the other, a simpler one, in a recently discovered sermon which he preached to a mixed congregation in Carthage, probably in 397, the very year when he was confessing.[8] They share some points with the interpretation which he ascribes to 386, but they lack the main theme which engaged him at that time. In his bedroom, he says, he understood Psalm 4 in terms of his former Manichaeism.

In his exposition in *c.*394, Augustine considered whether the resurrected Christ was speaking, but, on the whole, took the psalmist to be describing the experience of personal conversion: 'Thou hast set my heart at large when I was in distress,' he said (Ps. 4.1). This 'enlargement' from narrow 'sadness' to broad 'joy' is the psalmist's own, Augustine infers, and as a result he has God 'infused in his heart, with whom he can now speak inwardly'. However, Augustine suggests, the resurrected Christ might also be speaking here on behalf of the Christian faithful, the very least of whom can speak with God and, like Paul, have the Spirit diffused in their hearts.[9] The psalmist goes on to say, 'Be angry and do not be willing to sin . . . in your chambers feel compunction.' Here he himself must be speaking to us, Augustine thinks, and one interpretation is that he is telling us to be angry at our past sins and repent. This compunction must be done in our 'chambers', which are not our bedrooms, Augustine considers, but the inner chambers of our hearts.

The *Confessions* recall that at Cassiciacum, Augustine also read the psalm as the cry of a convert, one who had God in his inner heart. He did not read any of it as words of the risen Christ, but he certainly responded with 'anger' and compunction. In 386, there had been good reason for him to read the psalm in this way. He himself was poised between conversion and baptism, contrition and new hope. As he awaited baptism, he was rethinking his past sins and repenting of them. They were scaring him, he remembers, because they had not yet been effaced in the baptismal rite. He was angry with himself at his Manichaean past.[10] Amazingly, it was a past which the psalmist seemed to be addressing prophetically, centuries before Mani's lifetime.

Mani's followers sang their own psalms and ignored Psalm 4, a 'healing psalm of David'. In the *Confessions*, Augustine recalls that he was 'indignant at them with a vehement and keen grief' because they had never known a psalm like the one before him. He also develops a wish that they could have been in his bedroom without his knowing and could have overheard his exclamations as he read. This wish is rhetorical, and he has added it in 397. Nonetheless it dramatizes what he correctly recalls from 386, his anger and pity for the Manichaeans and his reading of phrases in the psalm as if they addressed his own errors while gripped by their 'vanity'. He was not addressing his confessions, as some have proposed, to Manichaeans in order to win them over. His imagined human readers are his fellow Christians, especially celibates and aspiring celibates. He was showing them, as elsewhere, how wrong he had been while a member of the Manichaean sect, a 'pest', he says, a 'bitter and blind barker' against God's scriptures. Manichaeans would not exactly like to read these words. His 'pity' of them was the lofty response of a Christian to his 'vain' and 'lying' former associates.[11] In 386 they included his patron, Romanianus, and the others whom he had converted to the sect in Africa.

The more Augustine read by himself in his room, the more Psalm 4 seemed to address his Manichaean past. He was 'terrified' by its relevance, he recalls; he 'shuddered in fear'; he 'boiled with hope'; he 'exulted' in God's mercy. His reading, therefore, was intense and emotional, befitting his mood in the night hours. 'Why do you love vanity and seek after falsehood?' the psalmist asked, while inspired, Augustine believed, by the Holy Spirit. Augustine had indeed loved Mani's 'vanity' and sought after a Gospel of Truth which was false. 'Know the Lord has magnified his holy one,' the psalmist then said, at least in Latin: Augustine read the words as proof that Jesus had been exalted to heaven, something which the Manichees denied, and that the Comforter, or Holy Spirit, which Mani confused with himself, had been sent long before Mani existed.[12] In the *Confessions*, Augustine amplifies the point with a web of phrases from the Third and Fourth Gospels and the Letter to the Ephesians. In the villa he was probably not yet able to interrelate these texts so readily while praying aloud, but the underlying point was evident to him. He therefore interpreted the words as a refutation of Mani's entire theology. He did not know that, in Hebrew, the psalmist had written nothing of the sort. His puzzling words are likely to have meant 'Know that Yahweh has shown great grace to me.' Nonetheless, Augustine read on in Latin, 'How long will you be heavy at heart?' and he 'heard and trembled' as he himself remembered his years of Manichaean error. He was 'angry' now not only with the Manichaeans but 'with myself'. He was 'unwilling to sin', himself personally, not a wicked implant in him which derived from the Manichaean Kingdom of Darkness. His response is yet more evidence that he was in no way still a crypto-Manichaean in 386.

The psalm led him to this remarkable interpretation because his Manichaean past was weighing on his mind while he revisited his sins at night. The *Confessions* have not invented it with hindsight. Neither his exposition in 394 nor his sermon in 397 has an anti-Manichaean thrust. The *Confessions*' recall of his running commentary is as valuable as if it was the summary of yet another text by Augustine in the villa. In *On Order*, he had briefly voiced his objections to Manichaeism. In the company of Psalm 4 at night-time, he gave a more detailed polemic, his first major riposte to Manichaeism, a theme which will dominate his written works for the next ten years.

There is still the question of why the *Confessions* chose to dwell on this particular psalm's meaning. As we will discover, allegations that Augustine had remained a Manichaean while awaiting baptism in Milan were to swirl around him less than a year before the *Confessions*. Their choice of Psalm 4 and its impact allows them to give a decisive anti-Manichaean answer to these slanders.

'Who will show us good things?' the psalmist continued and 'the light of your countenance is sealed on us'. Augustine understood the words in a most revealing way. They refer, he says, to the 'internal Eternal Light which I had tasted' and of which the Manichees knew nothing.[13] It is a crucial remark, but it does not refer to his conversion in the garden: he had not turned inwards there to 'taste' an inner light. It refers to his first reading of texts by Plotinus and to his prompt contact with God, the 'internal Eternal' who was both above him and within him. It confirms that in Milan he indeed believed that he had had an inner experience of God as a brilliant light. Although his exercises with the boys never mention it, he was acutely conscious of it in private.

The psalmist's 'good things' were 'within', Augustine exclaimed, in his 'chamber', the chamber of his heart. If he were to put the psalmist's question 'Who will show us good things?' to the Manichaeans, they would reply, he explains, by looking outward through their eyes to the sun. He means that they would turn to the sun, the direction of their daily prayers, and show it as the repository of 'good things', the liberated Light-particles of their God. He recalls that he 'gnashed his teeth' in his bedroom because he could not show Manichaeans the inner 'eternal' which he had 'tasted' and which was such a sweet dish, very different from their false foods. Manichaeans wrongly thought that Light-particles of God were inside themselves and did not realize that God Himself was personally illuminating them within. After describing the scene in the garden, the *Confessions* had praised God as 'sweeter than all pleasure, but not in flesh and blood, brighter than all light, but more inner than every secret part'.[14] Now we readers better understand the meaning of this 'inwardness'. The psalmist said, 'You had given joy in my heart.' Augustine recognized that 'God had begun to be sweet to me and give joy to my heart.' Conversion was already bringing him positive rewards.

He kept on exclaiming aloud, reading the psalm's words outwardly but recognizing them inwardly, where God, he had recently learned, was to be found. They seemed to speak to him of the abandonment of worldly ambition, exactly what he himself had renounced, and to promise a peaceful repose. In Latin, its psalmist then said, 'In peace, in "It Itself" I will go to sleep and take my slumber.' Helped by Plotinus' language for the One and Being, and perhaps by Porphyry's too, Augustine understood 'It Itself' to be nothing less than unchanging God. In a text which he wrote within two years of his conversion he uses the phrase to refer to God, and thereafter he uses it some 1,700 times with this reference in his writings. In fact, the Latin words (*Id Ipsum*) were based on a translator's misunderstanding of the Hebrew: it was an adverb which meant 'at once'.[15] 'I will go to sleep,' Augustine read on, oblivious. These words suggest to modern commentators that the psalm was composed as an evening psalm and was connected to a liturgy in the Temple (it talks of 'offering sacrifices'). Augustine, however, took the words to refer to repose after death in the future life. Again, the psalmist had meant nothing of the sort: he was referring to falling asleep without anxiety. 'You, Lord,' Augustine goes on, 'set me in hope', not among the multiplicity of worldly pleasures but as a single, simple One (*singulariter*). The word 'hope' mistranslated the Hebrew word 'safety'. If Jerome, and not a Manichaean, had overheard Augustine's commentary, he would have acidly dismissed it as based on a Latin translator's cluster of errors.[16]

Augustine was 'chatting with You, my distinction and my riches': God was now the replacement for the worldly rank and riches which he had formerly sought. Once again the Holy Spirit, he believed, was speaking to him through another's words, but it was speaking, we realize, through human misunderstandings. Unknown to Augustine, Latin 'howlers' were helping his tongue to run freely. However, like the psalmist, he had 'God infused in his heart' and could 'speak with Him inwardly'. Remarkably, we are seeing the start of the dynamic from which the *Confessions*, ten years later, will pour forth.

Within four months of his conversion, Augustine had found texts over which, once again, he and his heart could weep: not Virgil or mimes in the theatre, but the Psalms. Soon afterwards, their 'internal pricking' was joined by physical agony: he had raging toothache, a pain, he recalls, such as he had never known in his life. It made him unable to speak, let alone to pray aloud. He had to write down words of prayer on a wax tablet so that his friends could recite them to God on his behalf. On bended knee they did so, and promptly the pain stopped.[17]

For pagans and Christians alike, as Libanius' experiences remind us, ill health and recovery were manifest proofs of divine intervention. In his toothache Augustine experienced the 'harshness of God's lash', he tells us: presumably, he understood it as a chastisement for his past sins. 'I was scared out of my wits.' He offered a prayer and, wondrously, the pain disappeared. His views on God and man are usually traced from texts which he wrote, but they existed in a context of feelings and random experiences. In acute pain, the unbaptized Augustine had experienced God's sudden 'lash', followed by His 'mercy' or grace.[18] This intervention was much more clear-cut than the oblique signs through third parties which he had encountered in the garden. What God did to the body, surely He could also do to a man's inner life? 'Your inclinations had been insinuated deeply in me,' Augustine recalls, but instead of berating God's cruelty, he 'rejoiced and praised His name in faith'. They are the first such praises which the *Confessions* recall in his life. The two aspects of confessing had now occurred in it: confession of sins (through the Psalms) and praising God (through toothache).

24
Augustine With Augustine

I

Soon after recovering, Augustine embarked on the first original project in his career: he wrote a text for which he coined a new name, 'Soliloquies'. In it, he argued at length with a new dialogue partner: his own reason. It began, he tells us, when he was suddenly 'admonished', a word which reminds us again of his admonishment in the garden. Such promptings seem ultimately to be divine for him, although Augustine cannot decide if this one came from without or within.[1] We cannot decide for him, but the general point remains: his soliloquies, he believed, were prompted by God.

They were not so new or odd as they may seem. For some while Augustine had had a habit of going over matters with himself alone. In the *Confessions*, he presents himself as debating questions with himself after the death of his friend in Thagaste or before writing *The Beautiful and Apt* or when hesitating in the garden about giving up sex. In the villa he had already had plenty of time to do likewise, 'searching ceaselessly and intently', he tells us, 'for my own self and my good and what evil is to be avoided'.[2] Interior monologues remain a lifelong feature of his writings. Remarkably, this one is presented as a masterclass between himself and his own Reason, lasting two days.

One or two of the famous Greek philosophers were said to have argued only with themselves, but the implication of these stories was that their behaviour was very odd. Augustine would probably not have known that in some of his Greek dialogues Plato had recommended discussing questions with one's own soul.[3] The reason for Augustine's innovation lay in his circumstances. He wanted to engage with questions which were much too hard for the only partners around him, his mother and the boys. In Latin, philosophy was conventionally presented

1. Personified Generosity in Antioch, the virtue of the donors of shows and prizes to their cities, admired by Libanius and by rich patrons in Augustine's Africa. Yakto villa, Daphne, *c.*AD 450.

2. A mosaic floor (*c.*AD 280) from a villa at Daphne, near Antioch, showing personified Comedy with masks (*left*) and the comic poet Menander and his courtesan Glycera reclining on a couch for a *symposion*. Menander was author of scenes which Libanius deplored and which adult Augustine would deplore too.

3. The grand country home of Lord Julius in north Africa, much like the country homes of Synesius in Libya. Carthage, *c.*AD 400.

4. A mosaic floor (*c.*AD 370) from Complutum in Spain, about twenty miles from Madrid, showing the adultery of Jupiter, as a swan, undressing married Leda, the sort of scene that adult Augustine regretted having learned in school but which delighted diners in this villa, neighbours of grand Paulinus and his wife Therasia.

5. Three panels surrounding a big mosaic floor, now lost, from north Syria, probably from Antioch or its territory. Young Kimbros is whipped (*left*) by his tutor and then goes to his first schoolmaster (*centre*). The proposed date is *c.*AD 450, but may perhaps be as early as Libanius's lifetime. The best imagery of schooling as Augustine recalls it in North Africa.

6. Kimbros goes on to his grammar-teacher and is greeted by him with a kiss. His friends greet him on the right.

7. Kimbros and friends, now older, flank their teacher whom personified Education attends, while figures captioned as the first day of the school year (in October) and the last day (in August) stand on the right, the dates between which Augustine taught in Italy too.

8. Kimbros's friends appear to denounce Kimbros to his teacher. Kimbros (*right*) is taken away and held by the feet, evidently for a flogging.

9. Female Elect members of the Manichaean church, on silk fragments, tenth century AD, from Jinjiang, China. In Carthage young Augustine worshipped beside Manichaean females.

10. Manichaean scribes were important in the sect, as Augustine also knew. At work among music and song, from a book of Chinese paper, eighth to ninth century AD.

11. A Manichaean Hearer, like young Augustine, offers Light-rich fruits to the Elect at the Bēma Festival in spring. From a manuscript of Chinese paper, eighth to ninth century AD, Jinjiang, China.

12. A stone statue of Mani as Buddha of Light, re-erected in AD 1339 in a Manichaean temple in Jinjiang, China, the furthest point of his Gospel's travels and evidence of his followers' close contact with Buddhism.

13. Mani's Universe, newly identified in this South Chinese painting as showing the Kingdom of Light at the top, the ten heavens arching over, and, below, the five types of creature in the Kingdom of Darkness, all relating to items mentioned by Augustine many centuries earlier in Africa.

14. The Manichaean Seventh Heaven with Atlas and the King of Glory (in red) and the three wheels to extract Light from the world. The five sections below show snakes and other vile breeds of the Kingdom of Darkness, much as Augustine describes.

15. Mani's Lord of the Firmaments (in red) in the Seventh Heaven, with a demon of Darkness imprisoned in a chest below in the sixth heaven, recalling Augustine's references to the wars in the Universe.

16. The surviving half of an ivory diptych from Rome (AD 402), recently identified decisively as depicting the consecration of Augustine's patron in Rome, the pagan Symmachus, once a consul, and his soul's ascent to heaven. He processes in a fine chariot drawn by elephants, ascends and is held in the pagan heaven by two winds, beneath a monogram for the Symmachus family.

17. A mosaic portrait of Ambrose, from St Victor's chapel in Milan, incorporated in the big Basilica Ambrosiana. Made *c*.AD 450 but probably a good likeness of the famous bishop, who died in 397.

18. Idealized mid-sixth-century images from San Vitale, Ravenna of SS. Gervase (*left*) and Protasius (*right*), the famous couple whose skeletons were located and 'identified' by Ambrose and his diggers in Milan in May AD 386.

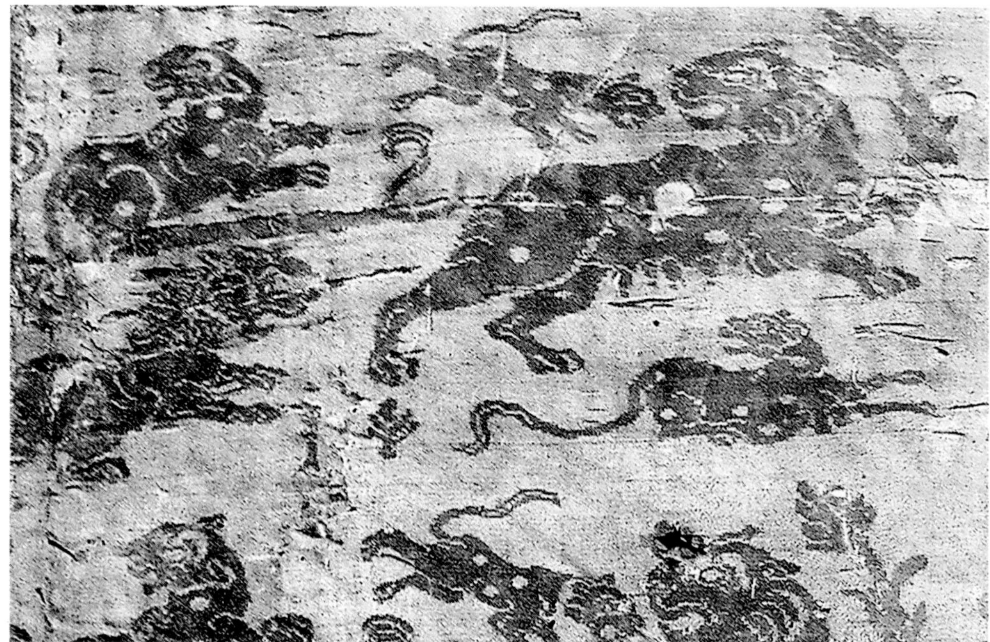

19. Detail of a big silk dalmatic, or robe, woven with scenes of a big lion hunt, preserved in Milan and surely worn by the city's bishop. Dated fourth to sixth century AD and perhaps going back to Bishop Ambrose's own lifetime.

20. An octagonal baptismal pool, almost certainly where Ambrose baptised Augustine at Easter 387, adjoining Milan's huge 'New Basilica', the medieval Santa Tecla, rediscovered in the 1960s beneath the modern Piazza del Duomo, Milan.

21. Peter and Paul, as brethren despite their quarrel in Antioch, about which Augustine and Jerome also disputed. Gold glass fragment, Rome *c.*AD 380.

22. The earliest surviving representation of Augustine, in St John the Lateran, Rome, early sixth century.

23. A marble portrait of an elderly intense philosopher, probably a Neoplatonist, fifth century AD, from Aphrodisias, Western Asia.

24. A bust of a sophist-orator in civic dress, a Libanius by trade, fifth century AD, from Aphrodisias, Western Asia.

25. A tomb mosaic for Valentia, giving our best image of a fourth-century North African Church, Thabraca AD 380–400.

26. A table top for feasting and honouring the martyrs, Matares necropolis, Tipasa, *c.*AD 400.

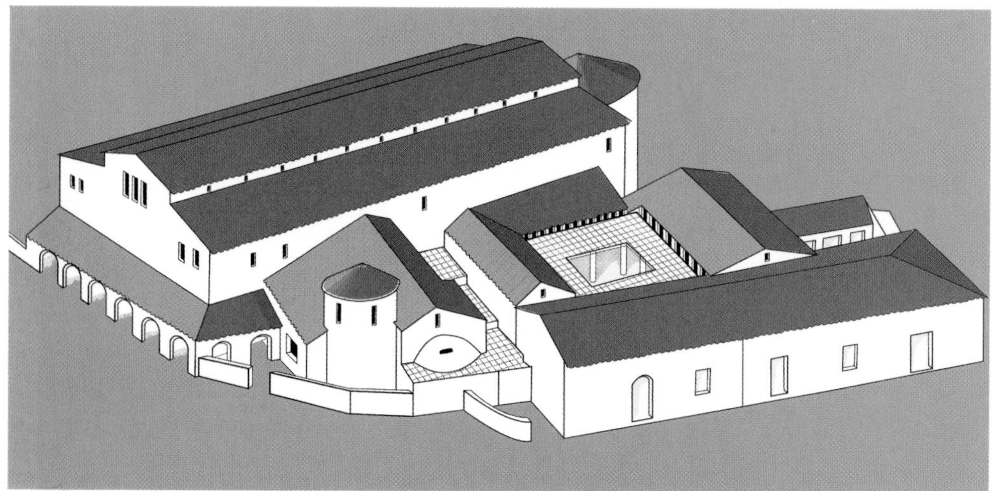

27. A reconstruction of the basilica at Hippo from a groundplan, arguably a Donatist one, late fourth century AD.

28. One half of a mosaic covering a double sarcophagus, showing a north African Christian, perhaps the accompanying girl's father, holding a pen and writing a list or calendar of Christian martyrs, Thabraca, east of Augustine's Hippo, *c.*AD 400.

29. The other half shows Christian Victoria, captioned as a 'Holy Girl', her head covered as a consecrated virgin and her hands held out sideways in a north African praying position.

30. Lazarus being raised by Jesus from the dead, an apt scene for this Christian sarcophagus in Rome, *c.*AD 300, but one which Augustine expounded in 394/5 as the soul's liberation from the desires of the body.

31. A mosaic from the floor of a basilica which it presents as Catholic, not Donatist, in the village of Beni Raschid, near Castellanum Tingitanum (now Chlef), west of Hippo, in Algeria.

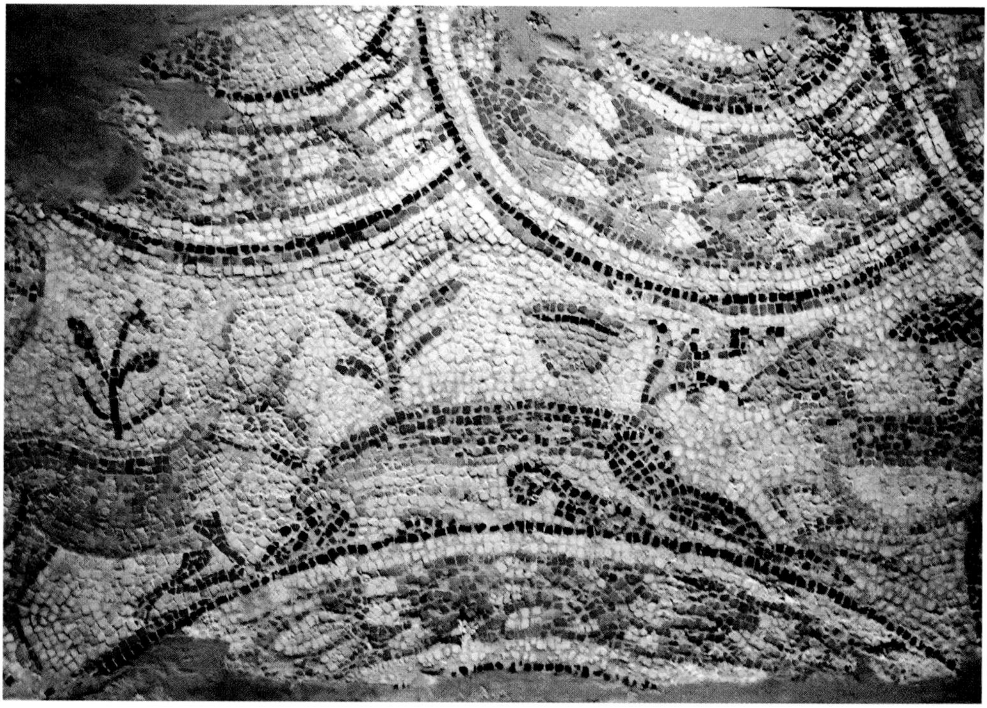

32. An apse mosaic of a stag and doe drinking from the four rivers of Paradise, alluding to Psalm 42, interpreted as a baptismal psalm and exploited by Augustine in *Confessions*, Book 13. Bir Ftouha, Carthage, *c.*AD 380–420.

33. Monnica, by Benozzo Gozzoli, fifteenth century, Sant'Agostino, San Gimignano.

in dialogue, and if Augustine wanted a dialogue, he had to argue the questions with the only partner available: himself. The questions are indeed difficult, especially those about 'imagination', illusion and truth.[4] They proceed by attempts at deductive argument and, like the boys in the dialogues, Augustine falters at times before Reason's relentless attack, what Licentius had well called the 'cold shower' of dialectics. There was another advantage to his new genre. A soliloquy caused none of the combative aggression and hurt feelings which arise in arguments between competitors. In the garden Augustine had recently read Paul's words denouncing 'quarrelling and jealousy'. In his poor state of health he was too sensitive, he recalls, to bear such tussles.[5] In a soliloquy he would battle only with himself.

At the very beginning, he presents his Reason as telling him not to dictate their debates: they are too intimate. They must be written down by Augustine personally. More than two centuries earlier, the pagan Emperor Marcus Aurelius had also compiled a personal text, one which was entitled in its early manuscripts *To Himself*. Nowadays we know it as *The Meditations* and, probably, Marcus himself wrote it down. The contrast with the *Soliloquies* is instructive. His text was composed over a long period of time without a title or a structure. It was a personal spiritual diary which was made up of spiritual exercises. Ever self-reproachful, Marcus had to try to live by them: they were not intended to circulate for others.[6]

Like Marcus, Augustine probes and reproaches himself, but his text was not written for his eyes only. Its division into books was carefully planned and composed. It was written deliberately for a suitable few, and included lengthy praises of the talent, intelligence and writings of none other than Theodorus and Zenobius, two of his 'greater friends' in absence. It would exercise their minds and, yet again, it would show them how Augustine, the lover of wisdom, was engaging keenly with his new philosophic role. Augustine even sent off the first two books before the third, *On the Immortality of the Soul*, existed: it survives only in the form of compressed notes which were written in the following spring. In a letter to Nebridius, Augustine hints that he will send him a copy and gives a foretaste of his latest 'little reasoning' about the soul, expressed in short questions and answers like parts of the *Soliloquies*.[7] The *Soliloquies* are indeed his first work to have a lasting impact. Five centuries later, in the 890s, the ageing English King Alfred chose to adapt and translate them. According to his biographer, 'day and night, Alfred would lament and sigh constantly to God and to his close friends that Almighty God had made him without divine Wisdom and the liberal arts'.[8] Born too late for Augustine's 'disciplines class' in the villa, Alfred attached himself to it by translating its most remarkable product.

In the *Soliloquies* we can read 'Augustine with Augustine', as he well describes it, arguing with himself in his own words. It is worth dwelling on the implications, ten years before the *Confessions*. Much of the text is an exercising of the mind, like the workouts which he had been imposing daily on the boys. It uses deductive reasoning, as befits Reason, its protagonist. In answer to Reason's questioning, Augustine states what he wants to know: 'God and the soul'. These concepts are not exactly at the heart of modern analytical philosophy, but they remain the focal points of Augustine's philosophizing for the next forty years. He had already stated this aim in *On Order* in the third week of November. It overlapped with themes in Ambrose's sermons, but they were not its impetus. It had been stated in Cicero's writings and had been learned by Augustine from his Neoplatonist readings.[9] In the mid-seventeenth century it still attracted the Cambridge Platonists, thinkers who were concerned, like Augustine, with the relations between faith and reason. John Smith, Fellow of Queens' College, even wrote discourses on Augustine's same subjects, *The Immortality of the Soul* and *The Existence and Nature of God*. They shared Augustine's premise that 'the best way to know God is by an attentive reflexion upon our own souls'. There is a direct line from Cassiciacum to dons in seventeenth-century Cambridge.[10]

Manifestly, Augustine's conversion had done nothing to dim his passion for philosophy and his admirable gift for hard reasoning. Big questions still stretched before him, fascinating his mind. His aim, he writes, is to possess wisdom without fear of loss, thereby realizing happiness within the terms he had first met in the *Hortensius*. Reason replies that 'there is not one road for reaching' wisdom, an echo of a famous phrase in Symmachus' recent plea for Rome's pagan cults. Do we know God, Reason begins by asking, in the same way in which we know concepts of, say, geometry? Both are invisible in this world and neither is known by sense-perception. The faculty of seeing is the same in either case, and yet the object seen differs. To see, or 'know', God, we must purify our souls as a starting point and be helped in the endeavour. Augustine's aim here too is a mystic contemplation of God.

Some people, Reason explains, have 'such healthy and vigorous sight that they can turn without fear towards the Sun as soon as they are opened'. They do not need a teacher but perhaps they need caution: they remind us of Augustine's second ascent to God in Milan. Others, however, are 'dazzled by the very gleam which they ardently want to see and, on not seeing it, return to the darkness': they remind us of Augustine's first, less successful attempt.[11] Yet, even in private, Augustine does not answer Reason by citing his own experiences. As in his classes with the boys, he accepts the need for prolonged mental exercise and applied study of the 'liberal arts' as the preparation for an eventual vision.

Reason then sets out the stages more precisely. There are three, as in every other vision: having eyes, looking and seeing. First, the soul must be wholly cured of bodily passion; then it must turn towards God, to look. These two stages require faith and hope. Then, the soul will see, yearning to do so by charity, or love. Seeing God, in this life, is 'knowing' Him, and then, in the future life of bliss, the soul will be wholly united to Him. In this future life only love will be needed, as faith and hope will be superfluous.

Just as in *On the Happy Life*, Augustine is linking Paul's 'faith, hope and charity' to an ascent to God. As the *Confessions* recall, he had read Paul immediately after his ascents in Milan and found that he made sense of them. The *Soliloquies* confirm that he had been continuing to think about them with Paul's help. In one of Porphyry's letters, 'faith, truth, love and hope' were specified as necessary elements in an ascent to God. Augustine may have noticed this overlap too between Paul and Porphyry's thinking and taken it to heart as another piece of the 'true philosophy'. Already, love is essential to his aspirations, love, not of a wife, but of 'wisdom' and God. In this life, Augustine states, 'seeing' is knowing, but he already accepts that a sustained heavenly vision is a prospect which awaits pure-minded, virtuous Christians most readily in the life to come. This prospect had been stated clearly by Paul and the Gospels, but it had also confronted Augustine in Cicero's *Hortensius* as a prospect for pagan souls after death.[12] It will remain essential to his aspirations and thinking throughout his life.

To begin to aspire to 'know God' the soul must be cleansed of moral failings. Reason therefore probes the 'health' of Augustine's mental state. His interests in 'God and the soul', he tells him, are laudable, but how healthy and single-minded are his own aims and vision? Physically, Augustine is still suffering chest pains and having difficulty in speaking at length. He is weakened. He is acutely aware of his failings. As he has already told us in *On Order*, he is praying 'almost daily' for the healing of his 'wounds'. He weeps frequently, assisted by his readings of those psalmists who 'nightly water their couches with their tears'. After thirteen years of sex whenever he felt like it, he has not felt a young female's softness, seen a girl naked or had sex with one for nearly four whole months.

With deadly accuracy Reason addresses Augustine's weak points. What does Augustine fear? Pain, he replies, after the recent experience of toothache; he also fears the loss of his friends, those constant companions along life's 'brightly lit boundary'; and, fairly enough, he fears death.[13] If only he could be healthy, he says, and his friends could be with him at leisure, he would then be happy indeed. Friends are bound together by their souls, and the soul is one of his basic subjects of study. He values friends, he says, for their reason: unintellectual qualities are less relevant. In fact, none of his friends had opted to stay with him in the villa and even the loyal Alypius was going to Milan from time to time.

Relentlessly, Reason persists. If Augustine could have money which would help his friends to study at leisure with him, would he be so indifferent to riches? Would he really regard them 'most prudently and cautiously', as Cicero had urged in his *Hortensius*? Suppose he could have a wife, 'a beautiful, chaste and accommodating wife' but also (significantly) 'an educated wife or one who would be easily educated by you'? What about a wife who would bring, not a big dowry, but enough of a dowry to ensure that 'she would not be a burden to your free time'? Augustine rejects this ever-seductive snare. Philosophers may marry, he says, but they do so only for the sake of having children (he is thinking of the Stoics here; other philosophers had forsworn marriage altogether). He himself, he says, is being more strict. He has decided never to sleep with a woman, because the risks of being undermined by the act are too great and then he will lose the 'freedom of my soul'. Sex, he says, is something which he looks back on with 'horror and disdain'.[14]

Again, Reason digs deeper. Suppose that Augustine's friends would pursue wisdom with him if he had public honours and if they had honour through his status? Would he not then desire rank and honours? And suppose the 'ample patrimony' of a wife was the only way in which Augustine could provide for his friends to live together with him? Suppose, even, that the wife herself favoured that aim? Suppose that the honours which were needed to persuade his friends to join him could only be gained with the help of this wife's noble family? Reason has an insider's knowledge of the role of patronage in the late Roman system of appointments. Reason also knows that students prefer teachers with a public title. In reply, all Augustine can say is, 'When would I even dare to hope for all that?'[15]

Despite Reason's sabotage, he insists that he has made progress. He is convinced that his mind can still triumph over his instincts. On rethinking the questions, he sees that he is no longer desiring 'riches, honours or a wife' (a conventional trio) for their own sake. If he still desires them, it is only so that he can pursue wisdom with his friends. In an answer pregnant with his future life, he states that his desire is that 'we can all at the same time and in concord of heart seek our souls and God'. It is his first-ever statement of the ideal of a celibate community. In it, he believes, the one who first discovers the soul and God will lead the others on to it. 'And if they do not want to?' Reason inquires, justifiably. 'I will make them want to,' he replies. Nobody is pretending it is going to be easy . . . This ideal of a community, led by Augustine, will dominate the next five years of his life and persist until his death. It is enshrined in his Rule for monks, still the foundational text for his celibate male followers.[16]

Night intervenes, but in the morning Reason returns to the target. 'Are you not aware how confidently we had announced yesterday that we are freed from all pollution, that we love nothing but wisdom and we seek or desire other things only for wisdom's sake?' Yesterday, the female sex had been written off. 'How vile, how detestable, how shameful, how dreadful we considered the embrace of a woman when we were inquiring among ourselves about the desire for a wife!' In fact, in the text, the discussion had not been so explicit and had not used such a sequence of damning adjectives. However, that very night, it had all begun to seem different. As 'we lay awake', and 'went over this again in our mind', you realized, Reason tells Augustine, how the 'imagined caresses of a woman and their bitter sweetness still titillated you'. Augustine had not been asleep. These bitter-sweet imaginings were not the inevitable turbulence of a wet dream. They had been going round and round in his wakeful head.[17]

Augustine begs Reason to be quiet. 'Why do you torment me? Why are you probing so deeply?' Yes, he desires these things, but he desires them very much less than he used to. He desires them nonetheless, and he cannot hold back his tears of remorse. Once again he starts to cry. Augustine was not a young, ignorant virgin when he vowed himself to celibacy in the garden. Nor was he an ageing veteran whose impetus was fading. He had given up sex while enjoying it at his peak. In response, he entrusts himself entirely to God: 'Let Him do as He wills . . .' he prays. 'I commend myself wholly to His kindness and guidance.'[18] Augustine's first appeals to God's 'grace' come not from theology or texts read on the subject: they result from toothache and his sexual drive.

II

On reading this remarkable dialogue, the 'greater friends' would have to give Augustine credit for his struggle. They would also give him credit for his intelligence. From one angle, he still seems close to an emotional breakdown. From another, he is admirably able to marshal his brain, sustain it in rigorous argument and approach a problem with high hopes of a cast-iron logical result.

Though he is self-taught, he is near the frontiers of his subject. Aristotle's *Categories*, his former conquest, is in evidence. He is commendably wary, the former sceptic, of the direction of Reason's questioning. He is aware that knowledge is not belief and that there is a distinction between a proposition and its reference. He sees that 'I think' is a necessary truth, long before Descartes made it the foundation of his search for truth and knowledge. He knows the classic sceptical arguments about the uncertainties of knowledge which claims to be based on sense-perception. Long before Bishop Berkeley, he is aware of the possibility that objects in the world may not exist when there is nobody present to perceive them. Problems of truth and perception, he knows, are posed by a straight oar apparently bent when seen in water, what the modern philosopher Bernard Williams has called 'the apparently bent stick situation'. Long before Descartes, it had been known to the sceptical Cicero and thus to Augustine. Manifestly, scepticism has intensified his skills of argument. Is truth eternal, he wonders, and if so, what will happen if the world ends? Truth will persist, he claims very neatly, because it will still be true that the world has ended.[19]

Professors of rhetoric like Libanius did not have the brains for this hard type of philosophy. If only Augustine could have joined Synesius in a masterclass in a major Greek city . . . Without one Augustine believes that he has proved more than he actually has. He is particularly pleased, he writes to Nebridius, with his reasoned argument for the immortality of the soul. It rests, modern logicians realize, on four implicit premises and inevitably it is a failure. When Reason drives him in pursuit of 'Truth', the arguments founder on yet another confusion, between 'true' and 'real', 'false' and 'fictitious', which Latin's single word *falsum* did not clearly distinguish.[20] Yet the enterprise remains much grander than its failings. Logical dialectic, the 'discipline of disciplines', is regarded as the route to certainty. When Reason asks him if he would be content to know God as Plato and Plotinus knew him, Augustine gives a revealing answer: 'even if they said true things, it does not necessarily follow that they knew them'. His point is not only that they were pagans. It is also, I believe, that they did not base all their knowledge on logical dialectic.[21]

These aims and ideals will only seem arid to readers for whom logical argument is too difficult. There is, however, another dimension. The *Soliloquies* occur after divine prompting, and in the course of them Augustine prays repeatedly for God's help. At a moment of progress, Reason even detects an 'inexplicable gleam of light' which is leading the argument onwards, surely a light from God. Augustine's tears will cease only when his love is 'granted what is loved', his new beloved, God.[22] Once again, it is clear that, from the very start of his life after conversion, love is essential to his aspirations.[23]

At Reason's prompting Augustine began his *Soliloquies* with a long prayer. Complex but fluent, it is the best evidence we have of his newly won capacity for speaking to God. Sentences pour out of him, addressing anything from God's order in the universe to the non-existence of evil, a truth which God shows 'to the few who flee to That which Is'. Recently in Milan, Augustine had himself been one of these few. Future themes of his writing rush past us, undeveloped, among phrases from Paul's epistles and the Fourth Gospel, the very sources with which the *Confessions'* account of his progress credit him in Milan. Conspicuously, phrases which, to us, are Neoplatonist dominate the second part of the prayer. As ever, Augustine is not a Neoplatonist at heart.[24] He addresses God as the Creator who has made the entire universe from nothing: Plotinus explicitly rejected that view. He presents his soul and its aspirations as of personal concern to God: they never would be of concern to the One at the summit of Plotinus' universe. God 'calls us back to the Way, leads us to the door', and, as in the Gospels but nowhere in Neoplatonism, 'opens it to those who knock'. He 'purges us and prepares us for divine rewards', wholly unlike Plotinus' One. 'Come to me, propitious, You . . . hear me out, hear me out, hear me out,' Augustine prays in insistent, rhetorically shaped language. 'Take back Your fugitive, O most merciful Father . . . now, now, may I have paid punishments enough . . . Receive me, Your servant.' He does not actually apply the word 'grace' to God, but it is implicit throughout. This prolonged prayer is not always analysed closely, but it is a remarkable testimony to Augustine's view of God and the soul before he has even been baptized.[25] In less than six months since his encounter with the Platonic books, his impassioned thinking has assembled an un-Platonic whole. The next four years will be spent thinking it through.

Carefully read, the *Soliloquies* confirm the *Confessions'* portrait of the Augustine of 386. He is sure that among the temptations, he is making progress. A masterclass in logical argument will cleanse his mind and help him to realize a vision of God. If we look back from the vantage point of the mature Augustine, this optimism may seem like a youthful illusion. Within a few years, his writings will be insisting on the contrary force of human habit and the legacy of original sin. Yet in 386 he was not one-sided or naïve. Already, by reading the Psalms, he was aware of man's dependence on the God who tests him. Among his logical reasoning, he was also a pious seeker, who was praying each day to God for necessary light and assistance. His opening prayer asks God to 'convert me within to You', to 'command whatever You wish' and to 'tell me where to attend, so that I may see You'. Without God's help, his soul will not be able to ascend to the spiritual world. Unlike Plotinus, Augustine does not consider himself to be self-sufficient. He speaks of a 'secret doctor', Christ, who is helping him to heal his sexual urges.

This hope of ascent to God was not confined to two days of soliloquizing. It shines through a letter which he then sent in late 386 to the ever-inquiring Nebridius. On reading the villa dialogues, Nebridius had written to Augustine and described him as truly happy or 'blessed'. At night while on his bed, Augustine wrote in reply: he has pondered the contents of Nebridius' letter, still 'soliloquizing'.[26] With false modesty, he claims only to be 'quasi-happy', but if Nebridius could read his *Soliloquies*, he says, then he would have to find a new word for him. He is evidently very proud of his tightly reasoned work. Questions are teeming in his mind, meanwhile. Why is the world not bigger than it is? Why is it in the place it is? He treats Nebridius to what he had said 'one day' to Alypius in extreme secrecy: perhaps he had said it in the third week of November. Objects in the world of the senses can be divided infinitely, but they cannot grow infinitely. The world of the intellect, by contrast, can grow to infinity, but cannot be divided infinitely, as it rests on a 'monad'. The reflections of images in mirrors, he thinks, point to the same conclusion: big mirrors do not make small objects bigger, but small mirrors will do just that. So do the pupils of our eyes. Behind this tortuous argument lies a tradition going back to Aristotle: once again, Augustine had encountered it in pagan Porphyry.[27] Behind everything which we see in the shadowland of this world lies a higher, invisible reality. Nebridius, Augustine says, must join him in thinking about it. There is every hope of success, because Augustine has prayed to God and is beginning to raise himself to 'what most truly exists'. He is not yet a fully grown wise man, but he is certainly making progress. So he sends Nebridius a 'proof' of the soul's immortality. It is essentially the proof given in the *Soliloquies*. 'We are boys,' still, he writes, in our mutual progress, 'but we are pretty boys, not naughty ones.'

A playful optimism runs through this letter, the optimism of a mind in love with its new tools. It is the direct sequel to the *Soliloquies*, and, in both, the object of this new 'love' is revealingly expressed. Augustine wishes to 'embrace' Lady Wisdom, to hold her as if she is naked with nothing interposing, to grasp her breasts, to gaze on her lovely face. This displaced erotic imagery is not mere literary convention. It reflects on Augustine's own predicament. He is in the habit, he tells Nebridius, of 'being sweet' to his new love, 'as if it is my one and only girlfriend': like her, it 'delights him too much'.[28] However, this love is no longer a girl. Beyond the visible world, Wisdom has become his erotic substitute, but she is a lover with a crucial difference. Unlike Augustine's previous girls, she is not a love for him and nobody else. The more she is loved in common by Augustine's other friends, the more he will love both them and her. She demands his entire love, but unlike a girl, she does not cause him jealousy. Sharing is of her essence.[29] The germ was already forming of the shared life in which his conversion would be lived out.

25
Born Again

I

These intense months in the villa were not an idyllic interlude, soon to be left behind. By the end of them, Augustine had found a new impetus for his tears, a new focus for his intelligence and a new object for his love. In due course he settled down to write on each of the 'disciplines', or liberal arts, as preparations for an ascent to God. He extended his first polemics against the Manichaeans. He began the text on 'true religion' which he had promised Romanianus. He compiled a dense, unfinished outline which was intended to be the *Soliloquies*' third book: it addressed the soul's immortality and the nature of reason. In a larger work, a year or so later, he then engaged with the soul's 'quantity'. It was another topic which went back to Cassiciacum. One day at the villa, he and the boys had cut up a centipede and watched while its pieces wriggled on a writing tablet. Was the soul divisible and was it, despite Plato, a material substance? The boys had been sent away to consider the matter and Alypius and Augustine had discussed it all afternoon.[1]

His project of ascent and vision would not disappear with the passing decades. Ten years later, ascents to God and the exercises which are required for them are the key to his long self-analysis in *Confessions*, Book 10. They persist in his subsequent thinking, in his big work on the Trinity, and in some of his sermons and biblical commentaries.[2] Only the timing of the vision shifts, from the possibility of one in this life to one in the life to come. In his first writings, Augustine still hoped for a vision in both.

In these first works after his conversion Augustine is nowadays credited with discovering 'interiority', the inner depths and scope of the human person. It is a dimension which we, his heirs, tend to ignore in life. We wonder, perhaps, about the mind and whether it is fully explained by the firing of circuits in the brain. We consider, briefly, the fact that we remember or that we are conscious. If we stop longer and think more closely about the range and scope of what we remember, let alone that our minds can think about themselves, the thinking soon becomes scary, even without considering the existence of the subconscious mind. Augustine did not consider these questions in terms of the analogies we draw feebly from computing science. He thought of them in terms of God.

His notes on the soul's immortality take the *Soliloquies* a stage further and engage closely with Platonists' theories on the topic. They have been argued, convincingly, to be based on a discussion by Porphyry in his *Miscellaneous Questions*.[3] Before and after his baptismal classes with Ambrose in Lent 387, therefore, Augustine was addressing arguments for the immortal soul by a thinker whom we know to have been an arch anti-Christian. Augustine's text mentions God only once and never alludes to any Christian scripture at all. This silence is not because his concerns are still basically 'pagan': they are entirely philosophical, like those of the source which lies behind them. Within six months of his conversion Augustine was also considering the problematic relation of time present, past and future: it will become a famous theme of the *Confessions* ten years later.[4] His thinking in the intervening years is characterized less by abrupt breaks than by a redistribution of emphasis onto themes which he had touched on earlier but left undeveloped.

All the while letters from the absent Nebridius were flooding him with excited questions about the immaterial world. Here, at least, was a worthy dialogue partner, keen to debate questions about memory and imagination, mental images and the sources of dreams.[5] This level of abstract questioning may seem curious for two young Christians, but it is here that Synesius makes Augustine and his friends seem less surprising. He would have been in his element as a third correspondent. Like them, he was a Christian who engaged with Porphyry's views on the mental life of the soul and the nature of dreams, topics which the scriptures had not much discussed. One night, he claims, he had even dreamed that he must write a book on the subject. On waking he spent the rest of the night composing the short text on dreams which we now have. The questions gripped him, just as they gripped Augustine and Nebridius in their night hours. How, Synesius wonders, does the consciousness of being an individual survive the death of a physical being? That consciousness depends on images stored up in the soul. When we dream, our past and present experiences sometimes resurface, but what about dreams of future events? How is the soul able to prophesy? Somehow, he believes, these events send out 'waves, in advance' of what is not yet present. Synesius thus inclines, unawares, to one of the answers which Nebridius had put to Augustine. Maybe the soul has a 'sensory faculty' of its own by which it absorbs impressions from the other senses, its 'gateways'.[6]

Synesius had had clear, personal proof of dreams' prophetic power. Once, he tells his readers, he had been on the point of abandoning a hunting expedition in the wilderness, as the animals were adept at avoiding him and hiding their intentions. A dream, however, told him to wait one more day and, sure enough, he was rewarded with an excellent bag of animals 'taken by the spear and taken in nets'. Hunting, that acid test of reality, was supported by theoretical study. Like Nebridius, Synesius shaped his ideas about dreams by reading Porphyry. Like Vindicianus, whom Augustine had once met in Carthage, he also assumed that the parts of the universe are linked as an interconnected whole and react to one another. The whole universe, therefore, 'breathes together and is in sympathy with itself'.[7] This sympathy explains the curious powers of sorcerers and diviners, people, Augustine would say, like Albicerius in Carthage. There was much here for the three of them to discuss. There was also something which had escaped the Latin-speaking Africans entirely, but which Synesius had studied with Hypatia: the esoteric *Chaldaean Oracles*. They were a Platonist poetic text about the gods, the ascent and descent of the soul, and the hidden powers and 'tokens' in the universe which allow the 'gods' to be manipulated. Repeatedly, Synesius cites this text in his book on dreams.[8] He is especially concerned by the 'imaginative spirit' which the *Oracles* and Porphyry present as accompanying the soul in its descent and ascent. Like Augustine at this time, he is unwilling to accept a crude notion of the resurrection of the body. Like Augustine's, the main thrust of his writing is spiritual and other-worldly. The main aim of philosophy is still the Platonists' aim, to purify the soul and allow it, by turning inwards, to sustain a vision of God. Just as Augustine had been telling his young pupils, Synesius states that this purification is achievable by 'the exercise of pious living'. However, he also refers to 'rites' which will assist it. Just as Augustine has allowed both for the helping 'direction' of God and for the autonomous 'disciplining' of the soul, so Synesius writes both of the soul's innate potential to ascend and the potential of rituals to restore it to its home. Both of them are keeping conflicting sets of ideas in tension in their thinking, Augustine as a Christian and a reader of the Platonists, Synesius as another, but also as a rapid writer who finished his text, he tells us, in a single night.[9] A 'conference call' with Augustine and Nebridius would have helped to expose and tighten up his loose ends.

Among his reverence for philosophy and Hypatia's mysteries, Synesius nonetheless submitted to Christian baptism. His long first hymn is best read as related to the event. In it, he addresses the 'King of gods' in abstract Platonist language but fits it cleverly to a metre of bounding anapaests. He has 'come to pay his due', he states, after his arduous and hateful years in 'Thrace' (Constantinople, the scene of his prolonged embassy on Cyrene's behalf). He calls on God to 'give Your seal, the token [for Synesius' soul] on its holy path to You': the hymn is set at the very time when the 'seal', surely of baptism, is imminent for Synesius now that he has returned home to Cyrene.[10] The rite, he says, will help his immortal soul to ascend beyond the snares of the material world. Awaiting baptism, Synesius thus composes a hymn of more than 700 lines and a second, related hymn of another 300, both on the ascent of the soul. At a similar time in his life, on a similar topic, Augustine preferred prose.

The classes in the villa were an interlude and Augustine still had to sort out a basic question: how was he going to live? During the next two years, we will follow him as he realizes an answer and then gains a confident voice in its role, before circumstances change yet again and he embarks on another life in parallel, a life of action beside his life of contemplation. First, however, an existing decision had to be carried further. From the villa, he tells us, he sent 'letters' to Ambrose in Milan: the plural suggests that he sent several. Unlike Synesius he did not accompany them with a poem: he included some autobiography, his first to be written. 'I acquainted' him (*insinuavi*), he recalls, with 'my former errors', the circuitous story which Ambrose, reading silently, had managed to avoid previously, and my 'present vow', the intention to be baptized. The 'errors' would include his years as a Manichaean, a point which Ambrose, however busy, would have to take seriously. He could not risk including a closet Manichee in his baptismal class in Lent. Augustine's letters surely emphasized that he had renounced Mani for good, and they also asked what he should best read to prepare himself for baptismal instruction. Ambrose told him to read the Book of Isaiah, but when Augustine tried it, he found it to be unintelligible. He put off reading the rest of it, he recalls, assuming that it would all be as difficult, but planned to try it again when he was 'more practised in the Lord's eloquence'. Ambrose, he thought, must have recommended the book because it was one which especially foretold the Gospel and the calling of the Gentiles.[11] After reading about Augustine's Manichaean years, Ambrose probably chose Isaiah as the text which most obviously linked the Old and New Testaments and prophesied the Nativity. Both were 'truths' which Manichaeans rejected.

Augustine's reason for writing these letters was not only a wish to be helped and better understood. Like all such letters they would be read aloud and become known to others. It was important for him as a former Manichee to make quite clear to Ambrose and his assistants that whatever Manichees in Milan might say, he had broken decisively with their 'vanity'. Baptismal candidates had to submit their names by the Feast of the Epiphany in early January, and Ambrose accepted Augustine's application: if he had heard that Augustine had given up reading Isaiah, he might have been less willing. As Lent began, Augustine, his son, Adeodatus, and Alypius were back in Milan, members of pre-baptismal classes, to be held twice daily by Ambrose himself.

In later life Augustine would appeal to 'witnesses' in north Africa of his baptism. Other Africans in Milan, it seems, had joined the group, including, perhaps, Evodius, a former Imperial courier who appears later, baptized, in Augustine's company. He is the third such courier known in Augustine's past year to have become a celibate Christian: Libanius expresses lively disgust at such officials' lives, their pimping and blackmail, their corruption and bearing false witness. His case was no doubt exaggerated, but it shows one side of their public image and may help to explain why such people were sometimes drawn to high-principled Christianity instead. Augustine himself was a more unusual candidate. He was still reading Porphyry, the anti-Christian, and like Synesius after him was obsessed with the soul and the vision of God. Twenty years later, in 406/7, he would reflect on similar cases. 'Sometimes, one sees a catechumen who gives up all sexual activity, who renounces the world, who abandons everything he owned, giving it to the poor, and who is even instructed, perhaps, in the saving doctrine beyond many of the faithful [the baptized Christians].' Such an applicant may wonder, 'What more am I going to receive? Look, I am already better than this or that one of the faithful.' He may even 'revile those whom he despises': it may 'seem to him to be of almost no value to receive what lesser men have received, because he already seems to himself to be a better man'. Sins, however, remain with such a man, and can only be dismissed by baptism. Without it he cannot enter the kingdom of heaven.[12]

Augustine came to Ambrose's classes profoundly conscious of his past sins. He had been lamenting them nightly in the villa and had written and spoken of them tearfully for months. Only in baptism could they be effaced.

II

In the *Confessions*, Augustine's recall of his baptism is famously brief: he describes himself as 'reborn', but he never even names Ambrose. His reticence has been variously explained. One reason may be that at baptism secrets were imparted to the candidates and Augustine would not wish to give them away in writing. However, the scope of this 'secrecy' is unclear and a more pressing reason may be that when he wrote the *Confessions*, he was surrounded by 'Donatist' Christians in north Africa who placed great weight on the purity of the baptizing minister and its relation to the effects of the rite. Augustine may have downplayed Ambrose his baptizer and the details of the rite in order to express the difference between these schismatics' view of baptism and his own. He is not silent because the rite meant little to him. Ancient authors, even Augustine, know how to express much by saying very little. Within a year, he would be writing how 'it is by this holy "bath" that the renewal of the "new man" begins, so that progress may bring him to perfection, more quickly for some, more slowly for others. Nonetheless, numerous are those who advance themselves in new life.' He classes himself among them: 'do we silence the testimony of our own experience,' he later writes, 'do we go so far as to forget how attentive, how anxious we were over what the instructors taught us when we were "seeking" the sacrament of the baptismal font?' Ten years later the final book of the *Confessions* will interpret parts of the first chapters of Genesis in terms of baptismal imagery.[13]

In later life, as we will see, Augustine makes a statement which shows that, once, he had 'anathematized' Mani and his teachings. An anathema was a formal text of abjuration which was pronounced in approved words to a clergyman and signed by the abjurer.[14] He alludes to no such 'anathema' before Ambrose, but if he had made one, he had no good reason to omit it ('How I cursed utterly the snare of the Devil,

Lord, before your holy minister and with what a vehement voice I testified to Christ, born of a virgin and crucified for our salvation,' he could have written). As the accusation that he had still been a Manichee when baptized was to be cast at him shortly before he began the *Confessions*, such an 'anathema' would be too valuable a counter for him to leave out. It belongs, I believe, later in his career, when he was under attack in north Africa.

By having their names accepted and joining the classes, Augustine, his son, Adeodatus, Alypius and the others became 'seekers', or *competentes*. Throughout Lent, they were participants in a strict routine of instruction and discipline. In order to recapture it, we can extract a pattern of practice from Ambrose's sermons and writings on the subject and assume that this pattern applied in 387. Pre-baptismal classes were an arduous business for him, as he took them in person, twice a day on at least thirty days in Lent. Candidates heard him in a new context, in a smaller group, intensified by prayer and exhortation. They were there to learn, the one context for 'instruction' in the Christian Church. It was very different from trying to hear Ambrose at a distance while he preached among the noise in the big basilica.

From Monday to Friday, at the third and the ninth hour of the day, 'seekers' attended services of worship, psalm-singing and Ambrose's sermons of instruction. He urged them to keep throughout to a strict diet and to abstain from sex, rules which Augustine and Alypius had already imposed on themselves for life. Every week, their naked bodies were inspected with the care of a modern army 'clap parade': they were checked for signs of demons.[15]

Ambrose would advise the candidates to read ethical books of the Old Testament: Ecclesiasticus (by the Jew Ben Sira), Proverbs (whose inner meaning he explained) and the Book of Wisdom. Exactly these books are sources of most of the verses from the Old Testament which Augustine's first works after baptism use. The actual subjects of Ambrose's Lenten sermons until Easter Week, 387, remain uncertain, because none of his surviving sermons can be dated securely to that period. However, the survivors from one or other Lent share features which are likely to have been part of his preaching to Augustine and his fellow candidates in 387 too. In such sermons Ambrose focuses on great persons in the Old Testament and allegorizes their stories into sermons on a moral virtue.[16] As a Manichaean, Augustine had deplored the immorality of the 'dirty old men' of Jewish scripture, but now Ambrose's 'keys' revealed a moral example beneath each story. Careful study of Augustine's later interpretations has now revealed two stories from the New Testament which he also heard from Ambrose in Lent. One was the story of the Samaritan woman of the Gospels, that heroic survivor of five husbands and a sixth adulterous partner. The other was the story of Lazarus when he 'came forth' bandaged from his tomb.[17] Ambrose presented both of these stories as tales of the soul's escape from sin and bodily desire. They became examples of conversion, fitting for his pre-baptismal audience. As we shall see, Augustine was not to forget them.

On Palm Sunday, 18 April, Augustine and the candidates were initiated for the first time into the words of the Creed. Ambrose presented it in three stages.[18] First, they signed themselves with the sign of the Cross and Ambrose recited the Creed with a general explanation. Then they recited it again together and Ambrose explained the words for them phrase by phrase. Then he broke it down into three groups of four, twelve sections in all 'like the twelve Apostles'. They had to learn them by heart, because the Creed was a secret and not something to be written down: the power of secrecy was exploited in both pagan and Christian initiations.[19] After learning it, the candidates were enjoined to recite it every day. On each day of Holy Week Ambrose would then preach a sermon. It is highly likely, in my view, that in Holy Week, 387, he preached *On the Six Days of Creation*, an allegorical tour de force. Its underlying biblical text, Genesis's first chapter, is one which Augustine would repeatedly interpret in his subsequent career, always aware of what Ambrose's published text said, a copy of which he owned.

On the Thursday before Easter, Ambrose had other business: it was his big day for reconciling penitent sinners to the Church. Then he returned to the baptismal candidates. Before dawn on Easter Sunday, the 'seekers' gathered for the awesome rite of immersion. Dressed in white, they were received by Ambrose with a rite of 'opening', the 'Ephphatha' uttered by Jesus in Mark's Gospel, in which the bishop touched their ears and nose to prepare them for what they were about to sense. Entering the baptistery, they were anointed by a priest and a deacon, as if they were preparing for combat against an 'adversary'. They faced west, renouncing the Devil and the world and its pleasures. Then they faced east, towards the rising sun. 'You face west,' Ambrose wrote, 'to sense your adversary whom you intend to renounce face to face: then you turn to the east, for whoever renounces the Devil is turned to Christ and sees Him in immediate clarity.'[20]

Next, the 'seekers' stripped naked. The women were kept separate and were perhaps taken to the smaller baptistery by the Old Basilica. Augustine stripped off his clothes, probably in the octagonal baptistery beside the big New Basilica: its plan is visible beneath the main piazza of modern Milan, where excavations revealed it during the twentieth century. It was a pillared building, sixty feet wide, with mosaics on its ceiling and a patterned black-and-white floor.[21] After stripping, the candidates were anointed with oil, 'like athletes', Ambrose reminded them. Ambrose would strip too, and then, lying perhaps in the shallow baptismal pool, each candidate would have their head submerged three times, once for each person of the Trinity; Ambrose explained that the second time was for 'Jesus and for His Cross'. So far the Crucifixion had not been prominent in Augustine's philosophical writings. Henceforward, he could hardly overlook it.

On leaving the water the candidates had their heads anointed. 'You entered, you saw the water,' Ambrose would write, 'and in case, perhaps, someone says, "Is that all?" you must remember that the water is the seat of "all piety, all grace, all sanctification".' When explaining the rite to them during the following week, he emphasized the role of the Holy Trinity and the unseen mysteries involved. 'Those things which are not seen are much greater than those which are seen.' Before the baptisms, Ambrose had exorcised the water.[22]

Next, Ambrose attended to each candidate's feet. He washed them, outside the pool, in a rite not practised in the Roman Church: even as a bishop Augustine never imitated it. Ambrose was not only recalling Jesus's foot-washing of his disciples during the Fourth Gospel's last supper, a text which was read out at this time. Explicitly, he was 'washing away the serpent's venom'. When Adam fell, so Ambrose believed, the serpent-devil had released venom onto Adam's feet so as to corrupt him. Baptism washed away a candidate's individual sins, but this foot-washing washed away 'hereditary sins'. Bending over Augustine, Ambrose cleaned off traces of original sin. In prayer, he then 'signed' each baptized Christian with the Holy Spirit, infusing them, he believed, with inner light.[23]

Sealed and washed, they were now ready to process from the Old Basilica (probably Milan's centre of worship from October to Easter) to the huge New Church (used, probably, from Easter until October). Dressed in white, the new Christians were compared by their bishop to the erotic imagery of the Song of Songs. They sang as they processed, probably singing Psalm 22 ('The Lord is my shepherd . . .').[24] The music, hymns and psalms of this baptismal week were an intense emotional experience for Augustine, one which he recalls in the *Confessions*. In 387, Ambrose's new musical programme was enjoying its first undisturbed Easter since the previous year's siege which had given it birth. Augustine recalls the impact with his usual exactness: the 'voices of your sweetly sounding church' were 'flowing into my ears' and 'truth was distilled into my heart'. The congregation's singing in unison 'moved' him and the combination of words and music, above all in the psalms, worked not just on his reason, but on his 'heart', as ever the seat of his feelings. It was very different from the superficial charm of a sweet worldly song, as he explains in later writings. 'The emotion of my piety was overflowing from it, and my tears were running.' For Augustine, tears are not only tears of entreaty or loss or penitence. They can also be tears of joy and devotion, a sweet gift from God on our pilgrimage through the world. For the first time in the confessions, he recalls tears that are joyous: 'and it was well for me, with them'.[25] As new Christians enter the basilica and prepare to receive the eucharist by the altar for the first time, the angels, Ambrose tells them, are spectators.

On each day of Easter Week, until the Saturday after Easter, Ambrose reassembled the group and gave yet more instruction. We can best follow it in his surviving texts *On the Sacraments* and *On the Mysteries*.[26] Throughout, the tone is heavily allegorical, emphasizing that there had been much more to the rites than the candidates had seen with their own eyes. Ambrose began by relating baptism to its prefigurations in the Old Testament and, by bold allegories, placed it as a rite even older than the rites of the Jews. Then, later in the week, he explained the eucharist, the rite which Augustine and his group had been qualified to take since Easter Sunday. He concluded with an explanation of the words of the Lord's Prayer which the new Christians had just learned for the first time: they could indeed call God their 'Father' now, as His true sons. The process had taken the better part of a fortnight and was quite unlike the brief sprinkling with water by a baptizing priest in a modern church. During it, Augustine had heard repeatedly about the Holy Trinity as an equal group of three. He had been infused, or illuminated, with inner light. He had been washed clean of the legacy of Satan and original sin. He had learned that when Jesus urged His disciples to pray 'indoors', He meant that they were to pray inside, in the 'inner recesses' of their heart. Inner illumination, original sin and the inward act of prayer will be central aspects of his subsequent Christian beliefs. Other sources helped to impress them on him, but during these baptismal days Ambrose had imprinted them firmly for ever after on his mind.

In the *Confessions*, Augustine recalls something else. 'We were baptized, and from us fled anxiety for our former life.'[27] All was wiped out, the sex, the heresy, the worldly ambition. In no way are the *Confessions* a plea for the sins of Augustine's past to be forgiven. They had already been washed away. It is surely Ambrose who composed the poem for Milan's baptistery which a later copyist preserved: 'Here, whoever wishes to lay aside the shameful crimes of their lives, let them wash their hearts and take on a clean breast . . . What can be more divine than that, that the sin of the people falls away in a brief moment?'[28] Libanius and his pagan friends would have deplored the message. They thought such a sudden wiping of the human slate to be a cause of 'dissipation, not admonition'. By promising a fresh start, it was an invitation for people to sin even more wholeheartedly before applying for it.[29] Unknown to them, young Augustine had been a prime example.

26
The Last Days of Monnica

I

Baptism did not resolve the practical question: how was the 'new man' to live? He had no job and his recent renunciations cannot have gone down well with his former pupils or in-laws-to-be in Milan. He had pictured himself presiding over a group of friends as fellow seekers of the 'true philosophy', but where were they to do it? If he had hoped for local support from the 'greater friends' to whom he had sent his first writings, none was forthcoming. The obvious alternative was to form a Christian community of his own. So Augustine began to consider the options. He recalls that he saw in Milan a 'lodging-place of [Christian] saints, not a few of them, over whom one older priest was in charge, an excellent and very learned man'. Probably it was the very lodging on the edge of the city which the visiting Ponticianus had described to him with such effect. It was a possibility, but Augustine himself was not a priest.[1]

After about four months, he returns to our view further south, in the harbour town of Ostia at the mouth of the River Tiber. With him were his mother, his brother and his son, but only one Christian friend from Milan, Evodius, the fellow townsman from Thagaste who had probably been baptized in his group. The boys and the country cousins had slipped away. In the *Confessions*, Augustine tells us that he has hurried over much in this phase because he is wanting to move on to a meditation on scripture. We would much like to know what he had been doing in and near Milan from Easter until late summer. He, Evodius and the others, he recalls, were 'intending to dwell together in holy resolve' and were looking for a place to be 'God's slaves, more usefully'.[2]

When he left Milan, there were other reasons for going south. By late summer 387 the spectre of civil war had crystallized. The usurper

Maximus had occupied some of the Alpine passes into Italy with his troops and by 8 September he took over Milan. The boy-emperor Valentinian's court had already dispersed and there was every reason for Augustine, the former public orator, to anticipate events and try to leave Italy. On arrival in Ostia, he and Monnica, he tells us, were 'tired' after a long journey, intending to go to north Africa and presumably to settle back at Thagaste. They had not travelled to Rome to try their luck and only later to Ostia when the political situation worsened: Ostia is fourteen miles from Rome, a journey of only a few hours. They had come directly from north Italy intending to take a boat from Ostia and return home.

It was from Ostia two years earlier that Jerome, about to sail east, had composed his 'answer to critics' and artfully sent it to Asella, the ultimate Christian nun in Rome.[3] Unlike Jerome, Augustine was not leaving Italy among slander from enemies: Ostia was to be the scene of a very different encounter. He had 'friends' there, he recalls, and so he and his family lodged in a house, not an inn. There were plenty of Christians in the Ostia of the 380s, but did Augustine have help from a 'greater friend'? The powerful family of the Anicii has been suggested, one of Italy's greatest Christian families, of which members in Ostia would exchange letters with Augustine some twenty years later. However, we do not know if a contact with these people went back to Augustine's earlier time in the town.[4] Simply to survive, Augustine and Monnica could turn yet again to fellow north Africans who were clustered there, as elsewhere. A former public orator and his elderly mother were no longer of much concern to the highest society in Italy.

In Ostia, Christians were only one group and pagans were still widely present. Scholars have suggested that the town had a meeting-place for Platonist philosophers, a bath-house in which a sculpted stone statue represented none other than Plotinus. The date and identity of this portrait's type have been revised by recent study and the 'philosophers' baths' have disappeared, except from guidebooks to the town.[5] Instead, while resting, Augustine found himself conversing with Monnica alone. What followed has remained of concern to all the *Confessions*' readers: it arose from the culture they brought with them, not from a new contact with philosophers in Ostia itself. Augustine and Monnica were sitting by the window of the house where they had lodged and were looking, once again, onto a garden. The sequel is beautifully described and touchingly related to Augustine's prayer of confession. He and his mother, he tells us, made simultaneous contact with divinity, with nothing less than God's Wisdom, the second person of the Trinity. They sighed and then fell away, back to the world of transitory speech and sound.[6]

Psychologically, a duet of mother and son and a simultaneous climax has seemed a rich subject for analysis. Historically, Augustine is clear how it arose. He and his mother had begun to talk of the nature of 'the eternal life of the saints'. No fleshly pleasures on earth, they agreed, could possibly compare with its delights. They continued to talk but also to 'ascend' by stages. They 'ambled on' beyond earthly realities and the heavens and still they kept ascending. They were talking still, but also 'thinking inwardly' and admiring God's works in the visible world. Then 'we entered into our minds and we transcended them too'. They were aiming to attain 'the region of unfailing riches', not the 'region of dissimilarity' which had frustrated Augustine's ascent in Milan. Still talking, they touched divinity, what Augustine interprets as God's eternal Wisdom. As in Milan, it was a brief, momentary touch, but was made with a 'total leap of the heart'. They sighed and fell away, but they had the sense, Augustine recalls, of leaving 'first fruits of the spirit', a phrase Paul had used when writing to the Romans, in the zone of eternity.[7] They left a little of their spirit, he surely means, as a preliminary to the life to come. Then they returned to the world of mortal speech, whose words belong in time and, unlike God's Wisdom, have a beginning and an end.

Unlike Augustine's ascents in Milan, this shared experience began from a Christian question, the nature of the life of the saints. Nonetheless, he describes it in the same sequence. First, there is a progress through the visible world, then an inward turn which transcends the thinking mind. The same words are used to describe it, an ascent by 'stages', 'lifting them up to It Itself', that Latin mistranslation of Hebrew scripture, and then the 'thinking inwardly' and the brief contact. Once again, this pattern of ascent is based on Plotinus' philosophy and describes an outward, then an inward turn of which the Christian scriptures had said nothing. This time, it was not conducted in silence: the climbers kept on talking even until they seemed to touch on God. As they returned to mundane reality, they promptly assessed the experience. If it could be sustained for ever, they agreed, then it would indeed be the eternal life of the saints. Augustine does not ascribe specific divine words or sights to it, no cry, this time, of 'I am who I am', no heavenly light. However, he writes that if it could be prolonged, it would be an undistracted vision as well as a direct hearing of divine words. For that reason the shared experience is justly known as the 'Vision at Ostia', although hearing was very important to it too.

This vision has been beautifully related to music by the modern composer Michael Tippett, but it has perplexed many Christian readers. Augustine was newly instructed and baptized, but the experience which he describes seems to many readers to be minimally Christian. As in Milan, his description weaves together much which derives from the non-Christian Plotinus, yet Monnica shared the experience and had never read a word of Plotinus in her life. What has happened to the programme of preliminary drilling in the 'disciplines' which had seemed, six months before in the villa, to be essential for a vision of God? She had not undergone it, either. Was this duet really a mystical experience and, if so, how was it shared by two people at once? Plotinus considered that our souls are parts of a common soul, but Augustine does not adopt this view. He describes two 'minds' which are the minds of separate individuals, himself and Monnica.[8] We still know moments of intuitive closeness between our own mind and someone else's, a child's or a lover's, a like-minded friend's or a fellow musician's. In intervals between speaking, this like-mindedness between two people can indeed come to one and the same conclusion. Was the 'Vision at Ostia' only what we would call a moment of 'insight'?

Augustine would not describe the experience in this way. It was to him a 'moment of intelligence', or understanding, but it involved an ascent and the sense of a brief contact with the divine beyond himself. In Milan, he had devoured the Platonist books at a time of intense personal stress. In Ostia, stress was not shaping the experience at all. He and Monnica were far from the madding crowd, at rest, chatting. In Milan, heaven-sent words had admonished him in his turmoil in a garden. In Ostia, he ascended to God while looking calmly over another garden, which lay beyond a window. Neither garden was a literary fiction: they were two real gardens, the settings for two different encounters with God.[9]

To express his experience, as in Milan, Augustine draws partly on Plotinus' language. In a magnificent paragraph, he then returns to it and enlarges it, prefacing it, 'we were saying therefore . . .' The words are too abstract, sometimes too reminiscent of Plotinus', to be Monnica's too. They are Augustine's elaboration of what, if at all, she may have tried to express. He describes what a sustained vision of the same type as their own would be like, but this time he links it with the precondition of silence before the outward and inward turns of the soul are made and there is an engagement with God's words 'not through the riddle of mere likeness', but directly. These stages were also prescribed by Platonists. When writing the *Confessions* Augustine did not stop to look up their phrases for them in his Latin translations. They were rooted in his mind and memory, intertwined with Christian scripture. They remained there, as we can again see from the recently discovered sermon which he preached in Carthage in January 404. In it he uses the same language to describe the Platonists' means of ascent to God.[10] It was easily found in their texts. 'Let us admire the world of sense,' Plotinus had indeed written, 'as we look out upon its vastness and beauty and the order of its eternal march . . . let us ascend to its archetype, to the yet more true and authentic sphere . . .' Silence will assist this ascent: 'let the imprisoning body be quiet for the soul and quiet, too, the surge of the body's passion: let all things be quiet that lie about her. Let the earth be quiet, the sea and the air quiet too and the heaven itself, pausing for a while.'[11] In the *Confessions*, Augustine adapts these fine words to the ideal type of the experience he had just shared. If it lasts, he concludes, it will last in the life to come, a point which Monnica might have made more simply. Plotinus considered that 'there will be a time when the vision will be continuous as there will no longer be any bother from the body', after death. In his *Soliloquies*, Augustine had already located the enduring vision of God in the future life. He and Monnica now reaffirmed it. It was to become a cardinal point in his aims and hopes for the rest of his life.

Augustine has interpreted this experience with hindsight in a brilliant tapestry of language, but, as in Milan, its core and conclusion are understood as Christian. It arises from a Christian question; it is prefaced with verses of Christian scripture on the future life which he and Monnica had perhaps been discussing at that moment. They were 'forgetting the past and reaching forward to what lies ahead' (Phil. 3.13), a life 'which neither eye has seen nor ear heard, nor has it entered into the heart of man' (1 Cor. 2.9). Their experience was not Neoplatonist. Plotinus never 'gaped' for Intellect with the 'mouth of the heart', as Augustine describes himself and his mother. Whereas Plotinus' soul returned upwards to its undescended layer and became flooded with light from that source, Augustine's soul was God's separate creation. It touched only briefly on the supranormal Wisdom which remained beyond itself. As Tippett well understood, Augustine's description is consistent with an opening and a shutting of the door of heaven, as could never be said of a Platonist's ascent. Augustine's placing of the

Ostia experience is what a careful reader of his villa dialogues would expect. It is understood as a part of the 'true philosophy', originally revealed by God, still partially known to Plotinus, and fully revealed by Christ. Like the prayer which began his *Soliloquies*, his description of it weaves what, to us, are Christian and Neoplatonist themes. To Augustine, they were parts of one and the same wisdom, personified by the Wisdom with which he and his mother made contact beyond their innermost minds.

Without any training in the disciplines and any prolonged purifying of her mind, Monnica shared his first successful ascent since a year or more before. Yet her success was not counter-evidence to Augustine's disciplined programme. It was evidence, Augustine would say, of Monnica's exceptionally devout soul, dedicated to God and chastity to a degree which is given to very few others. In the dialogues at Cassiciacum, she had shown her love of 'wisdom', her exceptional love of 'divine things' and her mind 'most intently focused on God'.[12] Conspicuously, her visionary experience at Ostia matches just what Augustine and the secretaries had recorded about her only ten months before. The experience was also, for them both, a part of God's hidden plan. Together, they had briefly been allowed to sense the bliss of the life to come. They had 'touched' it, no more, because, as Augustine later wrote, 'just touching God with the mind is great happiness: comprehending Him [or grasping Him all round] is completely impossible'.

By the window at Ostia, Augustine and his mother classed this moment of rapture in Christian terms: it was a trailer for the blessed life of the saints in heaven. In the *Confessions*, ten years later, he tells God that 'sometimes, You admit to me a state of mind that I am not ordinarily in, a kind of delight which would be hard to distinguish from the life to come if it could ever be made permanent in me'. What occurred in Ostia was not a rogue tremor. It was a type of experience which remained central to Augustine's spiritual aspirations, a touchstone for what he continued to strive to attain.[13]

Monnica had been at one with her son in this moment of shared presence. After it, she had no further interest in earthly life. Her son was a baptized 'Catholic' Christian: better still, he was now a celibate 'slave of God', despising earthly happiness. 'What I am still doing here and why I am here,' she told him, 'I do not know . . .' Within days her uncertainty was to be answered.

II

About five days after their shared experience, Monnica fell sick. In the course of her illness she lost consciousness and Augustine and his brother ran to her. She recovered at once and asked, 'Where was I?' She then looked them in the eye and told them, 'Bury your mother here.'

Augustine has a loving son's exact recall of his mother's last days and his own reactions to them. Two themes run through his confessions at this point: his mother's final resting-place and his own battles with his tears. Behind them, as he implies, lie others' ignorant criticisms. Why had he not brought Monnica back to Thagaste for burial beside her husband? Why had he stood stony-faced and not even wept at her last rites?

In Ostia, he tells us, Monnica had changed her mind about her burial. Previously, she had cared greatly that she should be buried beside her husband in the tomb which she had prepared in Thagaste. It would be a memorial to their 'decidedly concordant life together'. In Ostia she had then talked with some of Augustine's friends and taken a different line. She had held forth on 'contempt for this life' and the 'benefit of death'. As the latter is the subject of two surviving sermons by Ambrose, she had probably adopted this theme from her revered bishop in Milan. She was not afraid now, she told them, to be buried far from home. 'Nothing is far from God,' she remarked, 'nor should there be any fear that at the end of the world He may not know from where to raise me up.' By leaving her buried in Ostia, Augustine explains that he and his brother were observing her last wishes.[14]

There was no conflict unresolved between the two of them. In the final stages of Monnica's illness she kept calling the attentive Augustine her 'dutiful son'. With 'great love and affection', he recalls, she left him with the ultimate gift of a mother, the reassurance that she had never had a harsh or insolent word from him. It is the last we hear from her. Aged fifty-five, in autumn 387, she died in his presence, the woman whose social planning had done much to shape his first thirty-two years.

'I pressed her eyes shut', Augustine recalls, 'and a huge sadness flowed to my heart and began to turn itself into a flood of tears . . .' He fought them back with a struggle, but young Adeodatus burst into open lament. 'Restrained by us all, he fell silent.' Augustine mastered his own urge to weep, as Adeodatus was brusquely told to shut up. Evodius then took up the psalter and began to sing Psalm 101: 'I will sing to thee, O Lord, of mercy and judgement.' Many Christian brothers and 'religious women' had gathered when they heard what was happening in the household: evidently, Augustine and Monnica had been lodging in Christian company. While they made their customary arrangements for the last rites, Augustine stood to one side with those 'who thought he could not be left alone'. Solemnly, he discoursed on a 'topic suited to the occasion'.

It is a fine moment in his life, an Augustine who draws on his mental and spiritual reserves to talk gravely and coherently on a topic concerning death. No philosopher could have done better, not even Plotinus, who had written that 'even if the death of close friends and relations causes grief, it does not grieve the wise man. It grieves the part of him which has no rational intelligence, and he will not accept its distress.'[15] Psychologically, we would now say, Augustine was detached by shock from expressing his grief and was able to compartmentalize his mind. Admirably, he talked on a general theme as a reasoned distraction from his emotions.

He looks back on these emotions with two questions in mind. Should he, as others later said, have wept more? Why, though, had he wept at all when Monnica's death was not a wretched one and she had gone to a much better life? He answers by explaining his tears in terms of a persistent framework in his thinking: 'order'. Tears for the dead are part of God's 'ordered' universe and are an apt part for man's sinful place in it. Even Ambrose had been less austere. He had wept in public at his brother's funeral and defended tears as a mark of 'piety'. They are not always, he declared, a sign of faithlessness and weakness: 'I wept, I admit, even I did so . . . but the Lord Jesus wept too . . .'[16] Unlike Ambrose, Augustine grieves in the *Confessions* that grief continues to be inevitable, because it is a sign of the fallen state of man.

'Lo and behold,' he continues, Monnica's 'body was brought out': some of the women present must have prepared it for the funeral. It was escorted to the grave: 'we went, we returned, without tears'. In north Africa it was customary to bury the body and only then to hold the requiem. As the Christians who had gathered round him in Ostia were not north Africans, they followed their local practice. They prayed and celebrated the eucharist with Monnica, dead, beside them. Even so, Augustine still shed not a single tear. As if to answer critics, he explores his efforts to weep and defends his inability. All day 'I was gravely sad in secret', but God did not heed his prayers to send him relief. Augustine even went to the baths, probably the big Forum

Baths which are still visible in the town: he says he had heard that 'baths' were so called in Greek because they 'drive anxiety from the mind'. However, he did not 'sweat out his sadness'.[17] He slept, but still he did not weep.

In his concern for tears, their merits and their obstacles, Augustine seems unaware of the scriptural words of Ben Sira (Ecclus. 38.16–18), although Ambrose commended his book to baptismal candidates. 'My son, let thy tears fall over the dead, And as one that suffered grievously, begin lamentation . . . Make bitter weeping and make passionate wailing. And let thy mourning be according to his desert, For one day or two, lest thou be evil spoken of . . .' Instead, confessing Augustine looks austerely on grief for the dead as the grief of misplaced 'fleshly affection'. The sense of sorrowfully missing someone is a harsh reminder of the hold which 'long habituation' can exercise on our souls. Yet, as if answering critics, he remains keen to stress how strong his feelings were. When he awoke, a little refreshed, on the following morning, he recalled the words of Ambrose's hymn to 'God the Creator'. The words, not their music, were what mattered to him at this moment. After the night, they said, God refreshes us and is the One who can 'lighten tired minds and release the anxious from grief'. Sure enough, Augustine had awoken refreshed and was ready to be released from grief. 'Little by little', he began to think of Monnica as he formerly did, recalling her pious conversation to God and her 'kind and well-mannered, saintly conversation to himself'. So, at last, he wept, 'both about her and for her, about myself and for me'. However, his tears lasted only for 'a small portion of an hour' and were unseen, in private.

Others, he recognizes, may consider this brief and delayed weeping to be a sin. His response was very different from his response to the death of his unnamed friend in Thagaste. He had wept and wept at that loss, causing himself to wonder later where the pleasure of such weeping lies. At that time, he had been a Manichee. When losing Monnica, he was a Christian perfectionist, believing that all tears for a physical loss are a sinful weakness, a 'wound' or 'ulcer', as he later describes them.

Once again Augustine distinguishes between types of weeping, just as when he recalled his mother's weeping at his departure from Carthage four years before. Tears of mere fleshly affection, he insists again, are not tears heeded by God. The tears which accompany a prayer are different, especially if the prayer is being offered for the souls, not bodies, of the dead. Monnica herself had been adept at this tearful praying, believing that God was more likely to hear and heed it.

So, the books of confessional prayer which have revisited Augustine's past and his failure to weep at bereavement now rise to a grand finale. They present him weeping freely while praying in the present for forgiveness of his mother's sins.[18]

These tears, indeed, are real tears. We should picture Augustine weeping at this very moment in his confessing prayer. Monnica, he tells us, was only human, an heir to the sinfulness of Adam. In life, she always forgave and requited her debtors, and so in death may God forgive her 'dues'. Of course she sinned in life, as we all do, but may God forgive her, Augustine prays, rather than judge her. As a Christian, her debts have been paid by Christ. Doubtless God has forgiven her already, Augustine says, but may He approve his spontaneous prayer nonetheless.

As Monnica wished to be remembered at God's altar, may Christians remember her, he prays, together with her husband, 'whom she served' alone, no other. The *Confessions* hope to realize her wish more than Augustine's prayers ever can. The *Confessions* will cause 'Your slaves, God', my 'brothers', 'Your sons, my lords', to pray for Augustine's parents, far and wide. In them he is addressing fellow celibate 'slaves of God', the primary human audience for his text. He is not asking for his parents to be commemorated in prayers to be recited in the liturgy: he is asking for them to be remembered in people's personal prayers and thoughts.

It is a wholly remarkable finale, an author weeping and praying to God to forgive his mother's sins and asking his readers to pray for his own parents. In the early fifth century Monnica was indeed commemorated at Ostia, but not quite as Augustine anticipated. Verses were composed to honour her resting-place there by one Bassus, a member of the grand Anician family, probably the consul Bassus of AD 408. Perhaps a reading of the *Confessions* encouraged him to write his poem. Monnica was believed to repose in Ostia by the church in honour of St Aurea, a martyr in Ostian legend. Bassus' text was then reinscribed, probably in the seventh century. In 1945, while Italian boys were preparing a goalpost for a newly learned game of basketball, they hit on a fragment of its inscribed marble.[19]

Monnica had not gone to oblivion. In the fourteenth century supposed relics of her were still being brought home from medieval Ostia by pilgrims. In 1429 a Christian lady in the town asked for her body to be recovered. In 1430 the Pope, Martin V, agreed, and she was moved from the church of St Aurea in two processions to Rome. One brought her relics, the other her ancient sarcophagus. They arrived in Rome on Palm Sunday, and when a young boy was placed in the sarcophagus his paralysis was promptly said to have been healed. She came to rest in the fifteenth-century church of S. Agostino, home now to Caravaggio's boyish *Madonna of Loreto* and the tomb of Fiammetta, the mistress of Cesare Borgia. In her ancient sarcophagus, Monnica became a focal point for the order of Augustinian Hermits and for the 'sorority' of widows, spinsters and virgins which formed in her honour. Shrines for her were set up in Florence, Prato and Venice.[20] By the 1820s, her name had been given to Santa Monica, her continuing memorial in California.

Augustine was right. His confessions ensured her widespread remembrance, in places, however, which he never foresaw.

27
Authority and Love

I

After his mother's death Augustine went from Ostia to Rome, not to Africa as they had been planning. The decision was probably forced on him. Maximus' invasion of Italy had led to a naval blockade off the coast and shipping to Africa was interrupted.

His return to Rome by autumn 387 marks a change for all modern studies of his life. After Monnica's death, the *Confessions* no longer revisit people and incidents in his past. Instead, we have the many texts which he wrote on other subjects. Near the end of his life, he reviewed each one and left precious comments which explain their context and, sometimes, indicate their dates. Little in them is autobiographical, but just after his death a 'Life' of him was written by his younger follower Possidius which helps to fix some of his changes of place and aim. We also know about them from his letters: he has left another thirty or so up to the point when he begins the *Confessions* nine years later. In all this material, the themes which will most concern us are the relation of his past, especially his Manichaeism, to his present, his Christian progress to new ways of life, and the continuing thread of mysticism and ascent to God's presence. The thinking which emerges from them will eventually make the *Confessions* possible. First, however, he had to resolve the pressing question: how and where would he now live?

Augustine was to remain in Rome for about a year until autumn 388. We do not know whether he found lodgings with the help of a 'greater friend' from Milan or through a north African network in the city, but he no doubt went regularly to church, took communion, sang and prayed. Presumably he went to hear Rome's new bishop, Pope Siricius, but he never mentions him. In no way were these months an interlude in which his mind merely marked time. He continued to write texts on each of the disciplines, those pillars, he still believed, for raising young minds to God. He continued to explore the soul, writing *On the Magnitude of the Soul* to follow *On the Immortality of the Soul.* He began, at least, three works on other topics: *On Free Choice*, *On Genesis against the Manichaeans* and a polemical book, *On the Ways of the Catholic Church*, contrasting its virtue with the vices of the Manichaeans, whose Elect he would attack later in a second book.

Except for his books on the disciplines, each of these undertakings addressed questions which were central to the Manichaeans' teaching. *On the Magnitude of the Soul* and *On Free Choice* engaged with the problems it raised about the soul and evil. Is the soul a divine substance and, if so, what is its relation to God? Why do we do evil, out of free choice or necessity? His other texts, begun in Rome, attack the Manichaeans' hypocrisy and bad behaviour, their denial of the Old Testament and their misunderstanding of Creation and Genesis. They refute the insistence with which Manichaeans prioritize 'reason' before 'faith' and understanding. On each point, Augustine again shows the wide gap between his own beliefs and a Manichaean's. However, he would not be exploring these questions so deeply without his Manichaean past.

None of these books addresses a patron and we do not even know how he met the expenses of keeping alive in the big city. Their main target, Manichaeism, was a lively issue among 'virtuoso' Christians there. There had been a recent attempt to found a Manichaean 'colony' in a Roman household but it had collapsed in scandal and schism.[1] Aspiring celibates were still readily classed by critics as crypto-Manichaeans. Worldly Christian widows, according to Jerome, would look with disdain on any sad, pale-faced Christian virgin and call her 'miserable and monkish (*monacha*) and Manichaean'.[2] By attacking Manichaean morals and beliefs, Augustine was sure to find an appreciative audience. Perhaps he even hoped to find patronage and a place on the edges of Rome's Christian hierarchy. All he tells us is that he wrote his book on Christian 'ways' because he could not bear in silence the 'boasting' by Manichaeans of their 'false and deceitful abstinence' by which they 'rank themselves above true Christians in order to deceive the uninformed'. He disparages their 'chastity', but, importantly, he also disparages their teaching that reproductive sex is sinful. Just as Augustine had recently encouraged the married Verecundus, so he was not rejecting sex within marriage, although it was no longer his own chosen way. He remained approving of marriage because, as Paul said, it can bring one partner to the other's Christian faith and it can also produce Christian children.[3] He was not the implacable 'enemy of sex', the role in which modern outsiders sometimes choose to cast him: he was its implacable opponent only as it concerned himself and others like him.

Before writing this text, he need not have disputed with Manichaeans in person. His text *On Free Choice*, he tells us, arose from a debate with a 'Catholic' companion, although the subject was a mainstay of Manichaean teaching. Nonetheless, there was a shadow in the background: his sentencing in absence as a Manichaean about a year earlier. It was probably known by now through Africans visiting Rome from Carthage. By writing strongly against Manichaean beliefs, Augustine would make clear that he was no longer one of their group. He would also clarify his thinking on issues which Manichaeism raised. As a former insider in Mani's sect, he was better informed than any other opponent in the Latin West. However, he was not the first to refute its doctrines. In the 370s, the Christian Ephrem had taken them apart point by point in an excellent text composed in Syriac.[4] Augustine was unaware of this predecessor.

In Rome, meanwhile, he continued to widen his grasp of Christian thought, at least in Latin. Detailed study of his writing while in the city has now shown his range of references to previous Christian prose authors. He engages with Christian thinkers and preachers, including texts by Tertullian and the fourth-century Latin author whom we know as Ambrosiaster. It is probably from the latter that Augustine took a compelling use of the Old Testament text which he cites in *On Free Choice*: 'unless you believe, you will not understand' (Isa. 7.9). This text is cited twice in the parts of this book which he wrote in Rome and will remain fundamental to his way of thinking.[5] In the villa, he had already discussed two ways, 'reason' and 'authority'. Whereas Manichaeans scoffed at mere 'faith' and professed to offer reasoned truth instead, Augustine now argues that faith in authority must precede reason. Only then can reason go to work to explore it. *On Free Choice* is itself an example of this type of understanding. After citing Isaiah's authoritative words in its first book, it goes on in its second one to try once again to support God's existence by philosophical reasoning.[6]

Soon after leaving Rome, Augustine's first commentary, a long book on the opening verses of Genesis, is further evidence of his readings in Christian thinkers, including a few homilies by the great Origen, read in Latin translation. It repeatedly uses Ambrose's *On the Six Days of Creation*, arguably a compilation of the very sermons which the bishop had preached in the baptismal week of 387.[7] Rome had several Christian libraries and, plainly, Augustine made good use of them. Naturally, he would be keen to read his baptismal father's works.

As in the villa, philosophical dialogue was still his preferred literary form. He used it for *On the Magnitude of the Soul* and, again, for *On Free Choice*. In each, his dialogue partner was his north African Christian companion Evodius, a fellow celibate and baptized convert. Like the boys in the villa, Evodius begins *On Magnitude* by suggesting an unlikely thesis: perhaps the soul is 'like the wind'. Augustine then disabuses him in what becomes once again a mental workout.[8] He argues for the soul's magnitude by some theoretical reasoning from geometry, which is indebted to the pagan Porphyry and well worthy of his own arguments in the *Soliloquies*. The soul's homeland, Augustine explains, is God, who creates it, but He creates it from a distinct substance. It is immortal and is the closest item in Creation to God Himself. By implication, it is not a trapped particle of divine Light, as a Manichaean would assert. This point is an important point of difference, one to which his attacks on Manichaeans will repeatedly return. Created by God, the soul is not a part of God. It is 'formed' and is thus able to 'turn', or convert, to God, although it wavers and is unstable. This underlying pattern will be crucial to the *Confessions* nine years later. Turning to God, or 'converting' to him, is thus God's gift, not a fact of nature. We may be 'admonished' by Him (as Augustine himself had been in the garden), but it is we who choose to turn to Him. In doing so, we must be 'reformed' by the clemency of the One whose power and goodness have formed us.[9] We can then ascend, step by step, up to the seventh degree, the contemplation of God in the life to come. Already in Rome a ladder of potential achievement stretched before him.

This ladder is one which can usefully take us onwards and upwards too, as it recurs in his writings before the *Confessions*, and offers a vantage point from which to view their emergence. Its steps change their nature as the context of his life and writings changes too. Augustine seems to have found the idea of seven degrees of ascent to heaven in texts by the pagan Porphyry, but already in Rome he gave them a Christian dimension.[10] On the first step, he writes, the soul begins at the level of sensation, including sexual desire and being alive. It can then progress to 'art', the level of memory and interconnected information which enables artistic and intellectual achievement. Then it can go deeper, if it chooses, to the fourth level, virtue, where it realizes its superiority to the material world and can decide to focus on spiritual, not carnal, delight. Nonetheless, it is beset by fear, the fear both of death and of God's just punishment. Only when it has been cleansed of its sins and has adapted itself to God's order in the universe can it progress to the fifth step, tranquillity. Beyond it, the sixth step is 'entrance', what Plotinus called the 'porch of the Good'. Here the soul desires to understand Truth and to gaze on it, before reaching the seventh step, or abode, the contemplation of Truth.

These degrees are usually cited as evidence of an exceptionally optimistic phase in Augustine's thinking. Soon after baptism, he was writing as if 'great and good' souls can indeed attain tranquillity and a vision of God in this life. However, his first scheme presents the soul as unstable even when it reaches the sixth step, tranquillity. If it arrives there without being fully cleansed, it will be 'thrust away by the light of Truth' and will think that 'there is no good, but very much evil' in the light which it sees. In the *Confessions*, Augustine describes how his own soul had been 'thrust away', the very word, from its premature approach in Milan to the light of Truth. His sixth step, written up in Rome soon after his conversion, reflects his own experience.

On the Magnitude of the Soul also referred to the question of free will. *On Free Choice* then explores it in more detail, again in dialogue form, presumably with Evodius, although he is not now named in the text. The discussion is philosophical, but the difficulty is to know how much of the finished three books go back to actual debates in Rome. When reviewing the work later in life, Augustine tells us that he 'terminated' the second and third books while a priest in north Africa, at least four years, therefore, after their Roman beginning. Was he still working from his debates with Evodius in Rome or had the debates continued in north Africa, where Evodius was also with him? Was there a first Roman draft of most of the three books, or only of the first half? The questions are important for attempts to trace developments in Augustine's thinking from his surviving texts.[11] They are especially important because the final book of *On Free Choice* discusses original sin, our legacy from Adam, and tries, even, to justify the agonizing deaths of babies.

In my view, these chapters were not composed before 394/5, whereas the first book and most of the second were written in Rome itself. If so, Augustine certainly considered in Rome the problem of why infants had to be baptized. He admitted that it was a 'most obscure question' and that its 'benefits' will be discovered by 'reasoning' when 'they will have had to be investigated'. In later life he states that 'original sin' had always been in his thinking since his conversion. Scholars tend to disbelieve him, but I do not. 'Original sin' is Augustine's own famous phrase, first attested only after the *Confessions*, but a concept can long precede a name for it.[12] It was not Augustine's own invention. Up to seven previous Christian authors had referred to the notion, including the admired north African Bishop Cyprian. Augustine's compositions in the villa do not mention Adam's legacy or its sinful effect, but during his baptism Ambrose had brought it to the fore by washing the candidates' feet so as to wash away the 'serpent's venom'. Augustine would not forget this dramatic evidence of Adam's legacy, but the question remained whether the effects of such baptismal washing are permanent. Adam's sin had made the human body mortal, a punishment which not even Ambrose could wash out, but it had also affected the soul and here God's grace would be needed to cleanse and purify it. No Platonist had ever expressed that need.

In Rome, Evodius posed the blunt question, 'Tell me, I beg you, whether God is not the author of evil?' After some preliminaries, he and Augustine duly settled down to discuss 'what is it to act badly?' This direction to their argument matches Plotinus', in a treatise, *On What are Evils and Their Origin*, which Augustine had read.[13] First, Augustine tells Evodius how these questions had greatly troubled him in his own Manichaean phase. He then leads him through a long counterargument which retraces the sequence of his rejection of Mani's views. As in Milan, the arguments are abstract and philosophical, drawing on the Platonists' 'true philosophy'. Themes which will run through the *Confessions*' account of his progress through error and doubt to certainty are already present here in outline.

The first book establishes that we act badly only through a free choice of will: if original sin had been in Augustine's thinking at the time, it would, I think, be as a disposition to sin, but not as a necessity. Evodius therefore begins the next book with the difficult question of why God has given man this free will. This question later becomes entwined with the question of God's foreknowledge and whether sinning is indeed the result of necessity, but these further debates were probably written up later, in north Africa. First, Augustine turns the discussion to a prior question, whether the existence of God is itself certain and, if so, whether all that is good comes from Him.

Philosophically, the 'proof' of God's existence is invalid, but the dialogue, even in Rome, makes a profoundly un-Manichaean assumption, central to Augustine's thinking: an underlying 'order' and goodness in the universe.[14] If there is such an order, external, non-moral 'evils' must be understood as nothing of the sort. When seen in the context of the ordered whole, they become insubstantial. Moral evil, he tries to argue, results from a preference for worldly things over eternal realities. It is then punished justly by God, with apparent, not actual, evil. Indeed, as Augustine points out, we can will what is good simply by our act of willing, whereas worldly 'goods' cannot be acquired simply by wanting them. Why, though, are worldly goods any less good for that? The many thousands around him in Rome who were enjoying their daily horse races or the softness of a woman's embrace would pity him, rather, for all he was missing.

II

In these writings at Rome, ascent to God and contemplation of Him are still prominent. Since Milan and Ostia, Augustine has lost none of his mystical aspirations: they are present even in *On Free Choice*'s long demonstration of God's existence. It progresses from an intricate dialogue, enriched by Evodius, to a concluding exploration by Augustine of the 'marvellous beauty of God's Truth and Wisdom'.[15] His *On the Ways of the Catholic Church* then explains the familiar obstacle. If Reason draws near to God's presence, she 'turns herself away, she cannot last, she palpitates, she is in turmoil. She gapes at Him with love, she is beaten back by the light of Truth, and she is turned back to her familiar darkness, not by choice, but by exhaustion.'[16] Again, the words are strikingly similar to those he will use in the *Confessions* nine years later to describe his first experience in Milan. Augustine retained this language for so long because it best described what he had undergone.

It was not the language of a lingering Manichaean. Mani had taught that God can be known through a sudden moment of recognition, here and now in this life. By it, we can 'awake' from the contrary pull of our dark nature and have a perfect, immediate knowledge of God within us. In Augustine's view, we can ascend only step by step beyond the level of our daily consciousness. In the bliss of a future life, we will then reach the seventh step, the full contemplation of God. Months before, in

Ostia, he and Monnica had intuited this truth, briefly on the sixth step, and now, surely, she was enjoying the seventh degree beyond the grave.

After the events in the garden, the *Confessions* recall Augustine as arrow-pierced in the heart by God. In Rome, the two elements in this piercing now attract his close attention: the scriptures and love. The scriptures, he believes, are unified by the Holy Spirit, the agent of God's love. Manichaeans, therefore, are wrong to reject the Old Testament and to accept only the bits of the New which suit them. The authority of the scriptures gives 'shade' and guidance to us, gifts which help our reason not to be dazzled and repulsed when it tries to ascend to God.[17] Simpler minds, meanwhile, can find simpler truths in its words. In the villa, Augustine had taught the boys that disciplines classes in the liberal arts are the soul's proper preparations for ascent to God. Now, he adds a further, immensely important resource: the scriptures. Their very obscurity is one of their attractions. It arouses our minds and the more we have to search for understanding, the greater our delight when we find it.[18] As his soul had not been acclimatized in Milan by the scriptures' shade, it had been dazzled and 'thrust away' from the light which it briefly saw. In Rome Augustine was considering a 'step' on the ladder, the scriptures, which the Platonists had never included in sustainable ascents to God.

In the *Soliloquies*, Augustine had already applied Paul's words about 'faith, hope and charity' to the soul's love and yearning to see God. He now says more on the 'love' which such a vision requires and induces. Again, Plotinus had alerted him to this powerful way of thinking. For Plotinus, 'love' is inherent in the fallen soul's nature, but the One itself never shows the slightest hint of love for anything else. In Augustine's view, by contrast, God had commanded love to Moses ('Thou shalt love thy God . . .') and love is authorized by both the Old and New Testaments. Love, therefore, must govern our life's every purpose.[19] Plotinus had linked each of life's cardinal virtues to intelligent thought, but Augustine now sees them as dependent on love.[20] In Matthew's Gospel, Jesus linked the 'love of God' with 'love of one's neighbour'. Augustine duly prescribes 'love of one's neighbours' as a 'sure and certain' step towards God. It must be a love for them in their relation to God and their capacity for loving Him, but it is not only a spiritual love. It must also be expressed materially, in care for their bodily needs. Already, his ideal is not one of mere introspection which will give out nothing to those about him.[21]

As Augustine realized, Mani's Elect accepted Jesus's words about neighbourly love. However, their 'Father of Light' had concealed himself behind a veil so as to hide from the suffering of the world. He had not commanded love of Himself and our neighbours, whether or not they are members of his Elect. Augustine, by contrast, links love to the third person of the Christian Trinity, the Holy Spirit. For the Manichaeans, Mani himself was this spirit or 'comforter'. For Augustine, God's Spirit diffuses love into the hearts of everyone who turns to Him.[22] It is through the Spirit that the scriptures, old and new, are unified and through the Spirit, therefore, that we 'discern the mystery' in their hidden depths. This mystical engagement with the unity of scripture is profoundly un-Manichaean.

These powerful views on scripture and on love will be a crucial impulse behind the *Confessions*. Already in Rome, Augustine addresses what was to become one of his most frequent scriptural resources, the First Epistle of 'John'. In it, he knew the advice 'Do not love the world or the things in the world', which neatly matched his way of thinking. As he says, his text against the Manichaeans was not using words of scripture which Manichaeans rejected: he had therefore met these potent verses in 'John' while still in the Manichaean sect. Manichaeans would understand them as a warning against the evil which is teeming in the material world, but Augustine now understands them as advice not to love worldly things.[23] He still had to find the setting in which to live out this principle.

III

On first reaching Ostia with Monnica, Augustine and his group, he recalled, had already been resolved to cohabit as 'slaves of God' and were returning to Africa with that aim. In Rome after her death, their resolve was to be strengthened. Augustine's first book on Christian 'ways', completed in Rome, ends with a survey of the types of life being lived by perfectionist Christians in the contemporary world. Fascinatingly, he reviews the options before him. They were well known to Christians in Rome, as Jerome's notorious letter in praise of virginity had exemplified. Augustine's impressions are quite similar, but not so similar that he acquired them only by reading Jerome's text.[24] Evidently, stories about 'virtuoso' Christians circulated more widely. Some of Augustine's knowledge is based on hearsay.

There are some Christians, Augustine knows, who betake themselves away from other people's gaze and withdraw into the most deserted places. There, they live on bread and water and devote themselves to contemplating God. To us, the most famous of these solitaries is Antony in Egypt. They pray, he knows, which is to their credit, but he also knows that these lone perfectionists are often criticized. They are thought to have dropped out of useful society.[25]

As his *Soliloquies* have already shown, this solitary way of life could never be Augustine's own: for him, 'hell' was never 'other people'. In Egypt, he knows of an alternative. Big settlements of Christians have abandoned private property and are living together 'in common'. They work with their hands but are not hindered, Augustine believes, from focusing on God. They give the fruits of their labours to 'deans', each of whom oversees a group of ten. These deans allot food and clothes and attend to the sick. They send any surplus food in boatloads to the nearby poor.[26]

These Christians are the monks in big walled monasteries near the River Nile, communities which had been founded by Pachomius, a former pagan, from *c.*AD 320 onwards. By the 380s, they had grown into societies of up to 1,800 celibates on any one site. From their own texts, we can see that they did indeed split themselves into 'houses' of forty or so, each under 'housemasters', but Augustine's deans are not mentioned.[27] Nonetheless, Augustine has learned that as the sun sets, these Christians, still fasting, assemble to hear their presiding 'Father'. He is a great and virtuous person who is steeped in Christian teaching. He preaches to them and they listen with 'incredible keenness', responding with emotion to his words. 'Three thousand' or more of them gather, he believes, for such a meeting. They groan, they cry or they are 'quietly joyful'. Only then do they go away to eat, avoiding meat, wine and tempting foods.

Augustine's impressions of these meetings can be set beside a great treasure, the letter in which an Alexandrian visitor recalls his own glimpses of a big Pachomian monastery up the River Nile. He had visited it as a young man in the 380s, a contemporary, therefore, of Augustine's writings in Rome. He, too, saw monks seated in lines inside its walls. He, too, watched in amazement while their Father, Theodore, preached to them and elicited great gales of weeping and sorrowful compunction with the help of words of scripture. Individual monks, even, would stand before their Father and weep profusely as he gazed into their hearts.[28] Augustine seems unaware of a monastic Father's guidance by the Holy Spirit and the consequent power of his searching eye. He even believes that these walled-off Christians never show envy or hostility, but he also believes, correctly, that there are separate settlements for women. These women, he knows, weave woollen clothes which are given to the men's communities. No man can come closer to their settlement than to its threshold, even if he is a man of proven moral strength.

Augustine considers the life of these Christians to be 'most concordant and most intently focused on God'. Conspicuously, Synesius took a similar view of them after also living for a while in Egypt. He agreed that monks were devoted to contemplation, although, unlike Augustine, he thinks that mindless tasks like basket-weaving interrupt them and hinder the ascent to 'intelligible beauty', which is best attained by philosophy.[29] For monks in Egypt's monasteries, 'purity of heart' and a vision of God were indeed the ideals of their existence, but, as visitors observed, most of them were denied them. They were held back not by basket-weaving but by their intensified sense of their own sinfulness.[30]

There was no way that Augustine could found such a community himself. In Egypt a monastery's walls hemmed in hundreds of inmates, whereas Augustine's own group of 'friends and family' in Rome numbered perhaps six or seven. They had no land on which to build. In Rome, he had discovered another option, Christians who live in households and support themselves by work, both in the Eastern way and in accordance with Paul's words. They too live in 'Christian love', holiness and liberty. They are not under a priest, but under individuals who are distinguished by serious virtue and 'divine knowledge'. Many of them fast 'incredibly', sometimes for more than three days on end. Women also cluster together, but live separately under 'most serious women', older virgins and widows.[31]

Here was a possibility which suited Augustine's idea of his future. In the community which he was planning in north Africa, he could preside among male housemates as a virtuous and knowledgeable guide. In Verecundus' villa, when discussing 'order', he had already expounded 'precepts' for virtuous living, based on Varro, Pythagoras and the Gospels. In the *Soliloquies*, he had explained to Reason that he wanted his friends to live with him and 'in concord of heart seek our souls and God'. If they do not want to seek them, 'I will make them want to . . .'[32] By the time Augustine left Rome, the pieces of a new future had come together more clearly. His eventual Rule for monastic groups is distinctive in stressing love as its basis. Its emphasis on mutual help and its refusal to push members beyond their limits conform to what Augustine had learned while in the city.[33] It is evident from the first book of

On Free Choice that in Rome he had been reading the Acts of the Apostles, a book which the Manichaeans rejected.[34] In its fourth chapter, therefore, he had studied its words about the Christian community which formed in Jerusalem after Pentecost. Its members had 'all things in common' and, as Augustine interpreted the text, were 'most intent on God'. His book on 'Catholic ways' ascribes exactly these qualities to the contemporary monks in Egypt. He already considers, therefore, that the first Apostolic community is the model for Egypt's monasteries. Soon it will be the model for his own: in Rome, in these transitional months, its ideals were gaining a new depth.[35]

This image of monastic life was not shared by everyone. In Antioch, Libanius resented monks, their aggression and their dropping out 'in caves' from civic life. He characterized them quite differently: they were 'men dressed in black who eat even more than elephants'.[36]

28
Slaves of God

I

By early autumn 388 Augustine left Rome, returned to Ostia and at last took ship for north Africa. On 28 August the invading would-be emperor, Maximus, had been killed in north Italy and sea travel seemed to be safe again without the risk of civil war. The victor, Theodosius, was making the usual new appointments and, among them, new careers began to open for orators and men of letters. A north African, Aurelius Victor, was made the prefect of Rome, someone who is better known to us for a short history book on the Caesars. A Christian orator from southern Gaul, Pacatus Drepanius, delivered a Latin speech of praise on Theodosius' visit to Rome, calling him a 'god incarnate'. In return he was made the proconsul of Africa.[1] If Augustine had not resigned his job and had continued to 'sell lies for a living', would he have earned a post for some public flattery of his own? It might not have been so easy, as Libanius shows. The political changes impinged on him too, even in the East. Aged seventy-four, he was accused of having favoured Maximus: when envoys went off from Antioch to congratulate the victor, Theodosius, two of the three tried to slander him in the new emperor's presence. The third envoy, his pupil, made a speech in Theodosius' honour and saved the day: the emperor sent a letter in Libanius' favour.[2] If Augustine had had enemies in Milan, they could have used similar slanders to drag him down.

Instead, jobless, he returned to Carthage with very different aims: cohabitation with 'brethren' intent on God. First, he had a remarkable meeting on his arrival there, one rich in theological consequence. He called on Innocentius, an advocate in the provincial system of government, someone whom he knew, perhaps, through Alypius, who had had a legal career in the public administration.[3] The poor man was in agony, suffering from acute ulcers in his backside. Doctors had excised all but one of them and Innocentius was trying to avoid the extreme pain of a final cut. He had summoned an alternative surgeon; he was taking herbal remedies, and before his doctors could operate again, he was visited by important Christians, two bishops and a deacon among them. Augustine was present while they engaged in concerted prayer on Innocentius' behalf. Innocentius joined in, fervently: 'who could explain in any words,' Augustine recalls, even twenty-five years later, 'with what feeling, what emotion, what a river of tears, what groans and sobs, shaking all his limbs and almost blocking off his breathing', Innocentius prayed to God? Here were tears and groans of entreaty which not even Augustine could match. As often, he prayed silently in his heart, 'Lord, what prayers will You hear from Your people, if You do not hear these?' On the following morning the doctors prepared to excise Innocentius' final ulcer. As if by a miracle, they found it already sealed by a scar.

The assembled Christians had told Innocentius to 'trust in God and bear His will like a man'. In answer to prayer, God had shown grace, it seemed, from the very depths of His mercy. Indescribable 'joy and praise and thanks to all-powerful, merciful God' attended the discovery. Once again, God's grace and the power of prayer were not only abstract items, to be analysed in Augustine's writings and night-time thinking. They were living forces, verified in the world about him. Just as prayer and grace had healed his own toothache in Verecundus' villa, so in Carthage they healed excruciating pains in a government official's backside.

Nine years later, similar pains were to play an important role in the *Confessions*' own genesis. In Carthage, meanwhile, this physical crisis had brought some of the city's top Christians to an official's bedside. Their presence in the bedroom of a powerful man is notable. Among them was an older church deacon, Aurelius, whom Augustine saw for the first time. He, too, was to have a future in Augustine's career which neither could have guessed at the time.

II

From Carthage Augustine and his group returned to Thagaste, his home town. After the death of both his parents, the family house and farm were waiting for him and his brother, Navigius. For want of any other option, here was a place in which he could establish himself and his group as a celibate household, like the household-communities which he had discovered in Rome.

When Thagaste had last seen him, he had been a Manichaean. During his absence, in 386, he had been named as a Manichaean to a governor of proconsular Africa who was applying the laws and hounding down suspects. He had even ruled on Augustine's guilt. The sentences were then cancelled by an amnesty in early 387, but the case had not been entirely forgotten.[4] Augustine needed to establish that any group which he formed was not a Manichaean cluster in disguise. Twenty years and more later, he referred in letters to what he did. He 'despised his few little paternal fields', he writes, and 'turned to the free slave-service of God'. He had 'passionately believed' the words of Jesus, to the rich young man: 'Go, sell all you have and give to the poor . . .' Near the end of his life, he reiterated the point in a sermon: he had returned with his 'fellow Christians in poverty' and sold his 'little property' and 'few paternal fields'. He had a particular reason to emphasize what he had done: worldly property and its uses had become burning questions for his hearers. Members of his own monastery in Hippo had just been discovered to be betraying their ideals.[5]

On Augustine's return home, hard facts would force him not to be too hazy about his arrangements. In Thagaste Augustine and his brother were liable to tax, both to tax on their property and to poll tax which Augustine had so far avoided by his jobs abroad as a public teacher. Worst of all, his father, Patricius, had been one of Thagaste's lifelong council members, a status which passed automatically to his sons. Notoriously, it obliged them to take on costly jobs for their home town, including the horror of forcible tax collection from their fellow councillors. It made no difference what they intended to do, or not do, with their sex lives.

All over the empire, the costs and bother of these obligatory tasks were major problems for their holders. In Antioch, Libanius was famously articulate on behalf of the long-suffering councillors. He himself professed his own manifest 'love' for his home city, while claiming a highly contested immunity from the costs of being a councillor himself and also trying to secure immunity for his bastard son and others in his circle. In this very year, aged seventy-four, he was being accused of evading his civic obligations, a reason for the damaging allegation that he had favoured the usurper Maximus.[6] In Cyrene, Synesius would also engage in special pleading. At one moment he was himself liable for civic duties, at another he contrived to secure an exemption. In a brilliantly phrased letter, he made a similar plea on behalf of his brother.[7] As a bishop, Synesius was at last exempt from council service, but the law required his brother to take his place. So he wrote to the influential Hesychius, congratulating him on a novel appointment in Cyrene (probably as a 'defender of the city') and reminding him that they were friends, 'of old', bonded by their study of 'sacred geometry'. Evidently, they had once studied maths and philosophy with the great Hypatia in Alexandria. Could Hesychius therefore drop his inclusion of Synesius' brother among Cyrene's councillors and consider expunging the entire household from that 'wicked book, the list of town-councillors'? His brother had 'fled' to Alexandria, probably to escape council service. Could he also cancel a fine imposed on his brother's mother-in-law? Long ago, that classical Athenian, Themistocles, had regarded political office as a chance to help his friends. Hesychius should imitate Themistocles. He should look on Synesius' brother as one of his own brothers, linked to him through Synesius like the equal sides of the triangles which they had once studied together.

This artful request linked the classics, shared tutorials and a blunt plea for special treatment for 'friends and family'. It beautifully exemplifies the value of a shared education when soliciting men of power for illicit favours. Once again, Augustine had no such social network of 'good old boys' from his university days in power in proconsular Africa. As he could not use such pleas, his local obligations would ensnare him unless he took decisive action. A letter from his dear Nebridius is delightful evidence, not always recognized, that his actions had not been quite quick or clear enough.[8] Nebridius writes, with unusual brevity, to ask, 'Can it be true, my Augustine? Are you showing bravery and patience for the tasks of your fellow citizens and is that longed-for inactivity not to be restored to you?' Indeed, who are 'the men who are making demands of you, good as you are'? Plainly they do not know 'what you love', namely, 'God, serving God and adhering to God'. Nebridius offers to invite Augustine to stay with him in peace and quiet in the country. If he did so, he would not be called Augustine's 'seducer', he deftly concludes, because Augustine both 'loves and is loved by' his fellow citizens 'too much'.

Nebridius is playing neatly here with the language of civic obligation, and the obligatory councillor's professed 'love' for his home town. In fact, he is offering Augustine an escape from a fate worse than tax: let him come to Nebridius, retaining his 'love' for Thagaste while avoiding its impositions. Nebridius was in his own house near Carthage, living with his mother and brother, but as a rich man himself, much richer than Augustine, he was fully aware of the burdens of council membership. Reports had evidently reached him that, on his return home, Augustine was being snared into the worldly tasks of Thagaste's council.

In 386, in a recent law, the ruling emperor of the East, Theodosius, had banned councillors from selling their properties without the consent of their province's governor.[9] The law did not apply to Carthage, but it is a reminder that such sales were not officially encouraged. Augustine and his friends needed, nonetheless, to rid themselves of their assets so as to escape council service, but somehow to retain enough of a livelihood to be independent 'slaves of God'. The neat answer would be to give, not sell, property to a sympathetic owner, and to retain a share of its yearly revenues for their Christian group. Augustine's biographer Possidius duly tells of Augustine's return to his 'house and fields' and an 'alienation from himself', probably of the property, although the manuscripts of the text vary. 'Alienation' is a formal, legal term.[10] As one of Augustine's letters implies, the fields passed to the obvious beneficiary: Thagaste's 'Catholic' church. By accepting them, the church endorsed that he was no longer a Manichaean, a point which might be useful to him if malicious slanders started up.

Such an arrangement is discernible in other Christian cases, a surrender of ownership but not of a full interest.[11] At the time, Augustine owned only a share in his family property, others belonging to his sister and his brother. Neither will have opposed him, because his sister, obligingly, was to become a nun and Navigius was to join Augustine's monastic group. As for his son, Adeodatus, he was no obstacle, either: he was illegitimate and he was also to be one of God's 'slaves'. In Thagaste, this arrangement for 'slaves of God' was a novelty. Augustine's fellow citizens evidently still assumed that he could be obliged to show 'love' for the town and fulfil his inherited role. Hence Nebridius' letter.

Augustine was indeed resolved to show love, but it was love for God and his neighbours, his fellow Christian celibates. When reading the Acts of the Apostles in Rome, he had already encountered the idealism of the first community in Jerusalem. 'As many as were possessors of land and houses' were said to have sold them and laid 'the price at the apostles' feet'. They were then 'distributed to each, according to his need'.[12] As Augustine had made a gift, not a sale, there was no 'price' for him to distribute personally to the random poor. Any such distribution would be made by the Church and then only from its share of the future revenues. Augustine's community would live off the rest.

In due course, Augustine's fellow 'slaves of God' would do likewise. Like Augustine, they had property and Alypius was rich. Their former schoolfriends would not be so content. Alypius, Evodius and Augustine were people whom they had expected to share Thagaste's burdens with themselves. Instead, their possessions had gone to the Church, but priests and bishops were exempt from civic obligations. The other members of Augustine's age group were more exposed than ever to the costs of running their town.

III

Based in his family house, Augustine and his little group were not going to live an enclosed life. There were no walled monasteries as yet in north Africa. Living in chastity was, of course, familiar, being attested for men, widowers, virgins, widows and even, by his mature choice, for Bishop Cyprian. Chaste women were the most likely to live in a group, as they were physically vulnerable, and were best kept, therefore, in household groups under supervision. Here and there, males, too, may have grouped together for a shared life, but evidence, so far, is lacking. The word 'monk' derived from Greek (*monachos*), a fact which may have slowed its local reception. Augustine's group were to be monks in actuality, but not name. In Thagaste, they were probably the first male group to be so.[13]

Their monastic commitment was described by them as 'slavery to God'. The phrase was sometimes used loosely for ordinary Christians, but it was a phrase which Paul the Apostle had applied to himself. It was adopted by celibate Christian perfectionists, with the further twist, explained by Augustine, that this 'slavery' was true freedom. Like St Paul, celibate 'slaves of God' were not shut away. As Augustine and his fellow 'slaves' were not priests, they would have to go to their church frequently to receive the eucharist. By giving the Church their property, but depending on it for income, they were bound to its goodwill. From the start, they were not a detached group.

Inevitably, Augustine and his fellow 'slaves' faced a test whenever they went out in public. In church and in the streets a tempting presence was only too visible: women. Within a decade Augustine formalized the correct etiquette in the Rule which he wrote for his communities: it set out what had surely always been best practice.[14] When members are in the street or church they must walk and stay together. They may see women, but they must not catch their eye, attract a glance from them or receive 'letters or little gifts' from them. 'Lust for women is mutually fostered not only by touch and tenderness, but by a look, too': in his youth, in church and church porches, Augustine had known this as well as anyone. If any member sees a colleague with a roving eye, he must at once admonish him. If he sees that eye roving again, he must tell one or two others so as to have them as future witnesses. If the offender confesses, he will be pardoned. If he denies his offence, ultimately he will be whipped.

'Little women' had disrupted Augustine's plan for a philosophic commune back in Milan. Now, in Thagaste, he would aspire to unanimity, but in a group of men only who must avoid the female eye. When later he discusses the word *monachos*, he claims, revealingly, that it does not refer to 'one, alone' but to a group 'at one' with 'one soul'. God Himself, he believes, favoured the ideal. At Thagaste, he quotes the address to God in his Latin Psalm 67, 'You who make men of one mind to dwell in a house'.[15]

This house was quite different from the group at Cassiciacum. It was a house of 'brethren', not pupils. It was linked to the Church by a property-gift. It was not intended to be a short-term villa interlude. However, it was still a household of 'leisure' whose members aspired to be god-like. They would pray, fast moderately, and meditate on scripture 'day and night', according to Possidius.[16] No more than in Verecundus' villa, do we hear of manual labour by Augustine or the housemates. It would be good to know if the real slaves of Augustine's estate had passed to Thagaste's church with his property. The 'slaves of God' in his household-community were not nature's labourers. They grew to perhaps a dozen (we know the names of six, one being his brother, another his son). People like Alypius or Evodius were not obvious candidates for the work which monasteries were doing much to impose elsewhere: vegetable gardening.[17]

IV

Whenever Augustine quotes Acts' words about the first Jerusalem community, he usually adds a significant extra to the text: the members were 'intent', he says, 'on God'. His housemates were indeed to be 'intent', with welcome results for Augustine's own mental needs. Elsewhere, whenever students of philosophy in a big city left their teachers and dispersed to their distant homes, they were at risk to intellectual isolation. Synesius is a clear example of the difficulties, after returning to Libya from his time with Hypatia and his fellow students. The one means of continuing their debates was by letter. He writes, therefore, to encourage the student friends who had been closest to him, especially Herculianus and Olympius, a fellow horseman whom friends called the 'archer on horseback'. He implores his correspondents to continue to be philosophers, to 'think much' (a special greeting which he devised) and to aspire, through their reasoning, to God. Neither of them obliged him. It took at least five letters to make Herculianus even answer.[18] Synesius even ends one letter by quoting Plotinus' supposed last words to his pupils: 'raise up the divine in you to first-born Divinity'. Unlike Augustine, Herculianus failed to rise to the quotation.[19] Oratory was much more important than rarefied philosophy for well-off young men when they returned and found themselves forced to serve their cities.

After his studies in Alexandria, Synesius considered that his homeland, Libya, was suffering from 'philosophical sclerosis'. There was nobody willing to engage in dialogue. Augustine risked a similar plight in Thagaste. Unlike Synesius, he had never had the chance to befriend students in classes with a philosopher. His fellow philosophers abroad, the 'greater friends' in Milan, had dropped from his horizons. However, he was to be saved from 'sclerosis' by two very different partners: the 'brethren' in his newly formed community and the tireless Nebridius. Both have left enchanting evidence of their concerns.

Nebridius was cooped up in his country house near Carthage with a mother who expected him to look after her. Nonetheless, he continued to exercise Augustine with a deluge of questioning letters. We still have twelve of them, nine sent back by Augustine, three sent in by Nebridius, who wrote at least ten more, a 'pile', Augustine says, in his possession. As ever, Nebridius is acute and insatiably curious. Augustine's letters, he writes, 'sometimes speak of Christ, sometimes of Plato, sometimes of Plotinus'.[20] Like Augustine, Nebridius was reading Plotinus very carefully: both draw on Plotinus' *On the Descent of Souls into Bodies* in their letters. They were also continuing to read Porphyry, although Nebridius was a baptized Christian and a fellow slave of God. Like Augustine, Nebridius was surrounded by a group: he had converted all the members of his household.

There was no peace for his intellect, as his volley of questions shows. Like Augustine, he is fascinated by the inner workings of the mind.

What is the relation between the imagination and the memory? he writes to ask, taking his cue from Plotinus. How is it that we remember having learned or understood something? Do we only remember what we can represent in images? Does the mind generate such images or are they imprinted on it from outside? Is there a special 'imagining mind' as a separate part of the soul? These questions of imagination and illusion had been fascinating Augustine, at least since his *Soliloquies* two years earlier. In due course, they will resurface in the *Confessions*' long analysis of 'what I now am'.[21]

Once again, Synesius would have loved to join these discussions as an antidote to 'sclerotic' Libya. They were questions which intrigued him, as we have seen from his text *On Dreams*.[22] Nebridius and the two future bishops, Synesius and Augustine, were fascinated by the philosophy of mind, though they lacked the tools to make lasting progress in it. Augustine's first answer to Nebridius engages acutely with what the mind actually remembers (the perception of something, not the thing itself) and opposes the notion that memory depends only on mental images. Nebridius was still not satisfied and in yet another letter addresses problems raised by dreams. How can we represent in dreams the forms of bodily things which we have never seen? This very question would soon preoccupy Synesius.[23] So would Nebridius' next puzzlement, whether and how dreams are influenced by demons outside us: Synesius wrote on this same subject. Above all, the three Christian thinkers shared the same introspective ideal, one for which the consummation is ascent to God. 'I have well known your journeys upwards on high,' Augustine reminds Nebridius; 'convey yourself to your mind and raise it to God, as much as you can.' In letters, Synesius urges the same ideal on his friends, citing Plotinus. So does Augustine. Rather than worrying over an obscure, pointless question, 'should we not pray to God,' he suggests, 'and raise ourselves to the serenity of the supreme being?' Unlike Synesius, he had had his 'Milan experiences', and the lure of them lived on.[24]

When Nebridius was not posing questions of memory and illusion, he raised problems of identity. Why do he and Augustine do the same things, but are different persons, whereas the sun is a heavenly body, but does not do the same things as the other heavenly bodies, the stars? Nebridius liked long answers and to each of his increasingly impossible questions he hoped for a long letter in reply. He was almost asking too much when he sent in two fearsome questions at once, one on the so-called 'vehicle' of the soul (a most 'obscure' question, Augustine rightly replies, though Synesius would have much enjoyed it) and another on a hugely difficult problem: are there higher 'forms' of individuals (persons like you and me) or only forms of universals (mankind)?[25]

These questions were not questions from a half-hearted Christian: they merely fell in areas which the Bible had not clarified. Christian Nebridius also posed Christian questions, relating to what we now call 'neo-Nicene theology', the very teaching which he and Augustine had met in Milan. Why, he asks, was it the Son who became incarnate, not the Father? In reply, he received Augustine's most complex explanation to date of the unity of the Holy Trinity and the properties of each Person in it. Here, once again, Augustine drew on Neoplatonist language and thinking in order to explain a Trinity which scripture had never analysed.[26]

This questioning and answering presupposed time to think: the ideal, as both partners agreed, was 'to be made god-like in leisure'. This 'godliness' was not simply the self-acquired godliness of a Platonist wise man, exercising his own reason. It was a passive 'deification', which depended on the gift of God.[27] As Augustine quoted at the time from Psalm 45, 'Be still, and acknowledge that I am the Lord' (Ps. 45.11). 'Leisure', in this sense of 'stillness', is later endorsed in Augustine's Rule for his monks, with a characteristic reference to the Jerusalem community being 'intent on God'. No other monastic Rule in the Christian West has such an emphasis. It was already evident in Augustine's Thagaste phase: 'it is Augustine who makes monasticism "contemplative", at least in the West'.[28]

The prayer, the quiet, the meditation had the aim, so Augustine writes, of attaining 'familiarity with death'. A well-tempered Christian contemplative would have nothing to fear from death's sting. The ideal had already been aired in the villa at Cassiciacum, but within a year of Augustine's return Nebridius' questioning ceased and it was put to the test: after an illness, Nebridius died. He had begged Augustine to come to live with him, but Augustine had refused, saying that he had obligations which it would be 'sacrilege' to abandon. Nebridius' letters, he says, found him short of 'leisure' in which to answer them.[29] The reason for his commitment was his little community in Thagaste: they were looking to him for guidance and intellectual leadership, evidence that a group had indeed formed under his direction.

V

There are many hours in a day, and more in a sleepless night. Augustine described it as a 'sacrilege' for him to leave his brethren, but what exactly were they doing? The established monastic groups in Egypt suggest a general routine, although their details and leadership were rather different. Monks would listen to psalms being recited, up to twelve a day, and then they would pray in silence. One of their ideals was ceaseless prayer. Another ideal, shared by Augustine's group, was the contemplation, if possible, of God. It could only be attained in 'purity of heart', so monks would scrutinize their patterns of thought with an intensity which even Augustine's brethren do not seem to equal.

In the Egyptian monasteries, monks were conscious of specialized demons, each attempting to sabotage them with unsought 'thoughts'. The *Confessions* and Augustine's previous writings are almost wholly uninterested in such demons. They focus, rather, on God's hidden order in the world. Synesius gave demons more consideration. Unlike Augustine, he had read about them in the esoteric *Chaldaean Oracles*, which he had studied with Hypatia, and he had also heard about them from a real desert father while in Egypt.

In these desert communities the presiding fathers were awesome figures with a fine sense of demons. They were also gifted, their underlings believed, with penetrating spiritual insight into other people's souls. In the biggest monasteries, even to hear a great father approaching at night could cause a novice to break out in sweat. Monks would lay vexing patterns of thought before a father whose experience and insight could discipline and guide them. He was in every way the Superior. By contrast, there were no novices in Augustine's community. He himself was the acknowledged head, but he claimed none of the authority of Egypt's grand old men. His ideal was friendship between brethren, but it was not, in his mind, mere friendliness which helps an all-male common room to work smoothly. His ideal of friendship was more highly pitched. It required love, not just love from himself, but reciprocal love from the friend. Friends must be loved as oneself, but one truly loves oneself only if one loves God. Each friendship, therefore, must be an eternal triangle, in which two friends love each other and God.

Before his conversion Augustine had been schooled, paid and praised for performing and competing. His new community was to be anything but competitive: the brethren were equals, mutually correcting and assisting each other's spiritual progress. However, unlike the monks in Egypt, friendly Augustine still had a brilliant philosophical mind and a detailed knowledge of Plotinus and Porphyry's thinking. Fortunately, his brethren included Alypius, Adeodatus and Evodius, men who were able to engage with his spiritual and intellectual concerns. Their range is still visible in a remarkable series of questions which survive with Augustine's answers. Eighty-three in all, fifty of them surely belong to his Thagaste years. They were not the competitive quiz questions he had once known from schoolteachers in the town. They arose, Augustine explained, from discussions with the brethren, the celibate 'slaves of God' in his household.[30] When Augustine gave answers, some of his brethren took them down and preserved them. Six years or so later, as a bishop, Augustine arranged for the texts to be collected and issued in a book, apparently in chronological order. Besides them, we have twenty-one 'opinions', as the Middle Ages called them, which address separate topics, also in Augustine's name. Erasmus declared these opinions to be spurious, but their credit has recently been affirmed in a brilliant re-examination.[31] They are best explained as yet more statements by Augustine during his Thagaste phase which he did not collect into the book of eighty-three. They remained, therefore, as separate notes. They include bits of Plotinus in Latin and that metrical tour de force, the poem, in my view by Mallius Theodorus, which discusses the beauty of the universe. Perhaps Augustine had brought it home with him from Milan, a last reminder of his 'greater friends'.

Like Nebridius, the brethren combine an interest in the philosophy of mind with problems in Christian theology. 'Will we ever be able to see our own thoughts?' they ask. Augustine's answer was, 'Yes, but only in the next life.' 'Is the soul self-moving?' 'Can truth be perceived by the bodily senses?' What about the ideal Forms in Platonist thinking? More briskly, 'Why was Christ born of a woman?': Augustine replies to his male brothers that both sexes were intended to be saved and, as Christ was a man, it was reasonable, therefore, for a woman to give birth.[32] Like Nebridius, the brethren are puzzled by an utter mystery, the Trinity. Like him, they receive a complex account of it, based yet again on Platonizing concepts. They, too, are concerned by death, in connection with Christ's death on the Cross. In reply, Augustine explains that the Crucifixion demonstrated that death, even at its most fearful, is not something to be feared and that his own fears about dying are receding. Ambrose had called death a 'blessing', and in his instruction for baptismal candidates related Christ's crucifixion to redemption and atonement. Augustine's answer presents it as part of Christ's moral lesson: 'Christ became a man to show us how to live virtuously.'[33]

The brethren are much concerned by this question of 'living virtuously'. To help them, Augustine even gives them Cicero's long definition of the 'virtues'. Some of them were so pleased with it that they copied it into their notes, where it has survived for us. Augustine also explains the basic distinction between 'enjoying' something (as an end in itself) and 'using' it (as a means to an end). This distinction, found in Cicero, will remain central to his way of thinking. 'Fear', too, is explained and related to the fact that 'what is loved may be lost or might not be acquired', an idea which went back to the *Hortensius*. Love and its appropriate objects are then analysed in three successive answers.[34]

These questions reveal a thoughtful group of brethren, concerned with questions of introspection and Christian wisdom, but also with values and virtues. They are a community aspiring to live in harmony, but they are also contemplatives, 'intent on God'. As in the big monasteries of Egypt, so in Augustine's household, the 'brethren' are hoping for a vision of God. As 'some of the brethren were questioning me very closely on these topics' (visions of God), Augustine later recalls, he introduced them to a text by a pagan, Fonteius, at Carthage.[35] They liked it very much indeed. They even wanted its core to be written down among the questions, where we can still read it. The 'mind must be purified in order to see God', Fonteius had argued, but he also considered it at risk to a 'wicked spirit' which 'creeps in' through each of our senses and 'darkens them with dark emotions'. This 'spirit' was somewhat Manichaean, but it appealed to the Thagaste brethren, conscious of their continuing struggles and failures to see God.

Previously, the most prominent celibates in north Africa had been Manichaeans: it was Augustine himself who had first spread their Gospel among the clever young men of Thagaste. Now, he found himself giving very different answers to classic Manichaean questions, and stressing, instead, the role of free will. His *Opinions* address that Manichaean staple, the nature of Adam before the Fall.

Among Manichaeans, fictional questions and answers were given in books called 'Chapters' so as to settle topics which might trouble their rank and file. In Augustine's Thagaste, real questions, answers and 'opinions' preserve the perplexities which exercised his housemates. They were not men 'eating more than elephants'. They were concerned by scriptural and philosophical problems, by the soul, by visions, by questions made urgent by Mani, the alternative apostle of the celibate life. Similar 'slaves of God', both inside and outside north Africa, will be the primary human audience whom, nine years later, the *Confessions* address.

After returning to Libya, Synesius would lament that his fellow students in philosophy had behaved 'like swallows'.[36] After nesting beside their teacher, they had flown quite suddenly to other lands. In Thagaste, in the *Questions* and *Answers*, we still catch the thoughtful twitter of Augustine's 'brethren', nested round him in his parents' home.

29
True Religion

I

Aged thirty-four, Augustine had found a context for his life, a new focus for his love and a ladder for his aspirations. It was a small group of equals who nonetheless deferred to him. His ideals of friendship could be reapplied to his community of Christian brethren, beneficiaries of the good works and neighbourly love which the ladder required from its climbers. A lesser man might have stayed there, reading, contemplating and writing. However, Augustine was not detached from the world or his Church, nor were they entirely detached from him.

He still travelled, and for some while he was in Carthage, probably in autumn 390, when bishops from north Africa happened to be meeting there for a Council. Augustine was a layman and would not attend, but no doubt a bishop or two talked to him. He could be decidedly useful to them. From the family house in Thagaste, subject only to a supply of writing materials and copyists, he was beginning to send clusters of his books, re-read and corrected where necessary, to people who needed to be rid of Manichaeism.[1] He wrote to one that he hoped 'he will not be estranged from the Catholic [Universal] Church'. Significantly, he was putting the 'Catholic' case, although he had no clerical position.[2]

Formerly, young Augustine had returned to Thagaste and converted his friends to Mani's 'true Christianity'. Now, most of his meetings were intended to win members for his monastic community. When he followed up with letters, he could not count on succeeding. Some of the recipients of his books failed even to reply. Once, when he had hoped for dialogue, he was reduced to asking for his texts to be sent back to him. Augustine's voice is the predominant one to survive from north Africa, but it was not a voice which enthralled every African Christian at this time.

He was to remain based with his Thagaste housemates for just over two years. Sadly, they were another time of significant deaths. It was after scarcely a year that he lost his crucial sparring partner, dear Nebridius. Worse, in 390, he lost his highly intelligent son, Adeodatus, in only his seventeenth year. It must have been the most bitter blow, despite all that he had read and written about the 'blessings of death'. In Libya, philosophic Synesius would consider killing himself after the loss of the dearest of his children. 'You know how feminine I am about such suffering,' he writes to a fellow clergyman, 'beyond what is necessary . . .'[3]

Adeodatus is the last person to be written up in a formal dialogue with Augustine. Perhaps it was his fatherly tribute to this brilliant young son very soon after his death. From then on, it was hard for him to find a participant who had such intellectual ability. Dialogue continued, but was sustained more slowly, in the to-and-fro of letters.[4] He treats one recipient to the relation between a text, the understanding of it and the inner illumination of its reader: meanwhile he was arguing about this very topic in his longer work, *On the Teacher*. He treats another one, Celestinus, to a brief, clear statement about the hierarchical ordering of God, the soul and the body, in which the soul is poised midway, able to fall down in sin and worldliness or rise up to happiness and contemplation through free will: at the time, he was expounding this view in his first commentary on Genesis and in *On True Religion*. Views expressed in these letters are also similar to those he expounds in answers to his brethren's questions. From this concentrated phase emerge 'key themes' for what will become his confessions.[5]

Its three most significant texts address problems of meaning. Augustine was still at work on his interlinked texts on the disciplines, of which the main survivor is *On Music*, begun in Milan in 387.[6] Cast as a dialogue, the teacher (surely Augustine) is left anonymous and the pupil is also nameless, frequently saying no more than that he agrees. Its culminating subject is the ascent of the soul beyond the visible world. Music is a specially promising means by which to ascend because it is closely linked to the spirit and the senses and can sweep us out of the everyday. There is a risk that it may pull us back by the mere pleasures of sound, but if we turn ever inwards, grasping music's underlying rhythm, or 'number', and judging the sounds themselves, our soul will 'sense in the flow of melody the eternity of pure reason'.[7] A main topic of the book, therefore, is metre, or 'number', the underlying 'measure'. Augustine distinguishes mere pleasure for the senses, something which we share with animals, from the stimulus to our souls to 'ascend', which the best music inspires. The final book was completed only some twenty years later, but the core was already in place by 389. Its views would have fascinated Synesius, author of hymns with a rich musical imagery and a dazzling range of classic metres, including 'Anacreontics' and 'anapaestic dimeters'. Like Augustine, Synesius regarded metrical hymns as assisting the soul's ascent to God. Unlike him, Augustine examines the interplay of sense and reason, the role of underlying 'number', or modulation, and the relation between a melody and the words which are sung to it. In the *Confessions*, he will analyse at length the dangers in the pleasures of music, to which, he admits, he is very susceptible. He does not reject them entirely. During the baptismal service, in Milan, he had responded emotionally to the wholesome words which were sung in unison by the congregation. Musical chanting will remain a part of his idea of bliss in the future life, to be deployed in God's presence. The chant will be the sound 'Jubilee' and nothing else.

On the Teacher is a more demanding work. In serious dialogue with the clever Adeodatus, Augustine argues about the relation of words, or 'signs', to things and the relation between learning, intercommunication and knowledge. For the last time, there is a dialogue here as the months in Verecundus' villa had known one. First, Augustine establishes that words teach us. Then he engages in a tortuous, roundabout argument to 'exercise' the mind and show that words do not teach by their signs. How, then, do they teach? The question becomes the subject of a final exposition by Augustine himself. If they do not teach by signs, then they teach, he argues, by the inner Master whom we all share: Christ. Adeodatus thanks his father for anticipating 'all I had prepared' and for leaving him in no doubt.

A theory of language emerges here beside Augustine's now-familiar philosophy of mind.[8] He does not endorse a picture theory of language, the error of the young Wittgenstein, as if words simply picture things in the world. Conversely, he has much to say on words' inability fully to express meaning. As we communicate truths not by words or signs, but by an inner communication between minds, it follows that no human teacher teaches knowledge, least of all by talking to others while they listen. Lectures are decidedly insufficient. We learn, instead, by our inner reason. Augustine is concerned, not with the 'impossibility of dialogue' but with the conditions which make intercommunication possible. They are not conditions which logicians could accept nowadays. As in a true friendship, he thinks, there have to be three in the relationship: the two who wish to communicate and a third party, God. We understand one another by our inner reason, but only because this reason is illuminated by Christ within us. Just as the Gospel says, 'One is your master, Christ.'[9]

This fundamental item in Augustine's thinking seems odd to modern logicians, but it was not new or peculiar to him. The idea of an 'inner light' had been a cardinal point in the Manichaeans' teaching, albeit with a very different explanation. It was prominent in the Platonist books, the Fourth Gospel and Paul's letters, texts read closely by him in Milan. In the *Soliloquies*, he had already written that God's inner light was guiding his reason. Then, at baptism, Ambrose told candidates that they were being 'infused' or illumined by just such an inner light.[10] *On the Teacher* applies this idea to all knowledge, not to religious knowledge only. For something to be known, what matters is the inner understanding of our heart. In the *Confessions*, Augustine will show a notable wariness about words and the limits of logical reasoning ('dialectic'). Words are evasive or misleading. As they allow a speaker to lie or to express error, feeling something ranks above merely stating it. These penetrating ideas will recur in sermons which he will eventually preach to Christian congregations in Africa.[11] My words, he tells them, are the cause of your ears hearing sounds, but the cause of your intelligence and understanding is not me: it is Christ the 'inner Master' whom we all share. In Milan, he had identified the Intellect in Plotinus' philosophy with the Word and Wisdom of God, Christ. In the very first dialogues, in Verecundus' villa, he had done the same. It was easy for him, therefore, to make Christ the source of all our intelligence and understanding.

On the Teacher still interests philosophers of language, but the text from Thagaste which most interested the Middle Ages is *On Genesis against the Manichaeans*. Augustine's reading for it had begun in Rome in 388, but he finished it only by late 389.[12] Before doing so, at Thagaste, he added a second volume, *On the Ways of the Manichaeans*, to his *On the Ways of the Catholic Church*. In it, he deplored the low morals of the Manichaeans, with some lurid anecdotes: significantly, the Manichaeans in question are all members of the Elect. They were the rival celibate vanguard, the people whom newly celibate Augustine most needed to discredit.

His book *On Genesis* then refuted the Manichaeans' reading of an all-important text, the first two chapters of Genesis on Creation.

Revealingly, Augustine wrote in simple, clear Latin and summed up his refutations in an accessible final summary. He stated that Manichaeans mislead simple people as well as educated ones, and so, like none of his previous texts, his book is addressed to both audiences. Augustine already saw himself addressing a wider public and trying to confirm them in the truth.

Unlike Manichaeans, he interprets Genesis's opening chapters allegorically.[13] Much of what he discusses is not original to him. He is especially influenced by his baptismal father, Ambrose, whose various texts he has consulted, including his *Six Days of Creation*, which I believe he had heard in Holy Week, 387. The topic was also widely studied in the Greek East, but although Augustine shows similarities to Greek interpretations, including Origen's, they are most likely to have come to him second-hand through Ambrose.

To historians and biblical critics nowadays, his interpretations seem wholly misguided. Adam and Eve do not symbolize reason and sense-perception and their 'tunics of skin' do not symbolize mortality. When the text says, 'In the beginning, God made heaven and earth', it means 'in the beginning of time'. It does not mean, as Augustine claims, 'In Christ'.[14] However, his text is particularly important for us because the *Confessions* end with three books of meditation on exactly these chapters of Genesis.[15] They are allegorical and repeat many of the same interpretations. In 388–9, his objections to the Manichaeans are already clear and coherent. They deny the scriptures' hidden sense. They do not read them for their coherent meaning as a 'story' and as an intimation of the future. They fail to understand that God's Creation is His work from nothing and is shaped by His order. In 388, five years after his break with them, he would not be addressing these chapters of Genesis so closely without his Manichaean past, but he has no doubt whatsoever of the contrast between his views and theirs.

For the first time, he links God's 'order' in the universe to a scriptural trio from the Book of Wisdom, a text which had been part of his pre-baptismal reading: they are 'measure, number and weight'.[16] This trio will be important in the *Confessions*. Yet again, he emphasizes the need for love if we are to read scripture with understanding. His loving interpretation of the Creation and the Fall has a memorable scope. Paradise, he says, represents a state, 'happiness', but not a place. Adam and Eve united the rational soul (Adam) and sense-perception (Eve). When God was said to have breathed into their 'clay', He was not breathing in His own divinity, as a Manichaean would try to argue. He was breathing in the 'breath of life'. Adam and Eve were not yet liable to die. They lived in 'happiness' as embodied creatures, and although they did not have sex together, perhaps they spoke to each other with words from time to time. As they were sinless, God did not address them verbally: He communicated directly with their intelligence. They were sustained, therefore, as if a 'spring' of truth was spilling over in their innermost beings. They were the 'earth' which this 'spring' watered (Gen. 2.6) and the ground was 'dry' because it was without sin, and also, as yet, there was no rain.

Adam and Eve, those frail originals, fell when their souls succumbed to the arch-sin, pride. The serpent made a 'suggestion': Eve was 'persuaded' and she and Adam 'consented'. This same psychological sequence, from 'suggestion' to 'consent', is repeated daily in our own sins: it will remain very important for Augustine's analysis of why we choose to sin. The two of them then realize that they are 'naked', not in the sense of sexual shame, but 'bare', rather, of their former direct contact with God. They put on mortality, the 'tunics of skin', and God 'dismisses' them from the Paradise of happiness, because their sinning souls will now stray away from Him into worldly seductions. Crucially, He no longer speaks directly to their inner being. Thereafter, His words are present to their descendants only in the 'clouds' of scripture and in the words which Christ spoke when He assumed a 'cloud' of human flesh. The 'clouds' of the scriptures bring refreshing 'rain' to the world, but, like Adam and Eve, we must toil and labour to find the truth in them.

Meanwhile, mortality befalls us and, like Adam and Eve, we sin. However, although we have been dismissed from bliss, we have not been expelled for ever. By subjecting our body to our rational soul and by sustaining ourselves on God's words, 'squeezed' from the clouds of scripture, we can return to happiness and contemplate God once again, primarily in the next life. Since Adam's fall into sin, God very rarely communicates with mortals directly. He speaks to them through the medium of the scriptures, whose each apparent difficulty points to a deeper, divine meaning. To grasp it we need to 'turn' with love. 'Nobody can enter deeply into the scriptures without purifying his heart and turning himself towards the light of God.'[17] Seven years later, the structure of the *Confessions* will rest on this very point. First, it gives Augustine's purifying self-analysis, 'what I now am', and then it engages closely with the text of Genesis. Finally God speaks directly to the 'heart' of his lover, Augustine.

Near the end of *On Genesis*'s first book, Augustine considers the 'six days' of Creation in two related ways. They stand for six successive phases in our lifetimes and, once again, for six progressive 'stages' in Christians' lives, by which they progress from elementary faith to a 'stability' of thought and deed. On the seventh day, they too will find eternal rest. These neatly interrelated series are probably influenced by Ambrose's writings, but for the eventual thinking in the *Confessions* they are of special importance. Like the infant Augustine's life in the *Confessions*, every life begins with a stage of which we retain no memory, one of sensation, not reason. Six more stages follow, ending with an old age of undefined length. The third day of the seven is the day of 'adolescence', when a young man separates his mind from the taint and waves of fleshly temptations and stands like dry land separated from the 'turbulence of the sea'. In the *Confessions*, as we have seen, he presents the onset of his own adolescence in similar metaphors of turbulence, whirlpools and watery waves, but in this earlier text the virtuous young man of the 'third stage' prevails against the flood tide. He can even say with the Apostle Paul, 'In mind, I serve the law of God, but in the flesh, the law of sin' (Rom. 7.25).[18]

These words of Paul to the Romans are to have a profound interrelationship with Augustine's own journey to the *Confessions*. In our completed text of *On Music*, they and their sequel are cited twice in the final book.[19] They occur there as words with which Augustine is wholly familiar. The last book of *On Music* did not take its final form until nearly twenty years after his Thagaste phase, but, as the *Confessions* imply, he had been relating the words of Romans 7 to himself in Milan even before he went out into the garden. They also much interested the Manichaeans, in whose company he would surely have heard them as a younger man. Their appearance in *On Genesis* is the first in his surviving writings, and they serve there to illustrate virtuous adolescence. They were to exercise him ever more deeply, not least with their apparent reference to grace, the means by which we can overcome the 'law of sin'.

In the soul's six stages of ascent, the fourth now involves strengthening by Christian 'doctrine', or teaching through scripture. The fifth, the stage of 'tranquillity' in Augustine's first scheme in Rome, is now the stage of discernment and 'good works', done for the 'utility of fraternal society'. They are either acts of courage by which the 'waves of the worldly age' are despised or words which 'preach heavenly things'. As Augustine settled into a life against worldly temptations in the 'fraternal society' of his housemates, his interpretation of the seven stages had changed to match it. After absorbing the scriptures and a fifth day of action, the soul is no longer considered at risk to 'thrusting away' on the sixth day: its prospect is one of stability.

II

All the while, Romanianus, still a Manichaean, had been promised a separate book. Back in Milan, he had discussed Manichaean topics with Augustine, and in the villa Augustine had promised to send him a full answer to his mistaken 'assumptions'. They continued to exchange letters, and Romanianus continued to pose acute questions. Back in Africa, Romanianus then wrote to tell Augustine of his 'domestic joy', perhaps because he had surmounted his lawsuit. While welcoming the good news, Augustine wrote back warning him not to be pulled down by worldly fortune but to rise above it, like a bee above cloying honey. He would send him, at last, the book he had been promising.[20]

The result, *On True Religion*, is the most historically revealing work of Augustine's time between his conversion and his fraternal years at Thagaste. It has an ample scope and style and, centuries later, was to be one of Petrarch's favourites. The simple sentences of *On Genesis* have disappeared. A single sentence can now run on for a whole paragraph or be phrased as a series of rhetorical questions and answers. Augustine's oratorical training has not died with his worldly ambition. Nor was his choice of title new. Since *c.*200, Latin writers in north Africa had written of Christianity as the 'true religion'. Already in Rome, Augustine had been reading one of them, Lactantius, but unlike him he presents the 'true religion' in contrast to the Manichaeans' Gospel. He also presents it as divine wisdom, or philosophy, a category to which Lactantius had been less open: when he read the *Hortensius*, he had identified with Hortensius' praises of rhetoric.[21]

As the origins of this book go back to summer 386, it offers historians a priceless consummation of Augustine's thinking since that turbulent time. It is not only a riposte to Manichaeism. It presents the 'true religion', 'Catholic' Christianity, as the only means of attaining truth and the happy life. These questions had first been raised for Augustine, and also for Romanianus, by the *Hortensius* many years before. Above all, *On True Religion* states very clearly Christianity's superiority to the teaching and conduct of the Platonists. Romanianus had long had an interest in philosophy, and Platonism would have been discussed between him and Augustine often enough in Milan. So far from being written piecemeal, *On True Religion* is Augustine's first coherent 'apology' for Christianity's superiority on all fronts. It is a forerunner of his greatest, the *City of God*, which he will begin some twenty years later, but by then, he was an established Christian bishop.[22]

Against the Manichaeans, Augustine makes his now-familiar points. Creation was a creation from nothing; evil is not an eternal, contrary substance; God may use it to bring us back to Him. The soul is created by God, but is not a part of God; sin is the result of its free choice, not of an evil implant. The universe is an ordered, hierarchical unity. The Old and New Testaments are a unity and have not been distorted by 'Jewish' insertions. Adam and Eve sinned by choice, not inner necessity. Christ became a real man, one who truly suffered and died on the Cross. He was not an 'airy spirit' like Mani's 'Jesus'. Christ is the light within us which guides our reason, but this light is not a substance transmitted from a separate divine Kingdom.[23]

The work's philosophical thrust is more original. Augustine states firmly that philosophy is not one thing, religion another, an interrelationship which had already been a hallmark of his thinking at Cassiciacum and will remain so throughout his life. On reading the *Hortensius*, he had identified Christ with Wisdom, an identity which he reasserted in his first dialogue, *On the Happy Life*. It was as Wisdom, therefore, or as a 'true philosopher', that Christ came down among men. Traditionally, philosophy was considered to have three parts: physics, ethics and logic. As Wisdom, Augustine now claims, Christ fulfilled all three parts: physics (by His resurrection), ethics (by His example) and logic (by His teaching, no less). As a result, each of the three parts can cure one of the basic 'lusts' which afflict mankind: the 'lust of the flesh, the eyes and worldly ambition', specified in 'John's' first epistle, which Augustine had already cited in Rome (1 John 2.16). In scenes sculpted on contemporary Christian sarcophagi, Christ is indeed shown as a healer, wondrously curing the sick and the afflicted. In antiquity, it was the mark of an authentic philosopher to heal an afflicted soul. As Christ was now healing thousands, Augustine regards Him as manifestly the true philosopher and 'doctor'.[24]

In Augustine's view, the Platonists stand out from all other pagan philosophers because they have grasped two crucial truths: there is one supreme God and there is a higher spiritual world. However, they live with a glaring contradiction between their philosophy and their acts of worship. They pay traditional cult to idols and demons and they compromise with superstition. Indeed, Plato had expressed his views in the most 'seductive' style, as Augustine's trained literary eye appreciates, even if he mostly read Plato in Latin extracts among his 'many things of the philosophers'. However, these views were 'timid conjectures', out of line with his followers' conduct. Christians, by contrast, have a faith and a cult which are consistent and 'simple'. Christians have brought them to whole peoples and have democratized faith, in 'Christian times'. These times are the times since Christ's incarnation, our 'CE' or 'AD'.[25]

In an imagined interview, Augustine presents Plato as coming back to life, a notion which continues to appeal to students of his thought ('Plato Today'). If he did return, Augustine thinks, he would promptly convert to Christianity in view of what he would see around him. He would need to change 'only a few words' in his philosophy, Augustine dares to claim. Recent Platonists have indeed become Christians, he says, surely thinking of Victorinus, of whom he had heard in Milan. 'Hundreds' of Christians, Plato would find, are now living up to their ideals in deserts or on islands and adopting a sexless way of life. Plato, by contrast, had to defend himself from widespread criticism when he 'never married'. Augustine knows that Plato wrote verses to a handsome boy: Plato had defended himself in public, the story said, by sacrificing to the goddess Nature. Augustine implies that Plato was unmarried because he was homosexual. Christians, by contrast, are unmarried because of their religious ideals.[26]

Unlike Christians, Platonists rely on false guides, on pagan omens, divination and demons, the helpers which are solicited by Porphyry's followers. Christians, by contrast, admire the good angels, who contemplate God in a stable repose. They do not worship them with misplaced cult: they try to imitate them. Above all, they have a mediator, Christ, who came to earth in human form and whose life, teaching and death are their moral examples. Platonists propose that the soul, by its own natural power, can ascend back towards God. Christians, by contrast, have the experienced hand of Christ to help and guide them on their upward course. The very word 'religion', Augustine claims, derives from the word *re-ligare*, to 'bind back together'. Through the one true 'religion', Christ re-links (*re-ligat*) the soul to God.[27]

On True Religion presents the Platonists' deficiencies as exactly those which the *Confessions* will describe, six years later, as dawning promptly on Augustine in Milan. Platonists have no helpful mediator, no notion of an Incarnation and only a proud faith in false cult, false demons and blood sacrifice. These counterarguments are not the *Confessions'* invention eleven years later. Just as they claim, they formed in Augustine's mind very soon after his first encounter with the Platonist books in Milan. It was in summer 386 that *On True Religion* had begun to be planned.

Unlike the Platonists, Christians benefit from God's continuing 'dispensation' through time. Strikingly, Augustine presents all of us as participants in this dispensation's plot. We were bit-players in God's story until Christ, our mediator, took on human flesh and came down to set us an example and bequeath us His authority. As a result, we can now understand the plot in full, how it runs from Creation to Fall, from restoration to future resurrection. Platonists, by contrast, see only a confusing sequence of random episodes, like cuts, we might say, from a film. Christianity even existed, Augustine believes, before Christ came to earth and preached it. In the *Confessions*, likewise, he will discern Christian rites and ministers beneath the surface meaning of Genesis's words about Creation. Platonists, still playing short-sightedly, have no idea of the grand narrative which God's intervention in history has brought about.[28]

The progress of this 'dispensation' is not easy for us, because we are distracted by the three misplaced desires identified in 'John's' epistle. Augustine had already touched on the three in his recent texts *On Music* and *On the Way of the Manichaeans*. In *On Genesis*, he had seen them as symbolized, memorably, by the 'beasts' of the newly created world.[29] As, in my view, he first encountered this text by 'John' as a Manichaean Hearer, he would know that Manichaeans related it to the three seals on their conduct. By contrast, he relates it to three specific lusts: the pleasure of the flesh, misplaced curiosity and worldly ambition. In Greek, 'John' had referred to 'boastfulness', but Augustine's Latin Bible mistranslated it as 'curiosity'. This misunderstanding made the three lusts even more similar to those which he had renounced in his own conversion. In *On Genesis*, he had related them to the Serpent's three temptations of Adam and Eve. Now, he relates them, uniquely, to Satan's three temptations of Christ in the wilderness. Christ's resistance to them, he considers, is the model for us to resist all three.[30]

These three 'lusts' remain important to Augustine's idea of sin. They have even been seen as a deep structure which shapes his entire presentation of his sinful youth in the *Confessions*. Certainly, they underlie his presentation of 'what I am' in their tenth book. Nonetheless, they would not impress other 'slaves of God'. Far beyond the horizons of Augustine's housemates, experienced monks in Egypt recognized many more lusts than three. After spending time with the desert fathers, Libanius' ex-pupil from Antioch, Evagrius, listed eight: they were 'thoughts' which we cannot simply exclude from our consciousness. Each 'thought' is sent by the particular demon who specializes in its type. They include anger and 'listless boredom', besides thoughts of fornication, vainglory and pride.

How do such lusts fit into a world which has been created (supposedly) good? Here, Augustine enlarges on two themes which have been central to his thinking since Milan: once again, the 'hidden order' in the world and the relation of falsehood, illusion and imagining to the soul. On the first point, he asserts the role of God's 'providence'. Even our own vices, he emphasizes, are not wholly bad. By them, he claims, we are made aware of virtues, their opposites. 'Pleasure in the flesh' is an attempt to find 'apt' pleasure, but as its pleasure is brief and changeable, it alerts us to its contrary, unchanging pleasure, and the possibility of bodily 'peace'. That pleasure is God. As for worldly ambition, it aspires to an invincible freedom of action, out of pride, Adam's sin. We can indeed realize such freedom, but only by submitting to God's laws and 'imitating' His power with love. Curiosity, likewise, seeks knowledge, but it is misplaced knowledge. True knowledge is wisdom guided by the scriptures. This structure of sin and its misplaced aims will underlie the *Confessions*' analysis of Augustine's sins, from his youthful theft of pears, aspiring to equal God's power, to their tenth book's exploration of his sinful self, 'what I am'.[31]

In *On True Religion*, he stands back and, for the first time in his writings, sets the soul's instability in the context of Adam's first sin. Because of Adam's misplaced choice, we, his heirs, are drawn to fleeting, worthless ends. Instead of them, we should turn inwards and aspire upwards, to God. As he had explained to Caelestinus in a recent letter, there is an orderly hierarchy between body and soul. The body, being inferior, must submit to the soul, which is placed midway in God's 'order'. Unlike the body, it can therefore 'turn' or convert to God, the summit above it. By turning inwards, we can ascend to God, not descend into sins. We put off the old man, in Paul's optimistic metaphor, and become the new.[32] We must pass beyond our reasoning soul; we must transcend it and aspire to 'where the very light of our reason is lit up'. That source is God: He is the absolute Truth and Being whose traces are present in our minds already. He is the opposite of fleeting, transitory goods. In *True Religion*, Augustine identifies this Absolute Being with the personal God of Scripture, the One who stated as much to Moses when, from the Burning Bush, He proclaimed the enigmatic words, 'I am [the One] who I am.' For the first time in his writings, he uses this awesome text on God as 'Being', the one which his confessions relate to his ascent to God in Milan.

This ascent is possible for the soul because the inner mind, he believes, has the 'image', or imprint, of God's triple qualities (Being, Truth and Love). More than a decade later, his major work on the Trinity will explore this parallelism between God and His 'image' in each of us. Seven stages mark out the soul's progress, but it now needs 'temporal medicine' while on their ladder. This medicine is twofold: authority, which must precede reason, and grace, 'by which the soul is 'reconciled' to God.

Their role relates to his changed circumstances since 386. The Church is the 'Church Universal', as it is known, he observes, both by its members and by those outside it: it is not north Africa's other Church, the one which is called 'Donatist', but only by outsiders. The Church Universal is linked by a core of shared rites which are common to all peoples. As for the scriptures, they communicate God's hidden meaning. They are like the mud-plaster which Christ in the Gospels applied to the man born blind: beneath an outer coating they contain Christ's healing saliva. To discern it, we must apply the mental intelligence which God has given us. We must not bury this mental gift nor wrap it in a handkerchief, like the unwise hoarders in Jesus's parable of the Talents. These readings of items in the Gospel may seem startling, but they were shaped by Augustine's continued reading of Latin Christian Fathers.[33]

On True Religion had begun from discussions in Milan in 386. It shows that Augustine's thinking and aspirations have remained mystical throughout the subsequent four to five years. However, the final stage has now shifted. It will only be fully realized in the next life: 'nobody, indeed, in this life can live as a new and heavenly man', not even those 'great and good' who had once seemed to Augustine, newly baptized, to be able to do so.[34] The presence of 'original sin' postpones the necessary full cleansing of the soul. In the preparation for it, ideas of order and hierarchy still shape his entire thinking, but with another revealing twist. Just as the body must submit to the soul, its superior, so some people are placed 'above', by a correct use of their gifts. Those 'above' must help 'those below', who, in turn, must help those 'even lower'. Augustine's guidance of the brethren at Thagaste is, on this view, a precondition of his being helped by his own superior, Christ. Properly orientated, we will then love correctly, loving 'God and our neighbours'. However, as ever, we must not love somebody possessively nor even love a son as 'our' son. We must love only what links him to God and, by loving him, we must help this link to take effect.[35] In the *Confessions*, Augustine will present his relation to Monnica in this light. It is harder to believe that he looked on the recent death of his son, Adeodatus, only in the way he proposes.

Whatever would the opponents whom he targeted have made of this assured treatise? In older age Plato had indeed written that chastity was a supreme virtue and that he could see no way of enforcing it except by instilling the fear of God.[36] Christians, he might reply, had done exactly that. He would rebel, however, against the claim that he needed to change 'only a few words' in order to become a Christian himself. The 'few words' required him to accept something which, to him, would have been wholly preposterous: a resurrection of the body.

The polemic would not exactly persuade Manichaeans, either. Their 'three seals' curbed the scope of sin and evil, but sin goes far wider than a simplified trio of basic lusts. There are hundreds of sins, they believed, seething inside us from the Kingdom of Darkness. Manichaeans also aspired to return to Him. At their great spring festival, the very steps on the ceremony platform, or *Bēma*, symbolized the soul's ascent and return to Him. The soul could return because, quite literally, it was a fragment of God's own substance.[37] As for Augustine's allegories of scriptural texts, they would regard them as nonsense. The use of typology would seem no better: nothing in the Old Testament predicted anything in the New. Where, too, is the supposed 'order' in this allegedly 'good', created world? Augustine had even misquoted Paul's words to the Romans as if he had written, 'All order is from God.'[38] What is so good about a tidal wave or a famine, those instruments of mass destruction irrespective of their victims' sins? Where, indeed, is the 'will' or the misplaced 'judgement' in much of our basic lust? On seeing a naked, inviting young lover, do we stop to 'judge' or 'will' our actions or give orders to what Paul in a famous text called 'flesh' (Gal. 5.17)? Rabid desire sweeps us on like a tide, surely from the force of Darkness.

The worldly majority would be no more persuaded. The great and the good among them still went in pride and honour to the theatres and the arena. After cheering on the actors and the horses, they returned and rolled over beside their soft young concubines. Happiness, they realized, was not a steady, self-perpetuating state, but one which was to be found, then resought, in compelling multiplicity. Religion for such people was a passive presence, unless something went badly wrong or turned against them. Only then did they need an active means of aversion or explanation, the solaces which religion could provide. They had no sympathy, meanwhile, with what would strike them as monastic piffle about three sinful 'lusts' in their lives.

Augustine's *On True Religion* nonetheless had a remarkable range and confidence. It refuted the Manichees, gave an explanation of evil, engaged with the good and bad in the Platonic books, and explained the steps of an ascent to God and the related importance of the Incarnation. This sequence of moves was exactly the one which he himself had followed in Milan. Six years later, the *Confessions* will describe it biographically. From the vantage point of *On True Religion*, therefore, could he have gone straight on to compose his confessional masterpiece? Many of its elements were already in suspension in his thinking, but others were still only on the surface, the Psalms, the *Confessions*' formative language, and the depths of Paul's epistles, especially his words about grace and freedom.

Near the end of *On True Religion*, Augustine refers again to Paul's cry in Romans 7. For the first time, in a securely datable text, he cites both Paul's question and his answer and sees them as part of his wider struggle. 'Wretched man that I am, who will free me from this body of death?' (Rom. 7.24). In his original Greek, as in our English Bibles, Paul goes on, 'I thank God through Jesus Christ our Lord.' In the Latin translations which Augustine was using, the word 'I thank' had become the mistranslation 'grace' (*gratia*). The word seemed, therefore, to answer Paul's question: in Latin, 'the grace of God through Jesus Christ' would free a sinner from the 'body of death'. This passage would continue to shape Augustine's focus on 'grace' in much of his later thinking, but it was based on an earlier mistake, a fertile misunderstanding by a biblical translator.[39]

The 'grace' of which Paul (in Latin) seemed to be writing delivers us, Augustine now thinks, from pride. Pride deflects us downwards to bodily desires while we are travelling with our body in this life. Our deliverance from them is progressive, not instantaneous, and progress depends on the soul's submission to God. When we are resurrected we will attain full 'peace', but only if it has been our aim already in this life. Reason, therefore, must minimize lust during our life on earth.

There is a programme here for an entire Christian pilgrimage through life, but it is one which still takes relatively little account of the 'dark pools' in the human personality.

In a letter, Augustine remarks that at this very time, in late 390, he was thinking of a period of free time so 'we could get to know the scriptures'.[40] 'We' implies close study with his brethren. By 390/91, his 'answers' to his brethren were indeed beginning to address scriptural problems: as in Rome his focus was shifting decisively from the liberal arts and the disciplines. Throughout the scriptures, Augustine insists, God's wisdom 'reaches mightily from end to end', as the Book of Wisdom says, 'and "disperses" all things sweetly'. However, his own use of the Old Testament is still thin. He cites psalms and the beginning of Genesis, but, except for God's famous words from the Burning Bush, nothing from the narrative books, the Law or the prophets.[41] To ascend further, he will need to engage with very much more in the scriptures' unified 'shade'.

'Be at leisure,' he quotes in *On True Religion*, 'and you will recognize that I am the Lord.' It is a significant misquotation of Psalm 46.10. The word 'leisure' (*otium*) is his own insertion, the word for his contemplative ideal at this time.[42] It was about to be denied him by the real world.

PART V

He became a clergyman. Dear Jesus, how he groaned, how he howled, how he forbade himself food, how he fled from everyone's sight! For the first and only time, he was enraged with his uncle [the bishop who appointed him]. He kept on complaining that he could not bear it.

Jerome, Letter 60, on Nepotianus' ordination

The Country Parson is exceeding exact in his Life, being holy, just, prudent, temperate, bold, grave in all his wayes. And because the two highest points of Life, wherein a Christian is most seen, are Patience, and Mortification; Patience in regard of afflictions, Mortification in regard of lusts and affections, and the stupifying and deading of all the clamorous powers of the soul, therefore he hath throughly studied these, that he may be an absolute Master and commander of himself, for all the purposes which God hath ordained him. Yet in these points he labours most in those things which are most apt to scandalize his Parish.

George Herbert,
A Priest to the Temple (1632), Chapter III

30
The Reluctant Priest

I

Life in his monastic household had taken Augustine far from the lives of Synesius and Libanius at a similar age or similar time. They are reminders of quite other ways of negotiating man's 'triple lusts'. Since the year of Augustine's baptism, Libanius had been enjoying an Indian summer in his mid-seventies, which showed how pride, the pagan classics and worldly ambition did not exclude common human decency or banish efforts on its behalf from a public orator's career. In 387, he was able to invoke the high standing he had come to enjoy with the Emperor Theodosius in order to stop a vandal of a Roman governor from felling the superb cypresses of the god Apollo's famous grove in the hills above Antioch. Promptly, he was accused of treason by malicious enemies.[1] In 386, the year of Augustine's conversion, he had addressed a compelling speech to the same emperor, perhaps for actual delivery to him, on the fearful crowding and abuses in Antioch's city prisons: it remains one of his masterpieces. Next, in 387, during Antioch's fearsome 'Riot of the Statues', he used his contacts with courtiers and visiting commissioners to moderate reprisals against the city and his fellow councillors.[2] He owed his invaluable influence to two of Augustine's sinful 'lusts': 'curiosity', the source of his mastery of pagan texts and public speaking, and 'worldly ambition', which had assured him the favour of the emperor and the relevant officials. Throughout, he remained a tireless correspondent, writing artful references for his pupils to enhance their careers and giving them letters of introduction which they could take, when travelling, to important people known to him abroad and then 'sponge' on them for lodging and food, on the strength of a good word from their old tutor. Letters of reference and the provision of hospitality would eventually occupy Augustine too, but only after his eventual appointment to a bishopric.

At Augustine's same age of thirty-six, Synesius was living proof that Christianity and a commitment to Platonizing philosophy did not have to lead to withdrawal from the world. After returning from his long embassy on his city's behalf in Constantinople, he had followed 'pleasures of the flesh', married and continued to have sex with his wife. He then gave himself soon afterwards to the active military defence of his beloved Libyan countryside against invading tribal raiders, provoked, he said, by the corruption of a Roman military commander who had demoralized the local inhabitants. For seven years, Synesius found himself engaging with these 'terrorist' invaders, whose small warbands aimed to loot and retreat. He himself rode out from the local forts at the head of mounted archers, writing excellent letters afterwards for public circulation and bemoaning the corrupt commander's absence 'from the battlements beside Synesius the philosopher'. The wretch had dared to leave by ship with the payments he had extorted.[3]

Augustine was not to become a warrior-monk. However, as his *On Genesis* and his *On True Religion* show, he was already assured enough to put a wider case for the 'Catholic' Church. *On True Religion* had the fluent prose style of an impressive sermon in waiting. A letter from this very time shows his horizons were not only the state of his own soul. In a significant exchange, he writes to one Antoninus calling him 'your sanctity', a Christian, therefore, but not necessarily a cleric.[4] He thanks him for his praises of Augustine's continuing progress in 'slavery' to God. He even greets Antoninus' little son and hopes that he will grow up in accordance with God's saving precepts. He then gives Antoninus some advice about the 'weaker vessel', his wife. He must either instil in her a 'reasonable fear of God' or nourish her with readings from the scriptures and with serious conversation. If needed, Augustine himself will gladly become involved. A good guide will teach her the 'difference between "a sort of schism" and the one "universal" faith'. Antoninus himself is a 'Catholic' Christian (a 'Universal'), but his wife is inclining to the 'Donatists'. For the first time, Augustine's writings mention the lethal Christian schism in north Africa and even offer to intervene, like a priest in waiting.

Within months, Augustine was to be propelled into a role which his new voice almost seems to be anticipating. It was not, however, to be easy. After the formation of his thinking in the past five years, the next five are the story of an Augustine in action. They too bear significantly on our appreciation of the *Confessions*.

At the turn of the year 390–91, after finishing *True Religion*, he left Thagaste and travelled to the harbour town of Hippo (modern Annaba, in Algeria), nearly fifty miles to the north. Hippo was another ancient foundation, tracing back to Punic settlers a thousand years earlier. It had a huge main square, theatres, baths and an arena for games and bloodsports. As it lay between two rivers, it also had a favoured port, one of the main outlets by which the great cargoes of north African grain were shipped to Rome. It had its own bishop, the elderly Valerius, who was an unusual import into the crowded ranks of episcopal north Africa. In Hippo's port, Greek could always be heard, a language in which visiting sailors swore out loud. Valerius was an immigrant from the Greek-speaking world and he knew no Punic, a fact which limited his appeal in parts of Hippo's hinterland. His Latin was not particularly good, either; nor was his health. He was shrewd, however, and quick to realize how useful Augustine could be.[5]

The reasons for Augustine's journey are known only through his memories many years after the event. Near the end of his life, in a sermon, he recalls for his congregation how he came to Hippo looking for a site 'where I could establish a monastery in which I could live with my brethren'. It would not be a family home, but a monastery in name as well as purpose. Perhaps the brotherly house in Thagaste was now full, but was he still being bothered by compatriots who were wanting him to take up duties in his home town? He recalls that he had come to see a friend whom he hoped to 'win for God' so that 'he would live with us in the monastery', plainly the one to be begun in Hippo. According to Augustine's biographer Possidius, he was yet another Imperial courier, of the same rank, indeed, as Evodius or even Ponticianus, Augustine's fateful visitor in Milan. He had heard about Augustine and wished to talk with him personally. Ever a keen converter of others, Augustine kept on meeting the man, because he was promising from one day to the next that he would indeed take the big decision. He continued to dither, just as Augustine himself had dithered four years earlier.[6]

Augustine recalls that he had been careful to avoid cities in which there was no Catholic bishop. As his letters and texts circulated, his fame was growing and he did not wish to be coerced, like many others, into taking up a bishop's job. As Valerius was the bishop in Hippo, he felt safe enough to go to his church on a Sunday. However, Valerius knew about his talented visitor and began to speak to the congregation of his need for a priest to help him. The people responded by calling for Augustine in repeated acclamations. They pushed him forward from the nave to the bishop's throne, 'grabbing me', Augustine recalls, like a reluctant participant in a modern game show. The 'people', the *plebs*, were adept at chanting, or 'acclaiming', in everyday life, but they had no formal right in the process of selecting a priest. They could only hustle it along. It was Valerius who laid hands on Augustine in order to carry out the sacrament. He had managed a coup, but Augustine was distraught. He burst into tears. Onlookers tried to console him: they thought that he was crying because he had not been made a bishop.[7]

Augustine had not connived in his own choosing. We know as much, because within two months, perhaps less, he recalls his alarmed reactions to his appointment in a remarkable letter which he sent to Valerius himself. 'Force', he writes, had been applied to him and he can only conclude that it had been God's punishment for his sins. Among the storms of everyday Christian life, he had been forced to become the second-in-command of the ship's helm, although he had never even pulled an oar before.[8] As Augustine retained a deep fear of the sea, the image is eloquent about the dangers of being a priest: hence, he explains, his tears at his selection. Previously, he had criticized some of the clergy: was God punishing him for these hard words, he wonders, and forcing him to live among the reality? He certainly did not despise all clerics. In a letter to Nebridius and in his book *On the Ways of the Catholic Church*, he had already expressed admiration for priests who live up to the highest principles while serving a turbulent community. However, ordination made it much harder to maintain high standards. Celibate monks, he had written, act only 'where life is being lived', whereas priests have to act 'where people are learning to live'. He knew he would now confront a very difficult life-class.[9]

As his letter shows, this class promptly turned out to be far more difficult than he expected. He had thought that he knew himself, he writes, but he had underestimated the 'cunning and strength' which his new role required. It was perilous and he could not cope. Although he knew the Christian faith well enough and had a good grasp of some of the scriptures, he did not know how to apply them to the Christians who now confronted him. 'God laughed at me', he writes, in the words of Psalm 36, 'and wanted to show my self to me by real events.' In the *Confessions*, he will tell how God 'laughed' at his misplaced ambitions in Milan and obliged him to confront his true self.[10]

As a result he begs a favour from his bishop, Valerius. Some of the 'brethren', he writes, have already made a request on his behalf and now he wants to add his own entreaty. The very fact of sending a letter implies his willingness to have its case presented to a wider public. His whereabouts are unclear: he was not in Hippo, surely, and perhaps he was back in Thagaste among his 'brethren'. His letter is most insistent, even by the conventions of ancient letter-writing. 'Elderly Valerius' is his 'father'. 'Where is your kindly love?' he implores him. 'Surely you love me?' He even puts words into the mouth of God. Suppose that a piece of Church property was being disputed, he makes God say: surely Augustine would devote himself to saving it, would appear before judges and, if necessary, appeal for a further hearing outside Africa? If so, he would not be accused of the wrong priorities. It would be right, he makes God say, to drop everything for the sake of the laity and go away. If it is right to do so for land, how much more is it right to do so for the good of the people's souls.[11]

'Tell me what I should answer,' Augustine writes to Valerius, 'I beg you . . .' He is a newly appointed priest, but he is manipulating his bishop by asking him to answer what God would say in a lesser case. This ascription of words to God is most audacious, a sign that his crisis is urgent. Only at the end of the *Confessions*, about six years later, will Augustine presume to give words to God again.[12] His letter does not specify the details but it is not the only such letter from a man appointed to his first Church job. In Libya, for all his different lifestyle, Synesius has left one, a pearl among early Christian correspondence. It helps us to see in Augustine's case what had gone wrong, and why.

II

Nearly twenty-five years later, without any awareness of Augustine, Synesius found himself suddenly appointed bishop of the city of Ptolemais in Libya. It was a much grander job than Augustine's priesthood but, like Augustine's, it was the first Church job he had ever held. Although a commander of six years' standing against 'terrorists', he still considered himself a devoted philosopher, or 'lover of wisdom'. The Church appointment caused him, too, the gravest misgivings. We know them, because he wrote about them to his brother, a fellow lover of wisdom and a former student under Hypatia. Usefully, his brother was still in Alexandria, where Synesius intended his letter to circulate and be read by the city's archbishop and his council of clerical advisers.

Before accepting his 'priesthood', he wished to set out points which were non-negotiable and to state how he intended to address them. He could not then be blamed for them if and when he accepted the job.[13]

Synesius emphasizes much which Augustine emphasizes, although neither knew the other and there were no literary conventions for this sort of letter. He writes of his sense of personal failing when confronted with the 'burden' of ordination, his consequent examination of his inner self and his awareness of the temptation of believing others' praises of his merits, when these merits are due to God. Like Augustine, he describes himself as a 'lover of wisdom'. Unlike a bishopric, wisdom, he claims, is a 'light burden', although it is one which his fellow Libyans admire. He presents himself as having to betray this 'love' if he accepts the job. In fact, Synesius was a major landowner, rich and very well-born. He had already proven his worth as an ambassador to the emperor on behalf of his city and as a military commander with years of experience against raiders. His selectors would be more impressed by these worldly talents than by his professed love for Platonizing wisdom.

Like Augustine, Synesius sets a high value on the Christian ministry. He, too, claims to admire those who carry out their priestly duties without allowing their intelligence to be swamped. Nonetheless, like Augustine, he is afraid of the job's demands. An ordained minister does not live 'for himself', he states: he has to make himself available to one and all. Augustine makes the same point to Valerius, quoting Paul, characteristically, in support of it: he is 'not seeking what is useful for myself, but for many, that they may be saved' (1 Cor. 10.33).[14]

Both men are aware that, hitherto, they have lived a life among books while aspiring to God. Whenever Synesius goes into the busy world of the city, he finds that the existing 'stain' of his sins is multiplied. They trouble his conscience, whereas a priest must be above such 'stains' altogether and must eliminate them, indeed, from other people. Unlike Augustine in Thagaste, Synesius has lived a 'mixed' life of books and pleasure. He presents five obstacles to accepting his new job. They are his wife, three philosophical problems and his love of bloodsports.

Up front, Synesius states that he will refuse to part from his wife. After all, Archbishop Theophilus once blessed their marriage. He will certainly not live with her in a secret affair, as it would be impious adultery. He also intends to go on having sex with her. In the Greek East, Councils did not disqualify a man as a bishop if he had married before being ordained. However, Theophilus' predecessors in

Alexandria expressed the fashionable preference for bishops who gave up sex within their marriages when they assumed their role. Synesius refuses to comply. He wants 'lots of fine children': he was to father at least three.

In 390/91, this stipulation was no longer Augustine's concern, but some of the others were more pertinent. Synesius states that he refuses to teach that the soul is born later in time than the body: matters of the soul would then be inferior to bodily ones. Augustine was equally uncertain of the truth about this vexed point and remained so, even at the end of his life. For Synesius, the soul's priority has been 'established demonstrably by rational thinking', the Platonist thinking, he means, which he had learned from Hypatia. Secondly, although he is not troubled by the notion that God created the world, he will not teach that the universe and all its parts will be destroyed simultaneously in a single 'big bang'. Philosophically, he respects laws of nature. He also refuses to believe in a literal resurrection of the body. The notion was an absurdity to all Platonizing thinkers, and Augustine, too, would hesitate long and ponder deeply about its exact nature. Synesius thought it to be a 'holy mystery', but he would not adopt the most literal beliefs about its nature simply for the sake of the Christian 'crowd'. He will 'philosophize at home', he says, 'and mythologize in public'. These 'myths' for the public, he means, will be fictions, like Plato's inspiring 'myths' in his dialogues.[15] They will help Christians who lack sharp sight to move towards the higher truth. Unlike Augustine, Synesius believes that philosophy is beyond the uneducated person's mind. He was not going to dumb down, become a hypocrite or go against his conscience. He would not believe only the lowest common denominator and become a 'people's priest'.

Finally, there were his passions since childhood: weapons and hounds. How could a hunting and shooting enthusiast easily give them up? He had written charmingly on hunting. He had even described how best to outwit an ostrich and lasso it in the Libyan desert. He loved his hounds, he wins our hearts by insisting: must he never take them hunting again? If 'God commanded', he would have to obey Him, as a good bishop must. We do not know if God allowed him to hunt on.[16]

These demands are not 'eccentric', as they have often been described. Synesius had lived a mixed life with several sides to it. He was a Martha, not a Mary. He was a landed upper-class Christian who had paid for the best philosophy teaching but also enjoyed hunting in his Libyan homeland, like many of his class. Even Augustine was aware of the sport's seductions. As a priest, when the 'brethren' asked him to explain the deadening force of 'fleshly habit', he gave hunting as an example. Suppose a man is forbidden to hunt, he states, but hunts nonetheless. Pleasure in it 'steals gradually over the soul' and, as the pleasure has been chosen despite a ban, Augustine shrewdly believes that it is indulged with more shameless delight and becomes much harder for the soul to renounce it. To give it up will cause 'vexation and anguish'.[17]

Synesius would accept a ban on his hunting if necessary, but only a ban from God. From personal observation, he had seen the bitter backbiting which Christian appointments could provoke. As a confident upper-class voice, he decided to set out his position and stay true to his conscience. If his archbishop did not like it, Synesius was rich enough to go into voluntary exile and study philosophy elsewhere. Bishop Theophilus was perhaps not too concerned. As a practical churchman, he was more concerned with such mundane topics as the woman in the Gospels vexed by 'the issue of blood'. Six months passed and he did not even answer his Libyan outlier's letter.[18]

Augustine's problem was different. He was bothered by gaps in his knowledge, not by fears for kennels or a wife. His request to Valerius was for time off to study the scriptures. It was not that he was entirely ignorant of them: his writings at Thagaste are evidence to the contrary. Rather, he wanted to know how to apply them aptly to his new ministry. By praying, 'weeping' (as ever) and reading, he says, he will gain suitable strength of soul for such 'dangerous business'. He asks, therefore, for time off until Easter, perhaps for as much as two months.

Modern scholars have considered him to be undergoing a 'vocational crisis' or needing to 'heal his soul'. In fact, his letter refers to a crisis with even wider dimensions. It is a very serious business, Augustine states, a matter of life and death. 'At this time, above all', priests should not be easy-going and negligent: much, clearly, is at stake. Rearmed with the scriptures, a 'man of God' can 'either minister to ecclesiastical matters which are more orderly, or else', if not, he can at least 'live or die with a good conscience among the wicked'.[19] 'Disorder' and 'wickedness', therefore, have beset Augustine in extreme circumstances. His first attempts at ministering to Hippo's Christians have plainly been a flop.

Augustine does not descend to the details. More must have been at issue than a failure of his voice or so bold a use of allegory in a sermon that plain, blunt Christians walked away from it. His parishioners, he says, had been 'wicked'. One obvious wickedness would be their passion for shows and bloodsports. Another, soon to resurface, would be their devotion to feasting and drinking at the tombs of their saints and martyrs. However, the most evident local source of 'disorder' was the separate Christian community in Hippo, the 'Donatist' Church, which outnumbered Augustine's 'Catholics'. Augustine had never lived with such a predicament in Catholic Thagaste. Hecklers from Hippo's Donatist Church may well have come to challenge their rivals' much-vaunted new preacher and batter him with proof-texts about the Church, its ministers, its martyr feasts and its sacraments. If so, they would have used bits of the Old Testament which Augustine had never studied and to whose topics he had no scriptural answers of his own.[20]

'Are you ordering me to die, Father Valerius?' Augustine asks, revealing the scale of the crisis. Likewise, Synesius recalls how he had preferred death to accepting a bishopric. As an independent aristocrat, he would take on secular assignments, but they were jobs for a short while only. As he observes, he cannot drop in and out of a bishop's job, because it is an appointment for life, and therefore he must sort out his conditions first. Six months after he had been offered the job, he had still received no answer to his letter. He therefore wrote to a fellow 'lover of wisdom' in Alexandria, and told him that he would have to go 'far from Libya' so as to understand the full nature of the post. Only if it was indeed compatible with philosophy would he then take it up: evidently, he was planning to travel to Alexandria to settle his demands with his archbishop.[21] They were settled, in due course, because Synesius reappears as an ordained bishop in Libya. Yet, he still had misgivings, even when in office. When first appointed, he summoned the bishops in his diocese and asked them to go and organize prayers for him in the city, the fields and the village churches. They were to pray that his job would not be a retreat from philosophy, but an ascent to it. They were to pray that he would be a 'philosopher-priest'. If these parish prayers were ever offered, they rank among the most remarkable in history, even in the early Church.[22]

Like Augustine, Synesius had undergone a crisis. Soon after these prayers, he recalls in an address to his fellow bishops how, on first being ordained, he had been 'thoroughly cowardly, as never before'. In private, he repeatedly implored God, falling on his knees and begging Him. He preferred 'death to ordination', but God 'prevailed over me', he insists. He had tried to evade the job with 'all his strength and devices', but both his attempted evasion and his acceptance had been God's will: in Augustinian terms, God's grace had prevailed. One of his elderly priests tried to reassure him that God was indeed his shepherd and that 'the Holy Spirit is joyous and makes those who share in Him joyous too'. Synesius, so this priest said, had been an object of struggle with the demons, but now that he had joined the 'better part', they would not prevail. 'God will not cease to care for a philosopher ordained as His.'[23] Synesius was not persuaded.

Despite the phrases which his letter shares with Augustine's, its account of his drama is not empty rhetoric. Before his audience he was recalling real turmoil and negotiation, and his letter, he knew, would be widely read. Augustine expresses a similar response. Six years later, at the culmination of his confessions' account of 'what I am', he interrupts his praises of Christ as mediator, sent to heal us from sin and despair. At this high point in his prayer, he alludes to just such despair in his own past. 'I had been terrified through and through by my sins and the mass of my wretchedness and I had been agitated in my heart and I had thought of running away into solitude . . .'[24] Augustine is not referring to his conversion in Milan's garden: 'flight' had not been a part of it. Some of his scholars have thought that he is referring to his later appointment as a bishop, but flight was never his reaction to it, as we will see, nor to the controversy which it stirred up. The occasion was his ordination in Hippo whose first crisis he indeed considered to be punishment for his own sins.

Like Synesius, he believed that he was redirected by God and Christ. 'You prevented me and comforted me, saying, "Christ died for all, so that those who live, may no longer live for themselves, but for him who died for all" ' (2 Cor. 5.15). In his crisis, therefore, Augustine read words by Paul and took them, once again, to be words in which Christ, too, addressed him. In Milan's garden, he had been brought to choose celibacy by words from Paul's Letter to the Romans. In north Africa, he was brought to continue his priesthood by words from Christ in Paul's Second Letter to the Corinthians. Once again, he had almost abandoned a career by running away from it. For the past three years, he had been teaching admiring listeners in the setting of a study group in his former home. Now he had to cope with teaching and heckling in the open university of life. His first exposure to it had been fearsome.

31
Sinners and Seekers

I

Strengthened by Paul's words and a sense of God's guidance, Augustine returned to Hippo before Easter with the scriptural resources to resume his job. Like celibacy, the priesthood was to transform the range of his life. For the past five years, he had focused with his housemates on the hope of becoming 'god-like'. In the view of his great modern commentator, James O'Donnell, 'if we must put a moment of conversion somewhere in his story time, this is it'.[1] However, his crucial 'moment of conversion' occurred in Milan, whereas the priesthood was a charge imposed on him, not another conversion which he had chosen. Although conversions are still important in his life, they are conversions which he, the convert, will strive to encourage in others. Neither they nor the priesthood are conversions which will cause himself to regard 'the old way as wrong, the new way as right'.

From the start, Bishop Valerius looked on his new priest as the answer to his prayers. He gave Augustine what he had been seeking, a site for a new monastery. It was very different from his family house in Thagaste: it was a simple house, or sort of shed, in the garden which surrounded the Catholics' church. In north Africa, a church-based monastery was something new, but the idea soon caught on. Some twenty years later, Synesius would found one as a matter of course when taking up his bishopric in Libya. His sister would be installed to head the separate female community. Augustine's sister would head a female community at Hippo, but Augustine himself would never enter it to see her.[2]

Some of the Thagaste brethren transferred to the new garden site, but membership was never confined to them. In due course simpler Christians began to join the garden monastery, not all of them from

Hippo. Some of them were old men, some from a background of vagrancy or labouring. Before long, slaves became members too, but only when offered by their masters: masters being masters, most of these slaves were too old or feeble to work. The garden monastery would soon acquire a very different social profile to the household of brethren back in Thagaste.[3]

For Hippo's Christian majority, it was a deplorable innovation. Donatists complained that it was not scriptural at all: 'show us where the name of "monks" has been written in scripture.' A monastery was at odds with their image of a Church tightly united round 'pure' priests and bishops. Others would fear that it was, underneath, a hotbed of Manichaeism. Its rules are not clear to us, but from later practice in a related community and from the later 'Order' for Augustine's monks, we can infer that its meals were not always vegetarian. Meat, it seems, was permitted in moderation and wine was to be drunk, but perhaps only on specified days in the week.[4] This moderate practice, if followed, distinguished the monks, perhaps deliberately, from the Manichaean Elect, for whom meat and wine were strictly forbidden

The new context of a monastery will divide Augustine ever after between the world of action, as a clergyman, and fraternity, as a monk. Once again, the monks of Egypt are guides to what a life of introspection might continue to entail. While Augustine was with his brethren, another young man from the Latin West, John Cassian, was touring Egypt's desert fathers, from *c.*385 to 399, and attending to their aims and insights. He wrote up his accounts of them only several decades later, but the core of what he recalls is likely to be close to their teachings at the time. Prayers and sessions with the Psalms, he observed, were accompanied by prolonged fasting and constant scrutiny of 'thoughts'.[5] The monks lived on red alert for symptoms of inner turbulence.

The desert fathers were eloquent on the sin of 'greed', or excessive lust. Not only did it cloud 'purity of heart': it fed continuing flickers of sexual desire. For a frank veteran's view of the monastic predicament, John Cassian turns to the sayings of fathers Chaeremon and Theonas. Male chastity, Chaeremon explains, has six stages, from the resistance of 'carnal attack' while awake, through the restricting of any 'movement of the flesh, however simple', to the absence of 'delusion by alluring images of women even when asleep'. As this 'delusion' is not a voluntary choice, it is not 'sinful', but it is nonetheless 'an indication of a desire which is still deeply ingrained'.[6] Its images are 'filthier and more explicit', Theonas believes, in anyone who has made love in their former life. He enlarges on the problem. Unrestrained eating and drinking make it much worse. If a man drinks before going to sleep, he is more likely, the monks observed, to have an erection during the night. If he eats, he is more likely, they believed, to have a wet dream, because too much food produces too much sperm. The body and mind are both involved: if not controlled, the mind conceives erotic fantasies and the body, if unregulated, is ready to overflow. In the elders' opinion a wet dream every four months is the acceptable maximum. A four-monthly dream will originate from essential bodily overflow, not from erotic 'thoughts'.[7]

In the *Confessions*, wet dreams are the first signs of continuing sin which Augustine, aged forty-two, confesses to God in 'what I am'. He does not dwell at length on them. He confesses them as signs of disorderly 'imagining' and of the wide 'gap between the happenings and our will': it matters because it shows that his soul is not fully following him in his conversion, or turning, to God. States of the body do not cause the problem: desires and their fantasies impel the bodily response.[8] God's grace, therefore, can intervene and end them. At the time, Augustine believed that before the Fall Adam and Eve had lived chastely in Paradise. Later, he would argue that they had indeed made love, but Adam's erections had been under the full control of his will, a condition which has eluded his fallen descendants, old and young, albeit in differing ways.[9]

Unlike the monks in Egypt, Augustine's brethren did not bring their sins and 'thoughts' and lay them before their presiding father's penetrating gaze. However, sexual dreams could not remain entirely private. They disqualified a brother from taking the eucharist on the following day, an absence which other brothers would then notice.[10] As Augustine and his 'brethren' were equals before the eye of God, there was a strong belief in the value of intercessory prayer by the entire group for each individual's sins.

As in Thagaste, the group in the garden was not to be sustained by mere friendliness. Friendship was to be its bond, and as ever Augustine's view of it was a high ideal, aspiring to love God in a reciprocal triangle. Here, he risked expecting too much of others. He was not always free to choose, but some of his Hippo brethren proved well able to keep up low standards of human behaviour. One young brother, Antoninus, would turn out to be the biggest disaster in Augustine's career.[11] Somewhat optimistically, Augustine still had in mind the

Apostles' first community in Jerusalem: all recruits to his garden group were to give up their property to the monastery's use. He himself had set the example in Thagaste, and in Hippo there were supposed to be no exceptions. Here, too, the reality turned out, years later, to be rather different.

The aim, at least, was for all funds and assets to be applied to 'each according to his need'. Members must also work, if able, with their hands. Augustine would soon write to advocate regular work for monks, but with due respect for their social backgrounds. Those from better-off homes, he realized, could not be expected to labour like hardened workers.[12] The garden, no doubt, was a prime focus for members' efforts. All over the Mediterranean, monks were becoming known for productive gardening, often in the bleakest of sites. Augustine's brethren would still have to buy necessities in Hippo, but in the surrounding garden they could be of practical use. There were no novices in the community to do the dirty work. If Augustine himself ever gardened, it was surely in Hippo as a priest.

His ordination, therefore, did not require him to break entirely with his recent past. He was to be a monk-priest. It was a novelty in north Africa, but elsewhere the category was more familiar. Some two years after Augustine settled into his garden house, Jerome, now out in the Holy Land, wrote to give advice to just such a person, a newly appointed monk-priest in north Italy. Unlike Augustine, the young man, Nepotianus, was the nephew of the local bishop. Like Augustine, he had been well educated in the liberal arts. He had held down a job in the civil service, but then took to wearing a scratchy shirt of goat's-hair under his tunic. It was a prelude to a greater trial. Before long, he abandoned sex and worldly ambition.[13]

In his letter, Jerome urges the young Nepotianus to keep the scriptures always in his hands. Whatever he teaches must be learned from scripture. The ideal is to become a 'library of Christ'. It is 'the very worst habit in some churches', Jerome remarks, that priests stay silent and do not preach when the bishops are present. Nepotianus, therefore, must preach, but he must not rouse 'clamour' from his congregation. He must not engage in oratorical fireworks. He must be very learned in the scriptures and use them to 'season' his sermons. 'Let the groaning of the congregation then be aroused: let the tears of your hearers be your praises.'[14] Before long, such tears would be Augustine's praise too.

Augustine was to be a priest at Hippo very much in accordance with Jerome's letter. Like the young Nepotianus, he was to be marked out from other priests in north Africa by a plain, dark robe. Augustine indeed armed himself with the scriptures in order to minister to his flock. In his garden community, illiterate recruits were to be taught to read by studying scripture. Psalms were to be sung and prayers offered regularly.[15] As a priest, Nepotianus even took to doing the flowers in church, 'adorning the basilicas and the shrines of the martyrs with varied flowers, the leaves of trees and the young shoots of vines'. Augustine is not known for flower arrangements, but his sermons soon became celebrated. As Valerius knew the practice of Eastern churches, he invited Augustine to preach even when he himself was present. In north Africa, the invitation was an innovation. Truculent upholders of what Jerome was to call the churches' 'very worst habit' complained, but Augustine continued nonetheless.

His monastic base was still combined with travel, always on horseback (without stirrups), but as a priest he would have to engage with Christians outside his own group. In Hippo, he had already been made painfully aware of the Christian majority, or 'Donatists'. Manichaeans were also active in the city. On travels through the diocese, he had to attend to rural sites, where hearers needed assurance that Christ would care for what really mattered: cows and hens. Even in Hippo, his church was only likely to be crowded on one of the big festival days. At other times, it could seem like a stopover for nothing but widows and old ladies.[16] Some of his hearers came there hoping to pick up a girl, as the young Augustine had once hoped for himself. Others came only to please an all-important patron. Some staunchly ordinary Christians, therefore, have walk-on parts as the assumed hearers of Augustine's sermons. They are ardent fans of shows and bloodsports. They argue and litigate over bits of land and family wills. They require absolute fidelity from their wives, but by a familiar 'double standard' are unwilling to impose the same fidelity on their male selves. In several of the local parishes there were priests, as ever, who deserved to be defrocked. Spectacular sinners, therefore, live on through Augustine's writing, the bold cheats who dressed like monks and conned Christians into buying fake relics, or the heroic old man, aged eighty-four, who endured a sexless marriage with his wife, could bear it no longer after twenty-five years and bought himself a musical slave girl for a final duet in bed.[17]

Augustine's audience should not be judged only by such memorable outbursts of sin. The men in it had a strong sense of honour and of justice. They and their womenfolk could be readily roused to tears of compunction. They could also be coaxed onto a straightish, not-too-narrow path. Peter Brown has sketched well the sort of man for whom Augustine had to find a place 'in the Catholic church: a man with a few good works to his name, who slept with his wife, *faute de mieux*, and often just for the pleasure of it; touchy on points of honour, given to vendettas; not a landgrabber, but capable of fighting to keep hold of his own property, though only in the bishop's court; and, for all that, a good Christian in Augustine's sense, "looking on himself as a disgrace, and giving the glory to God".'[18]

Augustine's sermons in Hippo's church are only partial evidence for the laity at prayer.[19] Even on a crowded day, his church's space would contain merely a fraction of the town's population. Beyond it, there was a 'second church', visible in the meetings of ordinary Christians in cemeteries and around the martyr shrines.[20] Their sites were usually located on a city's margins or at a bracing, extra-mural distance. Here, many more Christian families would gather to feast, drink and dance than would come to church on any given Sunday. One focus for their worship would be the dead in their own families, to be honoured near their graves. Another was the abundance of named Christian martyrs. In Hippo, the church claimed to have as many as 220 of them. It tried to centralize their festivals into a single 'martyrs' day' in mid-November and, like most of north Africa, it also honoured the female St Crispina (on 5 December).[21] Throughout his career, Augustine would preach vividly at martyrs' shrines on 'martyrs' days'. Nonetheless, in the cemeteries outside them, Christians liked to celebrate individual martyrs in their own unregulated way. Bishops had to take notice of this 'second Church's' vigour. Away from Hippo, some 150 miles to the west, the cathedral-church at little Tebessa claimed the grave and funerary 'table' of St Crispina herself. While Augustine was a priest at Hippo, this church had been built up and adorned with a big colonnaded square and an approach way which ran past clear pools of water and on through a triumphal arch. It was all the project of Tebessa's bishop.[22]

In his own writings so far, Augustine had not fitted this cult for martyrs into his philosophical universe. Nor had he fully confronted the faith of simple believers, aware though he was of its value. In Tolstoy's *Confession*, a confrontation with 'ordinary' humanity was to be fundamental: 'I looked into the lives of the great masses of people past and present. And I saw that those who understood the meaning of life, who knew how to live and die, were not two or three or ten, but hundreds, thousands, millions . . . And I came to love these people, and the easier it became for me myself to live.'[23] Unlike Tolstoy, Augustine had no need now to find the 'meaning of life', but his increasing engagement with uneducated 'saints' and sinners was to run beside a deepening of his views on original sin and God's grace. His double role, as a monk and a cleric, is a reason for a constant duality in his writings. Always he professes humility and his own abject unworthiness before God, as his 'virtuoso' standard of Christianity impressed on him. However, he remains capable of bruising polemic and tactical involvement for his 'Catholic' Church. Both a 'lamb' and a 'lion', he combines opposites, well suited to his two roles.

II

For the moment, Augustine's pastoral duties were centred on the church services. When he was back again, recharged, in Hippo, Valerius ordered him to instruct the year's crop of 'seekers' as they began to prepare in mid- to late March for baptism at Easter. Fortunately, we still have a sermon which he preached to 'seekers', and although none of his sermons survives with the date and occasion attached to it by its transcribers, this one is almost universally agreed to be Augustine's first to survive. Though brief, it is an underexploited gold mine.[24]

On a first reading, it can seem compressed and bafflingly quick to change topics. However, it has been nicely appreciated as 'more musical than logical' and it needs to be read with an exact understanding of its context. Some ten years later, Augustine would write a short text to show how best to catechize 'raw' beginners. In it, he gives a long and short type of address which can be used for the purpose.[25] His first surviving sermon resembles neither of them, because it addresses a very different audience, 'seekers', already catechized, who had enlisted for baptism. Lent is far advanced and the seekers' bodies have just been inspected for traces of the Devil. They have been exorcized by a sharp blow of Augustine's breath which has 'blown out' the demons. They have stood, meanwhile, on rough goatskins, a north African custom. They have just been blessed in the name of the Trinity. Very soon, at Easter, they will be baptized and known thereafter as the 'faithful'.

At this point Augustine begins by telling them that he and the seekers are new recruits, all in it together. He will sow the seeds, but they must bear fruit. He has prayed and exorcized and, now, they must examine themselves and be contrite. Lively rhythmical phrases lead into some vivid everyday imagery. Faith and its rewards are up for sale, he tells them, like goods at an auction. The hearers must race like athletes in a public arena.[26] A long-hidden side of Augustine's style resurfaces: a popular, sing-song catchiness.

During Lent, as he had heard from Ambrose, seekers for baptism must renounce sex and at baptism they would become new 'children of God'. Augustine duly exploits this progression. Once again, the first letter of 'John' is a guide for him. 'If any man love the world, the love of the Father is not in him,' 'John' had written, before listing the three basic 'lusts'.[27] Augustine tells the seekers to transfer their 'delight', or love, from the world to God. They must put to death their fleshly desires and conquer a Pauline list of vices, whether fornication or covetousness, a vice which includes the worship of idols. They must scrutinize their hearts closely and show humble contrition, as Lent is the time for baptismal candidates' penitence. They must proceed on their journey, as the psalmist proclaims, letting 'tears be your bread day and night'. They are not tears of misery. They are tears sustained sweetly by a longing for God. Onlookers, meanwhile, will say scoffingly, 'Where is your God?' For seekers who had formerly been pagans this warning was especially relevant. All over the squares of Hippo there were statues of the pagan gods, the 'manifest presence' which old Maximus, back in Madauros, had once written to point out to Augustine.[28] To pagan onlookers this motley group of seekers were standing on bits of coarse goatskin, crucifying their sex lives and imagining they were advancing to a God who was nowhere to be seen. To them it would seem most peculiar.

'Do not be disheartened,' Augustine comforts the candidates, always sensitive, like Paul, to the risk of despair among Christians of mixed ability. God will come to them in due course, in the future land of peace where they will see not a localized god of war or healing, but the God of all Creation. They will pass from slavery to freedom, from debt to stability, from Babylon to Jerusalem, the 'two cities' which will later have a major role in his *City of God*.[29] They will leave the present 'power of darkness' for the 'kingdom of light'. Phrases which could have come straight out of his Manichaean past take on a new force in this baptismal setting, one wholly alien to the Manichaeans' Church.

There is a revealing lack of precision in the timescale of the journey which he presents. Seekers had to give up sex and be penitent throughout the weeks until their Easter baptism, but Augustine speaks as if they must continue on this path for life. Meanwhile, they are lying in the womb, he tells them, and must not hasten in impatience their birth down the still-narrow birth canal of Mother Church. This imagery of 'rebirth' in the baptismal pool was one which he had heard from Ambrose and which the *Confessions* will repeat.[30] Only then will they gain a new Mother, the Church, and a new Father, God, and leave their previous parents behind. Earthly parents, Augustine states, procreate us into 'eternal punishment because of the ancient guilt', a clear statement of the original sin which Adam's fall had imparted. A new birth as children of God and the Church will 'regenerate' the seekers and cause the 'punishment and guilt' to persist no longer. When washing the venom from Augustine's feet before baptism, Ambrose had presumably told him much the same.

In a pre-baptismal context, Augustine did not need to consider whether 'original sin' was really effaced for ever by the rite. He quotes Psalm 23 to support the idea of 'regeneration' and returns to moral exhortation. The seekers had been standing on goatskins, and henceforward they must continue to trample on coarse 'vices and skins of goats', especially sexual sins. Their journey would be a long one, and once again he describes it in the imagery of six steps, or stages, which he links to the six ages of man. Each step will bring out a new quality, from innocence through courage to a wise old age, suiting the moral context of his address. Each is carried forward to the sixth step cumulatively, before the seventh step, perpetual rest and quiet in eternal life.[31] Six years later, the *Confessions*' finale will use words of the same baptismal Psalm 23 and commend the same 'journey' and 'bread of tears' towards the same goal of eternal repose. To the candidates, Augustine, the monk-priest, speaks as if the Lenten self-scrutiny, the tears and renunciation must last lifelong. Ever conscious of his own conversion, he urges them to a similar one. His exhortation, like Ambrose's, is for life, not just for Lent.

This brief sermon quotes the psalmists seventeen times in all, a clear reminder of their increasing centrality in Augustine's life. As in Verecundus' villa, their words are taken to be addressing contexts quite different from those which we assign to the original Hebrew text. One psalmist, Augustine states, was speaking when 'fleshly desire' had already been conquered. Another is encouraging us to cry out with a chaste heart, when he says, 'It is good for me to adhere to my God.' He understands them to be speaking prophetically for Christian chastity.[32] The seekers are to turn and convert, but the dynamics are significant.

They can buy faith at bargain prices, a gratifying 'favour' (a literal Latin *gratia*) which is available to them 'free gratis'. By a wider, divine 'grace', however, God will help them to conquer the world. 'Run to Him and be converted, for it is He who brings back those who have turned away.' 'A-version' will become 'con-version', as God comes to meet His straying children like the gracious father of the Prodigal Son.[33]

Once again, Augustine is interpreting his Christian hearers' lives by interpretations of scripture and, at the same time, interpreting scripture by his hearers' predicaments. The *Confessions* will be driven by precisely this interplay. In them, the psalmists will speak to Augustine himself, the prodigal son whom God has brought back and in His grace 'converted' when he had so prodigally 'a-verted' and turned away.

Bishop Valerius is unlikely to have exhorted previous baptismal 'seekers' in Hippo with such a dense and high-pitched speech. No doubt they included people from the city's port and from the surrounding farms. They cannot have imagined they were hearing the first soundings of themes which, six years later, would pattern their priest's confessional masterpiece.

32
Faith and Error

I

Augustine had indeed recovered his confidence. As a priest, he now returned to what had made him a name, his answers to Manichaeans. Then he went into the attack, against Donatists, who had already opposed him, and against Christian practices which his admired Ambrose had not tolerated in Milan. At first sight these initiatives seem a remarkable course for someone who had recently despaired of his new job and who continued to profess his own humility. Adversarial writings then become such a feature of his work that they shape many modern impressions of his personality. Are they symptoms of another 'conversion', it has been suggested, one from patient persuasion to a new future, the targeted use of force? Or are they symptoms of a continuity which goes back, even, to the tensions of 'a violent father and relentless mother'?[1] Rather than presuming to know his hidden past, which Augustine himself knew that he did not, we can at least read what a former friend claimed to make of it. When the schismatic Bishop Vincentius wrote to him in 407/8, he remarked on just such a change in Augustine. In his youth, he said, he had known Augustine as a principled student of literary subjects, but since 'converting to the Christian faith', by which he means being baptized and becoming one of the 'faithful' Christians, Augustine, so he hears from the reports of 'many', has busied himself with 'legal disputations'.[2] However, Vincentius was arguing an artful case, that 'disputations' were regrettable and not really true to Augustine's nature. His point can be corrected. Augustine was never a quiet and uncompetitive student. For nearly twenty years he had competed in 'disputations' to be the best of public speakers, an aim which was beset with hard knocks, as Libanius exemplifies. Winners can be highly sensitive when similar aggression is turned on them. In Carthage, Augustine the former Overturner had hated being overturned. He remains conspicuously sensitive to unsolicited criticism, despite requesting it from many of those to whom he writes. He regards love, nonetheless, as the impulse of his heart and soul and as the ideal of well-directed friendship. Love may not seem particularly evident in his polemics against Donatists and Manichaeans, but he would always see himself as addressing them for their own good, with their relation to God in mind.

Early in his priesthood Augustine addressed a far from aggressive text, *On the Usefulness of Believing*, to someone with whom he had become a Manichaean way back in his youth. Honoratus had known Augustine's passion for 'truth' since the *Hortensius* had fired it in them as young men in Carthage. Unlike Augustine he still believed in Mani's Gospel. He was mocking the 'teaching of the Catholic faith' because it 'commanded' what people should believe. Augustine recalled how he and Honoratus had once fallen in with the Manichaeans 'only' because they spoke with such authority of how they would lead them to God and the truth by using reason, not fear. Neatly, he raises for Honoratus the question he has often pondered in the past six years: the relation of authority to reason, and of both to faith. Honoratus, Augustine thinks, is having doubts. He can solve them, he proposes, by informed study of the scriptures.[3]

Once again, Augustine the convert was aspiring to convert others. He had already written books on the Manichaeans' abuses of Genesis and on the low level of their morals. If Honoratus wanted, he could find more details on these questions there. Instead, *On the Usefulness of Believing* addresses two interconnected issues at a general level. One is the relation of faith and authority to reason and understanding. The other is the interrelation of the Old and New Testaments, a fact which Manichaeans ignore, Augustine says, by 'tearing' and shredding the texts. Some of the argument here is familiar from *On True Religion*, which had also been addressed to a Manichaean. Nonetheless, the text for Honoratus sounds significant new notes.

Faith, Augustine reasserts, has to precede all understanding. Faith must be 'used' as a means, allowing us to attain and 'enjoy' happiness as an end. This important distinction of use and enjoyment had already been explained by him in answer to a question from the Thagaste brethren. As faith rests on authority, the one manifest source of authority, he thinks, is the 'Catholic' Church. Its authority no longer rests on miracles, because, Augustine believes, they do not occur in his own time. As their effect depends on wonder, 'if they were common happenings, they would not cause wonder at all'.[4]

Instead, Honoratus should study the scriptures as a unity and read them in the right way. To do so, he needs to find an expert, Augustine tells him, someone who can show him their various levels of meaning. Augustine states that there are four such methods, a foursome which has not appeared before in his writings. They make up his first-ever theory, or 'hermeneutic', of scripture. Each of them is based on a Greek word ('analogy', 'aetiology' and so forth). They are not paralleled in other authors and do not last for more than two years in his thinking. As they are Greek, the neatest guess is that Augustine had just learned them from his bishop, Greek-speaking Valerius. If so, the shrewd old man will have discussed them with his new priest when he was worrying over how to apply the scriptures to his job.[5]

Halfway through the text Augustine suddenly refers Honoratus at length to his own example. It is a significant use of autobiography. Not only does its content closely anticipate the *Confessions*, Books 5–6. For the first time, a text by Augustine uses his own progress as an example and encouragement to someone else. It will be the explicit aim of his confessing six years later. In *On the Usefulness of Believing* he presents himself as a model whom Honoratus should follow. He tells of his former doubts, just as Honoratus is now having doubts himself. He tells of his own prayers and tears before God and of his finding, significantly, a bishop (Ambrose) whose arguments answered the Manichaeans' abuse of the Old Testament.[6] He stops his own story there, but not because the next episode, the Platonist books and their impact, would seem an embarrassment to his argument. He tells only the part of his life which relates to Honoratus' current predicament. Like Augustine in Milan, the doubting Honoratus needs to find an expert to guide him in the scriptures. The implication is that he needs an Ambrose of his own. Then, like Augustine, he will surely abandon his Manichaeism and surmount doubt.

To this end Honoratus must pray to God 'with groans and even with tears, if possible'. Here, Augustine says that he will be joining the tears of Augustine himself, who had 'groaned and wept' in Milan in his uncertainty.[7] Penitence and self-abasement, he means, are the apt accompaniments of prayer: they will soon accompany his own great prayer, the *Confessions*. Honoratus, he writes, is resolved to attain a 'happy life': he and Augustine had no doubt discussed this aim after reading about it in the *Hortensius*. If so, Augustine hopes that God will 'not desert him' and that Honoratus will join him on the path of wisdom. 'Day and night, I strive to look on Him,' Augustine tells us. He has not lost his mystical aim. However, he now realizes 'often, in tears', that he is unable to do so 'because of my sins and ingrained habits'.[8] It is a revealing insight into his state of mind within months of becoming a priest. He does not mention original sin, but it may be in his mind nonetheless. As *On True Religion* had already explained, a vision of God, the seventh step on the ladder, is attainable only in the next life. It requires the soul to have been cleansed, but the higher the ethical standards which Augustine, striving to be 'perfect', pursued, the further that state receded in his lifetime.

The ancients were well used to texts which deployed general reasoning to urge readers to turn, or convert, to a new course: they were 'protreptic'. Just as the *Hortensius* had been a protreptic text on philosophy, *On the Usefulness of Believing* is a protreptic to Christianity. Like all such letters, Augustine would expect it to be read to others besides its recipient. Soon afterwards, he wrote another reasoned text against Manichaean teaching, *On Two Souls*. It, too, moves at a general level, based on abstract reasoning, not textual controversies. It, too, ends on a protreptic note, appealing to significant others to follow its course.

Again, *On Two Souls* deploys an argument from Augustine's own experience. It begins by stating that he has broken 'the snares' of the Manichaeans and 'at last been restored to the bosom of the Catholic Church'. 'Now, at least', he wants to deplore that 'misery of mine'. He will deplore it with the 'help of God's mercy'. Again, the tone of the *Confessions* is remarkably close here, six years before their composition: the deploring, the misery, the mercy of God relate to the Manichaeans' 'snares', which will be the underlying subject of three of their books about his past.[9] Once again, he presents his own experiences as an example for others, this time by criticizing himself. In the past, he was young, foolish and ignorant. Now, he can supply the questions which he ought to have asked when he first fell in with Manichaeans. Others, he hopes, will learn from his older and wiser self. Just as he had urged Honoratus, they must find an expert to help them to understand the scriptures.

From the very first sentence Augustine makes it clear that he is not still a Manichaean: others in north Africa might indeed have been wondering. Most strikingly, he ends by urging his old and dearest friends since childhood, 'whose minds I have known well', to agree with his own religious faith. He even prays to God 'almighty . . . invisible' not to allow them to dissent from him.[10] He is addressing people whom he himself had won over to Manichaeism in north Africa during his youth. Once again, the text is protreptic. Similarly the *Confessions* will address his fellow brethren and 'slaves of God', encouraging them protreptically to the conversion which Augustine himself had followed.

Both the letter to Honoratus and *On Two Souls* were intended to be copied and sent to other wavering Manichaeans. Twenty-one years later, this same Honoratus would write to Augustine with five questions relating to specific points in the New Testament. Each was relevant to Manichaean teaching. By now, Honoratus the former Manichee had become a Christian hearer, just as Augustine had become in Milan and had urged on him in *On the Usefulness of Believing.*

II

For nearly a year and a half, from spring 391 to late summer 392, Augustine disappears from view as no texts survive to help us. No doubt he continued to preach, to assist old Bishop Valerius and to dispense the sacraments. He also continued to pray, sing psalms and teach among his 'brethren' in the Hippo garden. When he re-emerges, he is once again opposing Manichaeism. This time, fascinatingly, his opponent is a real Manichaean, confronted in a debate.

On Saturday, 28 August 392, an audience gathered in Hippo's Baths of Sossius to listen to the encounter. Augustine had known Fortunatus the Manichaean during his early years in Carthage. Now, the man was a Manichaean priest. He had continued to 'seduce many' in Hippo, Augustine later recalled, and this success was a reason why he was still living in the town.[11] For the first time, we can hear a north African Manichaean in his own words, thanks to the accompanying secretaries: they were taking down the debate in shorthand, the source of its surviving record. The spectators included both 'Donatist' and 'Catholic' Christians. They had sunk their differences in the face of Manichaeism, an even greater threat, and had asked for the debate to be held. Years later, Augustine's younger fellow monk, Possidius, would describe the debate as one about 'the Law'. The word 'Law' was particularly current among Donatists as a word for their Christian religion, a faith with very strong biblical roots.[12] At the time, the mixed Christian audience did not want the debate to become bogged down in bickering over bits of scripture. They wanted to hear the big issues addressed by the use of reason. Augustine had just reasoned in this way for Honoratus' benefit and, again, in his *On Two Souls*. It was an invitation for which he was well equipped.

Once challenged, Fortunatus would not refuse, either. Public debates were a chance for Manichaeans to correct false impressions and put their case at its best.[13] If Fortunatus declined, Augustine's star would continue to rise. Two sombrely clothed celibates thus confronted each other in a public bath-house. Fortunatus was an Elect. He would have eaten nothing before or during the debates and by the second day, a Sunday, he would be fasting all day long. Nonetheless, he was acute.

As in *On Two Souls*, Augustine begins by stating that, once, he had been a Manichaean, but it was all a bad mistake and he had given it up. His first remark leaves the audience in no doubt: 'I now consider to be an error what, previously, I used to think to be the truth.'[14] Some of those present may have been wondering about this very point, after Augustine's Manichaean youth in their city, his disappearance to Italy, his 'sentence' in absence by the governor in Carthage and then his installation at Hippo of a novel sort of community which was said to be living a celibate life. Artfully, Augustine invites Fortunatus to tell him, 'Am I right?' The debate was to turn on three crucial issues: the nature of evil, the nature of the soul and sin, and why, if God is beyond all harm, He responded to the onset of evil? If He is beyond corruption and suffering, why did He react? Six times in all, Augustine would bring the debate back to this crucial point. It was an old weapon, the very same conundrum which Nebridius had posed some ten years earlier in Carthage.

By recent re-readers, the result of the debate has been called into question. Augustine has been considered to be 'badgering' and over-insistent.[15] Some of his points can be queried, at least with our hindsight, and set against a deeper knowledge of what Manichaeans might sometimes believe. However, Fortunatus was evasive and Augustine's insistence was well-founded. It was Fortunatus, not Augustine, who made an unwise answer which he then struggled to retract. He survived the first day, but hardly as the winner. That day's ending, indeed, was over-interpreted by the scribes of the debate. Fortunatus quoted Paul's First Letter to the Corinthians (15.50) to answer Augustine's correct point that in Romans 1.1–4, Paul described Jesus as physically 'born of the seed of David'. The overseers then called a halt because Fortunatus was resorting to scriptural details, not to general principles. Thereupon, the audience divided into small groups and continued to debate among themselves. They wanted a general debate on the big question of 'evil'. In the published proceedings they are said to have discussed 'how far' Fortunatus was saying that the 'word of God' had been 'bound in the race of darkness'.[16] In fact, Fortunatus had said no such thing. Augustine was the one who had referred to it: the secretaries may have interpreted in Augustine's favour what the audience were discussing. Nonetheless, their error does not mean that Fortunatus was winning at the time.

Like Augustine, Fortunatus presents himself with care. He begins by trying to move the debate on to Manichaeans' conduct and wants to start by clearing up scandal and suspicion. He implies that, as a former Hearer, Augustine will surely know that the scandalous rumours are untrue. In reply, Augustine is cautious. He did indeed hear that the Manichaeans celebrated a 'eucharist', but as a mere Hearer, he says, he never witnessed it himself. 'Let it be discussed among your Elect,' he adds, 'if it can be discussed at all', a hint that it is a repulsive secret.[17] This sort of slur was what Fortunatus had most wanted to refute from the former Hearer's own mouth.

For similar reasons, Fortunatus presents himself in as Christian a way as possible. He says nothing about Mani's story of the universe or Primal Man or the demonic origins of plants and animals and their consequences for Elect Manichaeans like himself. Instead, he goes on record referring repeatedly to Christ. He states that he believes in a Trinity: God, the Son and the Holy Spirit. He quotes frequently from Paul's letters and the Gospels, especially John's, the Manichaeans' favourite. He claims that 'we too' accept that Christ was 'in suffering and death' and that He 'descended' into them.[18] He talks of souls' 'reconciliation', of their 'amending their sins', of their sinning 'spontaneously', of the value of 'good works'. He even refers to Christ leading 'souls' back to the heavenly kingdom. Christian hearers had to be alert to realize that he was referring only to souls, not to resurrected bodies.[19]

These apparently Christian assertions are important. They help us to see how the young Christian Augustine, twenty years earlier, could have been won over to Mani's Gospel. Teachers like Fortunatus will have presented it in Christian language. The listeners to the debate may have been surprised: if Manichaeans thought in this way, why were they being persecuted? Fortunatus even claimed that each item in his faith could be 'confirmed by the authority of the scriptures'. The Apostle Paul 'instructs us', he says, and he quotes cleverly selected fragments of Paul to illustrate Mani's teaching. He even quotes the words of John's Jesus, 'No one can come to the Father except through me', and Paul's words on Jesus 'humiliating' Himself and 'making himself subject even to death'. Again, the audience needed to attend very carefully to realize that Fortunatus never called Christ God's Son by Mary and that he said only that He showed 'the likeness of death' in Himself, not a real death at all.[20]

The two debaters had had time to prepare. At one point, Augustine draws on language from Mani's *Letter of Foundation*: had he consulted a text of it again, or was he drawing only on his long-term memory? His own counter-arguments had already circulated in the texts which he had written since his time in Rome. Had Fortunatus troubled to look at them? He makes a point similar to one made by Evodius in Augustine's *On Free Choice*: had its first two books already been circulating, or is the overlap a coincidence?[21] Nebridius' conundrum had already been deployed in Augustine's writings, but Fortunatus did not come forearmed with a good argument against it. Both men seem to have gone into the debate more assured of their own views than prepared against their opponent's.

When they debate the general issues, they make their points of difference very clear. Though abstract, they have important implications. In Fortunatus' view, the soul in each of us is not created by God. It is directly 'from' God and, as a divine substance, it can return to Him. While it is in the body, it is not being punished: 'God's actions are entirely liberating, not condemning', as Fortunatus' most recent defender has well observed.[22] God has not sent the soul into the universe with any 'hostile intent' against it. He sent it as part of His plan to 'set a limit' to evil. The existence of evil is not a problem. It is an eternal substance, like God Himself. God has not created it nor will He ever completely destroy it. God is the 'avenger' of evil, but He is not in any way responsible for it. He has created only the good.

Augustine answers each of these points, much as he has already answered them in his books, especially in those he wrote in Rome in 387/8 on the soul and *On True Religion*. The evil in the world is not a separate, eternal substance. God created the entire universe, not only the good 'part' of it. Evil is explicable in three ways. In general, what seems to us to be 'evil' in the world is not evil at all when seen in its total 'order' and hierarchy. There is, however, the 'evil' of sin and the apparent 'evil' of its punishment. Sin is not God's creation, but the soul is. Contrary to Fortunatus' notions, the soul is not 'from' God. It is weak, as we know from experience; it wavers; its choices are often misguided. This spiritual floating voter is wholly unlike a pure substance from unchanging God. God created the soul with the gift of free choice, but, as Adam promptly exemplified, a soul will often choose very badly. Original sin resulted from a free choice. God then punishes it, with 'evil' in our eyes, but with justice in His.

These two opposing views of the soul entail markedly different views of personal responsibility. Here, the audience would be most engaged with the debate, as we are when we read it. Fortunatus puts Mani's ideas most clearly. Until Adam learned from 'Jesus' the truth of his own composition, there could not be sin at all. Sin began only in the wake of this revealed knowledge.[23] The soul became aware, once again, of its true nature. It continues to be overpowered by the evil, contrary nature in our human make-up, but, as a self-aware soul, it now knows that it should be doing better. It needs to 'confess' these lapses, to outweigh them by good works and then continue. Cleverly, the Manichaeans and Fortunatus could appeal to what their favourite Gospel, John's, stated: 'If I had not come and spoken with them, they would not have sin. But now, because I have come and spoken and they did not wish to believe me, they will not have an excuse for their sinning' (John 15.22).[24]

Such a notion of 'sin' and 'reconciliation' is decidedly limited. As Augustine's *On Two Souls* had recently emphasized, it makes a nonsense of repentance. Augustine seizes on the point and insists that sin is always a choice. Sin cannot be involuntary. Hence God punishes it, always justly, and we, therefore, are responsible for the punishments which we suffer. For Augustine, all sin is rooted in 'lust', or concupiscence, just as John's Gospel states. For Fortunatus, as for Mani himself, the roots of evil are much broader. 'Lust' is only a 'tiny little bit of evil', he states.[25] The entire material universe is evil by its very substance. So are our bodily natures, their sexuality and their demonic desires. This dualism is what Augustine strongly denies.

Against it, repeatedly, he deploys Nebridius' old conundrum. If God cannot be harmed, why did He attack invading evil? Evil could no more damage Him, we might say nowadays, than surrounding disorder and waste-paper can damage the owner of a room. If God could be harmed, and reacted for that reason, then He is not an incorruptible, impassive God. Fortunatus tries to turn this objection against Augustine. If Augustine's God knew in advance that a soul with free will is almost certain to sin, why ever did He send it out into the world, obliging Himself to send Jesus later to 'redeem' it? Is God really so cruel? In support of evil as a pre-existing substance, Fortunatus appeals seductively to dark verses in Paul's epistles. 'The mind of flesh is the enemy of God: for it is not subject to the law of God, nor can it be' (Rom. 8.7). Above all, he quotes two statements by Paul which already have histories in Augustine's own thinking: 'Who shall deliver me out of the body of this death? . . . I myself with the mind serve the law of God, but with the flesh, the law of sin' (Rom. 7.24–5); 'The flesh lusteth against the Spirit and the Spirit against the flesh: for these are contrary to one another' (Gal. 5.11). Could dualism ever have been better stated than by these words of Paul, the Apostle whom Mani acknowledged?[26]

'I recognize' these texts, Augustine replies, as well he might. They were texts, surely, which he had encountered as a Manichaean. The latter two are exactly the texts which the *Confessions* connect with his struggle in Milan against his sexual nature. Already at that time, he had taken them as words which addressed his own dilemma. In his writings since then, he had continued to cite them and ponder them.

To each of Fortunatus' points, Augustine gives a clear answer. Indeed God would know in advance that the human soul is likely to fall into sin, but He is not therefore responsible for its sinning. He was not constrained by an opposed 'necessity'. Like a gardener, we might say nowadays, God was planting a plant which tends, as He knew, to be invasive, but He was not Himself responsible when it lived up to its habits and overran most of the flowerbed. As for the 'mind of the flesh' and the 'law of sin', they are not hostile substances. The words refer to fleshly 'habit'. The soul's free choice indeed confronts very serious obstacles, as we recognize in our daily experience. The soul is descended from Adam and so, like Adam's soul, it is prone to sin. By repetition, sin then becomes a habit in each of us. Yet, crucially, a habit is not a 'substance'. We can always choose to break a habit and replace a bad one with a good one, just as Augustine had chosen to break habit's 'chain' in the garden in Milan.[27]

For Fortunatus, Nebridius' conundrum was very much harder to answer. If God cannot be harmed, why ever did He send out His powers to be captured by the 'race of darkness' and then engage in the long combats of 'middle time' in order to free what He had never needed to dispatch in the first place? If He acted under necessity, He was not God. If He could be harmed, He was not an incorruptible God. For Augustine, such actions were quite different from God's sending Jesus down to suffer in human flesh and save sinners. Their sinning had not been inevitable, but when it occurred, God graciously intervened nonetheless. Fortunatus' replies had not brought Augustine up against an unexpected obstacle here. Augustine had already confronted this question in debate with Evodius in Rome four years earlier; he had an answer, and had already discussed the crucial text by Paul. Fortunatus was not, in that sense, the long-term 'winner' of the debate or the 'shock' which was to change Augustine's subsequent thinking.[28]

Nor was he the winner in the short term. He tried yet again to cite John's Gospel, as if it is God who says, 'I have the power to lay down my soul, and the power to take it up again.' Correctly, Augustine retorted that everyone knows that Christ said these words 'because He was about to suffer and be resurrected'.[29] Repeatedly, he has countered Fortunatus' selective scriptural quotations by putting them in their correct context. Fortunatus then makes a bad slip, saying God was indeed under 'necessity'. Augustine pounces on it, repeating it word for word for inclusion in the shorthand record. He then repeats Nebridius' difficult questions. 'What, then, am I to say?' Fortunatus concludes. Only his modern sympathizers read these words as words of frustration. As Augustine realizes, Fortunatus is now in an impasse. Augustine knows it, because it is exactly the impasse which he himself had once confronted as a Hearer: 'from it,' he says, 'I was admonished by God that I should abandon that error', Mani's 'Gospel'. He even offers to expound to Fortunatus the Catholic faith. Fortunatus does not brush him aside. He goes on record as saying that he will put Augustine's question to his superiors and if they cannot answer it, 'it will be in my considered contemplation' to come to the inquiry which Augustine is promising to give him.[30]

Unless the scribes have misrepresented Fortunatus, he acknowledged his difficulty. He was not convinced that he still had the answer, nor was he weary of being harassed by a repeated 'irrelevancy'. Augustine recalled more than thirty years later that Fortunatus did not become a Catholic, but at least he left Hippo.[31] The laws against Manichaeans had strengthened, but they cannot account for his departure: he had already evaded them for nearly six years. The reason was his public embarrassment. Augustine, by contrast, was soon receiving praise and public credit. It was due, in large part, to his perceived victory in the bath-house.

33
'Not in Rioting and Drunkenness . . .'

I

Six years before, in Verecundus' villa, Augustine had been in such a fragile state that he could not even bear to listen to the arguments of his young pupils if they became heated. Now, he had proved himself the master of a public debate which had been set up as a contest to be won or lost. As Fortunatus had kept on wandering away from what was put to him, Augustine had pressed the hard question, correctly. He won because he was the only priest who had been highly trained as a rhetorical arguer in his youth, had known Manichaeism from inside and had been writing books for the past four years against its errors.

For the next thirteen months, Augustine disappears again from view. He had not been forced by Fortunatus' arguments to go off and rethink his world-view. As before, the gap exists because the *Confessions* give no autobiographical detail about this phase. There is no need to stretch the dates of his writings on either side of this interval in order to reduce it. The Augustine who re-emerges is decidedly different from the Augustine who had been unnerved by ordination and his first encounter with Christians in the raw. Time had indeed passed: it is Augustine, now, who will urge a reshaping of a Christian congregation's conduct.

At an uncertain point between autumn 392 and summer 393, he reappears, answering a letter received from a very superior person, Aurelius, Bishop of Carthage. The two had met once, in poor Innocentius' bedroom in Carthage, and it is possible that they had not met since. Aurelius' letter does not survive, but Augustine's reply is conspicuously keen to play down the effects of unmerited praise. Aurelius' letter may have praised Augustine for his performance against Fortunatus and his continuing skill against Manichaeism. He can hardly have expected the letter which he received back from his younger star.[1]

Augustine begins by respectfully thanking Aurelius for his recent favours to the brethren, including his concession that Alypius should remain among them, evidently at Thagaste. Perhaps there had already been a move to promote Alypius, too, to a priesthood. Thanks to Aurelius, we can infer, Alypius would continue to preside over the housemates in Thagaste while Augustine would preside over the brethren in the garden of Hippo's church. Each community was being headed competently, albeit by two ex-Manichees.[2]

Augustine then makes a proposal that the 'fleshly foulnesses and sicknesses' which are tolerated in the African Church 'should be cured by the grave sword of Church Councils' and by Aurelius' authority as bishop. He wants him to address nothing less than a clean-up of north Africa's most popular form of Christian cult, the honours in churches and cemeteries for martyrs and Christians' family dead. For ordinary believers they were the night-time dates which made the Church's official syllabus bearable. At them, wine flowed freely; food was offered at the little tables in the dead's honour round which 'friends and family' might recline on couches, like guests at a Roman dinner party. There might even be holes in the table to take pourings of wine down into the grave beneath, after which the remainder would be drunk, chilled sometimes in nearby wells of water. There was then rhythmic dancing to notes of the cithara or the ensemble of an entire band while the sexes mixed indiscriminately after nightfall. It was the nearest that Christians came to a good night's clubbing with drinks all round. Inevitably, the celebrations could descend into drunkenness, scandal and dirty songs.[3] They occurred on a martyr's feast day in the calendar, but they also happened 'every day', Augustine remarks. In Italy (but not Rome), he had found that Bishop Ambrose forbade such practices. In Aurelius, he now saw an ally. Like Augustine, Aurelius had visited Italy. He had deplored these excesses while still a deacon, as Augustine reminds him. No doubt, he had complained of them four years earlier when he met Augustine in suffering, bed-ridden Innocentius' house.[4]

Augustine's main proposal is for a ban on riotous feasting in the martyrs' honour. It must be stopped at the tombs of the saints, he urges, in the churches and wherever the eucharist is celebrated. He is opposing drunkenness and disorderly conduct and he does not want celebrations to be held whenever someone chooses. He is not opposing church services which are held in the martyrs' honour, but he would presumably expect them to be limited to the services fixed in the Church calendar. He is at pains to insist that prevention must not be 'harsh' or 'rough' or 'imperious'. It must be done 'in the spirit of gentleness and kindness' which Paul's letters commend. It must be done 'more by teaching than by commanding, more by warning than by threatening', at least for the ordinary Christian crowds. 'Severity' must be applied only to the sins of a 'few': if threats are made, they are regrettable, but are best made by citing scripture, the word of God, which threatens His future vengeance. In that way, he observes, it will be God, not the bishop, who will be issuing the threats. The 'few' to be threatened are the 'spiritual' Christians by whom other Christians will be broken if they apply the 'most gentle but most insistent admonitions'. They are Christian priests and other bishops.[5]

Augustine was not suggesting the use of physical force. He is at pains to insist that the gentlest way is the preferable one, but on a matter so serious he realizes that something verbally more forceful will be needed.[6] He had explained recently to Honoratus that the Old Testament and its 'Law' had used threats because they were appropriate to man's sins at that time. Then Christ had come as a Saviour and replaced the Law with love and gentleness. Now, he detects useful 'threats' in the New Testament too, especially in Paul's letters. The 'pestilence', he advises, of unruly martyr feasts can best be cured by the 'sword' and 'authority' of a Council. Carthage, the big city, must give the lead.

Augustine is not targeting mere sins: he insists that these drinking parties are outright sacrilege. He takes this strong view because of words in scripture, which he cites in a highly significant text, Paul's words to the Romans at 13.13–14: 'not in rioting and drunkenness . . .'[7] They are the very words which he himself had read so fatefully six years before in the garden in Milan. He points out to Aurelius that in it Paul listed three vices which must be curbed: drunken partying, sexual misbehaviour and envious strife. Only one, he observes, is presently being prohibited by the Church: sexual promiscuity and 'impurities' which disqualify Christians from taking the sacraments. The others, drunkenness and rioting and 'contention and envy', continue unchecked.

Once again, Augustine is citing Paul as an authority for Christian practice. Conspicuously, he cites, but does not discuss, the very words which the *Confessions* describe as having had such an impact on his own life: 'put on the Lord Jesus Christ and make not provision for the flesh in its concupiscence'. To Aurelius, he says nothing about their importance in his own past, because it would have distracted from the point at issue, the banning of riotous cult. Later in the letter, he tells Aurelius that there 'are many things in my life and dealings with men which I weep over', but which 'I would not wish to reach you by letter'. Here, he is not, in my view, referring back to his conversion, but to continuing personal failings at the time of writing, weaknesses which are not fit to be included in a letter which would be widely read.[8] His conversion in the garden is one more reticence among others: his silence about it is not historically significant.

From a mere priest in Hippo, such an unsolicited suggestion to Carthage's bishop was not exactly standard practice. After wrapping it in professions of his own humility, he then repeats it in an even bolder form. Ordinary Christians do not only think that their partying 'honours' the martyrs: they also think it is a 'comfort for the dead'. As he says, it must indeed be thought to be effective, but it must not be allowed to be 'extravagant'. Here, despite modern uncertainty, it is clear that Augustine wants to reform not only the honours paid to martyrs, who needed little or no comfort after their glorious death, but also the honours paid by everyday Christians to their own family dead (*suorum*: 'their own').[9]

When Christians died, their deaths and burial places were honoured in a specific sequence of days. A brilliant letter from Synesius, when himself newly ordained, lights up the practice from another angle.[10] In Christian company the rites were often paid on the third and the seventh days, dates with a Christian, scriptural significance. To Synesius' disgust, he had watched a young bride-to-be in his family come only to the third-day celebration of a dead family member. She was dressed in a purple robe, earrings and finery, doubtless, he remarks tartly, so as not to disappoint her own fiancé. She had sat, luxuriously, on a silver-legged chair, complained that the dead man had not died sufficiently before or after her wedding and proclaimed that she would have to miss the seventh day's 'funeral feast', because she would be getting married. Thereupon, she drove off ostentatiously in a carriage drawn by mules at a time when the city's main square was packed with people. Synesius expresses distress at having such a person in his family and sympathizes with her noble and gentlemanly grandfather, a rival, he says, of the legendary old Athenian Cecrops. He ends with a superb sketch of the promiscuity of the girl's mother, an ex-slave, he claims, who had once been the concubine of a rhetor (it could have been the young Augustine . . .) and had ended up, in wrinkled old age, teaching a younger generation of girls how to be tarts like herself. No wonder her daughter did not know how to behave, when the identity of her father was uncertain and her mother was a prostitute.

Such insolent luxury was not all that Augustine had in mind. Families' annual offerings on the date of their members' decease brought food and wine to the little stone tables by the grave where they and their friends would recline and party in their family members' honour. Augustine does not want to ban these offerings altogether, but he wants them too to be tidied up. At present, they are sometimes offered 'with conceit' to those who request them: they are 'sold' for money.[11] He refers, it seems, to proud families who offer food and drink to their own dead and then sell some of it on to others. His proposal is that nothing should be sold. If money is to be offered in a religious rite, it is best given to the poor. Memorials for the dead are not to be banned entirely, but they must be rid of abuses and arrogance.

Augustine's role model, manifestly, is Ambrose. We do not know if Ambrose curbed excessive offerings to the family dead, but he certainly banned partying and private offerings in cemeteries in honour of martyrs. Any gifts involved, he ruled, were to be diverted as gifts to the poor, and the rites were to be celebrated with the eucharist by one of his priests. Augustine's impetus for a ban came from scripture, from reverence for the bishop who had deeply influenced himself, and from his own perfectionist ideals as a monk. He wished to clean up north African practice as Ambrose had once prescribed for his mother, Monnica.

After more disavowals of praise and his instinctive love of it, Augustine asked for Aurelius' elderly priest, Saturninus, to come down to Hippo. He knew him already and together they could discuss and follow through. No answer survives from Aurelius. However, he summoned a Council of north African bishops to meet on 3 October 393. A Council was not a novelty in his diocese. The novelty was the venue. It was to meet, uniquely, in Hippo, Augustine's parish.

II

By a lucky chance, we still have this Council of Hippo's canons, or resolutions. They were preserved by a Council which met four years later in Carthage and had to fill in time. Some of its bishops had arrived early, by mistake, so they busied themselves meanwhile by recording their predecessors' rulings.[12] Thanks to their work, we can address the question of Augustine's role. In 393, had Aurelius called the Council because of his priest Augustine's recent letter?

On the likeliest estimate, only about twenty bishops actually came to

Hippo in October. Nonetheless, they worked hard. There were prayers, speeches and, as usual, a recitation of the Creed. They then passed nearly twice as many canons as the great Greek Council of Nicaea.

The bishops were concerned with internal Christian best practice, not with external society. Suggestions were brought forward, and then they resolved on them. They listed canonical books of scripture, including some which we now call apocryphal. They ruled on details of the liturgy. They regulated the discipline and conduct of bishops and clerics and tidied up problems of title and precedence. A severe sexual ethic was thrust ever further down the Christian hierarchy: church readers, even, had to be brought into line with it. If they were sexually mature, they must marry and stay faithful or else profess chastity. If not, they could not keep their job.[13] 'If a reader has two wives . . .' he must be sacked at once, not, surely, for bigamy, but for remarrying, poor fellow, after his first marriage ended. Women, as ever, needed regulation too. Bishops and priests were not to have access to widows or to virgins unless clergy or 'serious Christians' were present as companions. If consecrated virgins were bereaved of their parent-guardians, a clergyman must commit them to the oversight of 'more serious women', or else they must be made to cohabit together in a community and guard each other 'so that they may not harm the Church's reputation by wandering all over the place': a nunnery was thus accepted as the solution for females' vulnerable chastity. Clerics, too, must be kept within bounds. They are not to move from one church to another and certainly not to go overseas without permission. They are not to be part-timers, earning second incomes as managers of teams of labourers and estates. They are not even to go to the pub: they 'must not enter a tavern for the sake of eating or drinking, unless they are obliged to do so by a journey'.[14]

Laymen's behaviour also needed to be cleaned up. The sons of bishops and clergymen must not give or watch public shows, an interesting comment on their inclinations. The eucharist must not be given to dead bodies, either, and it must be made quite clear to the 'infirmity of the brethren' that the dead cannot possibly be baptized.[15] These rules are not a macabre eccentricity. They address a central concern of ordinary Christians, that a friend or family member might die without Christian preparation and not have the best possible chance in the handicap race for salvation beyond the grave. To simple minds, the simple answer seemed to be to give such persons after death whatever they had been too busy or lax to receive in life.

None of these tidy rules addressed Augustine's proposal about feasts for the dead. Only after twenty-eight rulings did the bishops, at last, come near to it, but they promptly backed off. 'No bishops or clerics,' they ruled, 'may hold a party in a church', unless they happen to need to entertain visitors from elsewhere. The laity are to be 'banned from parties of this sort, as far as possible'.[16] Partying in a church building would take place in honour of martyrs or any other 'special dead' who were buried under the church floor or near the altar. However, a ban on parties in church did not explicitly ban parties in outlying cemeteries, the main locations for the drunken celebrations. Even in the churches and their surrounding precincts, the Council's ban was to apply only 'as far as possible'. Beyond that point, Aurelius and the bishops did not reform excessive offerings to the dead. They did not ban night-time 'clubbing' at martyrs' memorials. If they considered Augustine's proposals, they refused to pursue them. Not for another few years would Aurelius take Carthage's churches down such a route.

The Council at Hippo has sometimes been interpreted as Augustine's idea, proposed perhaps after a visit by Saturninus, in which Aurelius merely followed Augustine's lead. Its origins turn out to be more complex. Its primary business was not Augustine's idea at all. Aurelius had wanted a Council anyway, and, at most, Augustine's letter inspired him to hold one in Hippo: why not invite this clever Augustine to address the bishops and give them plenty to think about? As Augustine had explained, his parishioners did not want him to travel, so the Council would have to be called to Hippo if he was to speak at it. Augustine was invited to address it, not on the 'sacrilege' of martyr parties but on 'Faith and the Creed'. His address was such a success that some of the bishops asked him to circulate the text. It was a carefully considered speech which used formal prose rhythms to help to convey its message.[17]

An address by a priest to a Council was another novelty, but it belonged in a specific context. Councils regularly began with a recitation of the Creed in Latin.[18] Augustine did not need to teach the Creed's contents to his audience. Instead, he reflected on them and the perennial issues which they raise. He made valid points against heretics, including (naturally) Manichaeans and 'Arians' who deny the divinity of God's Son. He dwelt on difficult questions about the Holy Spirit and its divine status and that great complexity, the Trinity. He was fully aware that he and his audience needed to teach and uphold central Christian items against people who were ignorant and contentious. He therefore suggested how to do so. He dwelt on bodily resurrection, an item which is such a 'scandal', he knows, for Christians' pagan critics: he showed how to answer them. The audience was all male, but Christ's virgin birth from Mary could not be sidelined. After all, it was in the Creed. 'We must not allow the very thought of a female womb to undermine our faith,' Augustine assured his masculine hearers. It showed that females, too, could attain salvation. Jesus had not been affected by incubation inside His mother: a sunbeam can shine into the filthiest sewer without being polluted.

Among their rulings, the bishops tightened the boundaries of their 'Catholic' Church in significant ways. The sons of bishops and clerics were not to marry 'gentiles, heretics or schismatics'. Bishops and clerics were not to give or (probably) bequeath their property to 'people who are not Catholic Christians, even if they are blood-relations'. The rules have Donatists in mind, but Catholic clergy, they admit, are in very short supply, and some places in north Africa are entirely bereft of them. As a result, if clergy from the Donatist Church come over to the Catholic Church with their own laity, they are to be received as valid Catholic priests.[19] There was, however, one precondition: defecting Donatists must not have rebaptized any Catholics who had previously joined them. This sort of rebaptism was regarded as a very grave sin, but prayer, unity and love could perhaps surmount what Donatists were doing if they were 'following the authority of their ancestors'. The proposal was potentially controversial, so it was to be put out for consultation to the overseas Church, the one in Rome.[20]

These measures were, as yet, far from extreme. In his speech on the Creed, Augustine also referred to 'schismatics', the Donatists.[21] It was surely with the Council's encouragement that, shortly afterwards, he would engage directly with the schism which was tearing north Africa's Christians in two.

34
Seat of the Scornful

I

At the time of the Hippo Council, the 'Donatist' Christians had recently split within their own ranks. A saga of excommunication and clerical sentencing had broken out around their bishopric in Carthage, setting the bishop against his former deacon.[1] Aurelius cannot have missed the helpful implications for his own 'Catholic' Church. The bishops at Hippo surely discussed the possibilities.

Not long after the Council, Augustine was to apply his talents to yet another literary form: he wrote a popular rhythmic psalm.[2] Under their previous leaders, the Donatists in Hippo could be heard singing psalms of their own. Augustine now composed a reply. Nearly 300 lines long, his *Psalm against the Donatists* begins each of its sections with a letter of the alphabet, running from 'A' to 'V'. The short lines fall into two halves and end with rhyming assonance, usually with the letter 'e'. In his youth Augustine had composed prize-poems in Virgilian hexameters. Now, he deliberately abandoned classical quantitative verse so as to produce a popular chant, a forerunner of our Latin Romance poetry.

Whenever the Donatists sang in their church in Hippo, they could be heard in Augustine's church nearby. His psalm was a retort to them, to be sung by soloists but with a refrain for the congregation at the end of each alphabetic section: 'You who will rejoice in peace, now judge the truth . . .' Augustine had not forgotten his lessons in law court rhetoric. The psalm followed the formal pattern of a legal speech and ended with words from Mother Church to her children, like a family witness brought on to implore the judges at the end of a forensic oration.[3] Simple half-lines, meanwhile, gave a 'history' of the schism, based on a short book written by Optatus some thirty years earlier. Augustine himself had no experience of the past events involved.

His Christians were already adept at chanting and acclaiming. They were features of everyday life for those who ignored their preachers and attended the games and races and chanted in Hippo's arena. Augustine's psalm repeatedly called for 'peace' and 'unity' and even admitted that past wrongs lay on both sides of the schism. However, he also said that the Donatists' claim to be the 'pure' Church, an untainted society of saints, was mistaken. The great net of the Christians had always contained both good fish and bad. Only God would eventually separate them. Despite his psalm's pleas for 'unity' and 'peace', Augustine states that the first Donatists 'handed themselves over to the Devil'. Their present-day followers, meanwhile, are guilty of pride, hypocrisy and false accusations. Pride has bound them 'in the seat of pestilence', the 'seat of the scornful' in modern translations of Psalm 1.[4] The Donatists used the phrase against Catholics, but Augustine's psalm turned it back against themselves.

Such language was far more likely to strengthen the Catholic faithful than ever to win over a half-hearted Donatist. The enemy, it insists, has set 'altar against altar', thereby tearing the Church apart. Manifestly, Augustine's persuasion is one-sided and paper-thin throughout. The popular rhythm did not prevent him from including scriptural texts in support, verses from the Books of Kings on the mixed abilities of ancient Israel and others from the prophet Ezekiel on the example of 'marking' those Israelites who deplored their sinful brethren but (unlike the Donatists) never separated from their company.[5] The law and imagery of the Old Testament already permeated the entire schism. When applying it, Augustine was drawing, as usual, on verses which he had found in his readings in previous Latin Christian writers.

He intended his psalm, he later tells us, for the 'humblest of people, ignorant and unlettered'.[6] Items in it, nonetheless, reappear in a different context, a letter by him to a Donatist bishop, which is also best dated soon after the Hippo Council. At rustic Mutugenna, in Hippo's diocese, this bishop was said to have rebaptized a Catholic deacon who had defected to his Donatist church. Rebaptism, as the Hippo Council recognized, was an intolerable assertion that the baptism of the Catholics' Church was null and void. Augustine had previously ridden out to Mutugenna to verify the scandal on site. The rebaptized deacon was not available, perhaps unsurprisingly, but his parents confirmed that he had indeed become a deacon in the Donatists' church.[7]

Again, Augustine's letter reads on the surface like a masterpiece of heartfelt tact and entreaty. Perhaps the bishop will confirm that he has done no such thing; perhaps he will write a reply and allow their two letters to be read out together. It takes an effort to remember that Augustine is only a recently ordained priest, although addressing an established bishop. He is even writing in his own bishop's absence, without his instructions: other clerics, presumably, had asked articulate Augustine to intervene. He handles the traditional forms of address very deftly. He cannot address this Donatist as his 'bishop', because he is not, nor is he calling him 'Honourable' with the full meaning of that word in mind. Instead, he is 'Your Benevolence', an address which Augustine uses henceforward for other Donatist bishops: it has a hint of 'with all due respect' in English. As a Christian he will also call the bishop 'brother', and if his 'brother' has no objection, he will read out his letter to his own congregation. He will not, however, read it in the presence of soldiers, an unexpected element, the reason for whose presence in Augustine's church escapes us. They are a reminder of how forceful the crisis could become.[8]

At a deeper level, it is doubtful if Augustine expected the bishop to deny the rumour: he had presumably confirmed it in person when he himself visited Mutugenna. As a mere priest, he was most unlikely to receive an answer. His letter's long discussion on the validity of Catholic baptism and the iniquity of rebaptism is intended, rather, for his own faithful on the assumption that the Donatist bishop would not write back. Augustine's hint that he might have read the letter out to 'soldiers' is at least as telling as his assurance that he will not.

'Persuasion' is not quite the word for such a communication: a 'sword coated in honey' is better, a phrase which was later applied to his letters to opponents.[9] In previous months Augustine had been attacking the Manichees to good effect, while professing 'reason' and 'understanding'. Nonetheless, in his *On Two Souls* he had aired the possibility that Manichaeans rank as subhuman, and in the *Confessions* he will call them 'barking' and 'mad'.[10] With Donatists, the persuasion was all in one direction. Augustine gives no serious hint that Donatists might in turn persuade Catholics. It was perhaps in the spring of 394 that he went on the attack against a basic Donatist text, a letter of Donatus himself. In it, Donatus had tried to justify the case for rebaptism. Like the letter, Augustine's retort is lost to us, but it can hardly have confronted a cardinal fact. Rebaptism, deplored by the Hippo Council, had been endorsed by the great African Bishop Cyprian, an authority revered by Augustine's own Catholics since the mid-third century.[11]

II

Once again, there was a spiritual reason for these attacks. Like his Christian superiors, Augustine firmly believed that 'Donatists' were sacrilegious schismatics who were ripping apart the Christian community and thereby blighting their own and their followers' hope of salvation in the life to come. There was no liberal middle way: Donatists rejected the very name 'Donatists' and regarded the self-styled 'Catholic' Church as a minority, created by a wilful schism of its own making.

After his psalm, Augustine's letters fall silent for us, but in summer 394 we know he was present in Carthage.[12] At Hippo, the bishops had ruled that they would hold Councils thenceforward every year. On 26 June 394, in Carthage, they held their next one. Perhaps Augustine was in the city for that reason. When he next appears in action, he is back in Hippo during the month of May, surely May 395. Thanks to one of his most vivid letters, we can at last hear him interrelating with his own congregation in the town. Again, he is on the offensive, but, again, the target is not one of his own choosing.[13]

In 393, Hippo's Council of bishops had banned parties inside church buildings 'so far as possible'. The recent Council in Carthage may well have reiterated the ruling. There was a framework, therefore, for the drama into which Augustine now threw himself. Every year, from 2 to 4 May, Christians in Hippo celebrated 'days of joy' for their dead Bishop Leontius. The older of the town's two big Catholic churches was dedicated to Leontius, its founder and probably its former bishop. He was buried inside it, no doubt by the altar, and after a while he was remembered, perhaps mistakenly, as a martyr. The 'festival of joy' included the usual drinking and partying, but in spring 395 Augustine and Valerius announced that it would not now be held.

From the start, the announcement provoked 'tumult'. Alypius had been with Augustine in Hippo when it began, and when it had run its course Augustine sent him a letter recalling the outcome.[14] Across three days it gives the outlines of no fewer than four of his sermons. It is also evidence for the absence of a single 'Bible' in his textual armoury. In church he reached for one book after another from the hands of the reader who read the day's lesson: Exodus was in one book, Paul's epistles in another, 'Peter's' letters in another.[15] Throughout, Augustine believed that God was guiding him and suggesting his next move. His congregation, meanwhile, contained groups who contradicted him, complained and protested. They were sinners, not saints, but his most spectacular sermon moved them nonetheless to a great gush of tears. They ended up weeping at the 'sacrilegious' commemoration-partying which they had been enjoying for many years.

The scope of this drama has not always been recognized. Augustine was not still trying to ban every possible party in every available cemetery. The 'days of joy' for Leontius were commemoration-parties inside the 'great space of the basilica'. They were celebrated on exactly the same days by Hippo's Christian majority, the 'Donatists', in their own church nearby. Valerius and Augustine were simply applying the rule which the Hippo Council had laid down: no partying inside a church building.

On the first day of Augustine's campaign, the lesson in church happened to include Jesus's words about casting pearls before swine. Augustine elaborated on them, considering them heaven-sent, and made his 'swinish' audience blush at their fondness for partying and drinking.[16] It was perhaps as well that the congregation on this day was very small. Word spread, nonetheless, and stirred up opposition.

On the next day, many more 'swine' came into church, fearing that a reform to their beloved partying was imminent. The lesson for the day happened to be Jesus's cleansing of the Temple. When Augustine stood forward to preach, he began by reciting it all over again. Jesus had cleared the Temple of people who were selling items for its cult: how much more would He have cleared it of drunkards and sinners? Again, his emphasis was on partying inside the church's walls. He had come well prepared with texts. In all scripture, the Jews, he observed, had never been drunk in a place of worship, except in the episode of their Golden Calf. It was a fine flourish. Calling for the Book of Exodus, he read out the story and then added Paul's words on the 'tablets' inscribed in Christians' hearts. Then, 'piling it on', as he himself says, he attacked drunkenness itself. Paul's reproaches to the Corinthians were explicit: Christians should not even eat with people who were drunk. 'By their fruits you will know them,' Augustine quoted from the previous day's lesson, and after citing long lists of sinners in other verses by Paul led a prayer.[17]

This prayer was a virtuoso performance. In it, he evoked humility and the sufferings of Christ, the blows, the spitting on His face, the crown of thorns, the Cross, the blood. It was a chastening picture in words by which Augustine implored his hearers, reminding them of their shared danger. Their plight had been committed to him as their priest, he reminded them, and he was in danger, because he was answerable for them before God in heaven. They must therefore pity him and also remember the revered Valerius. If they went on sinning, God had spoken very clearly in the Psalms of how He would 'visit this iniquity with a rod and with a scourge'. Augustine applied all the 'strength' granted to him and in reply the audience began to weep. 'I did not rouse their tears by my own,' he tells Alypius, 'but I admit that I was overcome by their weeping . . .' Together, Augustine and his audience wept.[18]

At no point had Augustine used allegory, but on the following day protesters were still to be heard. Why change the practice now? Surely the people who had formerly partied for Leontius were Christians nonetheless? What about the Vatican Hill in Rome, where Christians were said to drink and party around St Peter's without any prohibition at all? Augustine tells us that he had prepared himself for an ultimatum. In church, if necessary, he would read Ezekiel's words on the watchman who is blameless if he warns his heedless hearers. Then he would tear his own robe and 'depart'.[19]

We will never know to what lengths he might have taken this departure. Before the morning service, the protesters came to see him. A few words, he tells us, sufficed to convince them, and the day's services could then go ahead without Ezekiel's words being read. Instead, he preached an answer to the main complaints. To 'Why now?' he replied, 'Why wait?' He explained the parties as temporary concessions, formerly made to the crowds of pagans who were joining the Church in previous decades. In this later age, he claimed, the concession had outgrown its purpose. As for the partying around St Peter's, Rome was a very big place which was packed with visitors. It was hard, therefore, for a bishop to exercise control. Instead, hearers should listen to the words of Peter himself, in the letter which bears his name and which attacks drunkenness and the licentious ways of the past. To conclude, Augustine urged his morning congregation to return in the afternoon for yet more readings and for psalms.[20]

The afternoon congregation was even bigger: the campaign was succeeding. Readings and psalms alternated, but when Valerius and Augustine appeared, Valerius asked Augustine, without any warning, to preach yet again. He thanked his hearers and was given a lucky cue by the nearby Donatists. Sounds of revelry and drinking in Leontius' honour became audible from their church: Augustine could thus contrast the orgies of these 'heretics' with the 'spiritual celebration' of his own church. Two verses from Paul's letters emphasized the fate of people who indulge in such a binge. The case was made, thanks, Augustine writes, to God's inspiration. The evening service was then held and Christians, male and female together, stayed on in the church building until dark, singing hymns long after their clergy had left. The chance to sing the Donatists to shame will have helped to motivate them, but there was no scope for a party to begin in the church meanwhile. The clergy's case was won.

Its orchestrator was no shrinking violet, no more than was the author of the anti-Donatist psalm or the writer of the letter to the bishop at Mutugenna. When first writing to Bishop Aurelius and asking for a general ban, Augustine had insisted on as 'gentle' a reproval as possible, with threats only where needed and only from scripture. In his own church, he had not used force, but when opposition began, he had at once used scriptural threats and entreaty. He had picked his way cleverly through scriptures old and new; he had prearranged exactly which scriptural texts he needed, and when. He had won where many others would have failed. His years of training in emotional, improvised rhetoric and his profound personal commitment to his cause had stood him in excellent stead. He had not picked a battle at random: he had been working with his bishop to carry out a Catholic Council's ruling. It had been a 'dangerous' time, he recalled, when the 'ship' very nearly capsized.[21] It also showed how far he had come since his priesthood's disastrous beginning. He knew now how to apply words of scripture to its challenges. It was he, now, who threatened to leave if thwarted, rather than running away when the going seemed tough. Inside the 'lamb' there was indeed a lion.[22]

PART VI

Oh let us not be condemned for what we are.
It is enough to account for what we do.
James Fenton, *Children in Exile* (1982)

What thou lovest well remains,
the rest is dross
What thou lov'st well shall not be reft from thee
What thou lov'st well is thy true heritage
Whose world, or mine or theirs
or is it of none?
Ezra Pound, Canto LXXXI (1948)

35
The Seven Steps

I

The five years of Augustine's priesthood have involved some stirring events, but none of them will feature in the *Confessions* only two years later. When he analyses 'what I am', he confesses sins which relate to his parallel life, his one of prayer, introspection and exposition among fellow monks. To follow him to the conclusion of his masterpiece, I will adapt his own idea of steps towards a spiritual goal. Seven lie ahead, as he always explained, but the seven will now be my concluding chapters, beginning on the 'step' of scripture and then ascending through steps of the Psalms and Paul's letters to three steps which involve him with others, not in good works but in unexpected contacts, scandal and suffering. The seventh remaining step is the one to which Augustine has aspired, contemplation in God's eternal presence. It is the step with which the *Confessions* end.

The first step, one of scripture, relates to the works which Augustine was writing while a priest. Between early 394 and mid-396, he worked on no fewer than seven. Only one, *On Lying*, was not tied wholly to a book of the Bible. He also continued to answer questions from the 'brethren' in his garden monastery, of which some thirty more survive from this phase. Most of them, too, are concerned with problems in scripture.

Five of his texts study texts which Christians still value as central to their faith and worship: the Psalms, Paul's letters and the Sermon on the Mount. Augustine sees in them mystical and penitent meanings which are very strange to their lovers nowadays, but which grow from his readings of Latin Christian predecessors and his own demanding way of life. Far from Hippo's garden, these three parts of scripture had already been items of intense study: they were read, learned and recited by monks in Egypt's communities.[1] Augustine, a monk-priest, had perhaps heard about this monastic precedent, but he was drawn to preach and meditate on them by the monastic context of his own life.

As the *Confessions* are now near, these books are especially important for the thinking which will emerge there. In old age Augustine revisited them, usually in the order in which he had begun them: we can thus place their beginnings, although their exact dates of completion between 394 and 396 remain unknown.[2] At first glance, few of them were long or successful. A 'literal' commentary on Genesis went no further than the first chapters. A commentary on Paul's Epistle to the Romans was given up after engaging with only a small fraction of the text. Nonetheless, in others, Augustine was to achieve his first detailed writing on parts of a Gospel (Matthew's) and his most detailed refutation of the Manichaeans' abuses of biblical proof-texts (*Against Adeimantus*). Only by comparison with the surge which followed, in 396–7, could he ever be said to have had 'writer's block' during these years.[3]

The fullest of these biblical commentaries, nowadays the least studied, is Augustine's interpretation of Matthew's Sermon on the Mount. It is full of interest, especially for the *Confessions*' puzzling final book. Just after Augustine left Milan, Bishop Ambrose had written a long exposition of Luke's Gospel, including the Beatitudes, and by 395 Augustine had read it. Ambrose had begun by discussing the eight Beatitudes in Matthew's Gospel, but then focused almost entirely on Luke's four. He linked both sets of Beatitudes with a familiar foursome, the cardinal virtues of pre-Christian philosophy.[4] Augustine had known these four virtues since reading about them in Cicero's *Hortensius*, but he interpreted the Beatitudes in a more penetrating way.

Ambrose's expositions of Luke had been delivered as sermons in church. Copies then circulated and in due course attracted sharp critical comment from Jerome in the Holy Land: wickedly, but justly, he mocked the book for being 'adorned in bright colours, stolen from other birds'.[5] Augustine had plenty of scope to do better. He chose the longer Beatitudes in Matthew, on which Ambrose had said less, and decided to count them as seven, not eight, because of words he had noted during his expositions of the Psalms. In Psalm 11.6–7, he had read that 'the words of the Lord are pure words, as silver tried by the fire, purged from the earth, refined seven times'. The psalmist stated that he would 'deal confidently' with them. As elsewhere, Augustine assumed the psalmist was being prophetic. His 'dealing confidently' could thus be linked to 'Jesus's teaching with authority', the words which conclude Matthew's version of the Sermon on the Mount. The Lord's words, mentioned in the psalm as 'refined seven times', could be related to the Sermon's seven Beatitudes.[6] They could also be related to the 'seven gifts' of the Holy Spirit, which had been listed prophetically by Isaiah (Isa. 11.2). In his long work on Luke, Ambrose had referred to the 'seven-fold gifts of the Spirit', but had not mentioned them when discussing the Beatitudes themselves.[7] He was not Augustine's source for this ingenious connection, which appears to be his own.

Ambrose had read the Beatitudes as a sequence of steps which were moral, leading from one virtue to another. A different septet had long fascinated Augustine, the seven 'steps' of an ascent to God. He now linked them ingeniously with the Beatitudes and Isaiah's seven gifts of the Spirit. There was also a 'seven' in Matthew's version of the Lord's Prayer, which stands at the end of the Sermon on the Mount. The great Bishop of Carthage, Cyprian, had already analysed the prayer clause by clause.[8] Augustine now broke it into seven sections and worked them into his seven-fold tour de force.

A mystical reading of these Christian cornerstones was not new. Among the monks in Egypt, the Beatitudes underpinned much of their perfectionist ideal. Not only 'Blessed are the poor . . .', but 'Blessed are those who mourn . . .': monks were great weepers and lamenters. 'Blessed are the pure in heart, for they shall see God . . .': monks strove for 'purity of heart', through their constant self-scrutiny and their meditations.[9] The light of a heavenly vision was indeed believed to have shone on the faces of a few of the greatest desert fathers who had attained true purity of heart. Like Augustine, monks chose the Beatitudes of Matthew's, not Luke's, Gospel. In Egypt and the Holy Land, they, too, used them as steps, or stages, on an ascent towards God.[10]

In Greek-speaking western Asia, the Platonizing Christian and mystic Gregory of Nyssa had also recently discussed the Beatitudes and the Lord's Prayer in a spiritual sense. Ambrose knew this work, in which Gregory counted the Beatitudes as eight and saw mystic meaning in the number 'eight'.[11] The book had eluded Augustine because it was in Greek, but he was much taken with number patterns, as his answers to his brethren's questions well show at this time. An allegorical meaning, he explained, was hidden in them.[12] So too, in Christ's Sermon, the mount, he explains, is a symbol of 'justice' and represents the 'height' of His teachings, higher than the Jews' lesser Law on Sinai. 'Heaven' means the soul and the 'earth' means the body, an allegory which will soon reappear in the *Confessions*.[13] As usual, Augustine's 'spiritual' readings were compounded by his use of a Latin translation of a biblical text. He refers occasionally to a Greek word, but he does not address the Gospel's original language systematically. He continues to believe that the scriptures are internally harmonious, unified by the Holy Spirit. He thinks, therefore, that Paul's behaviour must always have been consistent with Jesus's Sermon, even when often it was not.[14]

Out of this 'spiritual' manner of reading comes Augustine's insistence that scripture has a multiplicity of meanings, no one of which can be upheld as the right one so long as each is consistent with God's Truth.[15] It is a view which he had first expressed in 388/9, in his first work on Genesis: the *Confessions* will insist on it at a cardinal moment near their end. For Augustine, each of the Beatitudes corresponds to his recurrent theme, one of the seven steps towards God. The first step, now, is reserved for the 'poor in spirit', whether actually poor or not. The next step involves piety, based on submission to the scriptures. Mercy is the third step; contemplation and peace in the life to come are the seventh step.[16] While Monnica, surely, is on the seventh step in heaven, it is worth asking where Augustine would now place himself. Even when surmounted, each step endures in its climber's experience. Groaning and weeping, Augustine is still among 'those who mourn', but he has also climbed to the fourth step, among those who 'hunger and thirst' while trying, courageously, to free themselves from temptation. He is also on the fifth step, among the 'merciful' who help their weaker brethren and are helped, in turn, by someone more powerful than themselves. As the head of Hippo's garden monastery, Augustine was giving daily help to lesser brethren, while himself obeying his bishop. The fifth step, therefore, is his position. The ideal of a pure heart still lies ahead of him on the sixth step, with the promise of seeing God. Then, on the seventh step, repose and peace in heaven await him. As we can see from their sayings, monks in Egypt were similarly placed, with the same two ideals still beckoning before them.[17]

Since he first explored them in the wake of his baptism, his account of these steps have significantly changed, conforming to Augustine's changed pattern of life. There had been a hint of the change already in Rome as he looked around for a new way of life and then, in works written at Thagaste, it had become clear. In *On the Sermon on the Mount*, the second step involves the study of the scriptures and the humble submission of the soul to their teachings. There is no hint now of the 'liberal arts' as a purification of the soul's eye. Augustine's focus on scripture in his daily life has altered his idea of the ladder of ascent.

The steps, as he now understands them, will be an important pattern in the *Confessions*. Augustine will emphasize humility, the first step, and describe how he learned to submit to the mysteries of scripture, the second step. He then mourns his sins, the third step, continues courageously, the fourth step, and begs for mercy from his fellow sinners, the fifth step. The very words of the Beatitudes are then compressed at the start of the final book.[18] In *On the Sermon*, Augustine discusses at length Jesus's words on 'seeking', 'finding' and 'knocking so that it will be opened'. These very same words occur at the start of the *Confessions* and recur near the end, when Augustine himself meditates on scripture and 'knocks' allegorically on God's house in heaven in search of answers. The answers are then given as gifts of the Spirit, like the meanings which he discerned in the Beatitudes in 394.[19]

On the Sermon envisages a prolonged journey for Christian perfectionists who have renounced temptation and the world. This same journey will unify the *Confessions*. Already, Augustine is describing how Christians' past life rises up like cliffs on either side of their path. It is walled with those most unclassical items, temptations.[20] In order to journey onwards they must befriend their apparent enemy (in *On the Sermon*, God's word in scripture) and seek for help (in the *Confessions*, the help of Christ). They are most likely to receive such help if they show mercy to fellow travellers. They must also confess their sins, but not like the traitor Judas, who never confessed with humility, although he had a 'bad conscience', the phrase's first use in Augustine's works: it will, in turn, soon describe his own conversion.[21] Only when a heart is humble can prayer clean it thoroughly by excluding worldly desire and then it is best 'turned' to receive the light which God is always 'ready to give if we will only take what He has given'. His providence and His grace 'admonish' us by trials, but they also give us the seven gifts of the Spirit, by which we can fulfil the seven Beatitudes. We never deserve these gifts by our own merits, a cardinal principle in Augustine's imminent thinking about grace.[22]

This interplay of inner light and prayer, trials and humility, grace and gifts of the Spirit, will be central to the entire *Confessions*, itself a prayer in progress. In 394, Augustine presents the Beatitudes as the summation of a good Christian life, just as many Christians, at least nominally, still regard them. However, his interpretations are perfectionist and, ultimately, mystical. His monastic setting is essential to his expositions. Parts of *On the Sermon* address concerns of special significance for a small monastic community: anger and its problems and the best ways of correcting and helping a sinful brother.[23] When they discuss the un-monastic questions of marriage and divorce, including the further question of whether wives will have transfigured bodies in the life to come, the exposition is monastic nonetheless. Husbands, Augustine claims, hope very much that their wives will have bodies, because husbands love them, but they show by this hope that they 'hate' sex, because transfigured bodies will not engage in it.[24] Sin, too, is analysed with a perfectionist's discrimination. 'Suggestion' leads to 'delight' (no longer just to 'persuasion') and 'delight' to 'consent', stages which Ambrose had also distinguished, in his case while discussing the Psalms. Augustine even links three types of sin to the three different types of resurrection which are attested in Jesus's miracles in the Gospels. Through Christ, he is implying, we can conquer each of the three types of sin.[25]

Ambrose's exposition of Luke had been devised for sermons to his congregation. Augustine's *On the Sermon* probably began from oral preaching, but much of it would have been preached to members of his monastic garden group, and only bits of it to the mixed Christian membership of Hippo's church. Fellow 'slaves of God' are the people most likely to have then read the text when it was made available as two books. Into its making had gone Ambrose's example, faith in the hidden depths in scripture, the Platonists' ideas on ascent and the choice of a perfectionist life: they are exactly the elements which the *Confessions*, three years later, trace memorably in Augustine's past. Above all, it appeals frequently to the Apostle Paul. He is not Paul the visionary, who encapsulates the 'wisdom' preserved by Platonists, the Paul whom Augustine had recognized to such effect in Milan. During the recent ban on commemoration-dancing, he had been Paul the moral example. As he himself had told the Galatians, 'I beseech you, brethren: be as I am' (Gal. 4.12). Paul, in Augustine's opinion, is a model for a Christian's conduct in harmony with the Beatitudes. He also speaks to Christians' continuing struggles. When he asks in his letter to the Romans, 'Who will set me free from the body of this death?' he is crying out, Augustine believes, to individuals on their journey towards God.[26] The cry, he explains in *On the Sermon*, is the cry of Christians on the third step who are 'mourning' while their body and soul are in conflict. In an answer to his brethren, at around this time, he continues the interpretation.[27] 'Therefore, as for myself,' Paul says, 'with the mind I serve the law of God, but with the flesh, the law of sin.' This struggle is the struggle of Augustine himself, still battling with his sins' impact on his body since his conversion. The text brought Paul yet again into Augustine's personal experience: the *Confessions* will be the clearest testimony to the results.

II

So far from being 'blocked', Augustine's mind was ranging widely and ingeniously, even among his priesthood's practical demands. Before he finished the *On the Sermon on the Mount*, he had also begun to dictate expositions of the Psalms. In Verecundus' villa, his first reading of them had been intense, fired by love and even fear. They spoke very powerfully to him and his circumstances. He had continued to read them, and on becoming a priest his first surviving sermon in Lent showed the skill with which he could already interweave phrases from different psalms into a single theme. During his priesthood, he intensified what he had well begun. It is the next step in his progress to the *Confessions*, as the language and imagery of the Psalms had to become the 'formulae' for their oral composition.

This resource was only to be acquired by close, detailed labour. From 393/4 onwards, Augustine embarked on the massive undertaking of expounding each psalm, verse by verse. The first thirty-two expositions were finished before the end of his priesthood in summer 396. They were delivered orally and taken down by copyists in shorthand, like the *Confessions* soon afterwards. They are an extraordinary achievement. Phrase by phrase, and never more than two verses at a time, Augustine patiently considers the meanings which can be discerned. The first eleven expositions are a distinct group. They detect several voices in each psalm and offer alternative interpretations, whereas the next twenty-one proceed more simply and comment more briefly. Their audiences, therefore, differed.[28] The first eleven are best explained as expositions for the brethren in Augustine's garden monastery, where a cycle of Psalms 1–11 may have been integral to their daily worship. The next twenty-one address 'brothers and sisters' and were probably intended for Hippo's church as a whole. They were delivered after the singing of the psalm by a soloist, to which the congregation sang one verse as a response.*

The expositions thus span the same two audiences as *On the Sermon on the Mount*, the work in progress when they began. In the wider world, they would not convince critical experts. When Jerome looked at some of them, he dismissed them as superficial 'little commentaries'.[29]

* Augustine's psalter numbered the Hebrew psalms 9 and 10 as one psalm. His numbering of Psalms 9B to 147 is therefore one short of the numbering in modern bibles, which I have followed so far. The rest of this chapter follows his numbering so as to match his *Expositions*.

Unlike Jerome, Augustine still knew no Hebrew. His commentaries on the first nine psalms refer six times to words in their Greek text, but he has evidently taken these references from a handbook, not from his own reading of the Greek. He himself was commenting on a Latin text, not even the one which was used by Ambrose in Milan. In Charles Kingsley's *Hypatia*, the Jew Raphael listens and marvels in a rustic shelter while Augustine expounds a psalm to Synesius' fellow huntsmen. 'The common sense of David seemed to evaporate in mysticism . . . He was treating David as ill as Hypatia used to treat Homer . . .' Augustine applied allegory to each psalm, but when he gave a mystical exposition, it was not quite as Kingsley expressed it.

As he considers the explanations of each word, his youthful training in grammar and rhetoric comes to life before us. He sees important meanings in a change of tense or in the use of a word as a part, he thinks, for an unstated whole. He considers carefully who may be speaking in the text and in what person. However, his rhetorical training was not driving his interpretation. No grammarian or rhetor ever applied these tools so boldly. The Psalms were profoundly religious texts, needing profound religious understanding. Like Ambrose and others before him, Augustine considered the psalmists to be prophetic and to be guided, therefore, by the Holy Spirit. In Luke's Gospel, the risen Christ had explained to the disciples how the Psalms related to Himself. While dying on the Cross, He was also said to have applied a psalm to His own person. Following these and other examples, Augustine considered that the psalmists spoke of Christ or even that Christ or God was speaking in their words. Ambrose had understood the Psalms similarly and had centred his readings of them on Christ: 'Christ is all things to us,' he would state to his awed hearers. Augustine had certainly read Ambrose's expositions, even if he had not heard him preaching on each psalm under consideration. Without any help from the rules of rhetoric, Augustine came to see a complex interrelation between psalmists who were speaking for Christ, for the Church and for individual Christians.[30] In his letters, Paul had used the language of a 'body' to represent the relation of Christians, its 'members', to Christ, their 'head'. Augustine began to expound the Psalms with Paul's help and sometimes to apply the relation of Christ as 'head', the Church as 'body' and Christians as 'members'. The psalmists' words then gained wholly unexpected layers of meaning.

When a psalmist wrote beautifully, 'The Lord is my shepherd', the Lord, for Augustine, is Christ, and the shepherd His Church or 'body'.

When his Psalm 21 begins 'My God, my God, why hast thou forsaken me?', Jesus's use of these words on the Cross causes Augustine to expound the psalm as a text on Christ's salvation and its spreading outwards from the Crucifixion. When he comments for his congregation on their Psalm 30 ('In you, O Lord, have I put my trust . . .'), he assures his audience, who have just sung a response to it, that 'Christ is speaking here in the prophet; no, I will dare to go further and say simply, Christ is speaking.' This type of exposition multiplied the audible words of Christ in ways which were thrilling for his hearers. Through the psalmists Christ was speaking of emotions and tribulations which supplemented those in the Gospel stories. In his Psalm 21, he explained, the speaker, 'Christ' on the cross, spoke both in Adam's name and in the name of this own body. That body was also His Church and so, graphically, 'we were here'.

Augustine's expositions related to the prayers and liturgy of the community around him. They were not 'commentaries' written only in a study. The thoughts and prayers of their first hearers, his brethren, were focused intently on Christ and His presence. In Egypt, monks also believed that they could hear Christ speaking in the Psalms. They listened to them daily, twelve at a time, and would then bow and pray silently and meditate on what Christ and other speakers seemed to be saying to them. The Psalms were a 'mirror' in which they saw themselves. They helped them to understand their own inner 'thoughts' and memories.[31] Augustine's way of reading the text, peculiar though it seems to us, was not peculiar to him at the time. It drew on Ambrose and, through Ambrose, on Origen, the greatest Greek predecessor. Augustine also drew on a recent *Book of Rules* for interpreting scripture, composed by Tyconius, a dissident Donatist in Africa.[32] Up in Verecundus' villa, he had read Psalm 4 as an attack on Manichaeans. His *Expositions of the Psalms* now include attacks on Donatists too. Their leaders are fierce 'teeth' who tear the body of Christ and put poison in the milk of their childlike followers. While expounding Psalm 10, Augustine proposes that it should be sung against the 'heretics' who are inciting 'Catholics' to abandon the sinners in their 'Catholic' Church and come over to their 'Donatist' Church instead.[33] In his letters, meanwhile, he was making feline offers of discussion and dialogue to prominent Donatists in Hippo's diocese.

For readers of the *Confessions*, the *Expositions* are an anticipation of much which will feature there. As in Verecundus' villa, Augustine reads whole psalms as the cry of a penitent convert: his confessions will weave together language from the psalmists to express the trials and hopes of his own conversion. He expounds Psalm 6 as the cry of an individual soul which is condemning the pleasures of the flesh but which cannot surmount them without healing: perhaps he had already understood it in that way by night in Verecundus' villa. 'I have toiled in my groaning and I will wash my bed with tears every night.' Proceeding word by word, Augustine finds the tenses of the verbs to be suggestive.[34] First, groans have been in vain, but, now, tears will be more effective until 'In the morning I will stand before you and contemplate you.' The psalm thus traces a convert's progress which is like Augustine's own, both of them aspiring to the contemplation of God. Psalmists testify to the emotions and the difficulties of conversion.

If the psalmists are taken to be 'converts', confessing becomes an important part of their progress. They confess God's justice (Ps. 7.18: 'I will confess to the Lord in accordance with his justice'). Confessing, Augustine explains, is twofold, of sin or of praise. 'When things are going badly for us, in the midst of our tribulations, let us confess our sins; when things are going well for us, in our joy at God's righteousness, let us confess praise to God. Only, let us never give up confession' (his exposition of Ps. 29.10). The double dynamic of the *Confessions* is already present here, fixed in his mind through the Psalms.

So is the *Confessions*' underlying structure, a journey towards God's presence. Words in our Psalm 24 ('I have been waiting for you all day long': verse 5) remind Augustine that 'turned out of paradise by You, and wandering to a far-off country, I cannot return by my own strength unless You come to meet me in my wandering, for my return has been waiting upon Your mercy throughout the whole stretch of earthly time'. Once again, the Prodigal Son sums up the sinner's journey: 'through his humility he wins happiness, showing himself worthy by the very confession of his unworthiness' (Expos. 2 on Ps. 18), a model which Augustine will soon apply in the *Confessions* to his own prodigal self. 'One thing have I begged of the Lord, to live in the Lord's house all the days of my life, that I may contemplate the Lord's delight . . .' (Ps. 26.4): the words, Augustine thinks, express the hope that 'the delightful vision may appear to me, that I may see God face to face', exactly the hope which he will express at the end of the *Confessions*. Meanwhile, 'look upon my humility and my toil and forgive all my sins' (Ps. 24.18): they are the 'sins of my youth and ignorance, before I believed' (the sins of *Confessions*, Books 1–8), but also sins 'even now when I live by faith, whether through weakness or the dark clouds which obscure this life' (the sins of *Confessions*, Book 10, 'what I am').

Throughout, the Psalms are considered to exemplify that a Christian's life must be one of humility: 'You, Lord, redeem us that we may turn to You and help us that we may reach You', soon to be the keynote of the *Confessions*. The proud, by contrast, are habitual sinners whose minds are 'beaten back by the light of truth, because of the darkness of their own sins' (on Ps. 5.6): so, too, Augustine's mind had been 'beaten back' by God during his ascents to Him in Milan. The 'way of humility' 'is not to be found in the books of pagans or Manichaeans' (on Ps. 31), as the *Confessions* will also reiterate. It comes only from Christ. 'Be my helper, I beg: do not forsake me' (on Ps. 26.17): I too am on the way, Augustine explains, and I have received free will, but 'do not trust yourself: if God abandons you, you will stumble, you will fall . . .'

On their journey Christian pilgrims must think of the Apostle Peter when Jesus commanded him to walk towards Him on the water. Peter 'went bravely, trusting in the Lord', but when he began to sink Jesus stretched out a hand and saved him, hearing his cry and reproaching him for his loss of faith. 'Crying to God is not done with the voice, but with the heart . . . If you cry to God, cry inside yourself, where God hears': exactly this inner 'cry of the heart' had been expounded by Ambrose, and will soon shape the *Confessions*' form.[35] It must come from a humble, contrite heart, whose merits are not its own. 'Let him who boasts,' as Paul had written, 'boast only in the Lord' (1 Cor. 1.31), a text which will become centrally important in Augustine's writings and thinking as the *Confessions* draw near.[36]

While Augustine expounds the Psalms, one by one, phrase by phrase, he proposes multiple meanings, none of which is superior to the other. The Augustine whom we hear is quite unlike the 'dogmatic' Augustine of modern popular stereotypes. As the *Confessions* progress, they too will emphasize the existence of multiple meanings in scripture, none of which can be said by us to be more true than another so long as they are consistent with God's Truth. The *Confessions* have been described as 'an amplified psalter'. His expositions allow us to see him assembling the script and tone for their imminent broadcast.

36
Paul and Lazarus

While the expositions of the Psalms were going ahead, Augustine progressed to the next step on his path to the *Confessions*: close engagement with Paul's epistles. As ever, Paul had the power to transform people's aims and self-image. In later sermons, Augustine would even present himself as talking to Paul in person.[1] This sense of Paul's immediacy was not unique to him, even 300 years or so after Paul's death. In this same period, Libanius' pupil John Chrysostom was describing himself to his Christian congregation in Antioch as called by Paul's 'spiritual trumpet' and 'warmed with desire, recognizing the voice that is dear to me'.[2] This living 'voice' was now to lead Augustine to some new, but hard-won, conclusions.

Augustine had first become closely aware of phrases in Paul's letters during his nine years with the Manichaeans. In Milan, Paul's words were essential to his development, culminating in his conversion in the garden. Four years later, he was strengthened to persist in his priesthood by a sentence from Paul in which, he believed, its subject, Christ, spoke. Only now, from summer 394 to summer 396, does he comment in detail on parts of Paul's letters. First, he expounds statements in Romans, and then he expounds all of Galatians. At the same time, problems in Romans appear among his answers to questions posed by his monastic brethren. He then began a full commentary on Romans, but found it, he later recalled, 'too difficult'. After commenting on the opening verses and claiming to discover the Trinity in them, he gave up.

This renewed engagement with Paul was still in progress while Augustine was engaged with banning the partying of his parishioners in Hippo: texts by Paul were one of his major weapons in that contest. The eventual outcome of his engagement would be a new and deeper understanding of the role of God's 'grace' and His 'separation' of saints and sinners. This understanding will then shape Augustine's presentation of man's turning from darkness to light in the *Confessions*' final book and God's separation of the wicked from the faithful. In many scholars' opinion, it will also shape the *Confessions*' presentation of his own former life.

The questions on which Augustine now begins to write are questions which would one day engage Luther, his most responsive reader, and underlie the great upheavals of Europe's Reformation. Before embarking on this vexed ground, he had been reading up on the subject. After a long period of interpretative neglect in the Latin West, letters of Paul had been worked on by several Latin commentators since the 350s. They included Ambrose and the famed Marius Victorinus, both of whom Augustine read before forming his own opinions. In north Africa, the dissident Donatist Tyconius had engaged closely with Paul. Away in the Holy Land, Jerome had also commented on him, including on his letter to the Galatians.[3]

This surge of Latin Christian interest in Paul was not surprising. He could be enlisted in the West's arguments over the Trinity and Christ's relation to God. He had also written of the battle between 'flesh' and 'spirit'. The historical Paul had left no text about the renunciation of riches, but Augustine and his contemporaries considered the epistles to Timothy to be by Paul himself, and the first one stated firmly that 'the love of money is a root of all evil' and that 'those who desire to be rich fall into a temptation and a snare' (1 Tim. 6.9–10). Paul had also undergone a profound conversion and had written on marriage and virginity. Unlike Peter, he was not known to have married. These themes made him especially relevant to the West's new age of aspiring perfectionists. He had also founded and guided the first Gentile Churches. He was therefore a role model for Gentile Christian conduct, especially for anyone who found himself at the head of one of the West's new monastic groups. Meanwhile, Manichaeans were appealing to selected phrases in the epistles, making their interpretation an urgent question. In August 392, during their public debate, Fortunatus had tried to unsettle Augustine with well-chosen Pauline quotations. They sounded seductive, as if they endorsed Mani's radical dualism and axis of evil. Prominent among them was that ever-challenging cry, 'O wretched man that I am: who shall deliver me out of the body of this death?', and all that followed it (Rom. 7.23–5).[4]

In his previous writings, Augustine's responses to Paul's predicament had drawn on two main themes: heritage and habit. It is worth recapping them, before his interpretations go deeper. By sinning in

Paradise Adam had lost his effortless 'free choice' and had been punished by losing immortality. This original sin has not only caused our bodies to be made subject to death: our wills too, like Adam's, are easily drawn towards sinful choices. These voluntary sins then become bad habits which are very hard indeed to break.[5] To do so, we need God's grace, and God has made it freely available to us since the life and death of his Son on earth. This 'grace' inspires us with 'God's love' and makes us submissive to God's will. We are thereby freed from the 'law of sin and mortality'. If we so choose, we can turn and become 'converted' to righteousness, not sin. Our 'flesh', Paul wrote, once 'tormented us with punishments while we remained in sin', but in the Resurrection this flesh will be transformed and will no longer 'shake us with any adversity'. In Augustine's opinion, Paul meant 'habits' when he wrote of 'the prudence of the flesh', the 'enemy of God'. Habits can be unfrozen just as snow can be melted into water. The necessary solvents are grace, submission and God's love.[6]

In June 394, Augustine can be watched re-engaging with these questions. It was not, as sometimes suggested, that they had become urgent to him because Fortunatus had cited these passages of Paul to him two years earlier. At the time of their debate, the texts were not new to him and his answers had been fluent enough for Fortunatus to let them pass.[7] Nor was he returning to write on them as part of a carefully defined 'theological project'. He expounded them because Christian brethren happened to question him about them.

Augustine was in Carthage, he later recalls, presumably because a Council was again meeting there, but it happened that 'the Epistle to the Romans' was being read 'among those of us who were together at the time'. 'Brothers' in this reading group then asked him about particular points and requested that 'what I said, should be written down, rather than poured out without being written'. He answered 'to the best of his ability'.[8] The answers, given orally, show the pre-existent depth of his thinking, but without the brethren's questions he might never have set out his thoughts in a text. Some of these brethren had no doubt come with him from Hippo, but others were Christians in Carthage. Reasons for their group's reading of Romans are not specified, but the Manichaean presence is likely to be one. After his defeat in Hippo, Fortunatus may have gone off to Carthage and taught there. Even if he had not, other Manichaeans in Africa will have been using verses from Romans to discomfort 'semi-Christians'. Christian celibates also had reasons of their own for worrying what Paul meant. The 'law of sin', 'the body of death' and his cry for help were of passionate daily interest to them in their attempts to surmount 'lusts'.

Augustine's resulting *Exposition of Romans* conforms to its oral origins. It picks on a verse or two in the epistle, interprets them and then moves on to others. Nonetheless, Augustine considers the epistle to have a central theme: the 'works of the Law' and 'grace'. Among much else which he clarifies, they are the recurring issues and are crystallized, as ever, in Paul's cry at Romans 7.23–5: 'who will set me free from the body of this death?' Augustine is not unusual among Christian 'virtuosi' in focusing on these particular verses. They occur some thirty times in the writings of his contemporary, Jerome, and they also concerned monks in the Egyptian desert. However, their interpretations differed.

For Jerome, Paul's verses signify his struggle against desire and sex, and no further analysis, he thinks, is needed.[9] John Cassian recalls how some of the old desert fathers in Egypt also considered that Paul's words expressed their own condition: Paul's 'law in their members' was what distracted them by 'earthly thoughts' from their aim, the contemplation of God.[10] To Augustine, Paul's words suggested deeper questions of God's grace and its timing for all men. Since his own conversion, these questions had been formulated for him by his careful reading of Christian Latin authors. In 394, he was certainly not discovering the idea of 'grace' for the first time in his life. Mani's Gospel had emphasized God's grace in words which the young Augustine had known very well. Divine grace had been implicit in his villa dialogues, though held there in suspension beside his emphasis on the natural potential of the soul. *On True Religion* had stressed the importance of grace in the soul's reconciliation to God. He had already seen spectacular 'grace' in action, granted to himself when beset with toothache or to poor Innocentius when distraught with pains in the backside. In the north African churches, meanwhile, the festivals of martyrs continued to present him with lively proofs of it.[11]

The novelty is that during his priesthood he began to link grace more subtly to conversion. Two years earlier, he had told Fortunatus that grace 'turns' us, or 'converts' us, to justice from sin. Soon afterwards, at the end of *On Two Souls*, he prayed to God to convert his former Manichaean friends. When reviewing this text later in life, he observes that 'in praying thus, anyway', he was 'already retaining firmly in his faith that those who have converted to God are helped by His grace . . . to be perfected', but also that 'it pertains to the very grace of God itself that they should be converted to God in the first place'. He is quite clear here that he is not reading his subsequent thinking about grace back into the text. He had already prayed at the end of *On Two Souls* for these people's conversion: why else would he have prayed, he observes, if God's grace was not needed for it?[12] If he is right, the link between 'grace' and 'conversion' was already in his mind before many of his modern commentators see it dawning. In *On the Sermon on the Mount* and his *Expositions of the Psalms*, he had also stated explicitly that grace was not 'earned' by deeds.[13] In Carthage, he now links a defined stage of God's grace to conversion: he is prompted to this important step by Paul's complex text in Romans 7.

These questions have left no mark on the writings of his fellow philosopher and bishop, Synesius. There were good reasons for the difference. Synesius was not a monk and had never been a convert, except to philosophy in Hypatia's classes. He had had none of Augustine's prolonged engagement with Manichaeism and with the scriptural problems which it raised. Those problems had made Augustine, but not Synesius, aware of dangers in what Paul had written. As Manichaeans denied the unity of the Old and New Testaments, they seized on anything written by Paul against the 'old' Law. Augustine had recently attacked writings by one of Mani's early disciples, Adeimantus, and answered one by one his arguments that individual verses in the Old Testament were contradictory to verses in the New.[14] As his text had not discussed Paul's words in Romans, he now needed to relate them too to the question of the Bible's unity. He also needed to prevail on a long-contested battlefield, the scope and nature of free will, the item which Manichaeans particularly denied.

In June 394, there were two great puzzles which he had to confront in Paul's epistle. One, of course, was Paul's cry at Romans 7.23–5, complicated by its Latin translator's mistake about 'grace'. Here, he took up a new position. In a recent answer to his brethren, he had interpreted the Gospels' story of the Feeding of the Five Thousand by a fourfold scheme of 'times', one 'before the Law', one 'under the Law', one 'under God's grace' and a fourth, 'the future peace of the heavenly Jerusalem'. He now applied these four time-spans to Paul's cry. He could infer the first three of them by reading verses in Romans 6–7, and it was then easy for him to add a fourth, the life to come.[15]

As a result, Paul's cry for help fell into place for him. First, men had lived without the Law and so they sinned without knowing that they were sinning. Then, through Moses, God imposed a Law which nobody could hope to fulfil unaided. 'Under the Law', therefore, we first became aware that we were sinning and that we were unable to stop. We continued to be drawn by temporal sins of worldly ambition and sex, but, in due course, some of us cried for help. Through Jesus's mission on earth, God made grace available to any sinners who have faith and 'turn' and call to Him. In reply, therefore, He will bestow grace on those who cry out. If we call on Him, we become 'under grace', in the third stage, and our spirit is serving the law of God. Our flesh, however, still reacts to tremors of sin (misplaced hunger, perhaps, and, as ever, sexual dreams and unsolicited desire). Only 'in peace', the fourth stage of the future life, will our transformed and resurrected bodies allow us to be sinless and contemplate God in perfect order.[16]

In this perspective, the Law of the Old Testament becomes a necessary stage in a unified whole. Unable to fulfil it, Christians like Paul and Augustine 'turn' to God with a cry for help: neither Jerome nor the monks in Egypt ever proposed this interpretation of Paul's words. Even then, Augustine states, God's grace does not dispel all obstacles. In *On the Sermon*, Augustine was poised on the fifth step of seven; in his *Exposition of Romans*, he stands on the third step of four. Grace has enabled him not to sin persistently, but he is still subject to ambush by relapses which affect his untransformed flesh.

The question then becomes, which of us calls to God, which of us is helped by Him, and why? At Romans 9.9–14, Paul had already confronted the very hard question in scripture: why ever had God hated the unfortunate Esau?[17] As Paul knew, this hatred had already been remarked by the Hebrew prophet Malachi. It could not have been for anything which Esau had done. God hated Esau in the womb, before he was even born, whereas He loved Jacob at the same stage. As Manichaeans gleefully pointed out, it seemed a most capricious display of hostility and indeed it is one which occurs to few, if any, mothers nowadays, even when pregnant with a child against their wishes. Augustine needed an answer which left free choice open to the likes of the divinely hated Esau when he was born.

This question was not new to inquiring Christian readers. In the mid-third century Origen had already called it 'a famous problem' and recognized that it challenged the value of man's free choice. In 394, Augustine found an answer with the help of recent Latin commentators on Paul, 'Ambrosiaster' and, above all, the dissident Donatist Tyconius.[18] God, he argues, 'hated' Esau because of his 'foreknowledge'. He knew that Esau would not have faith in Him, whereas Jacob would.

Sure enough, when born, Esau had no faith, and he showed it by his exercise of free (but foreseeable) choice. Knowing this lack, God hated him justly in advance.[19] In no way does God's 'admissions policy' relate to His candidates' presubmitted work: it is based on their potential for faith. Those who have faith and turn in humility to God are rewarded with gifts of the Holy Spirit. They receive God's grace, not as a reward for what they have done, but as His gift of pure mercy which enables them then to do good and just works. A modern analogy may clarify the point. Like a parent in a shop who knows his children very well, God knows in advance what each of us will choose to buy: He leaves us to choose nonetheless. Then He bestows a present even greater than we children have expected.

An answer in terms of foreknowledge was not wholly new in Augustine's thinking. In the third and final book of his long text *On Free Choice*, Evodius posed exactly the question which he now addressed. If God knows in advance that we will do this or that, Evodius asked, how can we be responsible for our 'inevitable' choices and actions? The date of this part of *On Free Choice* remains uncertain, because the text was begun in Rome in 388 but only finished in north Africa during Augustine's priesthood.[20] This long third book may be the final section of the composition, written up from discussions with Evodius in north Africa after the *Exposition of Romans* had been finished. As this discussion shows, the answer was not given casually nor thrown off in the course of only one debate. It was reasserted in Augustine's exposition of Galatians. It was also repeated in yet another contemporary answer, one of his eighty-three, to brethren who were asking once again about Romans 7.21.[21]

Augustine's next work, his exposition of Galatians, shows how focused his thinking was becoming. Again, it interrelates with questions posed by his brethren at the time, preserved among the total of eighty-three: whole sections of the exposition of Galatians read like yet more such answers.[22] It regards Paul from several angles, both as an authority for reading the scriptures allegorically and, yet again, for the struggle of 'spirit' and 'flesh'. Again, Paul is presented as a guide and example for Christian conduct, especially in a male monastic community. Not only is the 'beauty of an attractive woman' a potential source of 'sinful delight'. As in *On the Sermon*, the Pauline topics of anger and anger management attract special attention.[23] Correction of a sinful brother is analysed yet again, another recurrent problem in a small community. At this very time, it is also addressed by a question from the 'brethren' about 'bearing another's burden' (Gal. 6.2). Against the evidence, Augustine even argues that Paul never uttered a curse, because cursing would be contrary to Jesus's teaching. When Paul wrote, 'I wish those who are troubling you would castrate themselves', it was not a curse, Augustine claims, to be taken literally: it was a blessing, as they would then give up sex . . .[24] The principles of good group behaviour are exemplified, Augustine argues, even in Paul's heated reproach to Peter in Antioch. Peter had timidly reverted to the Jewish food laws but his conduct in the ensuing argument shows yet again that it is not for 'merit' that God chooses his agents. Nonetheless, he received Paul's correction with humility, the mark of a true Christian. This vexed point will soon resurface in Augustine's own exchanges of letters.[25]

As the Galatians were no longer under the Law, they were under God's grace, Augustine thinks, in the 'third phase'. Again, he discusses the topic in terms of habit. Since Adam, we have a 'natural habit' which turns us to sin; the pleasures of sin thus lodge in the memory and addict us to sin's delights.[26] Unlike the Manichaeans' evil, this 'natural habit' is not part of our human nature: it is only a powerful tendency. His unfinished commentary on Romans then repeats once again that only a humble cry for help will assist us: people 'are not called because they are holy: they become holy once they have been called'.[27] The Gospel had talked of an 'unforgivable sin' against the Holy Spirit, one whose nature had greatly exercised previous Christian commentators. Augustine now locates this sin partly in the 'despair' which a sinner may feel while poised between the second and third phases of his progress: it is a 'despair' which his perfectionist hearers would readily recognize.

How despairing had Augustine himself become during his third stage 'under God's grace'? Again, the final book of *On Free Choice* is relevant. In his concluding monologue, Augustine repeats the imagery of a Christian's journey. On it, the aspiring pilgrims are at risk, as ever, to the downward pull of sin and bad habits. As mortal heirs of Adam, they are also subject to life's one certainty: death. If they are tempted to stray, they must remember the fate of the Devil, the angel who fell by his own free choice from the blissful contemplation of God. The choice, however, to turn and continue on the journey is theirs, and their aim is supremely rewarding: eternal happiness in the next life.[28] Meanwhile, they are part of that mainstay of Augustine's thinking, God's justly ordered world. Augustine even addresses the hardest argument against its existence: the sufferings and deaths of small children. They may be outweighed, he claims, by the joys which God reserves for them in the next life. The deaths may even chasten their elders and turn them to God. It is not his finest argument, and parents who continued to put up poignant memorials to their dead little children all over the Roman Empire would not exactly be persuaded.[29]

All the while, he states, Christians are travelling in a world of beauty and justice, arranged for the best. Augustine's optimism is still intact here, but the means to its end have altered since the first months after his conversion.[30] In Augustine's monastic groups, the road now stretched ahead for people who had opted to live for the rest of their lives like the first Apostles. They were not young students in a temporary reading party. They had embarked on their challenge without the previous experience of a priesthood and without any proven talent for sustaining a life 'intent on God'. Nonetheless, the fourth stage of the journey still beckoned ahead of them, the future life in which a mystic vision would indeed be realized. We are not witnessing the poignant results of a 'lost future', unique to Augustine and his group. The future, a contemplative vision of God, has not been lost: it has been relocated. Three years later, Augustine will express the expectation of this goal in his *Confessions*' soaring final book. Its impassioned tone is not one of despondency or a sad loss of hope.

In a bold interpretation, Augustine develops his image of man's predicament at this very time. Once again, he was answering some of his brethren's perplexities. What, they asked him, is the meaning of the Raising of Lazarus? The episode was one which Ambrose had explained in his pre-baptismal classes, but on point after point Augustine discerns an even deeper allegorical meaning in the Gospel's words. Buried in the tomb, Lazarus, he claims, symbolizes all mankind, whose souls are buried in earthly sins.[31]

'Where have you laid him?' Jesus asked the bystanders. He was not ignorant, Augustine explains. It is we who are ignorant: the question shows that our 'calling' occurs in secret. For the first time in any of his works, Augustine refers to God's secret 'predestination'. When God 'calls' us, he states, we do not yet know it, but God has known it all the time. In another answer at this time, Augustine explains to the brethren that we cannot even 'will' to turn to God unless we are 'called', either in 'secret', in our innermost heart, or externally, by some 'visible sign'. Exactly this type of calling will be the key to his confessions' understanding of his own conversion.

With her usual common sense, down-to-earth Martha observed of her dead brother: 'Lord, it is already the fourth day, and he stinks.' As 'earth' is the fourth element, Augustine claims, the fourth day's 'stink' is the stink of earthly, fleshly desires. As before, Augustine sees an analogy with Adam: 'You are earth,' God told him. The analogy links Lazarus to ourselves, sharers of the same human heritage.

In the tomb, Augustine claims, Lazarus signified the soul, lying 'dead' among vices of the flesh. The 'stone' of the tomb was then removed, a symbol of the obstacles to our converting and heeding God's call. One meaning of the stone, he suggests, may be the 'corrupt' Christians in the Church, people who cause their fellow Christians to stumble: they are a telling comment on Christian ideals of community. Nonetheless, by an act of unmerited grace Jesus summoned the soul, or Lazarus, to withdraw from fleshly sins. It came out, still wrapped in some of the bandages, thereby showing that as long as we are in the body, we cannot be wholly 'free from vexations of the flesh'. Lazarus was now 'under grace', but, unlike Christ on this earth, he did not leave all his bandages behind him in the tomb. He conforms, therefore, to Paul's famous cry in Romans, the very words which Augustine had just been explaining in his exposition: 'with my mind, I serve the law of God, but with my flesh, the law of sin'. He also comes out with a handkerchief covering his face. As Paul said, we see now 'through a glass darkly, but later, face to face'. Lazarus is not yet fit to contemplate God, but nonetheless Jesus ordered the onlookers, 'Loose him, and let him go.' After this life, all coverings, Jesus means, will be removed so that we may see face to face. We will reach what Augustine has been presenting as the fourth phase or seventh step: peace and contemplation in the life to come.

As usual, he had been reading his Latin predecessors' comments on the verses of scripture which concerned him. On Lazarus, his main debts were to Ambrose, through whom ideas of the great Greek interpreter Origen had filtered down to Augustine's thinking.[32] Nonetheless, the resulting whole was powerfully his own. While Augustine presented it, he and his celibate brethren were standing on his fifth step of seven, in his third phase of four, 'under grace'. Tattered bandages of carnal sin still attached to them and handkerchiefs still veiled their faces from the mystic vision, but nonetheless that vision was awaiting them 'face to face' in the life to come. The Lazarus of this answer to fraternal questioners will soon be the Augustine of the *Confessions*.

37
Postal Contacts

I

On the fifth step, in the third level 'under grace', Augustine would go on within two years to begin the *Confessions*. His texts so far had had a limited circulation. The recent works on Paul and the Sermon on the Mount addressed monastic brethren and were of little likely interest to anyone else. Romanianus had a copy of most of the others, but if they were ever to become known outside north Africa, they would have to be copied by hand, a slow and expensive business unless done by a church's retained secretaries. As Latin texts, they would be ignored by most readers in the Greek East. In 394/5, Augustine's fame was still local, among the priests and bishops in his part of north Africa and among the very few there who were drawn to the celibate life. His bishop admired his writings against the Manichaeans, but even they were not known in Latin-speaking Gaul and Spain.

Augustine's last book as a priest is no exception. It is his book *On Lying*. The subject is a daunting one, as the Bible is well stocked with lies which people had told and the ethics of lying remained, as ever, a complex tangle.[1] 'Every man is a liar,' the psalmist had well said (Ps. 115.11), but are lies sometimes permissible? In the Book of Exodus, the midwives in Egypt told lies in order to protect the Hebrews' newly born sons, but God then caused them to prosper. Augustine correctly distinguishes a lie from a falsehood and relates it to its utterer's intention. He then distinguishes eight different levels of lying in ascending order of gravity: a lie told to win a convert or to bring about good consequences is less serious than a lie for evil ends. Augustine is not a consequentialist, willing to justify any lie by its compensating results. He takes the strict view that lies are sins and therefore always wrong. Nonetheless, he distinguishes lying from being 'economical with the truth', a point which he had already made when expounding Galatians. Even Jesus, he well observes, had not told the whole truth to his disciples.[2] Only a year before his confessions it is tantalizing to find Augustine defending a refusal to tell all.

When he later reread this text, he found it obscure and 'thorny' and never published it with his other works. However, at the time of writing, it coincided with the beginnings of his impact outside Africa. This impact started in summer 395, but only through others' contacts, not his own. The results were to be decidedly mixed. Within two years, Augustine had fallen out with two of his new-found correspondents. One was socially the noblest Christian he had ever addressed. The other was mentally the best-equipped. The third was to pose a question so difficult that his attempt to answer it has been described as his 'second conversion'.

II

These contacts mark an intriguing change in our evidence. They are known through letters, not only Augustine's letters, but letters from his correspondents, as never since Nebridius' death. As usual, they were not 'strictly private', as if only for their recipients' eyes. Augustine, like others, had copies made of his letters before he sent them off, a reason for their survival among his records.[3] On arrival they would also be read aloud to others. They are fascinating sources, but we never have the full correspondence: we have to infer from the surviving letters what was said in items now missing. The chronology is also a challenge, as none of the letters survived with its date of composition. However, more pieces in the chronological puzzle have become clear recently and can be arranged into a coherent sequence. The prizes are high, not only the very words and concerns of Augustine's most able contemporaries but the crucial element, for some of his modern scholars, in his decision to write the *Confessions* soon afterwards.

The exchanges began in 395. The richest involves a figure of great social eminence, Meropius Pontius Paulinus, a man in his early forties, who had recently become the most notable convert to a perfectionist style of life in the entire Latin West. He had been born into a Christian family a year or so before Augustine and had gone through a similar 'liberal' education. However, he was a nobly born senator, superior even to Ambrose's family. He inherited land on a grand scale in Gaul and Spain, and in fertile Campania near the town of Nola on the main route from south Italy up to Naples: he is still known as 'Paulinus of Nola'. In his mid-twenties, he even held one of the suffect consulships at Rome and presided over the games which traditionally marked anniversaries of the 'eternal city'. Five years later, in 383, he travelled to his estates in Spain and in 384/5 married the well-born Therasia, a lady of Spanish background. They then returned to their properties in southern Gaul, but became caught up in the aftermath of Maximus' usurpation, the danger of which was also hanging over Augustine during his time in Milan. Before 389, Paulinus and his brother had been baptized in Bordeaux, but political turmoil then cost Paulinus' brother his life. It almost cost Paulinus his Gallic estates.[4]

In a politically perilous atmosphere, Paulinus and his wife withdrew again to Spain, where the ideals of social and sexual renunciation had recently been thrown into particular prominence.[5] Nonetheless, they continued to try for an heir and, by 392, produced a baby son. They lost him, however, when he was eight days old, and buried him beside the resting-place of two martyrs in the city of Complutum, near modern Madrid. After this sad loss and the perils surrounding their estates, they began to think of a new life. Aged about forty, Paulinus decided to abandon sex and live with his wife, Therasia, in a *mariage blanc*. In late 394, they announced an even more spectacular renunciation: they would dispose of their vast possessions and 'buy heaven and Christ for the price of their fragile riches'.[6]

Like Augustine, Paulinus presented these decisions as a conversion, but he had much more to lose: sex with a wife who was daily by his side, enormous riches and a noble standing in society. He was the first senator ever to have announced such a drastic decision, the 'anti-social event of the century'. Even beforehand, his old Christian friend and tutor Ausonius had considered it to be mad. He compared the possibility to the wanderings of mythical Bellerophon 'out of his mind' in an Asian cave. Surely Paulinus was being influenced by his wife, a second Tanaquil, the scheming queen in Rome's distant Etruscan past? 'Not my Tanaquil,' Paulinus well replied, 'but my Lucretia', the Roman wife famous for maintaining her chastity.[7] In Milan, Ambrose delightedly imagined top people's reactions: 'a man from such a family . . . of such great eloquence has abandoned the Senate and broken the continuity of a noble family: this cannot be tolerated!'[8]

On Christmas Day, 394, in Barcelona, Paulinus announced in church something even more stunning: the renunciation of his and his wife's riches. Promptly, he was obliged by the congregation to accept another novelty for a senator: a priesthood. No doubt they hoped that if he was going to sell up his goods and remain childless, the proceeds would be spent on his parishioners, themselves. However, unlike Augustine, Paulinus was powerful enough to insist on a condition: he would not hold his priesthood in that same diocese.[9] He was already intending to return to his family property at Nola. In 395 he re-entered Italy and pressed on south, stopping in Rome.

As an ordained but untethered ascetic, he was not warmly received on his triumphal progress by Siricius, the city's Pope: his intention to renounce worldly goods and honours was all very fine, but was it really going to be realized? After this 'arrogant separation' by Siricius, Paulinus made contact with north Africa's 'Catholics'. On one view, he himself began it by writing spontaneously to Bishop Aurelius in Carthage, perhaps because of his rebuff in Rome. Such a letter does not survive, but to judge from the ones which followed, it might have asked for assistance with the scriptures and related matters. He might have announced his intention of settling in Nola, his family town, by the shrine of his patron saint, Felix. He had been studying scripture since his baptism and, as a new convert to a monastic style of life, would wish to learn as much as possible. On another view, which I prefer, there was no such letter and the exchange was not initiated by Paulinus himself. For other reasons he had sent a courier across to Africa, perhaps because he had big estates there and was planning to sell them. His envoy might have had orders to contact the local bishops, the natural beneficiaries of any sales. Then, unprompted, one of them sent a letter back with Paulinus' courier. As Paulinus' reply to it attests, that bishop was Alypius, Augustine's close friend.

With his letter Alypius sent books by Augustine, a man unknown at the time to Paulinus. They were five, all of them texts against the Manichaeans. In return, Alypius asked for a copy of a historical work, Eusebius' *Chronography*, which had recently been translated into Latin and updated by Jerome. He may have realized that a friendship with this immensely rich new contact would help Africa's local churches and monasteries if and when his massive fortune was given away.

In his accompanying letter, Alypius told Paulinus that he had heard about him years before while he was in Milan in 386/7 and was preparing himself for baptism. He even knew one of Paulinus' hymns.[10] After a while, Paulinus found a manuscript of the requested work by Eusebius in a celibate Christian's house in Rome. In autumn 395, he directed it to Africa and, just as Alypius had suggested, sent a letter to Aurelius, Bishop of Carthage. He also sent letters to his two new discoveries: Bishop Alypius and the author of his anti-Manichaean reading, Augustine.

As none of them had ever met, their letters use extravagant flatteries to bridge their physical absence and emphasize the inner persons whom their written words reveal. Repeatedly in his opening sentences, Paulinus states his new 'love' for Alypius, a love which God has willed: He has 'predestined' them for Himself, he writes, since the beginning of the world. Paulinus has been 'provoked', he says, to reply to Alypius' unexpected letter, and he longs to know more. Alypius had created a personal 'desert' for himself by his 'abdication from the everyday world and his repulse of flesh and blood', words which mean the renunciation of worldly ambition and sex.[11] Paulinus had done much the same, as he describes in a brief account of his own Christian progress. He also explains that they share a reverence for Ambrose, with whom he had had contact, perhaps mostly by letter: he had even been asked to be one of the great man's outlying priests. Could Alypius please, he asks with an echo of Virgil, send an account of himself up to the time when he became a bishop? Could he also send back the text of Eusebius when it had been copied in Carthage? Its safe return was very important, and as Alypius' letter had suggested, Paulinus was writing to the two Christians in Carthage who would best attend to it. Above all, there had been the gift of Augustine's five books. They seemed to Paulinus like texts dictated by the Holy Spirit. He was therefore risking a letter to Augustine in person: would Alypius please put in a good word on his behalf?

By writing, Paulinus knew that his letter would be read out to Alypius' Christian brethren. His letter to Augustine would be no more private. It is indeed a remarkable text, in the joint names of himself and Therasia, although, as usual, she contributes nothing. For the first time in the Latin West, we can read two celibate perfectionists corresponding with one another. These new circumstances called for a new mode of address: the heading of Paulinus' letter presents himself and Therasia as 'sinners', as startling as if a modern letter were to end 'yours sinfully'. Like Augustine, Paulinus was trained in rhetoric, but his talent was for poetry, not philosophy. Nonetheless, his letter interweaves no fewer than twenty-five phrases from the Psalms and Paul's letters, Augustine's favoured resources. He even works in a line from Virgil's *Aeneid* for his benefit. He presents himself as a novice convert, obedient to words of Paul but an 'infant', he writes, who is still 'crawling' and in need of suckling compared with Augustine's own wisdom, experience and, possibly, greater age. He has put off his 'burdens' and 'garments', sex, property and worldly ambition, but if he 'boasts, he will boast only in the Lord'. Carefully chosen, these words of Paul are exactly the words which Augustine was cherishing at this time.[12]

If the two men had corresponded ten years earlier, the grovelling would have been entirely Augustine's. Paulinus was socially much grander, a 'hyper-opulent rich man', in Augustine's fine phrase for him.[13] However, renunciation had reversed their social ranking and Paulinus was sending 'the love of humility'. Augustine was the very 'salt of the earth', Paulinus wrote, a helper to him while he was shipwrecked on the seas of life. His five books, he tells him, overflow with the skills of the rhetorical schools but also with 'honey from heaven'. Paulinus will send them, like a new 'pentateuch', to help churches 'in many cities', but could Augustine please send any other texts which he had written against 'enemies of the Christian faith'? God had arranged their friendship 'in His providence': more mundanely, Paulinus was offering to be Augustine's publisher in Italy and the west.[14] Meanwhile, he sent his usual present: a loaf of bread. It was a token of unanimity: he had also sent one with his letter to Alypius.

In the absence of a private postal service, letters could travel only with individual couriers. When the bearers of Paulinus' letter arrived, their verbal comments would add personal details to what he had written. They would explain, no doubt, that he was planning to develop the shrine of St Felix at Nola. Before long, he would indeed have adorned it with gardens, water, paintings and a huge new basilica. The proceeds of his sales of property were to turn it into a second St Peter's, accessibly placed on the main road up from southern Italy.

On the fifth step of his arduous journey to God's presence, Augustine would be greatly taken by this unexpected new fan from high society. Exceptionally, Paulinus was asking to follow in his hard-won footsteps, as nobody else of his rank ever had. He was a highly educated man. Like Augustine, he had composed a panegyric on an emperor, in his case the Christian Theodosius and his heaven-sent victory in September 394. He had also engaged with the Psalms, as texts for Latin poetry, however, not as multiple voices about Christ and conversion.[15] Augustine could teach him much, but while the winter seas interrupted traffic, he waited several months before replying.

Meanwhile, fearing a mistake, the eager Paulinus was to write yet again, reiterating his humble respect and his oneness with Augustine's inner being. Could they please share a talk, like family members and brothers? Might Augustine even deign to pay Paulinus a visit? In fact, Augustine had sent a reply in spring 396, and the letters had crossed.

Augustine's letter respectfully calls Paulinus his 'holy Lord', although Paulinus was only a fellow priest. Spurred on by Paulinus' stylish first letter, he treats 'my good man and my good brother' to his own brilliant burst of rhetorical paradoxes.[16] Paulinus' letter has revealed his 'inner self', and Augustine even claims that it reveals his wife too, the silent Therasia. In it, he enthuses, the reader sees a wife who is not leading her husband to 'softness', meaning sex, but 'to fortitude, by returning into her husband's bones'. Here, Augustine was exploiting Genesis's words about Eve, the 'bone of Adam's bones'. So far from becoming 'one flesh' with him through sex, Therasia has returned in chastity to the 'bones' from which she had been created. Husband and wife are now one, without any need to be joined by sexual penetration.[17]

Augustine commends the 'milk and honey' of Paulinus' first letter and its praises of God, by whom Paulinus has been made a 'new man'. He explains, just as Paulinus intended, that the letter has been read out to his brethren 'repeatedly'. They have been 'seized' by it. It has given off the very 'scent of Christ', enhanced by its perfectionist author whose origins were very much grander than their own. In reply, Augustine consigned his own letter to a bearer whom Paulinus would know already by name. He was the man to whom *On True Religion* had been addressed, none other than Romanianus, Augustine's former patron.

As Romanianus owned copies of almost all Augustine's books, he would be able to let Paulinus have copies in due course. First, it seems, Augustine wanted Romanianus to read them through and check them over.[18] As Paulinus was planning to publish Augustine's texts more widely, Augustine was concerned, as ever, that copies should be taken only from an accurate original. He was planning to send both those which were addressed to people outside the Church and those to his fellow brethren. Paulinus, he hopes with careful modesty, will pray for their 'sins and errors'. Whatever in them is written with 'truth and sincerity', a phrase from Paul, Augustine says that he reads with 'exultation and trembling', but its merits are gifts of God and His grace. 'What,' as Paul says, 'do we have which we have not received?' (1 Cor. 4.7). It is Augustine's first-known quotation of a text which will be very important for his deepening insistence on God's grace.[19] Meanwhile, Paulinus must pray for him, he requests, because he himself deserves no praise at all.

Self-praise and its remedy, humility before God, will soon be prominent in the *Confessions*. In words pregnant with future significance, Augustine tells Paulinus how he is 'offering my entire self to you, not as one such as you think me already to be, but as one for whom you may pray that I may deserve to be such as you think me'. Augustine is also sending more of his books, aware that they contain what Paul called 'old leavening': he judges himself 'with grief' when he rereads it. Exactly this sort of rereading will typify his *Retractations*, his review of his own works in later life. Above all, Augustine invites Paulinus to pray for his imperfect self, the one which he is presenting to him in a spirit of love. The *Confessions* will call for this sort of prayer and love from fellow slaves of God, readers of Augustine's imperfect self, especially when he turns in the tenth book to present 'what I am'.

In spring 396, Romanianus was leaving 'suddenly' with this letter. A reason for his haste is still discernible: his son. Not long before writing to Paulinus, Augustine had received a poignant echo of his past: a letter from this young man, Licentius no less, whom he had once taught in Verecundus' villa. Still a poet, he had recently sent Augustine a long poem in hexameter verse. It fondly recalled their days in the sub-Alpine villa, the engagements with Varro's 'disciplines' and the 'pure minds' of the assembled company. The hexameters scan competently and their bombastic place-names are no worse than those used by other poets in the later fourth century, although composers of Latin hexameters will not overestimate Licentius's talent.[20] He asked for Augustine's text *On Music*, which had been written after the villa party had broken up: he hoped, no doubt, that it would help him with his rhythm and metre. He also revealed his intentions. He was going up to Rome, hoping for a prominent career. He was even intending to marry.

For Augustine, this news was a fearful betrayal. So much for the chaste Licentius who had once sung a psalm about conversion while sitting in the villa's lavatory. Augustine wrote back to tell him he was being 'per-verted' not con-verted, and 'dis-ordered', not ordered: here, he alludes to Licentius' former 'conversion' to the 'order' in God's universe, discerned in the days at the villa.[21] Stung by his ex-pupil's defection from the sexless option, Augustine's first thought was to mobilize his new-found friend, Paulinus. If Licentius were to go to Nola, he would learn first-hand what conversion and perfection really mean. Licentius refused, and meanwhile Romanianus set off 'quickly' to Italy. Presumably, he was intending to help his son's worldly ambitions in Rome. On the way he could at least stop off with Paulinus and deliver Augustine's letter to him. Augustine also enclosed his letter to Licentius and the boy's poem, hoping that they might prompt Paulinus to intervene of his own accord.[22] When Romanianus talked with Paulinus, perhaps he too might realize the value of a monastic life and go to work on his misguided son.

As Romanianus was leaving in a hurry, Augustine explained that he was unable to send the account of Alypius' conversion which Paulinus requested. Alypius had been too modest to write one, and so Augustine had volunteered to write it himself, but the job was not yet done. This exchange of letters between 'slaves of God' is extremely significant. They were conscious that great moments of choice had changed their lives and, as a result, they wanted to hear stories of their making. Augustine also believed that another man's awesome example might win back a former follower who was about to opt for a mundane life. Augustine, the reflective convert, was as ever a keen converter of others. Very soon afterwards, the *Confessions* will tell just such a story, his own conversion to chastity, with the explicit aim of engaging the hearts and minds of fellow 'slaves of God' and encouraging them in pursuit of the same ideals. Stories of Alypius' earlier life cluster there in a sudden digression, as if they are material which Augustine had recently assembled in his mind. They are the sort of stories which Paulinus had asked for in 395.[23]

Books and letters were not the only items to circulate between the two men. In response to Paulinus' special present, Romanianus was to take an equivalent over to Nola: another loaf of bread.[24] Blessed by Augustine, it was to have a consequence which none of them could have imagined.

III

Before Paulinus wrote to Augustine, he had been writing to a greater scriptural expert: Jerome, now in Bethlehem. Jerome had contacts in Gaul and Spain, and by mid-394 Paulinus had already addressed him from Spain.[25] He asked for guidance in reading the scriptures and gave the news that he might be considering abandoning his worldly goods.

Jerome answered promptly with a letter which, for him, was unusually effusive. As if to assert his credit as a biblical guide, he briefly reviewed each book of scripture, concluding with special praises for the

Book of Revelation: 'in every single one of its words, multiple meanings are concealed'. Paulinus must 'live among these texts, meditate on them, know nothing else . . .': to do so is to anticipate heaven on earth. Jerome even invites him to visit Bethlehem: he 'will welcome him with outstretched hands' and will try to answer all his questions.[26] Paulinus must also act decisively if he is thinking of selling up: he must sell or abandon everything in one fell swoop. No doubt Jerome hoped that this immensely rich new contact would then support his group in Bethlehem and help to pay for the copying of his works.[27]

In early 395, Paulinus wrote back to Jerome, enclosing his recent panegyric on Theodosius, the Christian emperor. Jerome duly replied, admiring Paulinus' style, but tartly reviewing previous Latin Christian writers (except Ambrose) and urging Paulinus to engage more deeply with the scriptures. By spring 395 Paulinus, both a priest and a monk, was staying in Rome on his eventual way south to Nola. Jerome insisted to him that the life of a monk could be lived only in the country, whereas the life of a priest was to be lived only in towns.[28] Rome, by implication, was not the place for Paulinus to waste his potential: the Holy Land would be more suitable. The letter was polite in what it said, but modern scholars have suggested a coolness in what it did not. With his own letter Paulinus may have sent Jerome four of his poems, three of which versified some psalms and the fourth, at length, praised the life of John the Baptist. If so, Jerome's reply never even referred to them. Revealingly, Paulinus never preserved his copies of his two letters to Jerome. One reason for discarding them would have been the literary snub which resulted from them.[29]

Paulinus' excitement on discovering Augustine may be related to his recent disappointment over Jerome's pointed silence. For separate reasons, Augustine was soon to write to Jerome too. He was already known to the Church in Carthage, as a recently discovered letter has unexpectedly revealed. In 391/2, when Aurelius had become Carthage's bishop, he had written to inform Jerome, whom he had met about nine years earlier in Rome.[30] He already had copies, he explains, of two of Jerome's Latin translations of biblical commentaries by the great Origen. In reply, Jerome sent Aurelius his own commentary on Psalm 10 and his text called *Hebrew Questions on Genesis*. It used the Hebrew text, not the Greek one, and included Jewish traditions about its meaning which Jerome had gathered from erudite Jews in the Holy Land.[31] They were wholly unknown to Augustine and the African Manichaeans. Their battles were being fought only over a mediocre Latin translation.

As Jerome pointed out, trained Latin copyists were scarce in the Holy Land and if Aurelius wanted any more of his texts, he must send people out to do the work. In due course Aurelius obliged, sending none other than Alypius, perhaps with helpers. Probably, this visit belongs in 394. Jerome had suggested that a whole year would be needed for the job, and we know that Alypius was back with Augustine in Hippo in April 395.[32] On his return he regaled Augustine with tales of this learned 'slave of God', who was settled near Bethlehem with female patrons from Rome and was yet another fascinating example of celibacy in action. Alypius had also brought more texts by Jerome back to north Africa, but it may well be that he did not yet have copies of them all for Augustine's use. They had been taken off to Carthage and would have to be copied there first.

In this very year, 395, Augustine was writing his own commentary on Galatians, in ignorance, I believe, of Jerome's.[33] Another year passed, and only then, in spring 396, did he write to Jerome himself. This revised date for his letter depends on a related advance in the chronology of Augustine's clerical life and helps to explain his letter's tone.[34] Initially, Augustine is self-effacing, as we would expect in a first approach to such a prickly expert. However, he then challenges Jerome and shows himself to be remarkably firm and sure of his ground. He has two objections: Jerome's insistence on translating scripture from Hebrew texts, not Greek ones, and his claim, which Augustine now knows, that in the notorious quarrel at Antioch (Gal. 2.11–21), Paul had rebuked Peter, but only apparently so, as if Paul was merely pretending to be angry in what he said.[35]

On the question of translation, Jerome, like modern scholars, would not be impressed by Augustine's objections. Whereas Jerome had translated from Hebrew into Latin, Augustine asserted his faith in the Greek translation, the work, he accepts, of 'seventy' translators who had all agreed, possibly because they were inspired. Their work had authority and unanimity, Augustine insisted, whereas Latin translators from the Hebrew were still trying to make sense of the biblical text and were still disagreeing among themselves. If things in the Hebrew are obscure, he remarks, then Jerome may be wrong about them like everyone else.[36] Jerome was not exactly persuaded by this feeble argument. As for the question of Paul's 'hypocrisy', it was not a new one. Jerome had adopted the idea from Origen, but the suggestion was especially important to Augustine at this time. His own discussion of the episode had already been finished, I believe, in his exposition of Galatians: it envisaged no such pretence by the Apostle. If Paul's words were to be read as insincere, where would the lies and hidden pretences in scripture end? Augustine's letter tells Jerome how he will demonstrate that each apparent case of lying in scripture is illusory. In spring 396, he had been working on exactly this subject, central to his book on lying, and hence his confidence that he could 'demonstrate' it.[37]

This insistence that Jerome was wrong was the insistence, in my view, of an Augustine who had already worked out his own answers to these very questions. With his letter he sent some of his other writings, including, it seems, his *Soliloquies* and his expositions of the Psalms, a sign of the value he set on them. As usual, he begged the recipient to correct him frankly 'with the severe judgement of a brother'.[38] However, the letter was never sent. Before it could leave, its carrier, Augustine's friend Profuturus, was appointed to be a bishop.

Delays and interrupted deliveries were to bedevil the two men's correspondence, but Augustine did not lose heart. With a letter, it seems, from Alypius, his next move was to include another letter with a question for Jerome about the great Origen. It arrived at the most unfortunate moment, just when Jerome had become plunged into a controversy about Origen's 'heretical' authority.[39] Unawares, Augustine then repeated the untimely request and added it to a longer letter in which he set out once again his objections to the notion that Paul had told hypocritical lies. This letter was also to have a chequered life, reaching Rome and stopping there when its bearer went no further east than Italy. Several years later, Jerome wrote in annoyance that a letter with such criticisms of him had been enjoyed on its journey east by his enemies in the 'eternal city'.[40] Relations between the two greatest writers in the Latin West were nearly sabotaged by a series of postal accidents.

One consequence is especially important. In spring 396, Augustine had read and approved two of Jerome's other translations of scripture: his two versions of the Book of Job, one from the Greek, the other from the Hebrew. Already, therefore, Augustine was reading this challenging book attentively. In due course, in 399, the notes which he wrote on his copy of the text were to be gathered and preserved as his 'notes on Job'. As the text which these notes use is the first of Jerome's two versions, Augustine's noting is likely to have begun as early as 396, when he had this text to hand from Jerome.[41] In his notes, Augustine explains Job's 'confession' as a confession of sins and a confession of God's praises: the word will be used with exactly this range in the *Confessions*. Seven echoes of Job's wording are discernible in the *Confessions'* first book alone, including its famous prayer that 'our troubled heart may find rest in You'.[42] The more Augustine studied Jerome's translation of Job, the more it was to become a resource for his own confessing prayer.

38
Amazing Grace

During these contacts by letter, Augustine's mind was as active as ever. Recent studies have enabled us to follow it at work in what had previously been regarded as a phase of failed attempts and frustrations. For one thing, he rethought his ideas on peace and rest for the saints. Until *c.*395, he had implicitly accepted 'millenarian' teaching, the widespread view that the Christian saints would rule with Christ on earth in a millennial phase of a thousand years before God's final Judgement. From now on, he postpones this phase of peace and rest until after death, when each good Christian will enjoy it, but in the next life only. This new view is not one of a 'lost future' so much as of a delayed one: it will go on to shape the ending of the *Confessions* and their reflections on the 'seventh day' of Creation.[1]

Augustine also stopped to give his considered thoughts on biblical sightings of God. By that memorable oak tree at Mambre, Abraham had once entertained enigmatic strangers who seemed to be now one, now three. Christian readers therefore identified them with their Trinity. When answering the Manichaean Adeimantus' book, Augustine explained that Christ had indeed been present, through the person of the angel whom the text mentioned. It was important to recognize Christ here, because He was a link between Old Testament times and the New, a link which Manichaeans like Adeimantus denied. As for divine visions in general, Adeimantus was wrong to claim that the two halves of the Bible are contradictory on the subject. Isaiah indeed says that he saw the Lord seated on a high throne, whereas the First Letter to Timothy calls the King of Ages 'invisible'. However, there are three distinct types of vision, with the eyes, the imagination or the spirit. God is of course invisible to our eyes, as 1 Timothy says, but Isaiah saw God in a vision of the imagination through which God was working. These three classes of vision were known to Augustine from Platonist writings and were to shape his thinking on this question for the rest of his life.[2]

Meanwhile, in 395/6, his expositions of the Psalms reached Psalm 22 and required it to be read very closely. 'My God, my God, why hast tthou forsaken me?' it began, the words which the Gospels give as Jesus's words on the Cross. Augustine's exposition of this psalm has recently been seen as a 'watershed in his career as a Christian reader of Scripture, and indeed as a Christian', one whose importance 'it is impossible to overstate'.[3] This claim emphasizes that Augustine's previous writings had been less concerned with our redemption by Christ's suffering than with the scope for a heavenly ascent, step by step, for which Christ, since His Incarnation, is a helping mediator. No Christian reader of Psalm 22 could miss the stress on Christ's agonizing death as a redemption of mortals' sins or as a proof of His own humanity. Did its words now induce in Augustine a second 'conversion', to a deeper sense of Christ's humanity and to what many Christians regard as its central point, the 'taking away of the sins of the world' and the belief that it 'was for us', as the Anglican hymn puts it, that 'He hung and suffered there'?

Augustine's careful interpretation of this psalm indeed expresses a new emphasis in his writings. However, it is mistaken to limit his spiritual understanding only to what he expresses in surviving texts. At baptism, Ambrose taught candidates, including Augustine, about the Cross and redemption. Ever since, Augustine had regularly taken the eucharist, thinking it to be Christ's body and blood 'shed for our sins'. When he reproached his congregation's partying in Hippo, he gave them a graphic account of Christ's human suffering.[4] He had not much emphasized redemption in his writings, but, so far, they had addressed perfectionists who were concerned with a different question, the steps of an ascent to God's presence. I do not believe that the exposition of Psalm 21 opened his eyes to a Christian dimension which he had not considered.

In 396 Augustine was to be forced onto new ground, but of a different kind. He was impelled not by a psalm, but by a letter. It was to take him ever further from the concerns of Synesius, no connoisseur of the human will, and of pagan Libanius, for whom 'grace' meant a helpful favour to a friend or dependant. The letter arrived from someone whom he already knew and revered, elderly Simplicianus, the priest in Ambrose's Milan. Ten years before, they had discussed Victorinus, the prominent convert from Platonism, and the opening of John's Gospel. Now, Simplicianus wrote to his former questioner with scriptural difficulties of his own. His letter does not survive, but its questions can be inferred from Augustine's answers. They concerned six problems from the Book of Kings, ranging from difficulties with the Witch of Endor to the reasons why David had 'sat before the Lord', and two problems in Paul's Letter to the Romans. Augustine was to answer these two from Romans 7 and 9.[5] Simplicianus, therefore, caused him to revisit the very problems which he had recently answered in his *Exposition of Romans*: Paul's cry about the 'law of sin' ('O wretched man that I am': Rom. 7.22–5) and God's contrasting treatment of the unborn twins ('Jacob I loved, but Esau I hated': Rom. 9.13). In Milan, as in Carthage, Manichaean teaching may have made these Pauline questions urgent.

Simplicianus had written to Ambrose about his difficulties, but Ambrose had told him simply to read Paul and all would be answered. His decision to contact Augustine probably arose through Paulinus, who was well known to the clergy in Milan and who would have told them that Augustine was an anti-Manichaean expert.[6] Augustine's replies are an impassioned re-engagement with the problems. They read like orally dictated arguments, in which 'we witness, by following him', Paula Fredriksen has well observed, 'the birth of an idea'. The interpretation of Paul, she points out, which he 'works so hard to repudiate . . . is not so much his enemies' as his own'.[7]

Not long before answering Simplicianus, Augustine had answered a similar question from his brethren: it, too, concerned Paul's words to the Romans, 'O man, who are you to answer back to God?' In his answer, Augustine discussed the 'lump of clay' from which God, like a potter, forms each of us (Rom. 9.19–20). This lump of clay, he told the brethren, is a 'mass of sin', since Adam's first sin in Eden. We must not 'want to be clay', Augustine tells them: we must strive to become 'children of God'. God will choose us, but He will choose us, Augustine still thinks, on the 'merit' of our response to His call to faith. If we do not respond, we remain in the 'mass of sin' and are duly punished. If we accept, God offers the Holy Spirit, but here too we can choose to accept the offer or not.[8]

When answering Simplicianus, very soon after this answer, he takes a crucial step: he decides that even the merit of responding to God's call is no longer relevant to God's choice. From our sinful clay, he now believes, God either makes vessels of beauty, as Paul had said, or vessels of lowly 'ignominy'. The choice is God's inscrutable decision, hidden from our understanding, and is not dependent on our merits at all.[9] In later life, even after his many writings on grace, Augustine still looked back on his answer to Simplicianus as a turning point.[10] For many of his modern scholars, until recently, it has indeed seemed to be so, marking a truly 'lost future' in Augustine's thinking and the end of an earlier optimistic view of man's potential. For some of his readers, it seems to mark the beginning of another Augustine, a conversion, no less. To both parties, this change in his views seems essential for his decision to write his confessions soon afterwards. No longer, on this view, could Augustine believe that reasoned philosophy and 'rapt contemplation' alone can bring Christians to God.[11] They also need God's grace which prevails on their free will and striving. However, this grace is not given to them all: this selectivity is beyond our understanding. For the first time, in the answer to Simplicianus, the phrase 'original sin' appears in Augustine's writings. As each one of us, he insists, is part of the 'mass of sin' or 'mass of condemnation' which has transformed human nature since Adam's Fall, the mystery is not why God 'hates' Esau or anyone else for being a sinner: we are all sinners.[12] The mystery is why He chooses to love those whom He does.

To pained modern liberal readers, this answer has seemed profoundly pessimistic and misguided. However, while Augustine pursued Simplicianus' questions, he was not thinking in isolation: he was being helped yet again by writings of the dissident Donatist Tyconius.[13] Carefully he took Simplicianus' questions about Paul one after another. First, he focused on Romans 7, answering, it seems, a general question by Simplicianus about the status of the old law. Little was new in his thinking here, although he emphasized the role of 'delight' in our decisions. His second answer was the novel one. In brief, it presented even faith itself as God's gift. No longer does Augustine see a convert as someone who turns freely to God and is then rewarded with grace and the gift of God's Spirit. Faith itself, he now proposes, is God's inscrutable gift in the first place.[14] As for God's hatred of the unborn Esau, it is explicable by the sinfulness which has been passed to us all, the 'mass of sin' since Adam. The problem is not God's hatred, but rather why God loved Jacob. It is here that Augustine can give no answer, except by referring his readers to God's 'most hidden' reasons and 'inscrutable' ways.[15] God, after all, is unknowable.

In his First Letter to Timothy, we might counter, 'Paul' had written that 'God our Saviour . . . wills that all men should be saved' (1 Tim. 2.3–4; compare Rom. 5.18). In later life Augustine evades the word 'all' in this text by claiming that it means 'many' or 'all sorts'. Had not

Christ said that 'many' (not 'all') are 'called, but few are chosen'?[16] Here, Augustine distinguishes between God's 'calling' (of all) and actual 'election' (of a few). In his answer to Simplicianus, he was concerned above all with what Paul had emphasized: we must attribute all our gifts to God and not to our own merits. This concern was not new: he had been stating it in letters, answers and commentaries during the previous two years, including his recent letter to Paulinus.[17] What now changed was its scope. It caused him to revise his views on faith and conversion.

Previously he had argued that God's choices were based on foreknowledge: God knew whether Jacob and Esau would freely choose to show faith, and so He treated them differently. However, if we explain God's choices only by His foreknowledge, surely they still depend on humans' merits, to be shown by their future actions, including the act of faith? It is this argument which makes Augustine change his ground. Faith and the will to believe, he now insists to Simplicianus, must be entirely gratuitous gifts of God's grace. In support, he cites Paul when writing to the Philippians: 'it is God who works in you both the willing and the doing, according to his good will' (Phil. 2.13).

In old age, when reconsidering his writings, Augustine recalls how 'there was a struggle for free will' in his answer to Simplicianus, 'but the grace of God prevailed'. He means that grace prevailed in the struggle, not that it prevailed entirely over free will.[18] His understanding of the role of grace and the will is still complex. He never calls God's grace irresistible, nor does he state that our free will simply disappears before it. Far from it: 'it remains,' he concludes, 'that wills may be chosen'.[19] According to one modern reading of his argument, God sets the 'environment of choice' and gives a persuasive, or 'congruent', call. He knows our inner dispositions and gives the 'call' which is suited to them and is most likely to induce delight and response in the will. The grace of a 'persuasive vocation', on this view, gains the consent of the will, but is not itself located in it. Even late in life, Augustine states that God acts in the hearts of men 'not so that men believe without willing to do so, which is impossible, but so that the unwilling may become willing'.[20] What 'delights' us and draws us to God is unpredictable, even inexplicable, and God's gift of it is what sets our will in motion. Free will, nonetheless, is present in the process.

Augustine's constant enemy in this period is Manichaeism, and he would not, even here, give an answer which obliterated free will. To modern critics, however, Augustine has seemed to be combining an insistence on humans' utter helplessness with inexplicable favouritism by God. No longer, as he once assured Alypius in Verecundus' villa, is divine aid available to all alike: God picks and chooses, inscrutably.[21] Augustine also seems to be sombre and pessimistic when consigning many of those in the 'mass of damnation' to damnation for reasons beyond their comprehension. To see this new view, however, as Augustine's loss of a once-clear future or as an absolute break with his past is to miss the role of God's guiding gifts and the limits on humans' free choice in his earlier writings. They had already been touched on in his *Soliloquies*' great prayer to God, ten years earlier, before he had even been baptized. Soon after, when commenting on Genesis, he had stressed that it is 'God's Spirit who moves us to pray when we groan to God' and that we act 'with the Spirit moving us'.[22] In the lively words of Carol Harrison, many passages in the earlier writings 'describe God's gracious action in imagery more appropriate to a steamroller than a sympathetic teacher'.[23] In 396 the heavenly 'steamroller' is not a new arrival on the road: it gains a new gear.

On any view of Augustine's new thinking, he was not reverting to a dark Manichaean past. Mani had indeed written that he had been called by the grace of God: his followers could even claim that God had 'predestined' them. However, a Manichaean's calling was not considered in terms of will or delight. It was the result of an assent to the Truth when presented by members of the sect. A Manichaean was then saved in varying degrees according to his care for his innate particles of divine Light. There was nothing inscrutable about his election, nor did a gift of the Holy Spirit follow to enable him to live in fondness and love: Mani himself was the Spirit, and his gift was his written Gospel, available to all.

As Augustine remarks, his own insistence on grace, not merit, was already to be found in north Africa's Christian icon, Bishop Cyprian. Original sin was not original to him either, although his name for it has made it famous. At this point in his career he supports it from Paul's First Letter to the Corinthians, 'for as in Adam all die, so also in Christ shall all be made alive' (1 Cor. 15.22). Only some fifteen years later does he emphasize another text, Romans 5.12, where he was misled by a Latin translator's error, like others before him. Paul's Greek meant that 'death spread to all men, *because* all sinned'. However, Augustine's Latin text did not specify 'death' as the subject and mistranslated 'because' or 'in that' as 'in *whom*'. Our Bibles still wrongly translate, '*As through* one man sin entered into the world, and death through sin, and so death passed unto all men', making Adam the object of 'through'.[24]

The bleakest element in Augustine's argument may seem to be his claim that we are all condemned as a mass and that God's hating or loving each one of us is inexplicable. However, God is not unjust, Augustine insists: we merely cannot see His reasons. Since Adam's sin, we must think of ourselves as debtors and of God as our creditor. If God punishes His debtors, He is just, but sometimes, like a kind creditor, He releases a debtor from his obligations. In our debt crisis, God and His divine powers, a threesome or 'troika', are not being 'endlessly punitive' for reasons which we can never grasp.[25] Always, He is just and, always, He is merciful. Since Adam's sin, we are being justly punished with mortality. As mortals, we cannot explain everything in God's will: as Paul insists, 'O man, who art thou that thou repliest against God?' While reading the Book of Job, Augustine would also confront this point, which is ascribed in it to God Himself.[26]

For all their novelty and tightly argued detail, the conclusions of Augustine's answer are not cogent. Their logic has been acutely questioned and, yet again, they are based on misunderstandings, not only by previous scriptural translators, which he was not alone in failing to recognize, but also of Paul's words in their context.[27] Only in the Latin Bible's mistranslation of Romans 7.25 did Paul seem to answer the cry for deliverance with the word 'grace': Augustine's Latin text misled him. At 9.13, when Paul discussed the problem of Esau and Jacob, he was discussing the calling of Israel and the Gentiles. He was certainly not discussing God's choosing of individuals here and now. Paul nowhere connected the twins' calling and rejection to Adam's sin and Fall. Cleverly, Augustine added another proof-text, the words of Ben Sira on how 'some of them God cursed and brought low . . . As the clay of the potter in his hand, all his ways are according to his good pleasure: so men are in the hand of him that made them' (Ecclus. 33.12–13). However, this text says nothing about Adam's Fall and a resulting 'mass of sin'. Augustine misread these and other texts because the questions of random grace and choosing were preoccupying his mind. One reason for his preoccupation was the Manichaeans' abuse of such texts, but another, we may guess, was the human diversity which was confronting him ever more clearly in the north African churches. His new thinking on grace did not emerge simply 'for' pastoral purposes, but it emerged, in part, 'from' pastoral realities. Near the end of his answer to Simplicianus, he remarks that a man 'stained only by the slightest sins', with a keen intelligence, 'polished in the liberal arts', seems to be the 'one to be chosen for grace'. Back in Verecundus' villa, we recall, he had asserted that his friends were people whom he loved for their reason and intelligence. Yet, in the 'true faith and true Church' there are people, he now observes, so 'tepid' that they are excelled in 'patience and temperance' but also in faith, hope and charity by the least likely people, by prostitutes or even by actors who have suddenly converted.[28] The university of life had indeed been teaching Augustine that humanity is full of surprises.

How would the new thinking in his letter to Simplicianus relate to his view of his own past? Many of his modern scholars have considered it to be a change so fundamental that it obliged him to rethink his own conversion and that the *Confessions* are the result. When answering Simplicianus, he indeed addressed the case of another convert, Paul.[29] The 'least of the Apostles' had been a fervent persecutor of Christians and had travelled down to Damascus intent on continuing the good work. By a blinding light and by words from God, he was suddenly turned forcibly in a new direction. He became a Christian, the most drastic example of God's 'operative grace' in action. Would not Augustine see his own conversion henceforward in Pauline terms, as a conversion due to God's operative grace, not the free exercise of his human will?[30]

This powerful view misses a cardinal point: the two men's conversions were very different. Wholly unlike Paul, Augustine had been born to be a Christian; he had imbibed the name of Christ with his mother's milk; he had become a catechumen while a little boy. In all his wanderings, whether through the *Hortensius* and Mani's Gospel or scepticism and Platonic 'ascents', he had absolutely refused to abandon his belief in God or Christ. From the earliest years, the strength of his belief ranks as faith, even if his understanding of God and Christ's nature was still very hazy. His conversion was not a decision to strengthen it and seek baptism: that decision had already been taken before he wrestled with his divided will in the Milan garden. Nor was he turning, like Paul, to Christianity after a lifetime of unbelief. Nor was his conversion a clarification of his ideas of the nature of God. As he explains, his ideas had already been clarified by his ascents in Milan. He had not needed to be 'more certain' *about* God: he needed to be 'more stable' *in* Him. Stability required the abandonment of sex and worldly ambition. This conversion had nothing in common with Paul's abrupt conversion from anti-Christian ignorance, nor with the discussions of 'grace' and the gift of 'faith' to unbelievers which Augustine was conducting for Simplicianus' benefit.

When Augustine reviewed his conversion in the *Confessions*, he did not think that it was due to his own 'merits'. However, this fact was surely evident to him long before he tangled with questions of God's 'congruent calling' and 'operative grace'. His description of his long path to conversion in the *Confessions* is a description of his own willing, 'pricked' by God and foreseen by him, but marked by dithering, delay and creative misunderstandings. His final leap to chastity was made within a framework of 'environmental graces' which had been set round him by God's providence and mercy. He had to will it, nonetheless: he was not forced or blinded like Paul on the road to Damascus, a conversion into which 'willing' had not entered at all.

Theologians tend to look for a theological shift to explain the birth of the *Confessions*, a sudden masterpiece. In my view, Augustine's new thinking on faith and grace, hard won for Simplicianus' benefit, does not shape their account of 'what I [once] was'. The word 'mercy' (*misericordia*) is much more prominent than 'grace' (*gratia*) in the first eight books. When he resumes after the scene in the garden, he recalls how it had become a joy to him to cast off his former trifling 'sweetnesses', meaning above all sex, and that 'You [God] were casting them out and entering instead of them, sweeter than every pleasure.' The tenses of the verbs are important here: 'You *were*' in the imperfect as a process, not a sudden overriding intervention in Augustine's inner life, like God's intervention in Paul's on the road to Damascus. His confessions exploit the relation of 'operative grace' and faith, not in his spiritual journey in Milan, but in their concluding meditation on Creation, which they conduct in dialogue with words from Paul's letters. Just as God divided light from dark, so He 'moves upon our inner dark and fluid nature in His mercy', making some of us into 'children of light' and others into 'children of darkness'. Here, Augustine believes, God alone can 'discern' us. The stress here is indeed on grace, mercy and the Spirit and it would not have been phrased in this way without the answer to Simplicianus. However, at the end of the *Confessions* its context is Christian baptism in general, not Augustine's personal type of conversion, the renunciation of sex and the world.[31]

In his pastoral work, meanwhile, he remained capable of laying ample stress on a newly gained convert's own will. A few years later, he remarks how some people come for their first instruction as Christian catechumens with hypocritical aims, for reasons of gain or money, perhaps, but not a genuine call to faith. By his instruction, a priest may nonetheless rouse in them a will to convert. His lessons initiate it,

Augustine states without adding any further reflection on the questions of God's inscrutable grace or gifts of faith.[32] His sermons, too, are generally reticent on the topic, continuing to stress the role of free choice.[33] In the world about him, meanwhile, ever more Christians were being born Christians, people to whom 'election' and the 'gift' of faith were irrelevant. They took their faith as a matter of course from their Christian parents and needed only to deepen it.

The pagan Libanius is worth comparing, even here. In his speech about his life, he repeatedly professes thanks to the random 'grace' of the goddess Fortune.[34] He did not consider himself to be this goddess's creation, nor did he live in a world to which she gave 'order'. The questions of unborn twins and of willing and humble receiving were of no concern to him whatsoever: he had never been a convert, and in his pagan world the only conversions were to philosophy, which he avoided. Yet, in presenting himself as Fortune's protégé, he related himself to inscrutable divine favour. Like Augustine, he could not explain why he, in particular, was being favoured. Justice, he thought, was exercised by Fortune, but with a significant difference: her justice was intermittent, affecting individuals in externally visible ways. Augustine believed, by contrast, that the justice of God is universal and continuous, though unfathomable to mortals.

We do not know what Simplicianus made of Augustine's arduous answers. For some scholars, our ignorance of their immediate reception in 396–7 is evidence that in Milan, north Africa and even Nola, his novel thinking was received in stony silence. To prove its truth, they suggest, Augustine then had to write his confessions and present his own past as an example of what he had just come to understand.[35] However, the book did not present his own past in quite that way. Controversy indeed broke round him, but it was not because of his new notions of grace. It was because of a change in his own circumstances. Before answering Simplicianus, he had been nominated to be a bishop.

39
Food for Scandal

I

The final piece in Augustine's career, a bishopric, was now to fall into place. His biographer Possidius claims that Bishop Valerius had already had to hide him from visitors who wished to carry him off to be the head of their Church.[1] Once again, he had shown himself fit for a job in the Church before it was imposed on him. This fame helps to explain the increasing insistence in his writings that, whatever we have, we owe not to our merits, but to God's grace. While he wrote, he was being persistently tempted by others' praises of his merits and by the dangers of pride, as if he was superior to his brethren.

In due course Valerius himself promoted him. The succession to a long-serving bishop always brought risks, not least that faction might split the Church and that its finances and assets would be promised as gifts to win support for one or other candidate in the election. Pre-empting the future, elderly Valerius arranged that Augustine should be nominated immediately as his own co-bishop. In fact, 'joint appointments' with an existing bishop had been called into question by Constantine's great Council of Nicaea in 325. Valerius had gone ahead regardless, thinking that precedents existed.[2] The date of this initiative has long been disputed by scholars. Some have put it in 395, others in 396, but careful study of its announcement in the letters of Paulinus has now settled the question: it occurred in summer 396. Augustine became co-bishop in Hippo less than a year before he began to compose his confessions.[3]

On hearing the news, Paulinus, in Italy, recognized that it was a 'novel' sort of appointment. Valerius, he assumed, had been wanting to have Augustine as his successor, but had been given a co-bishop meanwhile. Augustine's own letters tell a different story. It was Valerius himself who imposed the job on him: he could not refuse, he says, although a bishopric, as ever, is a 'burden'. He had been unwilling, but he was told that there were precedents, and, evidently, he did not know they were unsound. He was obliged by his 'love' for Valerius and the 'eagerness' of the people.[4] Clearly, the appointment had been carried through in public.

His biographer Possidius gives a more detailed story, some of which comes from Augustine's own letters, some of it, probably, from what he had heard from him in later life.[5] Valerius, he says, began by writing to Aurelius, Bishop of Carthage, pleading old age and infirmity and his wish to share his job with Augustine. Aurelius wrote back from Carthage and granted the request, whereupon Valerius took the initiative. The senior bishop of Numidia, Megalius of Calama, was visiting Hippo's church and other bishops 'happened' to be there at the time together with Hippo's priests and Christian laity. Valerius introduced them to his 'unexpected' wish, whereupon they all acclaimed it and 'forced and compelled' Augustine to accept. They reassured him with precedents both in Africa and 'across the sea' of which he was ignorant. Only 'later' did he 'say and write' that his appointment should never have happened, and he regretted it.

Possidius' version was composed for his posthumous biography of the great Augustine, with whom he had lived in his later years. He was also the successor to Megalius' bishopric at Calama and would not wish to speak ill of the former holder of his see. In fact, Augustine's appointment was considered irregular even by the standards of early Christian bishoprics and was angrily attacked. In 396, Megalius' presence in Hippo had not been fortuitous. In the diocese of Numidia, ordinations to a bishopric had to be conducted by the longest-serving bishop, with others in attendance, and in 396 the longest server was Megalius. As the plan to appoint Augustine needed his consent, Valerius had to write to him first, but Megalius was enraged. All that he had heard about Augustine made him an impossible choice. He wrote back, denouncing him.

We know that this letter existed because, inevitably, Donatist Christians acquired a copy of it and about four years later used it to blacken Augustine all over again. In reply, Augustine addressed five of their allegations, most or all of which go back to Megalius' outburst.[6] They show that he had accused Augustine of being an overeducated public speaker and of being an unrepentant Manichee. No doubt he cited Augustine's denunciation as an active Manichaean on which the governor of north Africa had pronounced in 386. He may also have complained that Augustine's monasteries were secret Manichaean cells. Augustine's Catholic baptism was said to have happened far away in Milan, but there was no record of it anywhere in Africa. One item, certainly, which Megalius cited was Augustine's dispatch of a sinister present: 'noxious love charms' to a married woman, whose husband somehow connived in the gift.[7]

Such allegations were extremely damaging, not least because Manichaeism was still a capital offence. Valerius would have had to summon Megalius to Hippo, the reason, therefore, for the visit which Possidius mentions, and Augustine would have had to answer face to face. He could cite testimonies from people like Alypius and Evodius, his former companions in Italy with whom he had been baptized. He could also point to his anti-Manichaean writings, especially to his debate against Fortunatus, a widely witnessed victory whose official reports he had circulated. It was on this occasion, I believe, that he anathematized Mani and his teachings by reading out a formal statement and then signing it in front of his fellow bishops.

The evidence for this underappreciated event lies eight years later in December 404, when Augustine was demanding that a Manichaean Elect, Felix, with whom he was publicly disputing, should conclude by abjuring Mani in writing.[8] Felix agreed, so long as Augustine would do the same in a form of words which he then proposed. Augustine did so on a 'piece of paper' using the present tense, which Felix also used ('I anathematize Mani and his spirit of error'), but he began by saying 'I *have* already anathematized' Mani, his doctrine and his 'blasphemies'. As usual in such a debate, his exact words were being taken down by secretaries. This previous 'anathema' in Augustine's past is mentioned nowhere else, not even in the *Confessions*, although an abjuration of Mani would have fitted excellently with its anti-Manichaean passages. As the *Confessions* say nothing about one, I do not believe that Augustine had abjured Mani in Milan before Ambrose or his priests when he applied for baptism.[9] The likeliest occasion is 396, when Manichaeism was alleged as a reason why he should not be made a co-bishop.

If Augustine wrote and signed a personal abjuration, we can well understand why Megalius' accusations collapsed. Before a Council, evidently the one in Hippo, he apologized, begged forgiveness and ordained Augustine as Valerius' co-bishop. The laity approved 'keenly', according to Augustine's letter written soon afterwards, and this time he was not 'compelled'. His hesitations were only procedural. When 'precedents' were cited to him, he took up office and threw himself into the job.

The scandal and the joint appointment remained notorious nonetheless and Megalius' accusations lived on like unjust accusations on the modern internet. Nearly fifteen years later Donatist spokesmen raised them again at the climactic Council of Carthage in 411, a turning point in their history. Their spokesman asked Augustine face to face: 'who ordained you to your bishopric?' The Catholic notes of the proceedings are Augustine's own: they record the malice in the Donatists' question and Augustine's 'intrepid' answer.[10] Then, so Augustine's notes claim, the subject changed back to other topics. However, the official records of the Council were taken down by scribes and are much less bland.[11] They record that the question about Augustine's ordination was indeed put to him, but he declared it irrelevant. Noisy interruptions followed and only when he was asked no fewer than three separate times by the Council's president did Augustine answer. He asserted, 'with God as my witness, I am a Catholic'. Megalius, he stated, had ordained him. 'Go on,' he concludes, 'make your slanders.'

The Donatists' question was malicious. To answer it, Augustine asserted his Catholic credentials and then, as the official records show, dared his opponents to say the worst, knowing that it was linked with Megalius. Among the slanders, the most curious allegations are those 'noxious love charms' supposedly sent by Augustine to the wife of a conniving husband. Such an allegation against the chaste Augustine seems preposterous. Scholars have tended to reduce it to farce, to a 'love potion', perhaps, or, according to Henry Chadwick, a 'love philtre' even, 'for a married woman whose marriage was in trouble, causing her to fall for another man'.[12] However, as Pierre Courcelle first pointed out, Augustine himself linked the accusation to a gift of blessed bread. Indeed, he had been sending just such a gift to a famous married couple. We can follow it going to and fro with his letters: it is that loaf of bread, blessed and dispatched to Paulinus and his wife in Nola. It had left from Hippo with his carrier, Romanianus, after a loaf from Paulinus and Therasia had already reached him in Hippo.

Augustine recalls and scorns the charge against him as one concerning bread which was misrepresented by 'poisonous foulness and madness'. Like the other allegations, it needs to be understood in a Manichaean context. In 'mad' Manichaean company, bread was indeed represented by their critics as 'foul' and 'poisonous'. As Courcelle delicately remarks, it was considered to be 'soiled bread' (*pain souillé*), linked to the foul rumours which outsiders told about the nature of the Elect's holy meal.[13] Flour, it was alleged, was scattered on the floor and an Elect and a young lady were then said to have sex on it. The couple's juices ran out onto the flour and, in obedience to Mani's teaching, the Elect withdrew in time to avoid conception and to 'enlighten' the flour with his Light-rich sperm. The flour was then mixed and made into bread, the ultimate seeded loaf.

Whatever the truth, these rumours were well known. As a bishop, Augustine himself would later sit on committees which investigated alleged cases of the foul rite. He even received reports on them from clerics who had investigated the truth, validated by internal examinations of young Manichaean females.[14] In spring 396, these rumours had been very far from his mind. Thanking Paulinus kindly for his loaves, he had reciprocated and sent his own gift of bread off to Nola. As we have seen, the marriage of its recipient and his wife, Therasia, was not in trouble, but on ice. They were aspiring to cohabit, not as one flesh, but as 'one bone' without sex.

To outsiders in north Africa, the swapping of bread was a novelty.[15] The loaf's carrier was Romanianus, but it never occurred to Augustine that his postman was a liability for being a Manichaean. Nor did he imagine that his letter's closing wish that 'the Lord may protect you from this generation for eternity' would be wickedly misrepresented by his critics as the prayer of a true Manichaean, that the Lord might protect Paulinus and his wife from the 'act of generation', meaning sexual reproduction.[16] Without any warning of its scope for scandal, the bread arrived at Nola, and no doubt the couple were much touched by it. They broke it, presumably, and ate it in their simple monastic cell, which overlooked the site of their basilica for St Felix. They had no idea of the rumours which were to erupt round what they swallowed. A month or two passed and then, back in Africa, the donor, Augustine, was accused of sexual harassment at long range.

II

Scandalous allegation of this atrocious kind would have hurt Augustine profoundly. It was totally untrue and yet, on his own admission, he was always sensitive to others' criticisms. He hated malicious gossip. On the table of the monastic community which he later founded in his episcopal house, he had lines of verse engraved which he himself, it seems, had composed: 'Whoever loves to gnaw away in words at the life of those not present, let him know that his own life is unworthy of this table.' His associate and brother, Possidius, recalled witnessing how Augustine once 'sharply' reprehended some of his most intimate co-bishops when they were speaking contrary to the precept. 'Much moved', he told them that either the verses must be deleted from the table or he himself would get up from the middle of the meal and go off to bed.

In letters of Augustine and Paulinus which relate to their gifts of bread, we can watch the impact which Megalius' accusations had. In late 395, Paulinus sent his first letter to Augustine on the strength of reading his 'five books': 'see how I acknowledge you as a friend, with what awe I admire you, with what love I embrace you, I who daily enjoy the conversation of your writings and am fed by the spirit of your mouth'.[17] Paulinus ended by commending to him the loaf of bread which he was sending with his letter as a token of unanimity. By spring 396, hearing nothing, he wrote again, reiterating his love and unity, 'since we are filled with one grace, live by one bread and walk in one way . . .' If only he could see Augustine in person, but, meanwhile, could Augustine perhaps send 'some gift of the grace given to you', evidently yet more books, by using Paulinus' couriers, two fellow monks from Nola?[18]

In fact, Augustine had belatedly answered the first letter while unaware that this second letter had already been sent to chase him up. With that reply, he had already dispatched the fateful gift, his own loaf of bread.[19] Not until later in the summer of 396, after a gap of several months, did Augustine then reply to Paulinus' second letter. There was nothing ominous about this delay: it was caused by his need to wait until Paulinus' two couriers were free to take the letter home. They were waiting in Africa until the text of Eusebius' *Chronicles*, on loan from Italy, had been copied at Carthage and could be taken back. When they were ready, Augustine wrote to Paulinus and Therasia in the friendliest possible terms.[20] He quoted back to them the words of their first letter about 'one grace, one bread, one way'. He sent his three-book work *On Free Choice*, because Romanianus, his previous courier, had not had a copy of it. He asked for books in return: Paulinus' *Against the Pagans* and, from Paulinus' collection, a book by Ambrose which he did not have in Africa: it attacked people who seriously claimed that Christ had plagiarized Plato. He also sent Paulinus a most interesting young man, Vetustinus, 'pitiable, even for non-believers', who had been promising to become a 'slave of God'. Unfortunately for us, Augustine discreetly leaves Vetustinus' problems unspecified in his letter, but its carriers would elaborate them orally when they arrived. Vetustinus' promise to 'enslave' himself, he merely writes, needs greater maturity and the 'passing of his present fear', which will be helped by time spent with Paulinus.[21] Above all, might Paulinus and Therasia agree to come and present their good example in Africa? They were examples 'in one and the same marriage for both sexes of trampling down pride and not abandoning the hope of perfection'.[22] No such example of a chaste duet was available among Augustine's sexually segregated brethren and sisters in Hippo. They were all unmarried individuals.

The letter included a polite nudge. Paulinus had presumably read in Augustine's previous letter about the errant Licentius, Romanianus' son: could he please now intervene? There was also some surprising news to share. Augustine had assumed the 'burden' which Valerius had imposed on him and had become, 'reluctantly', a co-bishop.[23] Even so, he had not forgotten his previous gift of bread: 'the bread which we sent will become a richer blessing by the love of Your Benignity in receiving it'. He was wanting Paulinus to acknowledge its arrival and appreciate it.[24]

In Italy, Paulinus had been hesitating only until he knew that Augustine had received his second letter without offence. The very day after he received this reply, he acted exactly as requested. In the joint names of himself and Therasia he wrote effusively to Romanianus, the previous 'postman'. He was rejoicing, he told him, at the news of Augustine's bishopric. God, he wrote, has 'raised a man of strength in his Church so as to break the strength of sinners', just as the psalmist prophesied.[25] The sinners are Donatists and Manichaeans, but Augustine was not alone in his new role. Paulinus had also received letters from two existing bishops, Aurelius and Alypius, and two new bishops, Augustine's fellow monks Profuturus (his former envoy to Jerome) and Severus, his long-standing companion. These new promotions were indeed significant, though they were only a drop in Numidia's episcopal ocean.[26] They were all perfectionist monks, trained by life in Hippo's monastery.

After receiving Augustine's five books, Paulinus now had contacts with five bishops, all in office in north Africa. As for the errant Licentius, Paulinus wrote first to Romanianus, his father, expressing the hope that Augustine's spiritual aims would prevail over the young man's lusts. In Verecundus' villa, ten years earlier, he recalls, Augustine had given birth to a son 'in letters', one worthy indeed of Romanianus. May he now in his correspondence 'bring to birth in Christ' a son worthy of himself.[27] To help this rebirth as a 'virtuoso' Christian, Paulinus also wrote to Licentius, exactly as Augustine's letter had requested. He urged the boy to 'hold fast to the prophetic footstep and apostolic discipline' of Augustine, just as Elisha had once held on to the prophet Elijah. Then, Licentius would be a true '*pontifex* and a consul', two desirable, historic honours to which a man could aspire at Rome. In the villa, Augustine had cradled him and suckled him, like a mother, on baby food. As Licentius is still a baby in study of the word of God, he must let Augustine guide him with the 'hand of a mother and the arm of a nurse'. Not long before, Paulinus had introduced himself to Augustine in similar baby language.[28]

Paulinus was also a skilled poet. As Augustine had already sent him Licentius' poem in school hexameters, he now answered it with a long poem of his own. It is a far more elegant effort than Licentius'. To deter the young man from his career path, he invokes the pressures of Roman high society, something which he knew very well as a former senator. 'Do not consider as "free" the nobles whom you now see carried on high, before the awe-struck city.' To please them, Licentius will have to bow before idolaters 'worshipping silver and gold with the name of God'. Licentius must keep 'father Augustine' always before his mind as he faces all the 'attractions of the city: gaze on him; hold him in your heart, you will be safe among the great dangers of this fragile life'. Licentius must bend beneath the 'gentle yoke and light burden' which Jesus had preached in the Gospels: by this yoke and burden Paulinus was referring to the abandonment of worldly honours and sex. Without an ambitious career or a wife Licentius will be free, without chains, and will be a 'slave' only to Christ. He can count on two helpers: Augustine, who is his 'father', and his kinsman Alypius, who is his 'brother'. Their 'kingdoms' can be Licentius' if 'two just men conquer one sinner'. His mind will then penetrate the heavens, and by renouncing a career he will enjoy one great advantage: he will not have to endure military service.[29]

Licentius has left no answer, but in Rome we have a Latin inscription marking the burial in November 406 of a 'Licentius who is most illustrious' (*clarissimus*: a member, therefore, of the Senate).[30] No other Licentius is known to us in high society of this period and if, as is likely, this Licentius is our same one, he paid no attention to these two apostles of worldly renunciation: he went on to a highly successful career. Nonetheless, Paulinus had done his best. He even sent the boy and his father his hallmark presents: five loaves of bread. They were 'five from the army of Christ's supplies, in whose army we fight daily for a frugal living'.[31]

Manifestly, Paulinus' two brethren, returned from Carthage, had not brought back the scandalous allegations against Augustine which had erupted in north Africa. Although they would have attended his episcopal ordination, afterwards they had carried his letter and his loaf of bread dutifully back to Nola. At first, therefore, the foulest details of Megalius' outburst had remained confined to Bishop Valerius and his inner circle. In late summer 396, Paulinus was still unaware of them, and so, it seems, was Augustine.

Augustine's awareness of the full story can be traced, I believe, in a subsequent letter. Writing to his dear Profuturus, he recalls a conversation which the two of them had recently shared 'while on a journey'.[32] In late summer or autumn 396, Augustine had gone to Cirta for Profuturus' consecration as a bishop. The two then travelled on further together, as they were concerned to investigate troubles concerning Donatists. On the way, we learn, Profuturus had told Augustine something which related to anger and the need to control it. The context in which Augustine refers to this anger is the news, no less, of Megalius' death.[33] The neatest guess, amply deserving such anger, is that Profuturus told Augustine for the first time about the vile slander contained in Megalius' initial letter to Valerius. Once known, there would be no containing it from the vicious twitter of Donatists and other suspicious bishops in Africa. Inevitably, it would swirl across to Italy and reach Nola.

Until late summer 396, Paulinus had been the most eager initiator of letters in Augustine's direction and extremely prompt to act on Augustine's requests. Now, abruptly, he falls silent. Time passes, and in autumn 397 Augustine, in some irritation, writes again. Paulinus and Therasia, he says, are 'daily' giving away their possessions, so why will they not pay him what they owe (a letter)? His dear friend and fellow bishop Severus is stopping over at Nola: two summers have passed now (396 and 397), and Augustine is still 'thirsting' in thirsty Africa, waiting for a reply to his last letter.[34] Is it that Paulinus is still writing his book *Against the Pagans*, of which Augustine had requested a copy in his previous letter? Some 'refreshment' would be welcome, nonetheless, even before the book is perfected.

Letters by Augustine and his correspondents are beset by gaps in the surviving evidence which usually prevent certainty about the missing pieces. However, in spring 398 (in my view) Augustine sent another letter and tried again. By then, north Africa was beset with political danger: one Gildo had been in armed rebellion, and as it ended Gildo's brother fled from Africa to Italy. The bishops of north Africa may have been fearing that he would exercise his malign influence against them. A courier left for Italy with a batch of clerical letters, including a letter from Augustine and Alypius to Paulinus which had hitched a ride in the postbag. It vouched for their courier's reliability, but did not write out his name, doubtless for fear that the letter might be intercepted at this time of political turmoil.[35] Yet again, Augustine wrote of his concern at Paulinus' mystifying silence. Has his former letter not arrived? Has a reply from Paulinus somehow been lost? Please will Paulinus send a copy of *Against the Pagans* if he has finished it? The 'more ardently we love you, the less we can put up with you not writing'.[36] From these remarks, it is certain that Paulinus had not sent other letters now lost to us. He had remained silent. Initially, it had been he who had pressed Augustine for letters. Now, Augustine was the one who was pushing.

Paulinus was not being detained by the problem of writing his book. For at least two years he had maintained silence. Modern scholars have sometimes wondered if he had been shocked by Augustine's recent writings on the grace of God. The reason for his silence was surely less abstract: he believed what he had heard, that he and his wife had swallowed Augustine's seeded loaf.

40
Shared Burdens

I

Among these scandalous protests, Augustine had continued busily. His appointment as a co-bishop in summer 396 led to a new range of practical responsibilities, but unlike his priesthood it did not precipitate flight. In one of his most recently found sermons, he remarks how the great Cyprian had had to show the 'innocence of a dove and the cunning of a snake' while Bishop of Carthage.[1] As co-bishop of Hippo, Augustine was still both lion and lamb; nonetheless he found time for a burst of writing and preaching, which, in my view, is the most concentrated in all Christian history.

Even when his appointment was misdated to 395, a year too early, this burst was still evident. It was confirmed by the review of his works in sequence which he carried out near the end of his life.[2] His first work as a co-bishop, he writes, was his reply to Simplicianus. He then wrote an attack on the Manichaeans' *Letter of Foundation*, a copy of which he owned. He wrote a book, in (for him) simpler Latin, *On the Christian Struggle*, aiming to instruct those who lacked high-flown Latin 'eloquence' themselves. He wrote three and a half books of his *On Christian Teaching*: like *Christian Struggle*, the text would be widely copied in medieval Europe. He also wrote two books against the partisans of Donatus. His review then lists the writing of the *Confessions*.

This surge is not the achievement of someone who was cowed by a new job or the allegations surrounding it. Many scholars therefore wonder if it could have been so concentrated: in old age was he, perhaps, listing the order in which he began these books, but not in which he finished them? In my view, he composed all these works, and more, in a single, awesome sweep of about twelve months. Painstaking modern scholars underestimate the fluency and speed of trained ancient composers when equipped with shorthand secretaries.[3] As a co-bishop, Augustine had secretaries freely available, more freely, even, than during his priesthood. They would take down whatever he preached or dictated.

Most of the texts written in 396/7 relate to his new episcopal role. *On the Christian Struggle* and *On Christian Teaching* were works to guide and instruct fellow Christians, especially preachers and teachers. They include attacks on Donatist and Manichaean beliefs which are the subject of two other works in the 'surge'. *Christian Struggle* begins with a presence previously minimal in Augustine's writings: the Devil. It then addresses 'precepts for Christian living' followed by the 'rule of faith' and gives answers to eighteen 'errors' about Christian belief. The text may simply have been developed from two sermons, taken down by scribes and originally conceived for baptismal candidates.[4] Its two categories, 'precepts' and a 'rule', are the titles of Augustine's foundational texts for his monastic communities. The date and origins of these texts, too, have been a major challenge for scholars, but it is now highly likely that both the *Rule* and the *Precepts* were Augustine's own work, the *Rule*, at least, being written in 396.[5] There was a good reason for him to write it then. When he became co-bishop, his daily relations to his brethren in the monasteries at Thagaste and in Hippo's garden would be interrupted by his other responsibilities. It made sense for him to write out a *Rule* of 'best practice', now that he would be present less often in person.

His text refuting Mani's *Letter of Foundation* was one more nail in the Manichaeans' coffin. It was also a well-judged text from a man who had just been accused of crypto-Manichaeism in the crudest terms. He was writing keenly because there was a job to be done. His senior bishop, Aurelius in Carthage, continued to wish to raise the standards of argument and understanding in his churches and, therefore, in barely eighteen months he appointed four celibate champions, Augustine and three of his fellow brethren, to bishoprics in his diocese. He also wanted to allow ever more priests to preach in church, the model which Valerius had assisted by ordaining Augustine.[6] Augustine's texts would help to raise these novice preachers' standards. Part of his surge of new writing, therefore, relates to an initiative agreed between bishops. In a letter, Augustine even refers to himself as 'doing what Aurelius had commanded' and asks him for advice as to how his text *On Christian Teaching* should proceed.[7]

The texts in the surge rehearse themes which the *Confessions* will develop. *Against the Letter of Foundation* is truly a 'sword in honey', addressed to Manichaeans with the offer of setting aside all arrogance and merely seeking the truth. 'Others can rage against them,' Augustine writes, and then describes the enraged complaints which they will raise, 'whereas' Augustine himself will do no such thing, having once 'sought with curiosity, listened with attention and defended with stubbornness' the Manichaeans' 'fictions', which are embedded in their daily way of life. He had wept for 'so long', he writes, in the hope that an 'unchangeable and incorruptible substance' would convince him 'within himself of its advent, while the divine scriptures agree, too, in harmony'.[8] This progress is the one he will soon describe in detail in *Confessions*, Books 3–7. He then goes on to consider 'memory' and why, containing so much, it cannot be a 'place'.[9] This same theme will be explored in *Confessions*, Book 10.

On Christian Teaching may have been aimed primarily at aspiring clergy and preachers, but it freely uses the first person, 'I'.[10] Again, Augustine addresses his own experience in ways pregnant for the *Confessions*. He denounces astrology, the contrary lusts of the flesh and Platonism. However, Christians can justly rob Platonists when they agree with the scriptures, just as the Israelites once robbed the treasures of the Egyptians.[11] Exactly this perspective will be applied to Augustine's own progress and Platonist encounters in the *Confessions*. *On Christian Teaching* insists that the scriptures must be read for their spiritual meaning, as Augustine had learned in Milan, and with expert help, as he had discovered there from Ambrose. They must be understood in faith, hope and, above all, love. The final book of the *Confessions* will read Genesis in exactly this way. Through the Holy Spirit, God has placed hidden meanings beneath the scriptures' text. The Holy Spirit then pours love into Christian believers' hearts and through this love they can then discern the scriptures' mysteries. The Bible is best understood through a 'loop' of love.[12]

All the while, Augustine was reading and noting his copy of the Book of Job in translation. When Job tells his friends, 'I do not seek help from you', Augustine commented that 'the "true man" seeks help from God and the "true man" is one that confesses. As John's Gospel says, "he that seeks the truth, comes to the light" '. These same words resound in the confessions. When Augustine starts to lay bare 'what I am', he states that he is setting out to 'do the truth, in my heart, in Your presence, in confession'.[13]

II

This surge of writing was punctuated by practical business. It is a telling contrast to the business which confronted Synesius after his ordination in Ptolemais about fifteen years later. Synesius was promptly drawn into the feuding of the magnates of Libya, even urging one of them to submit to judgement for a charge of murder. Within months he had himself mobilized a possible excommunication of the governor, no less, of the Libyan Pentapolis, officially on a charge of his denying fugitive slaves and others their legally recognized right of asylum in a church. The governor had also accepted his job contrary to the law that nobody should be a governor of the province which was his home. He was also accused of excessive and unjustified use of torture in collecting taxes and in other feuds which set him against Synesius' petitioners.[14] Importantly, these grievances were ones which would have come to Synesius as a local aristocrat even before he assumed his bishopric. By birth and background, he was well able to outface such people: he was still someone whom others would want to become involved. Augustine, by contrast, was only one bishop among the hundreds in north Africa, with no previous history of meeting his province's magnates on their own terms. The most urgent business for a Catholic bishop in north Africa was internal to the Christian community. As soon as they met in their new role, Valerius and his co-bishop could not fail to discuss the most manifest trouble in their diocese: the Donatist schism. Here, too, there are actions in 396/7 which suggest an agreed initiative.

In Hippo, Augustine's close friend and companion Evodius had tried to initiate debate. By chance, according to Augustine, he found himself in the same house as the city's Donatist bishop and together they discussed the 'heritage of Christ'.[15] According to Evodius, the bishop offered to discuss the schism with Augustine 'in the presence of good men'. Evodius was then believed to have made an offensive reply, as if right was all on his side. The Donatist bishop took umbrage.

On hearing of the meeting, Augustine wrote to the bishop to try to smooth over the offence. Evodius, he explained, had been 'rather too excited in defence': he was perhaps too 'confident', but he was certainly not 'arrogant'. It was such excellent news, after all, that the bishop was prepared to discuss their differences. If so, shorthand secretaries could take down the debate and keep it straight. If not, the two of them could write or meet individually and the results could then be circulated. If not, they could at least write to each other and then their letters could be read out to their respective congregations. This proposal was exactly the one which Augustine had suggested to another Donatist bishop three years earlier. Then, too, it had failed.

Augustine was writing to this bishop in Valerius' absence, but explicitly with his support.[16] Their plan was clear enough. Augustine would enter into a debate with the Donatist leaders, just as he had already debated with Fortunatus, the leading Manichee. Beneath the wish to persuade lay the intention to win remorselessly on point after point. No bishop who knew Augustine's reputation would readily submit to what would become a grilling. At first, the Donatist bishop of Hippo was believed to have agreed and even to have been willing to go on official record as saying so. His priest, however, backtracked.

Meanwhile, similar tactics had been applied further south in the diocese. We know of them only as part of a back story in Augustine's later letters, but it becomes clear that one encounter belongs in late summer or autumn 396. Augustine and Alypius, both now bishops, had been riding from Thagaste with some fellow Christians to another bishop's ordination, surely their friend Profuturus', out in Cirta.[17] They had stopped on the way, about twenty-five miles west of Thagaste, at Thurbursica Numidarum (modern Khamissa) in the mountainous hills which contain the source of the River Mejerda. In this upland town, the Donatist bishop, Fortunius, was an elderly man, but as he agreed to meet the two bishops, they went to his house and began to talk with him. The news spread, and crowds gathered, hoping to witness a pugnacious debate. They give us a clear insight into the depth and passion of the schism, even far away from bigger cities. For several hours, the two bishops debated in public, but were beset throughout by noisy interruptions from their spectators. They had agreed to use shorthand secretaries, but the only volunteers for the job were some of the 'brethren' with Augustine: they were harassed by all the noise and shouting and soon gave up. On finishing the debate, Augustine then sent a long letter of the proceedings to Fortunius, hoping that he would agree the record to be correct.[18] There is no evidence that Fortunius did so.

The debate covered plenty of ground: the historical origins of the schism, the relation between persecution and justice, even the Donatists' practice of rebaptizing Catholics, which old Fortunius admitted to be regrettable. He had brought a historic text to help his case: a copy of the acts of the old Council of Serdica, now more than fifty years in the past. Its contents certainly surprised Augustine. Fortunius' view of the schism's history was not wholly obdurate, and so, on the next day, debate resumed. However, Augustine, Alypius and their brethren then had to leave for the ordination ceremony before a clear conclusion could be reached. Before departing, Augustine asked to be allowed to mark in his own hand the copy of the Acts of Serdica he had been shown. He was aware that it might be replaced with a faked one as soon as he was gone. The request was refused, but it was a reminder that throughout the schism forged documents continued to bedevil the arguments.[19]

This marathon of many hours had been watched and barracked by a big Christian audience. It was to be followed by yet another popular debate elsewhere. This time, Augustine was less hurried. He had stopped in the town of Thiava, unknown to us on the map but evidently near to Thubursica, to whose bishopric it belonged.[20] Probably, he was returning from the ordination at Cirta. Yet again, records of past history were read out by the Donatists and, in reply, Augustine and his attendants sent for records from a nearby church: they took another two days to arrive. The debate on the schism's origins then endured from morning to afternoon, culminating in Augustine's reading of a letter from the Emperor Constantine which patently supported the Catholic party.

Out in the hilly reaches of the diocese, texts, letters and documents were still readily being assembled by unyielding Donatists, confident of their vision of the past. Once again, Augustine took pains to write a letter which set out the topics covered and which explained, for the record, the Catholic case. He then sent it to prominent laymen in Thiava, the same people to whom he sent a letter containing his recent debate with Fortunius. The letters were intended to persuade and be circulated as well as to record. Among his works, Augustine looks back in later life on two books written 'against the party of Donatus'.[21] They have not survived as independent texts, but surely they are the texts which survive in these two letters, as good as books of detailed argument. If so, his surge of entirely new writing in this phase is reduced.

It was, I believe, on this same journey, to and from Profuturus' ordination, that Augustine had a more testing encounter. He passed through Spanianum, also as yet unlocated on our maps, and heard a tale of shameless sin.[22] A deacon of the Catholic church had been fraternizing, against the rules, with two receptive nuns. He had been defrocked and, in anger, had gone over to the Donatists and been rebaptized. Two nuns then went with him, presumably the same two. They were said to have joined roving gangs of the thuggish Circumcellions and 'bands of women who have shamefully refused to have husbands for fear of having any discipline'. The ex-deacon was 'proudly glorifying in orgies of loathsome drunkenness'.

The stories were excellent ammunition with which to prompt reluctant civil officials in Hippo into action against Donatists. Out in the field, they had been matched by something more direct. In Spanianum, the daughter of a Catholic, a tenant farmer on Church property, had joined the Donatists 'against her parents' will'. She had been baptized and was now dressing herself as a nun. Augustine insisted that she should only be taken back into the Catholic Church if she freely wished, a view in keeping with his general dislike at this time of forced conversions. Her father, the farmer, tried to beat her into agreement, but Augustine 'totally forbade' him.[23]

Meanwhile, as he and his Catholic companions passed through Spanianum itself, they rode by the estate of a 'Catholic and laudable lady'. On it stood a Donatist priest who shouted abuse at the passers-by. He called Augustine and his Catholics 'handers-over' (of the scriptures in the Great Persecution) and 'persecutors'. He also shouted abuse at the lady who owned the farm. Augustine writes that he had to restrain himself from beginning a fight. He also had to pacify his companions.

Less than six months before his confessions, these encounters with 'life as it is lived' are significant. Despite his confessing image, Augustine had not become a meek, self-abasing introvert. Anger was a temptation which still beset him, as it beset many others in antiquity, to the point of almost beginning a punch-up. It was surely while Augustine and Alypius were travelling to this ordination that they also wrote to Bishop Aurelius in Carthage, asking him to send copies of the sermons which his newly empowered priests were preaching.[24] With them to hand, Augustine would better see how his *On Christian Teaching* might improve the new preachers. At the end of the letter, Augustine asks Aurelius for guidance on the work he is doing at Aurelius' 'command': what does he think of Tyconius' seven 'rules'? Tyconius was the dissident Donatist whose rulebook, or 'keys', for interpreting the scriptures had already helped Augustine in his biblical expositions. His *On Christian Teaching*, when finished, would discuss these very rules, but, as he later tells us, it was abandoned for more than twenty years at a point just before its discussion of Tyconius began. The reason, evidently, was that Aurelius refused to endorse any engagement with a

Donatist thinker, even one of Tyconius' dissident status. Either Aurelius refused to reply, or else he sent such a negative answer that Augustine did not preserve it. At this tense time, there could be no question of putting a Donatist author to use in a Catholic book.[25]

Augustine, meanwhile, was making feline advances to Donatist leaders both in person and by letter, reiterating his wish for a 'debate' in which he would reduce them to surrender. He had also written very long letters to show, point by point, that Donatists were the schism's guilty party. Out on the road, a Donatist had insulted him, and he had nearly hit back. Yet, the *Confessions* never even mention the Donatists' existence, let alone their name. They have been read as an implicit counter to Donatists' teaching and theology, but if Augustine wanted to compose such a counter, he had shown repeatedly that he could phrase and address one against them head-on.[26]

III

By early 397 many of the building blocks of the *Confessions* were in place: close engagement with the Psalms (deepened by writing the *Expositions*), a view of non-Christian writing as mere 'husks' for pigs, the progress into and out of Manichaean beliefs, the placing of Platonist wisdom in relation to Christian teaching, the interest in memory's capacities, the presentation of a Christian's life as a pilgrimage among sin and temptation (Augustine's theme since his very first sermon as a priest to baptismal candidates), the use of his own personal journey to God as an example for others (since his text to Honoratus, six years earlier), the three essential lusts in human nature (since *On True Religion*), the allegorical reading of Genesis (since 388/9), the relation between God's foreknowledge and a convert's free will (the texts on Romans since June 394), the multiple meanings in scripture and the need for them to be interpreted with love (the soaring theme of the *Confessions*' final book). In *On Christian Teaching*, he had just considered the relation of pagan and Christian texts and philosophy, a running theme of the *Confessions*' presentation of his early life and his response to meeting the Platonic books. He had also returned to the nature of the seven steps in a Christian's spiritual ascent. The third step, now, was the step of 'knowledge', acquired in the scriptures but leading to 'lamentation about oneself' while showing humble submission to the scriptures' authority. In the *Confessions*, it is through scripture that Augustine expresses such 'lamentation' about his own self. The reading of scripture both encourages lament and expresses it. In their final books the step of 'knowledge' is the step on which he is poised.

These themes had all emerged since his conversion in the garden, but they were not the results of yet more conversions. They were evolutions, rather, in the eleven years of his writing, thinking and action, whose course we have been able to follow as for no other early Christian. The *Confessions* were not a sudden break with Augustine's past. Nonetheless, they needed an impulse, or 'prompt'. Some have seen it in Augustine's contact with Paulinus and his request for details of his new-found friends' life-changing choices. However, relations with Paulinus had broken off abruptly since autumn 396. Others have seen it in the supposed coldness with which Augustine's new answers on grace and free will had been received. Others, even, have supposed a 'spiritual crisis' or a routine re-examination of his life, unsurprising, it is suggested, for a man in his early forties.[27]

In a remarkable letter, Augustine presents himself in a somewhat different predicament. Early in 397, perhaps in February, he writes to the man whom he calls his '*alter ego*', Profuturus, now a bishop, to tell him that he is acutely ill. He is in bed. He cannot sit and he cannot walk. He describes his condition by two words of Greek origin, implying an expert medical assessment. He has haemorrhoids, or piles (*exochadae*), and 'anal fissures' (*rhagadae*). 'As we are sure it is the Lord's will,' he writes, 'what also can we say, except that we are doing very well?' in body as well as in spirit. Augustine's faith in God's 'order' and goodness was being tested from the bottom up.[28]

Eight years before, on returning to Carthage, he had observed human agony and the grace of God at work in a bed-ridden government official, suffering similar pain in the backside. In his major commentary on the *Confessions*, James O'Donnell first aired the possibility that the book might have owed its origin to Augustine's time in bed with piles, but he left it merely as a possibility.[29] In the experience of modern clinical specialists, the most frequent cause of multiple fissures of the anus is dietary. Augustine's weekly fasting, maybe, was taking its toll on his colon. Might we be witnessing the crucible in which the *Confessions* began?

In his letter, Augustine asks Profuturus to pray that he may not 'use the days intemperately' and that he may 'tolerate the nights with equanimity'. He must pray, too, that 'even if we walk in the valley of the shadow of death, we may fear no ill'. Revealingly, Augustine is applying the first-person words of a psalmist to himself. He is in extreme pain, clearly: how better to divert attention from it than to compose and dictate a prayer of confession to God, kneeling while he did so, the position, unlike sitting or lying, which would cause him the least discomfort?

Confined to his room, he certainly had time free for dictation, the commodity which the past few months on the road had denied him. The *Confessions* are not the cry of a man in physical agony, but as he had realized in the suffering Innocentius' bedroom, there was no greater cue for a sense of God's grace than a sense of relief at escape from pains in the backside. Suffering is thus the sixth and last of my steps on the path to the *Confessions'* inception.

As his letter goes on to show, there was more to its context than O'Donnell's passing suggestion emphasized. The news, Augustine tells Profuturus, had recently arrived that old Bishop Megalius had died: he had been buried only three and a half weeks ago. Perhaps, he suggests, Profuturus knows his successor: he was to be Possidius, Augustine's devoted future biographer. 'There is no lack of scandals, but neither of refuge, too . . .': is Augustine recalling here the 'scandals' that Megalius had spread about his own elevation and implying that the choice of a friend to take Megalius' place would indeed be a welcome 'refuge'?[30] The Latin is unspecific, surely as intended. However, he goes on, enigmatically, to remind Profuturus that 'among these things' great vigilance must be shown to stop 'hatred' for anyone from entering the innermost reaches of his heart. A disquisition then follows on the perils of succumbing to anger and its way of taking over the 'shrine of the heart'. He concludes it by reminding Profuturus of the 'things which he had mentioned to him on their recent journey'.[31] In my view, they were the full range of Megalius' slanders, including Augustine's supposed gift of seeded bread.

Confined to his bedroom, Augustine had been brought to consider yet again the atrocious twitter which had attended him in the previous year and had deeply hurt him.[32] Recently, he and his friends had been asked by Paulinus to describe their making as 'virtuoso' Christians and their past. It would also encourage others. So in all humility he began to revisit 'what I once was'. Unlike the allegations at this time, the *Confessions* could hardly be more un-Manichaean, from their opening prayer to God to their final reading of Genesis's words about Creation. So far from showing him to be an overskilled secular orator, a complaint which Megalius appears to have made, they pour scorn on the rhetorical arts of his youth. As for 'noxious love charms' for a married woman, they were unthinkable from an author who had given up sex eleven years ago and was glorying in the new stability of chastity and his late-found love for God. 'What I once was . . .' took his story down to his departure from Italy, hiding nothing, it claimed, from its primary audience, God. It also happened to cover the very years to which many of the scandalous allegations had attached, implicitly correcting them on each point. So far from being a crypto-Manichaean before his baptism, Augustine explained that he had been reading Psalm 4 and angrily deploring their errors. As for 'what I am', Augustine does not present himself as the hammer of Manichees and Donatists, the man who had nearly come to blows with a rude Donatist priest only weeks before, who had proposed to ban fellow Christians' commemoration-parties and was now trying to improve their priests' preaching. Not at all: he is an introspective, aspiring perfectionist, still beset by the 'triple lusts' of Christian tradition, but hoping to re-establish contact with the Father who had briefly come within his sight and hearing.

'Great You are, O Lord, and greatly to be praised . . . You have made us so as to turn to You and our heart is restless until it finds rest in You . . .' The greatest prayer in Christian literature began to flow.

41
Confessing

I

A masterpiece like the *Confessions* cannot be reduced to the 'prompt' which set it in motion. It is propelled by much more, by hope and humility, a rhythmic skill with words, especially the words of God in scripture, and a love and longing which reach a climax in its concluding appreciation of God's grace. Illness may have been the cue for them, but their dynamic goes far beyond a need to distract from pains in the backside. 'You [God] arrow-struck my heart with Your love' and 'struck it through': this is the wound from which the *Confessions* arise. The recent slanders could still tempt Augustine to anger, but the *Confessions* are not reducible to timely self-defence, either. They contain some answers to critics, but Augustine has no illusions about his own continuing wickedness. So far from evading them or hiding it, he accuses himself throughout before God. He gives enough new material to allow critics plenty of scope.

The pace, shape and impetus of his work have been endlessly discussed by modern scholars. It does not reveal its secrets, and therefore any theory of them has to rely on inference and, to a degree, a subjective sense of how they came about. The prevailing scholarly view is one of prolonged composition, even piecemeal composition, put together over four to six years. My own view is sharply different, and in order to put it into context, I will draw on two sources, first, the other autobiographic work of this period, Libanius' long speech about his life, and then evidence which has emerged only recently in one of Augustine's hitherto unknown letters. I will then support the work's unity by adducing Augustine's general views about prayer, the *Confessions*' genre. Their beginning is placed by Augustine himself in what we now fix as the year 397, in his review of his own writings in old age. They do not stand apart, therefore, from his great surge of composition in 396–7. Scholars wonder how they could have been composed in full during a phase when much else had to be begun or completed. I believe that they emerge as its crowning achievement. Against all expectations, yet more of this surge has recently been discovered and, in my view, it concludes one of antiquity's most remarkable bursts of verbal activity, even by the standards of Christian preaching.

Every reader of the *Confessions* is puzzled by their structure: first, the nine books which revisit 'what I once was', the foundation of all Augustine's modern biographies, then the long tenth book on 'what I am', which focuses on memory and persisting sins, and then the three books which set out to meditate on the first chapters of Genesis. Two of these final books go no further than Genesis's first two verses, while the third concludes with Genesis 2.3 ('on the seventh day'). Modern critics have often explained this puzzling sequence as a combination of pieces, composed at separate times. Even so, they dispute the scope of the pieces: did the first eight books exist separately and were the last three written later with the long tenth book somehow added in? The composition of the whole is then proposed to have extended over three, four or, on one recent view, six years, ending only in spring 403.[1] Believers in such a long-drawn-out composition rest some of their case on verbal parallels which they find in Augustine's later, datable works and which match short phrases in the *Confessions*' text. These parallels are then claimed to precede the *Confessions*' integration of similar phrases into its bigger whole. However, parallels of thought and phrasing also exist in works finished long before the *Confessions* were begun, and nobody would argue that they help to date it.[2] Practised speakers and preachers in antiquity were well able to recycle previously used themes and phrases at later dates. Attempts to use them to fix a chronology would fail in many other cases, not least in the speeches and 'prefaces' of the classic Greek orator Demosthenes, whose contents were objects of Libanius' close study during Augustine's lifetime.[3] A related method is to study the *Confessions*' uses of particular verses of scripture and especially their uses of several in similar clusters, their 'scriptural orchestration'. Some of these clusters recur in later, datable works, suggesting that the *Confessions* may belong precisely when these clusters became prominent in Augustine's writing and preaching. However, as its exponents recognize, this method is at risk to the loss of many of Augustine's sermons, which may well have used a particular scriptural cluster earlier, and also to the demonstrable existence of early outlying examples long before a scriptural cluster is repeated. The method is admitted to deal only in probabilities and the 'convergences' of individual indicators. It risks deducing the probable from the uncertain. I will infer my preferred solutions partly from a subjective sense of the *Confessions*' own pace and texture, and partly, as we all do, by citing close parallels in other works in support, fragile though it is. There is no scientific method, but, nonetheless, there was once a date, a speed and a context for what we now read. In other contested cases in ancient history, the way to cut through to it is to be bold and pull the pieces into a whole, whatever the prevailing traditional view. Supporters of tradition may resort to a general scepticism about any close dating at all, especially one new to them, but that scepticism should also apply to the view they have been adopting.[4]

When Augustine reviews each of his works in later life, he comments that he wrote some of them in separate phases. He says no such thing about the *Confessions*. They were composed, he therefore implies, in a single continuous burst. They contain no fixed points which date them, but to emphasize their unified structure I will now contrast them with Libanius' use of autobiography, the work of a highly trained orator, the pagan equivalent of young Augustine until the age of thirty-two.

II

Libanius composed the first version of his exceptional speech on himself for public delivery in Antioch in 374. At that time, Augustine was a newish Manichaean Hearer in Carthage, aged twenty and living with his concubine and two-year-old son. Libanius, by contrast, was aged sixty. The original title of his speech is unknown, perhaps *On His Own Fortune*, but it shows what a text about oneself looks like if composed piecemeal over many years. The first text ran, as he himself says, until his sixtieth year, the time of its delivery. Manifestly, almost as much has been added subsequently because the later parts refer to events in his sixties and afterwards, spanning nearly twenty more years. At least two blocks of such material can be detected, although some modern scholars argue for the existence of as many as eight.[5] The connections are not subtle and have caused critics to suggest that Libanius was adding material at intervals to a master copy without ever declaiming it publicly as a whole. Whether he kept it to a few friends or not, the text as we have it ends on a resounding note in the year 393, when Libanius was 79. At that time, Augustine had been a priest in Hippo for nearly two years.

From the beginning, Libanius cast his autobiography in an artful form. He had already shown his skill at devising speeches in apparent self-defence: he had spoken *On My Not being Harsh and Disagreeable*, for instance, or on *That I am Not Senile*, two fascinating examples of the genre.[6] Cleverly, such speeches set up an accusation in order to refute it, thereby allowing him to praise himself. In similar style, his 'autobiography' discusses his life in terms of a balance sheet of Fortune, good and bad. Some people, he claims, consider him to be the most fortunate person, because of the 'applause' which his lectures elicit: this claim is a neat piece of oblique self-praise in the very first paragraph. Others consider him 'the most wretched' because of his constant 'dangers and ordeals'. Instead, he will show that he is neither, but that the gods 'mixed' the 'results of Fortune' and have given him both good and bad. The mixing of good and evil by the gods is a theme as old as Homer, but it artfully defines the autobiography's scope. Libanius' life in the public eye has been mixed, like everybody's, and while proving the point, he can dwell safely on its successes.

Such self-praise was not conventional in a speech in Greek literature. Classical orators had included material about themselves in speeches for courtroom settings, but none, not even the voluble Isocrates, had devoted an entire speech to his own life.[7] Moralists had discussed the role of 'fortune', but only in others' lives, especially Alexander the Great's. Libanius' oratorical role model, Aelius Aristides (*flor.* 150–80), had spoken and written personally, sometimes in answer to critics, but had not reviewed his entire life while doing so. On this point, Libanius' speech is unprecedented. He composed it consciously for an audience, most or all of whom would presumably be invited hearers, many of them his ex-pupils. They would know as well as Libanius himself that slander and vicious accusations had continued to dog his life. When their elderly tutor stood up to speak, connoisseurs of academic conceit and evasion would be hoping for a treat.

They cannot have been disappointed. On first reading the speech, moderns (since Gibbon) have found it vain, verbose and in too many places vindictive. There is far more to it. It is very well written in literary Attic prose, deftly drawing on the classics. It evokes its author's career as a public speaker even more vividly than Augustine's *Confessions* evoke his. It testifies to the enduring reception in Greek cities of speeches when delivered for display: elderly hearers, Libanius claims, used to stand up and cheer at his public performances, though crippled by such pains in their feet that he would try to persuade them to sit down.[8] The further his speech extends, the more memorably it presents his need to negotiate the whims of each Roman governor in Syria, men who were often boorish and self-seeking. In his letters to such people, Libanius shows himself master of the moral platitudes which attached to the image of the 'good governor' and which survive in honorific inscriptions in their honour: their justice, their hard work, their 'gentleness', their care for a city. In his *Autobiography*, he gives the other side, no doubt because such people were not present. One of the worst, Tisamenus, denied Libanius a favour in 386, the year of Augustine's conversion, but found himself 'punished' by never attending his speeches, and then by being posted away to the Eastern frontier on the River Euphrates, 'under the blazing sun', Libanius memorably concludes, 'always thirsting, always drinking . . .'[9]

Already, contrasts with Augustine, when confessing, are clear. Unlike Libanius, Augustine could never claim or dare to have outfaced a figure as powerful as a Roman governor. He never dwells on the endemic envy and malice which no doubt accompanied his youthful career. He evokes the classics of his youth, Virgil, Terence or Sallust, but he looks back on them as misdirected vanity. Libanius' speech, by contrast, is the most heartfelt witness to a continuing love of the immortal classics, especially two of their geniuses, the historian Thucydides and the comic playwright Aristophanes.[10] Augustine never read either of them, but they are the authors who would best have challenged his mature world-view, Thucydides by his sceptical views about appeals to the gods, Aristophanes by his combination of laughter and sex.

Like Augustine, nonetheless, Libanius reviews his life in terms of divine guidance. He relates it, as we have seen, to the goddess Fortune. Long before Libanius, Fortune's role in history had been debated by historians; she had also been used as the guiding thread in ancient novels, those complex tales of adventure and long-postponed sexual love.[11] Yet, personified Fortune was also honoured and appeased as a divine presence in everyday lives. She was honoured in this way by the 'confessing' pagan Emperor Marcus Aurelius, and for Libanius, likewise, Fortune was much more than a literary figure.[12] She was an actively concerned goddess. She is not merely the prominent civic goddess, well known from her statues and her big temple in Antioch. When Libanius composed his speech, public cult had probably been stopped in this temple.[13] His Fortune is a goddess without a cult-epithet which would tie her to one place or function. She is one active deity among others in the pagan heaven. She exercises 'care' and 'forethought' in a world which is full, Libanius assumes, of active gods. They have been his companions throughout his lifetime.

Why ever did he speak, and then continue to write, about himself in this way during so many years? When he began the first version of his speech, he set out to establish Fortune's 'providence' both from 'what pertained to me in the past' and 'from what is still now the case'.[14] The *Confessions* of his fellow providentialist Augustine adopt the same time frame: 'what I once was' and 'what I am'. Both are selective about what they recall. Both skip over a block of recent time. Augustine's *Confessions* omit ten years, as they admit, from his mother's death in Ostia in 387 to 'what I [now] am', an introspective perfectionist in 397. Without forewarning us, the first version of Libanius' speech omits almost everything in the ten years from 364 to 374, the greater part of the reign of the Emperor Valens, under whom he was speaking.

When Libanius first decided to speak about his 'fortune', he had lived through exceptionally perilous years. The Emperor Valens was a Christian who had frequently been based in Antioch since 371. In 366/7, Libanius had already been accused of writing a panegyric on a failed pretender to the empire. In 372, he had been extremely fortunate to escape the inquisitions and executions at yet another time of suspected conspiracies in the city. Valens' presence there intensified the number of Latin-speaking military men and attendants, Libanius' natural enemies, while as a Christian he had no sympathy with Libanius' beloved pagan gods.[15] Libanius' surviving letters cease in the dangerous year 365 and resume only after a gap of twenty years, when other usurpers were safely dead. In his autobiography, Libanius credits Fortune with removing the risk that his letters might be discovered by enemies and found to contain incriminating correspondence at the time of a particularly dangerous plot. Fortune, he says, arranged that 'in tens of thousands of letters', relating to the suspects, 'there was not one of mine'. In fact, Libanius had reviewed his own files and pre-empted Fortune by destroying the dangerous items.[16]

This artful crediting of Fortune should put historians on their guard: Libanius deliberately erased evidence. Why, though, did he compose and, surely, deliver a speech in 374 about himself? His first version has been interpreted as his valedictory lecture, his farewell to public speaking. When he first delivered it, evidence for his continuing public role is indeed lacking, but his destruction of his own letters prevents us from seeing what it may still have been. Possibly, he was in eclipse, but he was certainly not planning to retire. The next emperor, Theodosius, was to be addressed in no fewer than eleven panegyrics from him, and Libanius' public involvement in Antioch is never more evident than in the late 380s.[17] In his seventies, his pupils had dwindled, but in no way, even then, did he give up his active career.

Alternatively, the speech has been read as 'tactical self-glorification' (*autoglorification politique*).[18] An 'answer to critics' is the more apt term. Behind it have been seen some long-running battles, above all Libanius' attempt to remain immune from the dreaded expense of council service in his home city.[19] However, these familiar battles are not evident in or behind the text. By contrast, answers to critics are explicit and implicit and alert readers can detect how far they are likely to extend.

The speech's first version was delivered only some two years after suspicions that Libanius had been involved in treasonable plotting against the Emperor Valens. Perhaps, in part, it was a personal rehabilitation after the recent allegations. Personal matters were relevant too. Libanius skates elegantly over the reasons behind his early career moves, to and from Constantinople or to and from his beloved Nicomedia. He emphasizes his care and consideration for his teaching predecessor in Antioch, and yet his other speeches and letters show that the truth was rather different.[20] He defends his close friendship with the Emperor Julian and denies that he ever abused it for his own financial gain: evidently, others had said that he did. He even denies allegations that he wrote to Julian and urged him to act harmfully against Antioch shortly before Julian died.[21] He glosses over most of the dangerous years after Julian's death. He is extremely careful over the space he gives to Valens' reign, in progress while he spoke. While thanking Fortune that his correspondence did not incriminate him, he diverts attention brilliantly from the great inquisitions of the 360s and 370s to a personal matter of fortune, one joyously good and yet, by comparison, small.[22] He describes how he lost his beloved little text of the great historian Thucydides, a copy so dear to him because of its small, elegant script. Abandoning it for stolen, he regained it years later thanks to an alert friend. What a special gift from Fortune it all was . . . The story transports his audience far away from the recent difficulties of Antioch's civic scene. The first version of his speech then ends with a manifest apology. As we know from his other speeches, critics attacked

Libanius for having taught pupils who turned out to be, at best, second class.[23] He answers this perennial hazard of a tutor's life: the best of his pupils died young, he insists, and so the criticism cannot stand. Fortune may have given him back his copy of Thucydides, but it is simply his bad luck that she has left him with pupils only from the middle rank. Indeed his life is neither too good for others to bear to hear about nor too bad for himself to tolerate. Fortune has indeed mixed her favours and setbacks.

The updates added to his speech have an even stronger tone. Typically, they review the Roman governors and senior commanders who were active in and around Antioch from the mid-360s to the 390s, some twelve governors and five higher officials.[24] Few are spared devastating judgements on their uncouthness, their savagery, their duplicity to Libanius himself and their need, as Latin speakers, to use those ultimate proofs of barbarity, interpreters in the presence of Greeks. One of them, Festus, is a man known to us for his short Latin *Summary of Roman History*, but for Libanius this future governor of Asia was 'a misguided man who knew no Greek . . . I thank Fortune for his hatred.'[25]

Perhaps these additions were also read aloud to selected audiences: it would be surprising if Libanius added them over twenty years solely for his own gratification.[26] In them, he has seemed to some of his readers to 'lose control not only of his life but also of his telling of it'.[27] However, his tone has not drastically changed. He shows no sign of losing his trust in Fortune and the other gods. They still protect him, he believes, even from unruly horses or from such hazards as a stone-thrower who was roaming Antioch's streets. Although Latin is on the rise, 'the gods,' Libanius remains convinced, 'will prevail' and restore the rightful pre-eminence to Greek.[28]

His personal losses multiply in these years, nonetheless. He loses a close friend and ex-pupil; he loses his lifelong concubine and, worst of all, his dear brother. True, he wins a battle to assert the right of his bastard son, Cimon, to inherit from him, but he then finds Cimon obliged, as a result, to take on the costs of service on Antioch's council.[29] So he pushes for Cimon to be made a senator in Constantinople, a route to exemption from all local obligations, but Cimon dies before he can take up a government posting. In the face of so many deaths, 'it was impossible,' he found, 'to make use of the theatres' for his public speeches, 'but for those who were learning as pupils, all was still fulfilled according to the law'.[30] His text ends with words ascribed to one of his friends, as if the man was extolling the gods' vengeance on the death of Libanius' son. Like the Hellenes in ancient myths, he says, Libanius is being granted revenge, thanks to the goddess Demeter. For four months, famine has been ravaging Constantinople, the seat of those brutes who had failed to protect his son, Cimon. Like the priest Chryses at the start of Homer's *Iliad*, Libanius, also a priest of the pagan gods, is presented as being granted vengeance on his enemies.[31]

These ringing words of consolation conclude the speech on a high Homeric note. Augustine, by contrast, will end his confessions with the hope of peace in the life to come. Such an ending sums up Libanius' personal view of Fortune, but it does not explain why he wrote in this way in the first place. For an answer, the first version of the speech is the crucial one, as the rest of it was added piecemeal to a pattern which had been set. One of its recent scholars has considered it 'not the speech of someone who feels under attack', and that 'apology is only a sideline'.[32] Yet, at every turn, the speech alludes to hostilities, envy and others' accusations. Whether true or not, they needed to be answered. Some of them are specified by Libanius, whether that he used the black arts of magic and divination or even that he had bewitched the wife of a rival orator with a love potion.[33] At almost no time in Antioch as an adult was he immune from scandal, but only once can we see from external evidence the scale of the scandalous twitter which had swirled round him. About six years after his death, the pagan Eunapius reviewed Libanius' life, one among his several biographies of thinkers and speakers. He had not known him personally, but his account is essentially admiring. He takes a poor view of Libanius' declamations, which, he thinks, were 'feeble' and 'lifeless', to us an odd view of them, and puts them partly down to Libanius' inadequacy with his teachers in Athens and his failure to be taught by the best. Here he probably reflects, unwittingly, malicious stories about Libanius' student days which Libanius' autobiography implicitly answers. However, he considers his letters and other speeches to be full of charm and learning, as indeed they are. Libanius had a way of being 'all things to all men' and reflecting back to them the characters which they themselves had: he was 'multiform'. This comment is not critical, as readers sometimes misunderstand it: it relates to what Eunapius most admired, Libanius' letters, where his ability to relate himself to his correspondents and their tastes is indeed a talent. Nonetheless, despite his admiring tone, Eunapius remarks on a dark blot, how a 'slanderous accusation concerning young boys' was brought against him. It forced Libanius out of

Constantinople during his first stay in the city and then pursued him to Nicomedia: 'running beside him there', it rapidly forced him out of that city too. 'It is not right for me to write about this,' Eunapius claims, 'as I am directing my text to the recording of what is worth remembering', but he mentions it nonetheless.[34]

In his speech, Libanius ascribes his departures from these cities to quite other causes, to riots in Constantinople and to an official appointment which required him to return to Constantinople from Nicomedia. The only accusations which he mentions in either place are some fatuous charges of magic which he had supposedly deployed for heterosexual ends.[35] He even claims that Fortune wisely brought him back from Nicomedia to Constantinople: she wished to refute people there who were saying that his previous departure from the city was 'justly deserved punishment' and a 'decree of the city', whereas in fact it was due only to the 'insulting abuse of a clique'. By returning, Libanius was able, he said, to shine professionally and refute this sort of malice. Nonetheless, his other speeches and letters contain clear evidence that slanders dogged his entire career: the charge of pederasty evidently remained prominent among them, because it survived for Eunapius to know and repeat after Libanius' death. It is not important for the motives of his 'autobiography' whether or not these sexual charges were true. It is enough that they continued to circulate. Allegations of sexual harassment had driven Jerome out of Rome, that 'slanderous city' (*maledica civitas*), as he called it, and had caused him to send a long letter of self-defence, the one which he artfully addressed to Asella, the city's ultimate nun.[36] Foul allegations had beset Augustine in Africa only months before he began to address his confessions to God. The gravest charge against Libanius was child abuse. No doubt it contributed to his decision, aged sixty, to summon an audience of ex-pupils and others and treat them to a review of the good and bad fortune throughout his life. For Jerome, Libanius and Augustine, charges of sexual harassment preceded their uses of autobiography.

III

Augustine's *Confessions* have none of Libanius' visible additions, none of his open, though artful, self-praise, none of his vengeful remarks about others. Blowing one's own trumpet was not only a vice among Christians. It provoked malice everywhere, and long before Libanius and Augustine an essay by the moralist Plutarch (*c.*AD 100) had set out appropriate strategies.[37] Self-praise, he aptly observes, is especially common among the elderly or the military. It resembles boastfulness and is as disagreeable in ourselves, we must always remember, as it seems to us in others. It is forgivable only if it is intended to encourage others to rivalry and ambition. Such encouragement should include examples of action as well as argument 'so as to be alive and able to stir up its audience'. If rightly used, it 'sets beside us the hope that such ends are attainable and not impossible'. Self-praise will be toned down if its author includes a few 'failings, shortcomings or slight faults', so long as they are not entirely shameful or ignoble. Above all, speakers and authors should lay aside the burden of glory by referring part of it to Fortune, part to God.

Just as Plutarch suggests, Libanius refers his 'glory' to Fortune and Augustine refers his 'glory' to God's grace. Libanius deftly expresses the wish that 'others' might speak of his successes in competitions, because then they will be able to speak of them 'without any veil'.[38] He speaks of them nonetheless, crediting most of them to Fortune so as not to credit them arrogantly to himself. Augustine recalls his youthful prizes and brilliance, but discredits them with hindsight as worthless 'strayings' from God. By discussing his life in terms of Fortune, Libanius neatly avoided discussing his own failings: he talked only of externals, which the goddess Fortune hindered or helped. Augustine, by contrast, confesses personal inner failings and presents his renunciations for our imitation: the abandonment of sex and worldly ambition. They are indeed described so as to stir up others, just as Plutarch recommended, and to make them realize that 'such aims are attainable'. However, Augustine's guiding models were not Plutarch and his tradition. They were the Psalms and the scriptural imagery which he applied throughout to himself.

Unlike Libanius, he did not continue to add to what he composed: the *Confessions* contain nothing which can be diagnosed as an update. Like Libanius, he was a trained improviser, one whose skills should not be underestimated. Once, in a church service, the reader read the wrong scriptural lesson, and Augustine began his sermon by admitting that he was preaching on the lesson without being forewarned. What he then said was preserved as usual by copyists: it is long enough to have lasted for about an hour and a half without a break. He delivered it on the spur of the moment.[39]

One of his recently discovered letters has clarified how fast he could dictate on a predetermined topic. Between 11 September and 1 December 419, he tells us, he composed what we can calculate as amounting to 4,572 lines of our basic publication of the works involved, given in Migne's compendious *Patrologia Latina*.[40] He has done them, he tells us, 'among other business', his episcopal duties. On Saturday and Sunday nights, he also reveals, he had 'just' dictated six of his *Tractates* on the Gospel of John. His most scrupulous French editor, using this new revelation, has concluded that the six are our *Tractates* numbers 55 to 60. He proposes, persuasively, that they were composed on, at most, the final three weekends of November, a maximum of six nights' work. In the classic French series of octavo volumes of the text (the Bibliothèque Augustinienne), these six *Tractates* occupy 40 printed pages.[41]

In Migne's text, the *Confessions* cover about 9,300 lines, twice as long as Augustine's output from mid-September to the start of December 419. In the editions of the Bibliothèque Augustinienne, the *Confessions* take up about 440 pages. At the same rate as the six *Tractates* of late 419, the *Confessions* would have been dictated within sixty-six nights. Augustine's rate of dictation during the longer period in 419, from mid-September to 1 December, is only indicative, because it occurred, he observes, among 'other business', the arduous business of a bishop.[42] Even so, if that rate is applied to the *Confessions*, it would suggest an upper limit of about twenty-five weeks for the entire work's composition. In 397, however, Augustine began to confess when he was not swamped with active business at all. In my view, he was confined to his room, suffering 'in the shadow of death'. The nights and days loomed painfully ahead. He could not sit or lie down comfortably, but he could pray, at least, while kneeling or standing. At the rate of the *Tractates on John*, ten weeks would suffice to dictate the whole *Confessions*, but the *Tractates* were composed at night-time only. With both the days and nights free, anything from three to six weeks would, in theory, be enough to dictate the *Confessions*, between mid-February, say, and late March 397.

In an interesting letter, Ambrose observes that it was not his practice to dictate at night when he would be 'troublesome and a burden to others', the secretaries.[43] However, if he was sick or weak, he would not write in his own hand. Weakened by his pains, Augustine would not, I think, dictate by day and write in person by night: I assume he dictated throughout. Ambrose goes on to refer to the fluency of a dictated text but to say that he preferred in his older age to write with a pen so as to ponder each word and save himself embarrassment before a secretary. However, unlike Augustine he had never practised as a trained speaker and teacher of improvised oratory. By dictating, the expert Augustine could maintain the 'impetuous flow' which Ambrose remarks. Of course, the artistry of his texts differs. The *Tractates on John* were written on defined topics, verses in the Gospel of John, whereas the *Confessions* proceeded fluently over many different questions, some of which arose at a tangent to the main prayer. The *Confessions* are stylistically dazzling and much more intricately phrased than any of the *Tractates*: could they really have been composed by dictation at a similar speed? Augustine's sermons were indeed dictated and transcribed, but they do not have the same sustained brilliance and stylistic complexity. They go back over points already made; they digress and return before resuming the thread. Even when the *Confessions* wander or proceed by posing questions, they read more fluently. Editors and critics have therefore assumed that they were composed in careful, slowly polished stages. However, Augustine had already shown himself to be an astonishingly fluent composer of a complex improvised prayer. In early winter 386/7, he had composed the prayer to God which begins his *Soliloquies*: it amounts to a quarter of the entire debate on the first day. Unlike this prayer, which was written by his own hand, the *Confessions*, I believe, were dictated. No doubt he would go over the first draft of his dictation and tidy up its style, but a first dictated draft could attain a speed which even the handwritten *Soliloquies* could not. Oral composition was underpinned by Augustine's entire education and training as a public speaker, the subjects of the first parts of this book. Then, after his conversion and especially during his priesthood, they gained a new rapid resource, the scriptures. He absorbed them by heart and he recited them regularly with his brethren.

Composition in a single burst seems implausible to modern readers, but Augustine was not alone in a capacity for it. Synesius composed his entire book *On Dreams*, he tells his readers, in a single night. The Emperor Julian concluded his famous hymn to the Sun God by remarking that he had composed it in at most three nights: it is as long as the first two books of the *Confessions* combined. Jerome claims similarly rapid composition of some of his long letters, and although modern critics prefer to disbelieve this claim as mere 'convention', he would not have made it if his readers did not consider it plausible.[44] A similar speed-dating of the *Confessions* does justice, I believe, to the work when it is read as it was composed, out loud. The pauses, the various high points, the frequent passages of praise and abject confession then fall into place. As a prayer in progress, it has a unified momentum. It rises and falls, throws up questions and then circles round them for answers (the theft of pears, the puzzles about time) because it is pouring orally from its author and being transcribed. Parallel phrases in Augustine's sermons and texts between summer 397 and spring 403 are not clues to the date of the *Confessions*' beginning. They are echoes of confessions which had already ended.

IV

A speed-dating, compressed between late winter and spring 397, also helps to sharpen the context of the whole work. It means that Augustine was confessing his sins in the first ten books during Lent. As his first surviving sermon as a priest had shown, penitence for past sins was strongly emphasized in Lent to the 'seekers', or baptismal candidates, as they stood contritely on rough goatskins.[45] At the end of Lent 397, for the first time in his life Bishop Augustine was to give 'seekers' their final instruction and baptism. As ever, he was sensitive to role models, none more so in this context than Ambrose, the bishop who had baptized him at Easter ten years before. Ambrose had preached with flair on the six days of Creation, in my view in Easter Week, 387, the very Easter when Augustine was prepared for baptism. Certainly Augustine had acquired a published text of these sermons and had already read it very closely by 388/9.

If we apply the rates of dictation which he attests for late 419, Augustine would be composing the last three books of the *Confessions* when Lent 397 was far advanced and Easter Week was approaching. In these books, he meditates on Ambrose's same subject, the six days of Creation, at the very same moment, I believe, as the one at which Ambrose preached on it in the liturgical year. Even without Ambrose's example, Augustine had a reason to dwell on it at the end of Lent: the first chapter of Genesis was regularly read on the evening before Easter in the north African churches. It was not a new challenge for him. Back in 388/9, he had already written on it 'against the Manichees' after studying Ambrose's six-day sermons. Manifestly, they were in his mind again when he discussed the same scriptural verses and concluded his confessions.

By a lucky chance we have other comparable texts by him: a cycle of six Easter Week sermons, preserved in shortened extracts, which Augustine himself once preached. In 1963, the Benedictine scholar Cyrille Lambot emphasized their interest: they are a series of sermons on the days of Creation. However, Lambot did not suggest a year in which they were preached and did not comment on the remarkable coincidences, even in their much-shortened form, with interpretations of these same verses from Genesis in the *Confessions'* concluding book. In both, the 'firmament of heaven' is related to the scriptures, rolled out between our world and the world of the angels above it. The separation of 'bitter waters' from the 'dry land' is the separation of the worldly, or the 'wicked', from the saints on earth. On the fourth day, the creation of the sun stands for the creation of Wisdom, whereby God's word in scripture is understood. The moon and the stars signify the gift of knowledge and other gifts of the Holy Spirit. On the fourth day, the 'reptiles with living souls' are none other than the Christian sacraments.[46]

In the *Confessions* Augustine recognizes that these allegories may seem preposterous to others who 'contradict' him: 'surely I am not misleading my readers?' he asks.[47] The appearance of the same unusual allegories in these Easter sermons is therefore especially remarkable. The sermons also use texts from Paul on being 'sons of light', not 'sons of darkness' (Eph. 5.8; 1 Thess. 5.5) and on 'charity', or love, as the supreme spiritual gift. These same texts are used in the *Confessions'* final books. Similar themes, interpretations and scriptural phrases do not prove that texts were delivered at more or less the same time. There is the risk here too of 'deducing the probable from the uncertain'. However, Augustine's use of these themes in the Easter Week sermons sits neatly with the suggestion, supportable on other grounds, that the *Confessions'* final book was composed while Easter Day drew near. The neatest explanation is that the sermons were preached, and the book composed, while one and the same Lent came to an end: the Lent before Easter, 397. If so, the sermons draw on the same ideas as those in Augustine's mind at the same time, for the *Confessions'* culmination.[48]

Augustine's very first Lent sermon, six years earlier, had linked Paul's words on becoming sons of light, not sons of darkness, to Christian 'seekers' progress to baptism. In the *Confessions'* final book, these words are pervasive. Baptism is presented as symbolized in the 'Spirit's movement above the face of the waters' (Gen. 1.2). At a high point, Augustine then pauses and redirects his prayer with the words 'Holy,

Holy, Holy . . .' and links them explicitly to words of the baptismal rite.[49] He then exploits words of the very psalm which baptismal candidates would sing: 'As pants the heart . . .' (our Psalm 42). It concludes with words addressed to the soul: 'Why art thou cast down, O my soul, and why art thou disquieted within me? Hope thou in God, for I shall yet praise Him.'[50] The baptism of seekers would occur at Easter, conducted by Augustine himself. The baptismal imagery near the *Confessions*' ending does not require its final book to have been concluded as Easter Day, 397, approached.[51] But it sits very neatly with it.

If a speed-dating is correct, the work is indeed a unity, composed, in my view, between the start of Lent and Easter, 397. As the text is a prayer, obvious keys to its direction are Augustine's own views about praying, clearly expressed in his other writings. Anyone who prays, he says, must 'invoke' God, or call Him into himself. Nobody, he observes, would dare to invite such a grand visitor as God without cleaning up the place which is to receive Him. As we cannot clean it by ourselves alone, we must invite Him in to help us. In fact, we are 'in' God already and He is present 'with' us. We must therefore turn inwards, where the image of God is present in our soul, and by concentrating ourselves in 'faith, hope and love' we can then communicate with Him. Confession of our sins and testimony to His mercy will prepare us for His presence. Just as God speaks to us at several removes in scripture, so we can then speak directly to Him in prayer.[52]

These views on prayer help to explain the *Confessions*' unusual shape. They begin with a prolonged invocation of God; then they lay Augustine's past sins, or 'a-version', before Him so as to clean himself before God's presence. After his 'con-version', his confessions continue to turn inwards, exploring what 'I am', not as a sick man's self-analysis, but as the rigorous preparation of a perfectionist with the positive aim of ascending to God. He centres on the mysterious power and scope of memory, its 'immensity', its 'many forms', its 'vast capacity' like an enormous space.[53] He does so, 'seeking You', God, and he discovers Him deep in his memory: *memoria*, his Latin word, contains much more than the conscious mind can itself recall. Its storage and range fill him with 'wonder and awe'. He cannot explain them. His memory is a 'boundless sanctuary', related to God, and so he will 'pass beyond its power, so as to press on to You', God: he will 'ascend'.[54] As he does so, he becomes ready to meditate, with the Holy Spirit's help, on God's words. They are audible at two removes, through scripture's authors and translators. Now that Augustine's prayer has made him fit for

God's presence, God's continuing gift of His Spirit helps him to discern the 'mysteries' in God's words. The 'mysteries' in the words about Creation include the scriptures, the Church, the sacraments and baptism. Augustine then anticipates his future rest in God's presence, not in this life, but in the life to come.

As he turns to consider 'what I am', he describes, in the tenth book, his work's intended human audience beyond its primary addressee, God. He tells us he is writing especially for fellow celibate 'slaves of God' and for those who may aspire to join them. He asks them not to mock him when they read about his past sins, but to give thanks to God if they themselves have done nothing comparably sinful. They must praise God for raising someone like himself from such abject depths.[55] Prayer for a Christian brother's sins was practised on behalf of penitent sinners by ordinary baptized Christians during church services. It was endorsed in the first letter ascribed to 'John', an important scriptural resource for Augustine, but, above all, it was a practice rooted in monastic and Christian perfectionist company.[56] Intercessionary prayer helped to carry an errant brother onwards and upwards in groups who were 'all in it together'. In Book 9, Augustine asks for such prayers on behalf of his mother and father. In Book 10, he addresses 'what I am' and requests such prayers for himself.

His own circumstances are therefore relevant. In 396 he had been made co-bishop of Hippo, but by late summer 397 he had almost certainly become the sole bishop: his name stands alone as Hippo's bishop in the acts of a Council which was held in Carthage in late August. The name of his co-bishop, elderly Valerius, is absent, almost certainly because he had died, although we do not know in which month he did so. While praying and confessing in his room, Augustine was either aware that the full 'burden' of Hippo's Church was now his, or at least that it very soon would be. It would never be easy to combine prolonged meditation on scripture with a bishop's full workload. As he tells the *Confessions*' readers, he is hastening impatiently onwards to consider the words of scripture. If the bishopric was now to be his alone, Lent 397 might well be his last chance for prolonged engagement with scripture in the privacy of his own room.[57] Gratefully, he took it.

He was also impelled to revisit his past life. Here, suggestively, he was not alone. Fourteen years later, as a recently appointed bishop, Synesius was to do the same. Only months after his reluctant ordination, he addressed his fellow bishops, assembled at Ptolemais, with a long letter which included a survey of his previous life. Soon after his appointment as bishop, he was preparing for an intervention far beyond Augustine's social horizons: his intended excommunication of the governor, no less, of the Libyan Pentapolis.[58] To do so, he needed his fellow bishops' support in a Council, so he addressed them in a letter which recapitulated the high ideals which he had always held. Philosophy, he insists to them, has been his lifelong priority and it still is, just as he had told them at his ordination. He will merely 'descend' from time to time to pressing matters in the world of action, and if his bishops are dissatisfied with that, they can appoint a co-bishop or replace him. The offer was more rhetorical than real. He was revisiting his past, including his recent loss of a son, in order to forestall criticism about his political involvement and to assure his bishops that his highly public intervention, the excommunication of the governor, was not mere worldly manoeuvring or inconsistent with his declared ideals.[59]

Within Augustine's presentation of his past, there are implicit answers to critics.[60] As we have seen, he rebuts the notion that his mother drank too much or that he left Carthage for Rome in order to escape being sentenced under new anti-Manichaean laws. He defends his delayed resignation from his teaching job in Milan and he counters any impression that he was heartless or unemotional when his mother died in Ostia. Implicitly, he is the very opposite of a Donatist, both in his presentation of himself as a priest and an imperfect sinner and in his insistence that even when Christians have been baptized they continue to need Christ's help and mediation. He was not evading awkward truths about these points. He was indeed not a Donatist and he was not a Manichaean, either, when he confessed to God. When he turns to 'what I now am', he does not present his achievements in the ten years since his baptism. He confesses his persisting sins. He then proceeds to a long meditation on himself and scripture which is the culmination of the entire work. It pulls together thinking which we have watched emerging in the period since summer 386. It could hardly be further from the themes and horizons of Libanius' artfully self-defensive speech.

42
The Heaven of Heavens

Suppose Augustine had married and after baptism continued his oratorical career, perhaps ending briefly as a proconsul of Africa: he might have called his friends together one day in Carthage and, like Libanius, applied his rhetorical skill to a review of his life. He would have deplored his Manichaean phase and carefully explained how rioting students had caused him to move from Carthage to Rome as a young teacher. He would have praised his mother's 'customary' sobriety and reminded his audience in passing that, 'as you well know', lower-class concubines 'always' have to be dismissed. He might have glossed over the awkward fact of a panegyric he had once written for the brief-lived conqueror Maximus in Milan. He would have expatiated instead on his gratitude to Theodosius and his sons. He might have protested undying devotion to his Milanese wife, the still-young mother of their four children, to the point where no listener could possibly credit recent slanders that he had seduced a noble Christian widow in a palatial house in Utica. Throughout, he would have thanked the continuing providence of God.

This alternative is entirely fictitious: instead as a monk-bishop Augustine composed his confessions. They share Libanius' sense of providence, 'grace' and divine guidance, but throughout they profess the least Libanian quality, humility. They acknowledge his persisting sensitivity to criticism, the temptations of praise and self-praise and the 'lust of [self-]vindication'. Libanius' speech exemplifies the exact opposites: pride, self-praise and the gleeful settling of old scores.

Within their shared sense of a 'guided life', pagan Libanius and Christian Augustine have revealingly different ideas of God. Augustine's God is omnipotent and the Creator of everything in His universe. He is Augustine's transcendent Father and Mother, commanding him and calling him as a father would, but caring for him, suckling him and stroking him as a mother would too.[1] Like a loving parent, God has him always 'in His sight'. While he was still an 'infant', unfit for solid theological food, God fed him on milk through the words of His scriptures and the sayings of Christ incarnate. Whereas Libanius envisioned his gods in dreams, Augustine still yearned to see his God face to face, to stand stable in His presence and contemplate Him without being 'thrust away'. His God is eternally present, far above Augustine but also as deeply inside him as hidden, invisible DNA.[2] Augustine's soul had been formed in his 'image' and his God is 'God of my heart'.[3] He can be sensed with each of the human senses, but although He can be loved, He is not fully knowable. Briefly, contact had been made with Him, but He is seldom, if ever, to be seen in this life.

Unlike Libanius' Fortune, God 'turns' to His children, but most of them promptly turn away. Some of them are then brought to turn 'to' Him and 'convert', but they have to be chastized to do so. Unlike Fortune, God knows in advance what each of His children will do. He shows anger as well as love to bring it about. He laughs when they stray and torments them with pangs and 'prickings' so as to correct them.[4] He listens and is ever-merciful but He is unpredictable in the ways in which He shows His love. Through the scriptures, whose words He has inspired, He can be envisaged by simple metaphors. They refer to His hands or feet, but these terms are unworthy of His sublimity: they are suited only to beginners.[5] Unlike Fortune, God is not a person or a substance. He is infinite in power, not size, and He is a spiritual, not a spatial, Being. Discerning mortals can try to know Him through the 'one true wisdom' which He once revealed and which the Platonists have partly preserved. He is unchanging, the One whom His scriptures (at least in errant Latin) call 'It Itself' and who speaks as He once spoke to Moses: 'I am [the One] who Is.' Although He cannot be fully comprehended by His children, He is fully intelligible to Himself.[6] To mortals He is ultimately unknowable and inexpressible in words.[7]

A down-to-earth modern reader's first instinct would be to refer such a parent to the social services. He is, however, the God of the Bible, who is eternally acting for His children's good. When He is harsh, it is always for a purpose. Only when the 'unjust' withdraw from Him, as Augustine withdrew in Carthage, does He offer His 'rectitude' and cause them to fall onto His 'roughness'.[8] If they return to Him, He 'wipes away their tears'. He is called 'gentle', merciful and patient, but such words of emotion only approximate to His eternal nature.[9]

'Tell me by Your mercies, my Lord God, what You are to me,' Augustine's confessing prayer to God begins. 'Say to my soul, "I am your salvation." Speak to me so that I may hear. Look, the ears of my heart are before You, Lord. Open them and say to my soul, "I am your salvation." I will run after this voice and I will seize You.'[10] Augustine begins by praying to God to come to him, to speak to him, even to be seen by him. It is round this desire that the *Confessions* cohere as a unity.

Those who enjoy the first nine books' revisiting of Augustine's former sins then encounter the books of self-scrutiny and meditation and feel baffled. The tenth book begins by praying to God, 'May I know You even as I am known', Paul's famous words (1 Cor. 13.12). In search of God Augustine turns inwards to his great exploration of the 'innumerable caverns' and 'hidden receptacles' of memory in its different forms. Some of the same imagery was used for memory and the senses in Manichaean teaching, as we now know from one of their 'Chapters', preserved in Egypt. Augustine's main sources were Platonist and philosophical. First, he marvels at all that the 'caverns' of memory contain and at its 'great force'. Then, he inquires into the origins of memory's images and confesses himself 'bewildered' (*stupor*). The vastness of memory is a 'mystery' and in it there is much which 'not even a man's spirit knows'.[11] His awareness of man's hidden subconscious depths endears him especially to modern theorists of the human mind.

In the eleventh book, Augustine embarks on a close meditation on scripture, the opening verses of Genesis. However, he goes no further than the first words, claiming, like Ambrose before him, that the words 'In the beginning' do not refer (as they do) to time, but to the 'Beginning', meaning God's Word. How, though, does eternal God relate to Creation and the time-bound world? Augustine embarks on the problematic nature of time, addressing it through one of his circling sequences of questions which are an 'exercising of the mind'. First, he concludes very acutely that time only began when the universe began and that God, outside it, is eternal. There was never a time before He created or when, as Manichaeans argued, he was doing nothing. Augustine has more success in arguing God to be timeless rather than 'eternal', but he then turns to individuals' sense of time. His underlying source was probably Porphyry, whose views he had already read and considered in Rome while awaiting baptism, but he now addressed this question for reasons of his own: how does God's relation to time and Creation differ from an individual mind's relation to time present, past and future? The question confronts him with his own uncertainty about what time is and results in some of the most intelligent philosophical argument in his entire work.

His two main questions become: how can times be long, and how do we measure time anyway? He argues that no time can be long, because the past, like the future, 'is not' and the present is fleeting. After comparing the way in which we memorize a song which is to be recited and then recite it to the duration remembered, he concludes that a 'long past' is our memory of the past and a 'long stretch of the future' is our expectation of a long duration. 'Lengths' of time are therefore 'affects' or 'memories' of time in the mind. The argument does not fully satisfy modern philosophers, but his related argument about our measuring time is exceptionally acute. We remember durations, and our measurement of time depends on them, our retained memories of lengths of time, their 'affects' in our mind.[12]

The twelfth book then re-engages with Genesis's first verse and interprets its 'heaven' and 'earth' as a spiritual 'heaven of heaven', home of the angels, and as 'unformed' matter. They are God's first Creation, Augustine explains, a spiritual one which preceded the second Creation, our visible universe: this interpretation was in no way his innovation.[13] Augustine admits that some of these hidden meanings seem ridiculous to some of his critics, and so he stops to affirm the existence of many possible meanings in scripture. They are not confined to the intentions of their author, in Augustine's view, Moses. He even explores what a meeting with Moses himself might teach him if the barriers of language fell away and he was able to converse with a Hebrew. In his *Sermons*, the poet John Donne would later fasten on this notion and repeat it in his own person, imitating what Augustine had written.[14] Augustine concludes that the meanings discerned by readers of a text, but not necessarily by its author, are true if they are consistent with God's Truth. Applying this principle, he confronts God's command to 'Be fruitful and multiply', an awkward command for his celibate ideals, and interprets it as a command to 'multiply' fruitful meanings while pondering on scripture.[15] In no way is he a relativist or a post-modernist before his time. For him, these truths depend on an absolute objective Truth, God's.

His answer to his 'contradictors' is punctuated by remarkable invocations of God. He recalls his own turning away into darkness and yet 'I heard Your voice behind me' like the prophet Ezekiel: again, Augustine is enabled by scripture to express his own predicament. 'I am panting for Your fountain. Let nobody forbid me; let me drink it, let me live at it. May I not be my own life. I have lived badly from my own self . . . Speak with me, converse with me . . .' There is an urgency here not deployed since the approach to the garden scene. God duly speaks to him, in his 'inner ear with a loud voice'. He states that the 'heaven of heaven' is not itself eternal but Augustine continues to call on Him in intense, fascinating language. 'May I enter my chamber and sing a song of love to You . . . groaning with inexpressible groans on my journey to the heavenly Jerusalem.' It is there, Augustine now realizes, that 'the first-fruits of my spirit are, and it is from there I am certain of these things'. He asks God to reassemble his whole self from its 'dispersion' and take him there. We recall the Vision at Ostia where Augustine and Monnica had indeed passed briefly beyond the time-bound world and sighed and left the 'first-fruits of their spirit'. Now, we see that they left them in the heaven of heaven, home of the angels and blessed souls: Augustine is praying for a return.

The thirteenth book resumes his meditation on Genesis, which has as yet gone no further than the book's first verse. It covers the six days of Creation and the seventh, God's day of rest, but it discerns quite other references throughout. Beneath the text's surface Augustine finds references to the scriptures and the Christian sacraments (the 'fishes'). He discerns the Church and baptism, miracles (the 'whales'), the preachers and ministers of God's word and 'spiritual' Christians who are best able to judge and discriminate. The sequence of thought and the density of symbols here are a challenge to his readers, but the first day (the creation of light) and the sixth day (the creation of man) are the ones discussed at most length. He ends with a summary of the previous exposition, a final attack on foolish Manichaeans, some words as if spoken by God and a reading of God's 'seventh day of rest': it is 'without evening' because it is the eternal bliss of the life to come. Throughout, there is emphasis on the Holy Spirit.

After his memories of Monnica or Ambrose or the garden scene in Milan, these final books appear to be on a different plane. They are the biggest challenge to survive in Latin prose. However, if carefully read and reread, they are not additions to an 'autobiographical' work. The final books are the culmination of the entire work, a 'prayer overheard'. They connect with much we have followed in Augustine's writings in the years since his conversion: the 'triple lusts', analysed in *On True Religion*, the view that God's word, since the Fall, is accessible in scripture and has an allegorical presence beneath the verses of Genesis (*On Genesis against the Manichaeans*, already in 388/9) and, above all, the value of a meditation on scripture which is guided step by step by the Holy Spirit (*On the Sermon on the Mount*, in 393/4). The culminating book, the thirteenth, is not a 'commentary'. One of the favourite scriptural verses in the *Confessions* has been Psalm 18.15 and its words 'may the meditation of my heart be always in your sight'.[16] The thirteenth book is a meditation, one in which the underlying elements of Christian worship are Augustine's passionate concern. As in *On True Religion*, he considers them to have been planned since the very beginning of the universe. This interpretation, to us so bold, is propelled by love and the Spirit, active (Augustine believes) in his heart. In the great monasteries of Egypt, the 'masters' of the individual houses might receive letters from their community's head written in a mystic language which, even now, we cannot decode.[17] In Hippo, Augustine the monk-bishop concludes his confessions while guided by the Holy Spirit in an inspired surge of meditation which is unique in Latin Christian literature.

Connecting themes are visible in it, nonetheless. Modern Christian scholars detect the persons of the Trinity, one after another in the last three books or even the presence of the eucharist. Augustine would accept these readings, even if he never intended them, because they are consistent with God's Truth. However, they do not link the final books to the dynamic of those which precede them. Quite other themes draw the whole work together: pilgrimage and the search for rest; the 'steps', once again, in a Christian's ascent; the errors and folly of the Manichaeans; and, as ever, God Himself, especially the puzzling relation of His eternity to time.

In the tenth book, Augustine turns inwards, no longer to factual autobiography but to the mysteries of memory and the 'triple lusts' which still beset him. He confesses his lingering loves of scents and the beauties of sunlight, music, food and drink. Sexual desires still disturb him, albeit only slightly, and 'curiosity' still besets his mind. These sins are the sins of a scrupulous perfectionist, but Augustine is not engaged in this self-analysis solely as a 'therapy' of his condition. The book is not a sombre 'rain-soaked landscape'.[18] It is a spiritual exercise in action, one which begins with a confession of the sins which distract him from God: so, too, monks in Egypt's communities would dwell daily on their sins and intrusive patterns of thought. Augustine asks his 'brethren' to be charitable to him and hopes that they may be stirred to rise up to God by what he confesses. His book then describes an ascent towards God's presence, which is punctuated by repeated words of prayer like a refrain: 'give what You command and command what You will'.[19] They are words which were later to scandalize his fellow Christian Pelagius, the champion of free will.[20]

In the first nine books, the scriptures and their language have helped Augustine to confess.[21] After he has confessed his persisting sins in the tenth book, he is fit to contemplate the words which God has given in scripture. His confessions change from confessions of sins to confessions of ignorance. 'I do not know, I confess,' he says now of scripture's puzzling language. Repeatedly, he calls on God to speak the truth to him directly in his 'inner ear'. Origen, above all, had written of this inner 'ear', considering it to be one of our inner senses which are modelled on those of our outer body.[22] In due course, God will indeed address Augustine's inner hearing, 'shouting with a loud voice'. In his first explanation of Genesis, in 388/9, Augustine expounded how God communicated without words to the inner beings of Adam and Eve in Paradise. After the Fall, he wrote, God's words have remained accessible, but only at several removes, in the words which His human transmitters have written in the scriptures. Now, at the end of the *Confessions*, God is communicating with Augustine directly: he is becoming like Adam in Paradise.[23] The *Confessions'* final books are the words of a mystic who has returned to close communication with God.

First, God speaks to him three times 'with a loud voice'. He tells him that He is eternal, that He created all 'natures and substances', that the 'heaven of heavens' is not co-eternal with Himself but that it contemplates Him for ever without change or distraction. Augustine therefore realizes that a purified heart will enjoy this peace and contemplation in the 'heaven of heavens', God's 'house'. God speaks these words in Augustine's own heart while he ponders God's 'voice' in the opening words of scripture.[24]

In the final book he will hear more. It arises (Augustine thinks) from the gift of the Spirit, also given by God's grace. Because of it, he can see (he believes) the spiritual, hidden sense of scripture which the Spirit has laid below the surface of the words. It is a sense which takes him far from Genesis's literal meaning, but he supports it with other scriptural verses, especially those by Paul, because he believes that God's Spirit unifies the scriptures into a whole. Despite his critics, he insists that what he discovers in them is valid because it is a truth consistent with God's Truth. The 'stars' set in the firmament at Genesis 1.16–17 symbolize spiritual Christians, of whom Augustine himself is manifestly one. These spiritual Christians can judge and discriminate correctly: Augustine, a 'star', is discriminating the 'truth' in scripture, while to a modern text-critical eye, he departs entirely from its logical sense and reference.[25]

In Egypt, according to John Cassian, old Father Germanus had warned against what, at first sight, the *Confessions*' final book seems to modern eyes to exemplify. During meditations on scripture, 'the spirit rolls from psalm to psalm, leaps from the gospel to Saint Paul, from Paul to the prophets, from there to items of spirituality . . . It is tossed along through the entire body of scripture, unable to settle on anything . . . it is pulled, like a drunk, in every direction . . .'[26] Yet there is an orderly purpose to Augustine's finale. The words of Genesis, he explains, express the grace of conversion and the realities of Christian life in the Church. They point to the end of Augustine's pilgrimage, the journey which the previous books have repeatedly presented to God.[27] They have represented him as a prodigal son, or as a sinner straying like the errant sheep in the Gospels. Throughout, he has been following the journey which, for him, is foreshadowed in the psalmists' words: now, 'panting with desire', like the deer in Psalm 42, he is ascending towards 'my mother, Jerusalem', sustained day and night by the 'bread of tears'.[28] His journey has not ended with his conversion in the garden and certainly not with his baptism. His soul began its journey turned far away from God, but now, still journeying, he yearns to live 'in God's house all its days'. That house is the 'heaven of heavens', presented as God's first Creation.[29] He realizes that God's house is eternal, never travelling, never changing in the 'vicissitudes of time'. The God who made it has also made Augustine: his goal, therefore, is to return to eternal rest. In the *Confessions*' opening prayer he had spoken of the 'restlessness of our heart, until it rests in You'. In the final book he understands its place of rest: it is the 'heaven of heaven', in the presence of God eternal.

In the *Confessions*' first book and the sixth, Augustine has already talked of 'knocking, so that all else may be opened'. In the eleventh, he begins his meditation on Creation with a prayer that God may not 'shut' the door on those who 'knock' while they meditate on the hidden sense of scripture.[30] May he find 'grace', he asks, as he 'knocks' on the inner meanings of God's words. He goes on to 'knock, that he may find', knocking on the very door of heaven. In the previous books of his prayer, he has followed his own progress, step by step. In his *On Christian Teaching*, begun a few months earlier, he had written of four steps, not seven, in a Christian's ascent: fear (his state in *Confessions*, Books 1–6), piety, attained by submitting to scripture (as he began to learn from Ambrose in Milan), and mourning (nightly, alone in the villa, but also when scrutinizing 'what I am' in Book 10). Ahead lies the final step: knowledge.[31] In the *Confessions'* last three books he frequently confesses his lack of full knowledge but, meanwhile, a little of it increases our awareness of our imperfect life and multiplies our tears. Augustine then calls on God to speak to him inwardly and directly and guide him on his way.

This way is not at all a path to social isolation. Augustine interprets the 'fruits' which the earth is to produce (Gen. 1.12) as symbols of Christians' works of mercy. 'Aware of our own weakness we are moved in compassion to help those in need, just as we would wish to be helped if we were in their same distress.' We are to 'give bread to the hungry, a home to the homeless in need' and not to 'despise domestics of our same flesh and blood', words which echo the prophet Isaiah (58.7–8). However, we are to pass from this 'inferior fruit of action' to the 'delights of contemplation' and obtain the 'higher word of life'.[32] It is to be found in the scriptures, which are unrolled like the firmament above our heads. Those who wish to shine brightly in it like stars must follow Jesus's advice to the rich young man. First, they must keep the commandments, honour their father and mother and love their neighbours. Then they must destroy the 'thorns of avarice' which smother good works, the 'fruits' of the earth. They must sell all and give to the poor. Then they will shine with 'light', distinct from the 'darkness' of other Christian 'infants' and they will be 'perfect', but not yet angels.[33]

Augustine himself is such a star, writing to urge others to be stars too. Like those before them, the final books of the *Confessions* are protreptic, aiming to turn others to follow their path.[34] He is aware of the diversity among Christians and their differing levels of responsibility. He cites Paul's example to show that simpler Christians should support the 'stars', their ministers, with gifts. Among the stars, too, there are different talents, but the highest are those who contemplate and receive 'wisdom' from the Holy Spirit. Augustine sees the value of both the life of service and the life of contemplation, but the latter is the higher of the two.[35]

He had first met the distinctions between 'light' and 'darkness' and between the lives of active Martha and contemplative Mary in the Manichaean sect. However, his journey and his understanding of it are profoundly un-Manichaean. Manichaeans denied the existence of underlying spiritual meanings in scripture and ridiculed Genesis's literal sense. Augustine corrects them by dwelling on the deeper meaning of words like 'beginning' and 'heaven and earth'. Manichaeans denied the goodness of the world, whereas Augustine counts seven affirmations of this goodness by God in Genesis's first chapters alone, and an eighth when He calls His Creation 'very good'. Manichaeans denied that the world is entirely created by God: Augustine follows the Bible in assuming exactly the opposite. They assumed that God existed always in time: what, they ask, was He doing before He began to create? Augustine presents Him as eternal and time as beginning only with the creation of the world. Item after item in Genesis's text is then interpreted allegorically in a non-Manichaean way: the sun, the moon (so important to Mani's Gospel), the 'creeping things' and the firmament stretched out above us. It is not made out of the skins of demons from the Kingdom of Darkness. It symbolizes God's scripture, rolled out above us for our salvation.[36]

With the help, not of Mani the 'Paraclete', but of the true Holy Spirit, Augustine discerns allegorical meanings in the text. Manichaeans had ignored them and had denied the unity of the scriptures, old and new. Augustine corrects them implicitly by interpreting Genesis through words of Paul: 'Once you were darkness, but now light, in the Lord' (Eph. 5.8).[37] For Manichaeans, light and darkness have always coexisted and are intermingled in our very beings. For Augustine, 'darkness' prevailed on earth in God's first Creation, the spiritual 'heaven of heavens', when matter was formless and at risk of sinking into the void. However, it then 'turned', or converted, to God when it was given light by His heavenly grace.[38]

By the 'one true wisdom', bits of which they have retained, Plotinus and the Platonists help Augustine to address the questions of time and memory which his meditation raises. Unlike them, however, he insists that Creation was a creation from nothing. It involved a spontaneous 'conversion', the turning of formless matter to God. This cosmic conversion is the context for the first conversion of each individual's soul to Christian faith, a turning which is due to God's unmerited grace.[39] Unifying his prayer, Augustine refers back to the conversion which his previous books have traced: 'You were insistent, frequently, with voices of many kinds, so that I might hear from afar and call on You who were calling on me.' He turns to God in love, now that he is newly formed and 'renewed', as Paul says, 'to the recognition of God according to the image of the Creator' in his soul within.[40] Plotinus had written of the soul's 'love' and 'yearning' to return to the higher world, but it was a love rooted in the necessity which runs through the universe. Augustine, by contrast, has experienced conversion as a freely chosen 'turning' in answer to God's call.

His own past thus finds a broader context in the origins of the entire universe. His final book talks repeatedly of 'converting', but the culminating conversion in his confessions is cosmic. No Manichaean would ever say that evil matter and darkness had 'turned' to God's Light. They had lusted and fought for it and God's only 'call' was the call to Primal Man, so as to make him aware of the Light imprisoned inside him. Augustine's idea of conversion is entirely different.

In the past, Augustine turned away from God and into multiple sin. He was 'dis-tended' and distracted. In the tenth book, he 'at-tended' and concentrated on his inner self and present sins. In the final three books, he then looks forward in expectation to the future.[41] He becomes 'in-tent', his soul in balanced 'tension' with his body. In this triple scheme of time, God's place seems perplexing. He is eternal; He has created the 'heaven of heavens' in which the resident angels are outside time, and yet He has also created the universe on seven separate days, He has seen that what He has created is good. He also knows man's every impulse in the time-bound world of change. He acts there and He intervenes, but how can He be both eternal, beyond time, and yet present to each one of us within it?

For this reason Augustine begins by addressing, famously, the question of time itself.[42] He argues that time has a beginning and that it was created by God Himself. Time entails change; there was no change before the universe existed; there was therefore no time before the universe. It is nonsense, then, for Manichaeans to ask what God was doing before 'He made heaven and earth'.[43] As for our measurement of time, it depends on our ability to remember durations and to rehearse them in our mind.[44]

These arguments are complex, but Augustine then hears God answer the puzzle about Himself. At the very start of the *Confessions* he had told God that the 'ears of my heart' are before Him and has asked God to 'open them'.[45] Now, as never before, he ascribes unscriptural words to God, words which He is addressing 'with a loud voice to your slave, in his inner ear, breaking my deafness and crying: "O man, what My scripture says, I say."' Scripture, God says, speaks in time, but 'time does not attend on My word, because it exists with Me in equal eternity'. Whatever a man sees or speaks 'in the spirit', God also speaks and sees. He is both in eternity, He says, and present in time.[46]

At the end of his autobiography's first version, Libanius made his goddess Fortune speak. She told him about the excellence of his many speeches, which were everywhere in the hands of teachers and pupils.[47] At the end of the *Confessions*, God explains to Augustine His relation to time and eternity. Augustine is not at all a man with a poignant sense of a 'lost future'. He knows exactly where his future lies: it awaits him in the future life of bliss, where love alone will persist, as his *Soliloquies*, ten years before, had stated.[48] Throughout his meditation, Augustine has been impelled by love. Love is the very 'weight' of his soul, drawing it, like other 'weights', to its proper place in the orderly universe.[49] He has discovered this truth through the books of scripture, but they are only a temporary aid. In the future life they will no longer be needed. They will be rolled up and discarded and, instead, we will contemplate God in eternity, singing 'Jubilee' before Him with the angels for whom God is their 'book'.[50]

The questions behind this remarkable meditation did not disappear with Augustine. They continued to exercise Christian thinkers: they recurred in the birth of English literary modernism. In his *A Portrait of the Artist*, James Joyce addressed the relations of the soul and memory, in *Ulysses* a stretch of 'extended' time present and the perceptions of a day, and in *Finnegans Wake* the subconscious mind in our 'memory'. Meanwhile, Ezra Pound had begun to compose his *Cantos*. Like Augustine, he was acutely conscious of words' insufficiency: he was open to the possibility of direct communication by a word's form, not by its misleading reference. Like Augustine, he was aware of meanings which can be discerned by cross-references between texts. He was also aware of time's 'barb': beyond it, he aspired to a recovery of paradise through a study of literary echoes of its previous state.[51] In older age, when asked about his *Cantos*' achievement, Pound merely replied, 'I botched it.'[52] Augustine did not 'botch' his confessions' ending. It had already answered Pound's concerns, with the help of God and His absolute Truth. God spoke to his heart, directly, while he knocked on the door of eternity. Nine years before, he had already been there: he had touched on it in Ostia, in a shared experience with his mother, Monnica. The *Confessions* end with a return visit.

43
Epilogue

I

In my view, the *Confessions* end just before the tenth anniversary of Augustine's baptism. Unknown, as yet, to him, their ending was marked by something else: on Easter Saturday, 397, Ambrose, his baptizer, died in Milan. According to his deacon and biographer, Ambrose 'passed into the company of Elijah'. His body was escorted to Milan's cathedral, where once, as his modern biographer Neil McLynn reminds us, 'he had triumphed over another Jezebel', the Empress Justine.[1] During their vigil on Easter night the newly baptized 'faithful' then claimed to see Ambrose in visions, sitting on his seat in the cathedral's apse. On the next day, his corpse was carried out in procession to the tomb in the Ambrosiana church which he had prepared long before. 'Crowds beyond counting' came to escort it, headed by the newly baptized, who were dressed, like Augustine ten years earlier, in robes of white. 'Unbelievable' screams were heard from those possessed by demons. Spectators struggled to press handkerchiefs against the corpse.

Back in Hippo, before hearing this news, Augustine was to learn that an aggressive, ill-tempered young Catholic Christian, who had defected to the Donatists, had gone and been rebaptized, the ultimate sacrilege, in the Donatists' own church on Easter Day. In response, Augustine tried an illuminating new tactic. He appealed to a civil official in Hippo in the hope that he would intervene. He could cite some thoroughly bad behaviour: this young Catholic man had beaten up his mother.[2] Significantly, the official did not even answer. A second letter from Augustine was no more successful, but the attempts are landmarks in the schism. For the first time, Augustine was writing to a civil official, trying to persuade him to intervene in a religious affair. His attempt is evidence that, as ever, his humble confessions of personal sin and inadequacy coexisted with a firm grasp of tactics in external Church affairs. Intervention by the civil authorities would have to wait for a few more years before being applied.

Augustine's preaching and whereabouts over the next five months after Easter, 397, have become ever more fascinating questions because of recent discoveries of some of his long-lost sermons and a continuing controversy over their dates and contexts. By extraordinary good fortune, we can now read him, I believe, preaching his very first sermon to the Christians of Hippo on his recovery from the acute pains in his backside which had accompanied the beginning of his confessions. In 1994, François Dolbeau published a long-lost sermon by Augustine which he had recovered by brilliant scholarship from later manuscript-texts, above all a text in Heidelberg.[3] Its topic is 'health'. Unlike Dolbeau, I conclude that this sermon belongs in spring 397, before Easter Day, and marks Bishop Augustine's return to his Christian public before preaching (perhaps) those six sermons on the days of Creation during Easter Week itself. In it, he thanks the Lord God for his congregation's 'thanksgiving which I see flowing from the fountain of love'. This love is 'pure' and 'sincere' from brothers and 'sisters' alike. Augustine then preaches in answer to the psalm of the day: 'Give us help concerning tribulation, and vain is the salvation of man' (Ps. 60.11, in its Latin text). He concentrates on the tribulation of bodily pain and suffering and, after a shortish sermon, concludes: 'I must still spare my all too recent scar, which is perhaps not yet fully completed and shut over.'[4] This physical scar, I believe, was the scar on sores still healing inside his backside.

In his earlier letter to Profuturus, he had presented this agony as the 'Lord's pleasure': he could not walk or stand or sit, he wrote, but as it is the Lord's pleasure, what else must be said 'except that we are fine'? His first sermon after reappearing from his bedroom takes the same line. Pains and sickness are from God, who is always just and merciful, whereas health may sometimes be granted to our detriment. Let us not 'mutter under His whip', but let us 'freely suffer His care'. Augustine divides his argument into three distinct sections, each supported by scripture. They can only have been so well-organized because he had been marshalling them during his long weeks of agony. As often, he had been making sense of his plight by understanding it in terms of scripture. He uses phrases from three sources: the Psalms, Paul and the Book of Job, the continuing object of his annotations in 396–7. Throughout, God's inscrutable grace and justice are upheld, key themes of the *Confessions*.[5]

In 1931, the Benedictine scholar Donatien De Bruyne observed the existence of a cluster of thirty sermons in the list compiled by Augustine's close associate, Possidius, on the basis of texts in the library at Hippo. They had been preached, he observed, at Carthage between May and late summer. In 1935, his fellow Benedictine Cyrille Lambot observed that the group could be placed between Ascension Day in May 397 and the Council which met in Carthage four months later and was attended by Augustine on 28 August 397.[6] In 1990, in another great discovery, François Dolbeau found long-lost sermons in a collection in Mainz's cathedral library, thirteen of which, he realized, matched titles in the thirty which are grouped in Possidius' list. These thirteen, he proposed, belonged where Lambot had placed the others in the group, between Ascension Day in May 397 and the Council in Carthage in August.[7]

On this dating of the evidence Augustine was absent from Hippo, preaching in churches and at martyrs' festivals in Carthage and nearby places for more than three months. Like the *Confessions*, none of these sermons survives with a year date, a fact which has allowed scholars to query their dating to 397 and to propose alternatives up to twenty years later.[8] Without yet more evidence, the disputes cannot all be settled, but in my view Dolbeau is still right in more cases than not. Most of his sermons 'of 397' belong where he and, in principle, Lambot dated them. With the usual reservations about its strength, a supporting argument exists which Lambot did not point out: their coincidences with the *Confessions*, in my view a work already dictated and completed.

If so, Augustine was away from Hippo by Ascension Day in late May 397. On that day we now find him preaching on the word 'confession', no less, because it was present in his Psalm 117. He insists on its two senses, 'confession of sins' and 'confession', or testifying, 'in praise of God'. He quotes the psalmist, 'And I said, O Lord, have mercy upon me; cure my soul, for I have sinned against Thee' (our Psalm 41.4). He tells his hearers, 'You will be corrected by confessing your sins and the praise of God.'[9] The *Confessions*, which were already, I believe, dictated, turn on exactly these two senses of confession and on these same themes.

In early June, we hear Augustine again, addressing the topic which had concerned him as recently as spring 396 in his *On Lying* and his decisive letter to Jerome. When Paul reproached Peter in Antioch, was he only pretending? Augustine insists yet again that if lies and pretence are once admitted in the scriptures, they will spread far and wide. Like destructive moths or worms, he now says, they will consume whole chests of clothing until nothing but shreds remain.[10] While preaching, he engages vividly with a heckler whose interruption is preserved in the secretaries' transcription of the sermon. He then ends with a memorable disclaimer. His writings are not to be treated like scripture, although people have been reading them in church as if they are equal to 'the canon'. They are no such thing: 'we write by making progress, we learn every day, we dictate by investigating closely, we speak by "knocking" [for an answer]'. In the holy scriptures, he says, we learn to 'judge', but in Augustine's writings it is Augustine himself who is to be judged.[11]

Perhaps an extract from his *Commentary on Galatians* had been read out in the church after Paul's very words about the quarrel with Peter in Antioch had been read as the lesson for the day. Questioners still wanted to know how to take the story, perhaps because uncertainty had spread in Carthage since the arrival of Jerome's book in which he claimed that the 'quarrel' was only a sham. Since its rediscovery, this sermon has resisted attempts to re-date it later than 397. There is a further point: the Augustine who preaches it says that 'I preach to you standing, and I am infirm.'[12] Again, I believe, he is referring to the scars and sores in his backside which have left him enfeebled since the Lent of 397.

Augustine was outside Hippo when he preached this sermon. In summer 397 he can be credited with other such sermons among Dolbeau's discoveries, on love for God and one's neighbour, on God's all-embracing grace and on the 'image of God' in our souls. Each of these themes had been themes in his recently concluded *Confessions*, although they are not, of course, found only there.[13] On 15 July, at the festival of the martyr Catulinus, he takes martyrdom as his cue to preach on 'hating' one's parents and family so that they cannot 'distract us into offending God'. Wives, even, must be 'hated' if they try to distract a husband from a sexless spiritual marriage.[14] It made chilling listening for his audience.

On 18 and 21 August we can hear him preaching again in honour of martyrs.[15] On the 18th his sermon discusses 'the happy life' (with an implicit allusion to the *Hortensius*) and closely echoes the words on happiness in the *Confessions*' tenth book.[16] On a previous Sunday, perhaps 16 August, he had been preaching 'on the woman bent double for eighteen years'. Here, he explains the number 18 in terms of the six days of Creation multiplied by three stages of man, 'before the Law, under the Law and under grace'. Exactly these stages had been the theme of his *Exposition of Romans*, in 394. The 'six days' have just been the *Confessions'* concluding theme. Together, they gave him the cue for this remarkable play on numbers.[17]

These and other echoes of the *Confessions* in the 'Dolbeau sermons' are not, in my view, anticipations of a work about to begin. They arise from a work already completed. By mid-May Augustine had indeed left Hippo, healing but not fully recovered, and embarked on a surge of preaching, items of which have been recently restored to us by François Dolbeau's discoveries. These sermons are explicable as yet another part of the agreed episcopal programme. Like Bishop Valerius, Aurelius, Bishop of Carthage, had ordered his priests to begin to preach in church.[18] He wanted Augustine, therefore, to preach in his city so that his sermons could be taken down and preserved as examples for the new novice preachers. Hence we can account for Augustine's absence from Hippo. We can also account for the grouping of the sermons during this summer's surge in a section of Possidius' library-list. They were known to have been part of a single initiative.

II

On 28 August 397, Augustine attended the Council at Carthage as Hippo's signatory bishop. Valerius, presumably, had died.[19] Thirty-three years as sole bishop now stretched before him, covering a career which many of his Christian readers regard as his crowning achievement. After 404, attacks on the Manichaeans disappear from his main writings. From *c.*400 to 412 his textual battles are with the Donatist schism, and then from 412 to 413 until his death in 430 with the proponents of free will, Pelagius and his supporters, who provoke many of his late writings on grace and original sin. Meanwhile, in 410, 'eternal Rome' had fallen to barbarian raiders. The vast *City of God* was to be his literary response to the event, a review of the failings of paganism and the earthly city.

Augustine did not cause the 'death' of paganism nor even, despite his deft Conciliar leadership, the extinction of the Donatist Church. Manichaeans continued to lurk in north Africa, and nowadays many people, if faced with the choice, prefer the views of Pelagius and his followers to Augustine's on original sin. Nonetheless, his lasting influence has been through what he wrote, the main themes of which, I believe, had already been sketched by 397 and continued to underlie his thinking, whomever it ostensibly addresses. In the Western Middle Ages, his writings on faith and reason were to be central to the thinking of Anselm, Archbishop of Canterbury, and then to Thomas Aquinas and his contemporaries. His writings on grace, faith and free will were to be crucial for the entire Western Reformation and Counter-Reformation and the disputes across sixteenth-century Europe over 'faith' and 'works'. He did not invent the ideas of original sin and predestination by God, both of which could be found in the Latin New Testament, but his discussions of them were to influence Calvin and many others: they also disgusted the Enlightenment thinkers of the eighteenth century. It is as the 'Doctor of Grace' that he is a Doctor of the Catholic Church, but he has never been only a Catholic source. His writings played a seminal role in the thinking of Luther and the first Anglicans in England's post-Reformation Church. In parts of the modern world his linking of sexual lust to Adam's original sin has won him few friends, but his views on sex and marriage, though not theirs, were more moderate and humane at the time than some of his contemporary Christians, including Jerome.[20]

After the *Confessions*, he had no further conversions, but he continued to deepen his thinking in response to circumstances and others' contrary views. Those who had crossed his path importantly before 397 did not all disappear from its later course. After their interrupted relations he and Paulinus resumed friendly contact. The hostile twitter turned out to be untrue, and certainly by 404, though some think by 400/401, the two were again exchanging letters. In 404, Augustine even wrote to propose that Paulinus and his monks should move to north Africa to be safer at this time of Gothic invasions in Italy. Paulinus stayed resolutely at Nola, but not because the past scandal made him keep his distance.[21] Both men then settled down to nearly twenty more years of correspondence, discussing anything from miracles and the vision of God to the questions of free will which Pelagius made urgent. Paulinus was to outlive Augustine, but only by a year.

Jerome, meanwhile, continued to be the victim of irregularities in the delivery of his and Augustine's letters, but maintained a fractious correspondence nonetheless, failing to establish his superior views on the biblical text and his mistaken view of the quarrel of Peter and Paul. Their correspondence continued in bursts because Augustine himself wanted it, until Jerome's death ten years before Augustine's own.

For the others in my triptych, Libanius and Synesius, life's final years seem sadder. After losing his brother, his concubine and his son,

Libanius' updated speech on himself ends in 393 with a ringing endorsement of Homeric revenge on his enemies in Constantinople. Soon after 412 Synesius disappears too, also after losing those dear to him, his three children. To one of his most faithful friends he writes of his loss, citing words of the poet Euripides which moralists had long commended for the occasion. 'Alas . . . but why "Alas"? We have suffered what mortals do.'[22] To his icon, Hypatia, he then wrote what appear to be his last two letters. Still he calls her his blessed Lady, his 'mother and sister and teacher and benefactress in every respect'. Stretched on his bed, he admits that his physical weakness has psychological roots, his grief. He does not, however, 'confess' like the suffering Augustine: instead, an eternal student at heart, he sends best wishes to Hypatia's pupils in Alexandria, including the new intake, although they are unknown to him by name. Philosophy remains his ideal and his consolation. He regrets Hypatia's silence among his many sorrows, not the least of which is the loss of his children and 'the goodwill of one and all'. He had always hoped her 'most divine soul' to be his 'one defence against the abuse of demons and the tides of fate'.[23]

Both men had stood up for lifelong values. Among the quarrels, the pride and the slanders, Libanius remained the impassioned champion of Greek and Greek culture. So did Christian Synesius, asserting it in the face of uncultured Christian monks. Both men shared an ideal of educated culture, a bridge which would have united them despite their differences of religion. As a lifelong teacher Libanius remained admirably committed to the advancement of his ex-pupils and their interests. It made no difference if others ranked them as decidedly 'beta', in the middle second class.[24] Aged seventy-six, he was still writing to an old friend, the philosopher Priscus, then teaching in Athens, and fondly recalling it as the star among cities and his years with the Emperor Julian as a golden age.[25] We last hear him speaking in January 392, the year before his death: he was praising the festival of the Kalends of January, the start to each New Year, when 'even a prisoner has been seen by his guards to smile'.[26] It reconciles 'guest with guest, child with child, woman with woman', but it has lost its former rituals, recently banned by a Christian law. Previously, it had been what Libanius manifestly loved, a time of 'much fire, much blood and much smoke ascending from every quarter to heaven' so that the gods, too, could enjoy a brilliant banquet during the festival days. Libanius' attachment to the pagan gods had not dimmed in 'Christian times'.

Synesius, meanwhile, was building a monastery in later life, a 'place of ascetic effort' (an *asketerion*, the very word) beside a river near Ptolemais' church.[27] However, it was not to be his own refuge. He remained the self-professed admirer of spiritual Platonizing philosophy while showing, unlike Augustine, that he could combine this admiration with a practical, muscular career. Both before and after his appointment as bishop, it fell to him to lead military resistance to the Austurenses, tribal terrorists who were marauding southern Libya. He wrote from the very forts and battlements, a philosopher under arms. 'Hunting,' he regretted 'has had to go', because of the terrorist raids in open country, but horses were still vital, not least for the squadrons of mounted guards with whom Synesius himself was serving. This role came to him from his high social standing as a former active landowner, as it never would have come to Augustine: while fulfilling it, he was able to appeal to contacts he had made in earlier life on his city's behalf, including no less a person than the praetorian prefect of Constantinople, way above Augustine's horizons. Synesius is the only Christian bishop to have composed both metrical hymns on an ascent to God and a letter referring to his preparation of stone-throwing artillery and his need for straighter arrows for his soldiers' bows.[28] His later letters are indeed the texts from antiquity which were written while 'waiting for the barbarian'. He is abiding evidence that a philosophizing Christian did not have to be a monk.

The elderly Augustine looked back on no Hypatia in his earlier life. Instead, he had his mother. More than thirty years after her death, he remained unwaveringly sure of her former love and devotion. In 420/21, it is Monnica whom he cites as proof that the dead do not participate in the affairs of the living. 'There is my own self,' he writes, 'whom my pious mother would not fail to visit every night' if the dead really did engage with our lives. She was 'that mother who followed me by land and sea so that she might live with me. Far be the thought that she should have been made cruel by a life more happy, so much so that when anything troubles my heart she would not ever console in my sadness the son whom she loved with an only love, whom she never wished to see mournful.'[29] It is the most touching spontaneous tribute to her, eloquent about his memories of her even when he had reached the age of sixty-five.

He also had his confessions. Near the end of his life, he remarks that whenever he reads them, they raise his understanding and emotions to God. They had indeed remained a force in his subsequent writings. His great work *On the Trinity* develops the thoughts on the Trinity's presence in each human soul which the *Confessions*' final books had first advanced. Pierre Courcelle aptly detected in the *City of God* a 'meditation by Augustine on the process of his own conversion in order to put disciples of [the Neoplatonist pagan] Porphyry on the road to Christianity': such a meditation is heir to the *Confessions*' presentation of his own meeting with the Platonist books.[30] Late in his life Augustine undertook, like no previous author, to review each one of his prolific writings and correct them wherever he thought necessary. These *Retractations* have been well described as the '*Confessions* of Augustine's old age'.[31] On through his life, meanwhile, ran the prospect of mystical contact with God, the *Confessions*' unifying theme. He continued to aspire to it in spiritual exercises. He discussed it at length in letters to an aristocratic Roman lady who was concerned to know in what sense God could be 'seen'. His next major commentary on Genesis, after the *Confessions*' final books, addressed the varying types of such a vision in careful detail. In a sermon before sailors and simple folk in Hippo, he preached with passion on the scope for mystical ascent.[32] To Synesius such 'mysteries' had been fit only for the philosophically trained, the happy few.

One aim of the *Confessions* had been to encourage others to adopt a life of sexual and worldly renunciation. The text still inspires applicants to the Augustinian Order, but it also speaks to those who have embarked on a monastic life, from Petrarch and Teresa of Avila to the monks of today. In his old age, Augustine noted that the book had become widely read and enjoyed, but its immediate impact is harder to document. Except, probably, for Paulinus, its first-known readers are all enemies, Donatists who seized on his confessed sins and a Manichaean as subtle as Secundinus, who argued that Augustine had never understood Mani's Gospel at all.[33] The earliest known literary response is preserved in a recently rediscovered letter by Consentius, a cantankerous Catholic priest in the Balearic islands. He wrote to tell Augustine how he had first acquired the *Confessions* in 407, ten years, in my view, after their composition, 'so that I might confess simply to God'. However, he had been put off by 'the bothersome splendour of your sentences' and had not opened the text again for another eight years. When he returned to it, the *Confessions* evidently impressed him much more, because his letter to Augustine adopts a structure which they had taught him.[34] Not until a year before Augustine's death do we have a letter from someone actually asking for a copy of the book. In 427/8 an Imperial commissioner in north Africa, a man of blood and power, wrote to Augustine to request a copy of the *Confessions*, despite his military duties against the invading Vandals.[35]

This Imperial commissioner, Darius, perhaps found his 'heart raised up to God' as a result, but he was not alone in continuing to avoid the celibate life. The cousins and the young soldier in Verecundus' villa have disappeared from history: not one is known to have taken up Augustine's celibate cause. As for that 'greater friend', Mallius Theodorus, he was quick, when occasion offered, to abandon the study of philosophy and to rejoin the 'worldly ambition' of a career. By January 397, he was holding the prestigious Praetorian Prefecture of Illyricum, Italy and Africa and in 399 the consulship at Rome. His panegyrist, the poet Claudian, graphically imagined how Theodorus' consulship would involve a show of spectacular bloodsports in the Colosseum. 'May the sand of the arena be enriched, far and wide, with blood', the blood of bears, lions and leopards. 'Let us see people who hurl themselves through the air like birds' and build a human pyramid, on which a boy will dance as an acrobat.[36] When the elderly Augustine revisited *On the Happy Life*, he regretted its dedication to Theodorus, no doubt in light of this subsequent conduct and its misguided attempt to discover 'happiness' elsewhere.[37]

After arriving in Rome in 396, young Licentius made similar discoveries and, if the epitaph of the 'Licentius' there is his, became a 'most illustrious senator' by 406. Some twelve years later, his father, grand Romanianus, re-emerges memorably in one of Augustine's letters. His wife, Cypriana, had died and he had promptly taken up with a concubine. As a baptized Christian, he had evidently provoked scandal, so he wrote first to Paulinus in Italy, who refused, and then to Augustine, his dear former protégé, asking him for nothing less than a letter of 'consolation', praising his chaste wife, now dead.[38] Augustine rose to the occasion in a brilliant blend of phrases from Cicero's speech against dastardly Catiline and words from Paulinus' poem to Licentius, which Romanianus would have known well. He was indignant at his old friend's request. 'A crowd (*plebs*) of women keeps watch, all night, over the sides of your body: the number of your concubines grows day by day . . .' Romanianus is their 'slave, dissipated by lust for so many common call-girls . . .': how dare he ask for praise of the chaste Cypriana as if to soften his grieving and excuse his current behaviour?

Most ordinary Christian readers would admit that, as usual, it was Romanianus who was leading the enviable life. The 'slavery of God' to which Augustine devoted most of his life was too daunting for almost everyone else. In his seventy-sixth year, as he lay dying in his room in Hippo, he continued to confess. 'He had had the Psalms of David on penitence, which are very few, copied out,' his biographer Possidius recalled, 'and, lying in his bed, he had the pages, in fours, placed against the wall, and in the days of his weakness, he would gaze at them and read, and he would weep copiously and continuously.'[39]

'In the books of my *Confessions*,' Augustine had written to Darius, less than two years earlier, 'behold me, and do not praise me beyond what I am: in them, believe what I say of myself, not what others say of me.' Darius must praise God, not Augustine, 'if anything in me pleases you'. He must also pray for Augustine 'when you find me in those pages . . . that I may avoid "defection" and reach "perfection" ': he must tell others to do the same.[40]

However, without Romanianus, his patron and benefactor, there would have been no such Augustine, educated to write like a marvel, able to teach in Milan and to be present for the conversions which led to his striving for perfection. Two ways through life endure, as Augustine's own sermons stress. While in the Manichaeans' Church, he had first learned about them and their interrelated value. He continued to regard them in that light. Martha's life, he says, is valuable because she served the Lord in this life, but although it is good to attend to the poor, it is even better to attend to the needs of the saints. Martha's work is temporary and will pass away, whereas the work of her sister, Mary, will endure. For Mary focused on 'one thing' only, the contemplation which will be enjoyed for ever in the next world.[41] Augustine related the two lives to aspects of the life of the Church, but they also apply to individuals. Marthas in our multiplicity, most of us avoid the Mary within, but some of us know, from Augustine, that there, but for the grace of God, go we.

Extended Captions to the Plates

1. 'Generosity', a virtue applauded in very rich donors to public shows and blood-sports in the city's arena before crowds of spectators, personified in a famous mosaic in Antioch. She is handing out gold coins from a basket full of them. Libanius admired this same virtue, whereas Augustine deplored its equivalent in north Africa as wasteful pride and worldly ambition. It is the central image of a very big floor-mosaic, in the house of a grand donor, which also shows expert hunters in the arena who bear the names of mythical Greek heroes and are fighting fierce wild beasts. The floor was flanked by a border showing part of urban Antioch which can be matched to Libanius' speeches a century earlier. Yakto villa, Daphne, AD 450s. Now in Princeton Museum, reproduced with its permission.
2. Mosaic from the dining room of a private house in the green hill-suburb of Daphne above Antioch, *c.*AD 250–80. Personified Comedy, on the left, holds a theatrical mask and a stick, perhaps to represent a messenger-speech in a play. Glycera, mistress of the comic poet Menander, shown right, reclines in the centre. Comedies would be recited at drinking parties after dinner, part of the theatre culture in the big cities which Augustine looked back on with disgust and which Libanius did not usually praise, either. Archaeological Museum, Antakya, Hatay, Turkey. (Photo: Hatice Pamir)
3. The grand country home of Lord Julius in north Africa, shown in a floor-mosaic from his house at Carthage. Its strong walls and towers flank an arcade and the domes represent his villa's bath-house. Julius and his wife are presented here in the setting of their garden. Offerings signifying each of the four seasons are presented to the couple by their estate workers. At the top, centre, ducks, olives and a lamb are brought to her ladyship. At the bottom left, she leans elegantly on a pillar in front of a rose bush while her maid gives her jewellery and another attendant brings more roses, fit for her erotic beauty. At the bottom right, a messenger gives Lord Julius, beneath a fruit tree, a scroll marked with his name, thereby identifying him for the viewer, while another estate worker approaches him from behind, a basket on his back and holding in his left hand, by its back legs, a hare, presumably killed in the orchard. In the central scene, left, Julius rides up to his villa in official dress and, right, a hunting party sets out for a day's sport. In Libya, Synesius and his family enjoyed a similar style of life in similarly towered country houses, far grander than the home of Augustine's family at Thagaste. Carthage, *c.*AD 400, contemporary with Augustine's years of preaching in the city. Bardo Museum, Tunis. (Photo: J. Williams)

4. Zeus disguised as a swan pulls off the married Leda's robe before making love to her and fathering Helen of Troy. Mosaic floor, fourth century AD, from a private house at Complutum, near Madrid, where the earnest Paulinus and Thersasia also had a house and property. Guests will have much enjoyed the racy image, unlike Augustine, who after his conversion refers to the tales of Jupiter's adultery as 'filth'. (Photo: K. Schmidt)
5. Mosaic panels which give a unique representation of a schoolboy's ordeals. They are now in private collections in the USA, but once they surrounded a bigger floor in north Syria, surely in or near Antioch, and plausibly dated to the fifth century AD, although I have wondered if perhaps it was contemporary with Libanius in the fourth. Here, young Kimbros, left, is flogged and then taken to Marianos, seated, probably a primary grammar-teacher. Black-winged Disease (Nosos) hovers by the bed-ridden Apollonides, whom Marianos visits, perhaps as a fellow teacher, as Libanius sometimes did. With the help of C. Marinescu. (Photo: Stefan Hager)
6. On the left, Kimbros is offered a pen and a writing tablet and then brought to his next teacher, Alexandros, seated, whom he kisses in greeting. Friendship (Philia) then introduces him to new little friends, shown right, carrying scrolls or food towards him. (Photo: Stefan Hager)
7. Older pupils, perhaps carrying scrolls, go for a discussion (Diatribe) with and then an exposition by the seated teacher, Alexandros, whose mouth is indicated by personified Education (Paideia). To his right are the figures of two days, captioned by dates, our 14 October and 7 August, signifying the start and end of the oratorical school year, just as Libanius in Antioch and Augustine in Milan knew it. The summer vacation fell between them. (Photo: Stefan Hager)
8. Kimbros' friend Markianos, on the left, with the personified figure of Petitioning (Enteuxis) at his right. Kimbros and his friends are discussing, with a dog, below right, and then the personified figure of Informing (Menusis) reveals details to the seated teacher, Alexandros. Kimbros is then held by the feet and head by his two friends and in my view is to be flogged by the standing figure with a lash, a sort of ancient pandy-bat. The panels beautifully relate to the perils of schooling, friendship and flogging which are recalled by Augustine and Libanius in their own past. (Photo: Stefan Hager)
9. The best surviving image of female Elect members of the Manichaean Church, reassembled from fragments of a silk hanging used in a Manichaean place of worship. They are dressed in Far Eastern style, but have the serious look which also befitted the female Elect among whom young Augustine worshipped while a Hearer in north Africa. Tenth century AD from Jinjiang, south-east China. bpk/Museum für Asiatische Kunst, Staatliche Museen zu Berlin Inv. III 4815.
10. Manichaean scribes at work with their pens in a context of music and song, for which copies of hymn books and psalters were necessary. From an illustrated Manichaean book made of Chinese paper, 8th–9th century AD, found

at Chotscho, Jinjiang, south-east China. bpk/Museum für Asiatische Kunst, Staatliche Museen zu Berlin Inv. III 6368 verso. (Photo: Jürgen Liepe)

11. In this unique image, a Manichaean Hearer offers Light-rich fruits as a meal to the Elect, males on the left, females on the right, at the Bēma Festival in spring, just as young Augustine did in Africa. From a manuscript of Chinese paper, eighth to ninth century AD, found at the temple, Chotscho, Jinjiang, south-east China. bpk/Museum für Asiatische Kunst, Staatliche Museen zu Berlin Inv. III 4979 verso. (Photo: Iris Papadopoulos)
12. Stone statue of Mani as Buddha of Light, re-erected in AD 1339 in a long-lived Manichaean temple, the Cao'an temple, in Jinjiang, south-east China, furthest point of his Gospel's travels and survival. It is evidence of his worshippers' continuing close contact with Buddhism, one which began in Mani's own lifetime and which Mani, we have recently learned, was represented by his followers as having confounded before the Persian court. An inscription on the nearby rock reads: 'Purity, Light, Great Power, Wisdom, Supreme Perfect Truth, the Light Buddha of Mani'. (Photo: S. N. C. Lieu)
13. Mani's Universe, newly identified in a brilliant study by Yutaka Yoshida from photos of this astounding painting on silk, 136 cm long by 56 cm wide, surely once a temple-hanging but preserved in a private Japanese collection, though probably made in Ningpo, China. At the top is a deity, surely the Father of Light, with twelve surrounding female figures, surely the Ages or Aeons. Below them, two round discs represent the 'ships' of Light, the sun (shown red) on the right, the moon (pale yellow) on the left. Each ship has five rooms and contains the major figures in Mani's cosmology: Primal Man, Jesus the Splendour and so forth. Ten arches, or vaults, then represent the ten firmaments, each shown with twelve gates and 'Light ships' in which purified Light is shipped back up to the Kingdom of Light. Tiny details in these heavens have all been identified with items in Manichaean texts. The mushroom-shaped mountain below can be identified with Mount Sumeru, attested in Manichaean Sogdian texts. It has thirty-two little houses on it, the exact number of the towns on Sumeru in Manichaean texts. Demons are shown on either side. Below them again are five more bands, which show snakes, wild beasts, birds, fish and two-legged creatures, all members of the Kingdom of Darkness. Yutaka Yoshida has related the details which are visible in miniature to Manichaean texts and even to texts by Augustine. He therefore proposes, most excitingly, that the scroll was ultimately based on Mani's famous, but long-lost, Picture Book, whose imagery underlies the Far Eastern imagery we see here. Photos by courtesy of Yutaka Yoshida, whose initial study is now published in S. G. Richter, C. Horton and K. Ohlhafer, eds., *Mani in Dublin* (Leiden, 2015), 389–98. (Photo: Yutaka Yoshida)
14. The Manichaean Seventh Heaven in the big cosmological painting, with Atlas and the King of Glory (in red) and the three wheels which are to extract scattered Light from the world. The five bands below show snakes and other vile breeds of the Kingdom of Darkness just as Augustine describes. (Photo: Yutaka Yoshida)

15. Mani's Lord of the Firmaments (in red) in the Seventh Heaven, with a demon of Darkness imprisoned in a chest below in the Sixth Heaven, recalling Augustine's references to the wars in the Universe. From the cosmological painting above. (Photo: Yutaka Yoshida)
16. The one surviving half of a pair of little ivory panels, linked as a 'diptych', which grand Roman citizens would give to important friends, usually to mark a significant occasion in the family. This one is topped by the letters of the name SYMMACHORUM, carved in an intricate monogram. Its meaning has been variously discussed, but in a brilliant reinterpretation Alan Cameron has recently explained it, to my mind decisively, as an ivory issued on the death of Q. Aurelius Symmachus, the very famous pagan Roman senator who recommended Augustine for his job in Milan in 384. A chariot is pulled by four elephants and in it, therefore, Symmachus himself is shown sitting, holding a sceptre as a reference to his high offices, including the consulship. From a funeral pyre behind, two eagles ascend, a traditional sign of souls ascending to heaven, best known in the formal 'consecration' rite for a dead Roman emperor. In a four-horsed chariot beside them Symmachus ascends to the sky and above, in a lifelike representation of his features, he is shown lifted up by two winged Winds into heaven and the company of his family ancestors. It is a pagan ascension as the philosophic Cicero imagined one, compatible with ideas in his *Hortensius*. The second eagle refers, Cameron proposes, to the soul of a dead member of the family which was commemorated on the second, linked panel, now lost. He identifies him as the grand pagan Flavianus Nicomachus and dates the diptych to 402, the year of Symmachus' death. (Photo: The Trustees of the British Museum; inv. 1857, 1013.1)
17. Mosaic portrait of Ambrose, Bishop of Milan, Augustine's revered baptismal Father and role-model. From St Victor's chapel in Milan, incorporated in the big Basilica Ambrosiana. Ambrose died in 397 and this mosaic was only made *c.* AD 450 but it is the earliest known representation of the great man, perhaps based on local evidence. (Photo: Benedetta Campana)
18. Imagined representations of the two martyrs, Gervase and Protasius, whose bodies were dug up by Ambrose in Milan in June 386. They became martyr-saints at several north Italian churches, most of all at Ravenna in the basilica of San Vitale, their supposed father, where these round 'portraits' of the two are shown in mosaic on the inner surface of the great arch in the nave *c.*AD 530. (Photo: Thomas Cameron)
19. Rare silk damask dalmatic robe, newly restored in Milan and showing a lioness and her cubs in a bigger scene of hunting. Worn surely by a bishop of Milan and its dating (fourth to sixth centuries AD) does not exclude the possibility that this impressive piece was once worn by Ambrose himself before his death in 397. Courtesy of Prof. M. Petoletti and Prof. Dr Sabine Schrenk, University of Bonn, director of the conservation of the dalmatic, a great treasure. (Photo: Ulrike Reichert)
20. Baptismal pool in the S. Giovanni Baptistery by the basilica known nowadays as Santa Tecla, Milan. In this octagonal pool, about 5 m wide and only 80 cm

deep, with a bench around its interior, Ambrose almost certainly baptized Augustine at Easter, 387. Candidates perhaps sat or reclined on the low bench in the shallow pool, whose drainage hole still survives. (Photo: M. Stirling)

21. Gold representation on glass of the paired apostles Peter, left, and Paul, balding, right, beside a column shown as if studded with jewels and topped by the Chi Rho – CH-R-istos – symbol of early Christian imagery. Mid to late fourth century around the time of Augustine's visit to Rome, where Pope Damasus had fostered the cults of the Roman martyrs. Part of a glass drinking vessel deposed in honour of the two martyr-apostles, perhaps after prayers and a libation for their intercession at their presumed place of burial. Rome, now in the Metropolitan Museum, New York. (Photo C. R. Jenkins)

22. Earliest imagined representation of Augustine, dated *c.*AD 550, more than 200 years after his death. Fresco excavated at the site of St John Lateran in Rome, in what its excavator proposed to be a wing of the papal library. Accurate rendering of Augustine's features is unlikely so long after his death, but, aptly, he holds a book in one hand and beneath the painting run Latin verses saying 'Various fathers have said various things [but this one] Has said everything with Roman eloquence, thundering forth mystic senses [of the scriptures].' These lines are good evidence for the elevation of Augustine as a universal authority in papal Rome, where his works had been copied since the papacy of Leo I, *c.*450. St John Lateran. (Photo: J. Mitchell)

23. Sculpted portrait bust of a revered philosopher in white marble, projecting from a rounded shield-shaped surround, an honorific type. From Aphrodisias in Greek-speaking Caria, now south-west Turkey, where sculpting and Greek intellectual life remained strong in the early to mid-fifth century. The furrowed brow, the upturned eyes, and especially the beard and dress support the identification with a serious Platonist philosopher, projecting the image of such people as Synesius would have imagined them, a type which also applied to the great Platonists read by Augustine in Milan. From a room with other sculpted portraits of famous Greek figures, including Plato and Pythagoras, perhaps a room for lectures and intellectual discussions. Described by its first publisher, R. R. R. Smith, in 1990 as the image of 'an inspired, visionary philosopher, a man of the spirit, an impassioned thinker of divine thoughts', very much Augustine's view of Plotinus and Porphyry, whom he read from summer 386 onwards. Aphrodisias Museum. (Photo: Mehmet Ali Dogenci, R. R. R. Smith)

24. White marble bust of a Greek-speaking public dignitary from Aphrodisias, probably a near-contemporary of Synesius and alive *c.*AD 430–50. The overmantle and under-tunic are both shown correctly and the long hair, with a few strands pulled over a balding front patch, typifies an intellectual. However, although the eyes are excellently stylized, they are not upturned and the beard is not rough and thick, sure signs of a philosopher. Probably a highly educated orator and thinker, like some of the friends of Synesius or, earlier, Libanius, but not a committed Platonist as Augustine would imagine one. His first publisher, R. R. R. Smith, in 1990 considered him to be a 'living public figure . . . thoughtful, serious, reserved . . . with a certain hauteur'.

Aphrodisias Museum, displayed in the same room as 23. (Photo: Mehmet Ali Dogenci, R. R. R. Smith)

25. Mosaic on the covering of the tomb of a Christian lady, Valentia, *c.*AD 400, set near the apse of the 'Chapel of the Martyrs' at Thabraca (now Tabarka). It is our best contemporary visual evidence for a north African basilica, here captioned 'Church as Mother, Valentia In Peace', mother Church being a favourite phrase in north African Christian writings, exploited in Augustine's early sermon in 391 to baptismal 'seekers'. Showing both interior and exterior, the mosaic presents a six-columned nave, entered at the right side of the design. The floor is patterned with a mosaic of birds and flowers and the altar, set with burning candles, is shown between two columns about two thirds of the way up the nave. On the left of the design, steps are shown leading up to a triple arch into the presbytery and, behind it, to the apse, whose rounded arch has a circular window. Above the nave are a tiled roof and clerestory windows. Many of the churches in which Augustine preached will have looked much like this one. Bardo Museum, Tunis. (Photo: R. Jensen)

26. Table for meals and offerings in honour of martyrs and family dead, the Christian practice which Monnica observed in north Africa and tried to follow in Milan. Augustine as a priest wrote to Aurelius, Bishop of Carthage, in an attempt to have it curbed in his north African diocese. This one shows a fish, a Christian symbol, and is inscribed: 'In God. May there be Peace and Conviviality in Our Concord'. Dancing, music, food and drinking were part of it, both sexes participating far into the night, often with rowdy results. From the Matares cemetery, near Tipasa, about twenty-five miles west of modern Algiers; *c.*AD 380–400, contemporary with Augustine's concerns. Now in the Museum of Tipasa. (Photo: R. Jensen)

27. Basilica complex at Hippo, now in Tunisia, the city of Augustine's priesthood and bishopric. This image has coloured up the recent black-and-white axonometric drawing by E. Brown, itself based on the ground plan of the buildings as excavated by E. Marec in the 1920s and 1930s and modified by subsequent study. The basilica existed in AD 390 and has three aisles and a baptistery attached and also buildings which are perhaps a scribal writing and copying room, the bishop's residence and, though much disputed, a martyr's shrine, possibly the shrine of St Stephen, whose cult is important in Augustine's later ministry. Until recently scholars agreed that the basilica was the Catholic basilica and therefore used by Augustine, although there was some dispute as to whether it was the Basilica of Peace or the Greater Basilica, both being attested in Hippo by literary texts. However, a very strong case has now been published for it being the 'Donatist' basilica of Augustine's opponents, reminding us that their churches cannot be readily distinguished from Catholic ones by their ground plans and that their community was very prominent, being much the larger one in Hippo when Augustine arrived there in 391. (Photo: R. Jensen)

28. One half of the mosaic covering a double sarcophagus for two north African Christians, probably father and daughter as she is presented as a 'Holy Daughter', or virgin. The father, captioned 'In Peace', holds a pen and is

writing on a scroll or tablet words of which the letters 'MAR' are visible in order to show that he is writing a list or calendar of Christian martyrs. From the martyrs' chapel at Thabraca, east of Augustine's Hippo, *c.*AD 400, now in the Bardo Museum, Tunis. (Photo: N. Panayotis)

29. The other half of the mosaic shows fair-haired Christian Victoria, also buried in the sarcophagus. She is likely to be the man's daughter as she is captioned as a 'Holy Daughter', *Filia Sacra*, and her head is covered, implying that she is a consecrated virgin. She is praying, because her hands are held out sideways, a position for prayer in north Africa and one which Augustine would use, not least while dictating, in my view, the *Confessions*. These two Christians evoke the virtuous sort of Christians who would also feature in Augustine's mixed-ability congregations. From the martyrs' chapel at Thabraca, *c.*AD 400, now in the Bardo Museum, Tunis. (Photo: N. Panayotis)
30. Lazarus being raised by Jesus from the dead and told to 'come forth' from his tomb. An apt scene of resurrection for the Christian in this sarcophagus in Rome, the 'Jonah sarcophagus', *c.*AD 300, on whose lid it is sculpted. Augustine expounded this Gospel story in an answer for his brethren in 394/5 and explained it allegorically as the soul's liberation from the desires of the body, symbolized by the bandages which attach to Lazarus. The onlookers are Lazarus's sisters, Martha standing with raised right hand and protesting, correctly, 'he stinks', after his time in the tomb, and, kneeling on the right, the focused Mary, for whom, in life, 'one thing is necessary'. The two sisters were considered by the Manichaeans and later by Augustine himself to represent two levels of Christian life, the practical and the spiritual. Vatican Museum, Rome. (Photo: P. Tannenbaum)
31. Mosaic from the floor of a basilica whose central inscription, 'Peace For The Catholic Church Always', asserts that the basilica and its community are Catholic, not Donatist. In the village of Beni Raschid, near Castellanum Tingitanum (now Chlef), west of Hippo, in Algeria. (Photo: R. Jensen)
32. Apse mosaic of a stag and doe drinking from the four rivers of Paradise, alluding to Psalm 42, which was regularly interpreted as a baptismal psalm, befitting the baptismal candidates in Easter week. It was exploited by Augustine in this sense in the *Confessions*, Book 13, and in his *Expositions* of the Psalms. From the mosaic flooring in the baptismal area of the basilica at Bir Ftouha, Carthage, *c.*AD 380–420. This part of the mosaic flooring was removed to the Louvre, but a similar part is still in the Bardo Museum, Tunis. (Photo: N. Panayotis)
33. Monnica as imagined by Benozzo Gozzoli and helpers in the 1440s. From the face of the left column fronting the apse at S. Agostino, San Gimignano, Tuscany, and its great fresco-cycle of Augustine's life, the only one in Tuscany. The frescoes were commissioned by Fra Domenico Strambi, who had been away in Paris to study for his doctorate in theology at the Sorbonne but then went on to England as a collector of revenues, a job from which he no doubt earned the funds which paid on his return for Gozzoli's frescoes. Monnica's cult was publicized in Italy after the arrival of her 'relics' from Ostia to Rome with the fulsome endorsement of the Pope in 1430. (Photo: S. Horsfield)

Bibliography

The bibliography for Augustine grows yearly by several hundred titles. The *Revue des Études Augustiniennes et Patristiques* contains a yearly critical Bulletin which is the essential point of entry. The continuing *Augustinus-Lexikon*, appearing from Basel since 1986, contains excellent entries by major scholars with extensive bibliographies and references. Allan Fitzgerald, ed., *Augustine through the Ages* (Grand Rapids, 1999), and V. H. Drecoll, ed., *Augustin Handbuch* (Tübingen, 2007), are invaluable resources. Augustine was the first saint to have a webpage, www.georgetown.edu/faculty/jod/Augustine, with many helpful connections. www.augustinus.it is an excellent source of Augustine's Latin texts and Italian translations. www.findingaugustine.org is an excellent site for bibliographical research, as is www.augustinus.konkordanz.de.

The outstanding biography is Peter Brown, *Augustine of Hippo: A Biography* (1967), a work of genius, supplemented by a further important essay in its second edition (2000a) and by fine chapters on Augustine in a social context in Brown (2012) 148–84, which appeared when my chapters on those same aspects were already written and so I have merely corrected mine if necessary and left our slight differences of emphasis to stand. The brilliant groundwork by Louis-Sébastien Le Nain de Tillemont in the 1690s has been re-edited with modern notes by F. van Fleteren and G. C. Berthold (2010), and its first volume is a fascinating insight into how far we have, or have not, advanced since. Henry Chadwick, *Augustine* (Oxford,1986), is an exceptional short guide by one 'past master' about another. Chadwick's *Augustine of Hippo* (2009) is also excellent. Serge Lancel's fuller *St Augustine* (English translation, 2002) is particularly good on north African topics, but has little to say about Manichaeism, a gap I have tried to refill. J. J. O'Donnell is the author both of a major commentary on *Augustine: Confessions* (1992) in three volumes, essential for all close work on the text, and of a life study, *Augustine, Sinner and Saint* (2005), which is reviewed by F. van Fleteren in *Augustinian Studies* (2005) 447–52. Mark Vessey, ed., A *Companion to Augustine* (Oxford, 2012) has short chapters by many scholars on aspects of Augustine's life and work, including an interesting review by Paula Fredriksen of Peter Brown's biography. Short books abound, especially Gillian Clark on the *Confessions* (2005 edition) and also on Books 1–4 (1995), the great H. I. Marrou, *Saint Augustin et l'augustinisme* (1955), T. Fuhrer, *Augustinus* (2004), a good way into German scholarship and much else, and G. Catapano, *Agostino* (2010) (2012), a good way into important Italian scholarship. Augustine's thought is most penetratingly examined by Christopher Kirwan, *Augustine* (1989), a major contribution, and by G. J. P. O'Daly, specifically on Augustine's philosophy of mind (1987). E. Stump and N. Kretzmann's edited *Cambridge Companion to Augustine* (2001) also has good chapters on philosophical questions by various scholars.

A recent translation, which I like, is Philip Burton, *Augustine's Confessions* (London and New York, 2001). There are many others, including the free one, which I find too free, by W. Watts, used in the Loeb edition, the Penguin one by R. S. Pine-Coffin (1961) and the Oxford one by Henry Chadwick (1991) with valuable notes but a style which I find leaden and, at times, too far from Augustine's vivid Latin.

The French editions of Augustine's works in the *Bibliothèque Augustinienne* series (referred to in my notes as *BA*) are fundamental guides, still progressing and still being updated. Volumes 13 and 14 contain the fine translation of and commentary on the *Confessions* by Aimé Solignac, which are essential resources, my constant resort and the best place for French-speakers to read the text. Volumes from 50 onwards have greatly deepened and improved our understanding of Augustine's works from *c.*388 to 396 and have been invaluable to me. My greatest debt is to the writings of Goulven Madec, whose contributions to the yearly *Bulletin Augustinien* and to the subject in general are essential for all study of Augustine and his thought. They underlie many modern books, including much of mine. His *Lectures augustiniennes* (2001) are points of entry into his work and its incisive clarity. His *Le Dieu d'Augustin* (1998) is most illuminating, as is his *Le Christ de saint Augustin* in a valuable new edition (2001). His *Saint Augustin et la philosophie* (1996) is a clear introduction to his life-long work on Augustine and his relation to philosophy. P. Hadot's collected lectures on Augustine are unmissable (2010) and a tribute to a scholar whose writings have taught me much.

I have not set out to write parallel biographies of Libanius and Synesius but while this book was in its later stages, works of interest appeared on them both. Goldhill's brief sketch (2006) even paired them, as I was doing, but I do not share his view of Synesius and pagan tradition or his view of Libanius's writings on the gods as constantly in tension or 'negotiation' with the Christianity around him. On Libanius, the entry by H.-G. Nesselrath for *Reallexikon für Antike und Christentum* (2008) is especially valuable and is now published as a separate book (2012). The heroic labours of P. Petit on Libanius' students (1955) can be matched with R. Cribiore (2007a) on Libanius' school. There is more in Cribiore's recent study of Libanius and the gods (2013), some of which I have not followed here. J. Wintjes gives the best way into Libanius' political life, its prosopography and contacts (2005). A. F. Norman was for many years a lone English doyen of the study of Libanius. A new Companion by L. van Hoof (2014a) carries forward his work in many directions and includes a full bibliography. Norman's translated Libanius volumes for the Loeb Library series (1969–77) have invaluable notes and are essential, but I find that the style he adopted for the *Autobiography* (1992) is too chatty to do justice to the art of the speech. Scott Bradbury (2004) gives an excellent selection of letters and notes. I have followed the numbering of Libanius' Letters in R. Foerster's twelve-volume edition (1903–27).

Synesius' conversion is discussed in the monumental work by Tassilo Schmitt (2001), a mine of bibliography and detail, although one of its main theses, that Synesius converted to philosophy only after the failure of his embassy to Constantinople, has not convinced me or his reviewers. Bregman (1982) sees a transition from a pagan Synesius to a Christian one, which I do not endorse, but contains much else of accessible interest. I am most in sympathy with I. Tanaseanu-Döbler's study (2008), another vital resource, to be used with S. Vollenweider on Synesius' Neoplatonism (1965). H. Seng and L. Hoffmann have edited some valuable studies (2012), but the major advances remain those of Cameron and Long (1993). I have hesitated repeatedly over the date of Synesius' embassy to Constantinople but, on balance, have decided to follow their revision. The many puzzles of his speeches in Constantinople are not relevant to my theme. J. Vogt likes Synesius for reasons which I share and are visible in his collected studies (1986), a charming book. D. Roques is an indispensable companion, both for the setting in Cyrenaica (1987), disputable though some of his conclusions are, and for the letters (1989). There were several interesting English translations of bits of Synesius before A. Fitzgerald translated the letters and opened them up permanently to more readers (1926). Nowadays the Budé editions and French translations of the letters and other works, by C. Lacombrade, D. Roques, A. Garzya and others, are essential and are indispensably annotated in all five volumes (1978–2008). *On Dreams* has just received an excellent commentary by Russell and Nesselrath (2014). My hope is that my book may prompt more readers to go into depth and detail about Libanius and Synesius, not just their dealings with emperors. I do not share the quick judgements which outsiders tend to pass on them as people. Close readings of their vast combined works will temper some of the traditional views. Genre, as ever, is all-important.

My abbreviations of Augustine's works and modern journals are usually based on those adopted by the *Augustinus-Lexikon* and my abbreviations of other Greek and Latin authors are usually based on the listing in the *Oxford Classical Dictionary*, third edition (1996). My quotations from the Bible mostly follow the RSV. I have prefaced the notes to each main chapter with a selective bibliography which is especially relevant to its main issues.

Adams, J. N. 2013. *Social Variation and the Latin Language* (Cambridge).

Adamson, P. 2008. 'Plotinus on Astrology', *OSAPh* 35: 265–91.

Adkin, N. 1993. 'Ambrose and Jerome: The Opening Shot', *Mnemosyne* 46: 364–76.

Alcock, A. 2001. 'The Sale of Mani', *VigChr* 55 (2001) 99–100.

Alflatt, M. E. 1974. 'The Development of the Idea of Involuntary Sin in St. Augustine', *REAug* 20: 113–34.

Armstrong, A. H. 1973. 'Elements in the thought of Plotinus at variance with Classical Intellectualism', *JHS* 93: 13–22.

Asiedu, F. B. A. 2000. 'Paul and Augustine's Retrospective Self: The Relevance of *Epistula* XXII', *REAug* 47: 145–64.

—. 2001. 'Memory, Truth and Representation at Augustine's Conversion Scene: A Review', *Augustiniana* 51: 79–104.

Asmussen, J. P. 1965. *Xuastvānīft: Studies in Manichaeism* (Copenhagen).

Aubin, P. 1963. *Le Problème de la 'conversion'* (Paris).

Auerbach, E. 2003. *Mimesis: The Representation of Reality in Western Literature* (Oxford).

Ayres, L. 2010. *Augustine and the Trinity* (Cambridge).

Babcock, W. S. 1979. 'Augustine's Interpretation of Romans (A.D. 394–396)', *AS* 10: 55–74.

—. 1982. 'Augustine and Tyconius: A Study in the Latin Appropriation of Paul', *SP* 1209–15.

—. 1990. 'Comment: Augustine, Paul and the Question of Moral Evil', in W. S. Babcock, ed., *Paul and the Legacies of Paul* (Dallas) 251–61.

Baker-Brian, N. 2011. *Manichaeism: An Ancient Faith Rediscovered* (London).

Bammel, C. P. 1992. 'Augustine, Origen and the Exegesis of St. Paul', *Aug* 32: 341–68.

—. 1993. 'Pauline Exegesis, Manichaeism and Philosophy in the Early Augustine', in L. R. Wickham and C. P. Bammel, eds., *Christian Faith and Greek Philosophy in Late Antiquity: Essays in Tribute to G. C. Stead* (Leiden) 1–25.

Barnes, Jonathan. 2011. *Method and Metaphysics: Essays in Ancient Philosophy* I (Oxford).

Barnes, M. R. 1999. 'Rereading Augustine on the Trinity', in S. T. Davis, D. Kendall and G. O'Collins, eds., *The Trinity: An Interdisciplinary Symposium* (Oxford) 145–76.

Barnes, T. D. 1996. 'Christians and the Theater', in W. J. Slater, ed., *Roman Theater and Society* (Ann Arbor) 161–80.

—. 1997. 'The Collapse of the Homoeans in the East', *StPatr* 29: 3–16.

—. 2000. 'Ambrose and the basilicas of Milan in 385 and 386', *ZAC* 4: 282–99.

Baron, H. 1985. *Petrarch's 'Secretum': Its Making and Meaning* (Cambridge, Mass.).

Bastiaensen, A. 2001. 'Augustine's Pauline Exegesis and Ambrosiaster', in F. Van Fleteren and J. C. Schnaubelt, eds., *Augustine Biblical Exegete* (New York) 33–54.

Bavel, T. J. van. 1987. 'The influence of Cicero's ideal of friendship on Augustine', in J. den Boeft and J. van Oort, eds., *Augustiniana Traiectina* (Paris) 59–72.

—. 1995. '"No One Ever Hated His Own Flesh": Eph. 5:29 in Augustine', *Augustiniana* 45: 45–93.

—. 1997. 'Maternal Aspects of Salvation History According to Augustine', *Augustiniana* 47: 251–290.

—. 2003. *La Communauté selon Augustin* (Brussels).

—. 2009. *The Longing of the Heart: Augustine's Doctrine on Prayer* (Leuven; Eng. trans.).

Beatrice, P. F. 1989. '*Quosdam platonicorum libros.* The Platonic Readings of Augustine in Milan', *VigChr* 41: 248–81.

BeDuhn, J. D. 2000. *The Manichaean Body in Discipline and Ritual* (Baltimore).

—. 2009. 'Augustine Accused: Megalius, Manichaeism, and the Inception of the *Confessions*', *JECS* 17: 85–124.

—. 2010. *Augustine's Manichaean Dilemma*, Vol. 1: *Conversion and Apostasy, 373–388 C.E.* (Philadelphia).

—. 2011. 'Did Augustine Win His Debate with Fortunatus?' in J. van den Berg et al., eds., *'In Search of Truth': Augustine, Manichaeism and Other Gnosticism: Studies for Johannes van Oort at Sixty* (Leiden) 463–79.

—. 2013a. *Augustine's Manichaean Dilemma*, Vol. 2: *Making a 'Catholic' Self* (Pennsylvania) 122–63.

—. 2013b. 'The Manichaean Weekly Confession Ritual', in A. D. De Conick, G. Shaw and J. D. Turner, eds., *Practising Gnosis: Ritual, Magic, Theurgy and Liturgy in Nag Hammadi, Manichaean and Other Ancient Literature. Essays in Honor of Birger A. Pearson* (Leiden) 271–300.

—. 2015. 'Parallels between Coptic and Iranian Kephalaia: Goundesh and the King of Turan', in I. Gardner, J. BeDuhn and P. Dilley, eds., *Mani at the Court of the Persian Kings* (Leiden) 52–74.

BeDuhn, J. D., and G. Harrison, eds. and transs. 1997. 'The Tebessa Codex: A Manichaean Treatise on Biblical Exegesis and Church Order', in P. Mirecki and J. D. BeDuhn, eds., *Emerging from Darkness* (Leiden) 33–87.

Beierwaltes, W. 1981. *Regio Beatitudinis: Augustine's Conception of Happiness* (Villanova).

Belayche, N. 2006. 'Les stèles dites de Confession: une réligiosité originale dans l'Anatolie impériale', in L. de Blois, P. Funke and J. Hahn, eds., *The Impact of Imperial Rome on Religions, Ritual and Religious Life in the Roman Empire* (Leiden) 65–81.

Bennett, B. 2011. '*Globus horribilis.* The role of the bolos in Manichaean eschatology and its polemical transformation in Augustine's anti-Manichaean writings', in J. A. van den Berg et al., eds., *'In Search of Truth': Augustine, Manichaeism and other Gnosticism. Studies for Johannes van Oort at Sixty* (Leiden) 427–40.

Bennett, C. 1988. 'The Conversion of Vergil: The *Aeneid* in Augustine's *Confessions*', *REAug* 34: 47–69.

Beretta, G. 1993. *Ipazia d'Alessandria* (Rome).

Berg, J. A. van den. 2010. *Biblical Argument in Manichaean Missionary Practice: The Case of Adimantus and Augustine* (Leiden)

Bermon, E. 2001. *Le Cogito dans la pensée de saint Augustin* (Paris).

—. 2013. 'Nebridius', in C. Mayer, ed., *Augustinus-Lexikon* 4: Fasc. 1/2 (Basel) 191–4.

Beskow, P. 1988. 'The Theodosian Laws against Manichaeism', in P. Bryder, ed., *Manichaean Studies: Proceedings of the First International Conference on Manichaeism, August 5–9, 1987, Department of History of Religions, Lund University, Sweden* (Lund) 1–11.

Bickel, E. 1915. *Diatribe in Senecae philosophi fragmenta*, i (Leipzig) 288–420.

Bickerman, E. J. 1988. *The Jews in the Greek Age* (Cambridge, Mass.).

Birley, A. R. 1987. 'Some Notes on the Donatist Schism', *Libyan Studies* 18: 29–41.

Blois, F. de. 2005. 'New Light on the Sources of the Manichaean Chapter in the *Fihrist*', in A. van Tongerloo and L. Cirillo, eds., *Il Manicheismo: Nuove prospettive della ricerca* (Louvain) 37–45.

Bochet, I. 1982. *Saint Augustin et le désir de Dieu* (Paris).

—. 1998. 'Le statut d'histoire de la philosophie selon la *Lettre* 118 d'Augustin à Dioscore', *REAug* 44: 49–76.

—. 2001. 'Variations contemporaines sur un thème augustinien: l'énigme du temps', *RecSR* 89: 43–66.

—. 2004. *'Le Firmament de l'Écriture': L'Herméneutique augustinienne* (Paris).

—. 2006. 'Augustin disciple de Paul', *RechSR* 94: 357–80.

Boin, D. R. 2010. 'Late Antique Ostia and a campaign for pious tourism: epitaphs for Bishop Cyriacus and Monica, mother of Augustine', *JRS* 100: 195–209.

—. 2013. *Ostia in Late Antiquity* (New York).

Boissier, G. 1888. 'La Conversion de saint Augustine', *RDM* 85: 43–69.

Bonnardière, A.-M. la. 1986. 'Les deux vies. Marthe et Marie (Luc 10.38–42)', in A.-M. la Bonnardière, *Saint Augustin et la Bible* (Paris) 411–26.

Bonner, C. 1932. 'Witchcraft in the Lecture Room of Libanius', *TAPA* 63: 34–44.

Bonner, G. 1962. '*Libido* and *Concupiscentia* in St. Augustine', *StPatr* 6: 303–14.

—. 1963. *St. Augustine of Hippo: Life and Controversies* (London).

—. 1986a. 'Augustine's Conception of Deification', *JThS* 37: 369–86.

—. 1986b. *St. Augustine of Hippo: Life and Controversies*, rev. edn (Norwich).

—. 2004. Commentary on *Augustine of Hippo: The Monastic Rules*, trans. Sister Agatha Mary (Hyde Park, NY).

Booth, A. D. 1973. 'Punishment, Discipline and Riot in the Schools of Antiquity', *EMC* 17: 107–14.

—. 1979. 'Elementary and Secondary Education in the Roman Empire', *Florilegium* 1: 1–14.

Borromeo Carroll, M. 1940. *The Clausulae in the Confessions of St. Augustine* (Washington).

Botte, B. 1961. *Ambroise de Milan: Des Sacrements. Des Mystères. Explication du symbole* (Paris).

Bourke, V. J. 2001. 'Augustine on the Psalms', in F. Van Fleteren and J. C. Schnaubelt, eds., *Augustine: Biblical Exegete* (New York) 55–70.

Bouton-Touboulic, A.-I. 1999. 'De la mort de l'ami à la présence divine (*Confessions* IV, 4, 7–12, 19)', *VitaLat* 153: 58–69.

—. 2004. *L'Ordre caché: La Notion d'ordre chez saint Augustin* (Paris).

—. 2012. 'Dire le vrai selon saint Augustin: un impératif catégorique?', in A.-I. Bouton-Touboulic and F. Daspet, eds., *Dire le vrai* (Bordeaux) 93–112.

Bradbury, S. 2004. 'Libanius's Letters as Evidence for Travel and Epistolary Networks among Greek Elites in the Fourth Century', in L. Ellis and F. L. Kidner, eds., *Travel, Communication, and Geography in Late Antiquity: Sacred and Profane* (Aldershot) 73–80.

—. 2006. 'Reflections on Friendship in Libanius' Letters', in Á. González Gálvez and P.-L. Malosse, eds., *Mélanges A. F. Norman. Topoi*, Suppl. 7 (Paris) 243–61.

Brakke, D. 1995. 'The Problematization of Nocturnal Emissions in Early Christian Syria, Egypt, and Gaul', *JECS* 3: 419–60.

Braun, Thomas. 1998. 'The Jews in the Late Roman Empire', *SCI* 17: 142–71.

Bregman, J. 1982. *Synesius of Cyrene, Philosopher-Bishop* (Berkeley).

Brock, S. P. 1973. 'Early Syrian Asceticism', *Numen* 20: 1–19.

Broise, H., M. Dewailly and V. Jolivet. 1999–2000. 'Scoperta di un palazzo tardo-antico nella piazzale di Villa Medici', *RPARA* 72: 1–17.

Brown, P. R. L. 1969. 'The Diffusion of Manichaeism in the Roman Empire', *JRS* 59: 92–103.

—. 1981. *The Cult of the Saints: Its Rise and Function in Latin Christianity* (London).

—. 1988. *The Body and Society: Men, Women and Sexual Renunciation in Early Christianity* (London).

—. 1992. *Power and Persuasion in Late Antiquity: Towards a Christian Empire* (Madison).

—. 2000a. *Augustine of Hippo: A Biography. New Edition with an Epilogue* (London).

—. 2000b. 'Enjoying the Saints in Late Antiquity', *EME* 9: 1–24.

—. 2000c. 'The Study of Elites in Late Antiquity', *Arethusa* 33: 321–46.

—. 2002. *Poverty and Leadership in the Later Roman Empire* (Hanover, NH).

—. 2008. 'Alms and the Afterlife: A Manichaean View of an Early Christian Practice', in T. Corey Brennan and H. I. Flower, eds., *East and West: Papers in Ancient History Presented to Glen W. Bowersock* (Cambridge, Mass.) 145–58.

—. 2012. *Through the Eye of a Needle: Wealth, the Fall of Rome, and the Making of Christianity of the West, 350–550 AD* (Princeton).

Browning, R. 1952. 'The Riot of AD 387 in Antioch', *JRS* 42: 13–20.

Bruning, B. 1990–91. 'De l'Astrologie à la Grâce', in B. Bruning, J. van Houtem and M. Lamberigts, eds., *Collectanea Augustiniana: Mélanges T. J. van Bavel* II (Leuven) (= *Augustiniana* 41) 575–643.

Brunschwig, J. 1986. 'The Cradle Argument in Epicureanism and Stoicism', in M. Schofield and G. Striker, eds., *The Norms of Nature: Studies in Hellenistic Ethics* (Cambridge).

Brunt, P.A. 1974. 'Marcus Aurelius in his *Meditations*', *JRS* 64: 1–20.

Bucheit, V. 1968. 'Augustinus unter dem Feigenbaum (zu *Conf.* VIII)', *VigChr* 22: 257–71.

Burnaby, J. 1938. *Amor Dei: A Study in the Religion of Saint Augustine* (London).

Burns, J. P. 1980. *The Development of Augustine's Doctrine of Operative Grace* (Paris).

—. 1993. 'Augustine's Distinctive Use of the Psalms in the Confessions: The Role of Music and Recitation', *AS* 24: 133–46.

—. 2002. 'From Persuasion to Predestination: Augustine on Freedom in Rational

Creatures', in Paul M. Blowers et al., eds., *In Domenico Eloquio: In Lordly Eloquence. Essays on Patristic Exegesis in Honor of Robert Louis Wilken* (Grand Rapids) 294–316.

Burns, J. P., and R. M. Jensen, eds. 2014. *Christianity in Roman Africa: The Development of Its Practices and Beliefs* (Grand Rapids).

Burnyeat, M. F. 1967. 'Wittgenstein and Augustine *De magistro*', *ArSoc* 61: 1–24.

—. 1997. 'Postscript on Silent Reading', *CQ* 47: 74–6.

Burrus, V., M. D. Jordan and K. MacKendrick. 2010. *Seducing Augustine: Bodies, Desires, Confessions* (New York).

Burton, P. 2007. *Language in the* Confessions *of Augustine* (Oxford).

—. 2008. 'Revisiting the Christian Latin *Sondersprache* Hypothesis', in H. A. G. Houghton and D. C. Parker, eds., *Textual Variation: Theological and Social Tendencies* (Piscataway) 149–71.

Burton-Christie, D. 1993. *The Word in the Desert: Scripture and the Quest for Holiness in Early Christian Monasticism* (Oxford).

Byers, S. 2013. *Perception, Sensibility, and Moral Motivation in Augustine: A Stoic-Platonic Synthesis* (Cambridge).

Cabouret, B. 2002. 'Le gouverneur au temps de Libanios: image et réalité', *Pallas* 60: 191–204.

Cain, A. 2005. 'In Ambrosiaster's Shadow: A Critical Re-Evaluation of the Last Surviving Letter Exchange between Pope Damasus and Jerome', *REAug* 51: 257–77.

—. 2009. *The Letters of Jerome: Asceticism, Biblical Exegesis, and the Construction of Christian Authority in Late Antiquity* (Oxford).

—. 2013a. *Jerome and the Monastic Clergy: A Commentary on Letter 52 to Nepotian, with an Introduction, Text, and Translation* (Leiden).

—. 2013b. 'Two Allusions to Terence, *Eunuchus* 579 in Jerome', *CQ* 63: 407–12.

Cameron, A. 2011. *The Last Pagans of Rome* (Oxford).

— and S. Long. 1993. *Barbarians and Politics at the Court of Arcadius* (Los Angeles).

Cameron, Averil. 2013. 'Can Christians Do Dialogue?', *StPatr* 63: 103–20.

Cameron, M. 2009. 'Valerius of Hippo: A Profile', *AS* 40: 5–26.

—. 2012. *Christ Meets Me Everywhere: Augustine's Early Figurative Exegesis* (New York).

Caputo, J., and M. J. Scanlon, eds. 2005. *Augustine and Postmodernism: Confessions and Circumfession* (Bloomington).

Cary, P. 1998. 'What Licentius Learned: A Narrative Reading of the Cassiciacum Dialogues', AS 29: 141–63.

Casella, M. 2007. 'Les spectacles à Antioch d'après Libanios', *AntTard* 15: 99–112.

Catapano, G. 2000. *L'idea di filosofia in Agostino: guida bibliografica* (Padua).

—. 2001. *Il concetto di filosofia nei primi scritti di Agostino: Analisi dei passi metafilosofici dal* Contra Academicos *al* De uera religione (Rome).

—. 2005. *Agostino: Contro gli Accademici* (Milan).

—, trans. and ed. 2012. *Agostino: Sermoni di Erfurt* (Venice).

Cavadini, J. C. 1999. 'Ambrose and Augustine *De Bono Mortis*', in W. E. Klingshirn and M. Vessey, *The Limits of Ancient Christianity: Essays on Late Antique Thought and Culture in Honor of R. A. Markus* (Ann Arbor) 232–49.

—. 2010. 'Eucharistic Exegesis in Augustine's *Confessions*', *AS* 41: 87–108.

Cayré, F. 1956. 'Le livre XIII des "Confessions"', *REAug* 2: 143–61.

Ceresola, G. 2001. *Fantasia e illusione dai Soliloquia al De Mendacio*, (Genova).

Chadwick, H. 1976. *Priscillian* (Oxford).

—. 1983. 'New Letters of St. Augustine', *JThS* 34: 425–52.

—. 1990. 'The Attractions of Mani', in E. Romero-Pose, ed., *Plērōma. Salus Carnis. Homenaje a Antonio Orbe* (Santiago de Compostela) 203–22.

—. 1993. 'Donatism and the *Confessions* of Augustine', in G. W. Most, H. Petersmann and A. M. Ritter, eds., *Philanthropia kai Eusebeia. Festschrift für Albrecht Dihle zum 70. Geburtstag* (Göttingen) 24–35.

—. 1996. 'New Sermons of St Augustine', *JThS* 41: 69–91.

—. 2003. 'Self-justification in Augustine's *Confessions*', *EHR* 118: 1161–75.

—. 2009. *Augustine of Hippo: A Life.* (Oxford).

Charru, P. 2009. 'Temps et musique dans la pensée d'Augustin', *REAug* 55: 171–88.

Charry, E. T. 2012. 'Loving Near – Loving Far: Augustine's Psychology of Monovision', *ASd* 43: 89–107.

Chase, M. 2005. 'Porphyre et Augustin: Des trois sortes de "visions" au corps de résurrection', *REAug* 51: 233–56.

Chastagnol, A., and N. Duval. 1974. 'Les survivances du culte impérial dans l'Afrique du nord à l'époque vandale', in *Mélanges d'histoire anciennes offerts à W. Seston* (Paris) 87–118.

Christern, J. 1976. *Das frühchristliche Pilgerheiligtum von Tebessa* (Wiesbaden).

Cipriani, N. 1994. 'Le fonti cristiane della dottrina trinitaria nei primi Dialoghi di S. Agostino', *Aug.* 34: 253–313.

—. 1997a. 'Il rifiuto del pessimismo Porfiriano nei primi scritti di S. Agostino', *Aug* 37: 113–146.

—. 1997b. 'La dottrina del peccato originale negli scritti di S. Agostino fino all'*Ad Simplicianum*', in L. Alici, R. Piccolomini and A. Pieretti, eds., *Il mistero del male et la libertà possible (IV): Ripensare Agostino. Atti dell'VIII Seminario del Centro di Studi Agostiniani di Perugia* (Rome) 23–48.

—. 1997c. 'Le opere di Sant'Ambrogio negli scritti di Sant'Agostino anteriori all'episcopato', *La Scuola Cattolica* 125: 763–800.

—. 1998. 'Lo schema dei *tria vitia* (*voluptas*, *superbia*, *curiositas*) nel *De vera religione*: Antropologia soggiacente e fonti', *Aug* 38: 157–95.

—. 2002. '*L'altro Agostino* di G. Lettieri', *REAug* 48: 249–65.

—. 2003. 'Il Modello antropologico nel Libro I delle *Confessioni*', in *Le Confessioni di Agostino 402–2002: Bilancio e Prospettive* (Rome) 421–35.

Clark, G. 1994. 'The Fathers of Children', in D. Wood, ed., *The Church and Childhood* (Oxford).

—. 1995. *Women in Late Antiquity: Pagan and Christian Lifestyles* (Oxford).
—. 2004. 'City of God(s): Augustine's Virgil', *PVS* 25: 83–92.
—. 2008. 'Can We Talk? Augustine and the Possibility of Dialogue', in Simon Goldhill, ed., *The End of Dialogue in Antiquity* (Cambridge) 117–34.
—. 2011. *Body and Gender, Soul and Reason in Late Antiquity* (Farnham).
Colditz, I. 2009. 'Manichaean Time-Management: Laymen between Religious and Secular Duties', in J. D. BeDuhn, ed., *New Light on Manichaeism: Papers from the Sixth International Congress on Manichaeism* (Leiden) 73–99.
Conybeare, C. 2000. *Paulinus Noster: Self and Symbols in the Letters of Paulinus of Nola* (Oxford).
—. 2006. *The Irrational Augustine* (Oxford).
Couenhoven, J. 2005. 'St. Augustine's Doctrine of Original Sin', *AS* 36: 327–58.
Courcelle, P. 1943. *Les Lettres grecques en Occident: De Macrobe à Cassiodore* (Paris).
—. 1943–4. 'Les premières confessions de saint Augustin', *REL* 21–22: 155–74.
—. 1944. 'Quelques symboles funéraires du néo-platonisme latin', *REA* 46: 65–93.
—. 1951. 'Les lacunes de la correspondance entre saint Augustin et Paulin de Nole', *REAug* 53: 253–300.
—. 1957. 'Les exégèses chrétiennes de la quatrième Églogue', *REA* 59: 294–319.
—. 1968. *Recherches sur les* Confessions *de saint Augustin*, rev. edn (Paris).
—. 1969. *Late Latin Writers and their Greek Sources* (Harvard).
—. 1971. 'Le jeune Augustin, second Catilina', *REA* 73: 141–50.
—. 1972. 'Verissima philosophia', in *Epektasis: Mélanges patristiques offerts au Cardinal Daniélou* (Paris) 653–9.
Coyle, J. K. 1978. *Augustine's 'De Moribus Ecclesiae Catholicae'* (Fribourg).
—. 2001. 'What did Augustine know about Manichaeism when he wrote his two treatises *De Moribus*?', in van Oort, Wermelinger and Wurst (2001) 43–56 (reprinted in Coyle (2009) 307–28).
—. 2003. 'Saint Augustine's Manichaean Legacy', *AS* 34: 1–22 (reprinted in Coyle (2009) 307–28).
—. 2009a. *Manichaeism and Its Legacy* (Leiden).
—. 2009b. 'Characteristics of Manichaeism in Roman North Africa', in J. BeDuhn, ed., *New Light on Manichaeism: Papers from the Sixth International Congress on Manichaeism* (Leiden) 101–14.
—. 2011. 'Prolegomena to a Study of Women in Manichaeism', in P. Mirecki and J. BeDuhn, eds., *The Light and the Darkness: Studies in Manichaeism and Its World* (Leiden) 79–92.
Cragg, G. R., ed. 1968. *The Cambridge Platonists* (Oxford).
Cribiore, R. 2007a. *The School of Libanius in Late Antique Antioch* (Princeton).
—. 2007b. 'Spaces for Teaching in Late Antiquity', in T. Derda et al., *Alexandria's Auditoria of Kom el-Dikka and Late Antique Education* (Warsaw) 143–50.
—. 2013. *Libanius the Sophist: Rhetoric, Reality and Religion in the Fourth Century* (Cornell).
Criscuolo, U. 2011. 'Considérations sur le dernier Libanios', in O. Lagacherie and P.-L. Malosse, *Libanios, le premier humaniste* (Alessandria) 177–91.

Cross, F. L. 1961. 'History and Fiction in the African Canons', *JThS* 12: 227–47.

Crouse, R. 1981. '*In multa defluximus*: *Confessions* X, 29–43, and St. Augustine's Theory of Personality', in H. J. Blumenthal and R. A. Markus, eds., *Neoplatonism and Early Christian Thought: Essays in Honour of A. H. Armstrong* (London) 180–85.

Cumont, F. 1908. *Recherches sur la Manichéisme*, I. *La cosmogonie manichéenne: d'après Théodore bar Khôni* (Brussels).

Curran, J. R. 1997. 'Jerome and the Sham Christians of Rome', *JEH* 48: 213–29.

—. 2000. *Pagan City and Christian Capital: Rome in the Fourth Century* (Oxford).

Cutino, M. 1998. 'Filosofia tripartite e trinità cristiana nei *Dialogi* de Agostino', *REAug* 44: 77–100.

—. 2000. *Licentii* Carmen ad Augustinum. *Introduzione, testo, traduzione e commento* (Catania).

Daniélou, J. 1958. *Bible et liturgie: La théologie biblique des Sacrements et des fêtes d'après les Pères de l'église*, 2nd edn (Paris).

Dassmann, E. 1975. 'Ambrosius und die Märtyrer', *JbAC* 18: 49–68.

Day, J. 1992. *Psalms* (Sheffield).

De Bruyn, T. 1999. 'Flogging a Son: The Emergence of the *Pater Flagellans* in Latin Christian Discourse', *JECS* 7: 249–90.

De Bruyne, D. 1931. 'La chronologie de quelques sermons de saint Augustin', *RB* 43: 185–93.

De Hoz, M. P. 2006. 'Literacy in Rural Anatolia: the Testimony of the "Confessions Inscriptions"', *ZPE* 155: 139–44.

De Labriolle, P. 1926. 'Pourquoi saint Augustin a-t-il rédigé des *Confessions*?' *Bulletin de l'Association Guillaume Budé* 12: 30–47.

De Sainte Croix, G. E. M. 1954. '*Suffragium*: From Vote to Patronage', *British Journal of Sociology* 5: 33–48.

—. 1975. 'Early Christian Attitudes to Property and Slavery', *StChH* 12: 1–38.

Deakin, M. A. B. 2007. *Hypatia of Alexandria: Mathematician and Martyr* (Amherst).

Dearn, A. 2001. 'The *Passio S. Typasii Veterani* as a Catholic Construction of the Past', *VigChr* 55: 86–93.

—. 2004. 'The Abitinian Martyrs and the Outbreak of the Donatist Schism', *JEH* 55: 1–18.

Decret, F. 1970. *Aspects du manichéisme dans l'Afrique romaine: Les Controverses de Fortunatus, Faustus et Felix avec saint Augustin* (Paris).

—. 1989a. 'Aspects de l'Eglise manichéenne: Remarques sur le manuscrit de Tébessa', in A. Zumkeller, ed., *Signum Pietatis: Festgabe für Cornelius Petrus Mayer, OSA* (Würzburg) 123–51.

—. 1989b. 'L'utilisation des Épîtres de Paul chez les Manichéens d'Afrique', in *Le Epistole Paoline nei Manichei i Donatisti e il primo Agostino* (Rome) 29–83.

—. 1995. *Essais sur l'église manichéenne en Afrique du nord et à Rome au temps de saint Augustin: Recueil d'études* (Rome).

Demura, K. 2013. 'The Concept of Heart in Augustine of Hippo: Its Emergence and Development', *StPatr* 70: 3–16.

Desch, W. 1980. 'Aufbau und Gliederung von Augustins Schrift *De uera religione*', *VigChr* 34: 263–77.

Dickie, M. W. 2002. 'Synesius, "De insomniis" 2–3 Terzaghi and Plotinus, "Enneads" 2.3.7 and 4.4.40–44', *SO* 77: 165–74.

Diefenbach, S. 2007. *Römische Erinnerungsräume: Heiligenmemoria und kollektive Identitäten im Rom des 3. bis 5. Jahrhunderts n. Chr.* (Berlin).

Dihle, A. 1982. *The Theory of Will in Classical Antiquity* (Berkeley).

Dillon, J. M. 1996. 'An Ethic for the Late Antique Sage', in L. P. Gerson, ed., *The Cambridge Companion to Plotinus* (Cambridge) 315–35.

—. 1999. 'Plotinus on whether the stars are causes', *Res Orientales* 12: 87–92.

—. 2004. 'Philosophy as a Profession in Late Antiquity', in S. Swain and M. Edwards, eds., *Approaching Late Antiquity: The Transformation from Early to Late Empire* (Oxford) 401–18.

Dionisiotti, A. C. 1982. 'From Ausonius' Schooldays? A Schoolbook and Its Relatives', *JRS* 72: 83–125.

Dobell, B. 2009. *Augustine's Intellectual Conversion: The Journey from Platonism to Christianity* (Cambridge).

Dodds, E. R. 1960. 'Tradition and personal achievement in the philosophy of Plotinus', *JRS* 50: 1–7.

Dodge, B., ed. and trans. 1970. *The Fihrist of al-Nadīm: A Tenth-Century Survey of Muslim Culture*, 2 vols. (New York).

Dodgeon, M. H., and S. N. C. Lieu. 1991. *The Roman Eastern Frontier and the Persian Wars (AD 226–363): A Documentary History* (London).

Doignon, J. 1997. *Oeuvres de saint Augustin: Dialogues Philosophiques. De l'Ordre*, Bibliothèque Augustinienne 4/2 (Paris).

Dolbeau, F. 1994. 'Un sermon inédit de saint Augustin sur la santé corporelle, partiellement cité chez Barthélemy d'Urbino', *REAug* 40: 279–303.

—. 1996a. 'Un poème philosophique de l'Antiquité tardive: *De pulchritudine mundi*. Remarques sur le *Liber XXI sententiarum* (*CPL* 373)', *REAug* 42: 21–43.

—, ed. 1996b. *Vingt-six sermons au peuple d'Afrique (Augustin d'Hippone), retrouvés à Mayence, édités et commentés* (Paris).

—. 1997. 'Le "Liber XXI sententiarum (CPL 373). Edition d'un texte de travail"', *RechAug* 30: 113–65.

—. 2001. *Les Sermons augustiniens de Mayence: Bilan des travaux et mise à jour bibliographique (1996–2000)* (Paris).

—. 2002. 'Appendice', in *Sant'Agostino. Discorsi nuovi. XXXV/2 Supplemento II*. Testo, note e appendice di F. Dolbeau; traduzione di V. Tarulli, indici di F. Dolbeau, F. Monteverde (Rome).

—. 2003. 'Le Combat pastoral d'Augustin contre les astrologues, les devins et les guérisseurs', in P.-Y. Fux, J.-M. Roessli and O. Wermelinger, eds., *Augustinus Afer – Saint Augustin: Africanité et universalité. Actes du colloque international Alger–Annaba, 1–7 avril 2001*, 2 vols. (Fribourg) 167–82.

—. 2003. 'Un nouveau témoin du *Sermon* 20B d'Augustin sur la santé corporelle', *REAug* 49: 285–96.

—. 2004. 'Un témoignage inconnu contre des Manichéens d'Afrique', *ZPE* 150: 225–32.

—. 2005. *Augustin et la prédication en Afrique: Recherches sur divers sermons authentiques, apocryphes ou anonymes.*

—. 2009. *Augustin d'Hippone: Vingt-six sermons au peuple d'Afrique*, 2nd edn (Paris).

Dombrowski, D. 1980. 'Starnes on Augustine's Theory of Infancy', *AS* 11: 125–33.

Dossey, L. 2008. 'Wife Beating and Manliness in Late Antiquity', *P&P* 199: 3–40.

—. 2010. *Peasant and Empire in Christian North Africa* (Berkeley).

Downey, G. 1945 'The Pagan Virtue of Megalopsychia', *TAPA* 76: 279–86

Drake, H. A. 1996. 'Lambs into Lions: Explaining Early Christian Intolerance', *P&P* 153: 3–36.

Drecoll, V. H. 1999. *Die Entstehung der Gnadenlehre Augustins* (Tübingen).

—. 2001. '*Etiam posteris aliquid profuturum*: Zur Selbststilisierung bei Augustin und der Beeinflussung der eigenen Wirkungsgeschichte durch Bücher Bibliothek', *REAug* 47: 313–35.

— and M. Kudella. 2011. *Augustin und der Manichäismus* (Tübingen).

Dubois, J.-D. 2011. *Jésus Apocryphe* (Paris).

Duchrow, U. 1965. 'Der Aufbau von Augustins Schriften *Confessiones* und *De trinitate*', *ZThK* 62: 338–67.

Dulaey, M. 1973. *Le Rêve dans la vie et la pensée de saint Augustin* (Paris).

—. 2000. 'À quelle date Augustin a-t-il pris ses distances vis-à-vis du millénarisme?', *REAug* 46: 31–60.

—. 2002. 'L'apprentissage de l'exégèse biblique par Augustin. Première partie: Dans les années 386–389', *REAug* 48: 267–95.

—. 2003a. 'L'apprentissage de l'exégèse biblique par Augustin. Deuxième partie: Dans les années 390–392', *REAug* 49: 43–84.

—. 2003b. '*Scatentes lacrimis confessionum libros*: les larmes dans les *Confessions*', in *Le Confessioni di Agostino 402–2002: Bilancio e Prospettive* (Rome) 215–32.

—. 2005. 'L'apprentissage de l'exégèse biblique par Augustin. Troisième partie: Dans les années 393–394', *REAug* 51: 21–65.

—. 2007. 'Recherches sur les *LXXXIII Diverses Questions* d'Augustin (2) Questions 61, 64 et 65', *REAug* 53: 35–64.

Dunbabin, K. M. D. 1978. *The Mosaics of Roman North Africa: Studies in Iconography and Patronage* (Oxford).

Duncan-Jones, R. 2004. 'Economic Change and the Transition to Late Antiquity', in S. Swain and M. Edwards, eds., *Approaching Late Antiquity: The Transformation from Early to Late Empire* (Oxford) 20–52.

Dunn, G. D. 2008. 'Anicius Hermogenianus Olybrius', in C. Deroux, ed., *Studies in Latin Literature and Roman History* XIV (Brussels) 431–7.

—. 2009. 'The Christian Network of the Aniciae: The Example of the Letter of Innocent I to Anicia Juliana', *REAug* 55: 53–72.

Dupont, A. 2014. '*Fides* in Augustine's *Sermones ad Populum*: A Unique Representation and Thematisation of *Gratia*', *REA* 116: 105–32.

Duval, Y.-M. 1980. 'Pélage est-il le censeur inconnu de l'*Adversus Iovinianum* à Rome en 393? ...', *RHE* 75: 525–57.

—. 2004. 'L'entrée en relations épistolaires d'Augustin d'Hippone et de Paulin de Nole', in L. Nadjo and É. Gavoille, *Epistulae antiquae, I: Actes du 1er colloque 'Le genre epistolaire antique et ses prolongements'* (Louvain) 397–419.

—. 2005. *La* décretale *Ad Gallos Episcopos: son texte et son auteur*, Suppl. *VigChr* 73 (Leiden).

—. 2009. 'Sur trois lettres méconnues de Jérôme concernant son séjour à Rome', in A. Cain and J. Lössl, eds., *Jerome of Stridon: His Life, Writings and Legacy* (Farnham) 29–40.

Dysinger, K. 2005. *Psalmody and Prayer in the Writings of Evagrius Ponticus* (Oxford).

Dzielska, M. 1988. *Hypatia of Alexandria* (Cambridge, Mass.).

Eck, W. 1983. 'Der Episkopat im spätantiken Afrika: organisatorische Entwicklung, soziale Herkunft und öffentliche Funktionen', *HZ* 236: 265–95.

Edwards, M. J. 1988. 'Scenes from the later wanderings of Odysseus', *CQ* 38: 509–21.

—. 1992. 'The *Clementina*: A Christian Response to the Pagan Novel', *CQ* 42: 459–74.

—, trans. 2000. *Neoplatonic Saints: The Lives of Plotinus and Proclus by Their Students* (Liverpool).

—. 2013. *Image, Word and God in the Early Christian Centuries* (Ashgate).

Ennabli, L. 1997. *Carthage: une métropole chrétienne du IV siècle* (Paris).

Ettenhuber, E. 2011. *Donne's Augustine: Renaissance Cultures of Interpretation* (Oxford).

Evans, G. 1990. *Augustine on Evil* (Cambridge).

Evans Grubbs, J. 1995. *Law and Family in Late Antiquity* (Oxford).

—. 2007. 'Marrying and Its Documentation in Later Roman Law', in P. L. Reynolds and J. Witte, Jr, eds., *To Have and to Hold: Marrying and Its Documentation in Western Christendom, 400–1600* (Cambridge) 43–94.

Evers, A. 2010. *Church, Cities and People: A Study of the Plebs in the Church and Cities of Roman Africa in Late Antiquity* (Leuven).

—. 2011. 'A Fine Line? Catholics and Donatists in Roman North Africa', in O. Hekster and T. Kaizer, eds., *Frontiers in the Roman World: Proceedings of the Ninth Workshop of the International Network 'Impact of Empire', Durham, 16–19 April 2009* (Leiden) 175–98.

Fabre, P. 1949. *Saint Paulin de Nole et l'amitié chrétienne* (Paris).

Fattal, M. 2007. *Plotin face à Platon, suivi de Plotin chez Augustin et Farâbî* (Paris).

Feiertag, J. C., and W. Steinmann. 1974. *Questions d'un païen à un chrétien (Consultationes Zacchei christiani et Apollonii philosophi)*, Sources chrétiennes no. 401 (Paris).

Feldmann, E. 1975. *Der Einfluss des Hortensius und des Manichäismus auf Denken des jungen Augustinus von 373*, diss. theol. [masch], Münster.

—. 1987. *Die 'Epistula Fundamenti' der nordafrikanischen Manichäer: Versuch einer Rekonstruktion* (Altenberge).

—. 1994. 'Confessiones', in *Augustinus-Lexikon* 1: Fasc. 7/8 (Basel) 1134–94.

—. 1995. 'Der Übertritt Augustins zu den Manichäern', in A. van Tongerloo and J. van Oort, eds., *The Manichaean NOUS* (Louvain) 103–28.

—. 1997. 'Der junge Augustinus und Paulus. Ein Beitrag zur (manichäischen) Paulus-Rezeption', in L. Cirillo and A. van Tongerloo, eds., *Atti del terzo congress internazionale di studi 'Manichaismo e Oriente cristiano antico'* (Louvain) 41–76.

—, A. Schindler and O. Wermelinger. 1986. 'Alypius', in C. Mayer, ed., *Augustinus-Lexikon* 1: Fasc. 1/2 (Basel) 245–67.

Ferrari, L. C. 1970. 'The Pear-Theft in Augustine's *Confessions*', *REAug* 16: 233–42.

—. 1974. 'The Boyhood Beatings of Augustine', *AS* 5: 1–14.

—. 1975. 'Augustine's "Nine Years" as a Manichee', *Augustiniana* 25: 210–16.

—. 1977. 'The Theme of the Prodigal Son in Augustine's *Confessions*', *RechAug* 12: 105–18.

—. 1980. 'Paul at the Conversion of Augustine (*Conf.* VIII, 29–30)', *AS* 11: 5–20.

—. 1982. 'Saint Augustine on the Road to Damascus', *AS* 13: 151–70.

—. 1984. *The Conversions of Saint Augustine* (Villanova).

—. 1989. 'Saint Augustine's Conversion Scene: The End of a Modern Debate?', *StPatr* 22: 235–50.

Festugière, A. J. 1944–54. *La Révélation d'Hermès Trismégiste*, 4 vols. (Paris).

—. 1959. *Antioche païenne et chrétienne: Libanius, Chrysostome et les moines de Syrie* (Paris).

Février, P. A. 1977. 'À propos du culte funéraire: Culte et sociabilité', *CAr* 26: 29–45.

Fiedrowicz, M. 1997. *Psalmus vox totius Christi: Studien zu Augustins 'Enarrationes in Psalmos'* (Freiburg).

Finn, R. D. 2009. *Asceticism in the Graeco-Roman World* (Cambridge).

Fischer-Bossert, W. 2001. 'Der Porträttypus des sog. Plotin: Zur Deutung von Bärten in der römischen Porträtkunst', *AA*: 137–52.

Fitzgerald, A. D. 2002. 'Ambrose at the Well: *De Isaac et Anima*', *REAug* 48: 79–99.

—. 2009. 'When Augustine was Priest', *AS* 40: 37–48.

Folliet, G. 1961. 'Aux origines de l'ascétisme et du cénobitisme africain', *Studia Anselmiana* 46: 25–44.

—. 1962. '"Deificari in otio", Augustin, *Epistula* X, 2', *RechAug* 2: 225–36.

—. 1987. 'La correspondance entre Augustin et Nébridius', in *L'Opera Letteraria di Agostino tra Cassiciacum e Milano: Agostino nelle terre di Ambrogio* (Palermo) 191–215.

—. 1992–3. '*In penetralibus mentis adorare Deum* (Augustin, *Epistula* 10, 3)', *Sacris Erudiri* 33: 125–33.

—. 1993. 'La correspondance d'Augustin à Thagaste (388–391)', in '*De Magistro*' *di Agostino d'Ippona*, Lectio Augustini, Settimana Agostiniana Pavese (Palermo–Rome) 73–107.

—. 2003. 'Le Livre de Job et les *Confessions*', in *Le Confessioni di Agostino (402–2002): Bilancio e prospettive. SEAug* 85 (Rome): 265–88.

—. 2008. 'Les trois sens possibles des mots *confessio/confiteri* dans les *Adnotationes in Job* d'Augustin', *REAug* 54: 31–42.

Fontaine, J. 1976 'Prose et poésie L'interférence des genres et des styles dans la création litteraire d'Ambroise de Milan', in G. Lazzai, ed, Ambrosius Episcopus. Atti del Congresso internazionale . . . Milano 2–7 Decembre 1974 (Milano) 124–70.

Fontanier, J.-M. 1989. 'Sur le traité d'Augustin *De pulchro et apto*: convenance, beauté et adaptation', *RSPhTh* 73: 413–21.

Fredouille, J.-C. 1987. 'Conversion personnelle et discours apologétique, de saint Paul à saint Augustin', *Augustinus* 32: 121–31.

—. 1993a. 'Deux mauvais souvenirs d'Augustin', in *Philanthropia kai Eusebeia: Festschrift für A. Dihle* (Göttingen) 74–9.

—. 1993b. 'Les *Confessions* d'Augustin: autobiographie au présent', in M.-F. Baslez, P. Hoffmann and L. Pernot, eds., *L'Invention de l'autobiographie d'Hésiode à saint Augustin* (Paris) 167–78.

Fredriksen, P. 1978. 'Augustine and His Analysts: The Possibility of a Psychohistory', *Soundings* 51: 206–27.

—, trans. 1982. *Augustine on Romans: Propositions from the Epistle to the Romans, Unfinished Commentary on the Epistle to the Romans* (Chico).

—. 1986. 'Paul and Augustine: Conversion Narratives, Orthodox Traditions and the Retrospective Self', *JThS* 37: 3–34.

—. 2008. *Augustine and the Jews: A Christian Defense of Jews and Judaism* (New Haven).

Frend, W. H. C. 1942. 'A Note on the Berber Background in the Life of Augustine', *JThS* 43: 188–91.

—. 1988. *Archaeology and History in Early Christianity* (London).

—. 1989. 'Pythagoreanism and Hermetism in Augustine's "Hidden Years"', *StPatr* 22: 251–60.

Froula, C. 1984. *To Write Paradise: Style and Error in Pound's Cantos* (New Haven).

Fry, C. 2010. *Lettres croisées de Jérôme et Augustin* (Paris).

Fuhrer, T. 1997. *Augustin 'Contra Academicos' Bücher 2 und 3: Einleitung und Kommentar* (Berlin).

—. 2008a. 'Augustin in Mailand', in Fuhrer (2008b) 63–79.

—, ed. 2008b. *Die christlich-philosophischen Diskurse der Spätantike: Texte, Personen, Institutionen. Akten der Tagung vom 22.–25. Februar 2006 am Zentrum für Antike und Moderne der Albert-Ludwigs-Universität Freiburg* (Stuttgart).

—. 2013. 'The "Milan Narrative" in Augustine's *Confessions*: Intellectual and Material Spaces in Late Antique Milan', *StPatr* 70: 17–36.

Funk, W.-P. 2009. 'Mani's Account of Other Religions According to the Coptic *Synaxeis* Codex', in J. BeDuhn, ed., *New Light on Manichaeism. Papers from the Sixth International Congress on Manichaeism* (Leiden) 115–26.

Fürst, A. 1994. '*Veritas Latina*: Augustins Haltung gegenüber Hieronymus' Bibelübersetzungen', *REAug* 40: 105–26.

—. 1999. *Augustins Briefwechsel mit Hieronymus* (Münster).

—. 2003. *Hieronymus: Askese und Wissenschaft in der Spätantike* (Freiburg).

Gaans, G. M. van 2013. 'The Manichaean Bishop Faustus: The State of Research after a Century of Scholarship', in J. van Oort, ed., *Augustine and Manichaean Christianity* (Leiden) 199–227.

Gabillon, A. 1978. 'Romanianus, *alias* Cornelius: du nouveau sur le bienfaiteur et l'ami de saint Augustin', *REAug* 24: 58–70.

—. 1998. 'Redatation de la lettre 109 de Severus de Milev', in G. Madec, ed., *Augustin Prédicateur* (Paris) 431–7.

Gardner, I. 1993. 'The Eschatology of Manichaeism as a Coherent Doctrine', *JRH* 17: 257–73.

—. 1995. *The Kephalaia of the Teacher* (Leiden).

—. 1996–7. *Kellis Literary Texts* 1–2 (Oxford).

—. 2011. '"With a Pure Heart and a Truthful Tongue": The Recovery of the Text of the Manichaean Daily Prayers', *Journal of Late Antiquity* 4: 79–99.

—. 2013. 'Mani, Augustine and the Vision of God', in J. van Oort, ed., *Augustine and Manichaean Christianity* (Leiden) 73–86.

— and S. N. C. Lieu. 2004. *Manichaean Texts from the Roman Empire* (Cambridge).

—, A. Alcock and W.-P. Funk, eds. 1999. *Coptic Documentary Texts from Kellis*, Vol. 1 (Oxford) (= P. Kell. Copt.).

—, J. BeDuhn and P. Dilley, eds. 2015. *Mani at the Court of the Persian Kings* (Leiden).

Garnsey, P. 1996. *Ideas of Slavery from Aristotle to Augustine* (Cambridge)

—. 2004. 'Lactantius and Augustine', in A. K. Bowman and F. Millar, eds., *Representations of Empire: Rome and the Mediterranean World* (Oxford) 153–79.

Garzya, A., ed., and D. Roques, trans. 2000. *Epistles*, in *Synésios de Cyrène: Correspondance* (Paris).

Gavrilov, A. K. 'Techniques of Reading in Classical Antiquity', *CQ* 47 (1997) 56–73.

Geerling, W. 1987. 'Bekehrung durch Belehrung: Zur 1600 Jahrfeier der Bekehrung Augustins', *ThQ* 167: 195–208.

Geest, P. van. 2011. *The Incomprehensibility of God: Augustine as a Negative Theologian* (Louvain).

Gerson, L. P. ed.. 1996. *The Cambridge Companion to Plotinus* (Cambridge).

—. 1999. *Plotinus* (London).

Gerven, J. van. 1957. 'Liberté humaine et prescience divine', *RPL* 55: 317–30.

Gerzaguet, C. 2013a. 'Le *De Fuga Saeculi* d'Ambroise de Milan et sa datation: notes de philologie et histoire', *StPatr* 69: 75–84.

—. 2013b. 'Ambroise, Cassiodore et la série dite *de patriarchis*', *REAug* 59: 275–98.

Getty, M. M. 1931. *The Life of the North Africans as Revealed in the Sermons of St Augustine* (Washington).

Gibson, C. A. 1999. 'The Agenda of Libanius' *Hypotheses* to Demosthenes', *GRBS* 40: 171–202.

Gigon, O. 1985. 'Augustin "De utilitate credendi"', in C. Schäublin, ed., *Catalepton: Festschrift B. Wyss* (Basel) 138–57.

Goehring, J. E. 1986. *The Letter of Ammon and Pachomian Monasticism* (Berlin).

Goldhill, S. 2006. 'Rethinking Religious Revolutions', in Simon Goldhill and Robin Osborne, eds., *Rethinking Revolutions Through Ancient Greece* (Cambridge) 141–63.

Graf, F. 2012. 'Fights about Festivals: Libanius and John Chrysostom on the *Kalendae Ianuariae* in Antioch', *Archiv für Religionsgeschichte* 12: 167–86.

Griffin, M. 1997. 'The Composition of the *Academica*: Motives and Versions', in B. Inwood and J. Mansfield, eds., *Ascent and Argument: Studies in Cicero's Academic Books* (Leiden) 1–35.

Grilli, A., ed. 1962. *M. Tulli Ciceronis* Hortensius (Milan).

Grossi, V. 1998. "Sant'Ambrogio e sant'Agostino: Per una rilettura dei loro rapporti', in Pizzolato and Rizzi (1998) 405–62.

Gruber, H. W. 2010. 'Enduring Stereotypes: Rhetorical Education on the "Problem" of Marriage', *Journal of Late Antiquity* 3: 286–99.

Guignebert, C. 1923. 'Les demi-chrétiens et leur place dans l'Église antique', *RHR* 88: 65–102.

Gulàcsi, Z. 2009. 'A Manichaean "Portrait of the Buddha Jesus": Identifying a Twelfth- or Thirteenth-Century Chinese Painting from the Collection of Seiun-Ji Zen Temple', *Artibus Asiae* 69: 1–38.

—. 2011. 'The Central Asian Roots of a Chinese Manichaean Silk Painting in the Collection of the Yamato Bunkakan, Nara, Japan', in J. A. van den Berg et al., eds., *'In Search of Truth': Augustine, Manichaeism and Other Gnosticism. Studies for Johannes van Oort at Sixty* (Leiden) 315–38.

Gury, F. 1996. 'Le métier d'astrologue', in *L'Africa Romana: Atti del XI convegno di studio*, I (Ozieri) 231–59.

Hadot, I. 2005. *Arts libéraux et philosophie dans la pensée antique: Contribution à l'histoire de l'éducation et de la culture dans l'Antiquité*, 2nd edn (Paris).

Hadot, P. 1967. '"Numerus intelligibilis infinite crescit", Augustin, *Epistula* 3, 2', in *Miscellanea André Combes* I (Rome) 181–91.

—. 1971. *Marius Victorinus: Recherches sur sa vie et ses oeuvres* (Paris).

—. 1979a. 'La présentation du Platonisme par Augustin', in *Kerygma und Logos: Beiträge zu den geistesgeschichtlichen Beziehungen zwischen Antike und Christentum. Festschrist für C. Andresen* (Göttingen) 273–9.

—. 1979b. 'Les divisions des parties de la philosophie dans l'Antiquité', *MH* 36: 201–23.

—. 1979c. 'Porphyre', *Encyclopedia Universalis* 13: 356–8.

—. 1987. *Exercices spirituels et philosophie antique*, 2nd edn (Paris).

—. 1993. *Plotinus, or, The Simplicity of Vision* (Chicago–London; Eng. trans.).

—. 1998. *The Inner Citadel: The Meditations of Marcus Aurelius* (Harvard).

—. 1999. 'Être, vie et pensée chez Plotin et avant Plotin', in *Plotin, Porhyre: Études néoplatoniciennes* (Paris) 127–81.

—. 2010. *Études de patristique et d'histoire des concepts* (Paris).

Haeringen, J. H. van. 1937. 'De Valentiniano II et Ambrosio: Illustrantur et digeruntur res anno 386 gestae', *Mnemosyne* 3: 152–8 and 229–40.

Hargrove, H. L. 1904. *King Alfred's Old English Version of Augustine's Soliloquies* (New York).

Harmless, W. 1995. *Augustine and the Catechumenate* (Collegeville, Minn.).

—. 2004. *Desert Christians: An Introduction to the Literature of Early Monasticism* (New York).

—, ed. 2010. *Augustine in His Own Words* (Washington).

—. 2012. 'A love supreme: Augustine's jazz of theology', *AS* 43: 149–77.

Harper, K. 2010. 'The *SC Claudianum* in the *Codex Theodosianus*: Social History and Legal Texts', *CQ* 60: 610–38.

—. 2011. *Slavery in the Late Roman World, AD 275–425* (Cambridge).

—. 2013. *From Shame to Sin: The Christian Transformation of Sexual Morality in Late Antiquity* (Cambridge).

Harries, J. 1984. '"Treasure in Heaven": Property and Inheritance among Senators of Late Rome', in E. M. Craik, ed., *Marriage and Property* (Aberdeen) 54–70.

Harrison, C. 1992. *Beauty and Revelation in the Thought of Saint Augustin* (Oxford).

—. 2000. *Augustine: Christian Truth and Fractured Humanity* (Oxford).

—. 2006. *Rethinking Augustine's Early Theology: An Argument for Continuity* (Oxford).

—. 2013. *The Art of Listening in the Early Church* (Oxford).

Harrison, S. 2006. *Augustine's Way into the Will: The Theological and Philosophical Significance of* De libero arbitrio (Oxford).

Hattrup, D. 2003. 'Die Befreiung aus der Sorge: Augustinus liest den Psalm 4', *ThGl* 93: 196–207.

Haubold, J., and R. Miles. 2004. 'Communality and Theatre in Libanius' Oration LXIV, In Defence of the Pantomimes', in I. Sandwell and J. Huskinson, eds., *Culture and Society in Later Roman Antioch* (Oxford) 24–34.

Heidl, G. 1999. 'Augustine, *Contra Academicos* 2, 2, 5. Origen in the Background?', *Adamantius* 5: 53–91.

—. 2003. *Origen's Influence on the Young Augustine* (Piscataway).

Heil, H, and Christian Pirus 2013. Pear (*Pirum*),' K. Pollmann and W. Otten, eds, *The Oxford Guide To The Historical Reception of Augustine*, vol. 3 (Oxford) 1508–11.

Henning, W. B. 1942. 'Mani's Last Journey', *BSOAS* 10: 941–53.

Hennings, R. 1994. *Der Briefwechsel zwischen Augustinus und Hieronymus und ihr Streit um den Kanon des Alten Testaments und die Auslegung von Gal. 2,11–14* (Leiden).

Henrichs, A., and L. Koenen, eds. and transs. 1970. 'Ein griechischer Mani-Codex (P. Colon. Inv. Nr. 4780)', *ZPE* 5: 97–216.

Henry, P. 1938. *La Vision d'Ostie: Sa place dans la vie et l'oeuvre de saint Augustin* (Paris).

Herman, G. 2011. 'Greek epiphanies and the sensed presence', *Historia* 60: 127–57.

Hill, E. 1962. '*De Doctrina Christiana*: A Suggestion', *StPatr* 6: 443–6.

Holgate, I. 2003. 'The Cult of Saint Monica in quattrocentro Italy: her place in Augustinian iconography, devotion and legend', *PBSR* 71: 181–206.

Hollmann, A. 2003. 'A Curse Tablet from the Circus at Antioch', *ZPE* 145: 67–82.

Holte, R. 1962. *Béatitude et sagesse: Saint Augustin et le problème de la fin de l'homme dans la philosophie antique* (Paris).

—. 1994. 'Monica: The "Philosopher"', *Augustinus* 39: 293–316.

Hombert, P.-M. 1996. *Gloria gratiae: Se glorifier en Dieu, principe et fin de la théologie augustinienne de la grâce* (Paris).

—. 2000. *Nouvelles recherches de chronologie augustinienne* (Paris).

Homes Dudden, F. 1935. *The Life and Times of St. Ambrose*, Vols. I–II (Oxford).

Hoof, L. van. 2013. 'Performing *paideia*: Greek culture as an instrument for social promotion in the fourth century AD', *CQ* 63: 387–406.

—. 2014a. *Libanius: A Critical Introduction* (Cambridge).

—. 2014b. '(Self-)Censorship or Self-Fashioning? Gaps in Libanius's Letter Collection', *RBPh* 92.

Hopkins, M. K. 1961. 'Social Mobility in the Later Roman Empire: The Evidence of Ausonius', *CQ* 11: 239–49.

Horn, H. J. 1998. '*Discordia concors?* Zu einem Briefwechsel des Augustinus mit Maximus von Madaura', *JAC*, *Ergänzungsband* 28: 194–8.

Horsfall, N. 1995. 'Apuleius, Apollonius of Tyana, Bibliomancy: Some Neglected Dating Criteria', in G. Bonamente and G. Paci, eds., *Historiae Augustae Colloquium Maceratense* III (Bari) 169–77.

Hourani, A. 1991. 'T. E. Lawrence and Louis Massignon', in A. Hourani, *Islam and European Thought* (Cambridge) 116–28.

Hübner, W. 2011. '*E pluribus unum* bei Augustin', *REAug* 57: 137–44.

Hunink, V. 2011. 'Singing Together in Church: Augustine's *Psalm against the Donatists*', in A. P. M. H. Lardinois, J. H. Blok and M. G. M. van der Poel, eds., *Sacred Words: Orality, Literacy and Religion* (Leiden) 389–403.

Hunter, D. G. 1993. 'Helvidius, Jovinian and the Virginity of Mary in Late Fourth-Century Rome', *JECS* 1: 47–71.

—. 1994. 'Augustinian Pessimism? A New Look at Augustine's Teaching on Sex, Marriage, and Celibacy', *AS* 25: 153–77.

—. 2003a. 'Augustine and the Making of Marriage in Roman North Africa', *JECS* 11: 63–85.

—. 2003b. 'Between Jovinian and Jerome: Augustine and the Interpretation of 1 Corinthians 7', *StPatr* 43: 131–6.

—. 2007. *Marriage, Celibacy and Heresy in Ancient Christianity: The Jovinianist Controversy* (Oxford).

—. 2011. 'Clerical Marriage and Episcopal Elections in the Latin West: From Siricius to Leo', in J. Leemans et al., *Episcopal Elections in Late Antiquity* (Berlin) 183–211.

Jensen, Robin M. 2011. *Living Water: Images, Symbols and Settings of Early Christian Baptism* (Leiden).

—. 2014. J. P. Burns, G. W. Clarke, *Christianity in Roman North Africa: the development of its practices and beliefs* (Grand Rapids).

Jones, A. H. M., J. R. Martindale and J. Morris. 1971. *The Prosopography of the Later Roman Empire* I (Cambridge).

Joubert, C. 1992. 'Le livre XIII et la structure des *Confessions* de saint Augustin', *RevSR* 66: 77–117.

Jürgens, H. 1972. *Pompa diaboli: die lateinischen Kirchenväter und das antike Theater* (Stuttgart).

Kany, R. 1997. 'Der vermeintliche Makel von Augustins Bischofsweihe', *ZAC* 1: 116–25.

—. 2007. *Augustins Trinitätsdenken: Bilanz, Kritik, und Weiterführung der modernen Forschung zu 'De Trinitiate'* (Tübingen).

Karfíková, L. 2012. *Grace and the Will According to Augustine* (Leiden).

Kaster, R. A. 1983. 'The Salaries of Libanius', *Chiron* 13: 37–59.

—. 1984. 'A Schoolboy's Burlesque from Cyrene?', *Mnemosyne* 37: 457–8.

—. 1988. *Guardians of Language: The Grammarian and Society in Late Antiquity* (Berkeley).

Katô, T. 1966. 'Melodia interior: sur le traité *De pulchro et apto*', *REAug* 12: 229–40.

Katz, P. B. 2007. 'Educating Paula: A Proposed Curriculum for Raising a 4th-Century Christian Infant', in Ada Cohen and J. B. Rutter, eds., *Constructions of Childhood in Ancient Greece and Italy. Hesperia* Suppl. 41: 115–27.

Kehoe, P. K. 1984. 'The Adultery Mime Reconsidered', in David F. Bright and E. S. Ramage, eds., *Classical Texts and Their Traditions: Studies in Honor of C. R. Trahman* (Berkeley) 89–106.

Kelly, J. N. D. 1975. *Jerome: His Life, Writings and Controversies* (London).

Kenney, J. P. 2005. *The Mysticism of Saint Augustine: Rereading the* Confessions (London).

—. 2012. 'God as Being: Interpreting Augustine', *AS* 43: 77–88.

—. 2013. *Contemplation and Classical Christianity: A Study in Augustine* (Oxford).

Kienzler, K. 1989. 'Der Aufbau der *Confessiones* des Augustinus im Spiegel der Bibelzitate', *RechAug* 24: 123–64.

Kirwan, C. 1983. 'Augustine against the Skeptics', in M. Burnyeat, ed., *The Skeptical Tradition* (Berkeley) 287–318.

—. 1989. *Augustine* (London).

—. 2001. 'Augustine's Philosophy of Language', in E. Stump and N. Kretzmann, eds., *The Cambridge Companion to Aquinas* (Cambridge) 186–204.

Klingshirn, W. E. 2001. 'The Figure of Albicerius the Diviner in Augustine's *Contra Academicos*', *StPatr* 38: 219–23.

Klöckener, M. 1994. 'Conversi ad dominum', in *Augustinus-Lexikon* 1: Fasc. 7/8 (Basel) 1280–82.

Kloos, K. 2005. 'Seeing the Invisible God: Augustine's Reconfiguration of Theophany Narrative Exegesis', *AS* 36: 397–420.

Knauer, G. N. 1955. *Pzalmenzitate in Augustins Konfessionen* (Göttingen).

Koenen, L. 1978. 'Augustine and Manichaeism in Light of the Cologne Mani Codex', *ICS* 3: 154–95.

—. 1986. 'Manichaean Apocalypticism at the Crossroads of Iranian, Egyptian, Jewish and Christian Thought', in L. Cirillo and A. Roselli, eds., *Codex Manichaicus Coloniensis* (Cosenza) 285–332.

— and C. Römer, eds. 1988. *Der Kölner Mani-Kodex* (Opladen).

Kondoleon, C. 2000. *Antioch: The Lost Ancient City* (Princeton).

Kotula, T. 1988. '*Modicam terram habes, id est villam*: sur une notion de *villa* chez saint Augustin', *L'Africa romana* 5: 339–44.

Kotzé, A. 2001. 'Reading Psalm 4 to the Manicheans', *VigChr* 55: 119–36.

—. 2013. 'A Protreptic to a Liminal Manichaean at the Centre of Augustine's *Confessions* 4', in J. van Oort, ed., *Augustine and Manichaean Christianity* (Leiden) 107–35.

Krautheimer, R. 1983. *Rome: Profile of a City, 312–1408* (Princeton).

Kriekenbom, D. 2012. 'Kyrene und Ptolemais zur Zeit des Synesios', in H. Seng and C. M. Hoffmann, eds., *Synesios von Kyrene: Politik-Literatur-Philosophie* (Turnhout) 1–34.

Laes, C. 2011. *Children in the Roman Empire: Outsiders Within* (Cambridge).

Lagouanère, J. 2011. 'La notion de prochain dans les premiers écrits d'Augustin: esquisse de réflexion', *REAug* 57: 239–67.

Lamberigts, M. 1997. 'Some Critiques on Augustine's View of Sexuality Revisited', *StPatr* 33: 152–61.

Lambot, C. 1935. 'Un "ieiunium quinquagesimae" en Afrique au IVe siecle et date de quelques sermons de S. Augustin', *RB* 47: 114–24.

—. 1950. 'Le catalogue de Possidius et la collection carthusienne de sermons de saint Augustin', *RB* 60: 3–7.

—. 1969. 'Les sermons de saint Augustin pour les fêtes de Paques', *RB* 79: 148–72.

Lamirande, É. 1963. 'La signification de "Christianus" dans la théologie de saint Augustin et la tradition ancienne', *REAug* 9: 221–34.

Lammers, Ann Conrad. 2007. 'To Aurelius Augustinus from the Mother of His Son', in Judith C. Stark, ed., *Feminist Interpretations of Augustine* (Pennsylvania) 301–2.

Lancel, S. 1998. 'Modalités de l'inhumation privilégiée dans la nécropole de Sainte-Salsa à Tipasa (Algérie)', *CRAI*: 791–812.

—. 2002. *St Augustine* (London; Eng. trans.).

Lane Fox, R. 1997. 'Power and Possession in The First Monasteries', in H. W. Pleket and A. M. Verhoogt, eds., *Aspects of the Fourth Century AD: Power and Possession* (Leiden).

—. 2006. 'Augustine's *Soliloquies* and the Historian', *StPatr* 43: 173–90.

—. 2010. 'Astrology and Cognitive Dissonance', in C. Bonnet, C. Ossola and J. Scheid, eds., *Rome et ses religions: culte, morale, spiritualité. En relisant* Lux Perpetua *de Franz Cumont*, Supplemento a *Mythos* I: 83–96.

—. 2014. 'Early Christians and the garden: image and reality', in K. Coleman, ed., *Le Jardin dans l'Antiquité*, Entretiens Fondation Hardt LX: 363–400.

Laporte, J.P. 2010. 'L'emplacement de la Basilique de la Paix 'a Hippone', *CRAI*; 73–92.

Latham, J. E. 1982. *The Religious Symbolism of Salt* (Paris).

Law, V. 1984. 'St. Augustine's *De grammatica*: Lost or Found?' *RechAug* 19: 155–83.

Lawless, G. 1987. *Augustine of Hippo and His Monastic Rule* (Oxford).

Le Blond, J. M. 1950. *Les Conversions de Saint Augustin* (Paris).

Lefort, C. 2013. 'À propos d'une source inédite des Soliloques d'Augustin: la notion cicéronienne de "vraisemblance"', *StPatr* 70: 547–52.

Lenox-Conyngham, A. 1982. 'The Topography of the Basilica Conflict of AD 385/6 at Milan', *Historia* 31: 353–63.

Lepelley, C. 1979–81. *Les Cités de l'Afrique romaine au Bas-Empire*. 2 vols. (Paris).

—. 1987. '*Spes saeculi*: le milieu social d'Augustin et ses ambitions séculières avant sa conversion', *Congresso Internazionale su S. Agostino nel XVI centenario della conversion (Roma, 15–20 sett. 1986), Atti,* I (Rome) 99–117.

—. 1994. 'Africa: présentation générale', *Augustinus-Lexikon* 1: Fasc. 1/2 (Basel) 179–205.

—. 2001. 'Quelques parvenus de la culture de l'Afrique romaine tardive', in his *Aspects de l'Afrique romaine: Les Cités, la vie rurale, le christianisme* (Bari) 149–60.

—. 2005. 'L'Afrique et sa diversité vues par Saint Augustin', in S. Lancel, ed., *Saint Augustin, la Numidie et la societé de son temps*. (Bordeaux) 29–44.

—. 2005b 'Témoignages de saint Augustin sur l'ampleur et les limites de l'usage de la langue punique dans L'Afrique de son temps,' in C. Briand-Ponsart, ed., *identités et cultures dans l'Algérie antique* (Roven) 117–41.

Lettieri, G. 2001. *L'altro Agostino: Ermeneutica e retorica della grazia dalla crisi alla metamorfosi del* De doctrina christiana (Brescia).

Liebeschuetz, J. H. W. G. 1972. *Antioch: City and Imperial Administration in the Later Roman Empire* (Oxford).

—. 1985. 'Synesius and Municipal Politics of Cyrenaica in the 5th century AD', *Byzantion* 55: 146–64.

—. 1986. 'Why Did Synesius Become Bishop of Ptolemais?', *Byzantion* 56: 180–95.

—, ed. and trans. 2005. *Ambrose of Milan: Political Letters and Speeches* (Liverpool).

—. 2006. 'Libanius and Late Antique autobiography', in A. González Gálvez and P.-L. Malosse, eds., *Gens de culture en un âge de violence* (*Topoi*, Supplément 7) 263–76.

Lienhard, J. T. 1990. 'Friendship in Paulinus of Nola and Augustine', in B. Bruning, M. Lamberigts and J. van Houtem, eds., *Collectanea Augustiniana: Mélanges T. J. van Bavel* (Leuven).

—, E. Muller and R. Teske, eds. 1993. *Augustine: Presbyter Factus Sum* (New York).

Lieu, S. N. C. 1981. 'Precept and Practice in Manichaean Monasticism', *JThS* 32: 153–75.

—. 1985. *Manichaeism in the Later Roman Empire and Medieval China* (Manchester).

—. 1994. *Manichaeism in Mesopotamia and the Roman East* (Leiden).
—. 2004. 'Libanius and Higher Education at Antioch', in I. Sandwell and J. Huskinson, *Culture and Society in Later Roman Antioch* (Oxford) 13–23.
—. 2006. '"My Church is Superior ...": Mani's Missionary Statement in Coptic and Middle Persian', in *Coptica-Gnostica-Manichaica: Mélanges offerts à Wolf Peter Funk* (Quebec) 519–28.
—. 2010. *Greek and Latin Sources on Manichaean Cosmogony and Ethics* (Turnhout).
Lim, R. 1992. 'Manichaeans and Public Disputation in Late Antiquity', *RA* 26: 233–72.
Lössl, J. 1994. 'The One (*unum*) – A Guiding Concept in *De uera religione*: An Outline of the Text and the History of Its Interpretation', *REAug* 40: 79–103.
—. 1997. *Intellectus gratiae: Die erkenntnistheoretische und hermeneutische Dimension der Gnadenlehre Augustins von Hippo* (Leiden).
—. 2012. 'Augustine's Use of Aristotle's *Categories* in the Light of the History of the Latin Text', in E. Bermon and G. J. P. O'Daly, eds., *Le* de Trinitate *de S. Augustin: Exégèse, logique et noétique. Actes du colloque international de Bordeaux, 16–19 juin 2010* (Paris).
Louth, A. 1981. *The Origins of the Christian Mystical Tradition* (Oxford).
Luttikhuisen, G. P. 1985. *The Revelation of Elchasai* (Tübingen).
Lyotard, J.-F. 2000. *The Confession of Augustine*, trans. R. Beardsworth (Stanford).
MacCormack, S. G. 1998. *The Shadows of Poetry: Vergil in the Mind of Augustine* (Berkeley).
—. 2001. 'The virtue of work: an Augustinian transformation', *AntTard* 9: 219–37.
MacMullen, R. 2009. *The Second Church: Popular Christianity A.D. 200–400* (Atlanta).
Madec, G. 1970. 'À propos d'une traduction de *De Ordine* II.v.16', *REAug* 16: 179–86.
—. 1974a. 'L'Homme intérieur selon saint Ambroise', in Y.-M. Duval, ed., *Ambroise de Milan: XVIe centenaire de son élection épiscopale* (Paris) 283–308.
—. 1974b. *Saint Ambroise et la philosophie* (Paris).
—. 1976. 'Introduction', 'Notes complémentaires', in *Augustin: Dialogues philosophiques, De magistro, De libero arbitrio, BA* 6, 3rd edn (Paris).
—. 1977. '*Verus philosophus est amator Dei.* S. Ambroise, S. Augustin et la philosophie', *RSPhTh* 61: 231–47.
—. 1978. '"Ego sum qui sum" de Tertullian à Jérôme', in *Dieu et l'Être: Exégèses d'Exode 3.14 et de Coran 20.11–24* (Paris) 121–39.
—. 1981. 'Si Plato viveret ... (Augustin, *De vera religione*, 3,3)', *Néoplatonisme: Mélanges offerts à Jean Trouillard, Les Cahiers de Fontenay*, 231–47.
—. 1986a. 'Admonitio', in *Augustinus-Lexikon* 1: Fasc. 1 (Basel) 95–9.
—. 1986–94b. 'Ascensio, ascensus', in *Augustinus-Lexikon* 1: Fasc. 3 (Basel) 465–75.
—. 1986b. 'L'historicité des "Dialogues" de Cassiciacum', *REAug* 32: 207–31.

—. 1987. 'Le milieu milanais: philosophie et christianisme', *BLE* 88: 194–205.

—. 1988a. '"In te supra me": le sujet dans les *Confessions* de saint Augustin', *BICP* 28: 45–63.

—. 1989. *La patrie et la voie: Le Christ dans la vie et la pensée de saint Augustin* (Paris).

—. 1991. 'Introduction', 'Notes complémentaires', in *Augustin: La première catéchèse. De catchizandis rudibus*, *BA* 11/1 (Paris).

—. 1992. 'Augustin et Porphyre: ébauche d'un bilan des recherches et des conjectures', in M.-O. Goulet-Cazé, G. Madec and D. O'Brien, eds., *ΣΟΦΙΗΣ ΜΑΙΗΤΟΡΕΣ: 'Chercheurs de sagesse'. Hommage à Jean Pépin* (Paris) 367–82.

—. 1994a. 'Conversio', in *Augustinus-Lexikon* 1: Fasc.7/8 (Basel) 1282–94.

—. 1994b. *Petites études augustiniennes* (Paris).

—, comm. and ed. 1994c. *Sant'Agostino: Confessioni*, vol. III (*Libri VII–IX*) (Milan).

—. 1995. 'Thématique augustinienne de la Providence', *REAug* 41 (1995) 291–308.

—. 1996a. *Introduction aux 'Révisions' et à la lecture des œuvres de saint Augustin* (Paris).

—. 1996b. *Saint Augustin et la philosophie: Notes critiques* (Paris).

, ed. 1998b. *Augustin prédicateur (395–411): Actes du colloque international de Chantilly (5–7 septembre 1996)* (Paris).

—. 2000. *Le Dieu d'Augustin* (Paris).

—. 2001a. *Le Christ de saint Augustin: La patrie et la voie* (Paris).

—. 2001b. *Lectures augustiniennes* (Paris).

—. 2003. 'Exercitatio animi', in *Augustinus-Lexikon* 2: Fasc. 7/8 (Basel) 1182–3.

— and I. Bochet. 2012. 'Augustin et l'*Hortensius* de Cicéron: notes de lecture', in I. Bochet, ed., *Augustin philosophe et prédicateur: Hommage à Goulven Madec* (Paris) 197–294.

— and L. F. Pizzolato. 1994. 'Commento', in *Sant'Agostino,* Confessioni, Volume III (Libri VII–IX) (Milan).

Maltomini, F. 2004. 'Libanio, il camaleonte, un papiro e altri testi', *ZPE* 47: 147–53.

Mandouze, A. 1954. '"L'exstase d'Ostie", possibilités et limites de la méthode des parallèles textuels', in *Augustinus Magister* 1 (Paris).

—. 1968. *Saint Augustin: L'Aventure de la raison et de la grâce* (Paris).

—. 1969. 'Monique à Cassiciacum, *REL* 47, 131–41.

—, ed. 1982. *Prosopographie chrétienne du Bas-Empire*, Vol 1: *Prosopographie de l'Afrique chrétienne (303–553)* (Paris).

—. 1991. '"Au travail, les moines!" Mot d'Ordre de Saint Augustin', in F. Babinet, ed., *Convergences, études offertes à Marcel David* (Quimper).

—. 2013. *Avec et pour Augustin: Mélanges. Sous la direction de Luca Pietri et Christine Mandouze* (Paris) 363–74.

Mara, M. G., et al. 1996. *La* Genesi *nelle* Confessioni: *Atti della giornata di studio su S. Agostino (Roma, 6 dic 1994)* (Rome).

Marinescu, C. A., S. E. Cox and R. Wachter. 2007. 'Paideia's Children: Childhood Education in a Group of Late Antique Mosaics', in A. Cohen and J. B. Rutter, eds., *Constructions of Childhood in Ancient Greece and Italy* (Athens).

Markus, R. A. 1989. *Conversion and Disenchantment in Augustine's Spiritual Career* (Villanova, Pa), reprinted in his *Sacred and Secular: Studies on Augustine and Latin Christianity* (London, 1994) 1–42.

—. 2001. 'Evolving Disciplinary Contexts for the Study of Augustine, 1950–2000: Some Personal Reflections', *AS* 32: 189–200.

Marrou, H.-I. 1938. *Saint Augustin et la fin de la culture antique* (Paris).

—. 1955. *Saint Augustin et l'augustinisme* (Paris).

—. 1958*a*. 'La querelle autour du "tolle, lege"', *RHE* 53: 47–57.

—. 1958*b*. *Saint Augustin et la fin de la culture antique*, 4th edn (Paris).

—. 1963. 'Synesius of Cyrene and Alexandrian Neoplatonism', in A. Momigliano, ed., *The Conflict of Paganism and Christianity in the Fourth Century* (Oxford) 126–50.

—. 1978. *Augustin et l'augustinisme*, 3rd edn (Paris).

Markschies, C. 1987. 'Was ist lateinischer "Neunizänismus"? Ein Vorschlag für eine Antwort', *ZAC* 1: 73–95.

—. 1995. *Ambrosius von Mailand und die Trinitätstheologie: kirchen- und theologiegeschichtliche Studien zu Antiarianismus und Neunizänismus bei Ambrosius und im lateinischen Westen (364–381 n. Chr.)* (Tübingen).

—. 2003. *Gnosis: An Introduction* (London).

Martin, J., and P. Petit. 1979. *Libanios: Discours*, Vol. 1 (Paris).

Martin, T. F. 1997. 'Augustine on Romans 7, 24–25a', *StPatr* 33: 178–82.

—. 2001. *Rhetoric and Exegesis in Augustine's Interpretation of Romans 7:24–25A* (Lewiston).

Massignon, D. 2001. *Le Voyage en Mésopotamie et la conversion de Louis Massignon en 1908* (Paris).

Matthews, J. F. 1974. 'The Letters of Symmachus', in J. W. Binns, ed., *Latin Literature of the Fourth Century* (London) 58–99.

—. 1975. *Western Aristocracies and Imperial Court. AD 364–425* (Oxford).

—. 1989. *The Roman Empire of Ammianus* (London).

—. 2006. *The Journey of Theophanes: Travel, Business and Daily Life in the Roman East* (Yale).

—. 2009. 'Four Funerals and a Wedding: This World and the Next in Fourth-Century Rome', in P. Rousseau and M. Papoutsakis, eds., *Transformations of Late Antiquity: Essays for Peter Brown* (Farnham) 129–46.

—. 2010. *Roman Perspectives* (Swansea).

Mattingly, D., and R. B. Hitchner. 1995. 'Roman Africa: An Archaeological Review', *JRS* 85: 165–213.

May, R. 2006. *Apuleius and Drama* (Oxford).

McGuckin, J. A. 2001. *St. Gregory of Nazianzen: An Intellectual Biography* (New York).

McLynn, N. B. 1994. *Ambrose of Milan: Church and Court in a Christian Capital* (Berkeley).

—. 2004. 'The Transformation of Imperial Churchgoing in the Fourth Century', in S. Swain and M. Edwards, eds., *Approaching Late Antiquity: The Transformation from Early to Late Empire* (Oxford) 235–70.

—. 2010. 'Augustine's Black Sheep: The Case of Antoninus of Fussala', in G. Bonamente and R. Lizzi Testa, eds., *Istituzioni, carismi ed esercizio del potere (IV–VI secolo d.C.)* (Bari).

—. 2012. 'Administrator: Augustine and His Diocese', in M. Vessey, ed., *A Companion to Augustine* (Oxford) 310–22.

Meer, F. van der. 1961. *Augustine the Bishop* (London).

Meiggs, R. 1973. *Roman Ostia*, 2nd edn (Oxford).

Menn, S. P. 1998. *Augustine and Descartes* (Cambridge).

Michel, Anne. 2005. 'Aspects du culte dans les églises de Numidie : un état de la question', in S. Lancel, ed., *Saint Augustin la Numidie et la société de son temps* (Bordeaux) 67–108.

Miles, M. R. 1982. 'Infancy, Parenting and Nourishment in Augustine's *Confessions*', *JAAR* 50: 349–364.

—. 2007. 'Not Nameless But Unnamed: The Woman Torn from Augustine's Side', in J. C. Stark, ed., *Feminist Interpretations of Augustine* (University Park, Pa) 167–88.

Millar, F. 2007. 'Libanius and the Near East', *SCI* 26: 155–80.

Misson, J. 1914. *Recherches sur le paganisme de Libanios* (Louvain).

Mitchell, C. W. 1912. *S. Ephraim's Prose Refutations of Mani, Marcion and Bardaisan* (London).

Mitchell, M. M. 2000. *The Heavenly Trumpet: John Chrysostom and the Art of Pauline Interpretation* (Tübingen).

Moles, J. C. 1978. 'The Career and Conversion of Dio Chrysostom', *JHS* 98: 79–100.

Molloy, M. 1996. *Libanius and the Dancers* (Hildesheim).

Monk, R. 1990. *Ludwig Wittgenstein: The Duty of Genius* (London).

Moorhead, J. 1999. *Ambrose: Church and Society in the Late Roman World* (London).

Morgan, R. 1995. *Romans* (Sheffield).

Moriyasu, T. 2011. 'The Discovery of Manichaean Paintings in Japan and Their Historical Background', in J. van den Berg et al., eds., *'In Search of Truth': Augustine, Manichaeism and Other Gnosticism. Studies for Johannes van Oort at Sixty* (Leiden) 339–60.

Mratschek, S. 2002. *Der Briefwechsel des Paulinus von Nola: Kommunikation und soziale Kontakte zwischen christlichen Intellektuellen* (Göttingen).

—. 2011. 'Die ungeschriebenen Briefe des Augustinus von Hippo', in J. A. van den Berg et al., eds., *'In Search of Truth': Augustine, Manichaeism and Other Gnosticism. Studies for Johannes van Oort at Sixty* (Leiden) 109–22.

—. 2014. 'Augustine, Paulinus, and the question of moving the monastery: dispute between theologians or between actors of history?', in J. Hallebeek et al., eds., *Inter cives necnon peregrinos: Essays in Honour of Boudewijn Sirks* (Göttingen) 545–61.

Müller, C. 1998. 'Confessiones 13: Der ewige Sabbat. Die eschatologische Ruhe als Zielpunkt der Heimkehr zu Gott', in N. Fischer and C. Mayer, *Die Confessiones des Augustinus von Hippo: Einführung und Interpretationen zu den dreizehn Büchern* (Freiburg–Basel–Vienna) 639–47.

Müller, G. A. 2003. *Formen und Funktionen der Vergilzitate und -anspielungen bei Augustin von Hippo* (Paderborn–Munich)

Munier, C. 1974. *Conciliae Africae. A.45–A.525. CCSL*, CLIX (Turnhout).

Mutzenbecher, A. 1999. 'Diversis quaestionibus LXXXIII (De-)', *Augustinus-Lexikon* 2: Fasc. 3/4 (Basel) 508–16.

Myres, J. N. L. 1960. 'Pelagius and the End of Roman Rule in Britain', *JRS* 50: 21–36.

Napier, D. A. 2013. *En Route to the Confessions: The Roots and Development of Augustine's Philosphical Anthropology* (Leuven).

Nauroy, G. 1988. 'Le fouet et le miel: le combat d'Ambroise en 386 contra l'arianisme milanais', *RechAug.* 23: 3–86.

—. 2008. 'Les "Vies des patriarches" d'Ambroise de Milan: de Cassiodore au débat critique moderne', *REAug* 54: 43–61.

—. 2010. *Jacob et la vie heureuse* (Paris).

Newman, H. I. 2009. 'How Should We Measure Jerome's Hebrew Competence?', in A. Cain and J. Lössl, eds., *Jerome of Stridon: His Life, Writings and Legacy* (Farnham) 131–40.

Nixon, C. E. V., and B. Rodgers. 1994. *In Praise of the Later Roman Emperors* (Berkeley).

Nock, A. D. 1933. *Conversion: The Old and New in Religion from Alexander the Great to Augustine of Hippo* (Oxford).

Nodes, D. J. 2009. 'The Organization of Augustine's *Psalmus contra Partem Donati*', *VigChr* 63: 390–408.

Norman, A. F. 1965. *Libanius* Autobiography (Oration) *The Greek Text* (Oxford) (trans.) 1992.

—. 1992. *Libanius: Autobiography and Selected Letters*, Loeb Classical Library (Cambridge, Mass.).

—. 2000. *Antioch as a Centre of Hellenic Culture as Observed by Libanius* (Liverpool).

Norton, P. 2007. *Episcopal Elections, 250–600: Hierarchy and Popular Will in Late Antiquity* (Oxford).

Nussbaum, M. 2001. *Upheavals of Thought: The Intelligence of Emotions* (Cambridge) 527–56.

Nuttall, A. D. 1996. *Why Does Tragedy Give Pleasure?* (Oxford).

O'Connell, R. J. 1967. 'Alypius' "Apollinarianism" at Milan (*Conf.* VII.25)', *REAug* 13: 209–10.

—. 1968. *St Augustine's Early Theory of Man, AD 386–91* (Cambridge, Mass.).

—. 1969. *St. Augustine's* Confessions (Cambridge, Mass.).

—. 1973. '*Confessions* VII: Reply to Goulven Madec', *REAug* 19: 87–100.

—. 1996. *Images of Conversion in St. Augustine's Confessions* (New York).

O'Daly, G. J. P. 1987. *Augustine's Philosophy of Mind* (London).

—. 1992. 'Cassiciacum', in C. Meyer, ed., *Augustinus-Lexikon* 1: Fasc. 5/6 (Basel) 771–81.

—. 2001a. '*Anima*, *Error*, and *Falsum* in Some Early Writings of St Augustine', in his *Platonism Pagan and Christian: Studies in Plotinus and Augustine* (Aldershot).

—. 2001b. 'Remembering and Forgetting in Augustine, *Confessiones*, X: in his *Platonism Pagan and Christian: Studies in Plotinus* and *Augustine* (Aldershot).

—. 2007. 'Friendship and Transgression: *Luminosus Limes Amicitiae* (Augustine, *Confessions* 2.2.2) and the Themes of *Confessions* 2', in S. Stern-Gillet and K. Corrigan, eds., *Reading Ancient Texts: Aristotle and Neoplatonism. Essays in Honour of Denis O'Brien*, Vol. 2 (Leiden) 211–24.

O'Donnell, J. J. 1980. 'Augustine's Classical Readings', *RechAug* 15: 144–75.

—. 1992. *Augustine: Confessions III.* (Oxford).

—. 2005. *Augustine, Sinner and Saint: A New Biography* (London).

O'Meara, D. 1993. *Plotinus: An Introduction to the* Enneads (Oxford).

O'Meara, J. J. 1951. 'St. Augustine's View of Authority and Reason in AD 386', *Irish. Cath. Quarterly* 18 : 338–46.

—. 1954. *The Young Augustine: An Introduction to the* Confessions *of St. Augustine* (London).

—. 1968. 'Virgil and Saint Augustine: The Roman Background to Christian Sexuality', *Augustinus* 13: 307–26.

—. 1988. 'Virgil and Augustine: The *Aeneid* in the *Confessions*', *MaynR* 13: 30–43.

Ogden, C. J. 1930. 'The 1468 Years of the World-Conflagration in Manichaeism', in D. P. Sanjana, ed., *Dr. Modi Memorial Volume: Papers on Indo-Iranian and Other Subjects* (Bombay) 102–5.

Olivar, A. 1991. *La predicación cristiana antigua* (Barcelona).

Ollier, J. 2011. *Firmamentum narrat: La théorie augustinienne des 'Confessions'* (Paris).

Oort, J. van. 1987. 'Augustine and Mani on *concupiscentia sexualis*', in J. den Boeft and J. van Oort, eds., *Augustiniana Traiectina* (Paris) 137–52.

—. 1991. *Jerusalem and Babylon: A Study into Augustine's* City of God *and the Sources of His Doctrine of the Two Cities* (Leiden).

—. 1995. 'Augustine's Critique of Manichaeism: The Case of *Confessions* 3.6.10 and Its Implications', in P. W. van der Horst, ed., *Aspects of Religious Contact and Conflict in the Ancient World* (Utrecht) 57–68.

—. 1997. 'Manichaeism and Anti-Manichaeism in Augustines's *Confessiones*', in L. Cirillo and A. van Tongerloo, eds., *Atti del terzo Congresso internazionale di studi, 'Manicheismo e Oriente Cristiano antico'* (Turnhout) 235–47.

—. 2001. '*Secundini Manichaei epistula*: Roman Manichaean "Biblical" Argument in the Age of Augustine', in van Oort, Wermelinger and Würst (2001) 161–73.

—. 2004. 'The Paraclete Mani as the Apostle of Jesus Christ and the Origins of a New Christian Church', in A. Hilhorst, ed., *The Apostolic Age in Patristic Thought* (Leiden) 139–57.

—. 2008a. 'Heeding and Hiding Their Particular Knowledge? An Analysis of Augustine's Dispute with Fortunatus', in Fuhrer (2008b) 113–21.

—. 2008b. 'Young Augustine's Knowledge of Manichaeism: An Analysis of the *Confessiones* and Some Other Relevant Texts', *VigChr* 62: 441–66.

—. 2010. 'Manichaean Christians in Augustine's Life and Work', *CHRC* 90: 505–46.

—. 2011. 'Augustine's Manichaean Dilemma in Context', *VigChr* 65: 543–67.

—. 2013. 'God, Memory and Beauty: A "Manichaean" Analysis of Augustine's *Confessions*, Book 10.1–38', in J. van Oort, ed., *Augustine and Manichaean Christianity* (Leiden) 155–75.

Oort, J. van, O. Wermelinger and G. Wurst, eds. 2001. *Augustine and Manichaeism in the Latin West: Proceedings of the Fribourg–Utrecht International Symposium of the International Association of Manichaean Studies (IAMS)*, NHMS 49 (Leiden).

Paulus, C. G. 2003. 'Confession', in *Brill's New Pauly* (Leiden) 688–9.

Pedersen, N. A. 1996. *Studies in The Sermon on the Great War: Investigations of a Manichaean-Coptic Text from the Fourth Century* (Aarhus).

Penelhum, T. 1983. 'Skepticism and Fideism', in M. Burnyeat, ed., *The Skeptical Tradition* (Berkeley) 287–318.

Penella, R. J. 2008. 'Himerius' Orations to His Students', in T. Corey Brennan and H. I. Flower, eds., *East and West: Papers in Ancient History Presented to Glen W. Bowersock* (Cambridge, Mass.) 127–45.

—. 2012. 'Libanius the Flatterer', *CQ* 62: 892–5.

Pépin, J. 1951. '*Primitiae spiritus:* Remarques sur une citation paulinienne des *Confessions* de saint Augustin', *RHR* 140: 155–201.

—. 1953. 'Recherches sur le sens et l'origine de l'expression "Caelum caeli" dans le livre XII des *Confessions*', *ALMA* 23: 185–274.

—. 1964. 'Une nouvelle source de saint Augustin: le *Zêtêmata* de Porphyre "Sur l'union de l'âme et du corps"', *REA* 66: 53–107.

—. 1987. *La Tradition de l'allégorie de Philon d'Alexandrie à Dante: Études historiques* (Paris).

—. 1996. 'Augustin et Origène sur les sensus interiores', in M. C. Bianchi, ed., *Atti del Lessico Intelletuale Europeo: sensus–sensatio* (Florence) 3–23.

—. 1999a. 'La hiérarchie par le degré de mutabilité (Nouveaux schèmes porphyriens chez saint Augustin, I)', in *Documenti e studi sulla tradizione filosofica medieval*, X (Florence) 89–107.

—. 1999b. 'Pourquoi l'âme automotrice aurait-elle besoin d'un véhicule? (Nouveaux schèmes porphyriens chez saint Augustin, II)', in J. J. Cleary, ed., *Traditions of Platonism: Essays in Honour of John Dillon* (Aldershot) 293–305.

Perrin, M.-Y. 2007. 'Le témoignage des ralliés: une arme de la polémique doctrinale entre chrétiens dans l'antiquité tardive', in D. Tollet, ed., *La Religion que j'ai quittée* (Paris) 65–86.

—. 2008. 'Arcana mysteria ou ce que cache la religion: de certaines pratiques de l'arcane dans le christianisme antique', in M. Reidel and T. Schabert, eds., *Religionen – Die religiöse Erfhahrung. Religions – The Religious Experi-*

ence (Würzburg) 119–41.

—. 2009. 'Norunt fideles: silence et eucharist dans l'*orbis christianus* antique', in N. Bériou, B. Caseau and D. Rigaux, eds., *Pratiques de l'Eucharistie dans les églises d'Orient et d'Occident (Antiquité et Moyen Âge)* 2 (Paris) 737–63.

Petit, P. 1955. *Libanius et la vie municipale à Antioche* (Paris).

Pietri, C. 1976. Roma Christiana*: Recherches sur l'église de Rome, son organisation, sa politique, son idéologie* (Rome).

—. 1986. 'Damase, évêque de Rome', in *Saecularia Damasiana: Studi di Antichità cristiana* 39 (Vatican).

Pigler, A. 2002. *Plotin: Une métaphysique de l'amour. L'amour comme structure du monde intelligible* (Paris).

Pincherle, A. 1947. *La formazione teologica di Sant'Agostino* (Rome).

—. 1973–4. 'S. Agostino: tra il *De doctrina christiana* e le *Confessioni*', *Archeologia classica* 25–6: 555–74.

—. 1974. 'Intorno alla genesi delle "Confessioni" di S. Agostino', *AS* 5: 167–76.

—. 1975. 'Sulla formazione della dottrina agostiniana della grazia', *RSLR* 11: 1–23.

Pizzolato, L. F. 1972. *Le Fondazione dello stile delle "Confessione" di Sant'Agostino* (Milan).

—. 1974. 'L'amicizia in sant'Agostino e il *Laelius* di Cicerone', *VigChr* 28: 203–15.

— and M. Rizzi, eds. 1998. *Nec timeo mori: Atti del Congresso internazionale di studi ambrosiani nel XVI centenario della morte di sant'Ambrogio, Milano, 4–11 Aprile 1997* (Milan).

Plumer, E., ed. and trans. 2003. *Augustine's Commentary on Galatians* (Oxford).

Pollmann, K., and M. Vessey, eds. 2005. *Augustine and the Disciplines: From Cassiciacum to* Confessions (Oxford).

Poque, S., ed. and trans. 1966. *Augustin d'Hippone: Sermons pour la Pâque*, SC 116 (Paris).

—. 1986. 'Les Psaumes dans les *Confessions*', in A.-M. La Bonnardière, ed., *Saint Augustin et la Bible* (Paris) 155–66.

—. 1987. 'Un souci pastoral d'Augustin: la persévérance des chrétiens baptisés dans leur enfance', *BLE* 88: 273–86.

Power, K. 1995. *Veiled Desire: Augustine's Writing on Women* (London).

Prendiville, J. G. 1972. 'The Development of the Idea of Habit in the Thought of Saint Augustine', *Traditio* 28: 29–99.

Price, R. M. 2006. 'Augustine's *Confessions* VII: Autobiography or Apologetic?', *StPatr* 43: 221–6.

Primmer, A. 1998. 'Augustinus und der Astrologe: Zu *Enarratio in Psalmum* 61', in E. Dassmann, K. Thraede and J. Engemann, eds., *Chartulae: Festschrift für Wolfgang Speyer* (Münster) 253–62.

Puech, H.-C. 1949. *Le Manichéisme son fondateur, sa doctrine* (Paris)

—. 1979a. *Sur le manichéisme et autres essais* (Paris).

—. 1979b. 'Le Prince des ténèbres en son royaume', in Puech (1979a) 103–51.

—. 1979c. 'Péché et Confession dans le Manichéisme', in Puech (1979a) 523–621.

Quillen, C. E. 1991. 'Consentius as a reader of St Augustine's *Confessions*', *REAug* 37: 87–109.

Quiroga, A. 2007. 'From *Sophistopolis* to *Episcopolis*: The Case for a Third Sophistic', *Journal for Late Antique Religion and Culture* 1 (2007) 31–42.

Ratzinger, J. 1967. Review of A. Adam, *Dogmengeschichte*, *JAC* 10: 222.

Rebenich, S. 1992. *Hieronymus und sein Kreis: Propographische und sozialgeschichtliche Untersuchungen* (Stuttgart).

—. 1993. 'Jerome: The *Vir Trilinguis* and the *Hebraica Veritas*', *VigChr* 47: 50–77.

—. 2002. *Jerome* (London).

Rebillard, É. 1998. 'La figure du catéchumène et le problème du délai du baptême dans la pastorale d'Augustin', in G. Madec, ed., *Augustin prédicateur (395–411)* (Paris) 285–92.

—. 2005. '*Nec deserere memorias suorum:* Augustine and the Family-Based Commemoration of the Dead', *AS* 36: 99–111.

—. 2009. *The Care of the Dead in Late Antiquity*, trans. E. T. Rawlings and J. Routier-Pucci (Ithaca, NY).

—. 2013. 'Church and Burial in Late Antiquity (Latin Christianity, Third to Sixth Centuries CE)', in É. Rebillard, *Transformations of Religious Practices in Late Antiquity* (Farnham) 227–50.

Reeves, J. C. 1992. *Jewish Lore in Manichaean Cosmogony: Studies in the* Book of Giants *Traditions* (Cincinnati).

—. 1996. *Heralds of That Good Realm: Syro-Mesopotamian Gnosis and Jewish Traditions* (Leiden).

Reinhardt, T. 2008. 'Epicurus and Lucretius on the Origins of Language', *CQ* 58: 127–40.

Riddle, J. M. 1992. *Contraception and Abortion from the Ancient World to the Renaissance* (Cambridge, Mass.).

Riedweg, C. 2005. *Pythagoras: His Life, Teaching, and Influence* (Cornell; Eng. trans.).

Ries, J. 1976. 'La Fête de Bēma dans l'église de Mani', *REAug* 22: 218–33.

—. 1980. 'La Prière de Bēma dans l'église de Mani', in H. Limet and J. Ries, eds., *L'Expérience de la prière dans les grandes religions* (Louvain-la-Neuve) 375–90.

—. 2011a. *Gnose, gnosticisme, Manichéisme* (Turnhout).

—. 2011b. *L'Église gnostique de Mani* (Turnhout).

Rigby, P. 1987. *Original Sin in Augustine's* Confessions (Ottawa).

Riginos, A. S. 1976. *Platonica: The Anecdotes concerning the Life and Writings of Plato* (Leiden).

Ring, T. G. 1987. 'Die pastorale Intention Augustins in *Ad Simplicianum de diuersis quaestionibus*', in C. Mayer, ed., *Homo spiritalis: Festgabe für L. Verheijen* (Würzburg) 171–84.

—. 1994. 'Bruch oder Entwicklung im Gnadenbegriff Augustins?', *Augustiniana* 44: 31–113.

Rist, J. 1967. *Plotinus* (Cambridge).

—. 1969. 'Augustine on Free Will and Predestination', *Jth.S* 20: 420–47.

—. 1994. *Augustine: Ancient Thought Baptized* (Cambridge).

Rollero, P. 1958. *La 'Expositio evangeli secundum Lucam' di Ambrogio come fonte della esegesi agostiniana* (Turin).

Römer, C. E., ed. and trans. 1994. *Manis frühe Missionsreisen nach der Kölner Manibiographie* (Opladen).

Roques, D. 1987. *Synésios de Cyrène et la Cyrénaique du Bas-Empire* (Paris).

Rose, E. 1979. *Die manichäische Christologie* (Wiesbaden).

Rosen, K. 1997. 'Kaiser Julian auf dem Weg vom Christentum zum Heidentum', *JBAC* 40: 126–46.

Rousseau, P. 1977. 'Augustine and Ambrose: The Loyalty and Single-Mindedness of a Disciple', *Augustiniana* 27: 151–65.

—. 1999. 'Christian Culture and the Swine's Husks: Jerome, Augustine, and Paulinus', in W. E. Klingshirn and M. Vessey, eds., *The Limits of Ancient Christianity: Essays on Late Antique Thought and Culture in Honor of R. A. Markus* (Ann Arbor) 172–87.

Russell, D. A., and H.-G. Nesselrath, eds. 2014. *On Prophecy, Dreams and Human Imagination: Synesius,* De Insomniis (Tübingen).

Rylaarsdam, D. 2014. *John Chrysostom on Divine Pedagogy* (Oxford).

Sage, A. 1967. 'Péché Originel: naissance d'un dogme', *REAug* 13: 211–48.

Salamito, J.-M. 2005. *Les Virtuoses et la multitude: Aspects sociaux de la controverse entre Augustin et les pélagiens* (Grenoble).

Sandwell, I. 2007a. 'Libanius' Social Networks: Undersatnding the Social Structure of the Later Roman Empire', *Med. Hist. Rev.* 22: 133–47.

—. 2007b. *Religious Identity in Late Antiquity: Greeks, Jews and Christians in Antioch* (Cambridge).

— and J. Huskinson, eds. 2004. *Culture and Society in Later Roman Antioch* (Oxford).

Savon, H. 1977. *Saint Ambroise devant l'exégèse de Philon le Juif,* Vols. I and II (Paris).

—. 1997. *Ambroise de Milan* (Paris).

Saxer, V. 1980. *Morts, martyrs, reliques* (Paris).

Schipper, H. G. 2001. 'Melanothesia: A Chapter of Manichaean Astrology in the West', in van Oort, Wermelinger and Wurst (2001) 195–204.

Schmeling, G. 1994/5. '*Confessor Gloriosus*: A Role of Encolpius in the *Satyrica*', *WJA* 20: 207–24.

—. 2011. *A Commentary on the* Satyrica *of Petronius* (Oxford).

Schmidt-Dengler, W. 1968. 'Die "aula memoriae" in den Konfessionen des heiligen Augustin', *RE Aug* 14 : 69–89.

1969. 'Der rhetorische Aufbau des achten Buches der *Konfessionen* des heiligen Augustin', *REAug* 15: 195–208.

Schmitt, T. 2001. *Die Bekehrung des Synesios von Kyrene: Politik und Philosophie, Hof und Provinz als Handlungsräume eines Aristokraten bis zu seiner Wahl zum Metropoliten von Ptolemais* (Munich).

Schniewind, A. 2005. 'The Social Concern of the Plotinian Sage', in Andrew Smith, ed., *The Philosopher and Society in Late Antiquity* (Swansea) 51–64.

Schouler, B. 1973. *Libanios: Discours moraux* (Paris).

—. 1984. *La Tradition hellénique chez Libanios* (Paris).

—. 1994. 'Libanios et l'autobiographie tragique', in M.-F. Baslez, P. Hoffmann and L. Pernot, eds., *L'Invention de l'autobiographie d'Hésiode à saint Augustin* (Paris) 305–24.

Schroeder, J. A. 2004. 'John Chrysostom's Critique of Spousal Violence', *JECS* 12: 413–42.

Scopello, M. 2000. 'Hégémonius, les *Acta Archelai* et l'histoire de la controverse anti-manichéenne', in W. Sundermann and P. Zieme, eds., *Studia Manichaica* IV (Berlin) 528–45.

Seng, H., and Hoffmann, L. M., eds. 2012. *Synesios von Kyrene: Politik–Literatur–Philosophie* (Turnhout)

Shanzer, D. 1991. '"Arcanum Varronis iter": Licentius' Verse Epistle to Augustine', *REAug* 37: 110–43.

—. 1992. 'Latent Narrative Patterns, Allegorical Choices, and Literary Unity in Augustine's Confessions', *VigChr* 46: 40–56.

—. 1996. 'Pears Before Swine: Augustine, *Confessions* 2.4.9', *REAug* 42: 45–55.

—. 2002. '*Avulsa a latere meo*: Augustine's Spare Rib – Augustine, *Confessions* 6.15.25', *JRS* 92: 157–76.

—. 2005. 'Augustine's Disciplines: *Silent diutius Musae Varronis?*', in K. Pollmann and M. Vessey, eds., *Augustine and the Disciplines: From Cassiciacum to* Confessions (Oxford) 69–112.

Shaw, B. D. 1987. 'The Family in Late Antiquity: The Experience of Augustine', *P&P* 115: 3–51.

—. 1992. 'African Christianity: Disputes, Definitions and "Donatists"', in M. R. Greenshields and T. A. Robinson, eds., *Orthodoxy and Heresy in Religious Movements: Discipline and Dissent* (Lampeter) 5–34.

—. 2011. *Sacred Violence: Sectarian Hatred and African Christians in the Age of Augustine* (Cambridge).

Sims-Williams, N. 1985. 'The Manichaean Commandments: A Survey of the Sources', in *Papers in Honour of Professor Mary Boyce*, vol. 2 (Leiden) 573–82.

Sizoo, A., 'Ad August. Conf. VIII.XII.29', *VigChr* 12 (1958) 104–6.

Slyke, D. G. van. 2005. 'The Devil and His Pomps in Fifth-Century Carthage: Renouncing Spectacula with Spectacular Imagery', *Dumbarton Oaks Papers* 59: 53–72.

Smith, A. 1974. *Porphyry's Place in the Neoplatonic Tradition: A Study in Post-Plotinian Neoplatonism* (The Hague).

—. 1978. 'Unconscious and quasi-conscious in Plotinus', *Phronesis* 23: 292–301.

—. 2004. *Philosophy in Late Antiquity* (London).

Soble, A. G. 2002. 'Correcting Some Misconceptions about Augustine', *Journal of the History of Sexuality* 22: 545–69.

Soler, E. 2007. 'L'État impérial romain face au baptême et aux *penuries* d'auteurs et actrices dans l'Antiquité tardive', *AntTard* 15: 47–58.

Solignac, A. 1957. 'Réminiscences plotiniennes et porphyriennes dans le début du *De ordine* de saint Augustin', *ArchPhilos* 20: 446–65.

—. 1958. 'Doxographies et manuels dans la formation de saint Augustin', *RechAug* 1: 113–48.

—. 1988. 'Les excès de l'"intellectus fidei" dans la doctrine d'Augustin sur la grâce', *NRTh* 110: 825–49.

Somers, H. 1961. 'Image de Dieu. Les sources de l'exégèse augustinienne', *REAug* 7: 105–25.

Sorabji, R. 1983. *Time, Creation and the Continuum: Theories in Antiquity and the Early Middle Ages* (London).

—. 2000. *Emotion and Peace of Mind: From Stoic Agitation to Christian Temptation* (Oxford).

Springer, C. P. E. 1989. 'Augustine on Virgil: The Poet as *Mendax Vates*', *StPatr* 22: 337–43.

Stark, J. C. 1990. 'The Dynamics of the Will in Augustine's Conversion', in J. C. Schnaubelt and F. Van Fleteren, eds., *Collectanea Augustiniana: Augustine – 'Second founder of the Faith'* (New York) 45–64.

Starnes, C. 1975. 'Saint Augustine on Infancy and Childhood: Commentary on the First Book of Augustine's *Confessions*', *AS* 6: 15–63.

Stein, M. 2004. *Manichaica Latina*, Vol. 3.1: *Codex Thevestinus: Text, Übersetzung, Erläuterungen* (Paderborn).

Stein, M. 1980. *Greek and Latin Authors On Jews and Judaism* (Jerusalem).

Stewart, C. 1998. *Cassian the Monk* (Oxford).

Stock, B. 2010. *Augustine's Inner Dialogue: The Philosophical Soliloquy in Late Antiquity* (Cambridge).

—. 2012. 'The Soliloquy: transformations of an ancient philosophical technique', in I. Bochet, ed., *Augustin, philosophe et prédicateur: Hommage à Goulven Madec* (Paris) 315–47.

Stroumsa, G. G. 1984. *Another Seed: Studies in Gnostic Mythology* (Leiden).

—. 1992. *Savoir et Salut* (Paris).

—. 1999a. 'Purification and Its Discontents: Mani's Rejection of Baptism', in J. Assmann and G. Stroumsa, eds., *Transformations of the Inner Self in Ancient Religions* (Leiden) 405–20.

—. 1999b. *Barbarian Philosophy: The Religious Revolution of Early Christianity* (Tübingen).

Stroux, J. 1931. 'Augustinus und Ciceros Hortensius nach dem Zeugnis des Manichaeers Secundinus', in E. Fraenkel and H. F. Fränkel, eds., *Festschrift Richard Reizenstein zum 2. April 1931* (Lepzig) 106–18.

Studer, B. 1997. 'Ambrogio di Milano: teologo mistagogico', in *Vescovi e pastori in epoca teodosiana: Atti del XXV incontro di studiosi dell'antichità cristiana* (Rome) 569–86.

Stump, E., and N. Kretzmann, eds. 2001. *The Cambridge Companion to Augustine* (Cambridge).

Sundermann, W. 1986. 'Mani, India and the Manichaean Religion', *South Asian Studies* 2 (1986) 11–19.

—. 1995. 'Who is the Light-Nous and What Does He Do?', in A. van Tongerloo and J. van Oort, eds., *The Manichaean Nous* (Louvain) 255–65.

—. 1997. 'Manichaeism Meets Buddhism: The Problem of Buddhist Influence on Manichaeism', in P. Kiefer-Pülz and J.-U. Hartmann, eds., *Studies in Honour of Heinz Bechert* (Swisttal-Odendorf) 647–56.

—. 2007. 'God and His Adversary in Manichaeism: The Case of the "Enthymesis of Death" and the "Enthymesis of Life"', in F. Vahman and C. V. Pedersen, eds., *Religious Texts in Iranian Languages* (Copenhagen) 137–50.

—. 2009. 'Mani', at www.iranicaonline.org/articles/mani-founder-manicheism.

Swain, S., ed. 2000. *Dio Chrysostom: Politics, Letters, and Philosophy* (Oxford).

Szidat, J. 1985. 'Zum Sklavenhandel in der Spätantike (Aug. *Epist.* 10*)', *Historia* 34: 362–71.

Tanaseanu-Döbler, I. 2008. *Konversion zur Philosophie in der Spätantike* (Stuttgart).

—. 2012. 'Synesios und die Theurgie', in H. Seng and L. Hoffmann, eds., *Synesios von Kyrene: Politik–Literatur–Philosophie* (Turnhout) 201–30.

Tardieu, M. 1987. 'Principes de l'exégèse manichéenne du Nouveau Testament', in M. Tardieu, ed., *Les Règles de l'interprétation* (Paris) 123–46.

—. 2008. *Manichaeism* (Urbana; Eng. trans.).

TeSelle, E. 1970. *Augustine the Theologian* (London).

—. 1993. 'Serpent, Eve, and Adam: Augustine and the Exegetical Tradition', in Lienhard, Muller and Teske (1993) 341–61.

Teske, R. J. 1984. 'Spirituals and Spiritual Interpretation in Augustine', *AS* 15: 65–81.

—. 1992a. 'Augustine's *Epistula* X: Another look at *deificiari in otio*', *Aug* 32: 289–99.

—. 1992b. '"Homo spiritualis" in the *Confessions* of St. Augustine', in J. McWilliam, ed., *Augustine: From Rhetor to Theologian* (Waterloo) 67–76.

Testard, M. 1958. *Saint Augustin et Cicéron.* 2 vols. (Paris).

Theiler, W. 1942. *Die Chaldäischen Orakel und die Hymnen des Synesios* (Halle).

Tilley, M. A., trans. 1996. *Donatist Martyr Stories: The Church in Conflict in Roman North Africa* (Liverpool).

—. 1997. *The Bible in Christian North Africa: The Donatist World* (Minneapolis).

Tomlin, R. S. O. 1979. 'Meanwhile in north Italy and Cyrenaica ...', in P. Casey, ed., *The End of Roman Britain* (Oxford) 253–70.

Tomlin, R. S. O. 2012. '*Spes saeculi*: Augustine's Worldly Ambition and Career', in M. Vessey, ed., *A Companion to Augustine* (Oxford) 57–68.

Treggiari, S. 1981. 'Concubine', *PBSR* 49: 59–81.

—. 1991. *Roman Marriage* (Oxford).

—. 1998. 'Home and forum: Cicero between "public" and "private"', *TAPA* 128: 1–23.

Trout, D. E. 1988. 'Augustine at Cassiciacum: *Otium honestum* and the Social Dimensions of Conversion', *VigChr* 42: 132–46.

—. 1991. 'The Dates of the Ordination of Paulinus of Bordeaux and of His Departure for Nola', *REAug* 37: 237–60.

—. 1999. *Paulinus of Nola: Life, Letters, and Poems* (Berkeley).

Tubach, J. and Zakeri, M. 2001. 'Mani's Name', in van Oort, Wermelinger and Wurst (2001) 272–86.

Turcan-Verkerk, A.-M. 2003. *Un poète latin chrétien redécouvert: Latinius Pacatus Drepanius, Panégyriste de Théodose* (Brussels).

Uhle, T. 2010. 'Truth and Dialectics in Augustine's *Soliloquies*', *StPatr* 49: 223–8.

Van Fleteren, F. 1973. 'Authority and Reason, Faith and Understanding in the Thought of St. Augustine', *AS* 4: 33–71.

—. 1976. 'Augustine's *De vera religione*: A new approach', *Aug* 16: 475–97.

—. 1990. 'Augustine's Theory of Conversion', in J. C. Schnaubelt and F. Van Fleteren, eds., *Collectanea Augustiniana: Augustine – 'Second founder of the Faith'* (New York) 65–80.

— and J. C. Schnaubelt, eds. 2001. *Augustine: Biblical Exegete* (New York).

—, J. C. Schnaubelt and J. Reino, eds. 1994. *Augustine: Mystic and Mystagogue* (New York).

Van Reyn, G. 2009. '*Ad christianam fidem pigrius movebatur* (Conf. VII. xx(25)): Alypius' more reluctant move to the Christian faith (compared to Augustine)', *Augustiniana* 59: 191–225.

—. 2010. '*Ad christianam fidem pigrius movebatur* (Conf. VII.xx(25)): Alypius' more reluctant move to the Christian faith (compared to Augustine). Part 2: Between Conversion and Baptism', *Augustiniana* 60: 193–234.

Vannier, M.-A. 1997. *'Creatio', 'Conuersio', 'formation' chez S. Augustin* (Fribourg), 1st edn 1991.

—. 2011. *Saint Augustin: La Conversion en acte* (Paris).

Vaught, C. G. 2005. *Access to God in Augustine's* Confessions, *Books 10–13* (Albany).

Verheijen, M. 1949. *Eloquentia pedisequa: Observations sur le style des Confessions de saint Augustin* (Nijmegen).

Verschoeren, M. 2002. 'The Appearance of the Concept *Concupiscentia* in Augustine's Early Anti-Manichaean Writings (388–91)', *Augustiniana* 52: 199–240.

Vessey, M. 2005. 'History, Fiction and Figuralism in Book 8 of Augustine's *Confessions*', in D. B. Martin and P. Cox Miller, eds., *The Cultural Turn in Late Ancient Studies: Gender, Asceticism and Historiography* (Durham, NC) 237–57.

Veyne, P. 1999. 'Païens et chrétiens devant la gladiature', *MEFRA* 111: 883–917.

Visonà, G. 2004. *Cronologia ambrosiana. Bibliografia ambrosiana (1900–2000)* (Milan).

Vogt, J. 1985. *Begegnung mit Synesios, dem Philosophen, Priester und Feldherrn, gesammelte Beiträye* (Darmstadt).

Vollenweider, S. 2005. *Neuplatonische und christliche Theologie bei Synesios von Kyrene* (Göttingen).

Vössing, K. 1997. *Schule und Bildung im Nordafrika der römischen Kaiserzeit* (Brussels).

Walsh, P. G. 1988. 'The Rights and Wrongs of Curiosity (Plutarch to Augustine)', *G&R* 35: 83–5.

Ward-Perkins, J. B., and R. G. Goodchild. 2003. *Christian Monuments of Cyrenaica* (London).

Warland, Rainer. 2009. "Das älteste Bildnis des hl. Augustinus? Zum Wandmalereifragment eines spätantiken Autors im Lateran', in N. Fischer, ed., *Augustinus: Spuren und Spiegelungen seines Denkens*, Vol. 1: *Von den Anfängen bis zur Reformation* (Hamburg) 1.13–18.

Watson, G., trans. 1990. *Saint Augustine: Soliloquies and Immortality of the Soul* (Warminster).

Watts, E. 2006. *City and School in Late Antique Athens and Alexandria* (Berkeley).

—. 2015. *The Final Pagan Generation* (Oakland).

Webb, R. 2008. *Demons and Dancers: Performance in Late Antiquity* (Cambridge, Mass.).

Weismann, W. 1972. *Kirche und Schauspiele: Die Schauspiele im Urteil der lateinischen Kirchenväter unter besonderer Berücksichtigung von Augustin* (Würzburg).

Wilken, R. L. 1983. *John Chrysostom and the Jews: Rhetoric and Reality in the Late Fourth Century* (Berkeley).

Williams, M. S. 2008. *Authorised Lives in Early Christian Biography: Between Eusebius and Augustine* (Cambridge).

—. 2011. '"Beloved Lord and Honourable Brother": the negotiation of status in Augustine, *Letter* 23', in Christopher Kelly et al., eds., *Unclassical Traditions*, Vol. II, *PCPhS* Suppl. vol. 35: 88–101.

—. 2012. 'Augustine as a Reader of His Christian Contemporaries', in M. Vessey, ed., *A Companion to Augustine* (Oxford) 227–39.

—. 2013. 'Hymns as Acclamations: The Case of Ambrose of Milan', *Journal of Late Antiquity* 6: 108–34.

Williams, N. P. 1927. *The Idea of the Fall and of Original Sin* (London).

Williams, Rowan D. 2004. 'Augustine and the Psalms', *Interpretation* 58: 17–27.

Wills, G. 1999. *Saint Augustine* (London).

—. 2001. *Saint Augustine's Childhood* (London).

—. 2011. *Augustine's* Confessions*: A Biography* (Princeton).

—. 2012. *Font of Life: Ambrose, Augustine, and the Mystery of Baptism* (Oxford).

Winterbottom, M. 1982. 'Schoolroom and Courtroom', in B. Vickers, ed., *Rhetoric Revalued* (Binghampton) 59–70.

Wintjes, J. 2005. *Das Leben des Libanius* (Würzburg).

Wroe, A. 2011. *Orpheus* (London).

Yates, J. 2001. 'Was There "Augustinian" Concupiscence in pre-Augustinian North Africa?', *Augustiniana* 51: 39–56.

Yoshida, Y. 2015. 'Southern Chinese Version of Mani's Picture Book Discovered?', in S. G. Richter, C. Horton et al., eds., *Mani in Dublin: Selected Papers* (Leiden) 389–98.

Zelzer, M. 1998. 'Zur Chronologie der Werke des Ambrosius: Überblick über die Forschung von 1974 bis 1997', in Pizzolato and Rizzi (1998) 73–92.

Zum Brunn, E. 1978. 'L'exégèse augustinienne de "Ego sum qui sum" et la métaphysique de l'Exode', in *Dieu et l'Être: Exégèses d'Exode 3, 14 et de Coran 20, 11–24* (Paris) 141–64.

Zumkeller, A. 1986. 'Agone Christiano (De)', in *Augustinus-Lexikon* 1: Fasc. 1/2 (Basel) 222–7.

—. 1989. 'Die geplante Eheschliessung Augustins und die Entlassung seiner Konkubine: Kulturgeschichtlicher und rechtlicher Hintergrund von conf. 6, 23 und 25', in A. Zumkeller, ed., *Signum Pietatis: Festgabe für Cornelius Petrus Mayer OSA zum 60. Geburtstag* (Würzburg) 27–33.

Zwierlein, O. 2002. 'Augustins quantitierender Klauselrhythmus', *ZPE* 138: 43–70.

Notes

1 CONFESSION AND CONVERSION

1. Catapano (2012). **2.** Aug. *Sol.* 1.1. **3.** *Conf.* X, 1.1, 2.2. **4.** *Conf.* XII, 6.6; XI, 2.2; *En. Ps.* 44, 2. **5.** Harrison (2013) 8–9. **6.** Aug. *Simpl.* II, 4; Madec (2001a) 111–19: Aug. 'ne cite pas; il prie; il tutoie Dieu'; Aug. *Doctr. chr.* II, 26.103; Jensen (2014) 555, on prayer positions; Lamcel (2002) 213–7 is valuable. **7.** *Conf.* IX, 10.25. **8.** Knauer (1955); Poque (1986) 155–66. **9.** *Test. Reub.* 5.3; Bickerman (1988) 204–10. **10.** *SEG* 57 (2007) 1378. **11.** Paulus (2003) 688–9; Herondas 5, 27, with W. Headlam's excellent note, ad loc.; Nock, *Gnomon* 15 (1939) 19 n. 3. **12.** Petr. *Sat.* 75; 130, 1–2; Schmeling (1994/5) 207–24; Schmeling (2011) xxvi; Belayche (2006) 65–81; *SEG* 56 (2006) 2128, with excellent notes; De Hoz (2006) 19–144. **13.** M. Aurel. *Med.* 1, 17, esp. 1, 17.6; Hadot (1998) 277–88. **14.** Pl. *Resp.* 515D–16D; Sen. *Ep.* 6, 1–7. **15.** Aubin (1963) 26; Madec (1994a) 1282–94. **16.** Aug. *S.* M 51 = D. 19, 12, with Dolbeau (1996) 165–7 and Klöckener (1994) 1280–82; *Conf.* I, 6.7 and Aug. Ps. 70, 20; *Conf.* XII, 3.4; Vannier (1997). **17.** Le Blond (1951); Geerling (1987) 195–208. **18.** Nock (1933) 7; Tanaseanu-Döbler (2008) 16–26 surveys many alternatives. **19.** Edward Gibbon, *The Decline and Fall of the Roman Empire*, vol. 2, ed. C. Dawson (London, 1910) 413 and n. 4. **20.** Charles Kingsley, *Hypatia* (London, 1896) 237. **21.** Gore Vidal, *Julian* (London, 1964) 3. **22.** Baron (1985) 1–19. **23.** Monk (1991) 282, 366.

2 WORLDLY AMBITIONS

Brown (2012), Brown (2000c), Clark (1993), Brown (2002) and Harper (2011) study social divisions of the rich, not so rich, women, poor and slaves. Lepelley (1979–81) is essential on the continuing vigour of many north African cities, a nice pair for Kreikenbom (2012) on Cyrene and Ptolemais. Dossey (2010) draws a picture of north Africa which I do not altogether share. Cyrene is also studied in Schmitt (2001) with full bibliography and in Roques (1987), though his general conclusions have been challenged. Liebeschuetz (1985) looks at the *curiales* usefully through Synesius' letters. Antioch is well served by Liebeschuetz (1972) and, among others, by Matthews (2006), Kondoleon (2005), the studies in Sandwell and Huskinson (2004), and the texts translated by Norman (2000). Sandwell (2007b) gives a view of 'religious identity' in Antioch. After the many stirring studies by Frend, some of which are collected (1988), the 'Donatist' world can be entered with Tilley (1997) and is surveyed most recently by Evers (2011) and by Shaw (2011). Evers (2010) relates it to the plebs in the cities. Burns and Jensen (2014) give a richly illustrated and detailed survey of north African Christianity across the centuries.

1. *Conf.* I, 5.5 **2.** Evers (2010) 39–40 on cities' titles; Mattingly and Hitchner (1995) 165–213, esp. 199–200; Lepelley (2001) 85–104. **3.** Aug. *Acad.* I, 2; Lepelley II (1981) 178–82; Erfurt Sermon IV, 6, ed. Catapano. (2012) **4.** Chastagnol and Duval (1974) 87–118. **5.** Dunbabin (1978) 119–21; Brown (2012) 194 and 239. **6.** Kotula (1988) 339–44; *Vita Melaniae* 21. **7.** Aug. *S.* 356, 13; *Ep.* 126, 7; Lancel (2002) 6–7. **8.** Aug. *Ep.* 10*, 6. **9.** Lib. *Or.* 28, 13–14; 1, 225; Brown (1992) 29–31, 53–5. **10.** Lib. *Or.* 1, 2–4; 11, 158–62; 19, 45–6; 20, 18–20; Liebeschuetz (1972) 42–51. **11.** Syn. *Ep.* 41, 240; 113, 17; Roques (1987) 127–33. **12.** Roques (1987) 387–400; Cameron and Long (1993) 16–17; Schmitt (2001) 146–78; Kreikenbom (2012)1–34. **13.** Liebeschuetz (1972) 92–6. **14.** Lib. *Or.* 1, 144; 11, 178. **15.** Lib. *Or.* 11, 196–202, esp. 201; 44, 21, on the levy for the poor. **16.** Lib. *Or.* 49, 8; Liebeschuetz (1972) 182–6; Roques (1987) 133–4. **17.** Kondoleon (2000) 8 and 114–15. **18.** Downey (1945) 279–86; Petit (1955) 142, 382. **19.** Lib. *Or.* 53, 6–26; Festugière (1959) 198–210. **20.** Hollmann (2003) 67–82. **21.** CIL VIII, 12508; cf. 12504–10. **22.** *Conf.* X, 4.5. **23.** Jo. Chrys. *PG* LVIII, 630; Brown (2002) 14–16. **24.** Lib. *Or.* 7, 1. **25.** Jo. Chrys. *PG* LX, 547; Aug., *S.* 25, 8; Brown (2002) 64, 94–6. **26.** Finn (2009) esp. 147–50; Erfurt Sermons II–IV, esp. IV, 1 and V, 8, ed. Catapano (2012); *Conf.* VI, 6.9. **27.** Aug. *Ep.* 10* (Dijvak) of AD 428, with Harper (2010) 610–38 and (2011) 92–5. **28.** Lib. *Or.* 25, 66–7. **29.** de Sainte Croix (1975) 1–38; Harper (2011); Syn. *Ep.* 145; cf. Lib. *Ep.* 567. **30.** Aug. *Civ.* XIX, 15; Garnsey (1996) 84 n. 9 and 206–19. **31.** Millar (2007) 155–80, a fundamental study. **32.** Lepelley (2005b) 117–41. **33.** Lepelley (2005a) 29–42, esp. 31. **34.** Frend (1942) 188–91. **35.** *Cod. Theod.* XVI, 10.18; Aug. *S.* 25; Shaw (2011) 225–32. **36.** Braun (1998) 142–71, an excellent survey; Lib. *Ep.* 974, 1098, 1105 and others translated in Stern (1980) 580–99; Wilken (1983) 58–62. **37.** Fredriksen (2008). **38.** Shaw (2011) 66–194; Evers (2010) 137–206; Frend (1988); Tilley (1996). **39.** Michel (2005) 67–108 is especially important, with Laporte (2010) 73–92, refuting Marec's, 'Basilica of Peace' at Hippo **40.** Tilley (1997) 170, with 148–51. **41.** Bochet (1982) 284–97. **42.** Eck (1983) 266–95. **43.** Ward-Perkins and Goodchild (2003) esp. 5–13 and 6 n. 5. **44.** Aug. S. 361.11 on dung; Syn. *Ep.* 148, 78–129; Schmitt (2001) 299–304. **45.** Syn. *Ep.* 5; Schmitt (2008) 246–50 for the dating problems. **46.** Syn. *Ep.* 5, 255; Xen. *Anab.* I, 5.3. **47.** Greg. Naz. *PG* XXXVII, 993–4; XXXVII, 1038–9; McGuckin (2001) 49–53; Paulinus, *Ep.* 49 and

Carm. 24, 95–8; Ambr. *De. Exc. Fratr.* 1.43–8. **48.** Syn. *Ep.* 5.123–4. **49.** Aug. *En. Ps.* 32, 2.8 and 99, 4–10; Getty (1931); MacCormack (2001) 219–37; Aug. *Ep.* 7, 6.

PART I

3 INFANCY, ORDER AND SIN

Rigby (1987) is essential on the allusions to original sin in *Conf.* I, against Sage (1967), who tried to limit them to bodily mortality. Starnes (1975), Dombrowski (1980) and Wills (2001) comment in varying detail, and most recently Napier (2013) relates Augustine to Stoic patterns of thinking which do not seem to me to be pertinent. Cipriani (1997b) argues well that Augustine held a 'traducianist' view of the transmission of original sin in the 390s.

1. *Conf.* I, 6.8. **2.** Reinhardt (2008) 127–40; Napier (2013) 165–212. **3.** *Conf.* I, 6.7, with the implicit disapproval of Aug. *En. Ps.* 49, 22. **4.** Aug. *Tract.* 12, 3; van Bavel (1997) 251–90. **5.** Aug. *En. Ps.* 120, 12. **6.** *Conf.* I, 7.11; *Adn. Iob* 14, 4–5. **7.** Rigby (1987) 29–46 is correct, here with *Conf.* I, 7.11–12. **8.** *Conf.* I, 7.12; Rigby (1987) 33–8. **9.** Cypr. *Ep.* 64, 5; *De Hab. Virg.* 23; Aug. *De Sacr.* III, 1.7, and *De Myst.* 7, 32. **10.** Latham (1982) 96–103; *Conf.* I, 11.17. **11.** *Conf.* I, 8.13. **12.** Wittgenstein (1953) para 32; Burnyeat (1967) 1–24; Kirwan (2001) 186–204. **13.** O'Daly (2001b) xii. **14.** *Conf.* I, 6.1. **15.** *Conf.* I, 6.10. **16.** Auerbach (2003) 71; *BA* 13.215–17.

4 FAMILY SCARS

Clark (1994) discusses children in patristic sources and Shaw (1987) takes a forceful line on fathers. Studies on Monnica proliferate, but Mandouze (1969) and Holte (1994) are still valuable points of entry to Monnica in the dialogues and their relation to our other impressions of her. Brown (2012) 150–52 takes a similar view to mine of Augustine's remarks about his 'modest 'origins and puts them very well in context; Frend (1942) provokes thought.

1. *Conf.* II, 3.6. **2.** *Conf.* IX, 9.20. **3.** Schroeder (2004) 413–42. **4.** Lepelley (1987) 99–117. **5.** *Conf.* II, 3.5. **6.** *Conf.* IX, 12.30; X, 3.4. **7.** Frend (1942) 188–91. **8.** Marrou (1978) 177. **9.** *Conf.* V, 8.15; VI, 13.23. **10.** *Conf.* IX, 8.18. **11.** *Conf.* IX, 9.19. **12.** Holte (1994) 293–316; Conybeare (2006) 64. **13.** Lib. *Or.* 1, 13. **14.** *Conf.* III, 12; Dulaey (2003b) 215–32. **15.** *S. dom. mont.* II, 2.7; Brown (2000a) 224 n. 2. **16.** *Conf.* III, 4.8; Aug. *Acad.* II, 5: '*pueris insita est et medullitus implicata*'; Lamirande (1963) 221–34 is important, with his entry, 'Fidelis', in *Augustinus-Lexikon*. **17.** *Conf.* I, 11.17. **18.** Aug. *Cat. rud.* 7.11. **19.** *Conf.* I, 11.7; Matt. 23.9; Madec (2001a) 22. **20.** Fredriksen (1978) 206–27. **21.** Rebecca West, *St Augustine* (London, 1933) 34. **22.** Aug. *Ep.*

3. **23.** *Conf.* I, 11.18; Aug. *Ep.* 2*, 2–7; Harmless (1995) 47–61. **24.** *Conf.* II, 3.7. **25.** *Conf.* II, 3.8. **26.** Lib. *Or.* 1, 4. **27.** Tomlin (2012) 56–68; Ausonius, *Proem* 5, 23. **28.** Aug. *S.* 37, 6.7; *BA* 14.552; Hunter (2003a) 63–85, esp. 73–85.

5 'SO SMALL A BOY, SO GREAT A SINNER . . .'

Vössing (1997) is most meticulous about the dates and details of education in the Latin West, especially Augustine's own. Cribiore (2007a) is essential reading on Libanius' school, Kaster (1988) on grammar teachers. Müller (2003) is the fullest collection of material on Augustine and Virgil. Rebecca West (1933) 40 already claimed that 'certainly he confesses to homosexual relationships', but Soble (2002) corrects such certainty and is judicious on the heavily ploughed battleground of Augustine's early sexuality.

1. Aug. *Ps. c. Don.* 21, 14. **2.** Booth (1979) 1–14. **3.** Dionisiotti (1982) 83–125. **4.** *Conf.* I, 13.20–17.27; Fredouille (1993a) 74–9. **5.** O'Meara (1968) 307–26 and (1988) 30–43; MacCormack (1998); Müller (2003). **6.** Aug. *Acad.* II, 4.10. **7.** *Conf.* IX, 9.19; Virg. *Aen.* 7, 53. **8.** Aug. *Doctr. chr.* IV, 10.24; Adams (2013) 48. **9.** Cameron (2011) 591–4 on 'infallible Virgil', Kaster (1984) 457–8; cf. Aug. *Ord.* II, 12.37. **10.** *Conf.* I, 17.27; Virg. *G.* 2.60; Rousseau (1999) 172–87, for similar language in Jerome; Springer (1989) 337–43; Aug. *S.* 105.7. **11.** *Conf.* I, 13.20–21. **12.** Aug. *Ps. c. Don.* 14, 3; Virg. *Aen.* VI, 730–33. **13.** Aug. *Ep. Rm. inch.* 3; *Ep.* 104, 3; 137, 12; 258, 3; *Ps. c. Don.* 10.27. **14.** Knauer (1955) is essential. **15.** *Conf.* I, 16.26; Suet. *Vita Terent.* 2. **16.** Cain (2013b) 407–12, esp. 411. **17.** Brown (2000a) 23. **18.** Aug. *Beat. v.* 1, 4. **19.** *Conf.* I, 19.30; *Gn. litt.* X, 13.23. **20.** Ferrari (1974) 1–14; De Bruyn (1999) 249–90. **21.** Lib. *Or.* 2, 20, but also *Ep.* 555, *Or.* 62, 6, *Ep.* 1330; Booth (1973) 107–14. **22.** Garzya and Roques (2000) L–LXX. **23.** Lib. *Or.* 2, 49. **24.** Lib. *Or.* 1, 4–5. **25.** Marinescu, Cox and Wachter (2007) 101–14, with Lib. *Ep.* 1255–6, but they doubt the identification. **26.** Lib. *Or.* 38, 8–11, 58; Laes (2011) 113–22. **27.** Aug. *Ep.* 16. **28.** Aug. *Ep.* 17; Horn (1998) 194–8. **29.** Walsh (1988) 83–5.

6 UNFRIENDLY FRIENDSHIP

Le Blond (1950) 56–88 and Bochet (1982) 78–84 are acute studies of the pear theft; H. Heil and Christian Pirus (2013) 1508–11 give a fake 'reception history', which is hilarious even if their editor realized what they had done.

1. Lib. *Or.* 1, 5–6. **2.** *Conf.* II, 2–4. **3.** *Conf.* II, 2; III, 1.1; Verschoeren (2002) 199–240 supersedes Bonner (1962) 303–14. **4.** O'Daly (2007) 211–24 is now essential. **5.** Soble (2002) 545–69, a judicious survey. **6.** *Conf.* III, 8.15; Soble (2002) 545–69, esp. 551–63. **7.** *Conf.* III, 1.1, where I prefer 'amari'; Courcelle (1971) 141–50. **8.** Le Blond (1950) 56–88 and Bochet (1982) 78–84 are especially helpful. **9.** V. van Gogh, *Letters* (Van Gogh Museum,

2014) no. 638. **10.** Madec (2001a) 111–19. **11.** F. Nietzsche, *Briefwechsel: Kritische Gesamtausgabe* (Berlin, 1982), III, 3.34, dated 31.3.1885. **12.** *Conf.* II, 6.14. **13.** Aug. *Adn. Iob* 7.2. **14.** *Conf.* X, 4.5–6.

7 'TO CARTHAGE I CAME . . .'

On corrupting shows, *Conf.* III, 2–3, still repays careful reading as its sequence of thought is not quite what some expect. Nuttall (1996) is worth comparing, though he does not discuss Augustine. Van Bavel (1987) compares Cicero and Augustine on friendship. Lieu (2004) points to similarities in the school experiences of Augustine and Libanius. Madec and Bochet (2012) are now essential for the *Hortensius* and Augustine, as is Madec (1996b) 25–9, more briefly.

1. Aug. *Acad.* II, 2.3; *Ep.* 26 *Licentii Carmen* vv. 137–9. **2.** Quodvultdeus, G.S.13.16 (CCSL 60.220); Brown (2000a) 54. **3.** *Conf.* I, II, 1.1. **4.** *Conf.* III, 1.1. **5.** Ennabli (1997); van der Meer (1961) 46–56. **6.** Aug. *En. Ps.* 147, 7–8. **7.** Barnes (1996) 161–80; Aug. *S.* 241, 5. **8.** Webb (2006) 127–36; May (2006) 10–13, 137–9, 302–3 is excellent on mimes and Apuleius; Kehoe (1984) 89–106, on adultery mimes. **9.** Soler (2007) 47–58. **10.** Aug. *Civ.* II, 4, two goddesses, I think, despite *BA* 33.783–4. **11.** *Conf.* III, 2.3; for other Christians, Jürgens (1972) and Weismann (1972). **12.** Casella (2007) 99–112. **13.** Lib. *Or.* 1, 5. **14.** Lib. *Or.* 64; Molloy (1996); Haubold and Miles (2004) 24–34. **15.** Veyne (1999) 883–917. **16.** *Conf.* III, 3.6; Soble (2002) 545–69 is now fundamental. **17.** *Conf.* III,1.1 **18.** III, 3.5; Soble (2002) 559 n. 48. **19.** Dolbeau S.2 = M 5, 5.2.80–90. **20.** *Conf.* IV, 2.2. **21.** Lib. *Or.* 1, 278. **22.** *Cod. Theod.* IV, 6.4. **23.** Council of Toledo, canon 17; Evans Grubbs (1995) 309–16; Ambr. *De Abrah.* I, 3.19. **24.** Aug. *Nupt. et conc.* 2. 26. **25.** *Conf.* IV, 2.2. **26.** Leo Tolstoy, *Confession*, ed. and trans. P. Carson (London, 2014) 120–21. **27.** Aug. *B. coniug.* 5; Evans Grubbs (1995) 310–16. **28.** Riddle (1992) 87–100; Aug. *Mor.* II, 18.65; Coyle (2009a) 283–96. **29.** Lib. *Or.* 1, 13. **30.** Dzielska (1988) 28–43; Wintjes (2005) 71–3. **31.** Lib. *Or.* 1, 16; Greg. Naz. *Or.* 43.16; Himer. *Or.* 48.37 and 69.7; Eunap. *VS* 486; Olympiodorus F 28; Watts (2006) 43–7. **32.** Lib. *Or.* 1, 16 and 18–21. **33.** Bonner (1932) 34–44; Maltomini (2004) 147–53. **34.** Cribiore (2007b) 143–50; Watts (2015) 56 and 240 nn. 132–8. **35.** Quiroga (2007) 31–42. **36.** Syn. *Ad Paeon.* 3 (Budé edn, 2008); Lib. *Ep.* 1105. **37.** Zwierlein (2002) 43–70; Borromeo Carroll (1940). **38.** Lepelley (2001) 149–60; Winterbottom (1982) 59–70. **39.** Lib. *Or.* 1, 17; Eunap. *VS* 495. **40.** Lib. *Or.* 1, 8. **41.** *Conf.* III, 4.7–8. **42.** Madec and Bochet (2012) 197–294 are now essential: the best edition remains Grilli (1962), which I cite. **43.** Griffin (1997) 1–35, the essential study. **44.** Cic. *Hort.* F 59, 59B. **45.** Cic. *Hort.* F 114. **46.** Cic. *Hort.* F 1, 91–2, 106–9. **47.** Cic. *Hort.* F 84. **48.** Cic. *Hort.* F 114. **49.** Cic. *Hort.* F 111, 80, 112, 115. **50.** *Conf.* X, 23. **51.** Cic. *Hort.* F 93, 73, 84; *Conf.* VIII, 7.17. **52.** *Conf.* VIII, 7.17. **53.** Aug. *Util. cred.* 1, 1, with O'Donnell III (1992) 44. **54.** *Conf.* III, 5.9. **55.** Aug. *Gn. adv. Man.* II, 10.13–14, and *BA*

50 (2004) 544–7. **56.** Nock (1933) 164–86. **57.** Syn. *Ep.* 137, 9. **58.** Dzielska (1988); Beretta (1993); Tanaseanu-Döbler (2008) 181–90. **59.** Syn. *Ep.* 96 and 137–46. **60.** Syn. *Hymn.* 9, 33–6; Tanaseanu-Döbler (2008) 213–24, an important discussion which, basically, I endorse. **61.** Syn. *Dion* 1, 12–15; Swain (2000) 22–5. **62.** *Conf.* III, 6.1; already in *Duab. an.* 9, 11.

PART II

8 APOSTLE OF CHRIST

Lieu (1994), Gardner and Lieu (2004) 1–45 and Lieu (2010) study Mani's life and mission: Sundermann (2009) is an essential complement, using unfamiliar east Iranian sources. Tardieu (2008) and now Gardner, BeDuhn and Dilley (2015) also warn against treating every detail in the *CMC* and other sources as coherent history which we can reconcile into a true biography; the *CMC* is published by Koenen and Römer (1988) and its significance for Augustine is excellently discussed in Koenen (1978). On Manichaeism's milieu, Brown (1969) remains classic, and in the Latin West Decret (1995) is an important collection of his studies. Baker-Brian (2011) is a clear recent introduction in English.

1. Dodge II (1970) 987 ff.; de Blois (2005) 37–45. **2.** Tardieu (2008) 2–3; Dodge II (1970) 773–4. **3.** Tubach and Zakeri (2001) 272–86. **4.** *CMC* 3.1–12. **5.** Lieu (1994) 83–4; Luttikhuizen (1985) 169. **6.** *CMC* 96.8–97.18; Stroumsa (1999a) 405–20; Luttikhuizen (1985). **7.** *CMC* 22.2–13. **8.** Markschies (2003); Drecoll and Kudella (2011) 53–8. **9.** *CMC* 65.4–12 (the 'Letter to Edessa'). **10.** *CMC* 31.1–10. **11.** Sundermann (2009). **12.** Funk (2009) 121. **13.** Sundermann (1997) 647–56, more cautious, even, than Stroumsa (1992) 299–327 and (1999a) 417–20; *CMC* 98.9, for Mani's father as 'housemaster'. The 'monasteries' in Funk (2009) 120 are still of uncertain identity. **14.** Gardner and Lieu (2004) 109 and 266, for trans. **15.** Lieu (2006) 519–28, with trans. **16.** Moriyasu (2011) 339–60, esp. 360; above all, Yoshida (2015) 389–98. **17.** *Keph.* no. 76.187, trans. in Gardner (1995) 195. **18.** M3, in Henning (1942) 949–50, trans. in Gardner and Lieu (2004) 84. **19.** *Hom.* 59.1–10, trans. in Gardner and Lieu (2004) 87, on the weeping women; Psalm 226, 18.30–19.22, ed. C. Allberry, trans. in Gardner and Lieu (2004) 100–101. **20.** Lieu (1994) 28 and 30. **21.** *Coll. Mos.* 15, 3, trans. in Dodgeon and Lieu (1991) 135–6. **22.** P. Rylands 469, 12–35; Ambrosiaster, *In Ep. ad Tim.* ii, 3.6–7, with 2 Tim. 3.7; Coyle (2011) 79–92. **23.** Lib. *Ep.* 1253. **24.** *CMC* 66.4–20; *Acta Archel.* 65.5–6; Decret (1970) 293–4, 300–301. **25.** Aug. *C. Fort.* 3; Drecoll and Kudella (2011) 67–71; Decret (1970) 225–36. **26.** Aug. *C. Faust.* 1, 2.

9 THE LIVING GOSPEL

Ries (2011a) 23–419 gives a fascinating history of scholarship and Ries (2011b) an invaluable series of studies on Manichaean beliefs, liturgy and practice;

Puech (1949) remains inspiring and Puech (1979a) contains many of his most important studies and lectures, especially on the Manichaean meal. Sundermann (1995) 255–65 gives an alternative account of enlightenment to Puech's, using Eastern sources on the 'Light mind', which, however, is not prominent in Augustine or the Latin West. Lieu (2010) gives a valuable summary of the main teachings; articles in van Oort, Wermelinger and Wurst (2001) relate them to the Latin West and BeDuhn (2010) relates them to Augustine. Drecoll and Kudella (2011) give an excellent, but to my mind somewhat too rigorous, survey of what Augustine certainly knew. Like Feldmann (1987) 55–78, I accept that the account of Mani's cosmology and so forth which we know from Theodore bar Konai is derived from the *Letter of Foundation* which was read out and known to Hearers like the young Augustine. This important point reinforces my belief that already as a Hearer he knew the full story about the Beginning and the Middle of time. Brown (2012) 157 and n. 27 remarks in passing that in the *Confessions* Augustine implies that 'for most of the time, he had been a half-hearted adherent', but *Conf.* V 7.13 refers to a waning of his interest only after Faustus failed to answer Augustine's growing doubts. It does not refer to the years from 373 to 382. The range of young Augustine's knowledge has been reasserted decisively by van Oort (2008b), whose many articles are important and listed in my Bibliography.

1. *Conf.* III, 6.10. **2.** Gardner (2011) 79–99. **3.** Stein (2004); Decret (1989a); and Scopello (2000) 528–45, esp. 542–3. **4.** Gardner (2011) 79–99; BeDuhn (2015) 52–74 is also now important for the homogeneity of Manichaean teachings. **5.** J. Ratzinger, (1967) 22. **6.** Secundin. *Ep.* 3; van Oort (2001) 161–73. **7.** Stroux (1931) 106–18. 8 Aug. *Retr.* I, 22.1. **9.** Aug. C. *Fel.* I, 14 and II, 5.1; *Nat. b.* 44. **10.** *Conf.* III, 12.21. **11.** P. Kell. Copt. 19, ed. Gardner, Alcock and Funk (1999) 160; van Oort (2008b) 465 n. 106. **12.** Scopello (2001) 205–29; Aug. *C. ep. fund.* 3, 3. **13.** Coyle (2001) 43–56, decisively answered by van Oort (2008b) 441–66. **14.** Aug. *C. Fel.* 1, 9. **15.** Markschies (2003); Lieu (1985) 37–54. **16.** Dubois (2011) 199–210. **17.** Baker-Brian (2011) 15–24. **18.** Aug. C. *Faust.* 15, 5–6. **19.** Aug. C. *Faust.* 15, 6. **20.** Aug. *C. ep. fund.* 13: '*supra lucidam terram*'; *Conf.* IV, 16.31. **21.** Aug. *C. ep. fund.* 15. **22.** Puech (1979b) 103–51. **23.** *Conf.* III, 6.11; van Oort (2008b) 450 nn. 30–31 suggests '*imaginari*' at III, 6.10 alludes to 'pictures', which I doubt; Aug. *C. Faust.* 20, 10 denies the use of pictures in the West. **24.** Aug. *C. ep. fund.* 32. **25.** Coyle (2009a) 65–88. **26.** 1 Tim. 6.15–16. **27.** Aug. *Mor.* II, 13.1; Sundermann (2007) 137–50. **28.** Drecoll and Kudella (2011) 20–21. **29.** Aug. *C. Fel.* 1, 19; *C. Faust.* 15, 5 (the Aeons); *Keph.* 9, trans. in Gardner (1995) 43–7. **30.** Ps. 223, 10.3–4, ed. C. Allberry, trans. in Gardner and Lieu (2004). **31.** *Keph.* 9.39–40, trans. in Gardner (1995) 44–5. **32.** Gardner (2011) 79–99. **33.** Gardner (2011) 79–99. **34.** Schipper (2001) 195–204; *Conf.* XIII, 15.16, 18.22; Aug. *En. Ps.* 93, 5–6; and above all Bochet (2004), who does not, however, explore the contrary Manichaean imagery. **35.** BeDuhn (2010) 99; Madec (1995) 291–308. **36.** Aug. C. *Faust.* 15, 5; Lieu

(2010) xv–xvi nn. 40–42; Tardieu (2008) 84–5. **37.** Aug. *Nat. b.* 44. **38.** Aug. *Haer.* 46, 8. **39.** Theodore bar Konai, ed. A. Scher (1912) 311.20–318, with Cumont (1908). **40.** *Conf.* XIII, 30.45. **41.** Aug. *C. ep. fund.* 12. **42.** Aug. *Nat. b.* 46; *Haer.* 46 ('Saclas'). **43.** Aug. *Nat. b.* 46. **44.** *Keph.* 56–7 and text trans. in Gardner and Lieu (2004) 228. **45.** Reeves (1992); Stroumsa (1984) 153–65; Reeves (1996) 67–109. **46.** Puech (1979a) 287–9; Sundermann (1995) 255–65 points to a rather different role for Light Nous, however. **47.** Reeves (1992). **48.** Theodore bar Konai, Lib. *Schol.* XI.318, trans. in Gardner and Lieu (2004) 17. **49.** Aug. *C. ep. fund.* 11. **50.** Stroumsa (1999b) 282–91, but see van Oort (2010) 505–46 at 525; Aug. *Haer.* 46, 19 cites 'two minds', not 'souls'. **51.** Secundin. *Ep.* 2. **52.** Dodge II (1970) 785. **53.** Puech (1979a) 26–7. **54.** Aug. *C. Faust.* 20, 2 and 32, 7; *Conf.* IX, 13.35; *En. Ps.* 140, 12; Rose (1979) 89–103 on Coptic and Syriac sources, importantly. **55.** Wroe (2011) 223. **56.** *Keph.* 83, 202–4, trans. in Gardner (1995) 210–12. **57.** Pedersen (1996); Gardner and Lieu (2004) 221–6. **58.** Ogden (1930) 102–5; Dodge II (1970) 783 cites Mani himself here. **59.** Aug. *Haer.* 46.19; Koenen (1986) 285–332; Gardner (1993) 257–73. **60.** Aug. *Nat. b.* 42; *C. Fel.* 2, 16; *Haer.* 46, 19; Bennett (2011) 427–40.

10 BECOMING MARTHA

BeDuhn (2000) reassesses the Elects' meal and related practices and BeDuhn (2013b) revisits the issue of 'confession'. Ries (2011b) 139–211 is a valuable survey of Manichaean 'daily life'. Brown (2008) is important on the *Kephalaia* and on alms for the dead. Chadwick (1990) and Feldmann (1995) are excellent studies of the sect's attraction for Augustine.

1. Brock (1973) 1–19. **2.** Luke 10. 38–42. **3.** Stein (2004) 1; Coyle (2009a) 173–86. **4.** Aug. *Mor.* II, 10.19; Sims-Williams (1985) 573–82; Coyle (2009a) 283–96, with Aug. *Mor.* II, 18. 65. **5.** Aug. *Duab. an.* 6, 8; Lieu (1981) 153–75, at 161 n. 4. **6.** *Conf.* III, 10.18; Aug. *C. Adim.* 17, 6. **7.** Sims-Williams (1985) 573–82. **8.** *Keph.* 80, 193, trans. in Gardner (1995) 202. **9.** P. Kell. Copt. 31; Brown (2008) 148–9; BeDuhn and Harrison (1997) 33–87. **10.** Colditz (2009) 73–99; Henning (1942) 146–64. **11.** BeDuhn (2000) 127–62. **12.** BeDuhn (2013b) 271–300, an excellent up-to-date study, but individual confessions in the West are still not attested; Aug. *Ep.* 236, 2 is the nearest source. **13.** Asmussen (1965); BeDuhn (2013b) 271–300. **14.** P. Rylands 469, 25–8. **15.** Ries (2011b) 179–89, (1976) 218–33 and (1980) 375–90; Puech (1979a) 389–94; Sundermann, in *Encyclopedia Iranica*, s.v. 'Bēma', is also important. **16.** Bema Ps. 227.4 for roses and Aug, *Mor.* II, 16.39 for violets. **17.** Aug. *C. ep. fund.* 8. **18.** *CMC* 37.1; 39.4–13. **19.** Secundin. *Ep.* 2. **20.** Puech (1979a) 169–78 is essential; Aug. *Duab. an.* 14, 22; *Conf.* X, 30.92; 38.63. **21.** Puech (1979a) 238–41; Aug. *En. Ps.* 40, 2; *C. Faust.* 20, 11. **22.** Aug. *Haer.* 46, 9; *Nat. b.* 44–7; *Mor.* II, 66. **23.** Aug. *Haer.* 46, 9–10; Drecoll and Kudella (2011)

171 n. 156. **24.** *Keph.* 81, trans. in Gardner (1995) 203–4. **25.** *Keph.* 65, 163, trans. in Gardner (1995) 172. **26.** Aug. *C. Faust.* 20, 21; *C. Faust.* 5, 10, and *Haer.* 46, 12; *Haer.* 46, 12 and *C. Adim.* 12. **27.** *Keph.* 151, trans. in Gardner and Lieu (2004) 266. **28.** *Conf.* III, 10.18. **29.** Aug. *C. Faust.* 13, 1; *Keph.* 9; Gardner and Lieu (2004) 261. **30.** Aug. *C. Faust.* 3, 1. **31.** Aug. *C. Faust.* 30, 4; Coyle (2009a) 123–6; the Acts by 'Leucius' may be the 'Acts of John': 124 n. 10. **32.** *Conf.* III, 11.19–20. **33.** Gardner (2011) 79–99 **34.** Gardner (1995) xvii; Tardieu (2008) 52–3. **35.** *Keph.* 38, trans. in Gardner (1995) 94–5. **36.** *Keph.* 85, trans. in Gardner (1995) 222–3. **37.** *Keph.* 88, trans. in Gardner (1995) 227. **38.** *Keph.* 93, trans. in Gardner (1995) 242–4; *Keph.* 92, trans. in Gardner (1995) 241–2; *Keph.* 115, trans. in Gardner (1995) 277–8, with Brown (2008) 150–51. **39.** *Keph.* 91, 233, trans. in Gardner (1995) 240; Brown (2008) 145–58, an essential study. **40.** *Keph.* 90, 224, trans. in Gardner (1995) 232–3. **41.** *Keph.* 90, 225, trans. in Gardner (1995) 233. **42.** O'Donnell (2005) 47.

11 SELLING LIES FOR A LIVING

Sandwell (2007a) surveys Libanius' social networks in their wider context. Bouton-Touboulic (1999) is the best close reading of *Conf.* IV's difficult chapters on death, friendship and the presence of God. Van Bavel (2003) 41–70 gives an excellent and wide-ranging survey of Augustine's remarks about friendship from 386 onwards.

1. *Conf.* IV, 1.1; Ps. 26.6. **2.** *Cod. Theod.* XVI, 5.3. **3.** Aug. *Ep.* 93, 13. **4.** *Conf.* IV, 2.; Winterbottom (1982) 59–70. **5.** *Conf.* IV, 16.28; Lössl (2012); *Conf.* XII, 29.40. **6.** Apul. *Flor.* 20, 1–4; Vössing (1997) 394–5. **7.** *Conf.* IV, 16.30; Marrou (1958b) 127–57, 237–75. **8.** Shanzer (1991) 110–43; (2005) 69–112; I. Hadot (2005) 156–90, 333–73; Frend (1989) 251–60. **9.** Ferrari (1984) 18–49, esp. 40–41. **10.** Bruning (1990a) 575–643; Gury (1996) 231–59, for the image of astrologers. **11.** Adamson (2008) 265–92a; Dillon (1999) 87–92. **12.** *Conf.* V, 10.8. **13.** Aug. *En. Ps.* 140, 9; *Ep.* 246, 2. **14.** Aug. *Cat. rud.* 7, 11; *En. Ps.* 61, 25; Chadwick (1976) 191–204, with Primmer (1998) 253–62, on *En. Ps.* 61. **15.** Brown (2012) 159–60 is important. **16.** Aug. *Mor.* II, 19. **17.** Wintjes (2005) 71–3; Lib. *Ep.* 1223, 1458. **18.** Syn. *Ep.* 93 and 5.312–16. **19.** *Cod. Theod.* XIV, 9.1, with O'Donnell II (1992) 203. **20.** Lib. *Or.* 1, 26–7; 55, 15; and Kaster (1983) 57 n. 72; cf. Liebeschuetz (1985) 146–64, esp. 156, and Syn. *De prov.* 1253C, 1256C; *Ep.* 100. **21.** Aug. *Acad.* II, 2.3. **22.** Possid. *v. Aug.* 1, 2. **23.** Stein (2004) 48, on Tebessa Codex A. Col. 46. **24.** *Conf.* IV, 4.7. **25.** Schouler (1973) 63–78; Bradbury (2006) 243–61. **26.** Cic. *Att.* XII, 13–14; Treggiari (1998) 1–23, esp. 14–23. **27.** *Conf.* IV, 4.9. **28.** Cic. *Att.* XII, 15, with 12, 16, 18, 21, 23, 35. **29.** Lib. *Or.* 1.118; *Ep.* 33, with 26 and 338. **30.** Aug. *Acad.* II, 2.3; *Conf.* VI, 7.11; Kaster (1988) 106–34. **31.** Wintjes (2005) 71–3; Lib. *Or.* 1, 27. **32.** *Conf.* IV, 8.13–15.26, with esp. Bouton-Touboulic (1999) 58–69; Kotzé (2013) 107–35 sees more of a

Manichaean relevance than I do. **33.** Hübner (2011) 137–44. **34.** Syn. *Ep.* 143, 40–52. **35.** *Conf* iv, 8, 13. **36.** Lib. *Ep.* 435, 8; 354. **37.** *Conf.* VII, 2.3; Bermon (2013) 191–4; *BA* 40/A.213–27. **38.** Feldmann, Schindler, Wermelinger (1986) 245–67; *Conf.* VI, 7.11–12.21. **39.** *Conf.* IV, 5.10–13.20 **40.** Ps.-Luc. *Erot.* 47, which Augustine did not know. **41.** *Conf.* IV, 7.12. **42.** *Conf.* IV, 9.14; Lawless (1987) 75.1; van Bavel (2003) **43.** *Conf.* IV, 10.15; Job 38. 11. **44.** *Conf.* IV, 12.19. **45.** *Conf.* XII, 18.27; XIII, 9.

12 GUIDED ENCOUNTERS

Mandouze (2013) 347–62 traces a thoughtful way through *Conf.* V. Madec (1995) 291–308 and Bouton-Touboulic (2004) study providence and hidden order. BeDuhn (2010) 106–34 studies Faustus, but credits him with an 'idiosyncratic synthesis of skepticism with Manichaeism' (130) which I cannot see. Van Oort (2011) reviews the book with valuable comments. Madec (1996b) 31–6 discusses 'multa philosophorum'.

1. *PLRE* 1 (1971) 427–8 (Hesperius 2) and 887–8 (Thalassius 3). **2.** *Conf.* IV, 13.20. **3.** *Conf.* IV, 14.21. **4.** *Conf.* IV, 13.20–15.27; Cic. *De or.* III, 74, 205, 232. **5.** Solignac (1958) 113–48; Katô (1966) 229–40; Fontanier (1989) 413–21; *BA* 13 (1992) 660–72; *Conf.* IV, 15.24–5. **6.** Riedweg (2005) 82–90; Syn. *Hymn.* 1, 174–6; 2, 60; 2, 117–19; O'Donnell II (1992) 257–8. **7.** Riedweg (2005) 36–7 and Plut. *Mor.* 945 A–B. **8.** *Conf.* VI, 7.11–12. **9.** Klingshirn (2001) 219–23. **10.** Aug. *Gn. litt.* XII, 22.45; Klingshirn (2001) 22. **11.** *Conf.* III, 7.12. **12.** *Conf.* IV, 3.5–6; VII, 6.8; Vössing (1997) 282, 491, 525–33. **13.** Spina (1960) 239–43. **14.** Cameron and Long (1993) 44–9 is essential; Beretta (1993) 129 for the ultimate mystical aim. **15.** Syn. *Ad Paeon.* 5–8 (Budé edn, 2008); Deakin (2007) 102–6, 122–6. **16.** Ferrari (1984) 45–9. **17.** Aug. *Mor.* II, 8.11 **18.** *Conf.* VII, 2.3; Aug. *Ord.* II, 17.46; *Mor.* II, 12.25–6; *C. Fort.* 7, 8, 15, 20, 22, 28. **19.** Aug. *Mor.* II, 19.68–72. **20.** *Conf.* V, 33–VII, 13; BeDuhn (2010) 106–34. **21.** BeDuhn (2010) 110–23; van Gaans (2013) 199–227 for a survey of scholarship on Faustus. **22.** Aug. *C. Faust.* 12, 1.15, 17. **23.** Aug. C. *Faust.* 5, 1. **24.** *Conf.* V, 7.12–13. **25.** *Conf.* V, 7.13. **26.** *Conf.* V, 5. **27.** *Conf.* V, 8. **28.** *Cod. Theod.* XVI, 7.3; I differ from BeDuhn (2010) 135–44. **29.** Aug. *C. litt. Pet.* III, 25.30 for the '*sententia*'; BeDuhn (2009) 85–124. **30.** *Conf.* V, 8.14; Lib. *Or.* 1, 19, 21–2, 85, 241–2. **31.** *Cod. Theod.* XIV, 9.1. **32.** *Conf.* V, 8.15; Lancel (1999) 89. **33.** O'Donnell II (1992) 307–8, also citing Virg. *Aen.* 9, 287–9, which does not seem to me sufficiently close.

13 ETERNAL ROME

Brown (2012) 93–119 and 241–72 and Cameron (2011) are masterworks on fourth-century Rome; Curran (2000) gives a useful survey; Kelly (1975) on

Jerome is taken forwards by Rebenich (2002), Williams (2008) and especially Cain (2009); Fürst (2003) is a good synthesis. I have not followed Duval's timely scepticism (1980) about Pelagius' presence in Jer. *Ep.* 50, but I have admiringly adopted Cain (2005) on Jerome, Damasus and the latent Ambrosiaster. Matthews (2010) 215–53 is especially acute on Symmachus and his letters. On Gratian and the pagan cults, I agree with Cameron (2011) 33–56 against the minimalist views which have been followed by Brown (2012) 101–9.

1. *Conf.* V, 9.16; Brown (2000) 58 is more cautious. **2.** *Conf.* V, 8.15; V, 7.13; VI, 1.1. **3.** Lib. *Or.* 1, 77–8. **4.** Lib. *Or.* 1, 188; 73, 1; cf. 1, 150. **5.** *Conf.* V, 9.17. **6.** Brown (2012) 93–6 and 110–19 are essential; Broise, Dewailly, Jolivet (1999–2000) 1–17 for the Anician palace; Symm. *Ep.* 1, 52. **7.** *Conf.* VI, 10.16. **8.** Lib. *Or.* 48, 22–30. **9.** Lib. *Ep.* 1063. **10.** Matthews (1989) 478–9, despite the controversy since; Wintjes (2005) 26 n. 40 agrees. **11.** Amm. Marc. XIV, 6.9–19, esp. 16 and 18–19; Cameron (2011) 263 n. 5 and esp. 354–60. **12.** Amm. Marc. XIV, 6.12 and 14; XXVI, 3.1–3; XXVIII, 4.15; Matthews (1989) 419–20. **13.** Aug. *C. Adim.* 24. **14.** Curran (2000) 230–36. **15.** *Conf.* VI, 8.13. **16.** Lord Byron, Letter 280, 30 May 1817 (1830 edn). **17.** Cameron (2011) 66–8, for cogent doubts. **18.** Symm. *Rel.* 28. **19.** Pietri (1986) 31–58. **20.** Diefenbach (2007) 289–329; Brown (2012) 252–3; Aug. *Ep.* 29, 10. **21.** Matthews (1989) 422–3. **22.** Zos. XVII, 8, whose truth is ably contested by Cameron (2011) 51–6. **23.** Cameron (2011) 40–51 is now essential, correcting Brown (2012) 103–8; Ambr. *Ep.* 73. **24.** Cameron (2011) 42 and n. 34. **25.** Symm. *Rel.* 3, 9; Aug. *Sol.* I, 13.23. **26.** *Epigramm. Damasiana*, ed. A. Ferrua (Vatican City, 1942) no. 42; Curran (2000) 148–57. **27.** Pietri (1986) 31–58, at 45 on the Decretal 'ad Gallos', with Duval (2005), which I follow. **28.** Jer. *C. Helvid.* 3, 9, 11, 17–18; Hunter (1993) 47–71. **29.** Kelly (1975) 1–90; Williams (2008) 30–62 and *passim* is now essential, with Newman (2009) 131–40; Cain (2005) 257–77, on Jerome's dismissal of Ambrosiaster, *via* Damasus. **30.** Salamito (2005); Lane Fox (1986) 336–40; Jer. *Ep.* 123, 10, with Brown (1988) 430. **31.** Ambr. *De Virg.* III, 1. **32.** Jer. *Ep.* 32, where I am not dissuaded by the cautionary study of Duval (1980) 525–7. **33.** Williams (2008) 280, for chronology; Brown (2012) 268–72; Jer. *Ep.* 108, 3; 33; ? 55; 108; *PL* XXVI, 556A. **34.** Jer. *Ep.* 22; *Ep.* 107, 5, for the aunt; Cain (2009) 47–58. **35.** Curran (1997) 213–29. **36.** Brown (2012) 271–2; Harries (1984) 54–70. **37.** Jer. *Ep.* 38, 4–5; 39, 3. **38.** Jer. *Ep.* 23, 1; 29, 1. **39.** *Conf.* VI, 12.21–2. **40.** *Conf.* V, 10.19; Fuhrer (1997), esp. 37–44, 404–22; Catapano (2005) 46–51 for the vexed question of *Acad.*'s sources; Fuhrer (1997) 38 and Solignac in *BA* 13.95 agree on use of Cicero's *Lucullus*, my main point here. Of course Augustine continued to read widely in scepticism until 386. **41.** Griffin (1997) 1–35. **42.** *Conf.* IX, 2.2. **43.** Aug. *Acad.* II, 3–30. **44.** *Conf.* V, 10.19. **45.** *Conf.* V, 10.20. **46.** Penelhum (1983) 287–318 on the history of 'fideism'. **47.** Sext. Emp., *Outlines of Pyrrhonism* 128. **48.** Aug. *Util. cred.* 8, 20. **49.** *Conf.* VI, 10.16. **50.** Syn. *Dion* 15; Lib. *Or.* 9, 36, 9 and 13; 43, 6–13. **51.** Lib. *Or.* 3, 6; 36, 9; 43, 6; 52, 19–20. **52.** *Conf.* V, 13.23. **53.** Brown (2012)

97–109, with n. 26 (his palace), n. 28 (Campania) and p. 97 (Africa). **54.** Matthews (1974) 58–99. **55.** Symm. *Ep.* 1, 1.5; Brown (2012) 99. **56.** Brown (2012) 100–101; McLynn (1994) 266. **57.** McLynn (1994) 159–60, 169–70. **58.** Lib. *Ep.* 1004. **59.** Amm. Marc. XIV, 6.19; McLynn (1994) 273–4. **60.** *Keph.* 38, 99, ed. Gardner. **61.** Jer. *Comm. on Ecclesiastes*, prol.; Matthews (2009) 129–46. **62.** Jer. *Ep.* 39, 6–7. **63.** Jer. *PL* XXIII, 105; Kelly (1975) 112–14. **64.** Jer. *Ep.* 45, 6, also for scriptural models; Kelly (1975) 114–15; Duval (2009) 29–40 argues convincingly that Jerome was already thinking positively about retreat from the city before 385.

PART III

14 MILAN AND AMBROSE

McLynn (1994) is fundamental, with Fuhrer (2013) on Augustine's experiences in the city, with which I have not always agreed. Moorhead (1999) is a good short introduction to Ambrose's life and writings and Brown (2012) 120–47 on his social setting. Madec (1974b) is essential on Ambrose's thought and Madec (2001b) 27–42 is a brilliant study of its key themes, with a penetratingly chosen bibliography and an empathetic understanding. Studer (1997) 569–86 gives an appreciation of Ambrose's allegory, harder for historical sceptics like myself or critics like O'Connell (1968) 156. M. Cameron (2012) 23–42 tries to establish the importance of rhetorical concepts for Augustine's response to Ambrose's scriptural preaching, but I prefer to stay with what the *Confessions* actually say. Fontaine (1992) 11–123 is an excellent entry point to Ambrose's hymns. Nauroy (2010) adds to the problems of dating Ambrose's texts to one single date of delivery. Naturally, Courcelle (1968) 93–138 remains essential, even if challenged now on many points.

1. Aus. *Ordo Orbium* 7. **2.** McLynn (1994) 266, with 222–4. **3.** McLynn (1994) 154–66; Matthews (1975) 173–80; Ambr. *Ep.* 30, 4. **4.** Lib. *Or.* 59. **5.** *Conf.* VI, 6.9; Cameron (2012) 750–53. **6.** Aug. *C. litt. Pet.* III, 25.30. **7.** Lib. I, 219; *Or.* XXII, 2; I, 232. **8.** Lib. I, 75–6; Kaster (1983) 37–59. **9.** Syn. *Hymn.* 1, 435–40, 470–73. **10.** *Conf.* V, 13.23. **11.** McLynn (1994) 53–169; Savon (1997) 51–191. **12.** Rufin. *HE* XI, 11; Paulin. *v. Ambr.* 9–11; McLynn (1994) 5–52. **13.** Jer. *Ep.* 69, 2 and 9. **14.** McLynn (1994) 69–71; Brown (2012) 123–4. **15.** Markschies (1987) 73–95 and on 'Arianism' (1995). **16.** Pietri (1986) 31–58 and for the council against Auxentius of Milan, Pietri (1976) 733–6, 791–811; Barnes (1997) 3–16 for the East; McLynn (1994) 22–31. **17.** *Conf.* VII, 19.25. **18.** I disagree with Fuhrer (2013) 17–36, at 33–5, an important study otherwise. **19.** McLynn (1994) 264–75; *Conf.* V, 13.23 ('civitati'). **20.** McLynn (1994) ii, 2–3, 124–49. **21.** Krautheimer (1983) 67–92, 141–51; McLynn (1994) 226–37; I incline to the identification of the Portiana with the site of S. Lorenzo, with McLynn (1994) 176 nn. 72–3 for the problems. **22.** Dassmann (1975) 49–68; *Conf.* VI, 2.2, the '*communicatio dominici corporis* *illic*'. **23.** McLynn (1994) 161–4. **24.** Ambr. *De Virg.* III, 37; Brown (1988). **25.** McLynn (1994) 254. **26.** *Conf.* V, 13.23; VI, 3.4; Moorhead (1999) 213; Fontaine (1976) 124–70. **27.** *Conf.* V, 14.24; Savon (1977); Madec (1974b) 52–60 and 68 n. 241, 97 n. 420 on Origen. **28.** Aug. *Ep.* 1; *BA* 40/A. 521–3. **29.** Ambr. on Ps. 118, 8.59; *Conf.* V, 14.24; VI, 4.6. **30.** Ambr. *Ep.* 2, 3, with Madec (1974b) 193–7. **31.** *Conf.* VI, 4.6, with Aug. *Gn. adv. Man.* I, 22.23; II, 26.40; and O'Donnell II (1992) 351. **32.** Moorhead (1999) 71–81, 84–7, 96–101. **33.** *Conf.* XII, 18.27–25.34. **34.** *Conf.* V, 14.24. **35.** *Conf.* V, 14.25; VI, 4, 6. **36.** *Conf.* V, 14.25; Mandouze (2013) 347–62 is an acute commentary. **37.** *Conf.* V, 14.25; Madec (1994b) 105–19 on its future importance. **38.** *Conf.* V, 14.25. **39.** Markus (1989); Aug. *Ep.* 93, 31 ff. **40.** *Conf.* V, 14.25. **41.** *Conf.* VI, 1.1. **42.** *Conf.* VI, 1.1: '*placidissime et pectore pleno fiduciae*'. **43.** Syn. *Hymn.* I, 430–73. **44.** Aug. *Ord.* II, 20.52. **45.** Aug. *Per-sev.* 20, 53. **46.** M. Williams (2012) 227–39, esp. 238–9 is most recent and interesting. **47.** *Conf.* VI, 1.1. **48.** Homes Dudden II (1935) 442–6. **49.** *Conf.* VI, 2.2. **50.** *Conf.* VI, 2.2; Rebillard (2005) 99–111, and (2009) 146–7. **51.** Aug. *Ep.* 54. **52.** *Conf.* VI, 2.2: 'saepe erumperet'. **53.** *Conf.* VI, 3.3. **54.** Aug. *Util. cred.* 8, 20; Grossi (1998) 405–62, a full survey of his relations with Ambrose. **55.** Ambr. *Ep.* 30, 4. **56.** Ambr. *Ep.* 30, with Liebeschuetz (2005) 349–51 for dating question. **57.** Ambr. *S. c. Aux.* 29–30; McLynn (1994) 173–5, 179–80. **58.** *Conf.* VI, 3.3. **59.** *Conf.* VI, 3.3; O'Donnell II (1992) 340–42, 345. **60.** Gavrilov (1997) 56–73 and Burnyeat (1997) 74–6. **61.** Madec (2001b) 40 thinks of him reading Origen on the Song of Songs. **62.** Madec (1974b) 141–66. **63.** *Conf.* VI, 3.4. **64.** Somers (1961) 105–25. **65.** Ambr. *Hexaem.* 6, 41. **66.** *BA* 50.569–70 shows Aug. *Gn. adv. Man.* used Ambrose's *Hexaemeron* already in Books 1–2, works of 388; Easter 386 was too turbulent for the *Hexaemeron* to belong there. I therefore opt for 387. **67.** Visonà (2004) 58–138 for an overview; Nauroy (2010) 41–58 for problems of several oral sermons combined in one written one; Gerzaguet (2013a) 75–84, esp. 76 n. 8 on early 'Philonian' works; Fitzgerald (2002) 79–99, esp. 79–84 on possible orality and audiences. **68.** Ambr. *Hexaem.* 6, 41. **69.** Madec (1974a) 283–308. **70.** Madec (1974b) 32–4. **71.** Brown (1988) 348–55 is important. **72.** *Conf.* VI, 4.6. **73.** J. A. Froude, *Thomas Carlyle: A History of His Life in London, 1834–1881*, vol. I (London, 1884) 291. **74.** *Conf.* VI, 5.7. **75.** *Conf.* VI, 5.8. **76.** *Conf.* VI, 4.5.

15 'TORN FROM MY SIDE . . .'

Madec (2001b) 121–84 is the French version of his essential commentary on *Conf.* VII, originally published in Italian and unmissable (Madec and Pizzolato, 1994). On the concubine, Shanzer (2002) updates previous studies and gives an invaluable close reading, and Brown (2012) 150 considers she was not in any formal sense 'his "concubine"', because Augustine lacked the sort of 'high status' that late Roman laws on this topic were designed to protect. I am less sure. Certainly, earlier marriage laws as in the *Digest* affected Roman citizens outside the highest circles and, after all, Augustine was a potential 'curialis'. Differing from Shanzer, I do not think that marriage was realistically considered an option by Augustine and this woman. Treggiari (1991) is important on the social status of concubines, though mostly in earlier evidence. Zumkeller (1989) inclines to Augustine's side, but is still a useful survey of law and attitudes. Miles (2007) is a recent avowedly feminist reading.

1. *Conf.* IX, 3.5–4.7; Aug. *Ep.* 258, 1. **2.** De Sainte Croix (1954) 33–48; John Gay, *Poetry and Prose*, ed. V. A. Dearing, vol. I (Oxford, 1974) 2, ascribed to Lord Bolingbroke. **3.** Lib. *Or.* 1, 76; Petit (1955) 179–82, for Libanius' comments elsewhere. **4.** Lib. *Or.* 1, 23 and 14, 27; 1, 126, for evil *daimones.* **5.** Cribiore (2007) 108–10 for examples. **6.** Lib. *Or.* 1, 61. **7.** *Conf.* VI, 6.9–10. **8.** Conf. VI, 11.18, with VI, 10.16; Lib. *Or.* 1, 54. **9.** *Conf.* VI, 11.19; Tomlin (2012) 57–68 **10.** Lib., Opera, vol. VIII (Foerster) 550–56; Gruber (2010) 286–99. **11.** Jer. *Adv. Jov.* 1, 47–8 uses Theophr.; Seneca, *De Matrimonio*, ed. E. Bickel (1915) 288–420. **12.** *Conf.* VI, 12.21–2; Zumkeller (1989) 27–33. **13.** *Conf.* VI, 13.23: '*iam petebam*'. **14.** *Conf.* VI, 13.23; Treggiari (1991) 134. **15.** Virg. *Aen.* 11, 581–2. **16.** Treggiari (1991) 151; *CJ* 5.1.2. **17.** *Conf.* VI, 15.25; Shanzer (2002) 151–76, esp. 159–60, arguing that Augustine used 'latus' interchangeably for the Latin Bible's 'costa' at Gen. 2.21–2. I still am unsure. At least the woman escaped the poem for her by Lammers (2007) 301–2. **18.** *Conf.* VI, 14.24; Riedweg (2005) 111–12. **19.** Aug. *Acad.* II, 1.2. **20.** *Conf.* VI, 16.26, with Solignac, *BA* 13.572 n. 1, suggesting indirect knowledge of Cicero and the others.

16 GREATER FRIENDS

Solignac, *BA* 14.529–36, on the 'Milan circle' should be followed up with Lancel, *BA* 40/A.519–21, on the problems of prosopography and, above all, Madec (1987) on the problematic notion of a Church-centred 'circle'. On the riots, Liebeschuetz (2005) updates the big bibliography, of which Lenox-Conyngham (1982), McLynn (1994) and Barnes (2000) are especially important recent items. I follow Liebeschuetz 126–7 against McLynn in not dating Ambr. *Ep.* 75A and 75 after Easter 386. However, against Liebeschuetz, I date 75A to Easter Week, 386, because 75A, 8 implies a date on Palm Sunday, as M. Zelzer also observed in *CSEL* 82.10, p. xxxiv. I therefore do not accept the chronological table for January to late March 386 given by Liebeschuetz 135 in an otherwise invaluable chart. The datings and the identity of the various 'basilicas' in the texts are famously disputed, and I cannot go here into more detail on this classic battleground. Liebeschuetz 161 gives an outline of the sites.

1. L. Tolstoy, *Confession*, ed. and trans. P. Carson (London, 2014) 132–46 and 166–9; *Conf.* VII, 3.5. **2.** *Conf.* VII, 1.1, 3.4 and 7.11; Pl. *Resp.* 381b–c;

O'Donnell II (1992) 394–5. **3.** *Conf.* VII, 4.6 and 2.3; VI, 5.7–8; VII, 3.5; VI, 4.5. **4.** *Conf.* VII, 1.1; Virg. *Aen.* 3, 233; O'Donnell II (1992) 395. **5.** *Conf.* VII, 1.2; Madec (1974b) 66–71 is the essential guide. **6.** *Conf.* VII, 5.7. **7.** Ambr. *Hexaem.* I, 8.31, with Courcelle (1968) 99–100; Madec (1974b) 71–8, again an essential study. **8.** *Conf.* VII, 3.5; Cic. *Hort.* F 112 (Grilli). **9.** *Conf.* VII, 6.8–7.10; Courcelle (1968) 262, on Firminus and Milan; Adamson (2008) reconsiders Plotinus' changing views. **10.** Lane Fox (2010) 83–96, esp. 87–8. **11.** *Conf.* VII, 7.11–8.12; VII, 1.1. **12.** Aug. *Ord.* I, 7.20; *BA* 40/A. 526–7; *Sol.* II, 14.26. **13.** Aug. *Ep.* 1, with Solignac *BA* 14.535–6 and the important note in *BA* 40/A.519–20; the son of Faltonia Proba is too young, Dunn (2008) 429–64; the consul of 379 would probably be addressed as Olybrius, not Hermogenianus; others are only possibilities. **14.** Courcelle (1968) 155–6 and (1969) 134–40; *Gramm. Lat.* (ed. Keil) VI, 583; Claud. *Panegyr. Mall. Theod.* 67–9, 84–6, 96–111; Aug. *Ord.* I, 11.31; *Sol.* II, 14.26. **15.** Aug. *Beata v.* 1, 4; Solignac *BA* 14.535 is suggestive about Celsinus, against Courcelle (1968) 158 n. 5. **16.** Dolbeau (1996a) 21–43; Claud. *Panegyr. Mall. Theod.* 70–83. **17.** *Gramm. Lat.* (ed. Keil) VI, 585; Ambr. *Hexaem.* II, 1.1. **18.** Aug. *Ep.* 118, with Bochet (1998) 49–76 and Solignac *BA* 14.536. **19.** *PLRE* 1, 900–902; Matthews (1975) 74–6, 174, 192, 214–16; Claud. *Panegyr. Mall. Theod.* 24–32. **20.** Syn. *Ep.* 101; Cameron and Long (1993) 79–80, with n. 4, the essential discussion. **21.** Syn. *Ep.* 101 and 119; Cameron and Long (1993) 82–91; Syn. *De Dono* 307B, 308A, *Ep.* 119 and 101, with Budé edn, 357 n. 33. **22.** Schmitt (2001) 113–19 unconvincingly dates Synesius' conversion to philosophy to the aftermath of the failed embassy; *contra*, correctly, Tanaseanu-Döbler (2008) 285–6; Syn. *Ep.* 140, to a '*magister militum*'. **23.** Syn. *De Dono*, *passim*. **24.** Syn. *De Provid.*, with Cameron and Long (1993) 143–398, a much-discussed work; Schmitt (2001) 304–41 for the continuing controversy. **25.** Fuhrer (2013) 17–36; Courcelle (1944) 65–93. **26.** Courcelle (1968) 106–38, a synthesis. **27.** Ambr. *Ep.* 65, 1; Courcelle (1968) 154–6, 170–74; Solignac *BA* 14.529–36, with Madec (1987) 194–205, against a 'Milan circle'. **28.** Aug. *Beata v.* 2, 16: '*docuisti*'. **29.** Madec (1974) 68–71; Nauroy (2010) 127–83, esp. 133–7. **30.** McLynn (1994) 170–86; *Cod. Theod.* XVI, 1.4; Ambr. *Ep.* 76.12 and 76.18; Nauroy (1988) 3–86 remains essential too. **31.** McLynn (2004) 235–70. **32.** *Conf.* IX, 7.15; Ambr. *Ep.* 75, 75A and 76, trans. and comm. Liebeschuetz (2005) 124–73; despite a valuable counterargument by Barnes (2000) 282–99, van Haeringen (1937) 152–8, 229–40 decisively locates *Ep.* 76 in 386. **33.** McLynn (1994) 175–9 on the Portiana; *Conf.* IX, 7.15, with Homes Dudden I (1935) 293–7. **34.** Ambr. *Ep.* 76, 1–3. **35.** Ambr. *Ep.* 75A, 33, 36; 76A, 4 (Job), 17–18 (Naboth), 11 (invisible protectors); my dating of *Ep.* 75A to March 386 is not uncontroversial, but 75A, 8, on the reading of Luke 19.31, is one of my main, considered reasons. **36.** Ambr. *Ep.* 76, 6; McLynn (1994) 189–90. **37.** Liebeschuetz (2005) 163 n. 6 for the 'basilica', whom I follow against McLynn (1994) 190–92; Ambr. *Ep.* 76, 9–13 and 14–16 (Job) and 17 (women). **38.** Ambr. *Ep.* 76, 20, where I follow McLynn (1994) 193–4. **39.** I disagree slightly with Fuhrer (2013) 26–35, an important analysis; for

Eusignius, *PLRE* I, 309–10. **40.** Ambr. *Ep.* 76, 25–8. **41.** Ambr. *Ep.* 77, 1, with McLynn (1994). **42.** Ambr. *Ep.* 77; *Hymn.* 19, in *PL* IV, 1182–3. **43.** Ambr. *Ep.* 77, 2 '*ossa omnia integra, sanguinis plurimum*', and 77, 12; Courcelle (1968) 139–53. **44.** Ambr. *Ep.* 77, 14, 18, 21, 11. **45.** Ambr. *Hymn.* 19, in *PL* IV, 1182–3, with M. Williams (2013) 108–34, an important study. **46.** Ambr. *Exhort. Virg.* 2–8; McLynn (1994) 347–50. **47.** Schmitt (2001) 347–54. **48.** *Cod. Theod.* IX, 17.7; Courcelle (1968) 145. **49.** *Conf.* IX, 7.16; contrast Ambr. *Ep.* 22, 2. **50.** Syn. *Hymn.* 1, 449–73; Courcelle (1968) 151 for a different view of an '*intellectuel individualiste*'. **51.** *Conf.* IX, 7.15 and 16.

17 PLATO REBORN

Hadot (1993) and Dodds (1960) are profound classics. The fine Loeb Library edition and translation of Plotinus by his expert, A. H. Armstrong, is best approached after reading a survey of Plotinus' thought, Rist (1967), D. O'Meara (1993) and Gerson (1999) being especially helpful. Smith (2004) and Schniewind (2005) discuss social connections, including the intended readership. Edwards (2013) is a brilliant study of the roles of text and image.

1. *BA* 14 (1962) 534–5; Fuhrer (1997) 93–4; Heidl (2003) 35–6. **2.** Respectively, Plot. *Enn.* I, 6; I, 7; I, 8; III, 2–3; then later IV, 1–5 and 7; VI, 4–5. **3.** Porph. *Plot.* 2–3 and 8; Edwards (2000); Solignac *BA* 13.682–9 is still essential, with Madec (1992) 367–92 and bibliography; O'Connell (1969) also confines the 'libri' to Plotinus; Beatrice (1989) 248–81 differs. **4.** Porph. *Plot.* 14. **5.** Plot. *Enn.* I, 6.8; III, 2.13–14 and 17; III, 3.5; Edwards (2013) 121–4. **6.** Aug. *Acad.* III, 18.41. **7.** Van Geest (2011); Kenney (2013) 16–20. **8.** Plot. *Enn.* VI, 8.15; Pigler (2002), esp. 27–36; I quote Dodds (1960) 4. **9.** Plot. *Enn.* V, 4; VI, 5.12; Dodds (1960) 3. **10.** Plot. *Enn.* VI, 8.15; VI, 7.31. **11.** Plot. *Enn.* V, 8.7; Hadot (1993) 38–9. **12.** Plot. *Enn.* III, 2.13 and 14; Hadot (1993) 3–89; Armstrong (1973) 14–16. **13.** Adamson (2008) 265–91; Dillon (1999) 87–92. **14.** Plot. *Enn.* III, 9.3 and III, 4.1. **15.** Plot. *Enn.* VI, 7.22. **16.** Plot. *Enn.* V, 2.2. **17.** Plot. *Enn.* IV, 3.13. **18.** Plot. *Enn.* I, 6.8. **19.** Pl. *Resp.* X (611d). **20.** Dodds (1960) 5–6 is essential; Plot. *Enn.* IV, 8.8. **21.** Plot. *Enn.* V, 3.3; VI, 5.7. **22.** Plot. *Enn.* VI, 9.8. **23.** Edwards (1988) 509–21; Plot. *Enn.* I, 6.8; Festugière, IV (1954) 141–258 remains classic. **24.** Dodds (1960) 6–7; Plot. *Enn.* I, 6.6; I, 2 on virtues; I, 4.13 on Phalaris. **25.** Plot. *Enn.* II, 9.18. **26.** Plot. *Enn.* I, 2.7; Hadot (1993) 70. **27.** Plot. *Enn.* V, 8.9 and II, 9.17; Hadot (1993) 36–7. **28.** Plot. *Enn.* VI, 9.9 and VI, 7.31. **29.** Pigler (2002) 55–74. **30.** Plot. *Enn.* V, 8.4; V, 5.7–8; VI, 7.34. **31.** Plot. *Enn.* VI, 9.3 and VI, 9.7. **32.** Plot. *Enn.* VI, 9.9; VI, 7.36; Porph. *Plot.* 23; Kenney (2005) 27–35 is particularly clear. **33.** Armstrong (1973) 16 on Plotinus and drugs; Plot. *Enn.* VI, 9.9. **34.** Dillon (1996) 315–35, at 324. **35.** Schniewind (2005) 51–64, on Plotinus and 'ordinary men'; Plot. *Enn.* III, 8.4; Smith (1978) 292–301.

18 INWARDS AND UPWARDS

'Contextualists' and 'perennialists' frame the modern debate about historical accounts of mystical experience, presented by Kenney (2012). Kenney (2005) and (2013) are exceptionally clear and rightly aware of the differences between Augustine and Neoplatonism, but I differ by still believing that we can recover something of Augustine's original experience (a 'perennialist', here at least) and by thinking that Augustine's words like 'erexit se' and 'pervenit ad Id Ipsum' in *Conf.* VII, 17.23 are evoking a journey which is more than intense inner contemplation. At *Conf.* VII, 10.16 I take the 'qui' with the subjunctive ('viderem') to be generic, i.e. 'such a one as to', just as in *Conf.* VII, 17.23 ('qui cohaererem'). Throughout, such points of translation and reference are crucial. From a different standpoint, Dobell (2009) is an important study, with which I have disagreed at several points, after careful consideration. Madec (1994b) 51–69 and (1996b) 37–44 are essential for the (non-)place of 'Neoplatonism' in Augustine's thought. Madec (1996b) 168 is an important correction to Courcelle (1972) on the meaning of the 'truest philosophy'. Bochet (1998) studies Augustine's own history of philosophy. Mandouze (2013) 403–82 reprints a 1954 survey which is still worth reading. Price (2006) is an acute survey of various points but sees 'not an attempt at mystical union but an intellectual ascent'. In my view, it is so, but still mystical.

1. Aug. *Acad.* II, 2.5. **2.** Justin *Dial.* 2. **3.** Courcelle (1968) 157–67; *contra*, Kenney (2005) 59–60. **4.** *Conf.* VII, 10.16. **5.** Kenney (2013) 77–88. **6.** Aug. *Acad.* II, 2.5; Fuhrer (1997) 97–8; Catapano (2001) 83–4. **7.** Plot. *Enn.* I, 6.8; I, 6.9. **8.** *Conf.* VII, 10.16. **9.** Kenney (2005) 58–61, on the cognitive aspect. **10.** Aug. *Ord.* II, 4.13. **11.** Aug. *Ord.* I, 7.20; Dolbeau (1996a) 21–43. **12.** Ambr. *De Isaac* 7, 60–61; Nauroy (2010) 119–83 on Ambrose's use of Plotinus elsewhere. **13.** *Conf.* VII, 15.21 and 17.23. **14.** *Conf.* VII, 16.22; Plot. *Enn.* V, 1.1; Kenney (2013) 21–7. **15.** *Conf.* VII, 16.22–17.23. **16.** Fattal (2007) 149–72 on Plot. *Enn.* VI, 7.31, despite O'Donnell II (1992) 437–8, who only approves 1 Cor. 15.52. **17.** Herman (2011) 127–57, at 149, citing Dostoyevsky. **18.** *Conf.* VII, 21.27; Aug. *Acad.* II, 2.5. **19.** Ambr. *De Isaac* 4, 11; Madec (1974b) 283–308. **20.** Aug. *Gn. litt.* XII and Madec (2001b) 221–39. **21.** *Conf.* VII, 14.20. **22.** *Conf.* VII, 10.16; Aug. *En. Ps.* 72.25, with Madec (2001c) 131–9. **23.** *Conf.* VII, 10.16; Madec (2000) 104–7; Zum Brunn (1978) 141–64; Madec (1978) 121–39. **24.** Aug. *Vera Rel.* 49, 97; Madec (1978) 121–39 for Augustine's predecessors and Exod. 3.14. **25.** Madec (1994b) 51–69; (2001a) 101–7; Kenney (2005) 68–72, a masterly summary. **26.** Rom. 1.20; *Conf.* VII, 17.23; Kenney (2005) 68–9. **27.** *Conf.* VII, 9.13–15. **28.** *Conf.* VII, 9.15, where I take 'inde' to mean 'from Athens'; O'Donnell II (1992) 433–4. **29.** Aug. *Ep.* 118; Madec (1974b) 61. **30.** Courcelle (1968) 137; Madec (1974b) 61–2; Ambr. *On Isaac* 8, 79; *On Noah* 8, 24–6. **31.** *Conf.* X, 40.65: 'hoc me delectat'; Madec (1994b) 137–49. **32.** *Conf.* VII, 21.27; *BA* 71.548;

Madec (2001a) 184. **33.** Aug. *S. Mainz* 62, 61 (ed. Dolbeau), with A. Cameron (2011) 791–2 on its audience.

19 SEX, AMBITION AND PHILOSOPHY

Finn (2009) is outstandingly good on asceticism in a wider sense than chastity; Brown (1988) is fundamental on sexual renunciation, with Hunter (2007) and Harper (2013) on the change from 'shame to sin'. Synesius' dream-ascents are now very clearly analysed by Tanaseanu-Döbler in Russell and Nesselrath (2014), and his ascents in the *Hymns* are examined by Tanaseanu-Döbler (2008). Ries (2011b) 413–29 surveys older studies on Augustine's 'conversion' from 'Manichaeism to catholicism' and the historical value of the *Confessions*, not the conversion, however, which Book 8 recalls. M. S. Williams (2008) is an apt reminder that Augustine was not exactly the first Christian author to interpret his life by scripture, though he also interpreted scripture by his own experiences, the major theme of Bochet (2004) 157–325.

1. Wintjes (2005) 72 and n. 87 on Plato and Libanius' writings. **2.** Lib. *Or.* 1, 173, 243–50; 18, 172–3 and 296. **3.** Julian, *Or.* 7, 228B–235; Rosen (1997) 126–46. **4.** Julian, *Or.* 7, 232a, **5.** Syn. *Ep.* 139, 33. **6.** Syn. *De insom.* 4, 4. **7.** Syn. *Hymn.* 9, 1–15. **8.** Syn. *Hymn.* 9, 120–27. **9.** Syn. *Hymn.* 1, 697–729; 1, 593–4. **10.** Syn. *Hymn.* 1, 210–21; 9, 50–70, 81–2. **11.** Syn. *Hymn.* 1, 8; 1, 164; 1, 268; Vollenweider (2005) 184–7; Tanaseanu-Döbler (2008) 231–45. **12.** Tanaseanu-Döbler (2008) 217 n. 24, 253–60. **13.** Syn. *De insom.* 6, 2; 8, 1. **14.** Cameron and Long (1993) 29–32, 50–52; Theiler (1942). **15.** J. Barnes (2011) 510. **16.** Syn. *Ep.* 105, 104; 137, 23–36; 142, 7–8; 143, 12–15 **17.** Aug. *Io ev. tr.* 38, 9; cf. *En. Ps.* 134; Courcelle (1972) 653–9. **18.** *Conf.* VII, 18.24, 19.25; O'Connell (1967); Madec (2001a) 34–7, 41–4. **19.** Aug. *Beata v.* 1.4. **20.** Lib. *Or.* 1, 243. **21.** Lib. *Or.* 1, 246. **22.** Lib. *Or.* 1, 249. **23.** Maltomini (2004) 147–53. **24.** Lib. *Or.* 1, 250. **25.** Lib. *Or.* 19–23; 1, 252–3; Browning (1952) 13–20; Wintjes (2005) 213–18. **26.** Syn. *Dion* V, 2. **27.** Syn. *Ep.* 154, 3 and 48–51, with Roques (ed. Budé) II, 423–4 n. 7. **28.** Moles (1978) 79–100, but Cameron and Long (1993) 62 and 223 are cautious. **29.** Syn. *Dion* VIII, 5–7. **30.** Syn. *Dion.* a, 6–8. **31.** Syn. *Dion.* 4, 1. **32.** *Conf.* VI, 10.17. **33.** Hunter (2003b) 131–6. **34.** Chadwick (1976) 29–31, 71–3. **35.** McLynn (1994) 60–68. **36.** Ambr. *De Virg.* I, 32 and I, 64. **37.** Ambr. *De Virg.* I, 9. **38.** Adkin (1993) 364–76. **39.** Ambr. *De Virginit.* 130; *De Virg.* I, 57. **40.** Brown (1988) 349–543. **41.** Aug. *Ord.* I, 1.4. **42.** Feiertag and Steinmann (1997) 7–33. **43.** *Consult. Zacc. et Apoll.* 3, 1, 3. **44.** *Consult. Zacc. et Apoll.* 3, 3, 5–6. **45.** *Consult. Zacc. et Apoll.* 3, 3, 10–16. **46.** *Consult. Zacc. et Apoll.* 3, 2, 1. **47.** 1 Cor. 7.1; Aug. *Acad.* II, 1.2. **48.** Damasc. F 102 (ed. Zintzen); Dzielska (1988) 50–52. **49.** *Conf.* VIII, 1.1: 'nec certior de te, sed stabilior in te'. **50.** *Conf.* VIII, 1.2.

20 INTO THE GARDEN

Bochet (2004) 265–93 and Matthews (2010) 275–90 are particularly important recent studies. Vessey (2005) goes into 'fiction and figuralism' in *Conf.* VIII and Schmidt-Dengler (1969) re rhetorical shape. Research into the conversion is surveyed in Geerling (1987), up to the 1, 600th anniversary. I do not agree with the attempted Stoic interpretation by Byers (2013), nor with the relevance of Origen, though brilliantly pursued by Heidl (2003) 1–74. Bouissou in *BA* 14. 543–6 is still excellent on the literary style of the central account. Ferrari (1984) and (1989) are clear studies, in a more fictional direction than I would accept. Asiedu (2001) reviews the issues.

1. *Conf.* VIII, 2.3; Ambr. *Ep.* 1, 2; 36, 10. **2.** *Conf.* VIII, 2.3; Madec (1974b) 200–207. **3.** Aug. *Civ.* X, 29; on 'solebamus', against Courcelle (1968) 168–74, I follow O'Connell (1973) 87–100 and Madec (1994c) 195 and 244; for the probable reference to Victorinus, not the much earlier Amelius, *BA* 34.633–4. **4.** Plot. *Enn.* V, 1.6; 3.77. **5.** Porphyr. F 432 (ed. A. Smith, 1993). **6.** Madec (2001a) 37–40, 70–71, 144; Courcelle (1963) 59. **7.** *Conf.* VIII, 2.3; O'Donnell III (1992) 12–15, with Hadot (1971); *PLRE* 1, 964. **8.** *Conf.* VIII, 2.4. **9.** *Conf.* VIII, 2.5; Cameron (2011) 218–20, for a less dramatic view. **10.** *Conf.* VIII, 5.9–10; M. S. Williams (2008) 154–63. **11.** *ILCV* 104. **12.** *Conf.* VIII, 5.12, with Bochet (2004) 224: 'ipso experimento . . . legeram'. **13.** *Conf.* VIII, 5.11, with VIII, 9.21; Rigby (1987) 69–83; Bochet (2004) 205. **14.** Matthews (2010) 275–90; *Conf.* IX, 2.2. **15.** Cribiore (2013) 62–9, with 63 n. 154 and Lib. *Ep.* 1287. **16.** *Conf.* VIII, 6.14–15. **17.** *Conf.* VIII, 6.16; M. S. Williams (2008) 163–85. **18.** Courcelle (1968) 181–7, still brilliant. **19.** Ambr. *Hexaem.* 5, 80. **20.** *Conf.* VIII, 8.19; Plot. *Enn.* I, 6.8; Bochet (2004) 270–72, on 'fiction' and truth. **21.** Matthews (2010) 275–90 is important here. **22.** *Conf.* VIII, 11.27: 'quasi diceret'. **23.** Here, Byers (2013) is not convincing: Augustine is seeing, not hearing. **24.** *Conf.* VIII, 12.28; O'Donnell III (1992) 57–8; Aug. *S.* 89, with Asiedu (2001) 91 for argument. **25.** *Conf.* VIII, 12.29; Courcelle (1968) 299–310; O'Donnell III (1992) 62–3. **26.** O'Connell (1996) 219–23; Horsfall (1995) 169–77, wondering if pagans *followed* Christian 'bibliomancy': I think our sources are defective earlier, and SHA, *Hadr.* 2, 8 uses earlier material. **27.** Van Reyn (2009) 191–225, (2010) 193–234. **28.** Aug. *Ep.* 22, 2. **29.** Aug. *Exp. prop. Rm.* 69 and 77, with O'Connell (1996) 224–7. **30.** I disagree with Fredriksen (1986) 3–34, a seminal article. **31.** *Conf.* IX, 1.1. **32.** I follow Sizoo (1958) 104–6, despite Matthews (2010) 275–90. **33.** Morgan (1995) 120: 'another phrase suggestive of the corporate Christ. It may imply a great cosmic shirt enfolding all believers rather than an individual's Van Heusen.' **34.** O'Connell (1996) 219–23. **35.** Jo. Chrys., *Hom. on Romans* 24. **36.** Aug. *Ep.* 22, 2. **37.** Orig., *Fragm. on 1 Cor. xxxix* (ed. C. Jenkins) 510, which I owe to Brown (1988) 394 n. 30. **38.** *Com. Cant.* II, 4.28–30; Heidl (2003) 1–74, an ingenious study which has not persuaded me. **39.** Aug. *Mag.* 10, 33–11, 38.

40. Aug. *C. litt. Pet.* III, 10.29; 25.30 ('Messiani proconsularis *sententia*', the Donatists claimed); BeDuhn (2010) 191, 196.

PART IV

21 GENTLE WITHDRAWAL

Madec (1986b) is convincing on the Dialogues' historicity and the secretaries, but Conybeare (2006) still takes free composition as a starting point for her readings. Madec and Bochet (2012) and Shanzer (2005) are essential reading on the syllabus and Mandouze (2013) 363–74 on Monnica. The setting and dates are well surveyed by O'Daly (1992) in *Augustinus-Lexikon*, s.v. 'Cassiciacum', 771–81 and the history of scholarship on '*philosophia*' in Augustine is invaluably surveyed by Catapano (2000).

1. *Conf.* IX, 2.2–4; 5.13. **2.** Dulaey (2002) 267–95, at 288–9; Heidl (1999) 53–91; Heidl (2003) 93–5. **3.** *Conf.* VI, 11.20. **4.** *Conf.* IX, 3.6. **5.** *Conf.* VIII, 6.13 and IX, 3.5–6. **6.** *Conf.* IX, 2.3; X, 6.8; Aug. *Adn. Iob* 6; Demura (2013) 3–16, esp. 11–12. **7.** Aug. *En. Ps.* 119, 5; 143, 13, with *Cant.* 2, 5 and *En. Ps.* 44, 16. **8.** O'Daly (1992) 771–81, at 771–3. **9.** O'Daly (1992) 778–9; Catapano (2005) 9–10. **10.** *Conf.* VI, 14.24 and 16.26; Aug. *Ord.* II, 20.53–4; *BA* 4/2 (1997) 377–8; Madec and Bochet (2012) 197–294. **11.** Aug. *Ord.* II, 20.53–4. **12.** Madec (1986b) 207–31; Fuhrer (1997) 17–19. **13.** Aug. *Acad.* I, 1.4. **14.** Sulp. Sev. *Ep.* 3. **15.** Aug. *Beata v.* 1, 1–4; *Ord.* I, 11.31. **16.** Aug. *Ord.* I, 1.1; 2.4; 7.20; 9.27. **17.** Aug. *Acad.* I, 1.1–2; II, 1.1–3.9; 7.18. **18.** Aug. *Retr.* Prol. 1. **19.** Trout (1988) 132–46 and esp. Cameron (2011) 398. **20.** *Conf.* IX, 2.4 and 5.13; Aug. *Beata v.* 1, 4; *Ord.* I, 2.5; *Acad.* I, 1.3. **21.** *Conf.* IX, 4.7. **22.** Aug. *Beata v.* 1; *Acad.* I, 1. **23.** Aug. *Acad.* I, 1.1; Bouton-Touboulic (2004) 248–51. **24.** Aug. *Ord.* I, 11.31. **25.** Aug. *Ep.* 1 and 2. **26.** Aug. *Acad.* I, 1. **27.** Aug. *Acad.* II, 1.1–3.9.

22 VILLA LIFE

Among modern commentaries on the Dialogues, Doignon (1986) on *Beata v.* in *BA* 4/1 and (1996) on *De Ordine* in *BA* 4/2 are essential, with Fuhrer (1997) on *Acad.* II and III and especially now Catapano (2005) on the whole work. Kirwan (1983) and (1989) are essential on the validity, or otherwise, of Augustine's philosophical arguments. O'Connell (1996) is challenging on the 'Confessions at Cassiciacum' and Cipriani (1994) is the most thorough study of Christian thought in the Dialogues, even if I find it hard to believe Augustine had already had access to as much in writing as Cipriani's search for sources requires. Beierwaltes (1981) is most helpful on the idea of happiness, as is van Bavel (1995) on the body, while C. Harrison (1992) and (2006) discuss beauty, divine grace and free choice. Madec (1996b) 45–52, (2000) 67–71 and (2001a) 46–8 and 69–71 are brilliantly terse presentations of the topics, with valuable selected bibliographies.

1. *Conf.* VII, 20.26; Massignon (2001); Hourani (1991) 116–28, a brilliant essay. **2.** Aug. *Acad.* I, 15; *Ord.* I, 9.26; Cameron (2011) 463–4 and 625–6. **3.** Madec and Bochet (2012) 197–294, at 220–40; Aug. *Beata v.* 2.10. **4.** Aug. *Acad.* II, 4.10. **5.** Aug. *Ord.* II, 6.18. **6.** Aug. *Acad.* I, 1.3. **7.** Aug. *Ep.* 3, 2–4. **8.** Aug. *Ord.* I, 8.25–6; *BA* 4/2 (1997) 341–2. **9.** Aug. *Ep.* 26 *Licentii Carmen* v. 54. **10.** Syn. *Ep.* 11, 15; 100, 7–10. **11.** Syn. *Ep.* 148. **12.** Syn. *Hymn.* 1, 50–112, 619–20. **13.** Aug. *Acad.* I, 1.3. **14.** Aug. *Ep.* 26 *Licentii Carmen*, esp. vv. 1–15; Cutino (2000); Shanzer (2005) 69–112. **15.** I. Hadot (2005) 156–90 and 333–73; Madec (2001b) 221–39. **16.** Aug. *Beata v.* 3, 18. **17.** Aug. *Ord.* I, 3; 5.12; 7.22; 8.21; 8.24. **18.** Aug. *Beata v.* 2, 15. **19.** Aug. *Ord.* I, 3.6–8.21. **20.** Aug. *Ord.* I, 8.24. **21.** Cary (1998) 141–63. **22.** Mandouze (2013) 363–74 is still essential; Conybeare (2006) 64–92, 107–13. **23.** Aug. *Beata v.* 2, 10; 2, 11; 3, 19; 3, 21. **24.** Aug. *Ord.* I, 11.31–2. **25.** Aug. *Ord.* II, 17.45. **26.** Aug. *Beata v.* 3, 21; *Ord.* II, 7.22. **27.** Aug. *Ord.* I, 8.22–3. **28.** Aug. *Ord.* I, 10.29. **29.** Cic. *Tusc.* 4, 7–8. **30.** Marrou (1958b) 299–327; Madec (2003) 1182–3. **31.** Aug. *Beata v.* 2, 11. **32.** Aug. *Beata v.* 4, 34–6. **33.** Aug. *Mor.* I, 2 and I, 13.22 and it is indeed used by Fortunatus at Aug. *C. Fort.* 3; for Aug., cf. *Beata v.* 4, 34. **34.** Aug. *Beata v.* 3, 18. **35.** Kirwan (1989) 15–35, at 29. **36.** Aug. *Ord.* II, 20.54; Kenney (2013) 65–74. **37.** Van Reyn (2009) and (2010). **38.** *Conf.* IX, 6.14; O'Donnell (1992) 104–9. **39.** *Conf.* VIII, 12.30 and IX, 5.13–6.14. **40.** Aug. *Beata v.* 4, 35; *Conf.* VIII, 12.29; Madec (1986a) 95–9. **41.** Aug. *Ord.* II, 20.53–4; *BA* 4/2 (1997) 377–8. **42.** Aug. *Ord.* II, 11.31; 16.44; *Retr.* I, 3.2; I, 4.3. **43.** Jer. *Ep.* 127, 16. **44.** Aug. *Acad.* II, 1.1. **45.** Aug. *Acad.* III, 20.43; *Beata v.* 4, 35; *Acad.* III, 19.42. **46.** Aug. *Ord.* II, 5.16, with Madec (1970) 179–86 and (2001a) 68–9. **47.** Catapano (2000) 183–6, 234–8 helpfully summarizes the essential views of Holte (1962) and Madec, *passim.* **48.** Aug. *Beata v.* 4, 32–6; *BA* 4/1 (1986) 149–54. **49.** Van Fleteren (1973) 33–71; O'Meara (1951) 338–46. **50.** Syn. *Ep.* 105, 87–90. **51.** Syn. *Hymn.* 1, 370–400; 9, 101–36, with Tanaseanu-Döbler (2008) 213–24. **52.** Mandouze (2013) 363–74. **53.** Aug. *Ord.* II, 20.52.

23 'WATERING MY COUCH WITH TEARS'

Dulaey and others are fundamental now on the Psalms in *BA* 57/A, including 570–82 on Psalm 4, and 57/B and 57/C. Cameron (2012) 165–214 is also worth considering. Kotzé (2001) and Hattrup (2003) are valuable close readings of Augustine's Psalm 4, but not always followed in my text.

1. Ambr. *Ep.* 76, 20. **2.** *Conf.* IX, 4.8. **3.** Bouton-Touboulic in *BA* 57/A.51–79 is fundamental, with 570–73 and 577. **4.** *Conf.* VIII, 12.28. **5.** Jer. *Ep.* 127, 3; 108, 26; Brown (1988) 369. **6.** Jer. *Ep.* 39, 1. **7.** Day (1992) 53. **8.** Aug. *S. Dolbeau* 16, 6–8; *En. Ps.* 4; *BA* 57/A.179–81. **9.** Aug. *En. Ps.* 4, 2, more cautious and nuanced, perhaps, than Cameron (2012) 184 might imply. **10.** *Conf.* IX, 4.12. **11.** *Conf.* IX, 4.11; Kotzé (2001) 119–36 takes a different view. **12.** *Conf.* IX, 4.8–11. **13.** *Conf.* IX, 4.10. **14.** *Conf.* IX, 1.1. **15.** Aug. *En. Ps.* 4, 9; Solignac *BA* 14.550–52; Berrouard *BA* 71.845–8; Madec (2000) 128–31. **16.** Aug. *En. Ps.* 4, 10. **17.** *Conf.* IX, 4.12. **18.** Myres (1960) 21–36.

24 AUGUSTINE WITH AUGUSTINE

Lane Fox (2006) gives more detail on *Soliloquies*, to be supplemented by Ceresola (2001) and Stock (2012). Kenney (2013) 47–59 and 72–97 is especially helpful on the opening prayer and on the ideas of light and ascent. Bermon in *BA* 40/A, 213–29 gives an excellent survey of Nebridius and his letters, on which Folliet (1987) is essential. Russell and Nesselrath (2014) contains important essays which consider Synesius' interest in dreams and modern studies of it.

1. Aug. *Sol.* I, 1 **2.** Aug. *Sol.* I, 1. **3.** Stock (2012) 315–47. **4.** Ceresola (2001) 37–64 is excellent here. **5.** Aug. *Sol.* I, 1. **6.** Brunt (1974) 1–20. **7.** Aug. *Ep.* 3, 6. **8.** Asser, *V. Alfredi* 76; Hargrove (1904). **9.** Aug. *Sol.* I, 2.7; Plot. *Enn.* VI, 9.7; Madec (2000) 70. **10.** Cragg (1968) 75–6, 323–36. **11.** Aug. *Sol.* I, 13.23. **12.** Aug. *Sol.*I, 6.12; Porph. *Ep. ad Marcell.* 24; Cic. *Hort.* F 110 and 114 (Grilli). **13.** Aug. *Sol.* I, 9.16. **14.** Aug. *Sol.* I, 10.17. **15.** Aug. *Sol.* I, 11.18. **16.** Madec (1994c) 91–103. **17.** Aug. *Sol.* I, 14.25. **18.** Aug. *Sol.* I, 1.5. **19.** Lane Fox (2006) 173–90, esp. 181–2; Uhle (2010) 223–8. **20.** O'Daly (2001a) vii; Lefort (2013) 547–52. **21.** Lane Fox (2006) 173–90, esp. 186–7. **22.** Aug. *Sol.* I, 13.23. **23.** Bochet (1982). **24.** Madec (1996b) 15–24. **25.** Aug. *Sol.* I, 1.4–5; Kenney (2013) 47–59 is most helpful. **26.** Aug. *Ep.* 3, 1. **27.** Hadot (1967) 181–91, at 184; *BA* 40/A (2011) 530. **28.** Aug. *Sol.* I, 13.22; *Ep.* 3, 3. **29.** Aug. *Sol.* I, 13.22; Madec (1994b) 216–31.

25 BORN AGAIN

Madec (1994b) 105–19 asserts Augustine's engagement with Porphyry from November 386 until summer 387, rightly, despite the cautionary queries in Drecoll (1999) about the basic thesis of Pépin (1964). Kenney (2013) is valuable on the steps of ascent to God. Wills (2012) presents the setting of Augustine's baptism very clearly, but I do not follow him in using M. M. Colish's datings of Ambrose's treatises about the patriarchs to 387. The matter is much more complex, as Nauroy (2008) and (2010) show. On the rites and preparation Harmless (1995) 244–9 is preferable, with Jensen (2011) adding much comparative evidence.

1. Aug. *An. quant.* 31, 62–3. **2.** Madec (1986) 466–75. **3.** Madec (1994b) 105–19; Pépin (1964) 213–67. **4.** *Conf.* XI, 10.12–28.38. **5.** Aug. *Imm. an.* 3, 3. **6.** Russell and Nesselrath (2014) 97–124; Syn. *De Insomn.* 4, 136A; 15, 149D. **7.** Syn. *De Insomn.* 2, 132B; Dickie (2002) 165–74. **8.** Syn. *De Insomn.* 4, 5; 7, 3; 9, 1; Tanaseanu-Döbler (2012) 201–30. **9.** Gertz, in Russell and

Nesselrath (2014) 117–24, sees this clearly. **10.** Syn. *Hymn.* 1, 620; I disagree here with Schmitt (2001) 197–201 and prefer Cameron and Long (1993) 32–3. **11.** *Conf.* IX, 5.13. **12.** Aug. *Io. ev. tr.* 4, 13. **13.** Aug. *Mor.* I, 35.80; *F. et op.* 6, 9; Bochet (2004) 230–39 on *Conf.* XIII. **14.** Lieu (2010) 105–24 and 131–43, for such texts and practices. **15.** Ambr. *Explanatio Symboli* 1; Aug. *F. et op.* 6, 9; Harmless (1995) 79–106 and 244–96; Wills (2012) 1–16 and 85–113; Botte (1961) 7–40. **16.** Ambr. *De mysteriis* 1; Madec (1974b) 52 n. 162 on Ambrose's wish to compile 'une sorte de galerie des patriarches'; Cassiod. *Inst.* I, 5.4 and I, 6.6 for its (later) existence. **17.** Dulaey (2007) 35–64, esp. 51 and n. 111 and 62–3, two very important points. **18.** Ambr. *Explanatio Symboli*; *Ep.* 20, 4. **19.** Perrin (2008) 119–41; Perrin (2009) 737–63. **20.** Ambr. *De mysteriis* 7. **21.** Wills (2012) 3–16; Jensen (2011) 158–69, 195–8 and n. 512. **22.** Ambr. *De mysteriis* 8; *De sacramentis* II, 14. Jensen (2011) 137, on lying in the pool. **23.** Ambr. *De mysteriis* 42; *De sacramentis* III, 8–10. **24.** Ambr. *De mysteriis* 36; *De sacramentis* V, 12–13; Daniélou (1958) 240–58; Jensen (2011) 79–91; Aug. *Ep.* 55, 3 later opposes the practice. **25.** *Conf.* IX, 6.14. **26.** In *CSEL* 73 (ed. O. Faller, 1955). **27.** *Conf.* IX, 6.14. **28.** Wills (2012) 1–16. **29.** Julian, *Or.* 245C–D.

26 THE LAST DAYS OF MONNICA

Van Fleteren, Schnaubelt and Reino (1994) edit useful articles on Augustine's mysticism. Mandouze (2013) 377–402 is still the best analysis of the intertextual relations with Plotinus, but is not easy to decode. Henry (1938) remains classic.

1. *Conf.* VIII, 6.15. **2.** *Conf.* IX, 8.17. **3.** Jer. *Ep.* 45. **4.** Lancel *BA* 40/A. 519–21 weakens Brown (2000a) 121; Dunn (2009) 53–72, esp. 66–8, is more supportive. **5.** Fischer-Bossert (2001) 137–52. **6.** O'Donnell III (1992), 122–37. **7.** Pépin (1951) 155–201. **8.** Ayres (2010) 165–82; Plot. *Enn.* IV, 1.2; *Conf.* IX, 10.23–4. **9.** *Conf.* IX, 10.23–6. **10.** Aug. *S. Dolbeau* 26 = M 62, esp. 61. **11.** Plot. *Enn.* V, 1.4. **12.** Aug. *Ord.* I, 11.31 and II, 1.1; Mandouze (2013) 363–74. **13.** Vannier (2011), at 121–6. **14.** *Conf.* IX, 11.27–12.32. **15.** Plot. *Enn.* I, 4.4. **16.** Ambr. *De obitu Satyri fratris* I, 10. **17.** *Conf.* IX, 12.32; Saxer (1980) 150–52. **18.** *Conf.* IX, 13.34–6. **19.** Boin (2010) 195–209; Boin (2013). **20.** Holgate (2003) 181–206.

27 AUTHORITY AND LOVE

Dulaey (2002), (2003a) and (2005) are essential on Augustine's Christian readings in the period up to 395, as are her notes and introduction, with M. Scopello, to *BA* 50 on *Gn. adv. Man.*, a major advance in our understanding. Cipriani (1997c) is important on Augustine's early continuing use of Ambrose. Coyle (1978) adjusts one or two emphases in the still-classic study of Burnaby (1938)

85–92. Van Bavel (2003) is excellent on Augustine's ideals of friendship and community and Lagouanère (2011) on neighbours. Brown (2012) 161–72 is a brilliant study of Augustine's developing views of a community of friends, but I put more weight on Augustine's researches and hearsay in Rome about other monastic groups and less on the evidence of Plotinus and Cicero. The Manichaean *Kephalaion* 63.156 is an interesting reminder that 'love' was also considered a hallmark of the Manichaean Church and its God, as Augustine may have heard while in their company.

1. Aug. *Mor.* II, 20.74. **2.** Jer. *Ep.* 22, 13. **3.** Aug. *Retr.* I, 7.1. **4.** Ephrem, ed. and trans. Mitchell (1912). **5.** Aug. *Lib. arb.* I, 2.4 and II, 2.6. **6.** Aug. *Lib. arb.* II, 2.6; *BA* 6 (1999) 157–88 and 549–51. **7.** Dulaey (2002) 267–95, at 272–4. **8.** Aug. *An. quant.* 4, 6. **9.** Aug. *An. quant.* 1, 2–2, 3; 34, 77–8. **10.** Kenney (2013) 93–105; also Madec (1994b) 137–49. **11.** Aug. *Retr.* I, 9.1; *BA* 12 (1950) 567–8; *BA* 6 (1999) 157–62; Madec (2001b) 242–55. **12.** Madec (2001b) 242–55, esp. 250–52. **13.** Aug. *Lib. arb.* I, 1.1; Plot. *Enn.* I, 8.1; Madec (1994b) 121–35; *BA* (1999) 170–78. **14.** Aug. *Lib. arb.* II, 19.53; Bouton-Touboulic (2004) 310, 321; *BA* 6 (1999) 575–8. **15.** Aug. *Lib. arb.* II, 13.35–15.39. **16.** Aug. *Mor.* I, 7.11; *Conf.* VII, 10.16; Courcelle (1968) 52–3; Coyle (1978) 322–3. **17.** Aug. *Mor.* I, 7.11; M. Cameron (2012) 79–82. **18.** Aug. *Mor.* I, 7.12; *Sol.* II, 14.26; M. Cameron (2012) 81–2. **19.** Aug. *Mor.* I, 8.13–9.15; 26.48–28.58; Burnaby (1938) 85–92, a brilliant study, adjusted, however, by Coyle (1978) 248 n. 949, an important proviso. **20.** Plot. *Enn.* I, 2, with Aug. *Mor.* I, 19.35–28.57; *Ep.* 155, 4: 'imus non ambulando sed amando'; Coyle (1978) 345–6. **21.** Aug. *Mor.* I, 26.48–28.58, despite Nussbaum (2001) 527–56, on which see Charry (2012) 89–107. **22.** Aug. *Mor.* I, 13.23–16.29. **23.** *Conf.* XIII, 25.38–26.41. **24.** Aug. *Mor.* I, 31.65–33.73; Jer. *Ep.* 22.33–6; I differ from Coyle (1978) 208–24. **25.** Aug. *Mor.* I, 31.66. **26.** Aug. *Mor.* I, 31.67. **27.** Goehring (1986); Lane Fox (1997). **28.** *Letter of Ammon* 3–4; Goehring (1986) 160–1. **29.** Syn. *Dion* 7, 4. **30.** Syn. *Dion* 7, 1–3. **31.** Aug. *Mor.* I, 33.70. **32.** Aug. *Sol.* I, 12.20. **33.** Lawless (1987) 38–44; Aug. *Reg.* 3, 2, 8; 4, 19; 6, 2. **34.** Aug. *Lib. arb.* I, 3.7. **35.** Aug. *Reg.* 1, 2; *Reg.* 2, 4; *Reg.* 3, 1, 1–3; 1, 8; Lawless (1987) 40–44. **36.** Lib. *Or.* 30, 8.

28 SLAVES OF GOD

Van Fleteren, *AS* (2005) 452, protests that 'the translation [of *servus Dei*] as slave is tendentious and smacks of eighteenth- and nineteenth-century America. Servant is the usual translation', but, nonetheless, it is true to the force of the words in fourth-century Greek and Latin and so I have kept it. Folliet (1961) and Lawless (1987) 38–58 are essential surveys of the 'monastic' shape of Augustine's plans in this phase, also now with Brown (2012) 163–72, although I have let my slight differences of emphasis stand. Power (1995) gives a vigorous analysis of Augustine's subsequent writings on women.

1. Pacatus Drepanius, *XII Pan Lat.* (ed. Mynors) 4, 5, transformed by Turcan-Verkerk (2003), approved by Cameron (2011) 227–30. **2.** Lib. *Or.* 1, 257–8; *Or.* 32; Wintjes (2005) 232. **3.** Aug. *Civ.* XXII, 8.3. **4.** Aug. *C. litt. Pet.* III, 16.19 and 25.30; *Cod. Theod.* XVI, 5.7 and 7.3; BeDuhn (2009) 85–124; Beskow (1988) 1–11. **5.** Aug. *S.* 355, 2; *Ep.* 126, 7; Lawless (1987) 50–51. **6.** Lib. *Or.* 32; Petit (1955) 418–19. **7.** Syn. *Ep.* 93. **8.** Aug. *Ep.* 5. **9.** *Cod. Theod.* XIV, 3.18. **10.** Possid. *v. Aug.* 3, 1. **11.** Mratschek (2002) 140–62, 251–3; Brown (2000a) 169. **12.** Acts 4.32–4; Lawless (1987) 45–60. **13.** Folliet (1961) 25–44; Dearn (2004) 1–18. **14.** Aug. *Reg.* 4, 1–11; Lawless (1987) 89–93. **15.** Aug. *En. Ps.* 132, 6; *Reg.* 1, 2; *Conf.* IX, 8.17. **16.** Possid. *v. Aug.* 3, 1. **17.** Lane Fox (2014) 363–400, esp. 385–8. **18.** Syn. *Ep.* 96–9 and 137–46; *Ep.* 140, 25, with Roques, ed. (2000), 404 n. 11. **19.** Syn. *Ep.* 139, 33–7, with Roques, ed. (2000), 403 n. 22. **20.** Aug. *Ep.* 6, 1; *BA* 40/A (2011) 213–27; Folliet (1987) 191–215; Folliet (1993) 73–107. **21.** Aug. *Ep.* 3–14; *Conf.* X, 28.32–39.64; Ceresola (2001). **22.** Russell and Nesselrath (2014) 108–10 (Sheppard); 111–24 (Gertz); and esp. 125–46 (Tanaseanu-Döbler), with Aug. *Ep.* 13 and *BA* 40/A.587–95. **23.** Syn. *De Insomn.* 134A–5D; Aug. *Ep.* 7–9 **24.** Aug. *Ep.* 13, 2; cf. *Ep.* 4, 2. **25.** Aug. *Ep.* 13–14. **26.** Aug. *Ep.* 10; M. R. Barnes (1999) 145–76, on the background. **27.** Folliet (1962) 225–36; Bonner (1986) 369–86; Folliet (1992–3) 125–33; Teske (1992a) 289–99. **28.** Aug. *Vera rel.* 35, 65; Lawless (1987) 51. **29.** Aug. *Ep.* 10, 1 ('nefas'); 14, 1. **30.** Aug. *Retr.* I, 26.1; Mutzenbecher (1999) 508–16. **31.** Dolbeau (1997) 113–65. **32.** Aug. *Div. qu.* respectively 47; 8; 9; 46; 11. **33.** Ambr. *De sacramentis* II, 2.6; Aug. *Div. qu.* 25. **34.** Aug. *Div. qu.* 33–4; Cic. *Hort.* F 67 (Grilli); Aug. *Beata v.* 4, 26. **35.** Aug. *Div. qu.* 12. **36.** Syn. *Ep.* 138, 18–19.

29 TRUE RELIGION

Madec's notes and introduction to *Lib. arb.* and *Mag.* in the revised *BA* 6 (1999) are now the essential studies, with full bibliographies on both of these difficult works. S. Harrison (2006) discusses in detail the will in *Lib. Arb.*. Kirwan (2001) is an important survey of Augustine's 'philosophy of language'. Bochet (2004) 333–84 is fundamental on *Vera Rel.*, on which Van Fleteren (1976), Desch (1980) and Lössl (1994) are also worth reading, with Madec (1994b) 189–213. Garnsey (2004) gives a valuable comparison between Augustine and Lactantius.

1. Aug. *Ep.* 15; 18; 19. **2.** Aug. *Ep.* 19. **3.** *Conf.* IX, 3.6 (Nebridius) and 6.14 (Adeodatus); *BA* 40/A (2011) 218; Syn. *Ep.* 79, 100–103. **4.** Averil Cameron (2013) 103–20, an important paper. **5.** *BA* 40/A (2011) 612–13; Aug. *Ep.* 18, 2, with *Vera rel.* 18–19; 24; and *Ep.* 19, with *Mag.* 13, 45–14, 46. **6.** Marrou (1958b) 199–204, 266–73, 292–307; Charru (2009) 171–88. **7.** Aug. *Mus.* VI, 11.29–14.48; Syn. *Hymn.* 2, 275–91 and 9, 1–50; *Conf.* IX, 6.3; X, 33.49–50. **8.** Kirwan (1989) 35–59; *BA* 6 (1999) 538–40, 543–5. **9.** Aug. *Mag.* 11,

38 and 14, 46; Mat. 23.10. **10.** *BA* 6 (1999) 543–5; Ambr. *De sacramentis* I, 6.22. **11.** *Conf.* X, 6.10. **12.** Aug. *Gn. adv. Man.* is now in a new text edition in *CSEL* 91 (1998); *BA* 50 (2004) is fundamental. **13.** Dulaey in *BA* 50.50–58, on 'spiritaliter intellegere'. **14.** Aug. *Gn. adv. Man.* I, 2.3; *BA* 50.507–9. **15.** Bochet (2004) 238–48. **16.** Aug. *Gn. adv. Man.* I, 16.26; Wisd. 11.21; O'Donnell II (1992) 356–9. **17.** Aug. *Gn. adv. Man.* I, 3.6. **18.** Aug. *Gn. adv. Man.* I, 25.43. **19.** Aug. *Mus.* VI, 5.14 and 11.33. **20.** Aug. *Ep.* 15. **21.** Bochet (2004) 377–85 is fundamental here; Aug. *Vera rel.* 16, 30–17, 33, 42, 79; Lactant. *Inst. div.* I, 1.5–6; I, 1.19; III, 6 on philosophers' contradictions, with Bochet (2004) 381–2; Lactant. *Inst. div.* 3, 21. **22.** Madec (1994b) 189–213. **23.** Aug. *Vera rel.* 9, 16–23, 44. **24.** Aug. *Vera rel.* 16, 31–17, 33, 39, 72–54, 106. **25.** Aug. *Vera rel.* 1, 1–3, 5; Madec (1994b) 189–213. **26.** Aug. *Vera rel.* 3, 5; Hadot (1979a) 273–9; Madec (1981) 231–47; Riginos (1976) 162–4 on stories of Plato's sexuality. **27.** Aug. *Vera rel.* 55, 111–13. **28.** Aug. *Vera rel.* 7, 12–18, 14. **29.** Aug. *Vera rel.* 38, 70; *Mus.* VI, 14.44; *Mor.* II, 11.23; *Gn. adv. Man.* I, 20.31; II, 18.26–7; and *BA* 50.523. **30.** Aug. *Vera rel.* 38, 70–71; Dulaey (2003a) esp. 54–61. **31.** Aug. *Vera rel.* 45, 83–52.101; *Conf.* II, 4.9 and X, 28.39–39.64. **32.** Aug. *Vera rel.* 52, 101. **33.** Aug. *Vera rel.* 50, 98–54, 106; Dulaey (2003a) 43–84, at 45–61. **34.** Harrison (2006) 185–6; Aug. *vera rel.* 26. 49 **35.** Aug. *Vera rel.* 46, 86–9. **36.** Plato, *Laws* 8, 838C; 841C. **37.** *Bēma Psalm* 222, 6 (ed. Würst); Ries (2011) 181–2 and esp. 188. **38.** Aug. *Vera rel.* 41, 77 quoting Rom. 13.1, corrected in *Retr.* I, 13.8. **39.** Martin (1997) 178–82, esp. 178; Bochet (2004) 186–7 and n. 152. **40.** Aug. *Ep.* 21, 3. **41.** Dulaey (2003a) 43–84, esp. 82–3. **42.** Aug. *Vera rel.* 35, 65; Dulaey (2003a) 44.

PART V

30 THE RELUCTANT PRIEST

O'Donnell (2005) 24–6 places Augustine's 'flight' where I have put it too. His view has been well amplified by Fitzgerald (2009), another important study to which I am indebted. Marrou (1963) is the classic study of Synesius' hesitations. M. Cameron (2009) helpfully surveys Valerius.

1. Lib. *Or.* 1, 255, 262–3; Wintjes (2005) 212–13. **2.** Lib. *Or.* 45, 19–23; Wintjes (2005) 213–17. **3.** Syn. *Ep.* 130, 40–56. **4.** Aug. *Ep.* 20, 1–3. **5.** Lancel (2002) 148–52. **6.** Aug. *S.* 355, 2; Possid. *v. Aug.* 3, 3–5. **7.** Possid. *v. Aug.* 4, 2. **8.** Aug. *Ep.* 21, 1–3. **9.** Aug. *Ep.* 10, 2; *Mor.* I, 32.69. **10.** *Conf.* VI, 6.9 and VIII, 7.16. **11.** Aug. *Ep.* 21, 4–6. **12.** *Conf.* XIII, 29.44. **13.** Syn. *Ep.* 105; Marrou (1963) 126–50, esp. 144–9. **14.** Aug. *Ep.* 21, 4. **15.** Syn. *Ep.* 105; Marrou (1963) 126–50, esp. 148–9, is essential; Syn. *Dion* 4, 3, on the '*philomuthos physis*' as the promise of the 'philosophic end'. **16.** Syn. *Ep.* 105, 113–18; the earlier interruption in Syn. *Ep.* 130, 31–9, had a military cause. **17.** Aug. *Div. qu.* 70. **18.** Syn. *Ep.* 96, 14–15; despite Liebeschuetz (1985) 149–50, I do not think he had withdrawn to Athens or anywhere else. **19.** O'Donnell

(2005) 19–26, esp. 25. **20.** Fitzgerald (2009) 37–48. **21.** Syn. *Ep.* 96. **22.** Syn. *Ep.* 11, esp. 18–24. **23.** Syn. *Ep.* 41, 139–51. **24.** *Conf.* X, 43.70.

31 SINNERS AND SEEKERS

Madec (2001b) 59–74 is an essential survey of Augustine's work and writings as a priest with Lienhard et al. (1993). Madec (2001b) 63 and 68 gives the case, a compelling one, for Sermon 216, but not 214, being Augustine's earliest known sermon as a priest. I do not place it in 397 when Aug was first a bishop during Lent. Harmless (1995) 265–74 appreciates it well.

1. O'Donnell (2005) 26. **2.** Possid. *v. Aug.* 26; Aug. *Ep.* 211, 4. **3.** Mandouze (2013) 485–500; Aug. *S.* 355 on slaves in monasteries; Aug. *Ep.* 64, 3; Chadwick (2009) 70–75. **4.** Possid. *v. Aug.* 22, 2–4, with Pellegrino, ed. (1955) 214. **5.** Jo. Cassian, *Confer.* 1, 16–17, 19; 24, 1 and 6; Brown (1988) 373–5, 420–23. **6.** Jo. Cassian, *Confer.* 12, 7, esp. 7, 4. **7.** Jo. Cassian, *Confer.* 12, 9 and 11, 4; 23, 3–6, 8. **8.** *Conf.* X, 30.41–2; Brakke (1995) 419–60. **9.** Aug. *Gn. litt.* IX, 9.17; *Civ.* XIV, 23–5; Brown (1988) 416–19. **10.** Jo. Cassian, *Confer.* 22, 7. **11.** Aug. *Ep.* 20; McLynn (2012) 310–22. **12.** Aug. *Op. mon.* 25, 33. **13.** Jer. *Ep.* 52, with Cain (2013a). **14.** Jer. *Ep.* 52, 7. **15.** Possid. *v. Aug.* 22. **16.** van der Meer (1961) 412–52; Chadwick (1996) 69–91; Chadwick (2009) 69–79. **17.** Aug. *Op. mon.* 28, 36 and *Contra Iul.* III, 11.22. **18.** Brown (2000) 349. **19.** Munier (1974) 12–18. **20.** MacMullen (2009); Février (1977) 29–45. **21.** MacMullen (2009) 51–67. **22.** Christern (1976) is very important. **23.** Leo Tolstoy, *Confession*, ed. and trans. P. Carson (London, 2014) 177. **24.** Aug. *S.* 216; Madec (2001a) 59–74; however, Dulaey, *BA* 50.530 opts for 'probablement 395–6'. **25.** Aug. *Cat. rud.* 16, 24–5, 49 and 26, 52–27, 55 respectively. **26.** Aug. *S.* 216, 6; Harmless (1995) 262–74. **27.** 1 John 2.16 and 3.2; Aug. *S.* 216, 2. **28.** Aug. *Ep.* 16, 1. **29.** Aug. *S.* 216, 4; Madec (1994c) 189–213 **30.** Jensen (2011) 247–56, for parallel sources. **31.** Aug. *S.* 216, 8. **32.** Ps. 72.27–8; Aug. *S.* 216, 5. **33.** Aug. *S.* 216, 11.

32 FAITH AND ERROR

Bochet (2004) 116–32 is an important analysis of *Util. cred* after Gigon (1985). BeDuhn (2011) and (2013) 122–63 consider Fortunatus hard done by, and influential, in his debate, but I do not. Van Oort (2008a) also considers him sympathetically. Decret (1970) 50–72 is still important.

1. Brown (2000a) 203. **2.** Aug. *Ep.* 93, 13. **3.** Aug. *Util. cred.* 1, 2–2, 4; Bochet (2004) 115–32 is essential. **4.** Aug. *Util. cred.* 16, 34. **5.** Aug. *Util. cred.* 3, 5–4, 11; Dulaey (2005) 22–6. **6.** Aug. *Util. cred.* 8, 20. **7.** Aug. *Util. cred.* 8, 20 and 15, 33. **8.** Aug. *Util. cred.* 2, 4. **9.** Aug. *Duab. an.* 1, 1; *Retr.* I, 15. **10.** Aug. *Duab. an.* 15, 24 ('*quibus mihi a pueritia . . .*'). **11.** Aug. *Retr.* I, 16. **12.**

Possid. *v. Aug.* 6; Brown (2000) 207–21. **13.** Lim (1992) 233–72. **14.** Aug. *C. Fort.* 1. **15.** Fredriksen (2008) 142–54; BeDuhn (2011) 463–79, esp. 464 and n. 3. **16.** Aug. *C. Fort.* 19. **17.** Aug. *C. Fort.* 3. **18.** Aug. *C. Fort.* 3; 7; 20; 21. **19.** Aug. *C. Fort.* 7. **20.** John 14.6; Phil. 2.5–7; Aug. *C. Fort.* 3; 7. **21.** Aug. *C. Fort.* 20; *Lib. arb.* III, 2.4–4.11; van Gerren (1957) 317–30. **22.** BeDuhn (2011) 463–79, esp. 478. **23.** Aug. *C. Fort.* 21; John 15.22. **24.** Aug. *C. Fort.* 20. **25.** Aug. *C. Fort.* 21. **26.** Bochet (2004) 186–228; Aug. *C. Fort.* 21. **27.** Prendiville (1972) 29–99, esp. 57–61 and 67–71. **28.** Despite Markus (1989) 1–42. **29.** Aug. *C. Fort.* 33–4. **30.** Aug. *C. Fort.* 36–7. **31.** Aug. *Retr.* I, 16.

33 'NOT IN RIOTING AND DRUNKENNESS . . .'

Rebillard (2005) is an important and rather complex study, but I think I differ from his pp. 103–6 by taking Aug. *Ep.* 22, 6 ('*suorum*') to refer not only to families' worship of their dead but also to a proposed reform of it, relocating it 'in church' and not just 'tolerating' it (Rebilland, 2009, 148–51). MacMullen (2009) is a lively evocation based on material evidence. Cross (1961) is the summation of long and careful thought about the respective Councils and their evidence. Madec (2001a) 168–9 crisply transforms understanding of the context and nature of Aug. *F. et symb.*

1. Aug. *Ep.* 22. **2.** Aug. *Ep.* 22, 1. **3.** Aug. *En. Ps.* 32, 1, 5; 69, 2; MacMullen (2009) 51–67; Rebillard (2005) 99–111; *S. Denis* 13, 4; Février (1977) 29–45; Saxer (1980) 133–40, still essential. **4.** Aug. *Ep.* 22, 3–4; *Civ.* XXII, 8.3. **5.** Aug. *Ep.* 22, 5–6. **6.** Aug. *Ep.* 22, 5 ('*lenissimis sed instantissimis admonitionibus*'). **7.** Asiedu (2000) 145–64. **8.** Aug. *Ep.* 22, 9; Bochet (2004) 273–4. **9.** Aug. *Ep.* 22. **10.** Syn. *Ep.* 3. **11.** Aug. *Ep.* 22, 6. **12.** Cross (1961) 227–47; Munier (1974) 20–53. **13.** *Brev. Hip.* 18. **14.** *Brev. Hip.* 26. **15.** *Brev. Hip.* 4. **16.** *Brev. Hip.* 29. **17.** Despite Brown (2000a) 135. **18.** Madec (2001b) 71–2. **19.** *Brev. Hip.* 37. **20.** *Brev. Hip.* 37. **21.** Aug. *F. et symb.* 10, 21.

34 SEAT OF THE SCORNFUL

Saxer (1980) is the essential companion to the practices, with important thoughts about the status of Leontius. Brown (1981) 28–49 is important on the motives for these celebrations which Augustine adduces, wrongly in Brown's view. As a Manichaean, Augustine also heard polemic, surely against 'semi-Christians' tomb cult': Mor, I, 34.75.

1. Aug. *Ep.* 43, 9.26; *Cresc.* IV, 8.10–9.11; *Emer.* 9. **2.** Nodes (2009) 390–408; Shaw (2011) 475–89; Hunink (2011) 389–403. **3.** Aug. *Ps. c. Don.* 271–92; Nodes (2009) 390–408, at 396–7. **4.** Aug. *Ps. c. Don.* 123; Ps. 1.1. **5.** Aug. *Ps. c. Don.* 172 and 192 (Ezek. 9.4 and 1 Kings 19.18); Dulaey (2005) 21–65, at

41–5. **6.** Aug. *Retr.* I, 20. **7.** Aug. *Ep.* 23, 2. **8.** Aug. *Ep.* 23, 7. **9.** Jer. *Ep.* 105, 1.2 (= Aug. *Ep.* 72, 1.2). **10.** Aug. *Duab. an.* 7, 9 ('*si tamen homines invenirem*'); *Conf.* XIII, 30.45; cf. V, 8.14; VI, 11.18; VII, 14.20. **11.** Aug. *Retr.* I, 21; cf. Cyp. *Ep.* 69; 70; 73. **12.** Aug. *Retr.* I, 23.1. **13.** Aug. *Ep.* 29. **14.** Aug. *Ep.* 29, with Saxer (1980) 176–9 on Leontius' uncertain status. **15.** Aug. *Ep.* 29, 4–5. **16.** Aug. *Ep.* 29, 2. **17.** Aug. *Ep.* 29, 3–7. **18.** Aug. *Ep.* 29, 7. **19.** Aug. *Ep.* 29, 8. **20.** Aug. *Ep.* 29, 10. **21.** Aug. *S.* 252, 4. **22.** Drake (1996) 3–36.

PART VI

35 THE SEVEN STEPS

It is easily forgotten that one side of Augustine was working in a daily monastic context and so I have tried to remind us of it by alluding to contemporary practices and meditations in monastic groups in Egypt. Brown (1988) 241–58 and 366–86 is full of comparative material as are Dysinger (2005) and, above all, Harmless (2004), a survey written with a conviction based on the author's own experience in north Africa, as he well explains. Lancel (2002) 221–34 is a valuable summary of Augustine's monastic life. Bochet (2004) 160–86 is essential on the relevance of the *En. Ps.* 1–32 to the *Confessions*. Rowan D. Williams (2004) gives a Christian theological appreciation which is more abstract.

1. Harmless (2004) 244–7, 388–91; Burton-Christie (1993); Dysinger (2005); Stewart (1998) 55–7. **2.** Aug. *Retr.* II, 18–23. **3.** O'Donnell I (1992) xlii–xliii. **4.** Ambr. *Expos. ev. Luc.* 5, 47–71; Rollero (1958) 21–46. **5.** Jer. *Didymi in Spir. Sanct.*, praef. = *PL* XXIII, 105; Kelly (1975) 143–4. **6.** Aug. *En. in Ps.* 11, 7; *BA* 57/A.616. **7.** Aug. *S. Dom. m.* I, 4.11 and II, 25.87. **8.** Cypr. *De Dom. Or.* 9–28. **9.** Harmless (2004) 389–90. **10.** Jo. Cassian, *Confer.* 1, 10.5, 14.9; and esp. 11, 12.2–5. **11.** Greg. Nyss., *PG* XLIV, 1193–1302, esp. 1292–3. **12.** Aug. *Div. qu.* 55–7. **13.** Aug. *S. Dom. m.* I, 2 and II, 23. **14.** Aug. *S. Dom. m.* I, 19.58, 21.71, 17.57. **15.** Aug. *S. Dom. m.* I, 8.20, 11.32, 19.61. **16.** Aug. *S. Dom. m.* I, 3.10–11. **17.** Jo. Cassian, *Confer.* 11, 12.2–5 and esp. Burton-Christie (1993) 241. **18.** Aug. *S. Dom. m.* I, 3.10–12, 11.32, 11.38; Duchrow (1965) 338–67; *BA* 11/2.503. **19.** Aug. *S. Dom. m.* II, 21.71–3; *Conf.* XII, 1.1 and XIII, 38.53 ('*ad te pulsetur*'); cf. *Conf.* XI, 2.3–4. **20.** Aug. *S. Dom. m.* I, 18.55. **21.** Aug. *S. Dom. m.* I, 22.74. **22.** Aug. *S. Dom. m.* II, 3.11–14 and 4.16 on grace, not merit. **23.** Aug. *S. Dom. m.* I, 9.24–6. **24.** Aug. *S. Dom. m.* I, 15.41–2. **25.** Aug. *S. Dom. m.* I, 11.34–5. **26.** Aug. *S. Dom. m.* I, 12.36; II, 6.23, 11.38. **27.** Aug. Div *qu.* 65 and 66. **28.** *BA* 57/A, 57/B, 58/A have transformed the subject and are essential: *BA* 57/A. 36–45 and 57–63 on the contrasts of Pss. 1–11 and 12–32. **29.** Jer. *Ep.* 5, 5; *BA* 57/A 30 n. 64. **30.** Madec (2001b) 27–42, memorably, for Ambrose; Fiedrowicz (1997); *BA* 57/A.60–63, 72–3, 589–90; M. Cameron (2012) 165–212. **31.** Dysinger (2005), esp. 62–9; Athanas. *Ep. ad Marcell.* 12. **32.** Aug. *En. Ps.* 30, 2.1, with *BA* 58/A n. 23 for a clear use of Tyconius. **33.** Aug. *En. Ps.* 10, 1, 5;

BA 57/A.615–16. **34.** Aug. *En. Ps.* 6, 7; Bochet, in *BA* 57/A.80–87 and 91–4, is essential here. **35.** Aug. *En. Ps.* 30, 2–3, 10. **36.** Thombert (1996) 19–24.

36 PAUL AND LAZARUS

Bochet (2006) gives a lucid survey of the 'generation of Paul' in the later fourth century, with *BA* 11/2.562–80 on Tyconius in Augustine's writings at or near this time. Bammel (1992) discusses Origen too. Fredriksen (1982) and (2008) give a very clear account of the changing interpretations of Romans, on which see also Martin (2001), but the fundamental account now is Bochet (2004) 186–228. On the thorny questions of grace, free choice and original sin up to 395–6 the most helpful up-to-date survey of the vast literature is now Karfíková (2012), esp. 35–65, concluding that this phase is 'the first, accomplished and, in my opinion, very fortunate form of his doctrine of grace, not as a mere stage leading to his later teaching', the latter part of which conclusion is my view too. Burns (1980) with his updating (2002), esp. 294–302, is also a fundamental analysis, whose emphasis I have mostly accepted.

1. Aug. *S.* 168, 7–8; 85, 3; 154, 2; 256, 1–2. **2.** Mitchell (2000); Rylaarsdam (2014) 157–93. **3.** Bochet (2006) 357–80; Babcock (1982) 1209–15. **4.** Aug. *C. Fort.* 21. **5.** Aug. *C. Fort.* 22; 25. **6.** Aug. *Exp. prop. Rm.* 38–41; Prendiville (1972) 29–99. **7.** Aug. *C. Fort.* 21–2. **8.** Aug. *Retr.* I, 23.1. **9.** Jer. *Ep.* 21, 3; 22, 5; 77, 3; 79, 5; 125, 7; 133, 1–2; and Paula, when ill, 108, 21. **10.** Jo. Cassian, *Confer.* 22, 14–15; 23, 11–13. **11.** Brown (2000b) 1–24. **12.** Aug. *Retr.* I, 15.8. **13.** Aug. *S. Dom. m.* II, 4.16; *En. Ps.* 18, 8. **14.** Aug. *C. Adim.*; van den Berg (2010). **15.** Aug. *Div. qu.* 61, 7; *Exp. prop. Rm.* 12. **16.** Aug. *Exp. prop. Rm.* 12; 27; 38; 43; 45. **17.** Aug. *Exp. prop. Rm.* 52–3. **18.** Babcock (1979) 55–74; Bastiaensen (2001) 33–54. **19.** Aug. *Exp. prop. Rm.* 52. **20.** Aug. *Lib. arb.* III, 2.4; *BA*. **21.** Aug. *Exp. prop. Rm.* 52–3; *Lib. arb.* III, 2.5–4.11; *Exp. Gal.* 46–7; *Div. qu.* 66. **22.** Plumer (2003), esp. 76–80, is essential. **23.** Aug. *Exp. Gal.* 56, 17; 49, 6 (women); Plumer (2003) 77–80. **24.** Aug. *Div. qu.* 71; *Exp. Gal.* 42, 19–20. **25.** Aug. *Exp. Gal.* 15, 6–17, with Plumer (2003) 145 n. 49. **26.** Aug. *Exp. Gal.* 49, 5–7; Plumer (2003) 246. **27.** Aug. *Ep. Rm. inch.* 7. **28.** Aug. *Lib. arb.* III, 25.74–7, where I do not take the passage as sombrely as Fredriksen (2008) 172. The 'torments of the Devil' are the Devil's own after his Fall, I think, not 'torments' which he imposes on us. **29.** Aug. *Lib. arb.* III, 23.66–8 **30.** Madec, in *BA* 6.575–8 ('*optimisme augustinien*') and 578–83 ('*condition malheureuse*'). **31.** Aug. *Div. qu.* 65; Dulaey (2007) 35–64, esp. 52–64, is essential. **32.** Dulaey (2007) 57–63; Ambr. *De Exc. Frat.* 2, 32 and *De Bon. Mort.* 11, 49.

37 POSTAL CONTACTS

Mratschek (2002) is essential on the letter networks of Paulinus and related matters. Trout (1999) and Conybeare (2000) approach Paulinus in a more literary-theoretical way and Lienhard (1990) is still valuable on 'friendship'. Courcelle (1951) remains fundamental, with the important adjustment by Duval (2004), too late for Mratschek (2002) to consider. Fürst (1999) is lucid on Jerome's letters and Fry (2010) is rightly attentive to postal mishaps. Trout (1991) really does re-establish 396, not 395, as the date of Augustine's bishopric.

1. *BA* 2.237–43; Kirwan (1989) 196–204. **2.** Aug. *Men.* 13, 21–21, 42; *Exp. Gal.* 10, 3; *En. Ps.* 5, 7; BeDuhn (2009) 85–124, at 104–21. **3.** Mratschek (2002) 410 n. 16. **4.** Trout (1999) 64–7; Mratschek (2002) 56–60. **5.** Trout (1999) 67–95; Mratschek (2002) 56–7. **6.** Paul. Nol. *Ep.* 1, 1. **7.** Paul. Nol. *Carm.* 10, 189–92. **8.** Ambr. *Ep.* 58, 3. **9.** Paul. Nol. *Ep.* 1, 10. **10.** Courcelle (1951) 253–300, a brilliant study, but on the opening move Duval (2004) 397–419 is preferable; Paul. Nol. *Ep.* 4. **11.** Paul. Nol. *Ep.* 3, 2. **12.** Paul. Nol. *Ep.* 4, 2–4; 2 Cor. 10.17. **13.** Aug. *CDiv.* 1.10. **14.** Paul. Nol. *Ep.* 4, 2, with Mratschek (2002) 478–9. **15.** Paul. Nol. *Carm.* 7–9. **16.** Aug. *Ep.* 27, 1. **17.** Aug. *Ep.* 27, 2. **18.** Aug. *Ep.* 27, 4; Mratschek (2002) 478–80. **19.** Aug. *Ep.* 27, 4. **20.** Aug. *Ep.* 26 *Licentii Carmen*; *BA* 40/A 625–8 is more impressed than I am by the versifying ; Cutino (2000) is most helpful, with Shanzer (1991) 110–43. **21.** Aug. *Ep.* 26, 4. **22.** Aug. *Ep.* 27, 6. **23.** Courcelle (1951) 256–300; Aug. *Ep.* 27, 5; *Conf.* VI, 7.11–10.16. **24.** Aug. *Ep.* 31, 9. **25.** Jer. *Ep.* 53, 1; Trout (1999) 90–103. **26.** Jer. *Ep.* 53, 9–10. **27.** Jer. *Ep.* 53, 11; Mratschek (2002) 90–96; Brown (2012) 280–82. **28.** Jer. *Ep.* 58, 4–8. **29.** Trout (1999) 96–101; Mratschek (2002) 548–50. **30.** Aug. *Ep.* 27*, 1, with Duval, *BA* 46B.560–68. **31.** Aug. *Ep.* 27*, 2. **32.** Aug. *Ep.* 27*, 3; 29, 1 for Alypius' return in 395. **33.** Plumer (2003) observes no demonstrable use of Jerome by Aug. *Exp. Gal.*, but accepts it nonetheless. **34.** Trout (1991) 237–60: Augustine became bishop in 396, not 395. Fürst (1994) and (1999) are essential, with Hennings (1994). **35.** Aug. *Ep.* 28, 3–4. **36.** Aug. *Ep.* 28, 2. **37.** Jer. *Ep.* 112, 3; Aug. *Exp. Gal.* 15. **38.** Aug. *Ep.* 28, 5–6; Jer. *Ep.* 112, 3.4. **39.** Aug. *Ep.* 40. **40.** Jer. *Ep.* 105, 1. **41.** Folliet (2003) 265–88, esp. 265–6, with Aug. *Ep.* 71, 3. **42.** *Conf.* I, 1.1 and 4.4; V, 6.18 and 20; 6.7; 6.10, 7.11 and 12; Folliet (2003) 265–88 is essential.

38 AMAZING GRACE

Fredriksen (2008) 155–89 gives an admirably lucid summary of her important views on the changes of thought visible in *Simpl.* I, 2, on which I agree with Ring (1994), not Flasch, and am closer to Burns (1980) than to C. Harrison (2006). Cipriani (2002) well discusses Lettieri's claim (2001) for 'un altro Agostino' from now on. Again, Karfíková (2012) 78–87 gives an excellent overview of the great debates in modern scholarship, in which Drecoll (1999) rightly warns against isolating Augustine's answers as 'the' theory of Grace which he then follows exactly ever afterwards. Original sin is helpfully followed through by Couenhoven (2005), among many others. Madec (2001b) 64–7 has tempered

Peter Brown's influential idea of a 'lost future' in Augustine's thinking, to my mind advisedly. Kirwan (1989) 104–28 gives the most philosophically searching analysis of Augustine's views on freedom of the will and grace, concluding, importantly, that 'on this difficult matter Augustine was among those theologians [who] are insufficiently reluctant to contradict themselves' (128).

1. Dulaey (2000) 31–60. **2.** Aug. C. *Adim.* 28; Kloos (2005) 397–420; Madec (2001) 221–40. **3.** M. Cameron (2012) 197–9, esp. 197. **4.** Aug. *Ep.* 29, 7. **5.** *BA* 10, 411–643. **6.** Ambr. *Ep.* 54; Paul. Nol. *Ep.* 20, 3. **7.** Fredriksen (2008) 175; Hombert (1996) 99–103. **8.** Aug. *Div. qu.* 66, 5–6. **9.** Aug. *Simpl.* I, 2.16–17; Karfíková (2012) 71–88 is a clear, up-to-date survey. **10.** Aug. *Retr.* II, 1.1; Madec (1994b) 85–9; Harrison (2006) 151–4; Aug. *Persev.* 20, 52–4. **11.** Brown (2000a) 139–50, esp. 140; much discussed, esp. by C. Harrison (2006) 14–18 and esp. 129–63, with Madec (2001b) 241–55. **12.** Aug. *Simpl.* I, 2.16 and 19 ('massa peccatorum'); *Exp. prop. Rm.* 62; *Exp. Gal.* 42; C. Harrison (2006) 187–8 and n. 79. **13.** Babock (1990) 251–61, esp. 254–6, is most valuable. **14.** Aug. *Simpl.* I, 1–7; II, 1.2–9. **15.** Aug. *Simpl.* I, 2.16, with Rom. 11. 33; Hombert (1996) 46 and C. Harrison (2006) 278–80 see anticipations in Augustine's earlier works. **16.** Aug. *Ench.* 27, 103. **17.** Aug. *Ep.* 27, 4. **18.** Aug. *Retr.* I, 28.1. **19.** Aug. *Simpl.* I, 2.22; I differ slightly from the important study of Rist (1969) 420–47. **20.** Burns (1980) 38–50 is essential; Harrison (2006) 274–6 criticizes it, but I am not convinced by all the citations she picks out, esp. those linked to Rom. 9.16; at *Simpl.* I, 2.21 'unless God moves and rouses us' (*movente atque excitante*) we would not be able to 'will' (*velle*), but the point is that we do still 'will', without being 'steamrollered'. Burns (2002) 294–316 revisits his earlier views, without retracting. Aug. *Gr. et lib. arb.* 2, 2–4 is still not denying 'free choice' in 426–7. **21.** Aug, *Acad.* III. 19. 42 **22.** Aug. *Solid* 1. 1. 3, *Gn. adv. Mar.* II. 8, 10, II. 19, 29–20, 32. **23.** Harrison (2006) 286. **24.** Kirwan (1989) 131–2; 138–9; Williams (1927) 379: 'of his five proof-texts, three are mistranslations'; Madec (1998) 11–13, on Rom. 5.12. **25.** Aug. *Simpl.* I, 2.16; Fredriksen (2008) 183. **26.** Rom. 9.20; Job 7.17, with, however, 42.2–6. **27.** Solignac (1988) 825–49 is essential here. **28.** Aug. *Simpl.* I, 2.22. **29.** Aug. *Simpl.* I, 2.22: '*voluntas, refracta saevitia, retorqueretur*'. **30.** Fredriksen (1986) 3–34 is fundamental for this approach. **31.** *Conf.* XIII, 13.14. **32.** Aug. *Cat. rud.* 5, 9. **33.** Dupont (2014) 105–32 surveys the sermons for this topic. **34.** Lib. *Or.* 1, 18 (Fortune's 'gifts'); 1, 20 (her foreknowledge); 1, 24; 1, 60; esp. 1, 78–9 (her 'saving' by adversity); 1, 95 (random chastening) as in 1, 117 and 133, 152 and 155. **35.** Hombert (1996) 112–14; more generally, Drecoll (1999) 263–8 and Lössl (1997) 211.

39 FOOD FOR SCANDAL

I have set out in the online edition of the *New York Review of Books* for March 10, 2016, available at www.nybooks.com/articles/2016/03/10/difference

-over-augustine/, the main texts and modern scholarship which support the exchanges presented in this chapter.

1. Possid. *v. Aug.* 8, 1. **2.** Council of Nicaea, c. 8; Aug. *Ep.* 213, 4; however, Kany (1997) 116–25 reopens the question interestingly. **3.** Trout (1991) 237–60, at 238, is essential; Mratschek (2002) 320 and 346; Lancel (2002) 500 n. 6 shows reluctance but is not persuasive in adducing Paul. Nol. *Ep.* 7, 1 as a list in chronological order. **4.** Aug. *Ep.* 31, 4. **5.** Possid. *v. Aug.* 8, 1–5. **6.** Aug. *C. Cresc.* III, 80.92. **7.** Aug. *C. litt. Pet.* III, 16.19. **8.** Aug. *C. Fel.* II, 22. **9.** See my ch. 25, pp. 347–8 Perrin (2007) 65–86, on testimonies and abjurations. **10.** Aug. *Brevic.* III, 7.9. **11.** *Gest. conl. Carth.* III, 245–7. **12.** Chadwick (2009) 64 for his final variant. **13.** Courcelle (1951) 255–300, esp. 256–9 and 261 n. 5; cf. the acute Bonner (1986b) 121 n. 2. **14.** Aug. *Haer.* 46; Possid. *v. Aug.* 16; Arnob. Iun. *Praedest.* I, 16; Dolbeau (2004) 225–32. **15.** Mratschek (2002) 428–30, showing Gallic, but not African, precedents. **16.** Aug. *Ep.* 31, 9. **17.** Paul. Nol. *Ep.* 4, 2. **18.** Paul. Nol. *Ep.* 6, 2–3. **19.** Aug. *Ep.* 27 and 31. **20.** Aug. *Ep.* 31. **21.** Aug. *Ep.* 31, 3 and 7; Mratschek (2011) 109–22, esp. 113. **22.** Aug. *Ep.* 31, 6. **23.** Aug. *Ep.* 31, 4. **24.** Aug. *Ep.* 31, 9. **25.** Paul. Nol. *Ep.* 7, 2. **26.** Brown (2000a) 193. **27.** Paul. Nol. *Ep.* 7, 3. **28.** Paul. Nol. *Ep.* 8, 1. **29.** Paul. Nol. *Ep.* 8, 3. **30.** *CIL* VI 32009; Mratschek (2002) 116. **31.** Paul. Nol. *Ep.* 7, 3. **32.** Aug. *Ep.* 38, 2. **33.** Aug. *Ep.* 38, 2. **34.** Aug. *Ep.* 42, 1. **35.** Aug. *Ep.* 45. **36.** Aug. *Ep.* 45, 2.

40 SHARED BURDENS

Lancel (2002) 187–220 is a particularly good survey of the many problems of dating and location which my chs. 40–42 interrelate, at times differing from his views. Bochet (2004) 92–115 is important on *Doctr. chr.* and the *Confessions*, as is much of her commentary in *BA* 11/2. Hill (1962) is still much to the point. Folliet (2003) and (2008) are essential on Job.

1. *Erfurt Serm.* 6, 1. **2.** Aug. *Retr.* II, 1–6. **3.** Madec (1996a), on the problems of dating and the *Retractationes*. **4.** *BA* 1.437–509; Zumkeller (1986) 222–7. **5.** Aug. *Agon.* 1–14 and 15–34, with *Retr.* II, 3; Lawless (1987) 121–51. **6.** Aug. *Ep.* 29, 7; 41, 1; Possid. *v. Aug.* 5, 2. **7.** Aug. *Ep.* 41, 2 and 17–18; *BA* 11/2.11–12, importantly. **8.** Aug. *C. ep. Man.* 1, 1–3, 3. **9.** Aug. *C. ep. Man.* 17, 20. **10.** Bochet (2004) 94–115. **11.** Aug. *Doctr. chr.* II, 20.30–40.60. *BA* 11/2.29–36, 471–3 and 528–46 are fundamental here. **12.** *Conf.* XII, 32.43; XIII, 8.9. **13.** Aug. *Adn. Iob* 6, with Folliet (2008) 31–43, esp. 37. **14.** Syn. *Ep.* 50; Liebeschuetz (1985) 146–64; Syn. *Ep.* 57 and 58; 72, 73, 78; Liebeschuetz (1986) 180–95, esp. 188–91. **15.** Aug. *Ep.* 33, 2. **16.** Aug. *Ep.* 33, 3–4. **17.** Aug. *Ep.* 44 and 6, 13. **18.** Aug. *Ep.* 44, 1.1–2. **19.** Aug. *Ep.* 44, 2.3–6.13. **20.** Aug. *Ep.* 43. **21.** Aug. *Ep.* 43, 2.3–5; *Retr.* II, 5. **22.** Aug. *Ep.* 35, 2. **23.** Aug. *Ep.* 35, 4. **24.** Aug. *Ep.* 41, 2. **25.** Aug. *Doctr.*

chr. III, 25.35 and *BA* 11/2.562–83, now essential. **26.** Chadwick (1993) 24–35 is important, but to my mind makes the 'silence' about Donatism too deliberate. **27.** Brown (2000a) 157; Pincherle (1947) 195. **28.** Aug. *Ep.* 38, 1. **29.** O'Donnell II (1992) 298 n. 2; (2005) 108 n. 200. **30.** Aug. *Ep.* 38, 2. **31.** Aug. *Ep.* 38, 2. **32.** Chadwick (2003) 1161–75 surveys them.

41 CONFESSING

Chronological uncertainties are presented by Hombert (2000) 9–24, who argues correctly for the absence of certainty, but I still hold on to what seem to me, subjectively, to be probabilities. Solignac in *BA* 13.45–54 remains an important study for all proponents of a later date than mine, but I do not accept his well-chosen arguments for a dating between 397 and 401. Gabillon (1998) is of course most congenial to my argument, though Hombert (2000) rightly observes that he cannot give a cast-iron, non-circular proof of his case. On the work's speed of composition my main ally in print is Harmless (2012), to whom I am grateful for encouragement. Van Bavel (2009) well surveys Augustine's views on prayer which I emphasize as essential to the *Confessions*' unity. Duchrow (1965) and Knauer (1955), a classic work, are especially valuable on the question of the *Confessions*' unity and remain starting points for all future discussion. Wills (2011) surveys the subject very clearly. The work's unity has now been interestingly discussed by Ollier (2011), emphasizing the themes of scriptural interpretation and interpretation of oneself. Cavadini (2010) emphasizes the eucharistic sub-plot which is present, he thinks, in Books 12–13. Both are obviously indebted to the example of Bochet (2004) 92–4 and 229–324, which is fundamental. As for Lib. *Or.* 1, it is commented on by Norman (1965), discussed in terms of its aim and method by Liebeschuetz (2006), and surveyed most recently by van Hoof (2014a), with a full bibliography. Cribiore (2013) 53ff. argues boldly that in *Or.* 1, Libanius 'was concerned with presenting himself as a sort of superhuman being' and she considers that he wrote in full awareness of the life of such a Christian saint as Antony. I do not agree. She takes 1.96 to present Libanius himself as a benign spirit or *daimōn*, but I take the Greek to say only that 'the opinion occurred that one of the kindly *daimones* had come in [to the prison] with me', i.e. as a traditional pagan 'divine companion'. The gods favour Libanius, but he is certainly not himself 'the "kindly spirit", emulating benevolent Zeus' (Cribiore (2013) 54). I do not therefore think that Christian hagiography has anything to do with *Or.* 1 and I differ from Cribiore's stimulating argument that Libanius shows 'a desire to listen to and incorporate all the voices of the times' (Cribiore (2013)74). To me, he is fascinating, and admirable, for doing exactly the opposite.

1. Hombert (2000) 9–23, a brilliant review of the subject and a new theory which does not convince me. **2.** An example is *En. Ps.* 36, emphasized by Hombert (2000) 15–22: there are many others, of course. **3.** Gibson (1999) 171–202. **4.** Hombert (2000) v–ix, and 'orchestration scriptuaire' as a criterion. **5.** Lib. *Or.*

1–155; 155–285; I disagree with Martin and Petit (1979) 3–17 and even Norman in the Loeb edn, I (1992) 8–10. **6.** Lib. *Or.* 2 and 4. **7.** Liebeschuetz (2006) 263–76 overemphasizes, I think, Isoc. *Antidosis* as a model. **8.** Lib. *Or.* 1, 88. **9.** Lib. *Or.* 1, 251; *Or.* 33. **10.** Lib. *Or.* 1, 9; 1, 148–50; and Schouler (1984) 522–35. **11.** Edwards (1992) 459–74, esp. 466–9. **12.** M. Aur. *Med.* I, 16.4; Norman (1965) xviii–xix and Cribiore (2013) 53 disagree with me and Misson (1914) 50–60 and, I think, Liebeschuetz (2006) 263–76, esp. 269–72. **13.** Julian *Or.* 346B refers to sacrificing in the temple of Fortune, but its persistence into the 380s is not at all clear. **14.** Lib. *Or.* 1, 1. **15.** Wintjes (2005) 191–7. **16.** Lib. *Or.* 1, 175, reconsidered, however, by van Hoof (2014b); I still prefer Norman (1965) 201. **17.** Wintjes (2005) 191–232. **18.** Schouler (1994) 305–24, esp. 311. **19.** Liebeschuetz (2006) 267–8. **20.** Lib. *Or.* 1, 96–106, with *Ep.* 391 and 405 and Cribiore (2007a) 93. **21.** Lib. *Or.* 1, 121–32 and esp. 136–8; Wintjes (2005) 109–33. **22.** Lib. *Or.* 1, 148–50. **23.** Lib. *Or.* 2, 50; 35, 25; 62, 53; *Or.* 1, 154–5. **24.** Wintjes (2005) 191–237; Cabouret (2002) 191–204, for governors' vices and virtues. **25.** Lib. *Or.* 1, 156–8; *PLRE* s.v. Festus (3). **26.** Cribiore (2013) 79–89, opposing Petit (1955) 479–509, esp. 488–9. **27.** Cribiore (2013) 40. **28.** Lib. *Or.* 1, 216, 234, 237, 244, 270, 283: no 'grey paganism' here; despite Cribiore (2013) 160–222, I do not see various individual gods becoming 'empty for him'. **29.** Lib. *Or.* 1, 195–6, 279–80, 283–4; *Ep.* 1000, 1003, 1011. **30.** Lib. *Or.* 1, 280: *Ep.* 1039 for his enemies' glee. **31.** Lib. *Or.* 1, 283–5. **32.** Liebeschuetz (2006) 266. **33.** Lib. *Or.* 1, 43–8, 62–3, 67–9, 74 and esp. 79. **34.** Eunap. *v. Soph.* 495; Penella (2012) 892–5, but I think Eunapius refers to a quality of Libanius' letters, not to his 'flattery'; cf. Socr. *HE* 3, 1, 1; contrast the tone of Lib. *Or.* 53, 8–18. **35.** Lib. *Or.* 1, 43–4, 62–6, 74; I do not think he intends us to understand the '*aischron*' at 1, 79 as 'pederasty'. **36.** Jer. *Ep.* 127, 3 and 45, 4. **37.** Plut. *Mor.* 539B–547F; cf. Aug., *Ep.* 27, 5. **38.** Lib. *Or.* 1, 37. **39.** Aug. *En. Ps.* 138, 1; *S.* 352, 1; Olivar (1991) 606–11. **40.** Aug. *Ep.* 23/A*, 3, with M.-F. Berrouard, *BA* 46B.545. **41.** *BA* 74A (1993) 17–26. **42.** Syn. *Ep.* 154, 105–7; Julian, *Or.* 4, 157C. **43.** Ambr. *Ep.* 4. **44.** Syn. *On Dreams*; Julian, *Or.* 4, 157C; Jer. *Ep.* 446 and 117, 12. **45.** Aug. *S.* 216, 4 and 11. **46.** Lambot (1969) 206–14; a reprint of a 1963 artide; Aug. *S.* 229R–V; Hombert (2000) 20–22, esp. n. 50 and 53, adding 'les points de contact sont innombrables', endorsing the overlap with *Conf.* XIII, but not putting both in 397. *S.* 229V 3, 5 is 'anti-Donatist', as he observes, but it can belong in 397 nonetheless. For the 'firmament', see Lambot (1969) 208. **47.** *Conf.* XIII, 20.27. **48.** *S.* 229R–V coincide especially with *Conf.* XIII, 12.13–31.46; Madec (1998b) 21–2, a confessed 'chronosceptic', notes the close overlap, but considers a simultaneous dating 'plus risqué'. **49.** *Conf.* XIII, 12.13; Bochet (2004) 231–7 is essential. **50.** *Conf.* XIII, 13.14–14.15. **51.** Bochet (2004) 229–37 brilliantly exploits the imagery but refrains from a dating. **52.** Van Bavel (2009), esp. 27–58 and 59–63; *Conf.* V, 47.7; Aug. *En. Ps.* 30, 2, 3–4. **53.** *Conf.* X, 17.26; Madec (1996) 85–91. **54.** Madec (1994b) 121–35. **55.** *Conf.* X, 4. **56.** 1 Jo. 5.16. **57.** *Conf.* IX, 4.7; XI, 2.2. **58.** Syn. *Ep.* 41 and 42; Liebeschuetz (1986) 180–95, esp. 188–91. **59.** Syn. *Ep.* 41, 90–205. **60.** Chadwick (2003) 1161–75 surveys the 'apologies'.

42 THE HEAVEN OF HEAVENS

Madec (1998a) is essential on Augustine's God. Madec (1996b) 85–91 is incisive on *memoria* and Madec (2001b) 185–95 is an important contextualization of the discussion of time. Hadot (2012) reprints valuable summaries of discussions of Books 11–13. Vaught (2005) is an especially helpful companion to Books 10–13 to which I owe much. Volumes IV (Cristiani and Solignac) and V (Pépin and Simonetti) of the Fondazione Valla commentary, *Sant'Agostino: Confessioni* (1997) are invaluable commentaries by masters of the subject. Müller (1998) is important on Book 13, but my major debt is still to Cayré (1956), an inspiring and essential response to Book 13 which opens it up for modern readers.

1. *Conf.* IV, 1.1; VII, 14.20; Aug. *En. Ps.* 26, 2.18 is explicit here. **2.** *Conf.* III, 6.11; Aug. *Vera rel.* 39, 72. **3.** *Conf.* IV, 2.3; VI, 1.1; Ps. 73. 26. **4.** *Conf.* VI, 6.9; VII, 8.19; IX, 2.3 and 4.7. **5.** Aug. *S.* 53, 7; *Conf.* III, 11.9; IV, 16.31; VII, 8.12. **6.** *Conf.* III, 7.12; VII, 14.20; VII, 10.16. **7.** *Conf.* I, 4.4; Madec (2000) 110–12; Aug. *Doctr. chr.* I, 6.6. **8.** *Conf.* III, 3. and IX, 4.12. **9.** Aug. *C. Adim.* 11; Madec (2000) 147–8. **10.** *Conf.* I, 5.5. **11.** *Conf.* X, 8.12–15 and 17.26; van Oort (2013) 155–75 compares a Manichaean Kephalaion, but also see Schmidt-Dengler (1968) 68–9 and esp. *BA* 14.557–67, an essential study. **12.** *Conf.* XI, 14.17–29.39, with esp. Kirwan (1989) 151–86; Madec (1996b) 95, on Porphyry. **13.** *Conf.* XII, 8.8–13.16; Pepin (1953) 185–274 is essential. **14.** *Conf.* XII, 16.23–26.36 and XI, 3.5; Ettenhuber (2011) 121–7. **15.** *Conf.* XIII, 24.35–7. **16.** *Conf.* XII, 10.10. **17.** *Conf.* XII, 16.23. **18.** *Conf.* VI, 2.2; VII, 8.12; VIII, 1.1; 12.28; IX, 1.2; XI, 2.4; XII, 11.11. **19.** Pachom. *Vita Prima* 99; Harmless (2004) 131 and 153–4. **20.** *Conf.* X, 29.40–35.57; Brown (2000) 174; Madec (1986–94b) 466–75; *Conf.* X, 4.5. **21.** *Conf.* X, 29.40 and 37.60. **22.** Pépin (1996) 3–25; Madec (2001b) 39. **23.** Aug. *Gn. adv. Man.* II, 4.5. **24.** *Conf.* XII, 10.10–11.12, 15.18; XIII, 29.44. **25.** *Conf.* XIII, 18.23; Bochet (2004) 254–61 is essential on the relation here with Paul. **26.** Jo. Cassian, *Confer.* X, 13–14. **27.** *Conf.* XI, 29.39; XII, 14.15, 15.21; XIII, 9.10; Duchrow (1965) 338–67. **28.** *Conf.* XIII, 9.10–13.14. **29.** *Conf.* XII, 8.8–13.16; Pépin (1953) 185–274. **30.** *Conf.* I, 1.1; VI, 4.5, 11.18; XI, 2.3–4. **31.** Aug. *Doctr. chr.* II, 7.9–11; *Conf.* XIII, 15.17; and esp. Bochet (2004) 101–3. **32.** *Conf.* XIII, 17.21–18.22; cf., earlier, Aug. *Gn. adv. Man.* I, 25.43. **33.** *Conf.* XIII, 19.24. **34.** *Conf.* XIII, 25.38; Feldmann (1994) 1134–94, esp. 1162–75. **35.** *Conf.* XIII, 18.23, with Bochet (2004) 257–8 on the parallels in *S.* 229T and U (I suspect, contemporary), preached in Easter Week. **36.** *Conf.* XIII, 15.16 and esp. Bochet (2004) 237–47. **37.** *Conf.* XIII, 2.3, 8.9, 10.11, 12.13, 14.15; Bochet (2004) 231–2, noting the link to Easter preaching. **38.** *Conf.* XIII, 2.3. **39.** *Conf.* XIII, 3.4. **40.** *Conf.* XIII, 1.1–2.3, 23.32–23.33, 26.40; Paul, Col. 3.10. **41.** *Conf.* XI, 1–2.3; XIII, 9.10, 35.50–38.53. **42.** *Conf.* XI, 10.12–28.38, with esp. Kirwan (1989) 167–96, Bochet (2001) 43–66 and Madec (1996b) 93–9, with helpful bibliography. **43.** *Conf.* XI, 13.15. **44.** *Conf.* XI, 27.36–28.38. **45.** *Conf.* I, 5.5. **46.** *Conf.*

XIII, 29.44. **47.** Lib. *Or.* 1, 155. **48.** Aug. *Sol.* I, 7.14. **49.** *Conf.* XIII, 9.10. **50.** *Conf.* XIII, 15.18; *En. Ps.* 32, 2.1, 8, and 46, 7. **51.** Ezra Pound *Canto* V and Froula (1984) 11–52. **52.** Daniel Cory, memoir in 1968, in J. P. Sullivan, ed., *Ezra Pound* (Harmondsworth, 1970) 375–6.

43 EPILOGUE

1. Paul. Mil. *v. Ambr.* 47; McLynn (1994) 367. **2.** Aug. *Ep.* 34, 2–3. **3.** Aug. *S. Dolbeau* 28 (*S.* 20B); Dolbeau (1994) 279–303; Dolbeau (2003b) 285–96. **4.** Aug. *S. Dolbeau* 28 (*S.* 20B) 11. **5.** Folliet (2008) 31–42, esp. 39–40 on Job 9.17. **6.** De Bruyne (1931) 185–93; Lambot (1935) 114–24; Lambot (1950) 3–7; Dolbeau (2005) 64–70. **7.** Aug. *S. Dolbeau* 8–20; Dolbeau (2002) 845–75 for second thoughts on datings, with (2009) 617–18 for hesitations over the datings of some of them **8.** Hombert (2000) 544–6; Dolbeau (2002) 845–75, at 847–8; Dolbeau (2009) 617–18. **9.** Aug. *S. Dolbeau* 8 (*S.* 29B) 7. **10.** Aug. *S. Dolbeau* 10 (*S.* 162C) 13–14. **11.** Aug. *S. Dolbeau* 10 (*S.* 162C) 15. **12.** Aug. *S. Dolbeau* 10 (*S.* 162C) 7; alternative dates of 405 (Hombert) and 418 (Drobner) do not persuade me. **13.** Aug. *S. Dolbeau* 11 (*S.* 90A), 17 (*S.* 110A), 14 (*S.* 352A), 16 (*S.* 72). **14.** Aug. *S. Dolbeau* 13 (*S.* 159A) 13. **15.** Aug. *S. Dolbeau* 14 (*S.* 352A) 4. **16.** Aug. *S.* 30B; *Conf.* X, 20.29–31; Dolbeau (1996b) 274–5. **17.** Aug. *S. Dolbeau* 17 (*S.* 110/A); despite Bochet (2004) 197–9, I accept with Hombert (2000) that *S.* 145 is much later than 397. **18.** Aug. *Ep.* 41, 1–2. **19.** *Conc. Africae* (ed. Munier, *CCSL* 149) 49. **20.** Brown (1988) 366–427 is the essential study; also, Hunter (1994) 153–77. **21.** Aug. *Ep.* 80; *Civ.* I, 10; Mratschek (2014) 545–61. **22.** Syn. *Ep.* 126; Liebeschuetz (1986) 193–5 suggests Synesius lived on into 415, which I do not accept. **23.** Syn. *Ep.* 10 and 16; *Ep.* 81. **24.** Lib. *Or.* 1, 153. **25.** Lib. *Ep.* 947; Criscuolo (2011) 177–91. **26.** Lib. *Or.* 9, with Graf (2012) 167–86. **27.** Syn. *Ep.* 126, 20–21. **28.** Syn. *Ep.* 14, 62, 77–8; esp. the *Catastasis*, *PG* LXVI, 1566–74; *Constitutio*, *PG* LXVI, 1574–8; Tomlin (1979) 253–70 evokes it all admirably. **29.** Aug. *Cura mort.* 13, 16. **30.** G. Bardy, *BA* 12 (1950) 217. **31.** Courcelle (1943) 168. **32.** Aug. *Ep.* 147; *Gn. Litt.* XII, 7.16–8.22, with Madec (2001a) 221–39; Chase (2005) 233–56; Aug. *S.* 52, 16–17. **33.** C. *Secundin.* 1, 3; *Conf.* III, 6.10; Courcelle (1968) 237. **34.** Aug. *Ep.* 12*, 1; Quillen (1991) 87–109 is important. **35.** Aug. *Ep.* 230, 4. **36.** Claud. *Pan. Cos. Mall. Theod.* 294–310, 320–32. **37.** Aug. *Retr.* I, 2. **38.** Aug. *Ep.* 259, 1; Gabillon (1978) 58–70 is, in my view, correct. **39.** Possid. *v. Aug.* 31, 6. **40.** Aug. *Ep.* 231, 6. **41.** Aug. *S.* 104, 3; La Bonnardière (1986) 411–26.

Index

ROBIN LANE FOX is Emeritus Fellow of New College, Oxford and was until 2014 Reader in Ancient History in Oxford University. The author of *The Classical World* and *Alexander the Great*, Lane Fox lives in Oxford, England.